PICTURING
BLACK
HISTORY

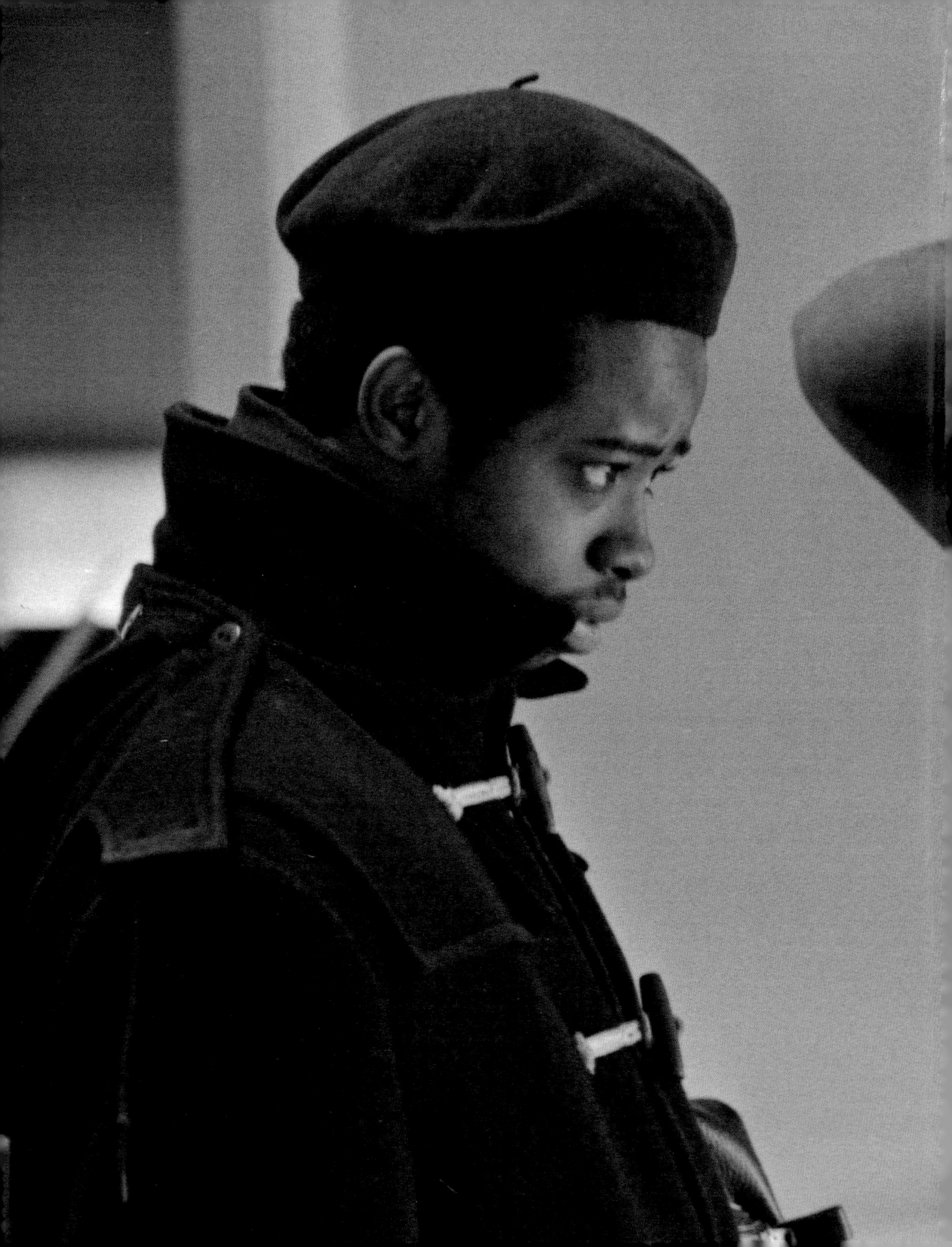

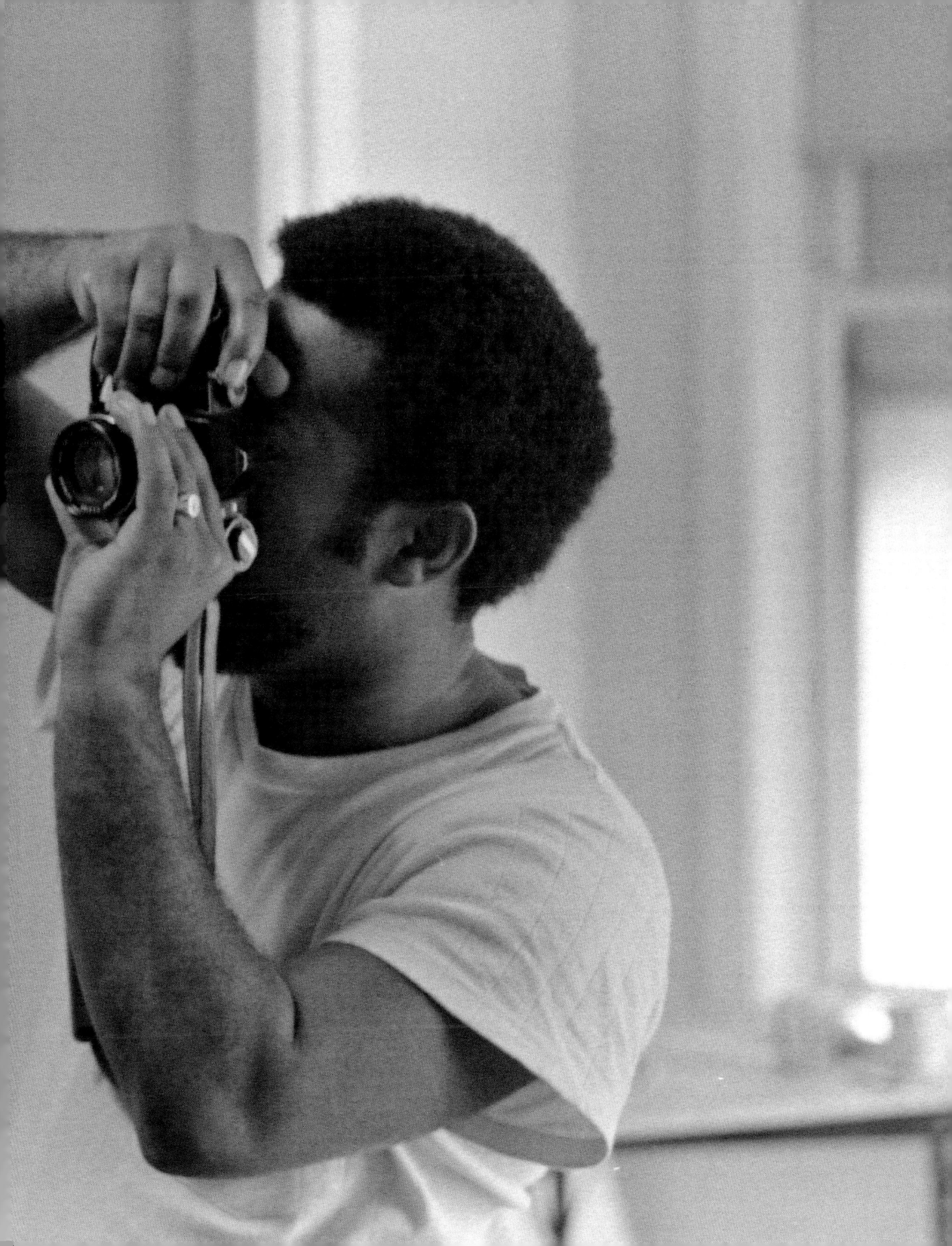

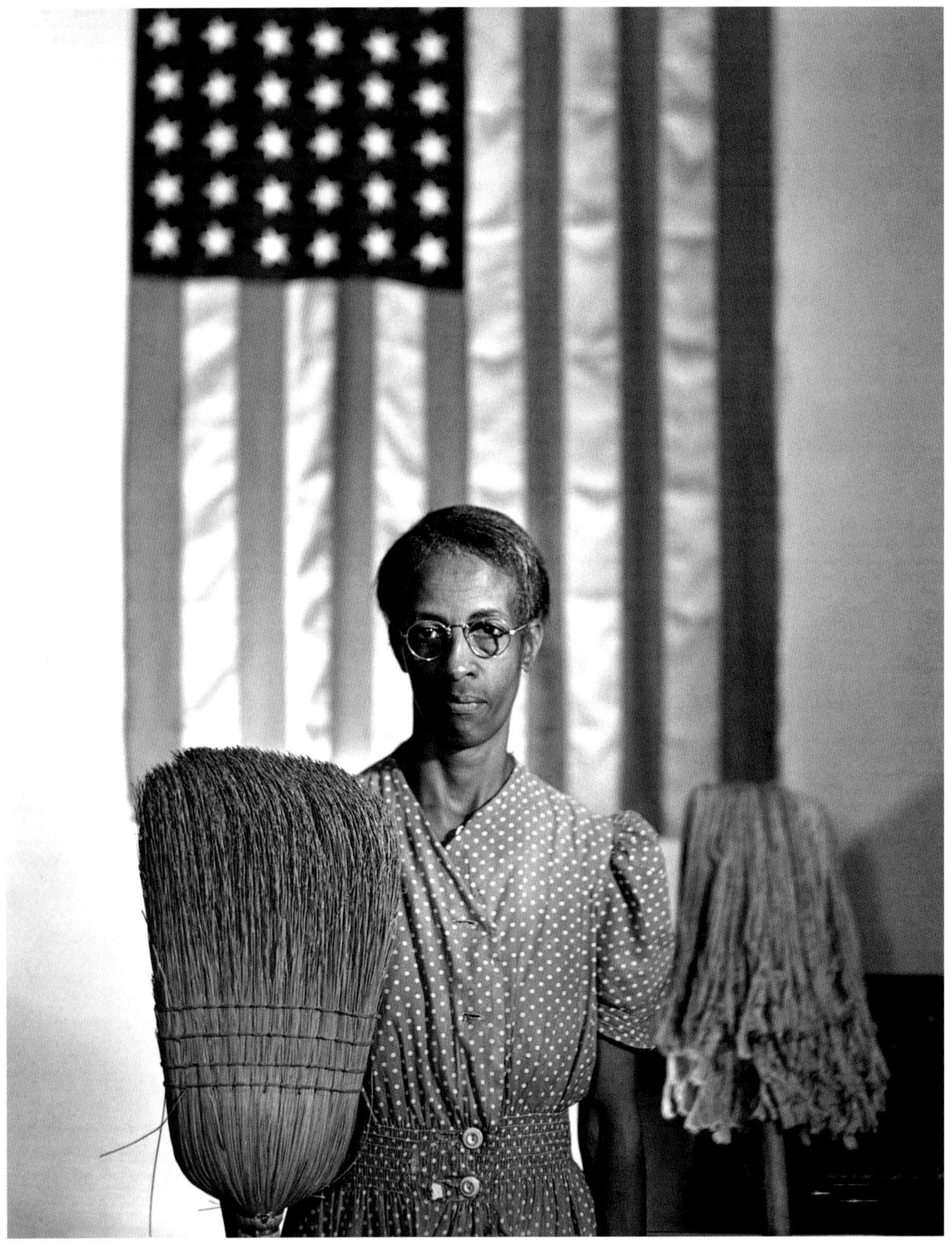

PICTURING
BLACK
HISTORY

PHOTOGRAPHS
AND STORIES THAT
CHANGED THE WORLD

Edited by Daniela Edmeier, Damarius Johnson, Steven Conn, and Nicholas B. Breyfogle
IN COLLABORATION WITH GETTY IMAGES

ABRAMS, NEW YORK

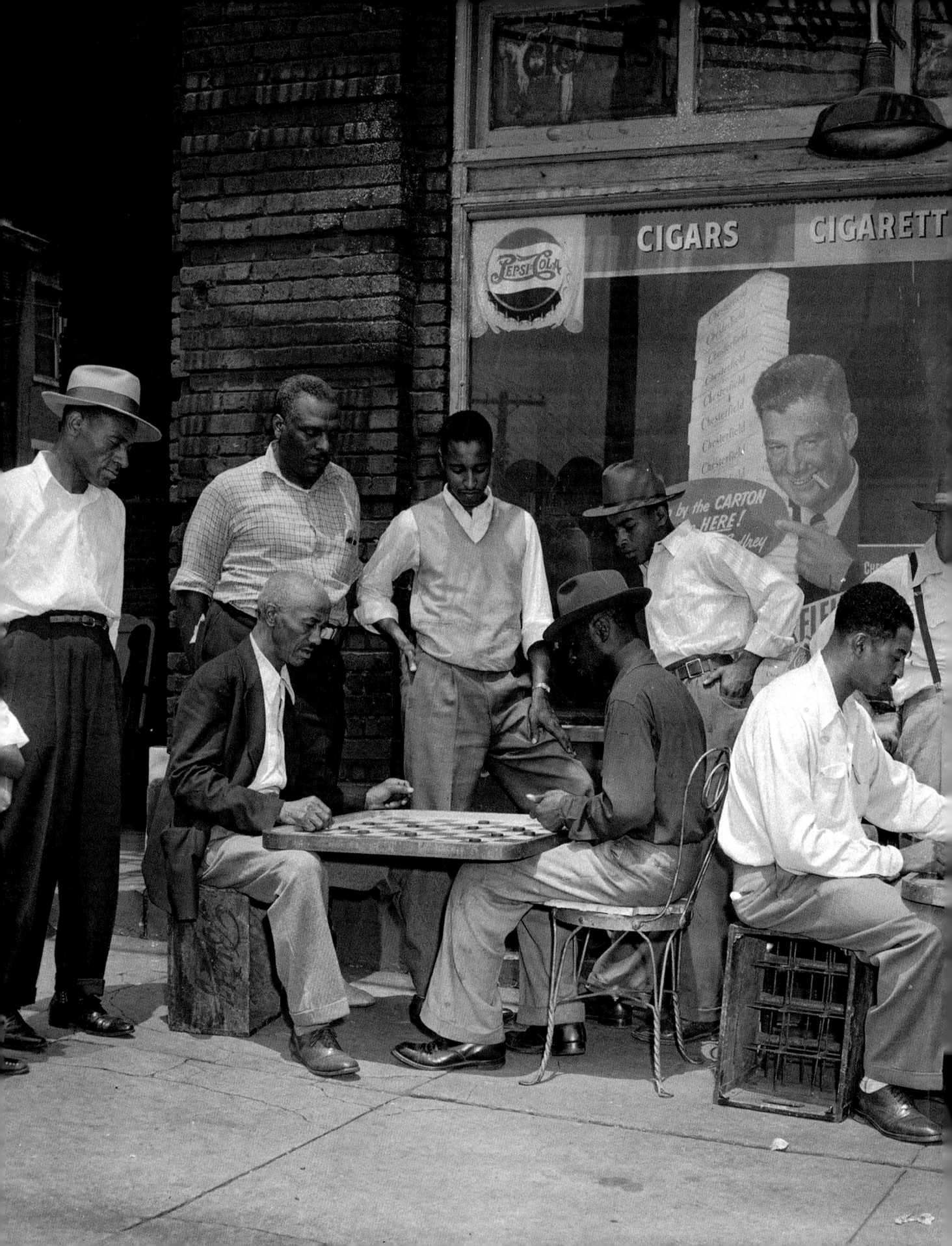

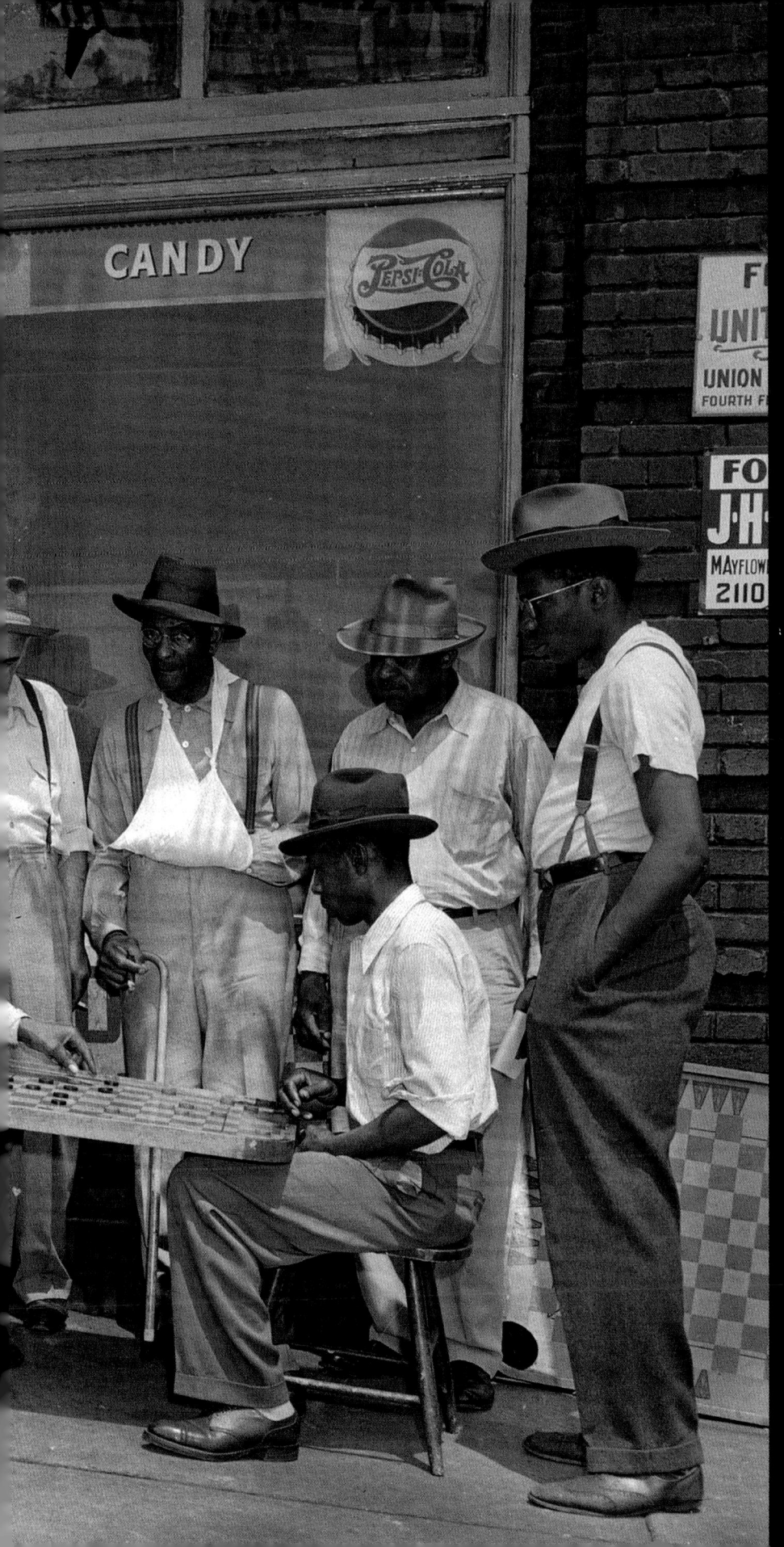

FRONT COVER: *American Gothic*, 1972-style. In Los Angeles and Black. Photo by Barbara DuMetz.

PAGES 2–3: In this image, photographer Robert Sengstacke Abbott captures Billy "Fundi" Abernathy photographing musician Joe Brandon in Chicago in 1967.

TITLE SPREAD: In another rendition of *American Gothic*, "charwoman" Mrs. Ella Watson poses with a mop and broom in front of the American flag in 1942.

LEFT: Residents of Pittsburgh's Hill District watch two games of checkers in front of Babe's Place in this photo by Teenie Harris taken in 1949.

CONTENTS

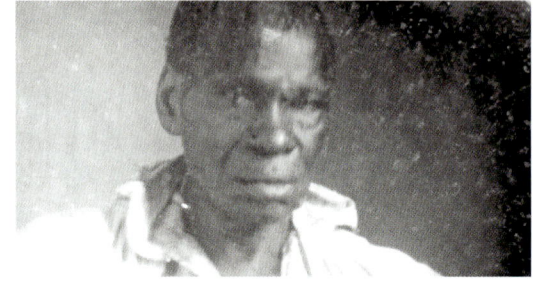

I.   PORTRAITS ^{OF} BLACK HISTORY · 25

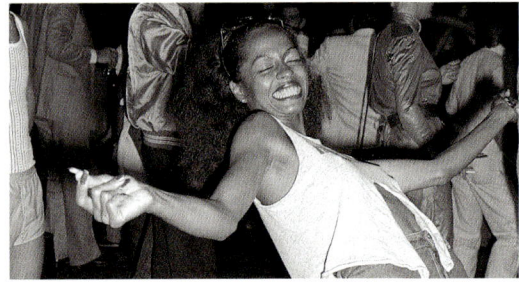

IV.   BLACK CULTURE ^{AS} PEOPLE POWER · 145

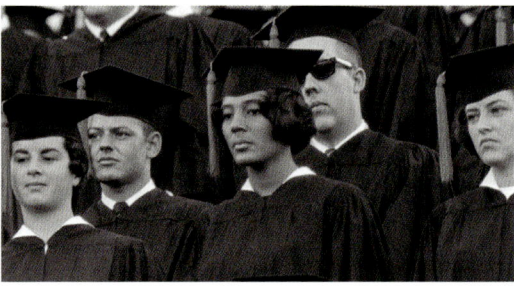

V.   BLACK EDUCATION ^{AS} RESISTANCE · 179

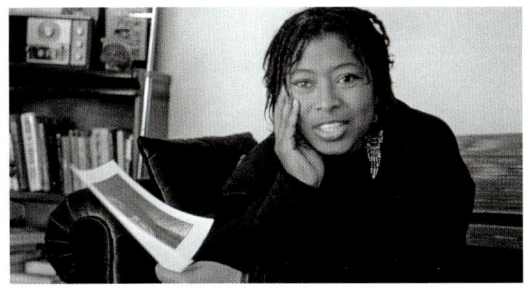

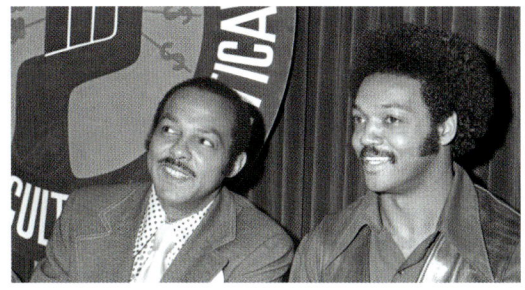

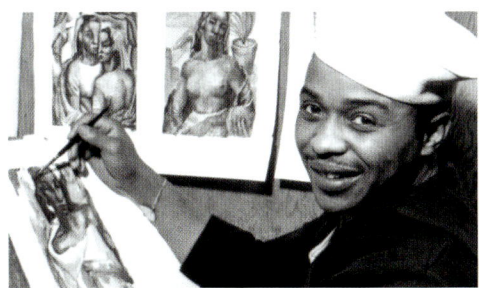

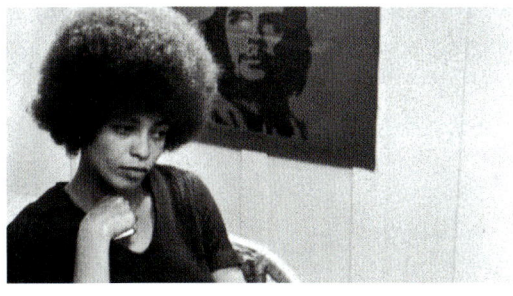

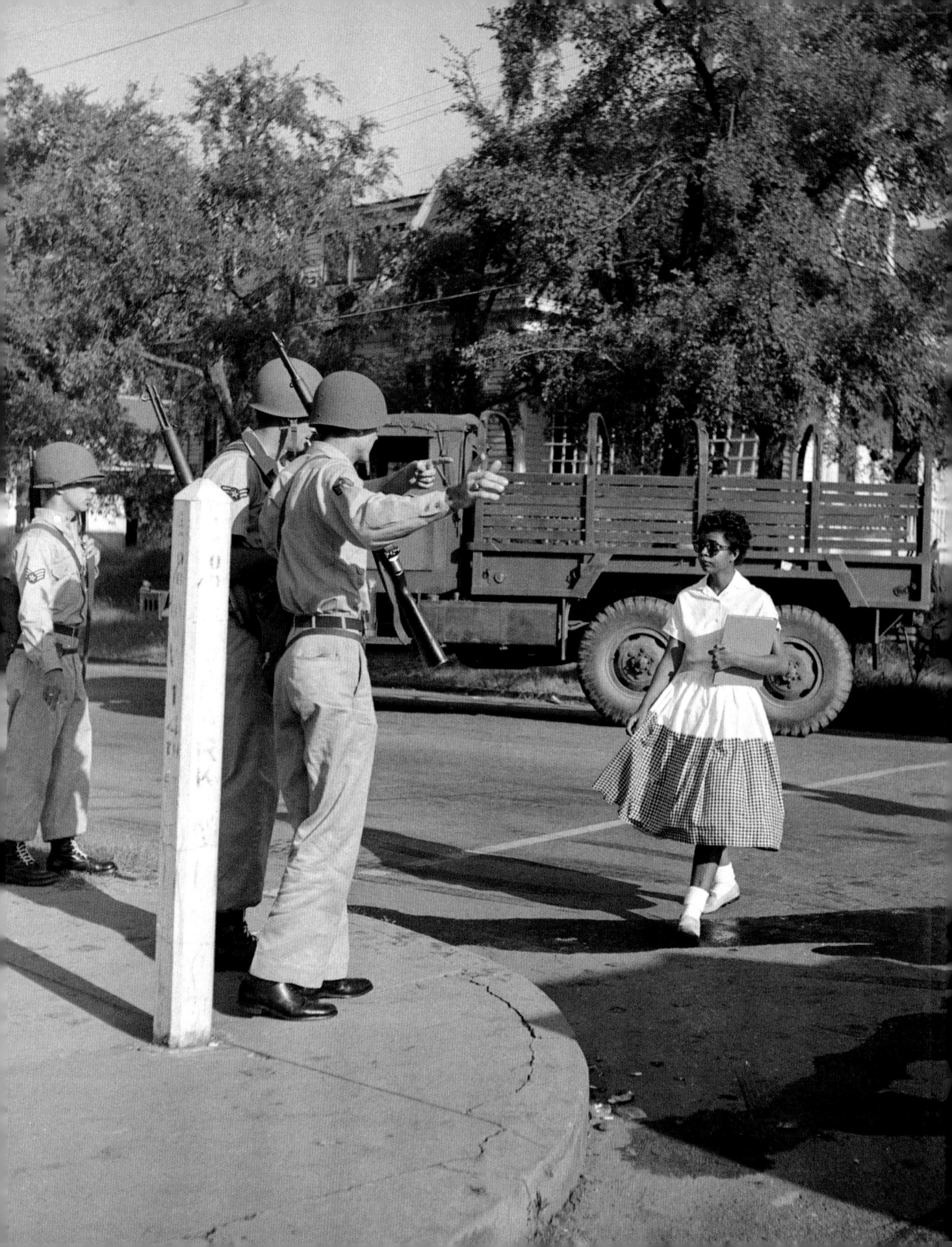

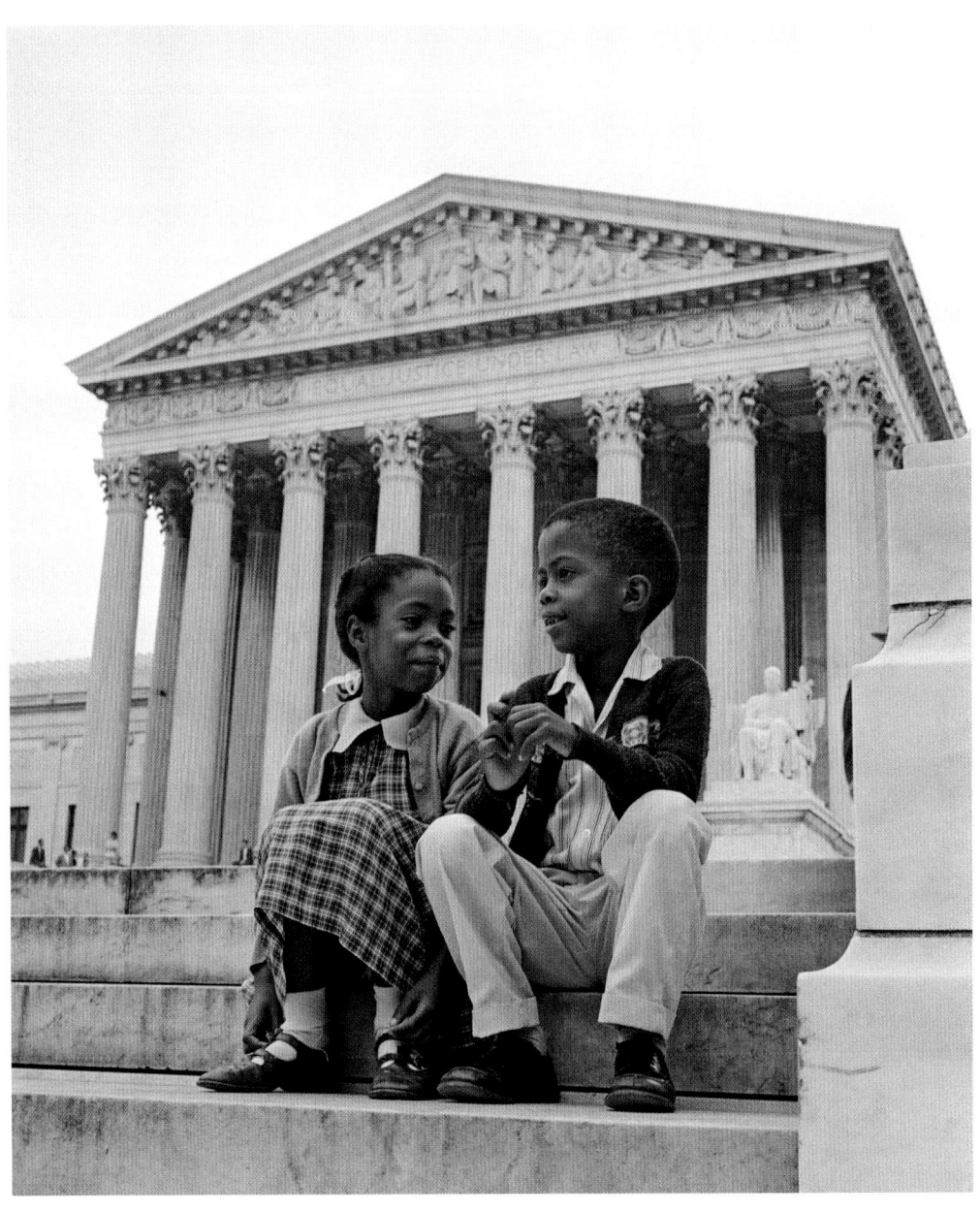

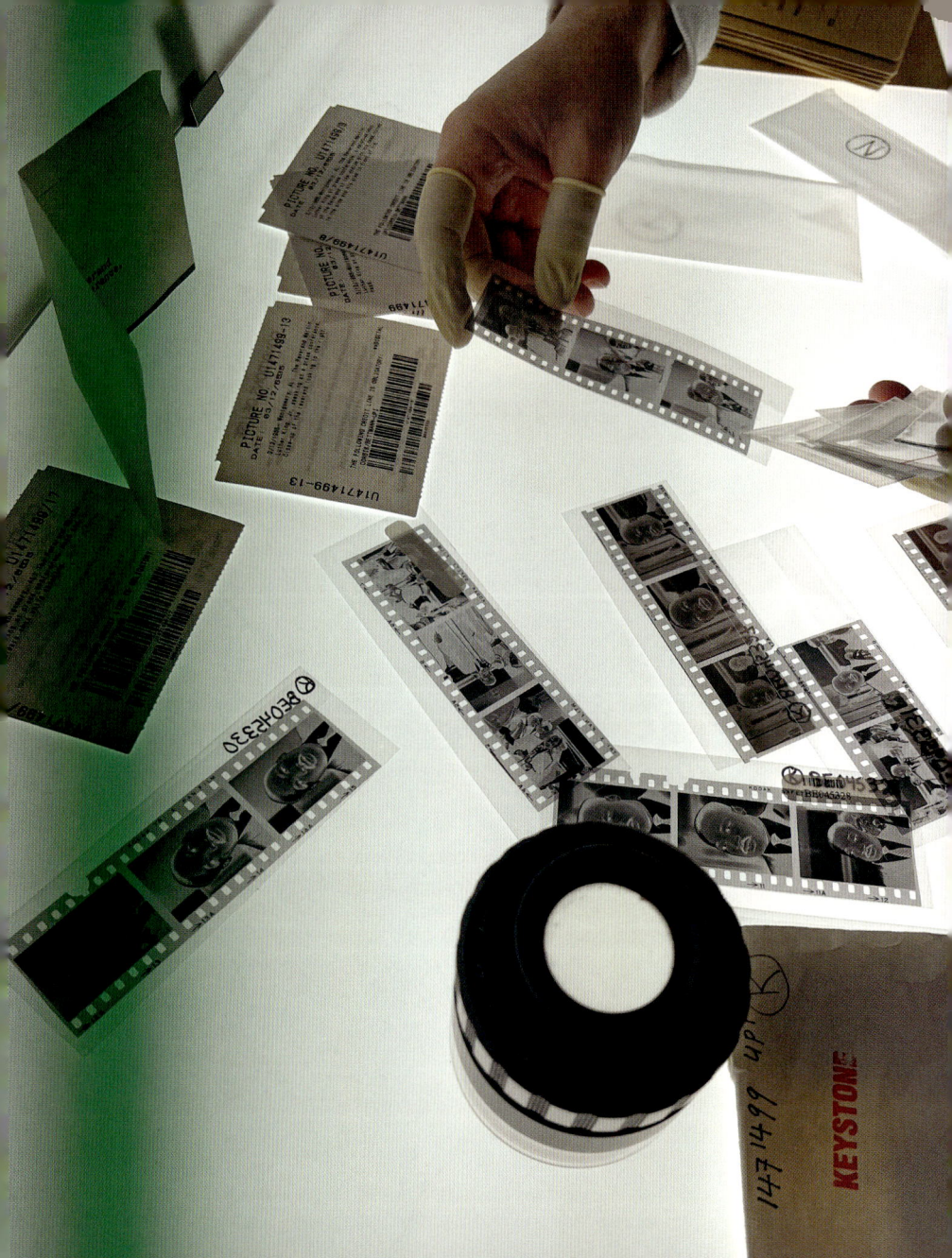

THE POWER OF IMAGES AND STORIES

DANIELA EDMEIER & DAMARIUS JOHNSON

June 2023—Deep underground in rural Pennsylvania, inside the security goliath known as Iron Mountain, our team of historians, archivists, and photography experts gathered around light boxes. We carefully passed around negatives and contact sheets from the 1963 March on Washington, searching in the Getty Images–run Bettmann Archive to unearth photographs for the book you now hold in your hands. Few people have the opportunity to see, much less touch, these precious artifacts of the Civil Rights Movement. Our work that day, in the freezing cold storage where such items are kept, in many ways embodies the spirit of this book: to uncover and publicize previously unseen and underappreciated dimensions of Black history.

Our two-hundred-foot descent into Iron Mountain reminds us that history lost or unseen in the American cultural memory is not forgotten or unknowable. Discovering and sharing these previously overlooked aspects offers a radically reshaped understanding of our past, present, and future—and what is *not* preserved sometimes tell us as much, or more, about our past.

PREVIOUS SPREAD, LEFT: Before she even got to the front door of Central High School in Little Rock, Elizabeth Eckford was turned away by Arkansas National Guardsmen called out by Governor Orval Faubus to keep the school from being integrated in 1957.

PREVIOUS SPREAD, RIGHT: Two children sit in front of the Supreme Court as justices hear arguments of school desegregation in Little Rock, Arkansas.

LEFT: All works of history begin with research in the archive. Here, a member of the Picturing Black History team reviews negatives from Getty Images' archive in Western Pennsylvania.

RIGHT: In 1979 the Dance Theatre of Harlem performed at the Sadler's Wells Theatre in London. These images capture dancers rehearsing for the ballet *Allegro Brillante*.

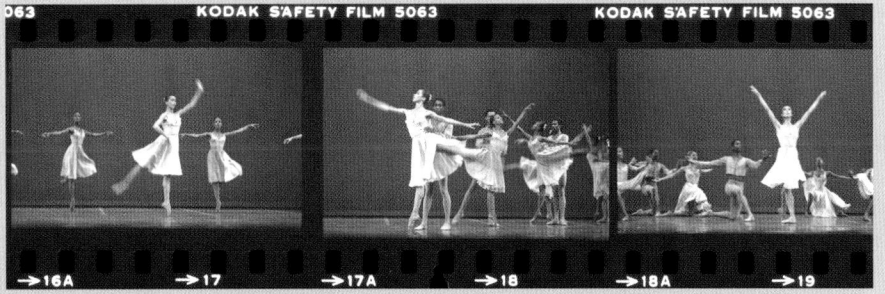

One of our main ambitions is to both uncover and better contextualize Black history in photographs. As a team, we descended into the old mines of Iron Mountain to revisit these files with a contemporary agenda: to seek out stories that may have been overlooked for decades. The whole process of discovering photographs for this book was a richly rewarding collaboration among authors, editors, archivists, and photography specialists.

Bringing these photos and stories to light is critical work. It ensures that we remember Black histories in all their diversity—from stories of oppression and resistance, perseverance and resilience, to freedom dreams, imagination, and joy.

From the nineteenth century to the present, whether defined as Negro history, Black history, or African American history, the study of African-descended communities in the United States has faced perennial obstacles and opposition. Yet Black history has been much more than simply a catalog of stories, figures, and events in the struggle against racial discrimination. It has offered a toolkit of strategies for confronting the persistent difficulties of everyday life and a context for imagining new possibilities for African Americans in American society.

Contemporary Black history is the product of two distinct but overlapping approaches to defining and studying Black life in the United States. The earlier Black history tradition emerged from community-centered reading groups, festivals, and cultural events that traced the interconnected histories, cultures, and lived experiences of African populations across the globe. In 1926, Negro History Week, today known as Black History Month, transformed this celebration of the African world into an annual event to commemorate, retain, and study Black history by celebrating Black youth.

Later, in the mid-twentieth century, African American history emerged from African American historical specialists. As the number of African American historians with PhDs has swelled since the 1960s, the field of

TOP TO BOTTOM:
Photographer Gordon Parks captured these two boys at the Frederick Douglass Dwellings in the Anacostia section of Washington, DC.

Broadway performer Sheila Ellis splits an ice-cream cone with her son after a performance of *Your Arms Are Too Short to Box with God* in 1980.

Harlem, 1972.

Gordon Parks was working the U.S. Office of War Information when he caught this woman and her dog looking out of their apartment window in Harlem in 1943.

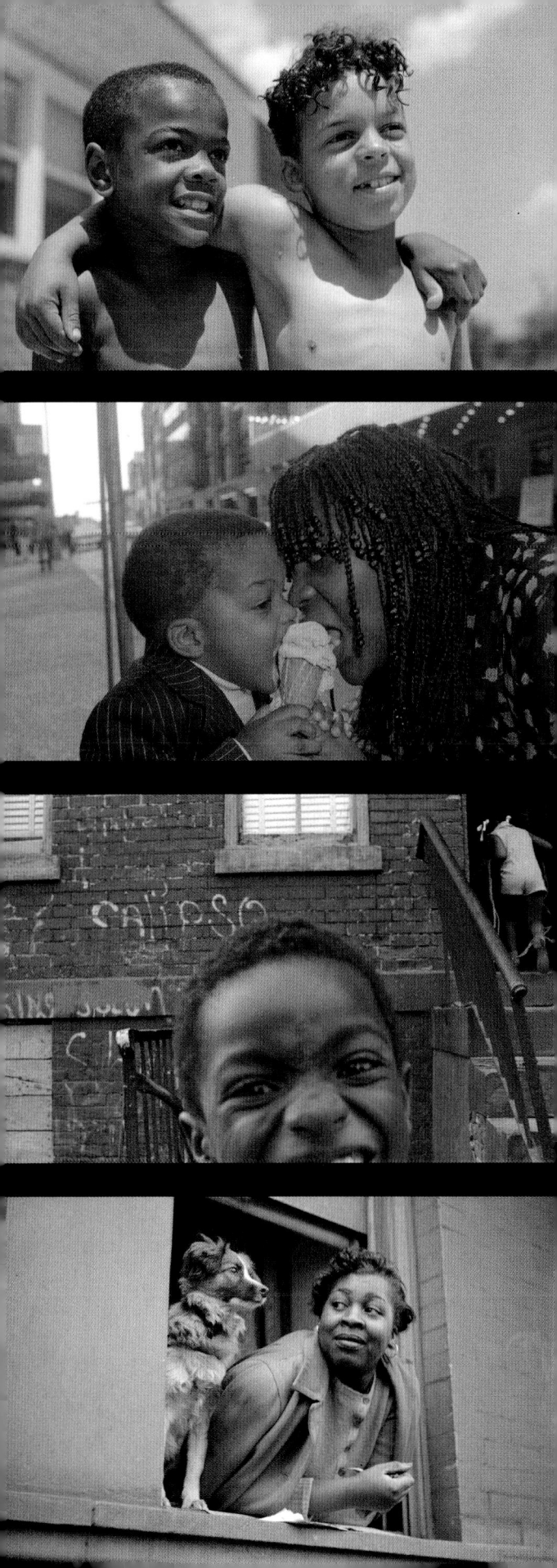

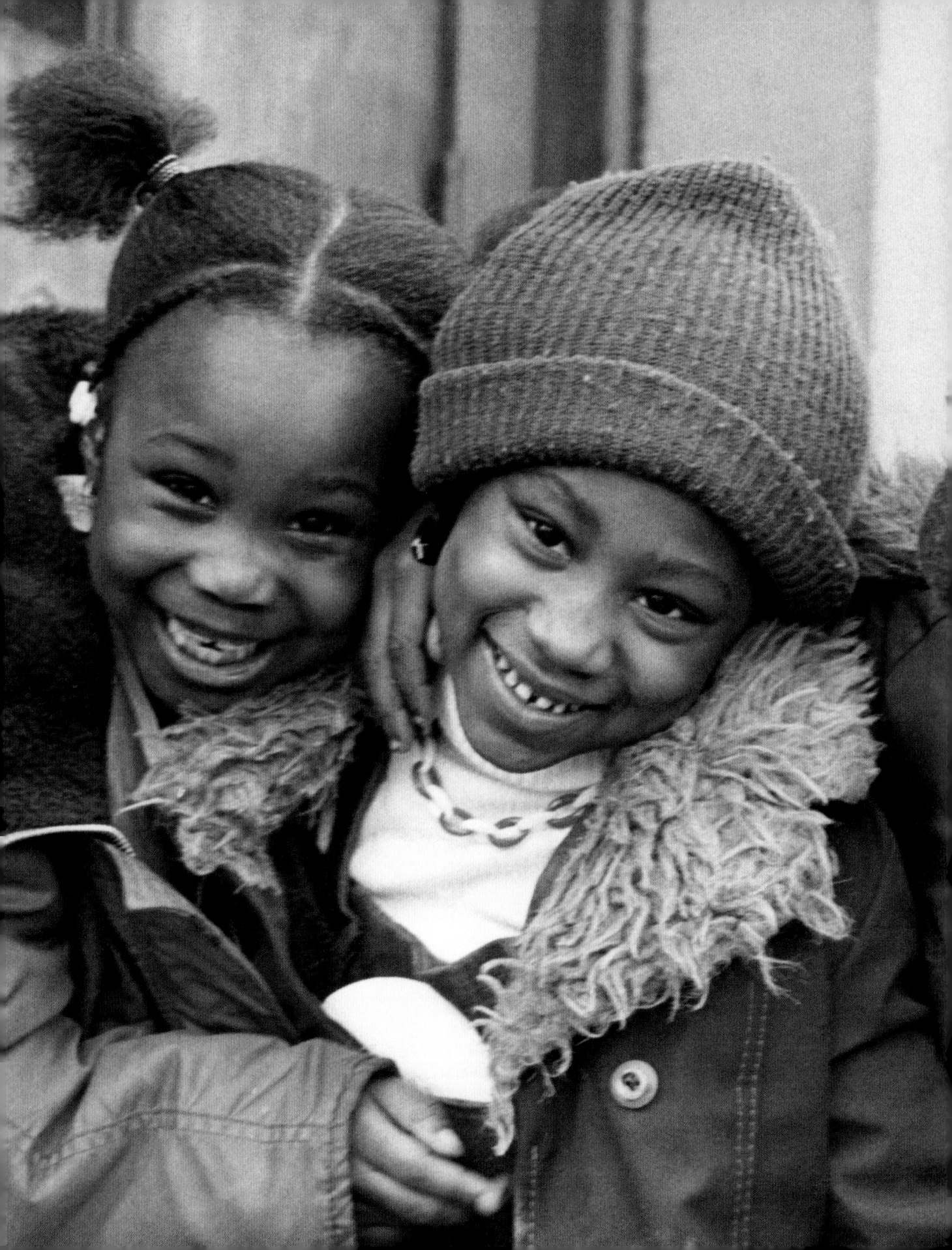

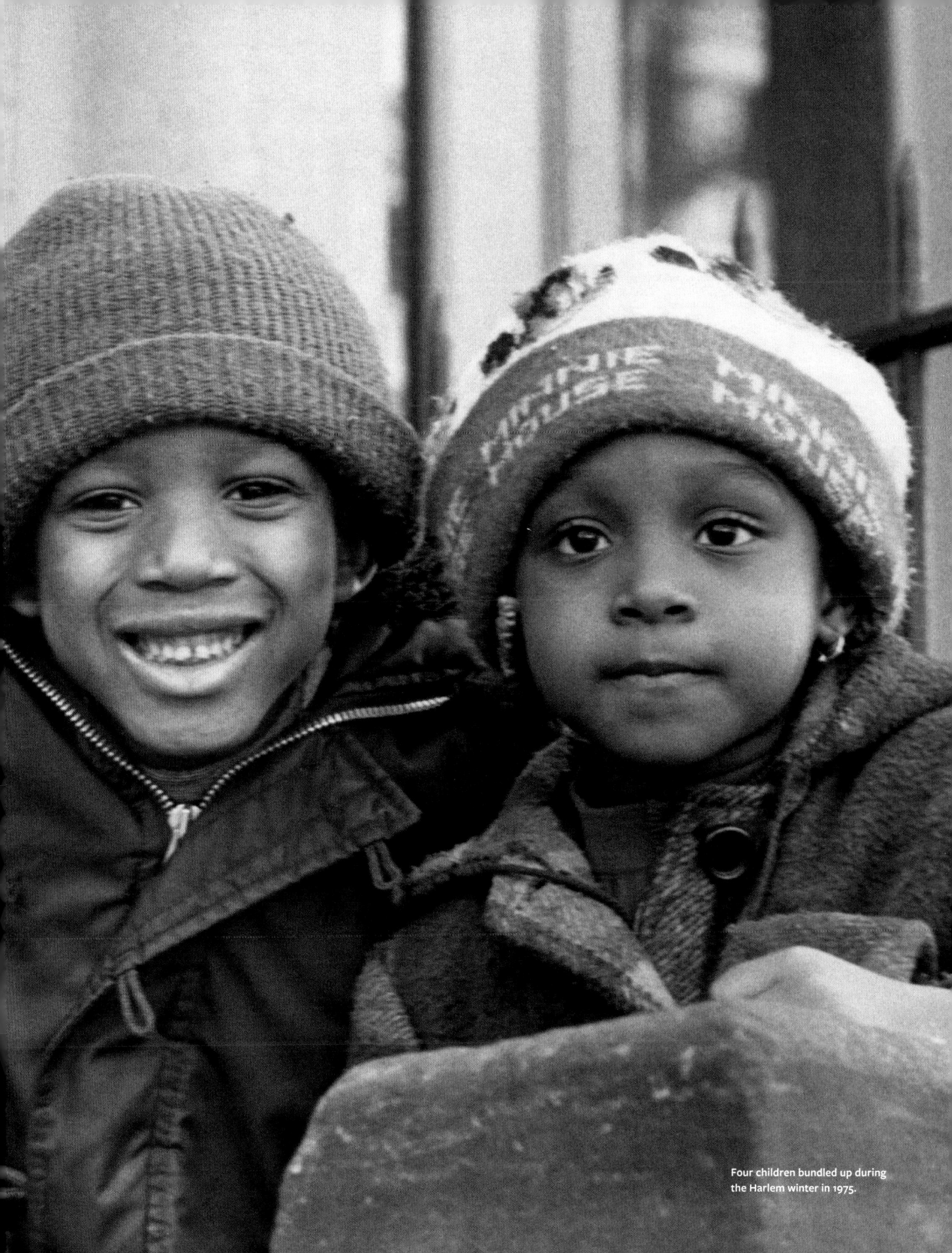

Four children bundled up during the Harlem winter in 1975.

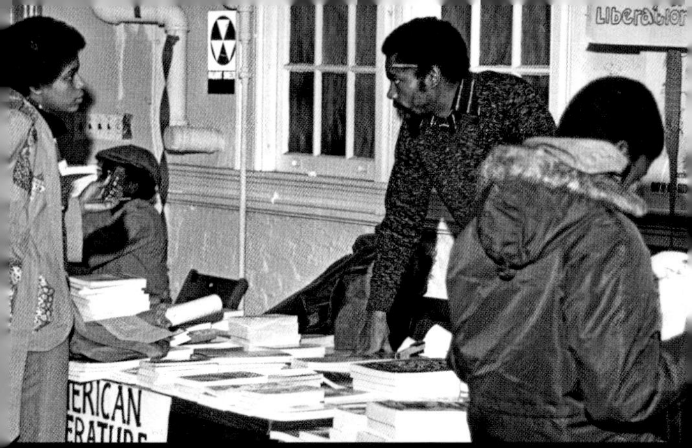

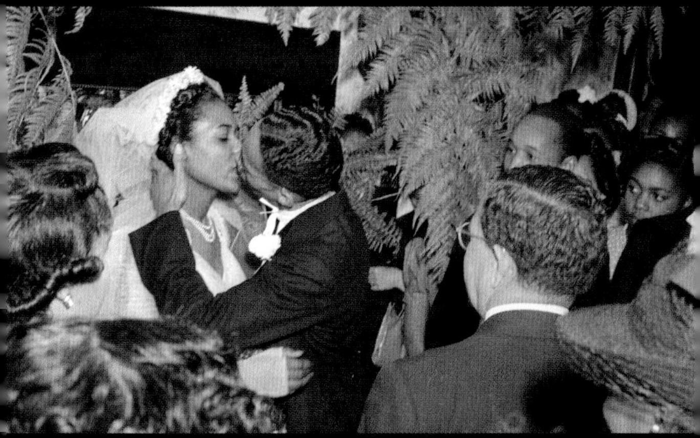

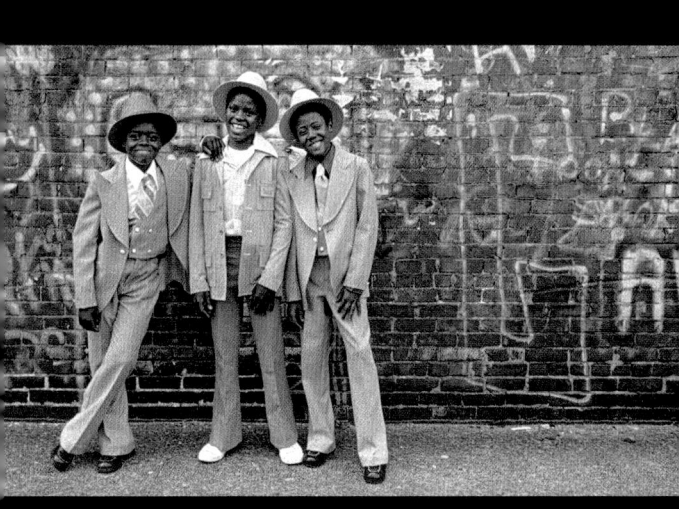
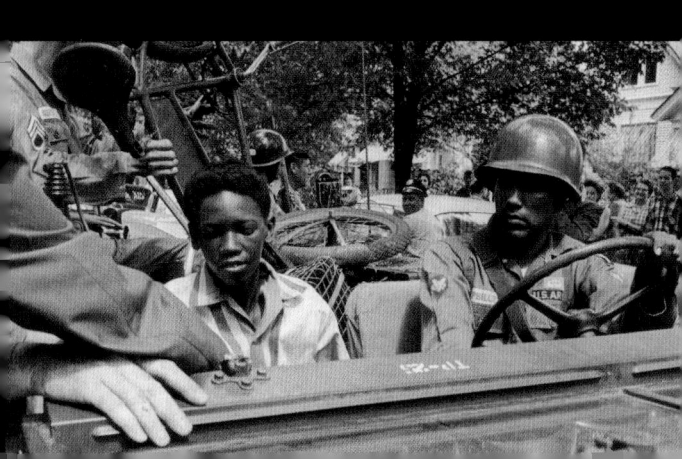

African American history developed a standardized curriculum within higher learning institutions. John Hope Franklin's *From Slavery to Freedom* (1947) constituted an early survey of African American history that established a framework for teaching African American history. Although African American history emerged from the work of professional historians, it was never confined to reading and writing in university classrooms.

In developing a history of the African American experience in its variety, community members and scholars alike embraced photography as a visual record of the enduring connections that sustained Black folk.

Pioneering photographers were both documenting and creating history in making Black life their subject. Photographers like James Presley Ball, James C. Farley, Augustus Washington, and the Goodridge Brothers recognized the significance of the events evolving around them and the urgency of capturing them on film. Generations of Black photographers have followed in their footsteps.

Much like the process of photography, wherein the photographer and subject collaborate, there, too, is a symbiotic relationship between photography and Black history. Photography introduced a new era of self-representation, previously unavailable to African Americans, who had usually been forced to rely on prevalent racist caricatures in the art and media of eras past.

The opening of Black-owned photography studios as early as 1847 reveals the importance that photography played for African Americans—both as subjects and as creators. Figures such as Frederick Douglass and Sojourner Truth—like so many Black people since—were able to use photography as a medium to represent themselves.

Nevertheless, more than 150 years of photography, visual culture, and archival preservation are laden with inherent biases. From the outset, most photographic and film technology was developed around capturing white skin; early photograph developers, such as Eastman Kodak, used white-skinned models to establish norms for a "perfectly" lit and colored image, known as "Shirley cards." Even through the 1990s, film developers were still using

TOP TO BOTTOM:
A book fair featuring titles on Black history and liberation to celebrate Black History Month in 1980.

Lilas King and Clarence Morton seal their wedding in May 1941 in a moment captured by photographer Teenie Harris.

Not yet five feet tall but still looking fine, these boys pose on a street in Harlem in 1975.

Children had to be escorted by National Guard troops to desegregate Central High School in Little Rock.

"Shirley cards" to color-balance photos. As such, these color-balancing practices distorted the variety and complexity of darker skin tones; consequently, events in African American life appeared less frequently, and often were muddled.

We also acknowledge that no matter how methodically we search archives for all the wonders and vagaries of African American life, much was simply left uncaptured. After all, the dominant paradigm of white-owned mainstream media and news coverage, which contributed to Getty Images' collection, did not prioritize Black history. Our hope is that this book will act as a reminder of the living nature of archives—both photographic and literary—and the power of knowledge to forge a more equitable and just future.

We are fortunate to partner with Getty Images, which oversees some 135 million photographs, to visualize our efforts. For while Getty Images are the custodians of the world's largest privately owned commercial archive, only a fraction of their analog catalog has been digitized; the yet-digitized archives provided many new opportunities to explore imagery of Black history. There is a powerful conversation between text and images in this book, exploring the web of intersections among the structural, social, and subjective experiences of the African American past.

Picturing Black History is a photography book that interprets Black history in thirty-five essays across seven major themes. This book features more than 250 photographs from the Getty Images archive, some perhaps familiar to you, and some previously unseen. We sought a balance of the stunning and the everyday, the familiar and the lesser-known, as entry points to learning, studying, and capturing Black history.

Discovery is at your fingertips.

TOP TO BOTTOM: Cooling off on a hot day in July 1983 in the public pool in Astoria, Queens.

Three friends, all smiles.

Toni Morrison won the Nobel Prize in Literature in 1993. Here she basks in the applause of Oprah Winfrey, Angela Davis, Maya Angelou, and others.

President Joe Biden made Juneteenth a federal holiday in 2021. The following year, these three celebrate Juneteeth with some double Dutch in Fort Greene Park, Brooklyn.

FOLLOWING SPREAD: Dancers from the Dance Theatre of Harlem rehearsing and in motion in 1983.

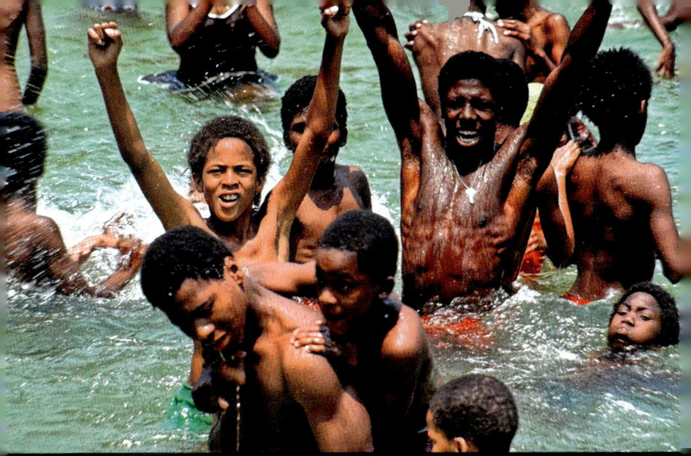

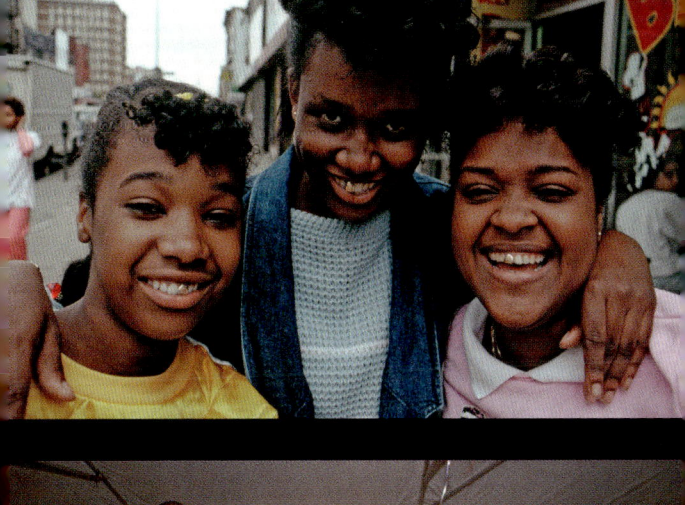

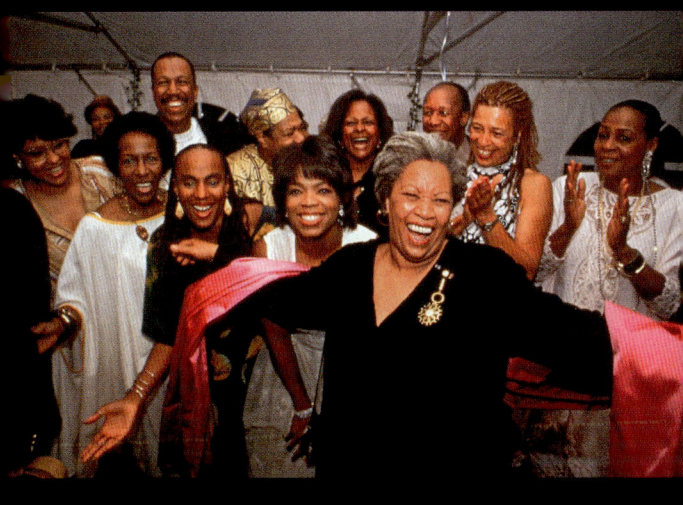

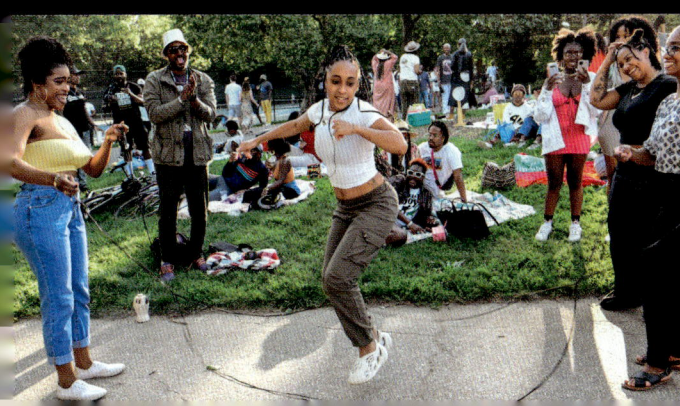

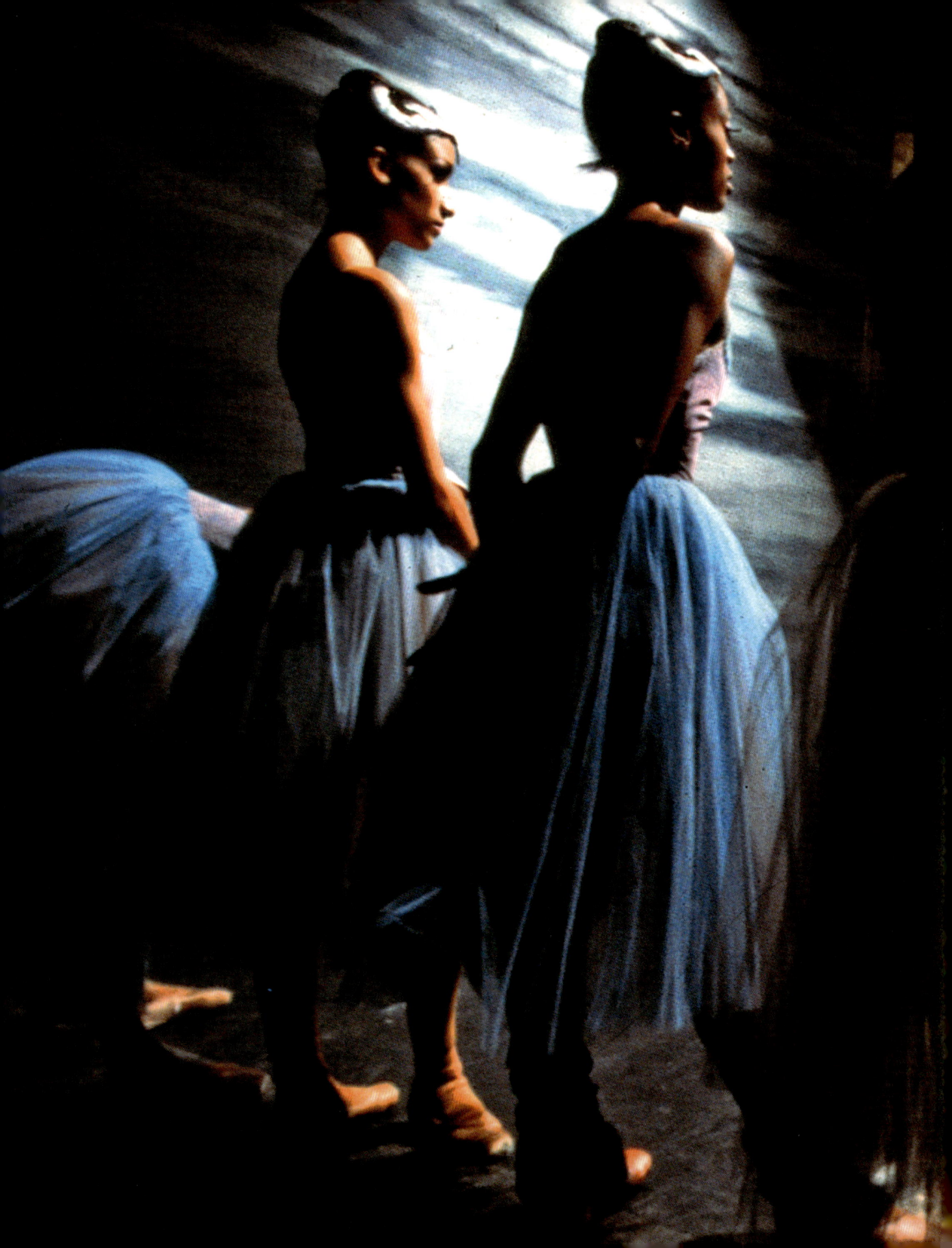

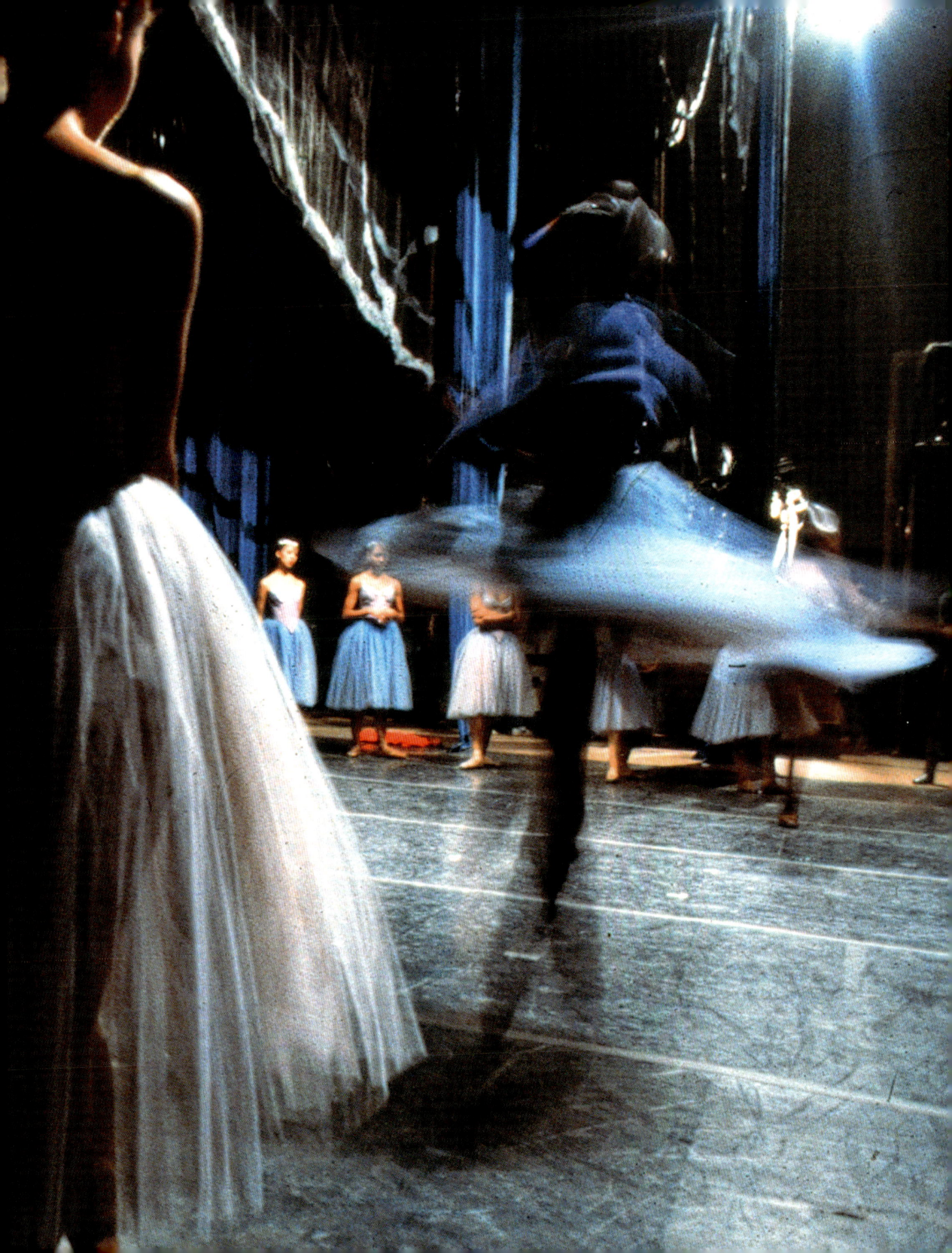

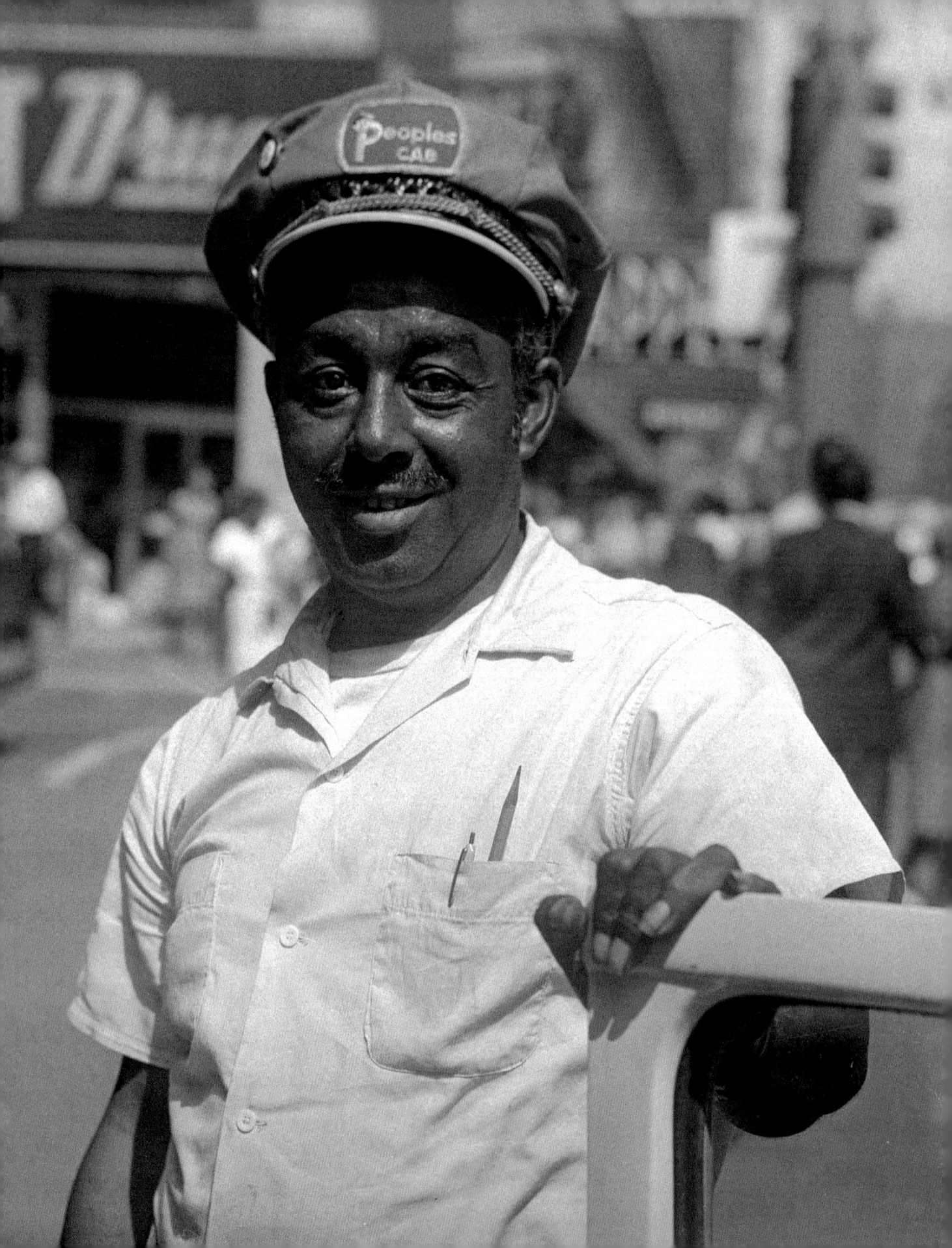

I.

PORTRAITS OF BLACK HISTORY

TODAY, WITH THE ADVANCEMENT OF DIGITAL CAMERA AND CELL CAMERA PHOTOGRAPHY, MANY OF US WALK AROUND WITH SOPHISTICATED CAMERAS IN OUR POCKETS. Though today we often use them to capture the minutiae of daily life, historically, capturing moments on film was more involved. More notable than the requirements of time and money were the conscious decisions about *who* and *what* were worthy of documentation.

African peoples in what would become the United States of America were critical to the foundation of the nascent country, yet photographic evidence of their contributions remain slim. As cameras became more readily available, representation of Black people—from their larger roles in society, to their daily lives in their communities—became ever more pressing and remained so. Photographing key events and lesser-known quotidian moments of Black life has radically shaped American history—and has the potential to radically reshape how we view our nation's history.

What do photographers signal to their viewers by choosing to make something the subject of their photography? How has photography been used, or at times not used, to document the relationship between African Americans and broader American society? How does photography create, or falsify, history even as it documents it? This section is an invitation to investigate the historical and ever-evolving relationship between photography and Black history.

OPPOSITE: Teenie Harris took this picture of cabdriver Edgar Moore in downtown Pittsburgh in August 1960.

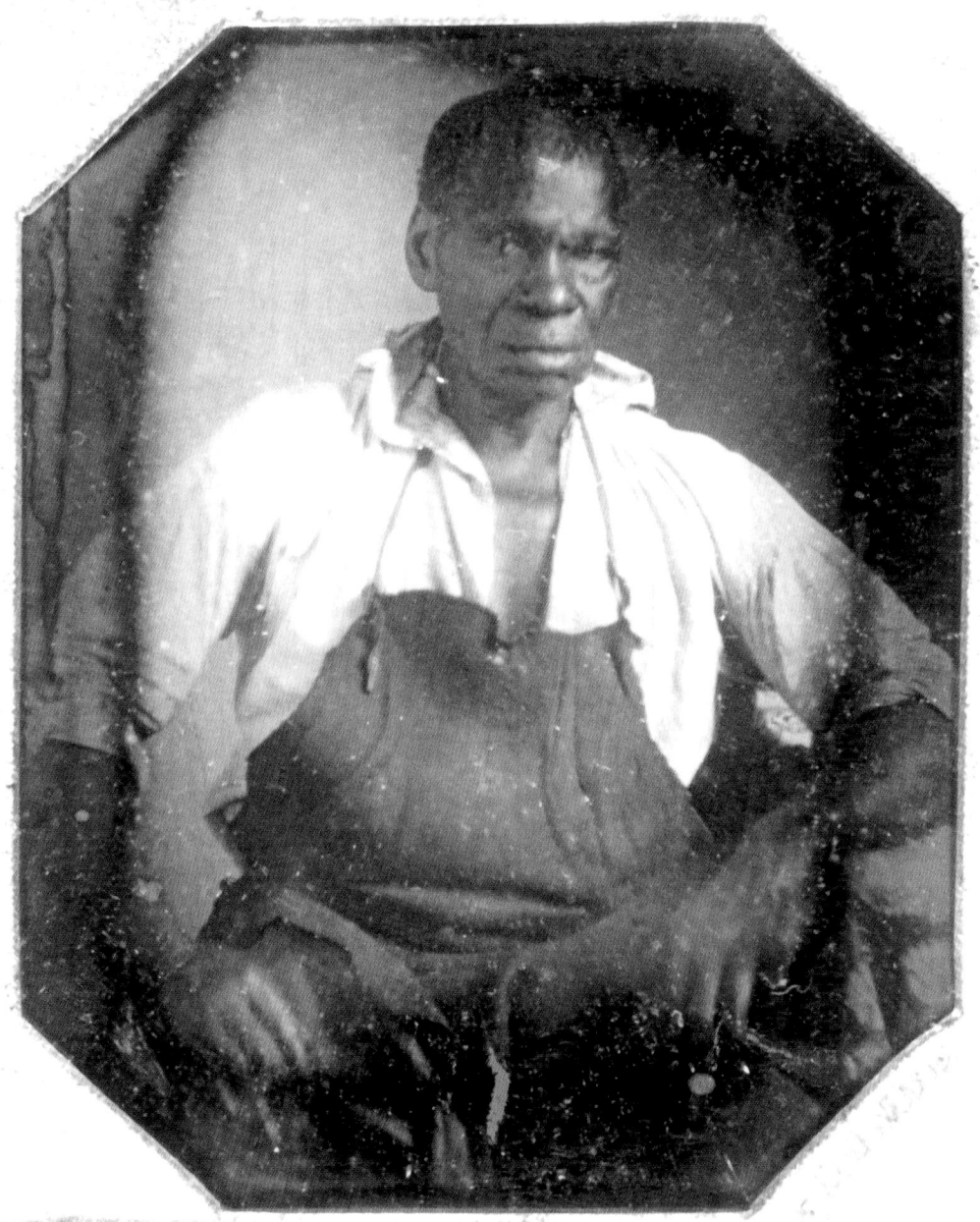

THE BLACK FOUNDERS OF THE UNITED STATES OF AMERICA

LAGARRETT KING

Freedom and agency—critical aspects of U.S. identity throughout its history— were promoted and galvanized by the nation's Black Founders.

The phrase "founding fathers," first coined by Senator Warren Harding, referred to the men who framed and adopted the documents that shaped the United States. These statesmen and politicians attended the Continental Congresses, signed the Declaration of Independence, participated in the American Revolution, and wrote and signed the Constitution.

However, the concept of founding fathers gives short shrift to all the other persons who built the nation: the poor, migrants, soldiers, women, Native Americans, and Black people who have shaped what became the United States of America that we know today. Just as critical to our nation's formation were Black Founders, who set a precedent for freedom for Black Americans and consequently for all Americans across our shared history.

WHO ARE BLACK FOUNDERS?

Black Founders were men and women of African ancestry who lived during colonial times. Their ideas and actions helped form economic systems, win freedom from the British, establish social institutions, and fight racial prejudice in the emerging United States.

Black Founders did not necessarily hold the same philosophical principles as their white counterparts, and in many cases their ideas and practices contradicted white Founders' beliefs about race and democracy. Given their racist exclusion from the larger American society, Black Founders were more concerned about building a country *within* a country—one for Black people.

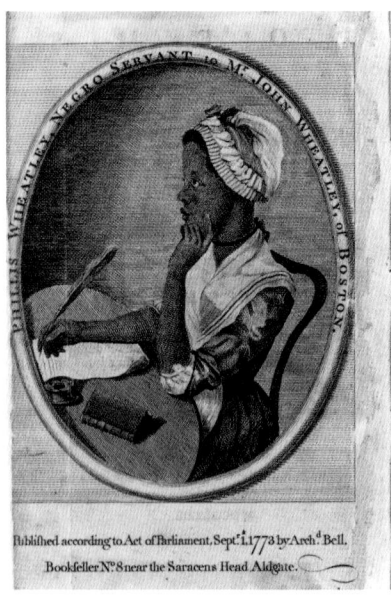
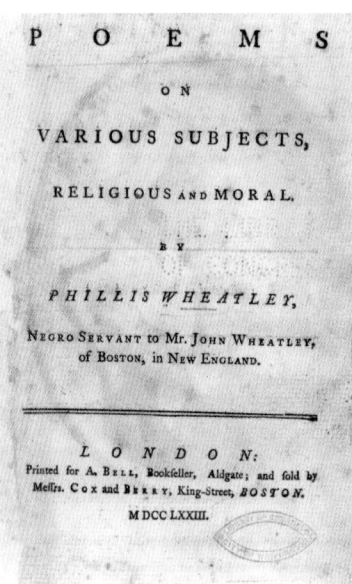
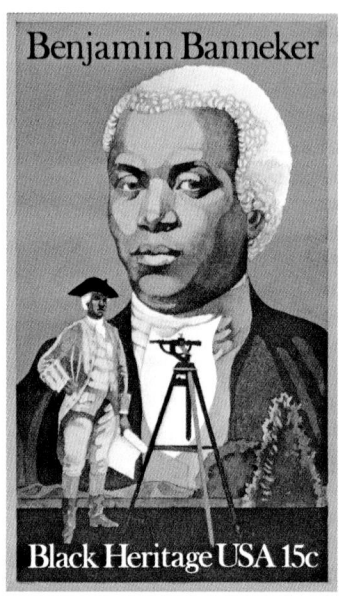
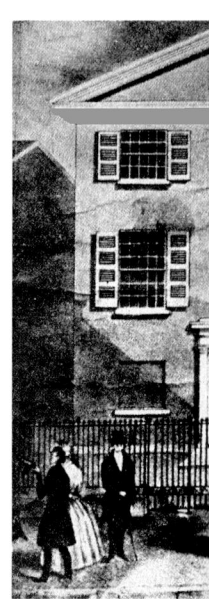

We can classify Black Founders into four groups: the enslaved; revolutionary soldiers; institution builders; and race leaders.

THE ENSLAVED

Enslaved Black people's labor developed the nation's economy. These people sacrificed a great deal for the United States and helped make it a global economic power.

U.S. enslavement yielded considerable profits from cotton, sugar, tobacco, and rice crops. Enslaved Black people also built the infrastructure of this country, including constructing Washington, DC, the nation's capital. And they created their own culture, mixing the practices of various African cultural groups, like the way that African foodways influenced Southern cuisine, which continues to shape American life today.

THE BLACK REVOLUTIONARY SOLDIER

Black persons were instrumental in the American Revolution as soldiers, guides, messengers, and spies. Their presence as soldiers was significant for several reasons.

Their actions repudiated the racist ideas that Black people were not brave or capable of military service. Their presence in arms demonstrated physical strength and required a certain mental capability.

Their military participation also complicated the idea of patriotism—Black soldiers were patriots in the conventional sense of the term. Black revolutionary soldiers were fighting for freedom, not for the thirteen colonies but for themselves individually and for the race as a whole.

For Black revolutionary soldiers, freedom and liberty carried very different meanings than they did for their white comrades. Black American revolutionary soldiers were fighting the "African Americans' Revolution," a separate cause from their white counterparts.

SOCIAL INSTITUTIONS

Black Founders established social institutions for Black life throughout the late 1700s and early 1800s, including religious, social, political, and economic institutions. These places served as safe spaces, allowing Black people to be among their kind without fear of racism.

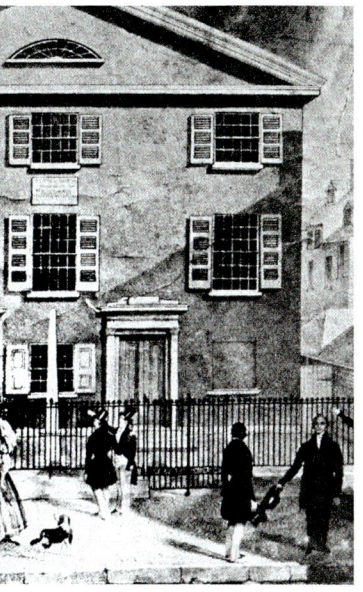

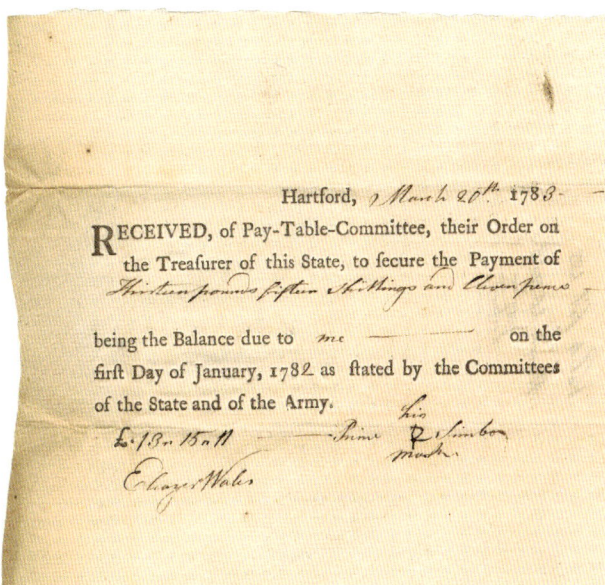

Some examples of these institutions include the African Methodist Episcopal Church, founded by Richard Allen and Absalom Jones and which traces its roots back to 1787, the very year the Constitution was drafted; the *Freedom's Journal*, edited by Samuel Cornish and John B. Russwurm and first published in 1827; and the African Masonic Lodge established by Prince Hall in 1784. Black women, too, founded their own organizations, such as the African Female Benevolent Societies.

RACE LEADERS AND CRITICAL INTELLECTUAL AGENCY

The fourth category of Black Founders comprised race leaders who promoted what I have termed *critical intellectual agency*—how Black Founders challenged the philosophical, social, and moral underpinnings of United States' alleged egalitarianism. Critical intellectual agency was an intellectual space for Black Founders to promote racial justice and repudiate white Founders' views about Black Americans and race.

Throughout the eighteenth and nineteenth centuries, Black Founders wrote speeches, pamphlets, and newspaper articles about their rights to full citizenship, cleverly and sometimes subversively using the same ideas promoted by white Founders. According to the Black Antislavery Writings Project, more than 1,500 documents were written by Black people about their rights to freedom and ideas about race. Persons such as David Walker, Daniel Coker, and Phillis Wheatley promoted racial justice and contradicted the era's prevailing racial "theories."

Benjamin Banneker's letter to Thomas Jefferson, written on August 19, 1791, articulates a view of race that stood in opposition to the prevailing one of the times. Banneker—a scientist, inventor, and astronomer—was best known for his contribution to surveying Washington, DC, and for his almanacs. His 1792 almanac contained a rebuttal letter to then Secretary of State Thomas Jefferson about his writings on race. Jefferson wrote about his conflict with race, stating that the institution of slavery was evil, but he also wrote that Black people were naturally inferior to white people.

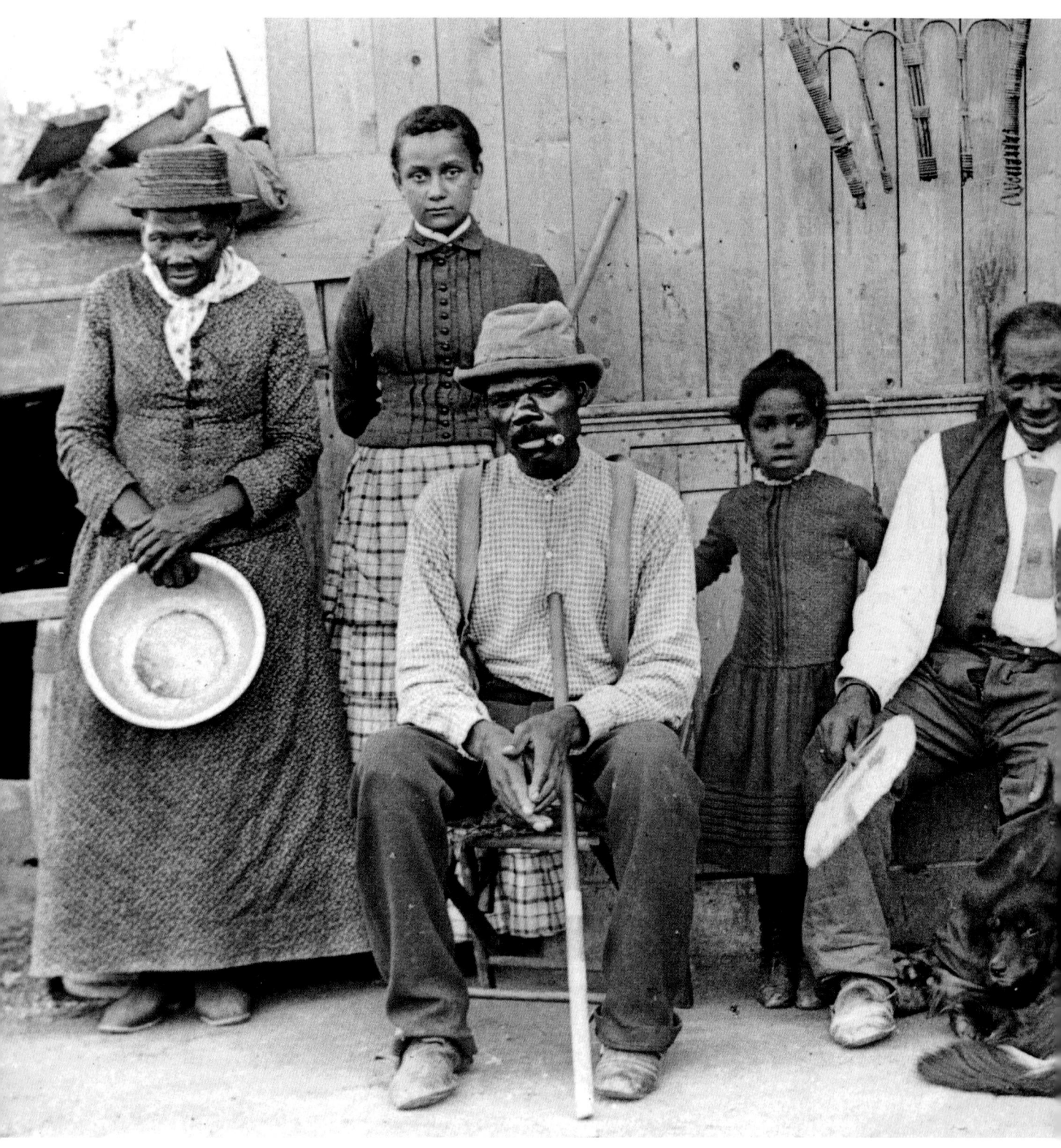

PORTRAITS OF BLACK HISTORY

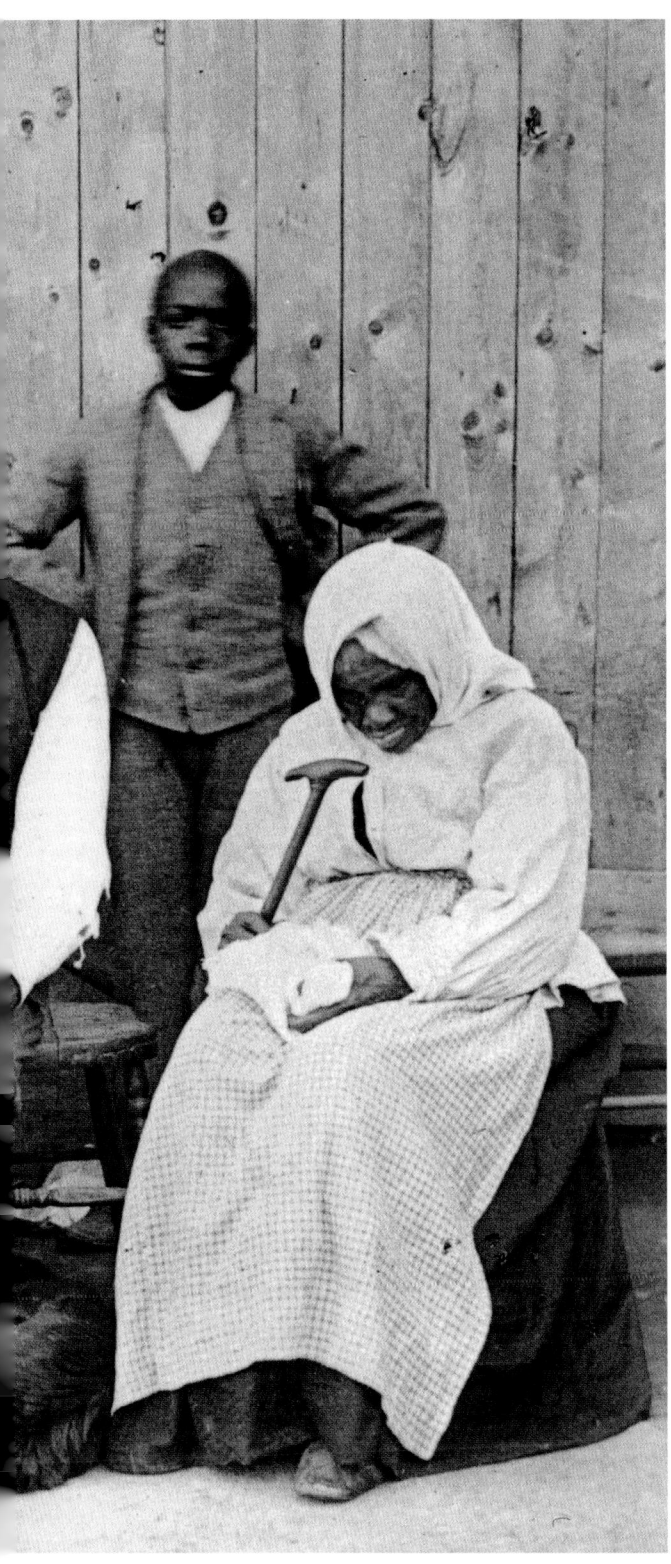

Banneker challenged Jefferson to rescind his proslavery stance, support abolition, and reevaluate his thoughts about Black people's intellectual capacities. He chastised Jefferson's moral authority as well. Banneker's letter became a commentary on the egregious racialization in America and established the antecedent for antislavery advocacy.

Black Founders such as Banneker set a precedent for social justice. They understood that the country founded on the principle of equality was, in fact, deeply racist and did not apply that principle to all. They attempted to fix that error. They challenged white Founders' misguided racial prejudices and made their voices heard. Black Founders established what we can think of as a separate nation within a nation, and in so doing they were uniquely American.

LEFT: Friends and family gathered on Harriet Tubman's porch in Auburn, New York, sometime in the 1880s. Tubman stands at the far left.

FOLLOWING SPREAD: In 2019 artist Dread Scott organized a reenactment of the 1811 slave rebellion in St. John the Baptist Parish, Louisiana. The blue banner is decorated with cosmological symbols that slaves brought with them from Kongo.

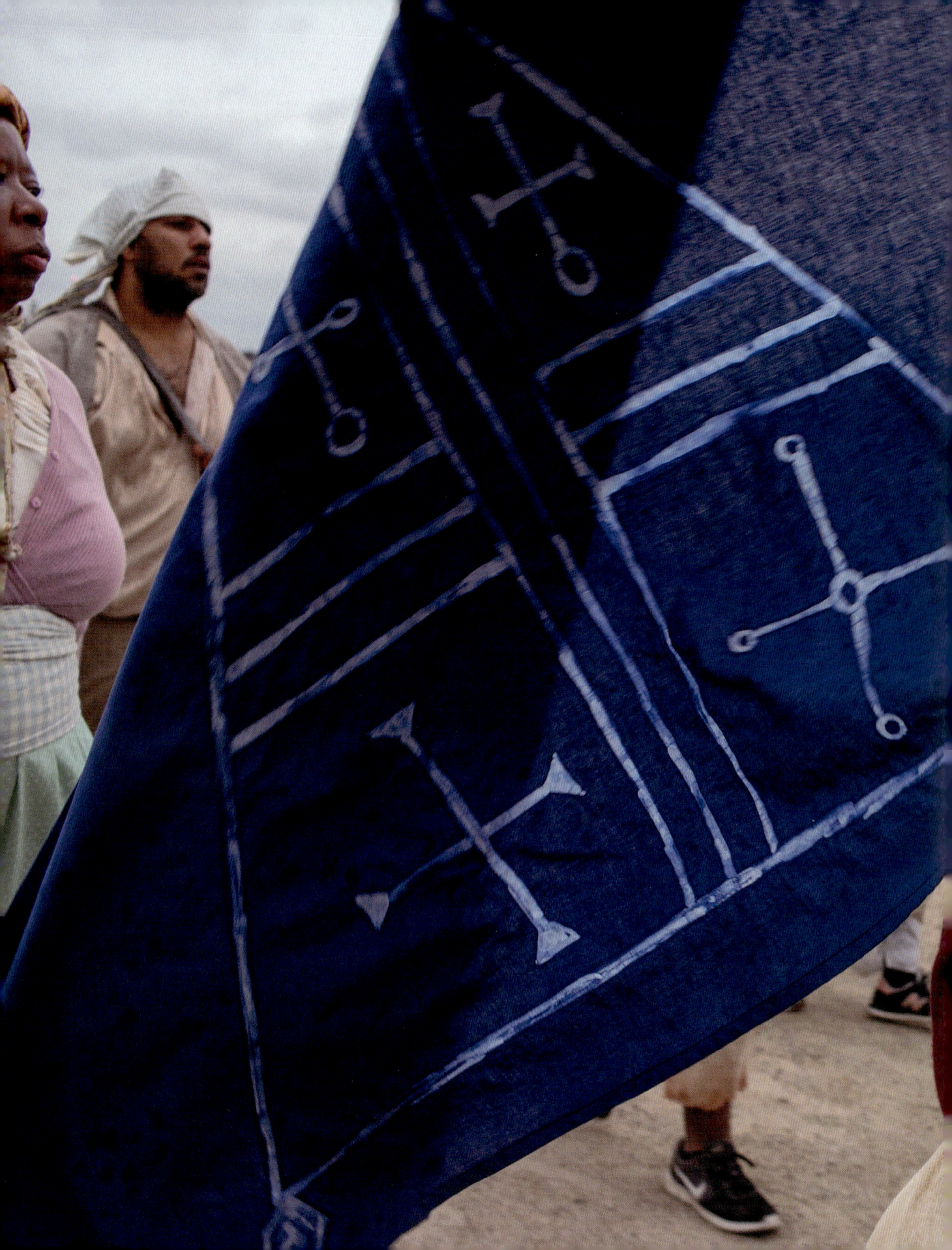

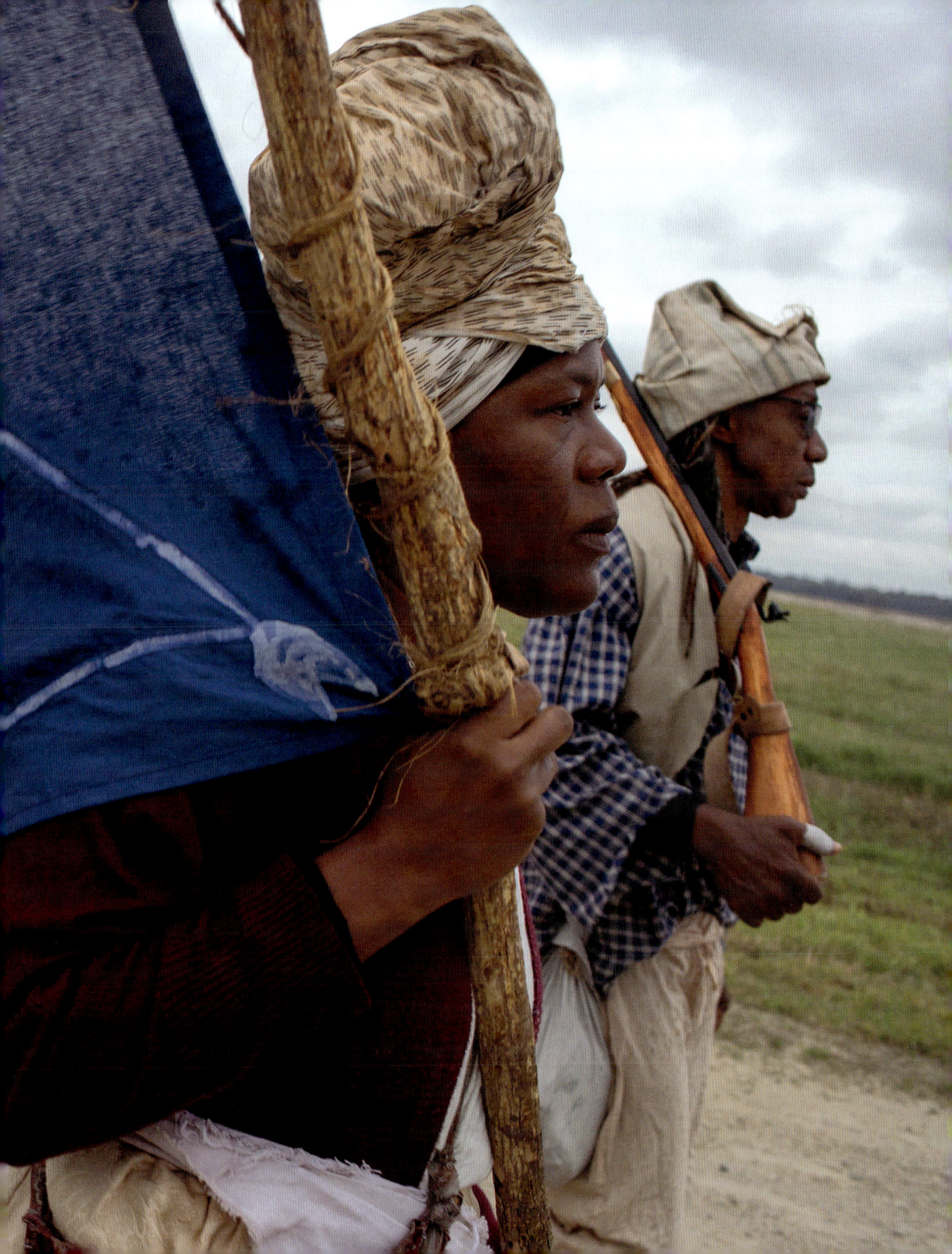

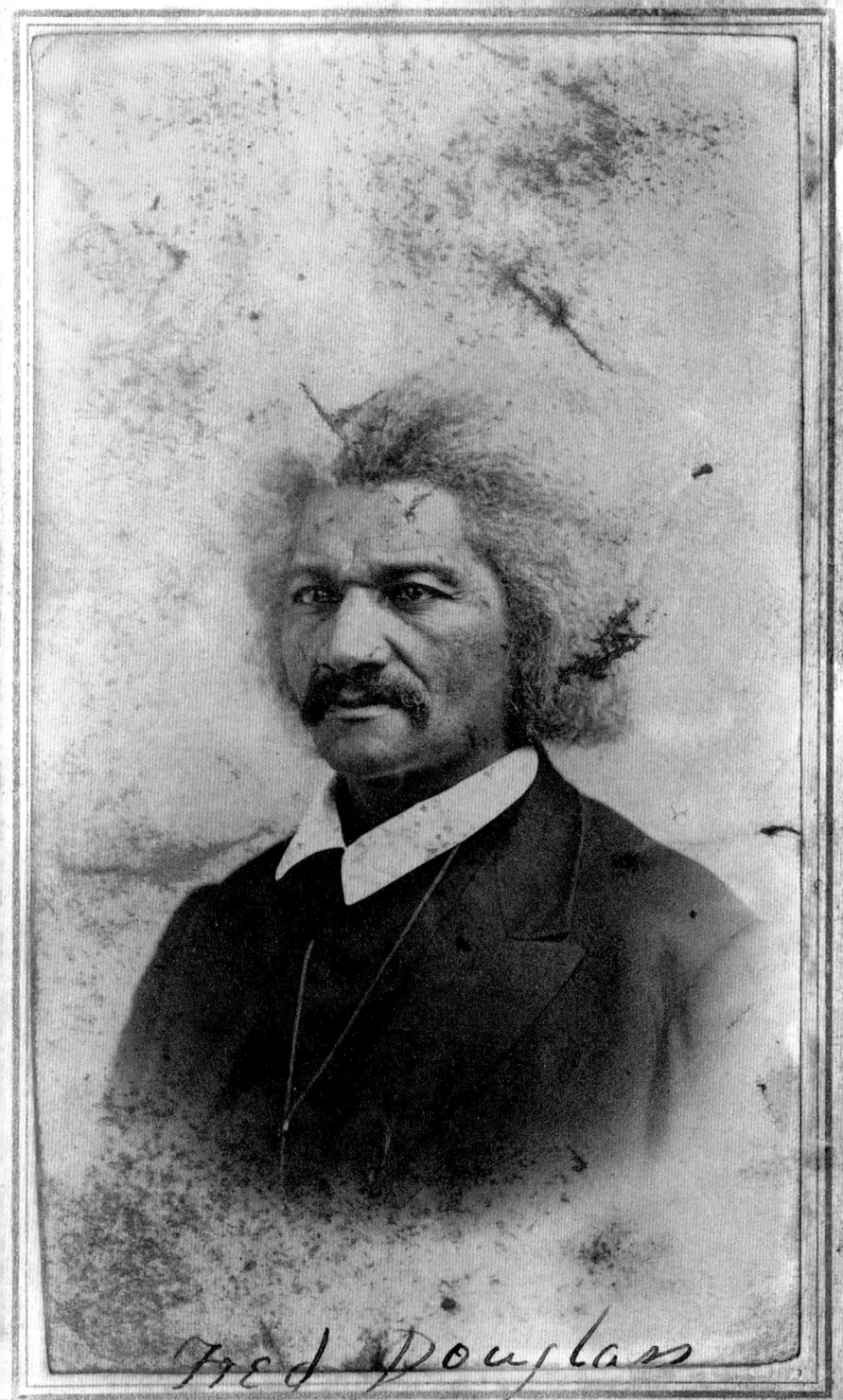

Fred Douglass

PORTRAITS OF A BLACK DAGUERREOTYPIST

CEDRIC ROSE

The photographer, activist, and entrepreneur James Presley Ball
helped many see themselves anew.

In his life and work, the Black daguerreotypist James Presley Ball (1825–1904) embodied the power of self-representation made available to Black people, through photography, for the first time in nineteenth-century America.

Photography's power was also put into words by one of Ball's subjects, Frederick Douglass, who sat for a portrait by Ball in Cincinnati, in January of 1867 (facing page). Douglass must have had many questions for Ball while the photographer set up his camera for the long exposure required to create this image. Photography fascinated Douglass. It was the subject he had chosen to speak about at Boston's Tremont Temple on December 3, 1861.

"The humblest servant girl may now possess a picture of herself such as the wealth of kings could not purchase fifty years ago," Douglass said in an 1861 lecture, "Pictures and Progress," the first of four lectures he delivered on photography.

While those words seem prescient of the digital age, Douglass was talking about the carte de visite, of which this portrait is an example. The affordability and availability of these photographic calling cards allowed Black people agency over their personal image, standing in stark contrast to commonly used derogatory pictures that perpetuated their subjugation. Douglass understood the value images lent to a sense of identity—an opportunity Ball enabled at the many studios he owned and operated.

Ball was born in Frederick County, Virginia, to free Black parents. He learned daguerreotyping from another "freeman of color," the Boston-based John B. Bailey. After working as a traveling daguerreotypist, Ball settled in Cincinnati in 1848, opening studios and galleries close to the neighborhoods of Bucktown and Little Africa, where many Black people's homes sometimes served as stops on the Underground Railroad.

35

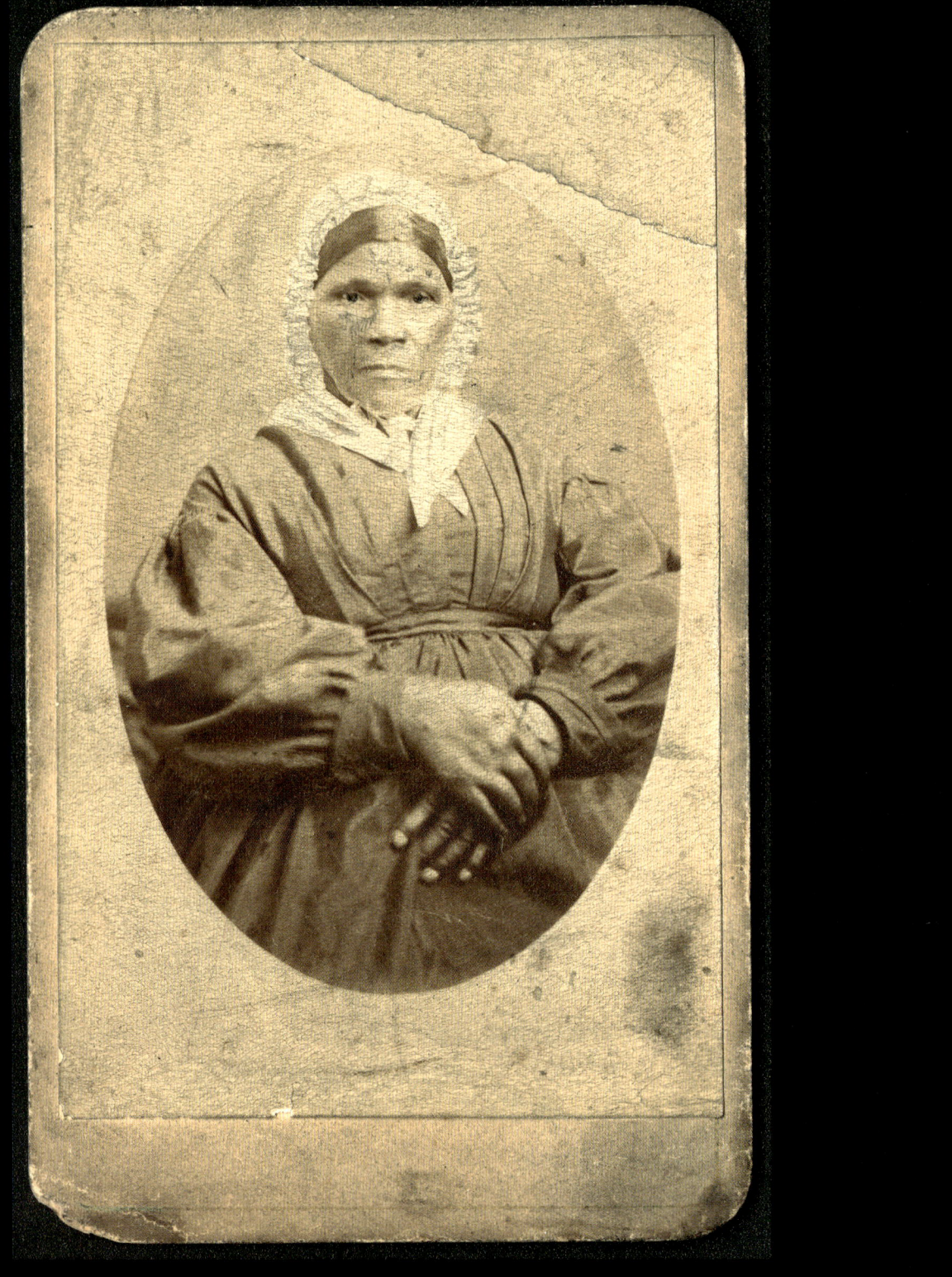

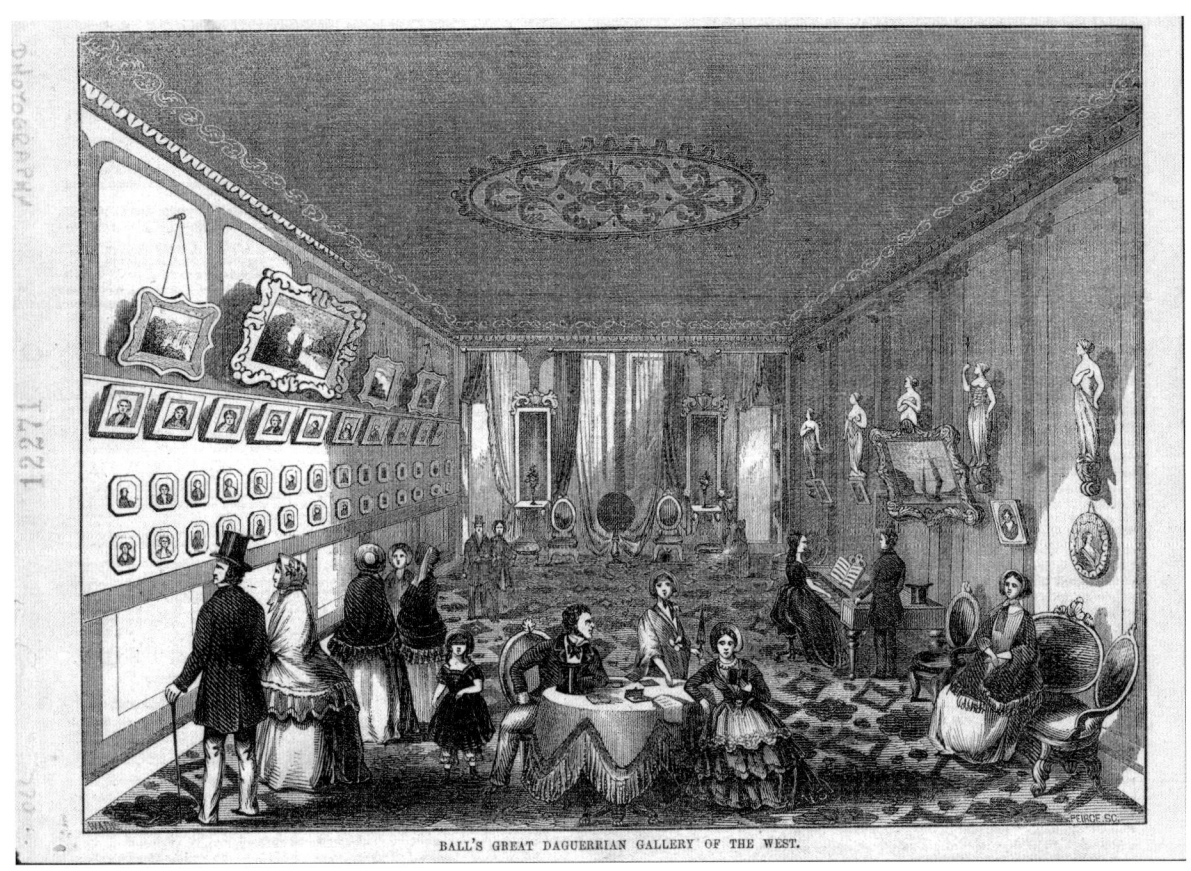

BALL'S GREAT DAGUERRIAN GALLERY OF THE WEST.

Ball brought his extended family to Cincinnati, including his mother, Susan Ball, pictured here. Ball's brothers Thomas and Robert G. Ball, and brother-in-law Alexander Thomas, became business partners.

"Ball's Great Daguerrean Gallery of the West" opened on New Year's Day, 1851. It quickly earned a reputation as the finest photographic gallery west of the Alleghenies. He photographed P. T. Barnum, the Swedish opera singer Jenny Lind, and members of Ulysses S. Grant's family. While traveling in England, *The London Times* reported, Ball photographed the likes of Queen Victoria and Charles Dickens.

With success came the means to support the antislavery cause. In collaboration with other Black artists, including the landscape painter Robert Seldon Duncanson, Ball created a panoramic, 2,400-square-yard scrolling canvas depicting the horrors of slavery. Originally shown in Cincinnati and Boston, this work is now lost, but is described in an 1855 pamphlet printed by the abolitionist Achilles Pugh.

Ball's support of Black artists extended to other mediums. He adopted and financially supported the musical education of Ella Sheppard, who fled to Cincinnati fearing re-enslavement. Sheppard went on to be a founding member of the Fisk Jubilee Singers and a confidante of Douglass's. Ball was also involved in an unsuccessful scheme to bring the blind piano prodigy "Blind Tom" Wiggins north. After emancipation, Wiggins remained in the custody of his enslaver.

This portrait of Wallace Shelton Polk typifies Ball's work. The young man's stance is relaxed against a formal, neoclassical backdrop. He projects precociousness and promise in the face of whiteness. Ensconced in opulence, he stands on par with royalty.

Financial difficulties led to Ball's departure from Cincinnati in the 1870s. He opened studios in Minneapolis, Minnesota, and Helena, Montana, where he recorded events such as the hanging of William Biggerstaff, convicted of a murder for which he claimed self-defense. Ball's photo-documentation of the execution rebuked a system that routinely perpetrated violence against Black bodies.

Ball lived briefly in Seattle, Washington, establishing studios there with his son J. P. Ball Jr. while the latter established a law practice. Poor health prompted Ball's final move to Honolulu, Hawaii, where he died on May 4, 1904.

Ball reclaimed Black image-making from white hegemony. The studios he founded and Black photographers and artists he nurtured continued a legacy of wielding the camera as a weapon against bigotry.

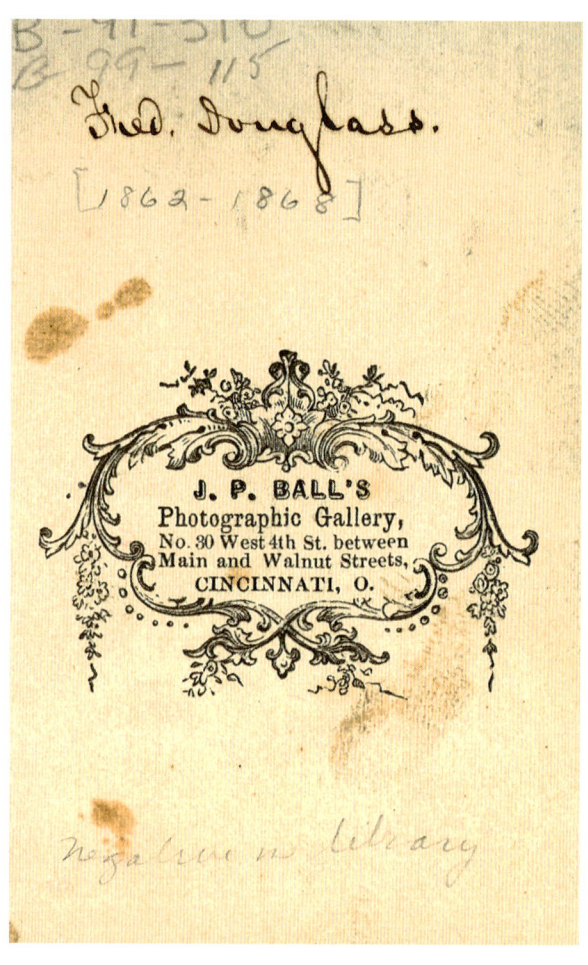

ABOVE: The backside of the 1867 photo of Frederick Douglass at the beginning of this chapter, showing Ball's studio stamp.

RIGHT: Young Wallace Shelton Polk stands for his portrait on a plush chair in the 1870s.

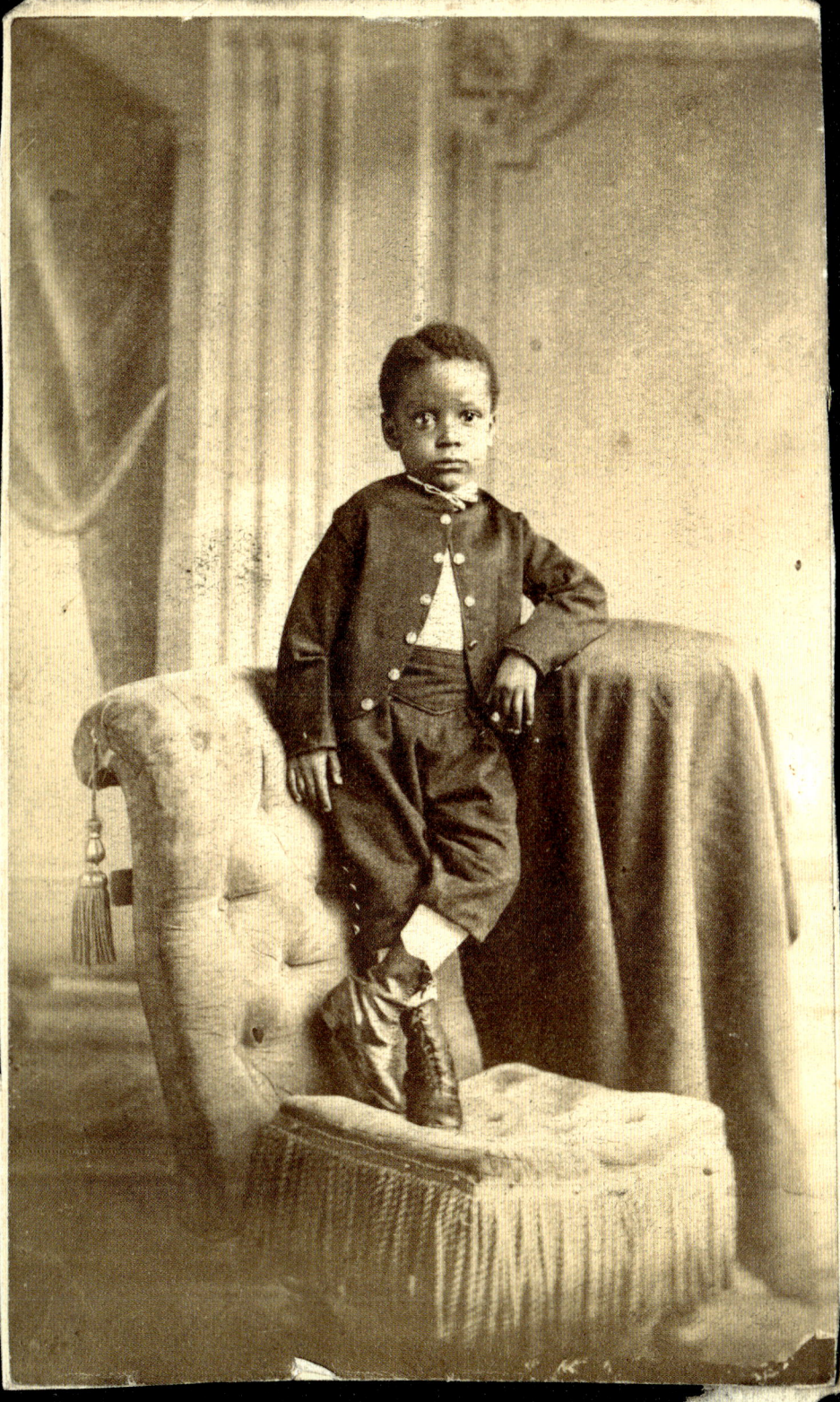

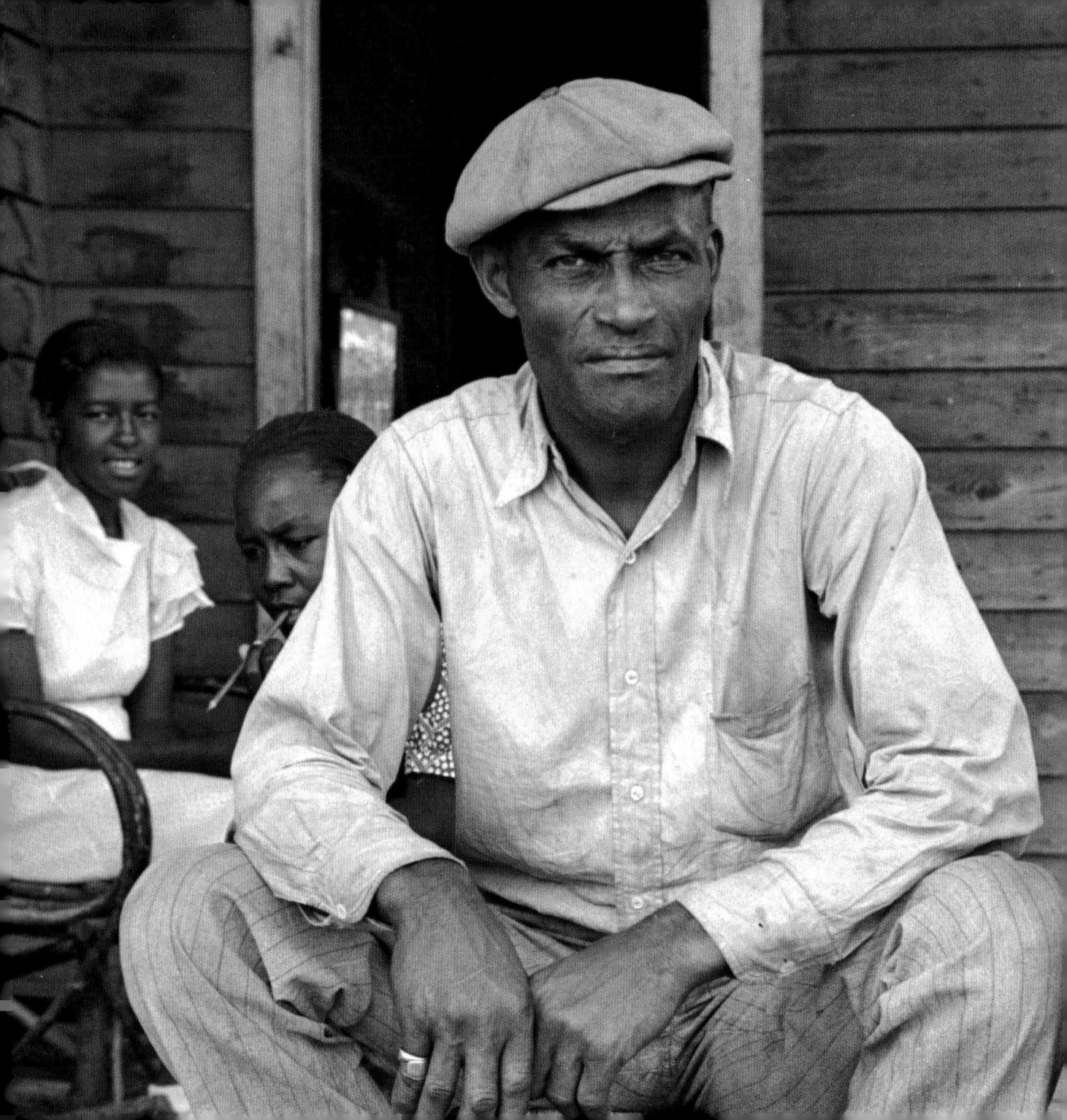

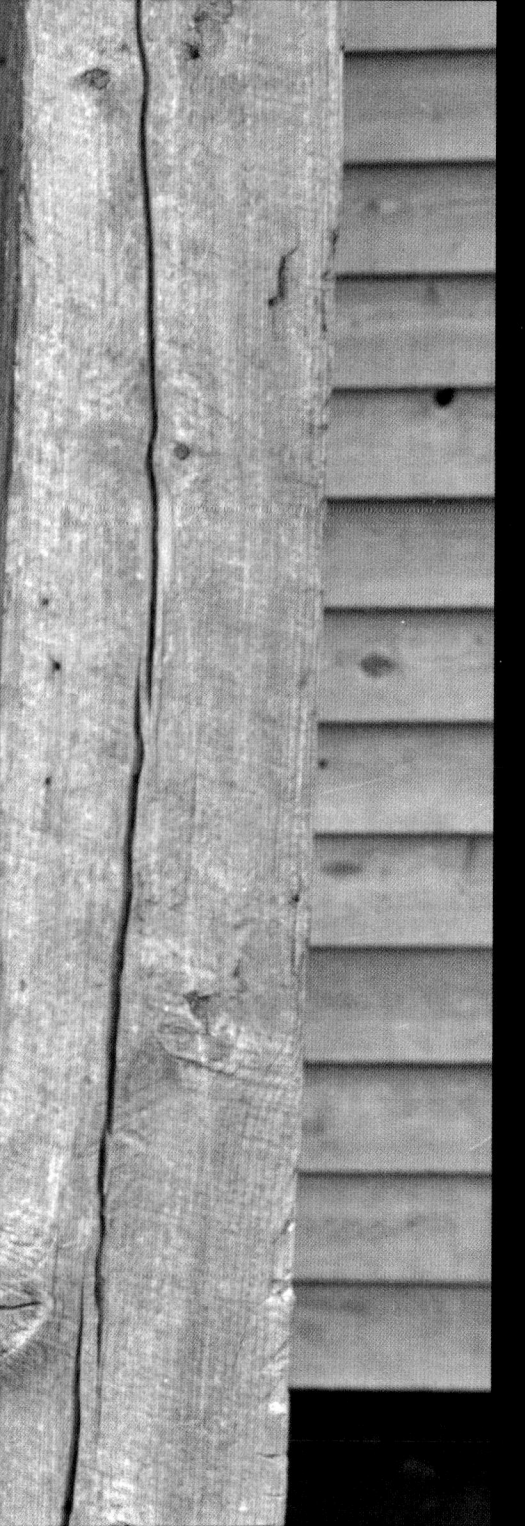

A SHARECROPPER'S FAMILY

ALEX LICHTENSTEIN

*Photographer Ben Shahn captures the lives of
Black sharecropper families in Little Rock, Arkansas,
one Sunday in 1935.*

During the Great Depression of the 1930s, America "discovered" the Southern sharecropper. As journalists, photographers, filmmakers, labor organizers, and government officials fanned out across the United States, many of them documented the lives and labors of the nation's rural poor. If, as President Franklin D. Roosevelt insisted in his second inaugural address in 1937, one-third of Depression-era America remained "ill-housed, ill-clad, ill-nourished," the landless tenants and sharecroppers in the cotton South represented a huge proportion of this submerged population.

Although the sharecropping system had emerged from the wreckage of Reconstruction as a system designed to keep Southern Black farmers poor, landless, indebted, and dependent on white landowners, it soon ensnared many poor whites as well. The catastrophic collapse of cotton prices in the late 1920s drove many small landholders—Black and white alike—from an already precarious tenure into the swelling ranks of the landless.

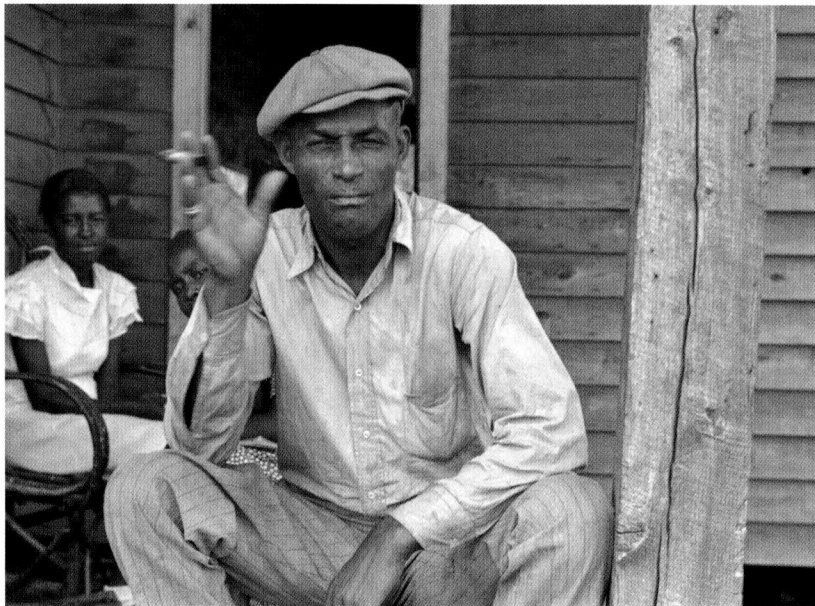

PREVIOUS SPREAD:
Ben Shahn took this photo of a Black sharecropper in Arkansas on a Sunday in 1935.

LEFT: Another version of this portrait.

RIGHT: Arthur Rothstein took this photo of a young girl in Gee's Bend, Alabama, in 1938.

The deepening rural impoverishment remains familiar almost a century later in the indelible images captured by photographers working for the New Deal's Farm Security Administration—Dorothea Lange, Walker Evans, Marion Post Wolcott, Arthur Rothstein, Ben Shahn, and others.

And yet, even sharecroppers didn't work on Sunday—and that's when Shahn caught up with this large African American family near Little Rock, Arkansas, in fall 1935.

The prototypical representation of Black and white sharecroppers found in most Farm Security Administration (FSA) photography emphasized poverty, loneliness, destitution, and grinding work. After all, these "sociologists with cameras" were tasked with demonstrating the necessity of government rural rehabilitation programs to alleviate poverty.

Ramshackle dwellings usually crowd the frame (as in the photo at right): interiors are often windowless, exteriors eroded or collapsing; individuals in the field are dwarfed by endless rows of cotton; mules, rather than tractors, pull the plows; backs are bent; clothes, ragged; faces lined with worry.

But Shahn saw something very different on this Sunday.

The first photograph (page 40) depicts a "sharecropper on Sunday," sitting on the porch in front of his home. Simply yet well dressed, filling the frame, he appears both relaxed and alert, fully in command, if somewhat skeptical of his interlocutor. In a second, closely related photo (above, likely shot a few moments later), he gestures with his right hand while holding a cigarette, as if recounting a story to the viewer—in this case, Shahn.

Sharecropping was, above all, a family business, and most sharecropping families were large, like the one shown in the top photograph on page 45. The head of the household—usually, but not always, male—was not paid a wage for working in the fields. Instead, he contracted his entire family's labor in return for a portion of the proceeds of the final crop.

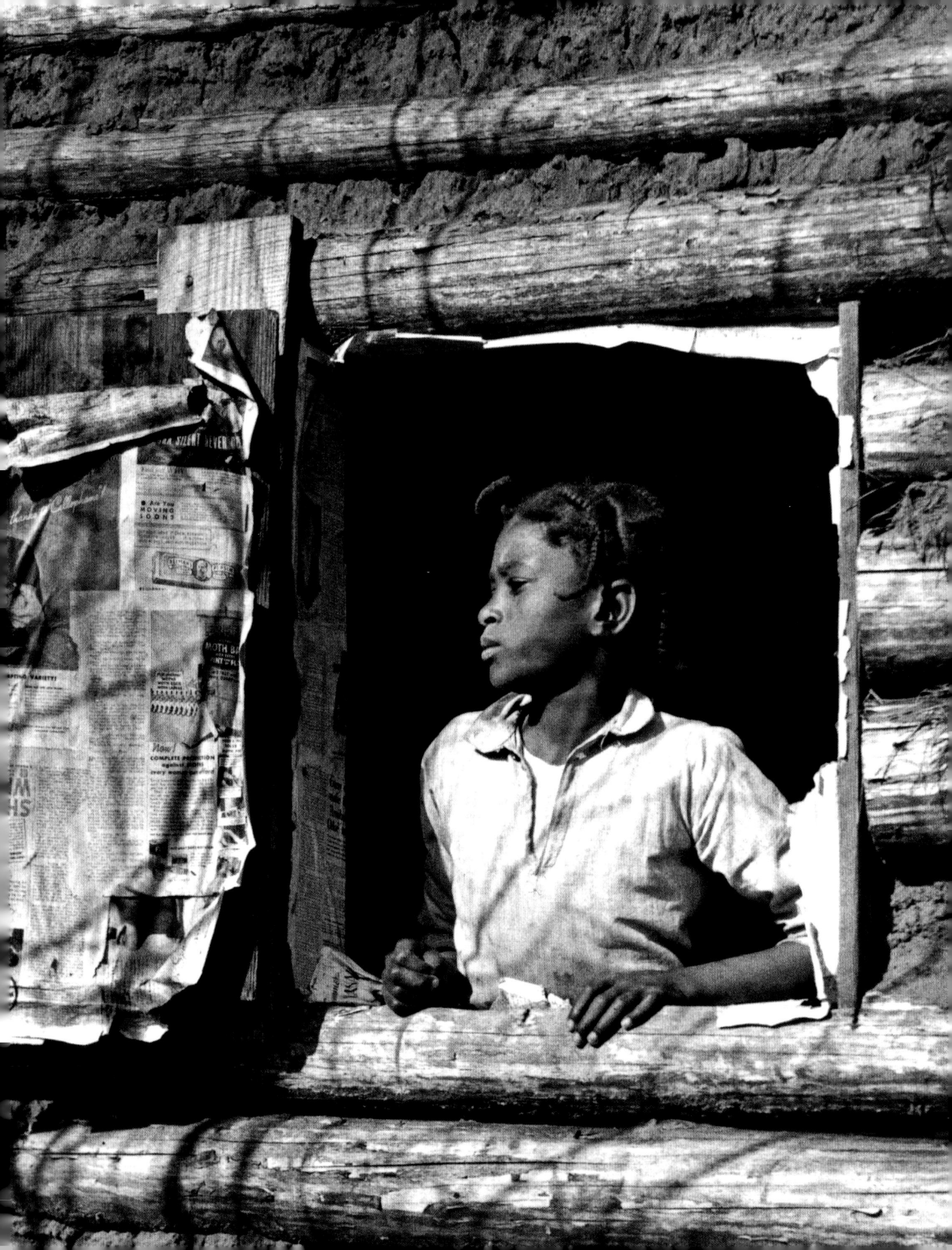

The more labor that family could deliver, the better, which put a premium on getting as many children into the fields at as young an age as possible. A larger crop—at least until the bottom dropped out of cotton prices—might mean a better "settle" at the end of the year. Accumulation meant escaping from the vise of debt and maybe, just maybe, purchasing your own plot of land someday. But that aspiration, dating back to the broken Reconstruction promise of "forty acres and a mule" and requiring constant labor, would not interfere with a Sunday's rest.

But if the Black sharecropper brought his family's labor to the bargaining table with the white landowner, another tool was required to ensure a fair settlement: a pencil. The school year was short for Black children needed in the fields, but the person—often the sharecropper's wife or eldest daughter—who could keep written track of loans, expenditures, and sales proved a valuable asset to the family. We cannot tell what the young woman just behind the sharecropper is writing or calculating, but her thoughtful expression and her grasp on her writing implement suggest its importance.

The older children in the picture (opposite, top) taken the same day seem to be dressed in their Sunday best. Store-bought shoes certainly were a luxury for sharecroppers, yet only the three youngest in this photograph remain barefoot. Jaunty hats, suspenders, and nice slacks also suggest that this particular Black Arkansan sharecropper's family spent what little income there was at the end of the year on Sunday clothing (or the cloth to make it). The relaxed and open pose of this family stands in notable contrast to the display of rural hardship and desperation one finds in many portraits of Southern Black life in the Depression era.

In a another group portrait of sharecropping children (opposite, bottom; probably more than one family in this case), we see a similar set of markers of dignity and Sunday pride: erect posture, faces up to the camera; hats, jewelry,

shoes, eyeglasses, nice dresses, even a full suit worn by the eldest boy. Indeed, generational ranking stands out in this photograph: it seems clear that as children grew older, they acquired more trappings of respectability.

At least one child, however, seems willing to directly express her impatience with the photographer and his demands. We can also see here the family's pencil holder and her older sister from the first photograph, second and fourth from the left in the back row.

Shahn's Sunday images remain striking for another reason; in contrast, for example, to Dorothea Lange's famous photograph of a Mississippi plantation owner dominating the frame in which he clearly wields power over his Black subjects, Shahn's photographs privilege Black experience without any visible white presence or interference.

To be sure, any Black sharecropper living in the Arkansas Delta in the 1930s remained beholden to powerful whites—his landlord, the local merchant, the sheriff, even his poor white neighbors and fellow sharecroppers. Yet the presence of those white authority figures does not intrude on this Sunday morning interlude.

It is a shame that Shahn failed to record the names of these children and their family, for it would be illuminating to learn what happened to them in the coming decades. Agricultural "reform" during the 1930s destroyed the last tenuous hold Black families like this held on the land; war jobs called the young men and women away from the fields to Little Rock and Memphis, or to tank factories in Detroit and shipyards in Mobile and Oakland. Tractors would soon displace family labor.

Those who stayed scrounged work as agricultural day laborers; many departed in the Second Great Migration to Chicago, Los Angeles, or St. Louis. There were many good reasons for rural Blacks to leave the South behind, but these photographs remind us of what else was lost in their departure.

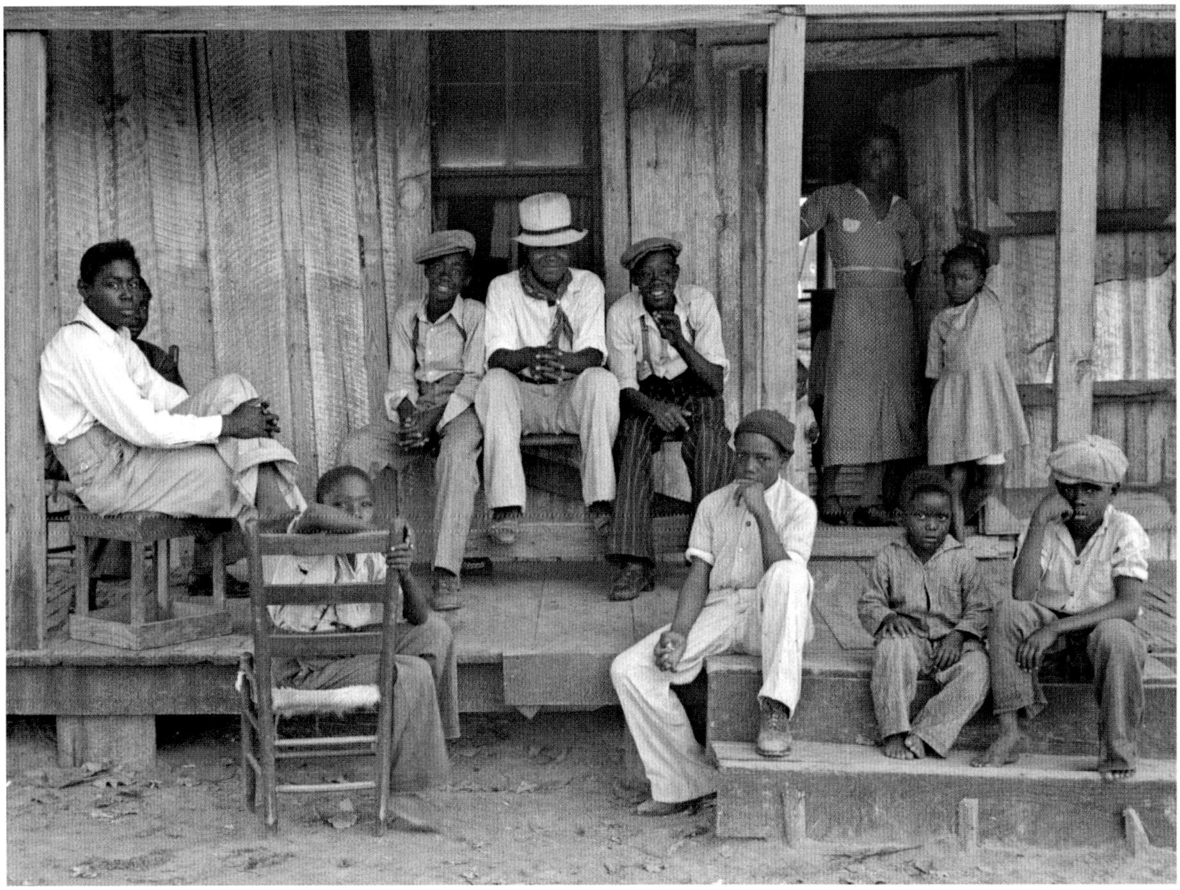

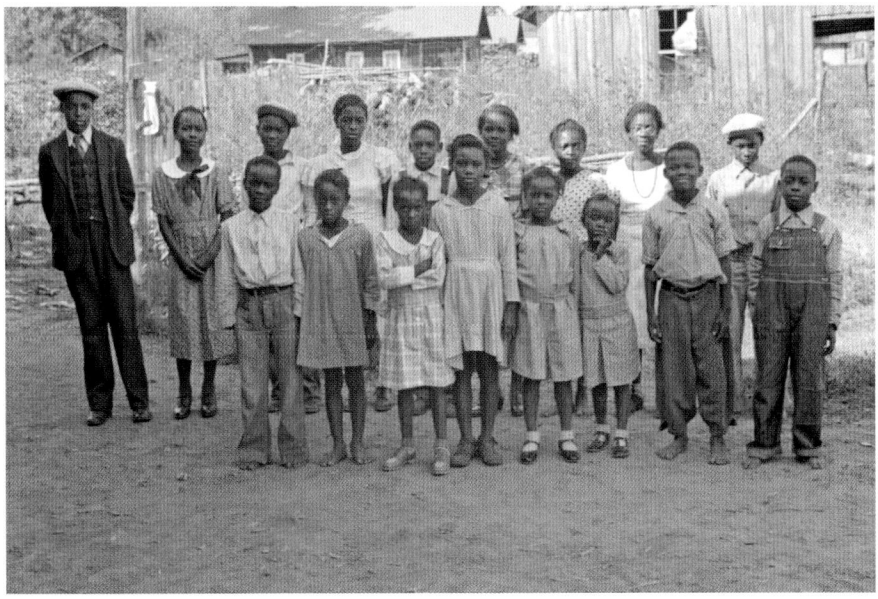

LEFT: Sharecropper's children assembled for this portrait by Ben Shahn.

ABOVE: Shahn also took this photograph of an extended family enjoying a Sunday's rest on the porch.

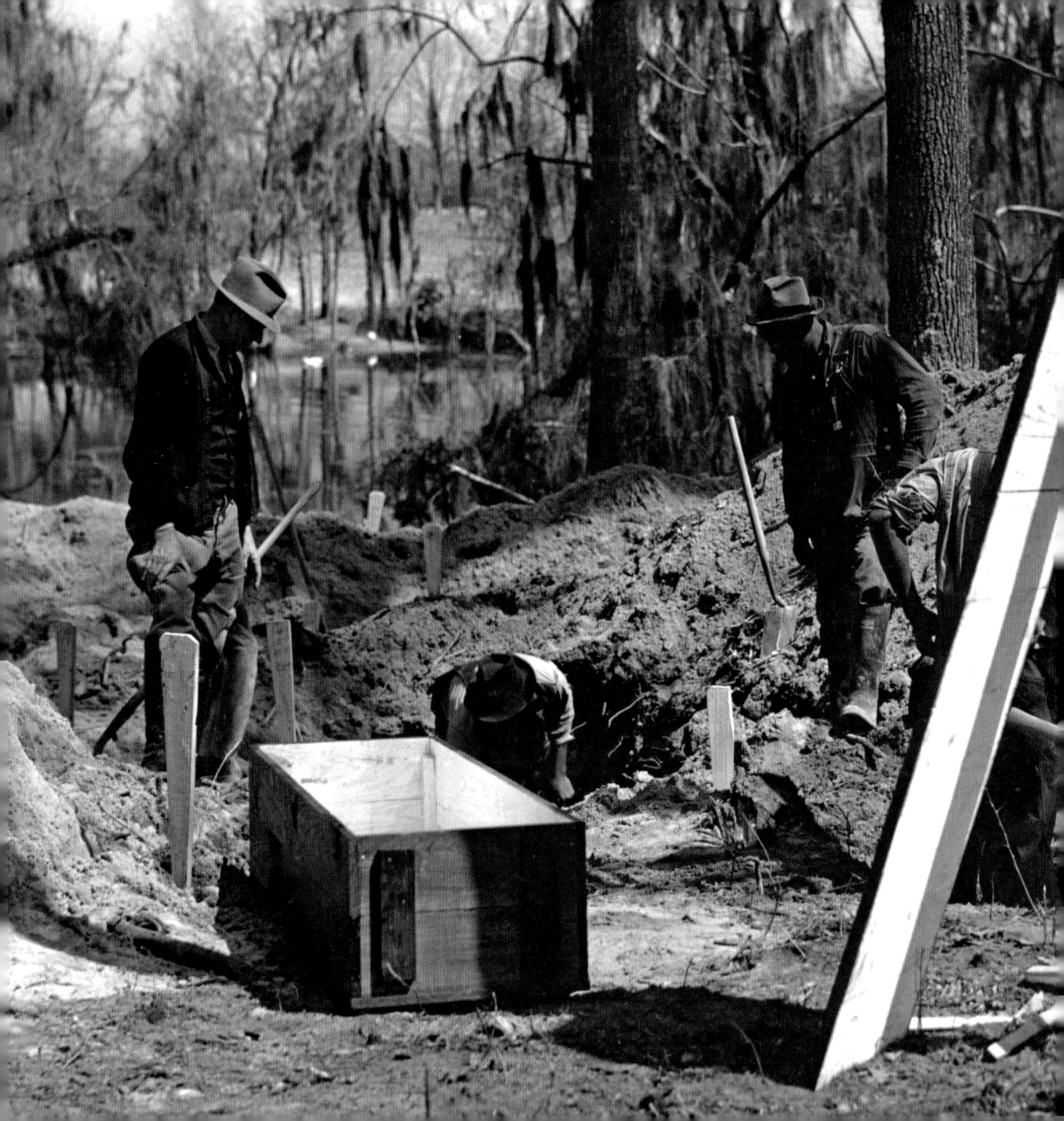

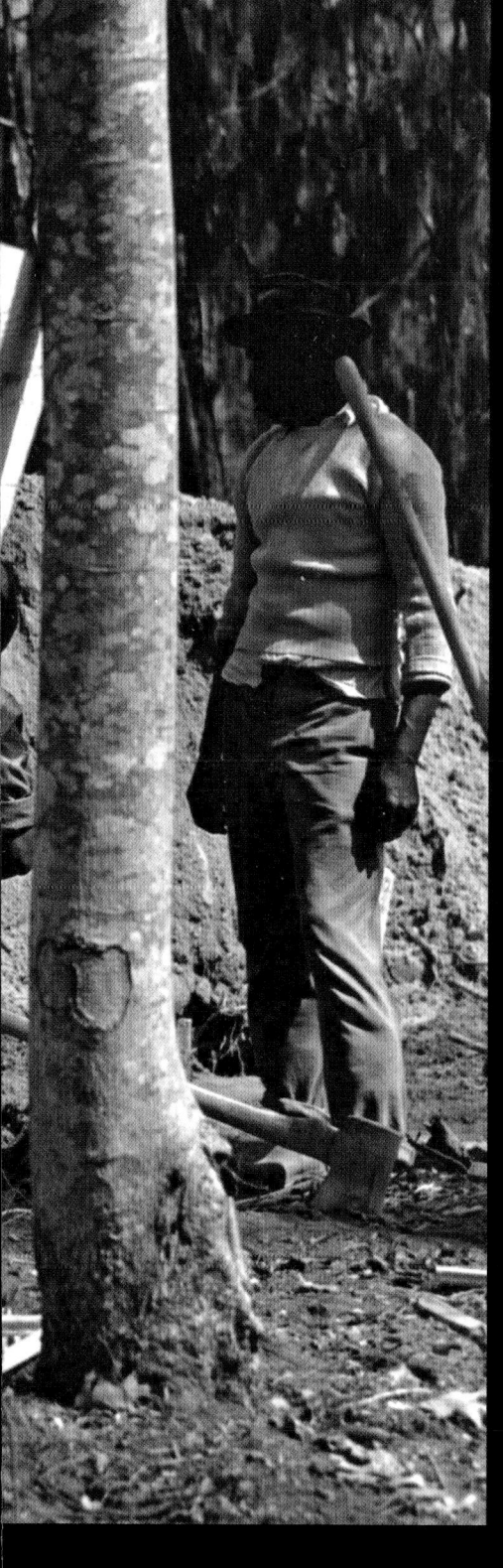

TWICE BURIED

KELSEY A. MOORE

*How the Santee-Cooper Project
disregarded the dead and the living.*

Across the Jim Crow South, New Deal projects designed to modernize rural areas took a tremendous spiritual, epistemic, and ecological toll on Black communities. Nowhere was it more so than in the Santee-Cooper Basin.

In 1934, the South Carolina General Assembly established the South Carolina Public Service Authority. The Authority was granted power to build canals, dams, and power plants, to divert the waters of the Santee River, to set rates for electricity it produced, to borrow money, and to issue bonds.

After lengthy court battles that postponed the start of construction, the Authority began work on the Santee-Cooper Hydroelectric and Navigation Project in parts of Berkeley, Orangeburg, and Clarendon counties. Once known for its prosperous rice, indigo, and cotton plantations, the area had felt the impact of the Great Depression, and its residents suffered from intense poverty. State and federal officials saw the Santee-Cooper Project as a solution to the area's economic problems.

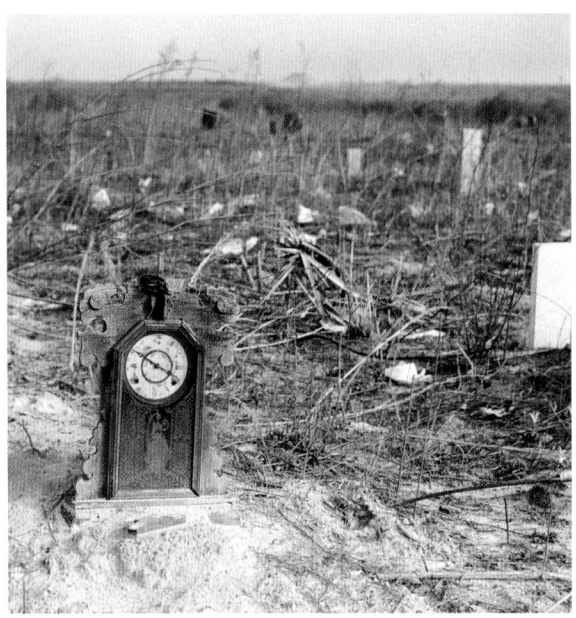

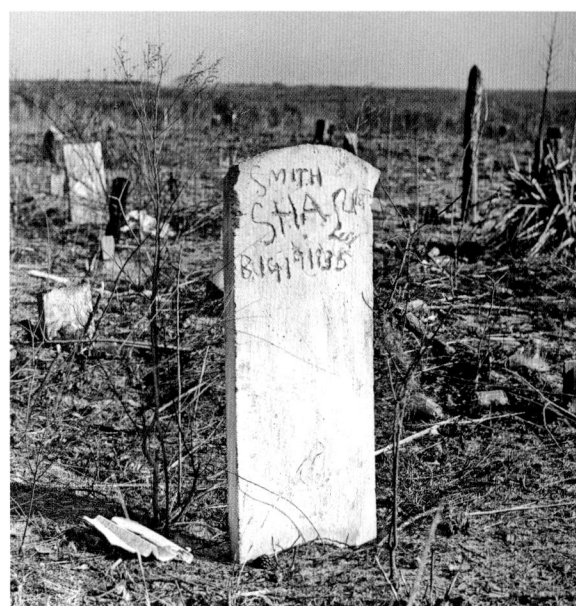

The project had three main goals: to extend electricity to rural communities, to trigger economic growth, and to improve the public health of the area. As a part of larger New Deal initiatives, the Santee-Cooper Project received funding from the Public Works Administration (PWA) while the Works Progress Administration (WPA) supplied labor. Known as "South Carolina's Tennessee Valley Authority," the Santee-Cooper Project gave hope that the South, the region that President Franklin D. Roosevelt called the "nation's number one economic problem," could be redeveloped.

But to complete the project, the Authority needed to determine the fate of nearly nine thousand graves in over 150 cemeteries. Most of the cemeteries were found either on old plantations used by enslaved Africans and their descendants or in Black churchyards established during Reconstruction. Various Indigenous mounds were also found.

Between 1938 and 1941, the Authority hired investigators, engineers, and lawyers to ascertain the number of graves, judge each cemetery's condition, and determine the fate of each. Cemeteries would be either reinterred, inundated, or left alone. Nearly five thousand graves of enslaved Africans and their descendants were removed—not, however, at the request of living relatives.

Engineers determined that some of the cemeteries' locations were between elevation heights that were in danger of erosion. The Authority hired, among others, four Black men—James Thompson, Alex Clark, Robert Butler, and Robert Graham—as "cemetery helpers" and "laborers." Some of the men, like Clark, were not from the area, coming from as far away as Lexington County. In the photograph on the previous spread, we see Clark, Thompson, Butler, and Graham along with another man as they remove remains to be reinterred on other land recently purchased by the Authority or other landowners.

Authority officials determined that at least three thousand Black graves would be left "undisturbed" and thus flooded under the two reservoirs, Lake Moultrie and Lake

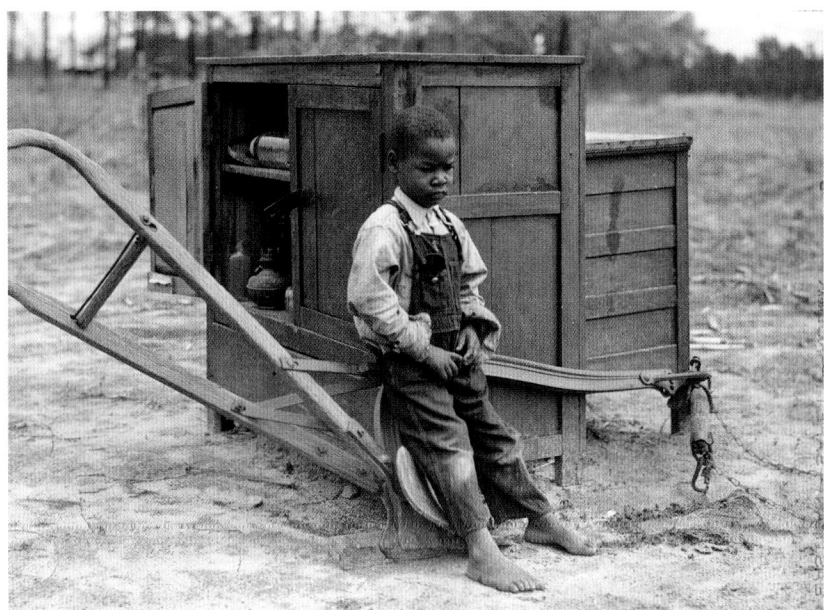

Marion, that would be created by damming the Santee and Cooper rivers. Ultimately, cemetery investigators did not fully account for all the graves, and the number of inundated graves might have been greater.

Many of the cemeteries found in the Santee-Cooper Basin existed among the swamps and forests that covered the area. It was common for Black South Carolinians to use this environment to bury their dead. What the Authority saw, however, were burial grounds that appeared neglected. They did not look like "proper" cemeteries, which, in their view, should resemble a fenced park or garden with manicured rows of headstones.

But these cemeteries were not abandoned. Community members still interred bodies in them. In fact, many Black residents continued to bury their deceased relatives in these areas even after the cemetery investigators made their initial surveys. In addition, residents acted as stewards of the cemetery, detailing intimate knowledge of persons buried in cemeteries even when headstones were not present.

The disruption of graves violated long-standing mortuary beliefs held by Black South Carolinians in the Santee-Cooper Basin. Many descendants of enslaved Africans in South Carolina carried traditions from the Kongo, where graves acted as a meeting place between the living and the dead. Many Black South Carolinians believed that cemeteries needed to exist in forests and swamps to hinder access by those who were not related to the deceased. What was viewed as neglect was in actuality quite intentional. What we do not see in the photographs is how the removal of the dead impacted the lives of residents in the communities they belonged to.

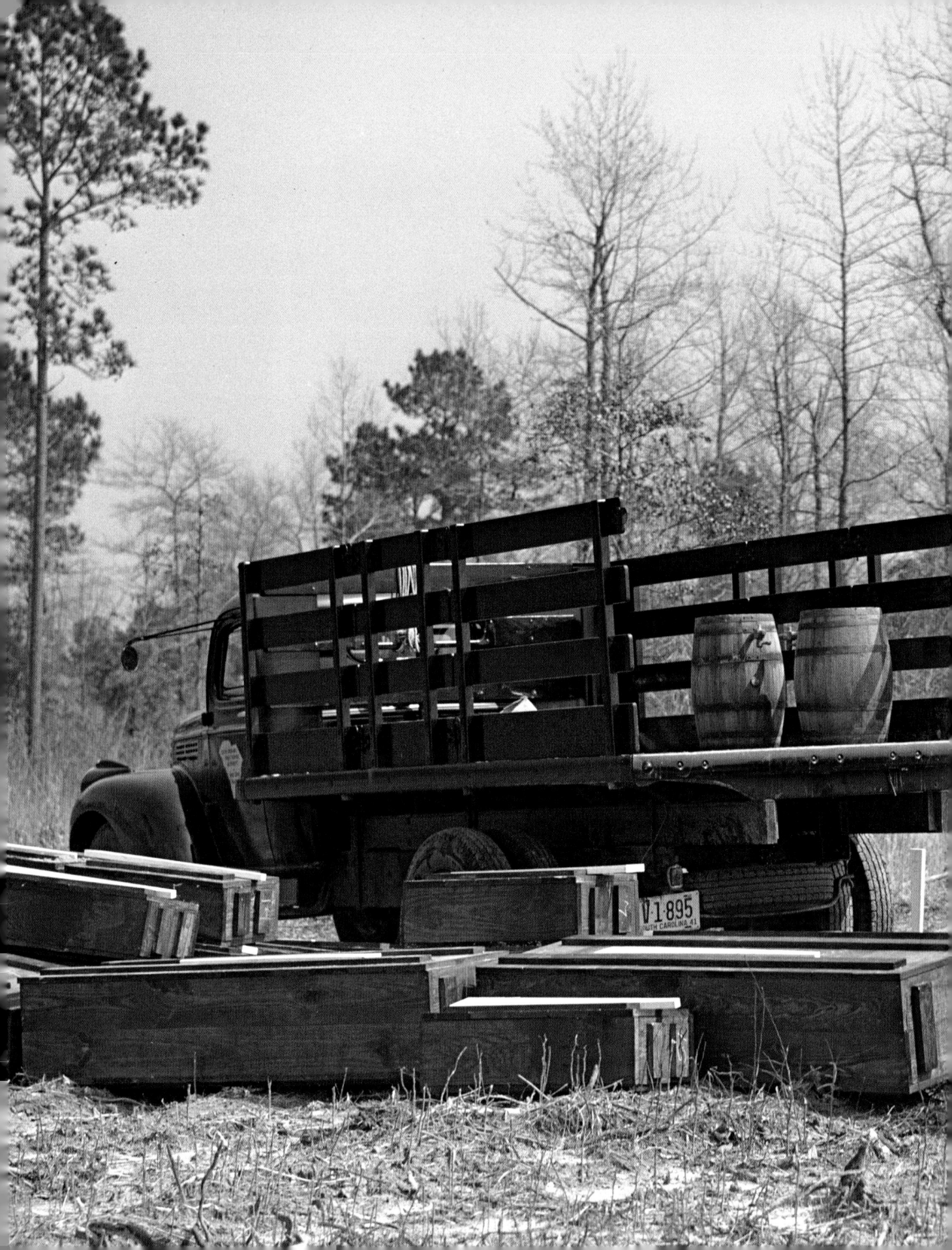

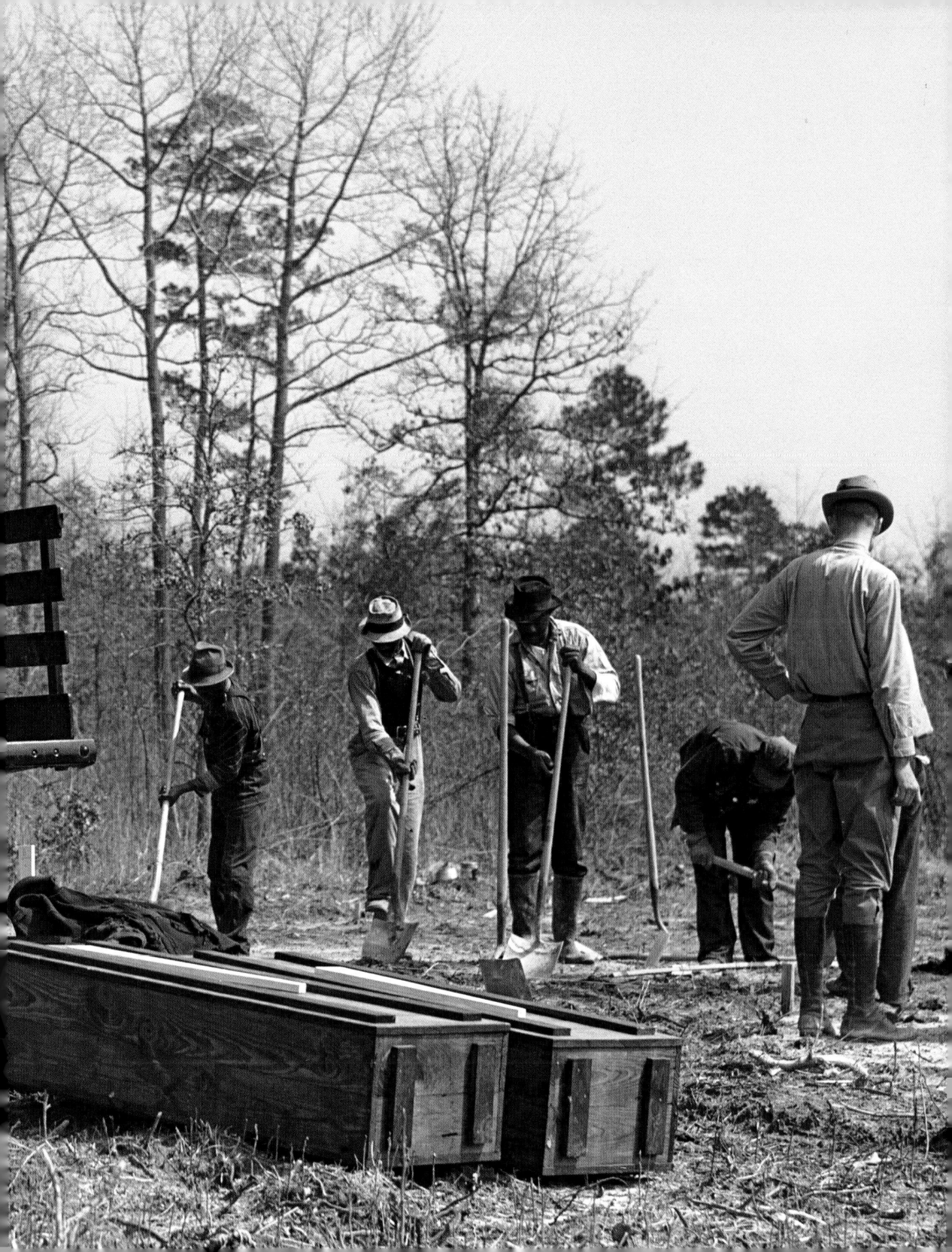

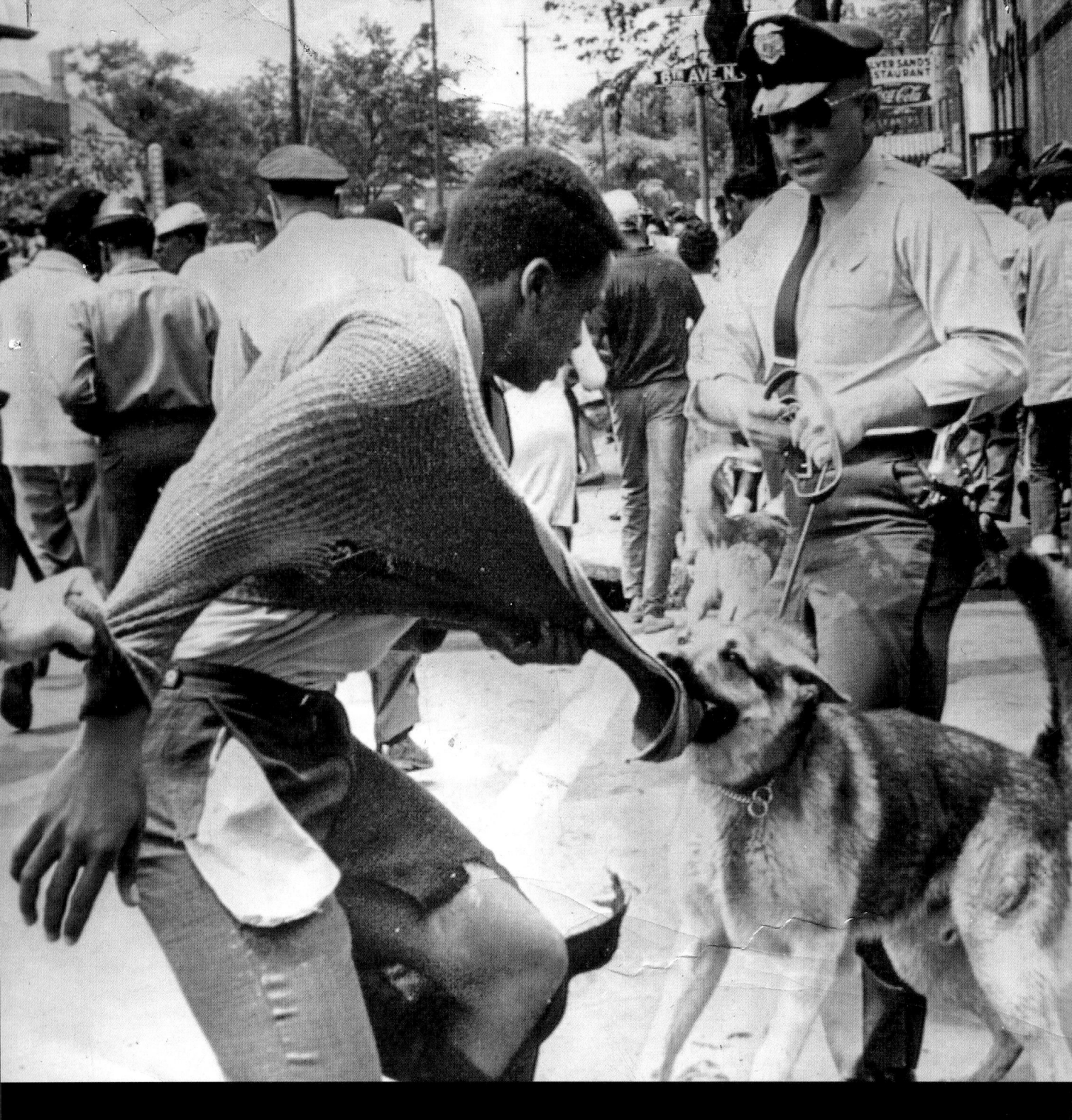

PHOTOGRAPHING HISTORY IN THE MAKING

MICHAEL M. SANTIAGO

*How I captured the final crossing of
civil rights legend John Lewis.*

I have always been passionate about U.S. history. As an immigrant to this country from the Dominican Republic, my learning about the past events of my new home fascinated me.

In middle school, as we began our study of the Civil War, I read everything I could. Though the textbooks contained photography, I only glanced at the pictures—the words were far more important to me then. I didn't yet fully appreciate how photographs expanded the context of the words. That was until I took my first photography class in tenth grade and started to become more aware not only of the photos in our history textbooks but of the photographers who had captured them. That was all more than twenty-five years ago.

I became a photojournalist because I wanted to document history in the making. As my photojournalism career has fully convinced me, the images my colleagues and I make in the present are vital to the continued telling of our country's true story.

Reporters have long recognized the power of photojournalism, and photography was and continues to be one of the most powerful tools to disrupt the powers that be and to help implement change. In his 1993 memoir *Leaving Birmingham*, Paul Hemphill, a journalist and former resident, described the 1963 photograph by Bill Hudson that depicts Walter Gadsden being attacked by a police dog in Birmingham, Alabama, as "an image that would burn forever." (The image here captures the same moment, by a different photographer at the civil rights demonstration.)

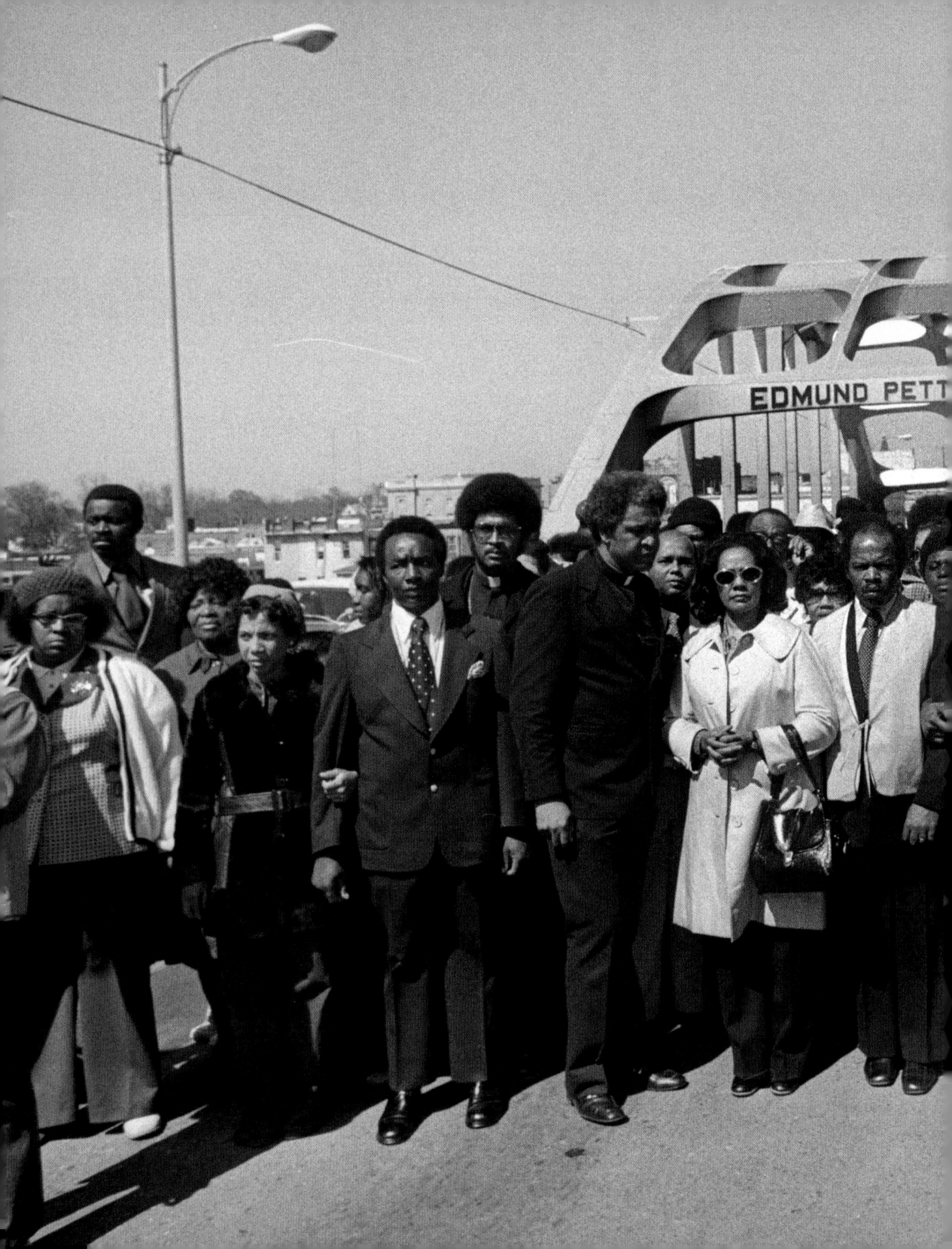

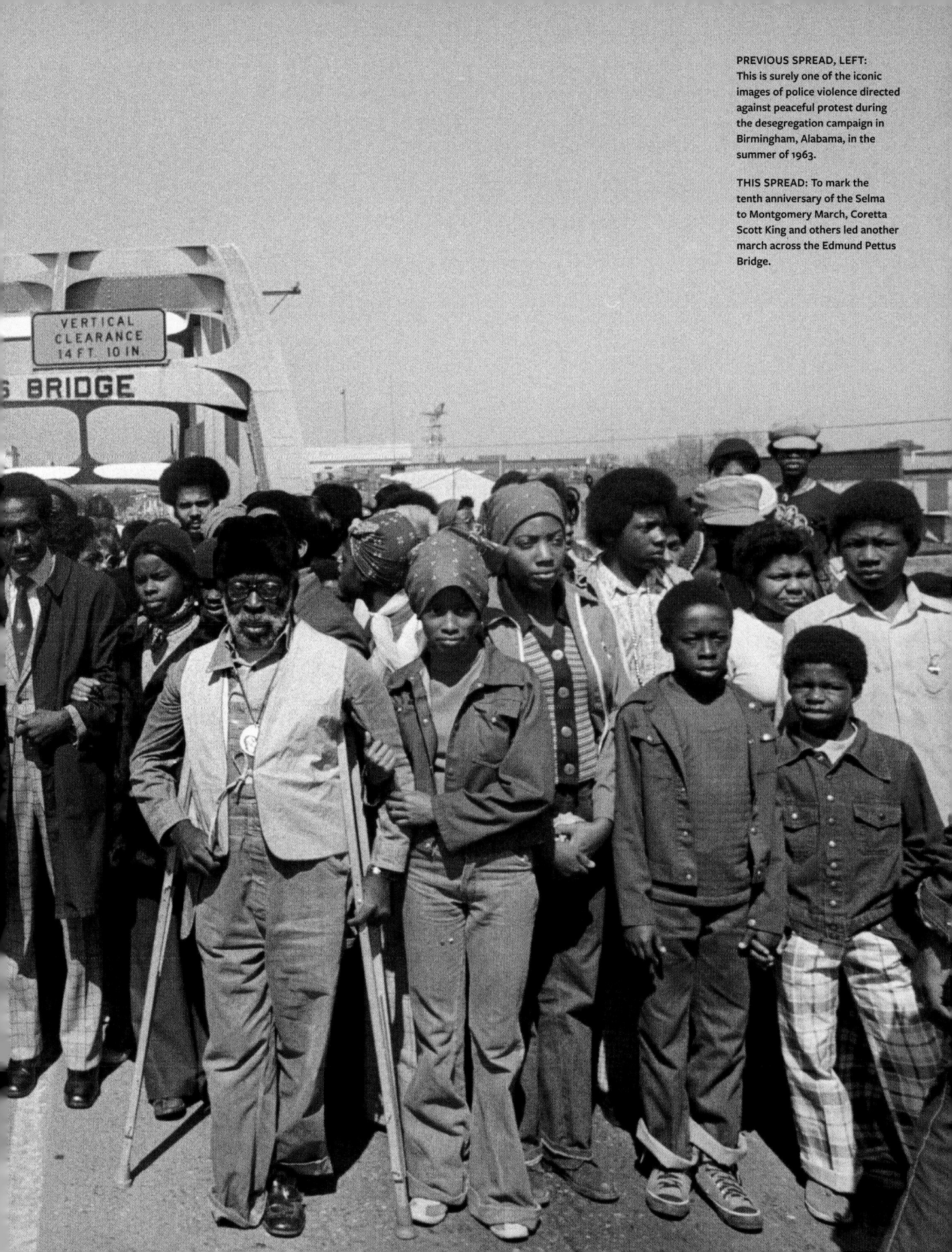

PREVIOUS SPREAD, LEFT: This is surely one of the iconic images of police violence directed against peaceful protest during the desegregation campaign in Birmingham, Alabama, in the summer of 1963.

THIS SPREAD: To mark the tenth anniversary of the Selma to Montgomery March, Coretta Scott King and others led another march across the Edmund Pettus Bridge.

VERTICAL
CLEARANCE
14 FT. 10 IN.

5 BRIDGE

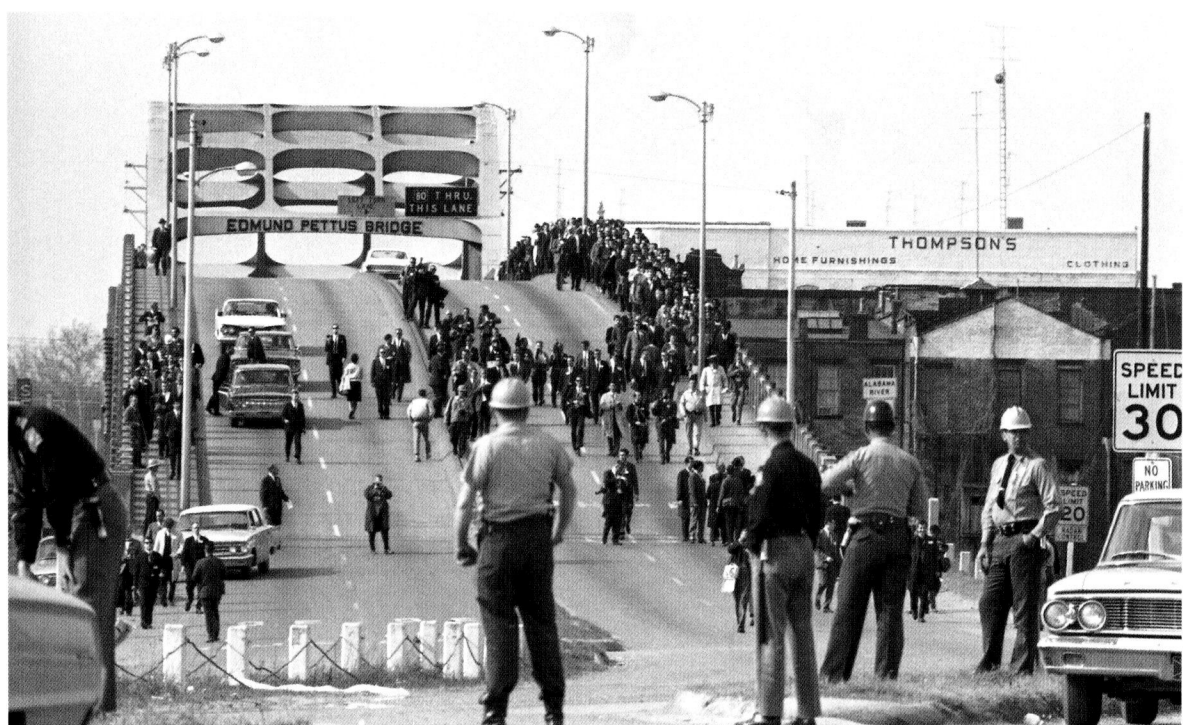

U.S. leaders understood the power of Hudson's image to transcend language and send a global message. "What a disaster that picture is. That picture is not only in America but all around the world," President John F. Kennedy reportedly said of Hudson's work. The photos of African Americans being attacked by police with K-9 dogs and hosed in the streets shocked and moved Northern white people and contributed to the passing of the monumental Civil Rights Act of 1964.

But the photos from Selma of twenty-five-year-old civil rights activist John Lewis and six hundred other marchers under attack by Alabama State Troopers on "Bloody Sunday" ensured a monumental change in this country.

The images of state troopers beating the marchers attempting to cross the Edmund Pettus Bridge—named after a Confederate general and reputed grand dragon of the Alabama Ku Klux Klan—for the audacity to demand their constitutional rights have been seared into the mind of every American since that fateful day.

Meanwhile, many Americans were tuning in to the television premiere of *Judgment at Nuremberg*, a film depicting the war crimes of the Nazis and the moral accountability of those who followed orders and didn't speak out against the Holocaust. The film was soon interrupted by breaking news of the troopers brutally beating these protest marchers in Selma—ironic, given that the Nazis had modeled the Nuremberg Laws on Jim Crow laws.

What happened in Selma helped to change public opinion, and Congress would go on to pass the Voting Rights Act with President Lyndon B. Johnson signing the law on August 6, 1965.

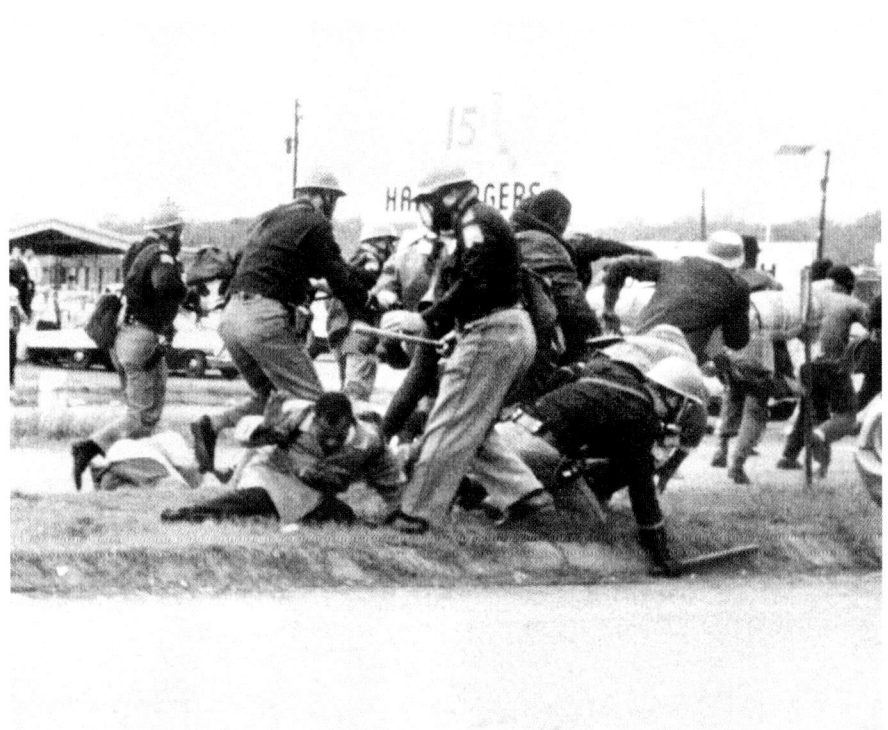

For me, an indelible photograph is that of John Lewis on the ground attempting to stop a white state trooper from clubbing him over the head. That image renders significant an image I took of Black state troopers saluting the casket of John Lewis as a horse-drawn carriage prepares to bear it across that very same bridge where he had risked his life a little over fifty-five years earlier.

I always wanted the opportunity to photograph John Lewis while he was alive. He was an icon, someone who will live on forever in our history. I wanted the opportunity to add to the collective preservation and historical documentation of his life. Sadly, I did not have that opportunity, but I jumped at the chance to photograph his funeral services back in Selma and Montgomery.

Though, I was nervous about it. Not only was this my first big assignment for Getty Images, but it was one the nation would be watching. I focused on making sure that the images matched the historical significance of the moment.

I could not fully experience the moment like all the others who gathered to see Lewis cross that bridge for the final time because I was responsible for ensuring that those who could not witness this themselves had an opportunity to see it through my eyes. My hope was for images that would evoke the emotion of the procession. Looking at the images had to make one feel as if one was there seeing it for themselves.

I spent the morning scouting the best locations. Most photographers positioned themselves to capture the crossing of the casket on the side of the bridge that leads out of Selma. But my instincts told me shooting the casket as it prepared to cross it would be the better choice. I placed myself in a spot that felt suitable, I took mental notes of

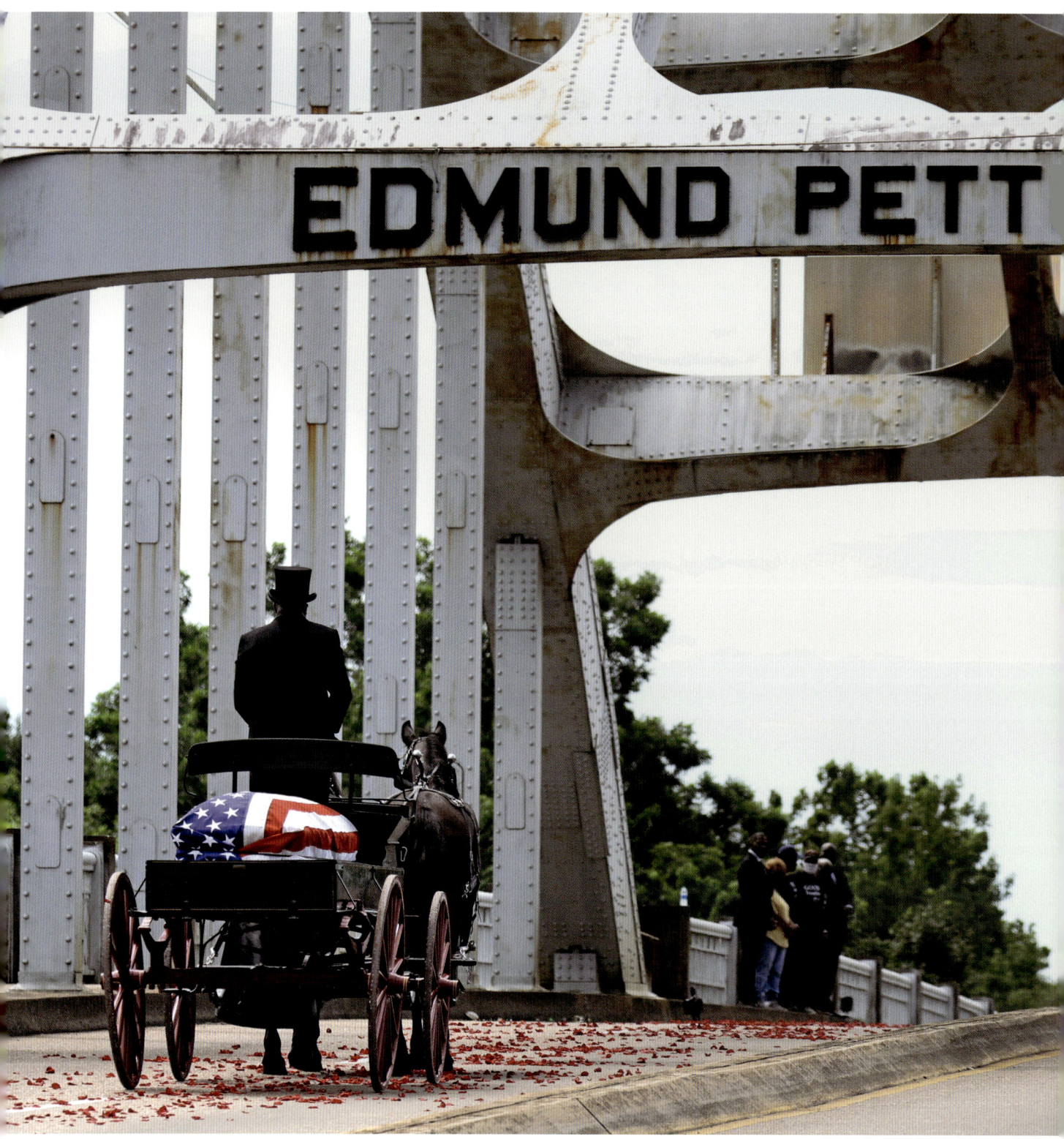

PORTRAITS OF BLACK HISTORY

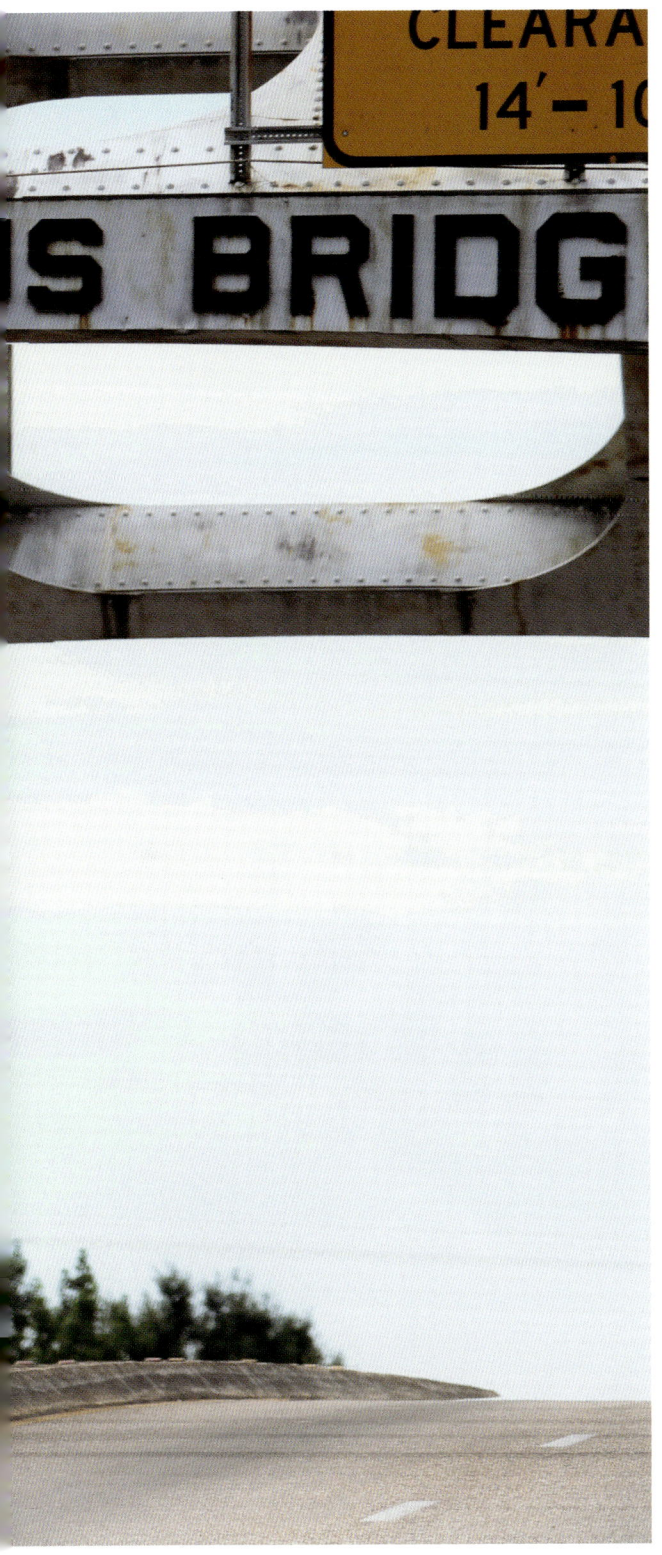

where I wanted my "perfect photo" to be, and I took test shots with different lenses and various focal lengths.

As I began to prepare, three young men began to place wreaths at the foot of the bridge and spread rose petals on the ground leading to the bridge and onto the other side. The petals were meant to represent the blood that was spilled on Bloody Sunday. Before I knew it, Broad Street, which led to the bridge, was swarmed with people on all sides.

My perfect spot was now taken over by folks hoping to have one last look at Lewis and to say their goodbyes. I had to adjust and did so with just enough time before news started to spread that he was on his way. Excitement filled the air once everyone saw the horse and carriage. I began to hear singing and saw people across the street swaying in unison. The state troopers stood at attention, and I was able see their salutes as the horse and carriage arrived. Fifty-five years after we saw white troopers halt his march and beat Lewis, we now saw Black troopers saluting his casket as it embarked upon its final passage.

Once the horse and carriage were in an ideal place, I began to snap away. Since the crowd was larger now, I climbed on top of a structure ensuring a higher vantage point for my shot. To me, spiritually, at that moment heaven's gates were opening and Lewis was stepping into heaven.

That photo would go on to be the A-1 photo of the following day's *Washington Post*. It would also be my defining picture of that year. To me, it was the one photo that mattered. It is the one photo of mine that I believed would make it into the history books. One that could possibly land in front of my daughter at school, where she would see my name and proudly tell her class, "This is my daddy's photo!"

In this essay, photographer Michael M. Santiago describes how he was able to get this shot.

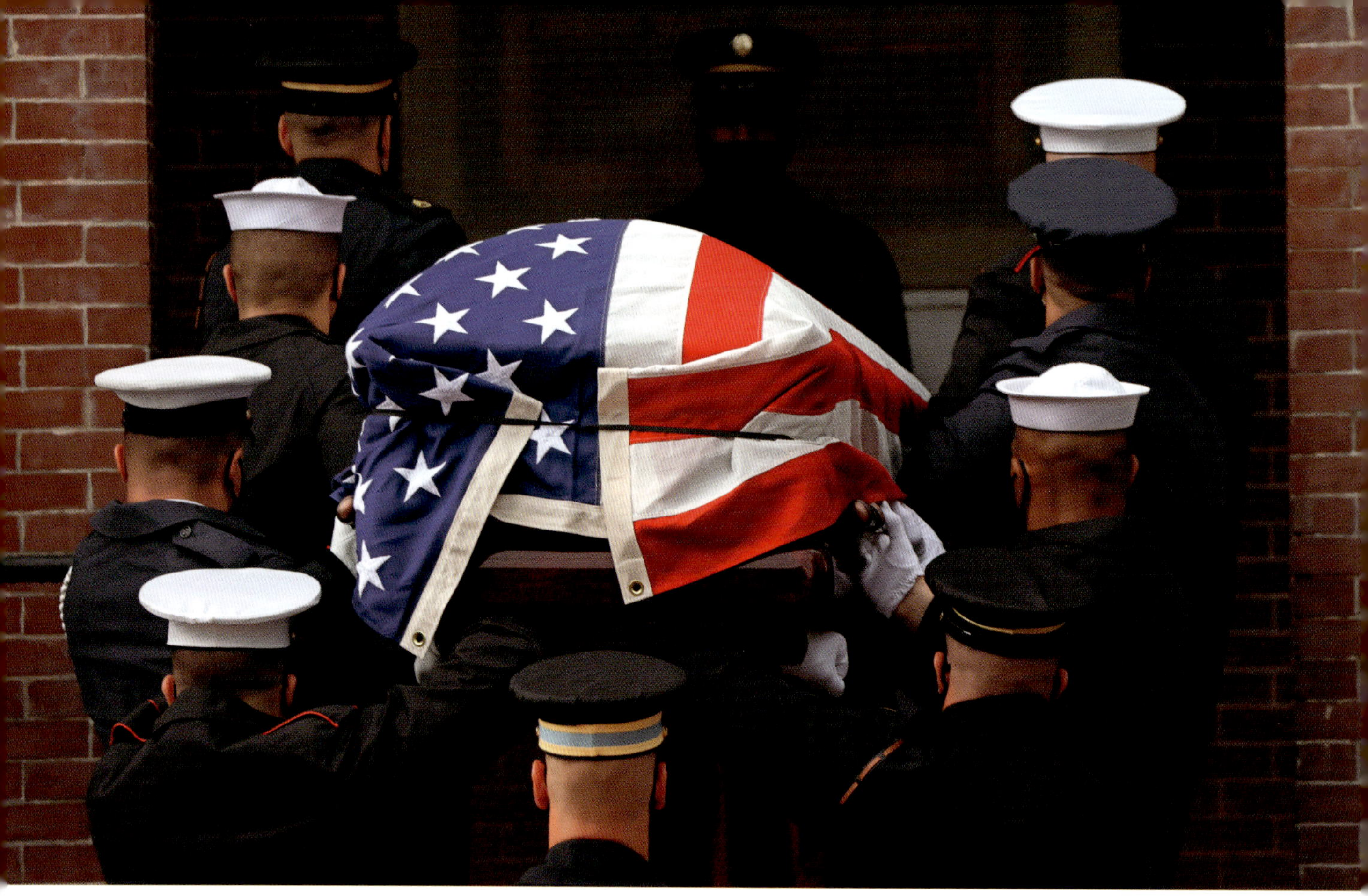

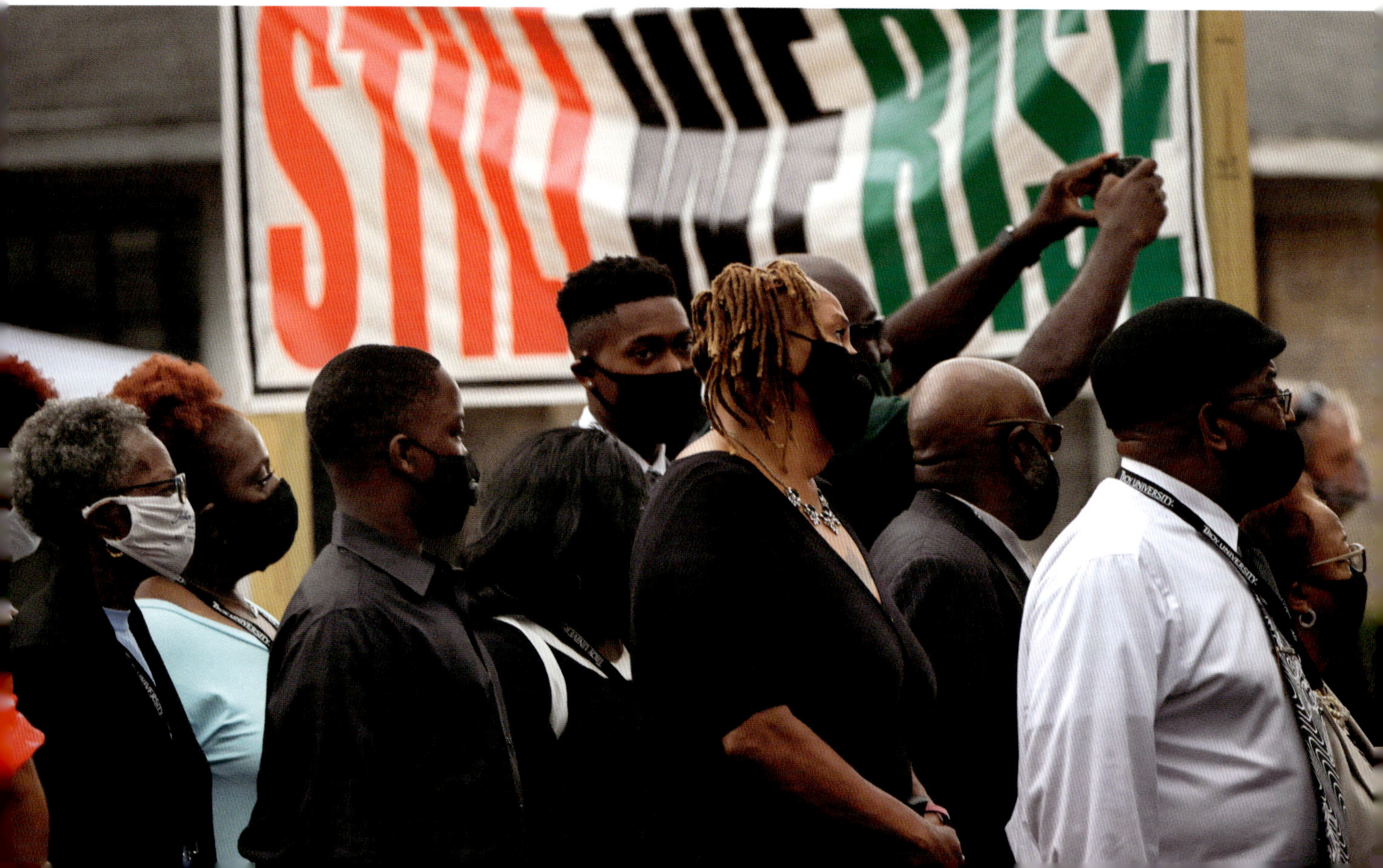

OPPOSITE, TOP: Military pallbearers carried the casket of John L. Lewis into the Brown Chapel AME Church on July 25, 2020.

OPPOSITE, BOTTOM, AND AT RIGHT: A few among the thousands who turned out to celebrate the life of John L. Lewis and to send messages to the world.

FOLLOWING SPREAD: The hearse carrying the flag-draped casket of John L. Lewis prepares to cross the Edmund Pettus Bridge on July 26, 2020.

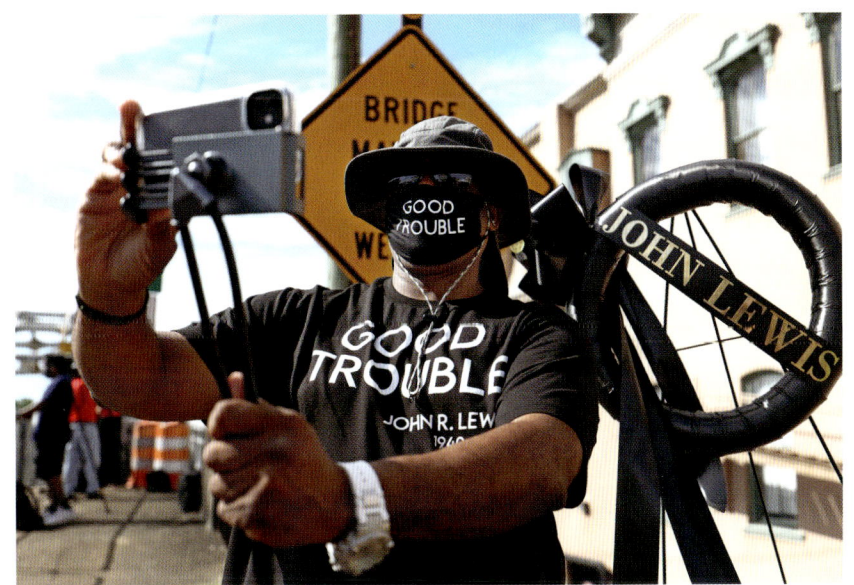

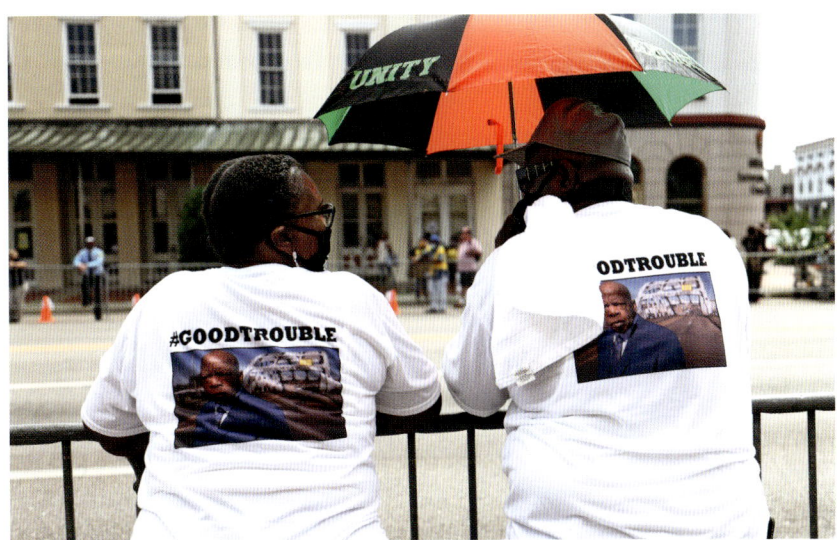

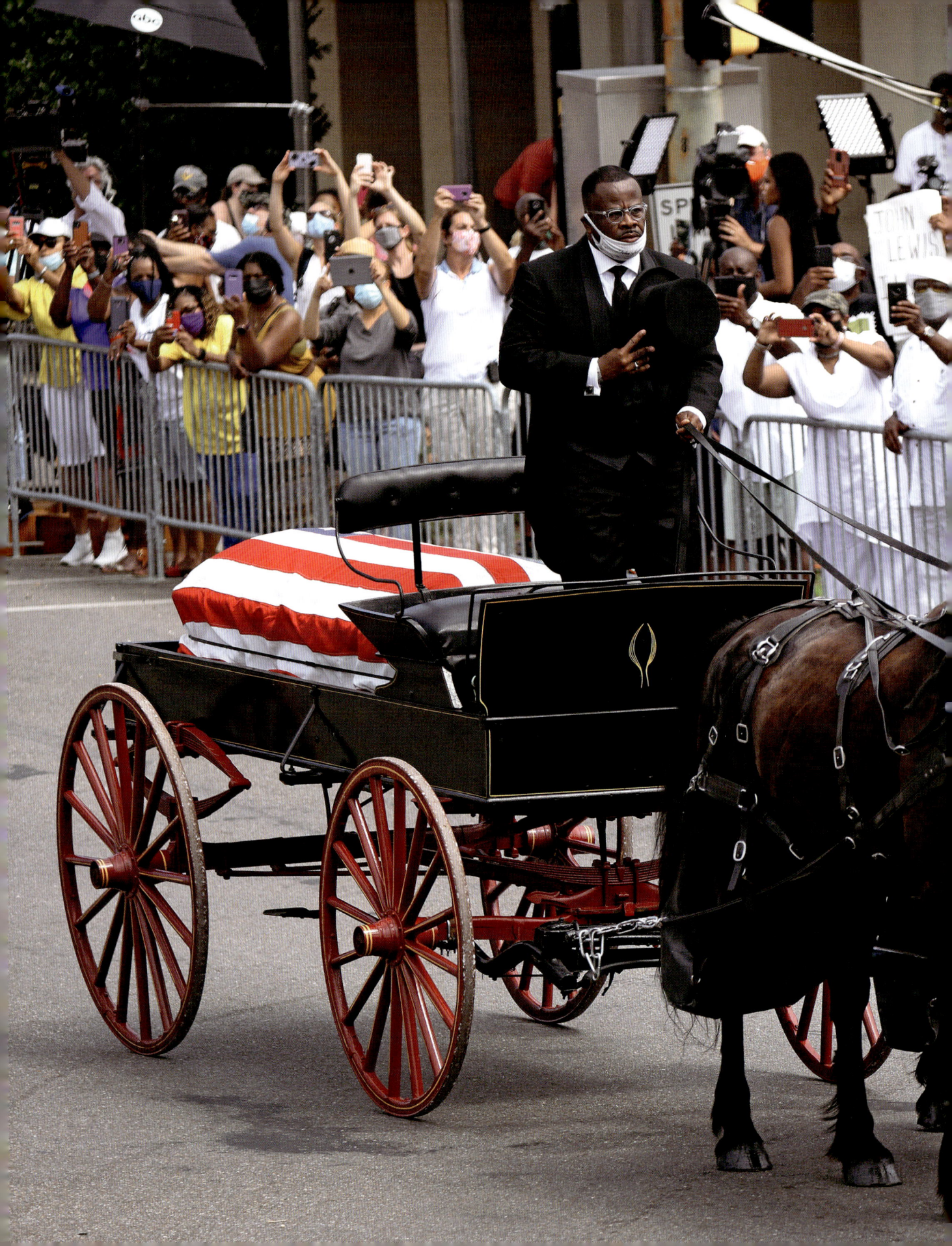

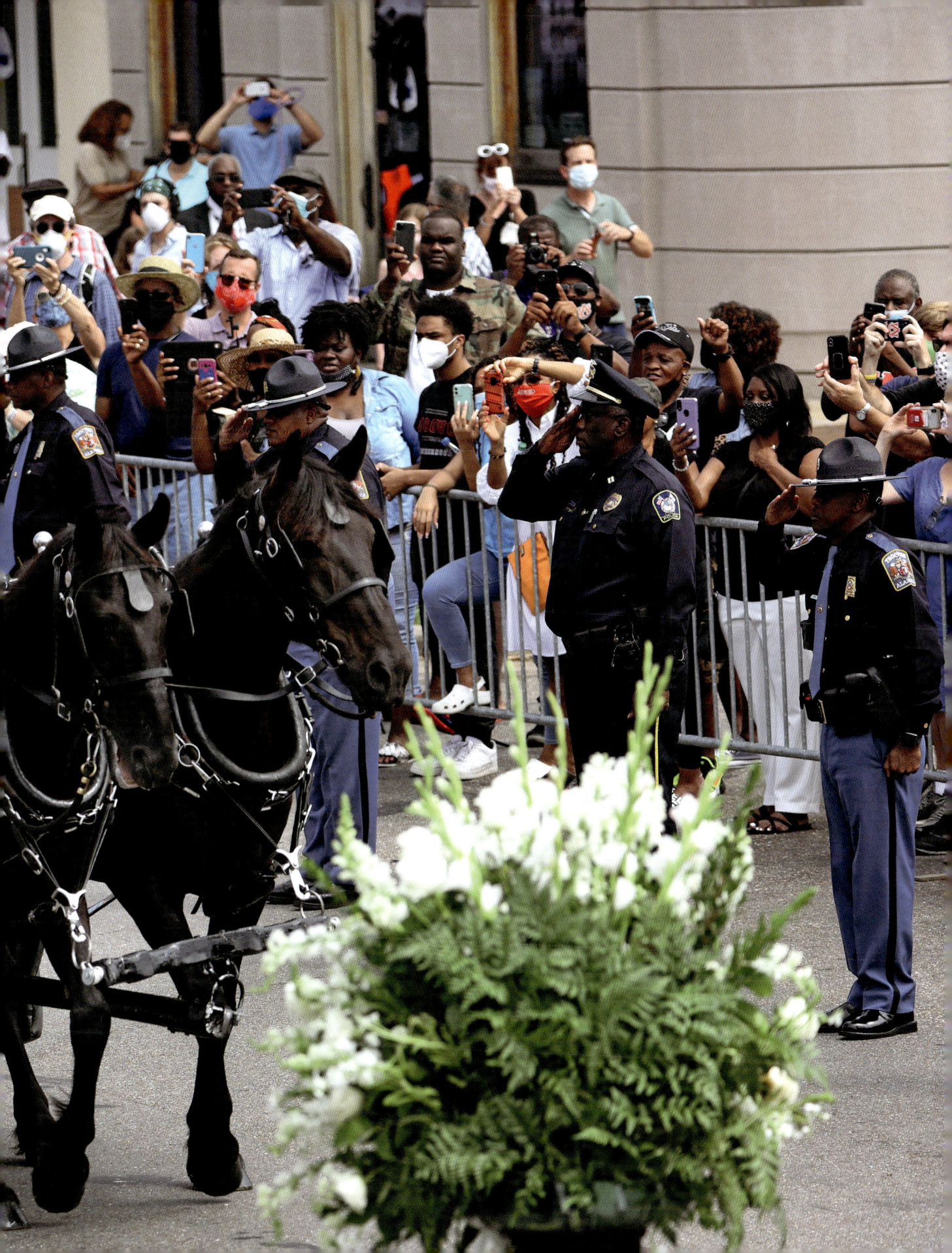

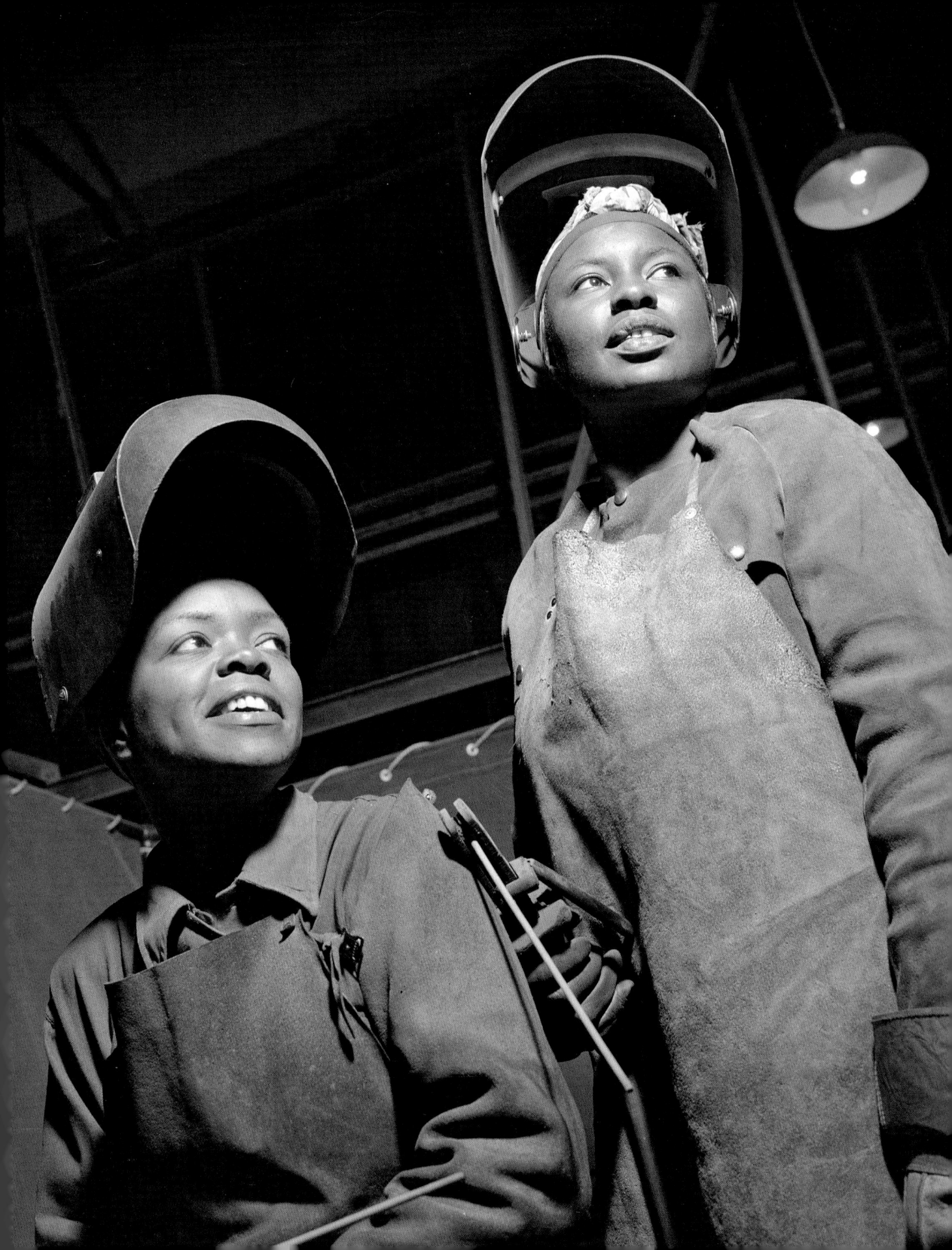

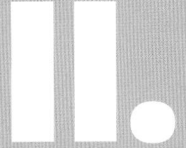

II.

BLACK WOMEN: ACTIVIST LIVES <u>AND</u> LEGACIES

BLACK WOMEN HAVE ALWAYS PLAYED A CRITICAL ROLE IN SOCIAL MOVEMENTS IN THE UNITED STATES. They fought for the abolition of slavery, engaged in interracial activism for women's suffrage, sought to end segregation and enact civil rights—all while caring for their families and cultivating community. Their unique experiences of oppression as Black women—their social exclusion and roles within Black communities as women and their exclusion from white society as Black people—transformed their activism. Despite Black women being the primary keepers and conveyors of Black history, they were frequently confined to history's margins.

The Black women and girls highlighted in these stories and photographs demonstrate the diverse ways they have demanded freedom and justice and fought against systems of racism and sexism. They remind us that women's activism is not confined to easy, predictable narratives. While these women each approached the challenges of their eras differently, what unites them is their courage and profound resilience.

OPPOSITE: These two welders contributed to the war effort at a plant in New Britain, Connecticut. They were photographed by Gordon Parks.

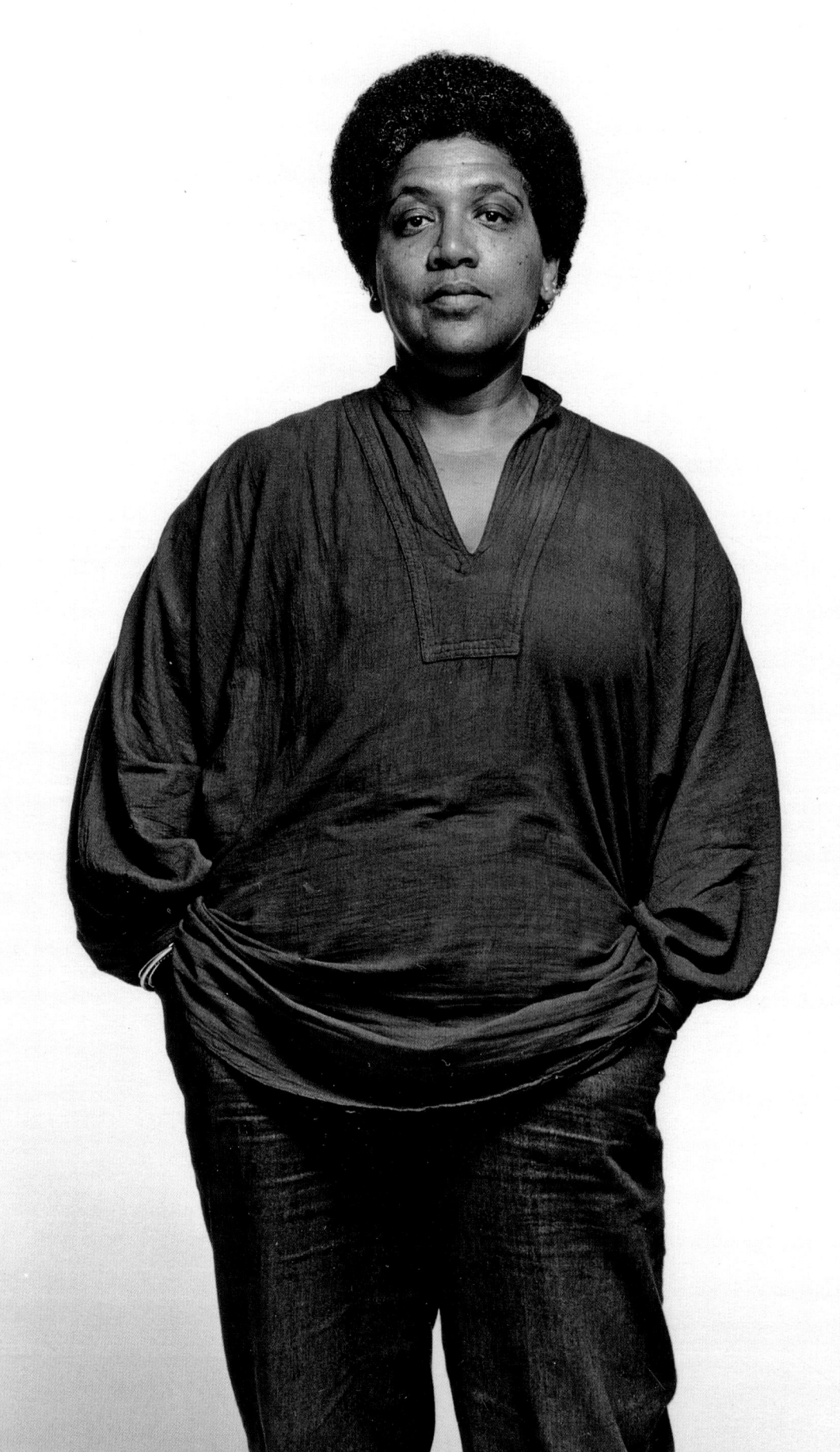

THE REVOLUTION OF BEING

CHET'LA SEBREE

Black women and girls being fully present in our bodies,
our lives, our laughter, our heartache, our joy, our friendships,
our family, ourselves is revolutionary, and it's on record here.

I love the beautiful revolution of Black women and girls being in our bodies, in celebrating our joy, in existing fully in ourselves in a world that has proven itself to be fraught, unwelcoming, and dangerous.

In 2015, Black women were removed from the Napa Valley Wine Train for laughing loudly—a humiliating and demoralizing experience for the group gathered for an afternoon of book-club sisterhood. They were removed for the audacity of their joy.

They filmed as they were escorted from the train, surrounded by police, and challenged what was happening, garnering national attention; they were revolutionary in refusing to allow their joy to be silenced, filing a racial discrimination suit against the company in response.

When I think of incidents like this one, the close of Audre Lorde's "Litany for Survival" echoes in my ears:

So it is better to speak
remembering
we were never meant to survive.

Lorde has always been a model for me of living fully in oneself—both in joy and pain. In *The Cancer Journals*, the self-proclaimed "black, lesbian, mother, warrior, poet" wrote, the day before her mastectomy, "And I think I am prepared to lose it . . . because now I really see it as a choice between my breast and my life . . . and yet if I cried for a hundred years I couldn't possibly express the sorrow I feel right now." The vulnerability of Lorde's work is one of its many incredible powers.

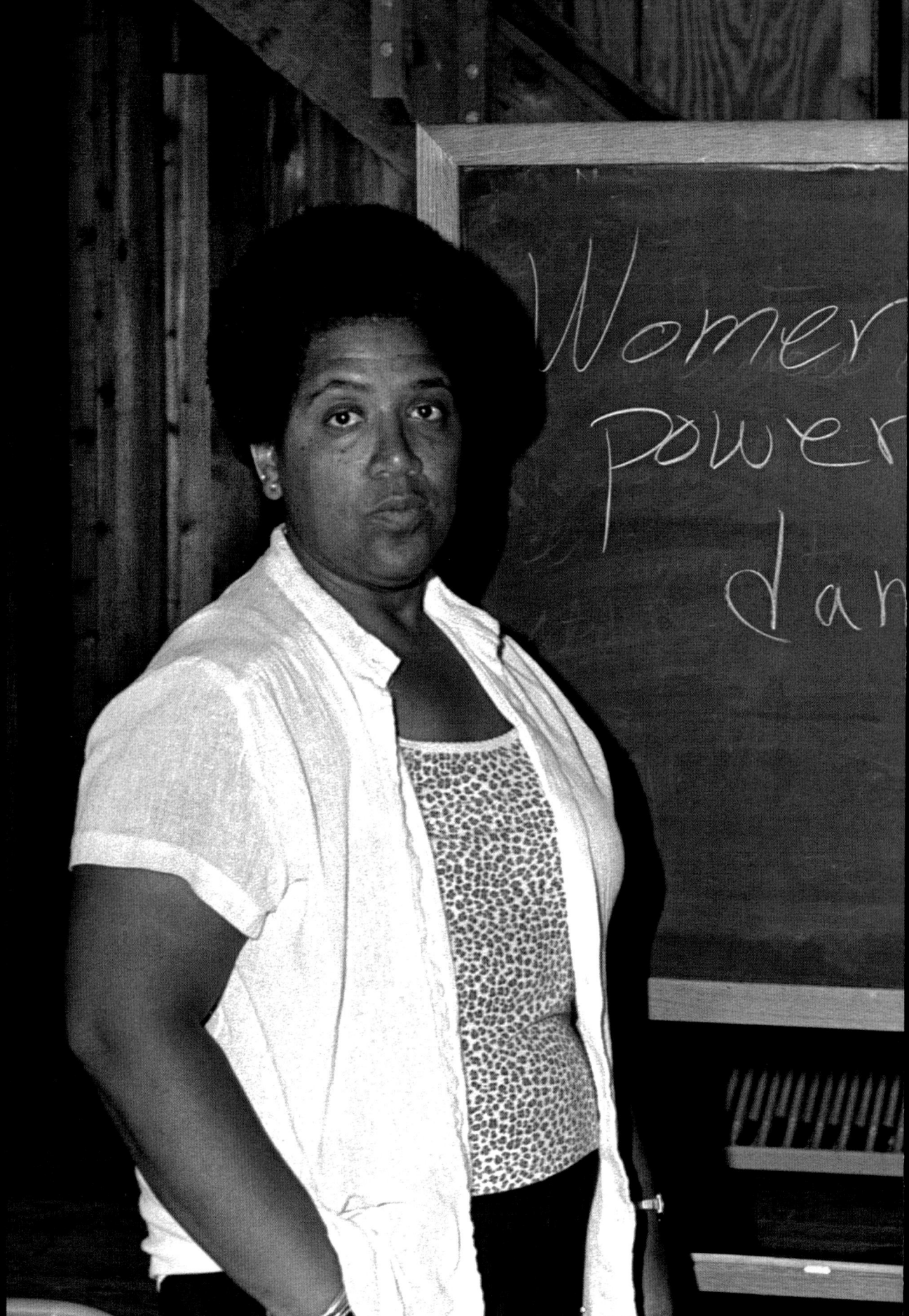

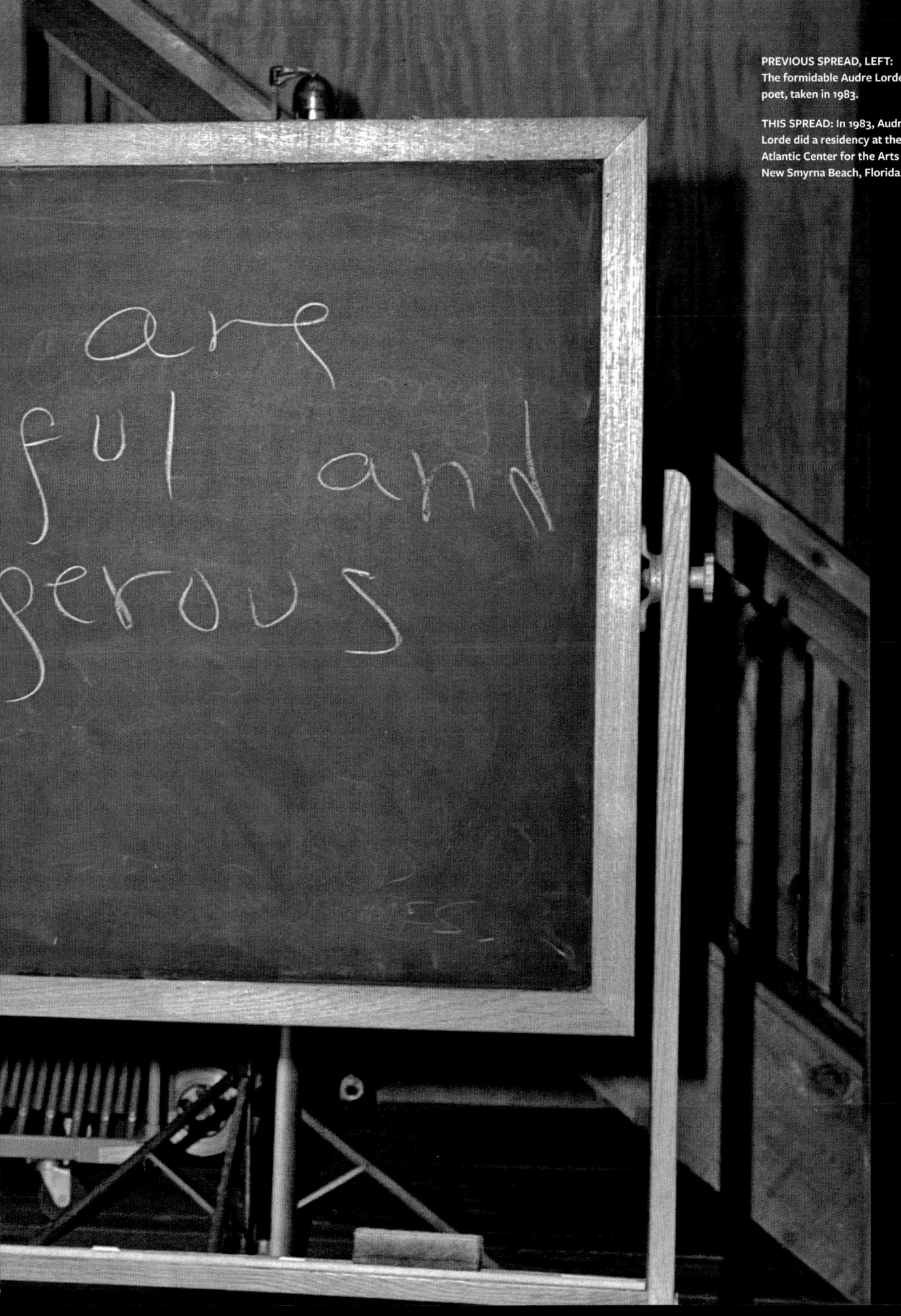

PREVIOUS SPREAD, LEFT:
The formidable Audre Lorde,
poet, taken in 1983.

THIS SPREAD: In 1983, Audre
Lorde did a residency at the
Atlantic Center for the Arts in
New Smyrna Beach, Florida.

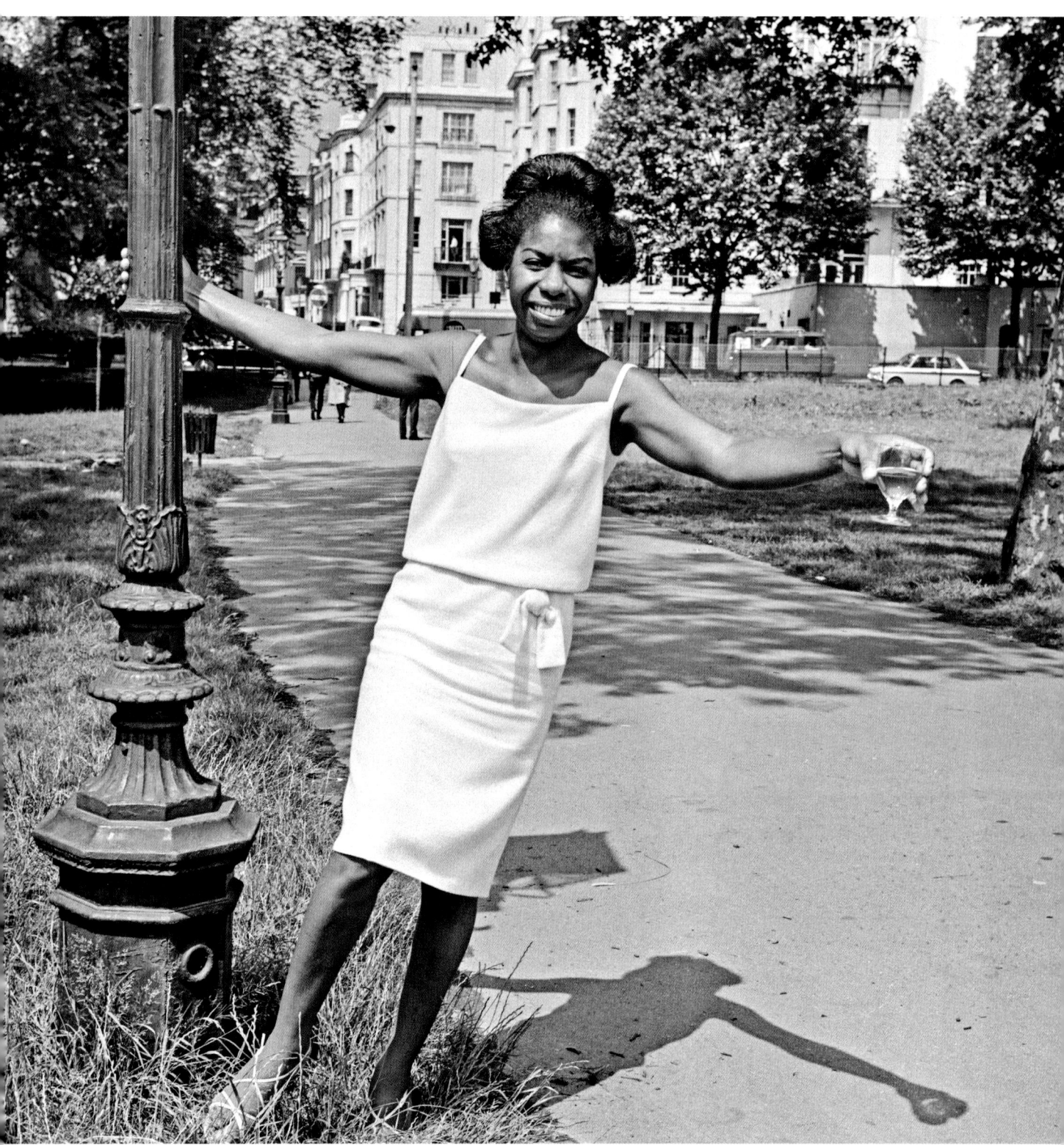

I think of that visceral vulnerability, of this willingness to speak and be seen, when I see the photo of Lorde by Jack Mitchell (page 66)—which was rendered into a mural by Rico Gatson, immortalizing her life in the 167th Street subway station in the Bronx.

In the mural, light radiates from behind her core. In the original photo, taken five years after her mastectomy, there might not be multicolored beams, but Lorde is radiant. She's regal. I see her fully present in both her fierceness and vulnerability—a complex intersection at which many of us find ourselves, particularly women at the helm of artistic, feminist, and Civil Rights Movements.

Daughter of the Depression and the Jim Crow era, Nina Simone was on her first European tour when she was swinging from a lamppost in London during the summer of '65 (photo at left). We know Simone—born Eunice Kathleen Waymon in Tryon, North Carolina—for her powerhouse music of a movement, songs like "Four Women" and "To Be Young, Gifted and Black." Rarely, in my mind, do I see her lighthearted as she is in this photograph—celebrating what it is to be alive, making art, and pursuing dreams unattainable to our ancestors.

Despite the national horrors she wrestled with in the early sixties—the bombing of the 16th Street Baptist Church in Birmingham, Alabama, and the murder of Medgar Evers, which shifted the nature of her music and career—here, she's photographed looking free. I imagine her champagne slightly sloshing out her glass in later shots, her laugh, her interacting with the world walking by with glee and merriment.

Similarly, I try to imagine what's just outside of the frame in this photo of Ruby Bridges, another Civil Rights Movement icon. The 1954 *Brown v. Board of Education* Supreme Court decision rendered segregation in public schools illegal, but many Southern states were slow to integrate.

LEFT: Glass in hand, Nina Simone enjoys a London park in 1965.

Bridges was six in November 1960 when U.S. Marshals escorted her to and from William Frantz Elementary School. She made history by being the first Black student at the all-white school in New Orleans.

The act: revolutionary. But Bridges: just a girl. This state of existence—girlhood—is one far too few Black girls truly get to enjoy. As Rebecca Epstein, lead author of *Girlhood Interrupted: The Erasure of Black Girls' Childhood*, reported in 2017, "adults think Black girls as young as five need less protection and nurturing than their white peers."

In the contemporary imagination, it's easy to remember Bridges surrounded by suited men as in Norman Rockwell's *The Problem We All Live With*. But I prefer her here, outside of what looks to be a family home, in a collared dress with her hands high on her hips as she smiles up at something or someone just outside of the frame. I see not the brave young woman marching among men paid to protect her; I see a jovial little girl.

In 2010, Bridges told Michel Martin, of NPR's *Tell Me More*, she was unaware of the gravity of the situation. "I really wasn't aware of what was going on," she shared. "I was . . . told . . . that I was going to attend a new school and that I should behave." She recalled feeling like she'd "stumbled into the middle of a Mardi Gras parade"— unaware the crowd was for her. In this monumental moment, she was protected, nurtured.

I love the story of her parents letting her remain a little girl. Unfortunately, this innocence was short-lived. Soon, she'd come to understand that what unfolded was because of the color of her skin, hastening her march toward adulthood. But I love a story of a girl, a Black girl, getting the opportunity to remain that way, even in the face of insurmountable change, even under the threat of violence. We have been told so many stories where the narrative is different.

In Birmingham, Alabama, on September 15, 1963, white supremacists murdered Addie Mae Collins (fourteen years old), Cynthia Wesley (fourteen), Carole Robertson (fourteen), and Carol Denise McNair (eleven) in the 16th Street Baptist Church bombing. Those four little girls, as many of us know them now, are immortalized in their youth by the brutality of their deaths. They have been the subject matter of documentaries and inspired songs like Simone's "Mississippi Goddam." Their images aren't part of this essay. It's not because their faces, bodies, lives aren't important. They are; they'll always be.

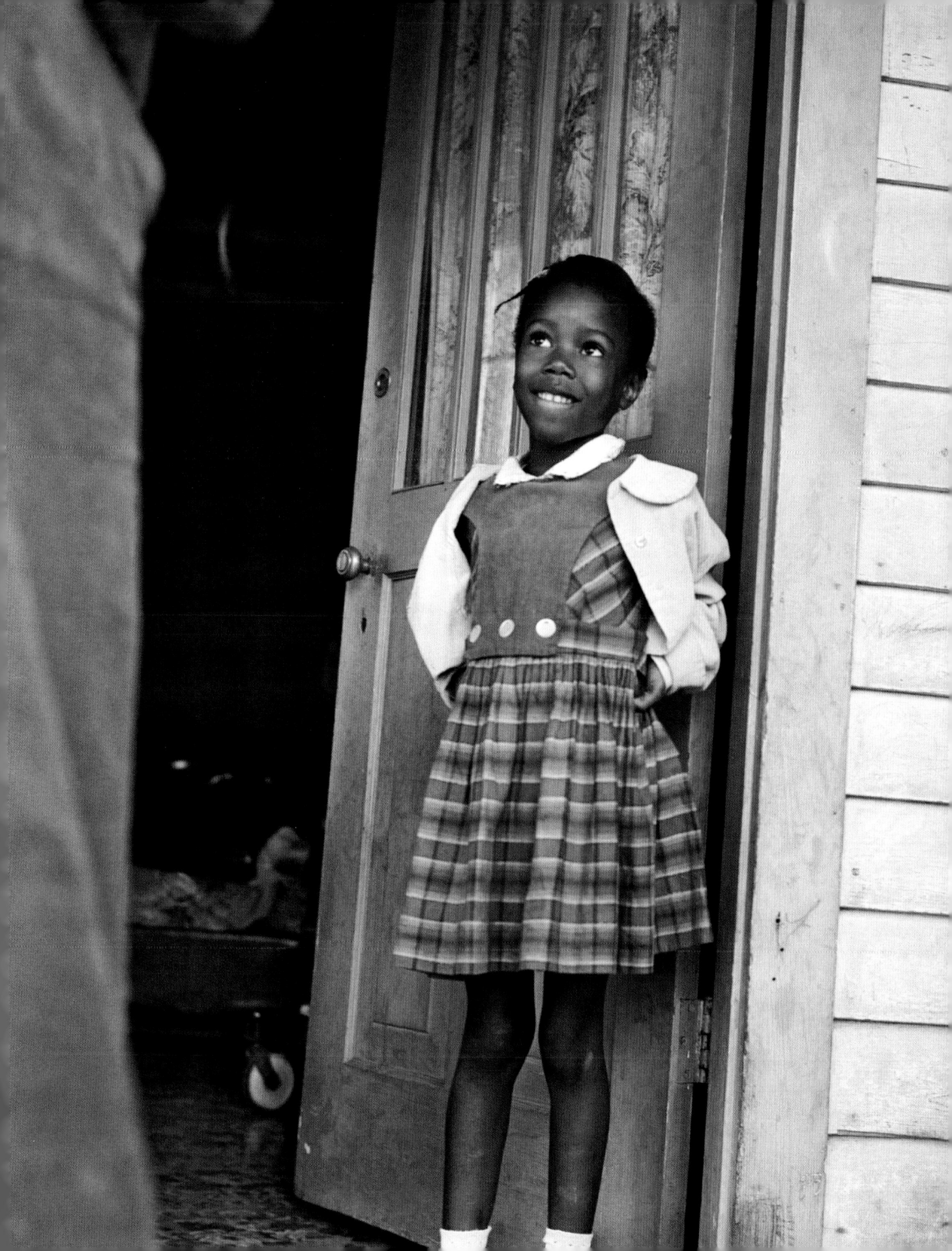

Instead, I've chosen to feature four girls cooling off from the summer sun in the Woodlawn neighborhood of Chicago. Their names have not been recorded in the archive. I do not know their ages. And though my mind drifts to the possibility of their likenesses being captured without their permission, there's a part of me that feels tender about their names not being recorded.

These four little girls, frolicking just ten years after the immortalized ones, are anonymous in this archive because, at least in the moment photographed, their lives weren't marred by national tragedy—the horrors of racism and injustice hadn't been mapped on their childhoods here. They weren't in a church basement in Birmingham, Alabama, or slammed on the ground at a pool party in McKinney, Texas. I hope it wasn't mapped on their adulthoods either, that they weren't "laughing too loudly" together in Napa Valley or startled from their sleep in Louisville, Kentucky.

However, the girls in this photo in 1973 are just that: girls holding one another up in a moment of embrace of both each other and the day. These girls are youthful. And that is revolutionary: their laughter, their joy, their camaraderie.

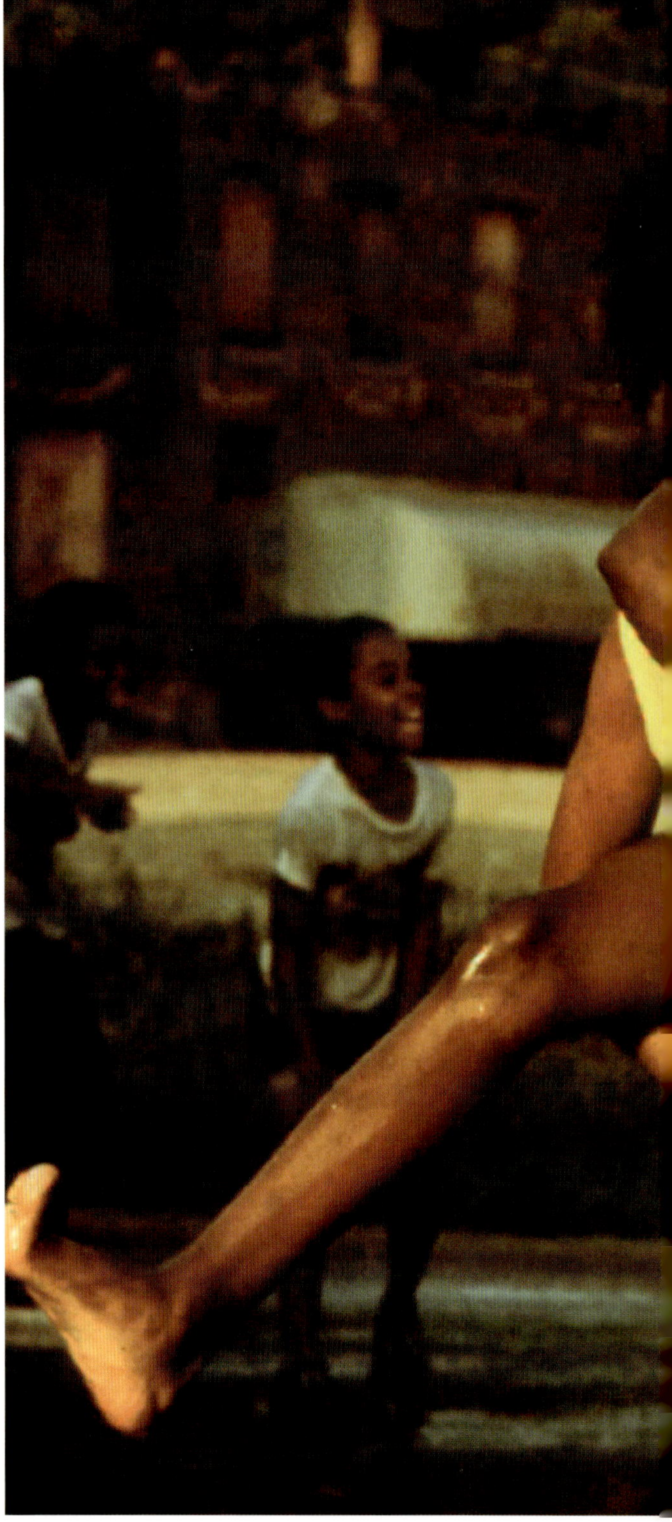

RIGHT: Fun on a hot summer day in Chicago in 1973.

FOLLOWING SPREAD: In front of the Metropolitan Opera House in New York, these three show an audience how double Dutch is done.

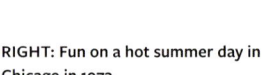

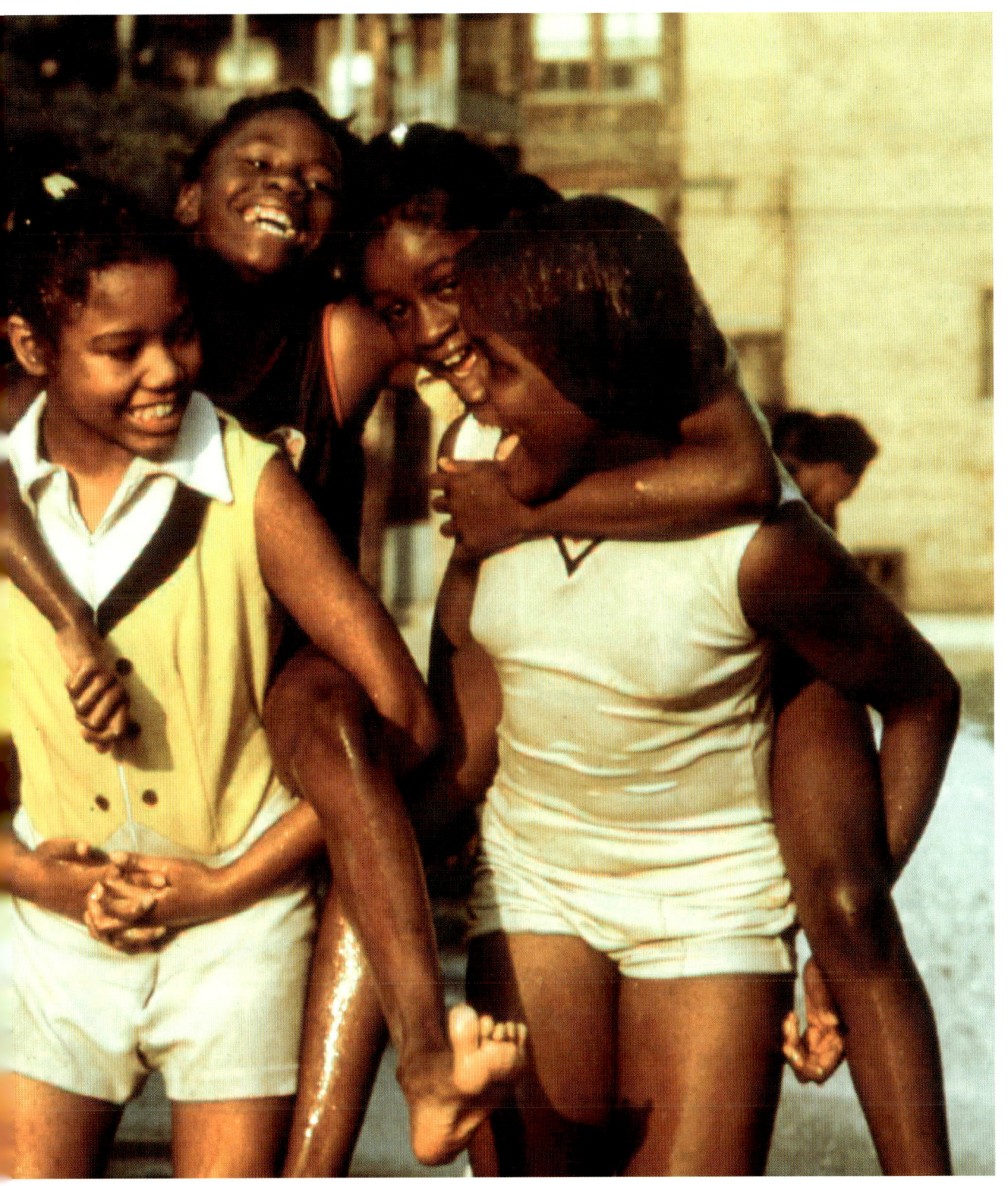

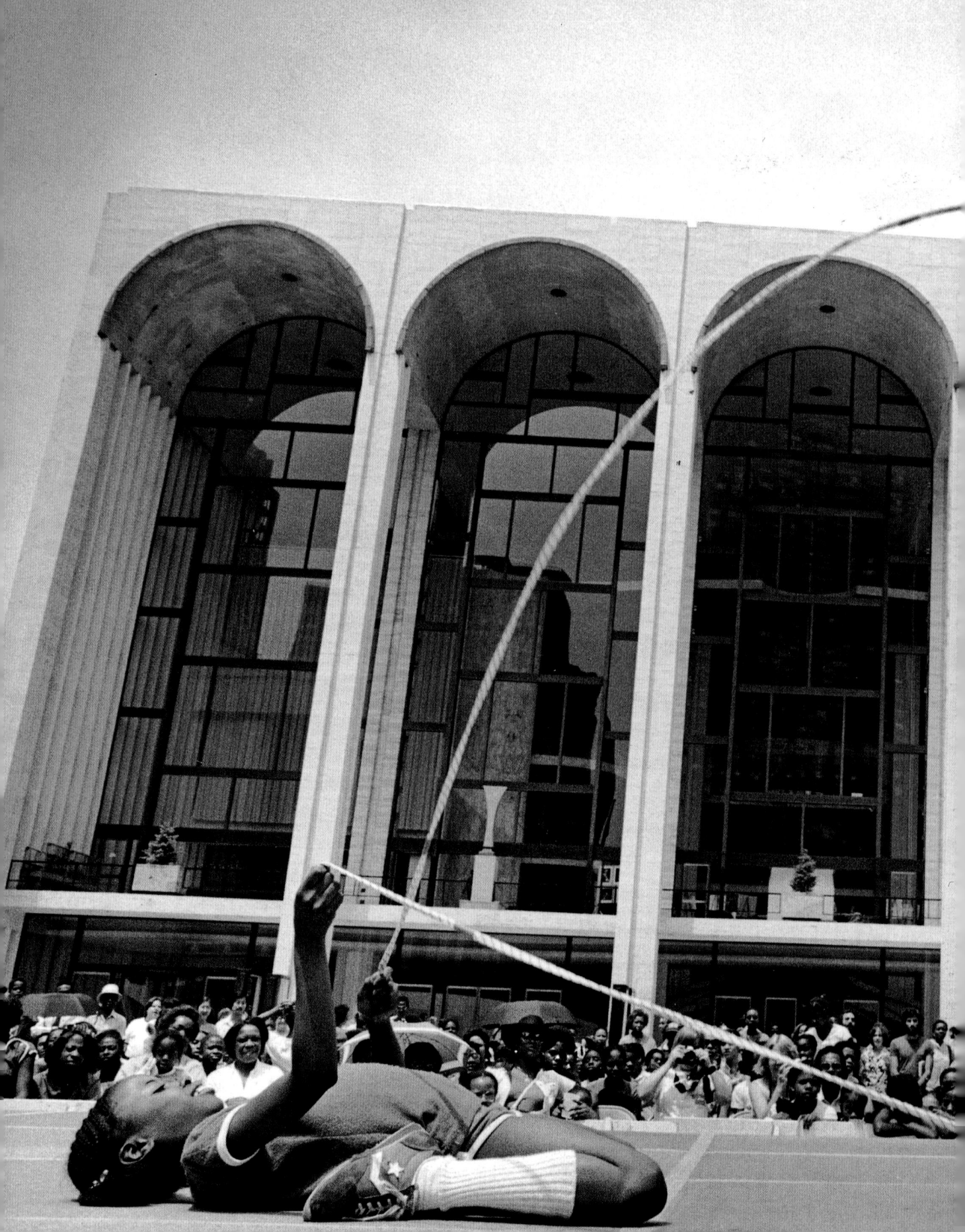

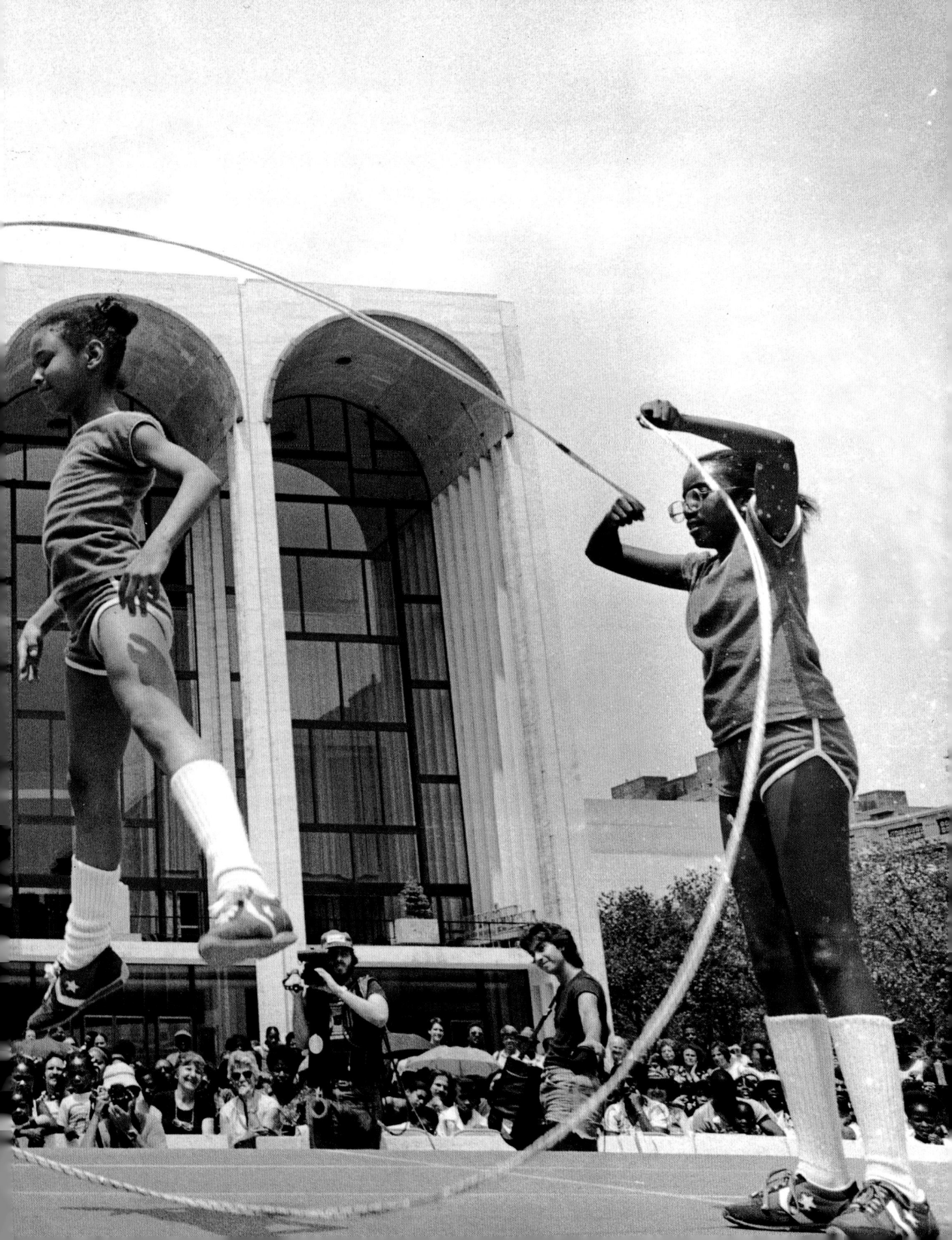

A MOTHER'S POWER

SIERRA L. PHILLIPS

The bravery of Mamie Till-Mobley.

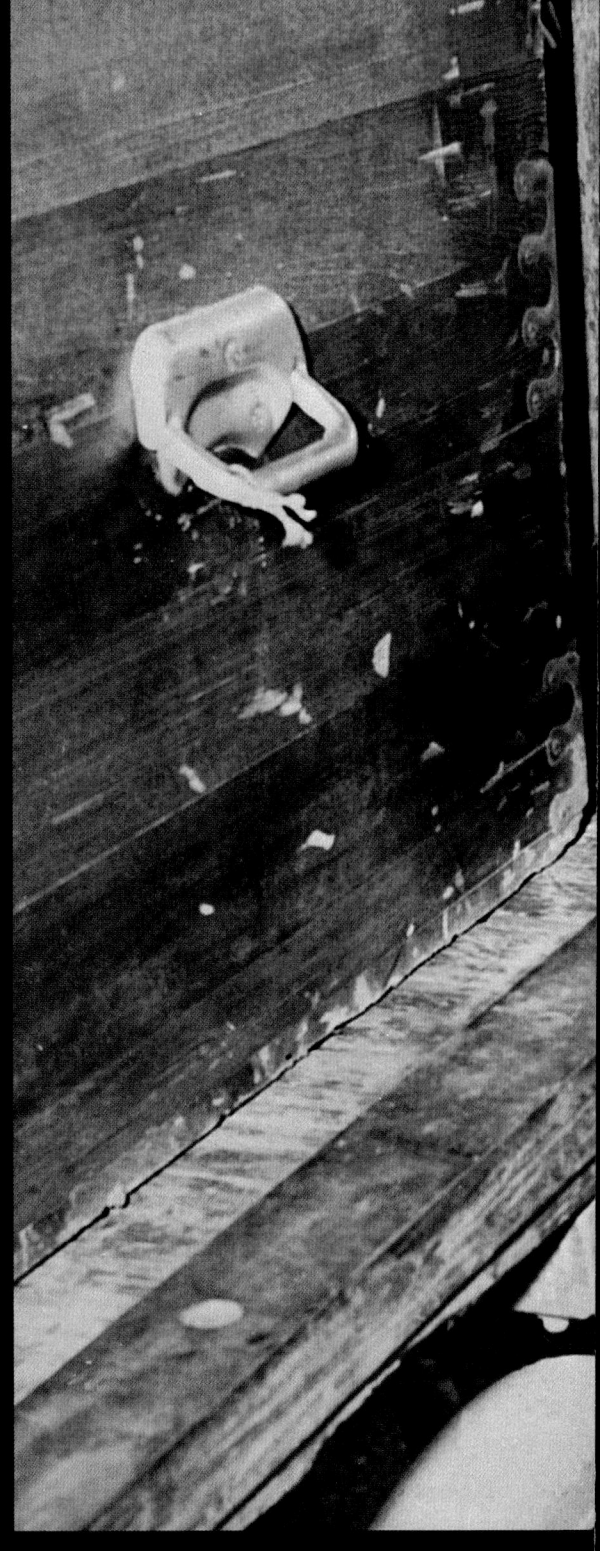

Mamie Elizabeth Carthan was born an only child on November 23, 1921, in Webb, Mississippi. When she was a young girl, her father moved their family north to Argo, Illinois. She married Louis Till in 1939 (later divorced), and two years later, on July 25, she gave birth to their only son, Emmett Louis Till.

In the summer of 1955 while visiting family in the Mississippi Delta, Emmett was accused of whistling at a white woman. A month and three days after his fourteenth birthday, Emmett was kidnapped and brutally murdered by two white men who proclaimed they were upholding the "purity" of white womanhood. Mamie never imagined this trip would result in her son's untimely death, yet she turned her grief into action, which ultimately added momentum to the Black struggle for freedom in the United States.

Clarence Strider was the sheriff of Tallahatchie County, where Emmett's decomposed body was found floating in the county's river on August 31, 1955. His body was badly disfigured, and Sheriff Strider knew he had to conceal this brutality from the public quickly.

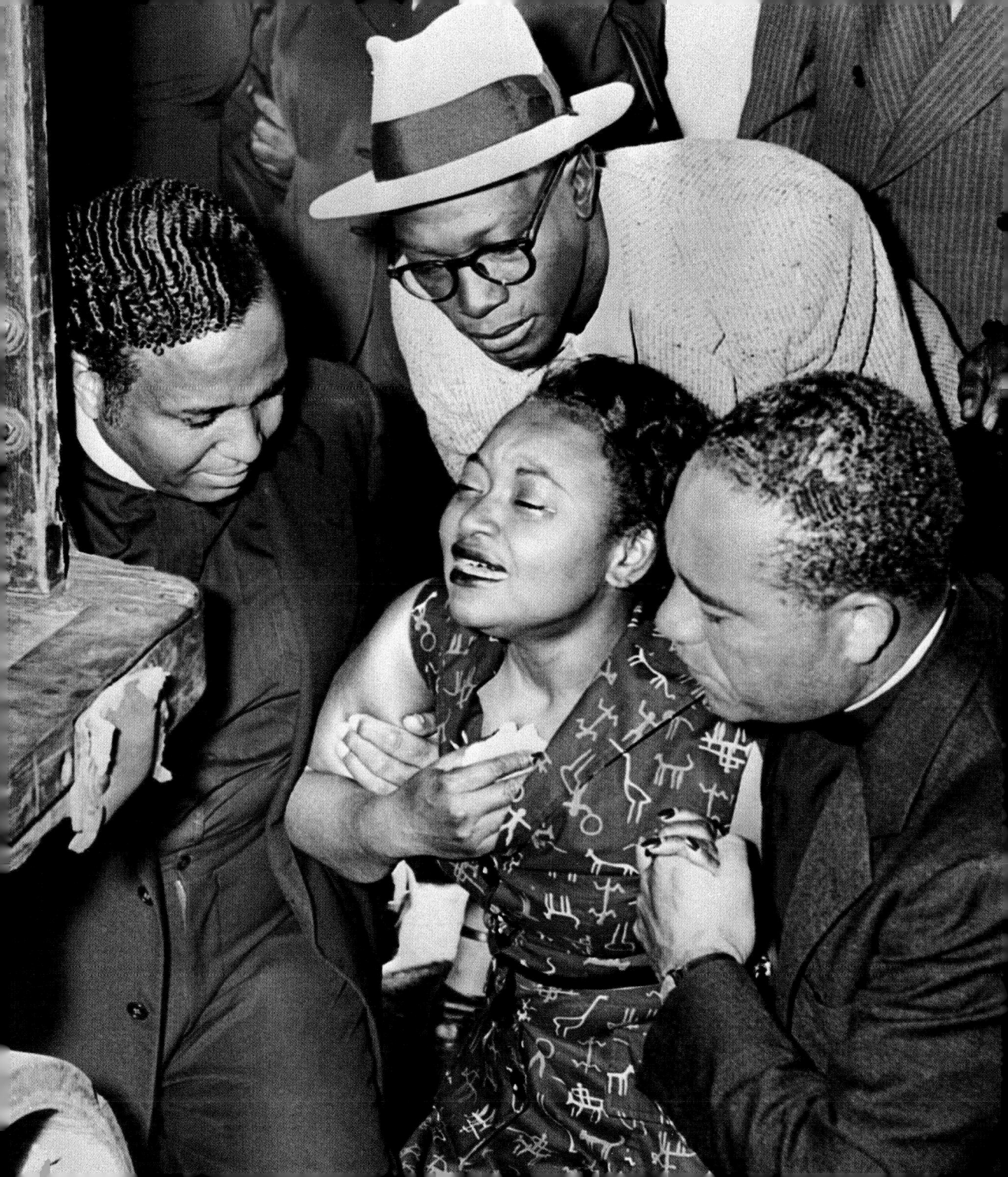

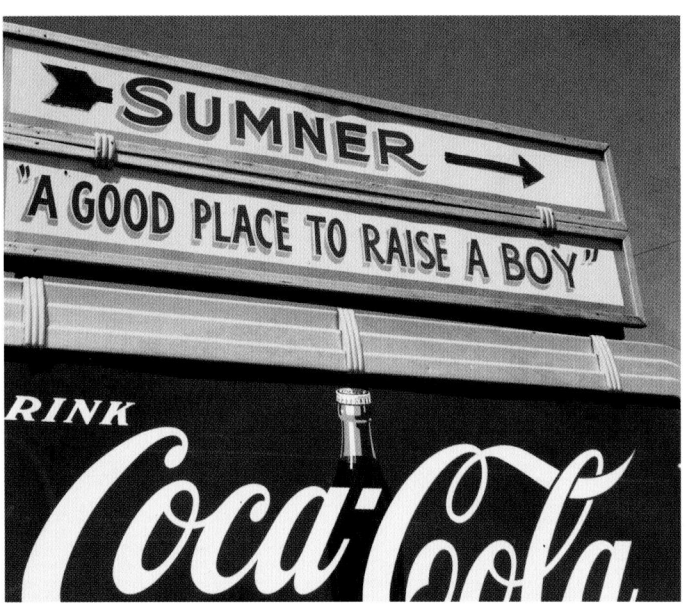
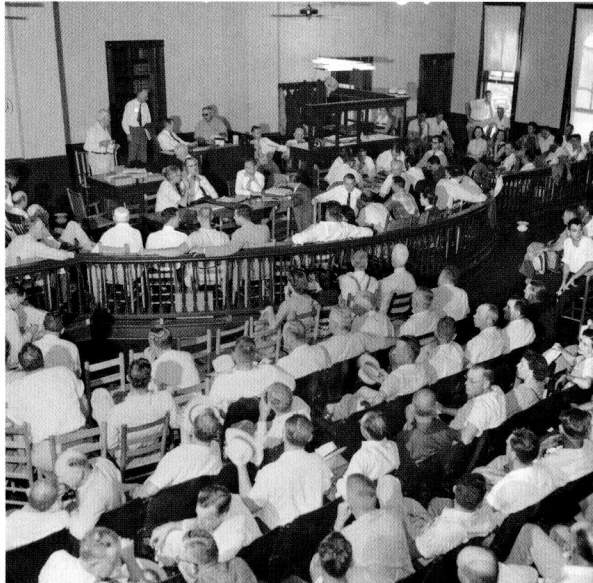

In an interview with The Chicago Project in 2003, Till-Mobley discussed how the sheriff attempted to cover up this deadly act by directing Emmett's family to bury his body by nightfall. When Mamie found out, she demanded her uncle halt the burial and ship her son back to Chicago immediately.

Before Emmett's body was transported home, the undertaker of the "Hospitality State" sealed the box with Till's remains and his Mississippi relatives were ordered to sign affidavits agreeing that at no point would they open it. It was not until the body arrived in Chicago that Mamie found out the true nature of her son's murder.

When Emmett's remains finally arrived in Chicago on September 2, 1955, three men accompanied the grieving mother to Central Station to meet her son's remains: the man who would later become her second husband, Gene Mobley (behind), Bishop Louis H. Ford (left), and Bishop Isaiah Roberts (right), both of Roberts Temple Church of God in Christ in Chicago.

The men are seen supporting Mamie perhaps emotionally, but certainly physically, as it appears that she was beginning to collapse. A crowd gathers behind them. The large wooden box, scraped and scratched, was placed on a flatbed truck. The handle can be seen at the top left of the photograph with the wheels of the truck.

Mamie was overcome with emotion when confronted with the direct, visual evidence that her "Bobo" had not returned home alive. In her memoir *Death of Innocence* (2003), Till-Mobley wrote: "What was I about to witness?" How could she know what awaited her inside the sealed box?

Despite opposition, and disregarding the signed affidavits, she demanded the box be opened. When she finally saw her son, he was unrecognizable. Rather than be consumed by grief, she insisted on an open-casket funeral and public viewing of Emmett because she wanted the world to bear witness to the brutality of white supremacy. On September 2, 1955, the *Chicago Sun-Times* reported her famous words: "Let the people see what they did to my boy."

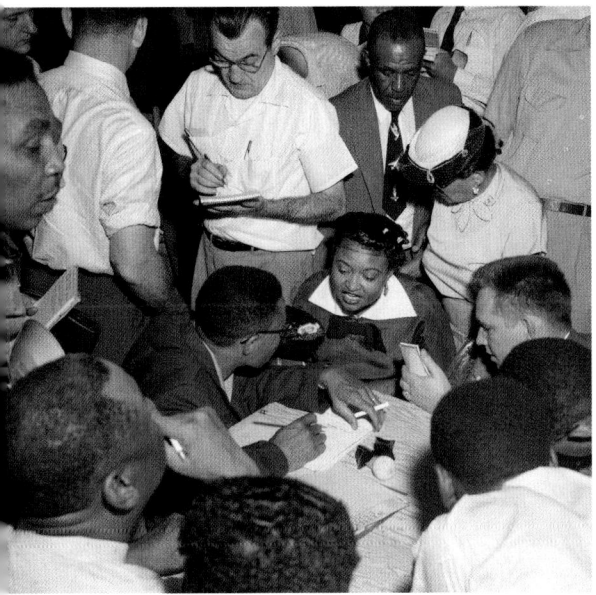
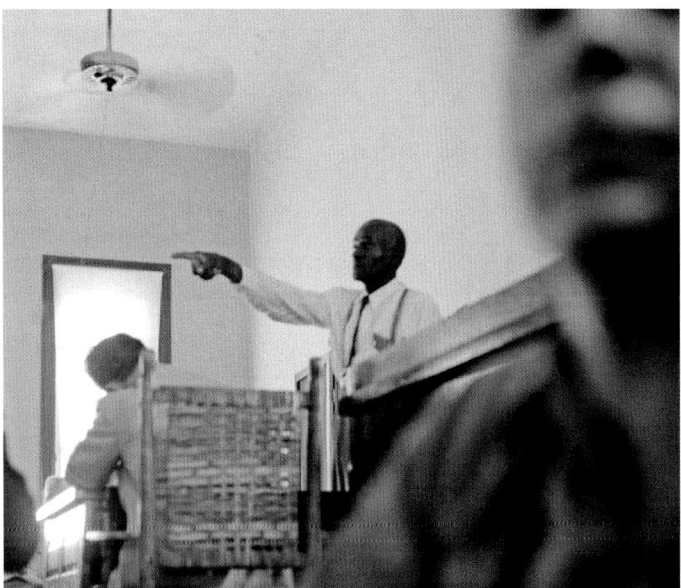

Although the assailants were never convicted of their crime, Emmett's death and the collective action of the Black community added momentum to the Civil Rights Movement. After brothers J. W. Milam and Roy Bryant were acquitted, Black residents in Tallahatchie County boycotted their grocery store and drove it out of business. Black people also sent letters to the White House demanding justice for Emmett Till.

Mamie's determination inspired those who were not already involved in the movement to engage in collective action and demand Black people be treated like citizens. The Montgomery Bus Boycott began less than four months after Emmett's lynching. Rosa Parks said she refused to give up her seat because "I thought about Emmett Till and I could not go back."

In her memoir Mamie states: "they were moved to action in ways they hadn't been before." Without Mamie's bravery, would the nation have known the brutality and inhumanity that targeted Emmett Till?

PREVIOUS SPREAD: On December 2, 1955, the body of fourteen-year-old Emmett Till arrived by train in Chicago. His mother, Mamie Till (Bradley), sinks to her knees surrounded by supporters.

ABOVE, LEFT TO RIGHT: Sumner, Mississippi, where the trial of Till's murderers was held.

J. W. Milam and Roy Bryant went on trial for the murder of Emmett Till in a segregated courtroom with an all-white jury and an almost entirely white crowd in attendance.

Mamie Till-Mobley traveled to Sumner for the trial of the two men accused of murdering her son. She speaks to a scrum of reporters outside the courtroom.

Emmett Till's great-uncle, with whom he was staying, stands up in court and points his finger at the men who took Till away.

FOLLOWING SPREAD: Emmett Till lying in his bed in Chicago the year before he went to visit family in Mississippi.

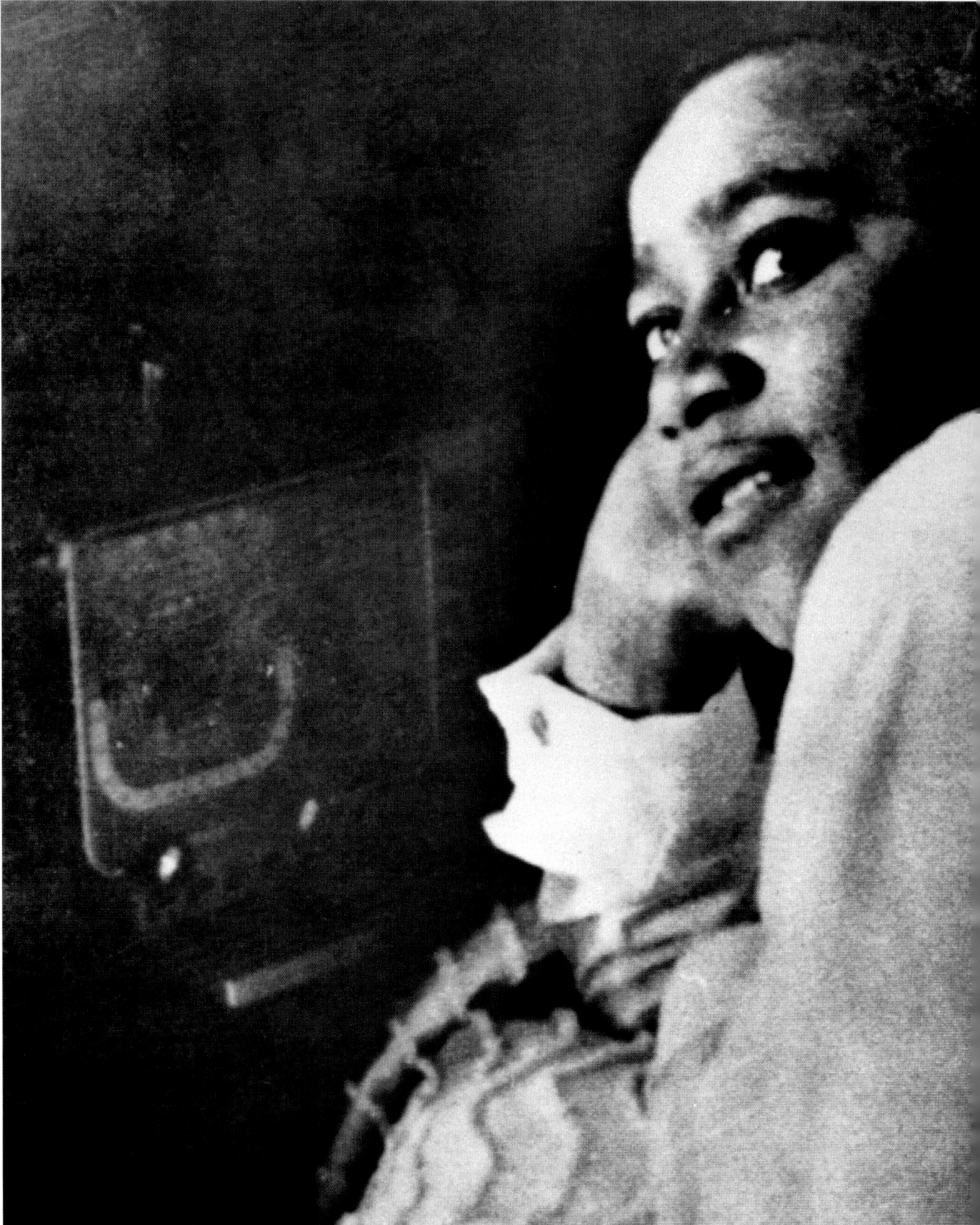

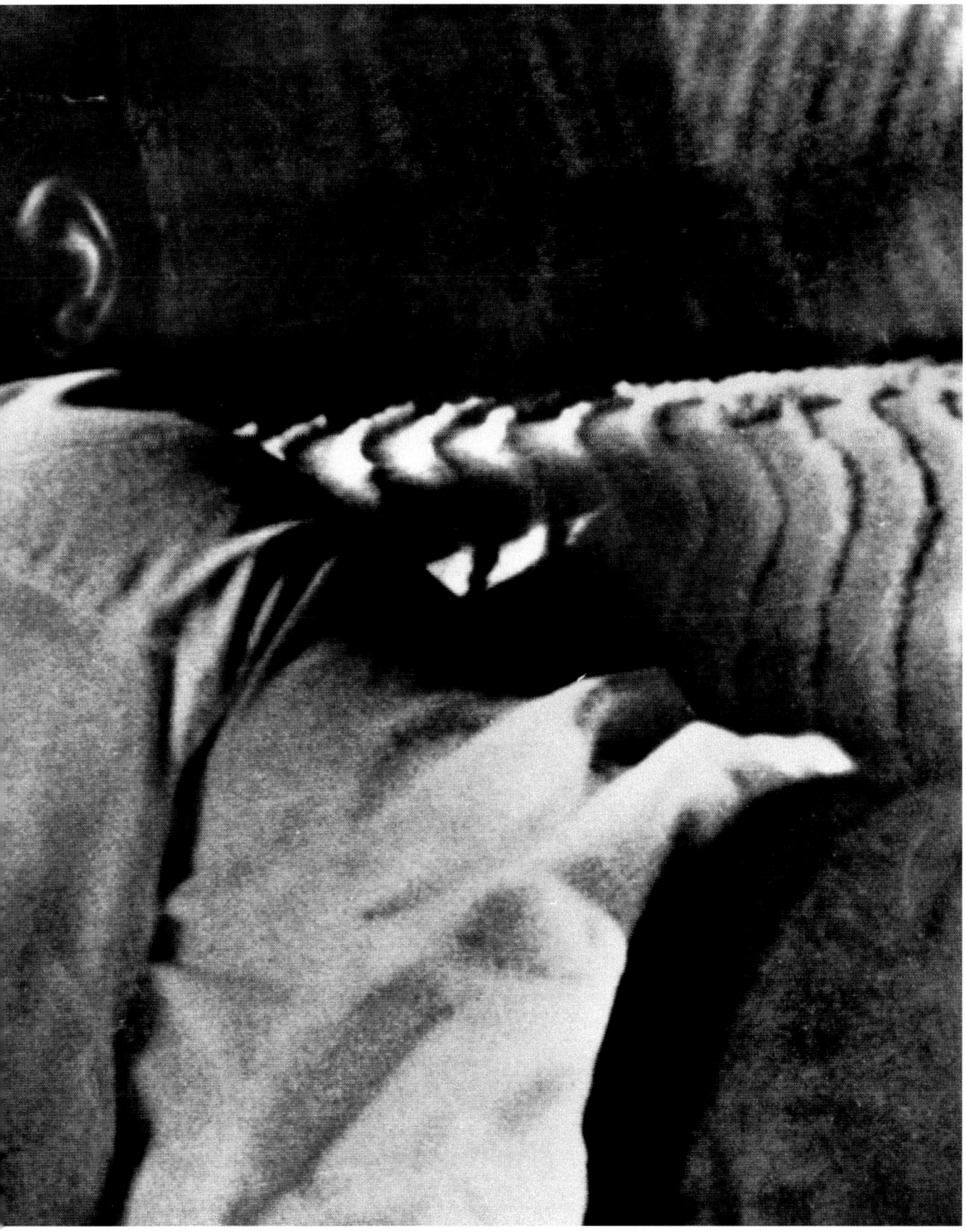

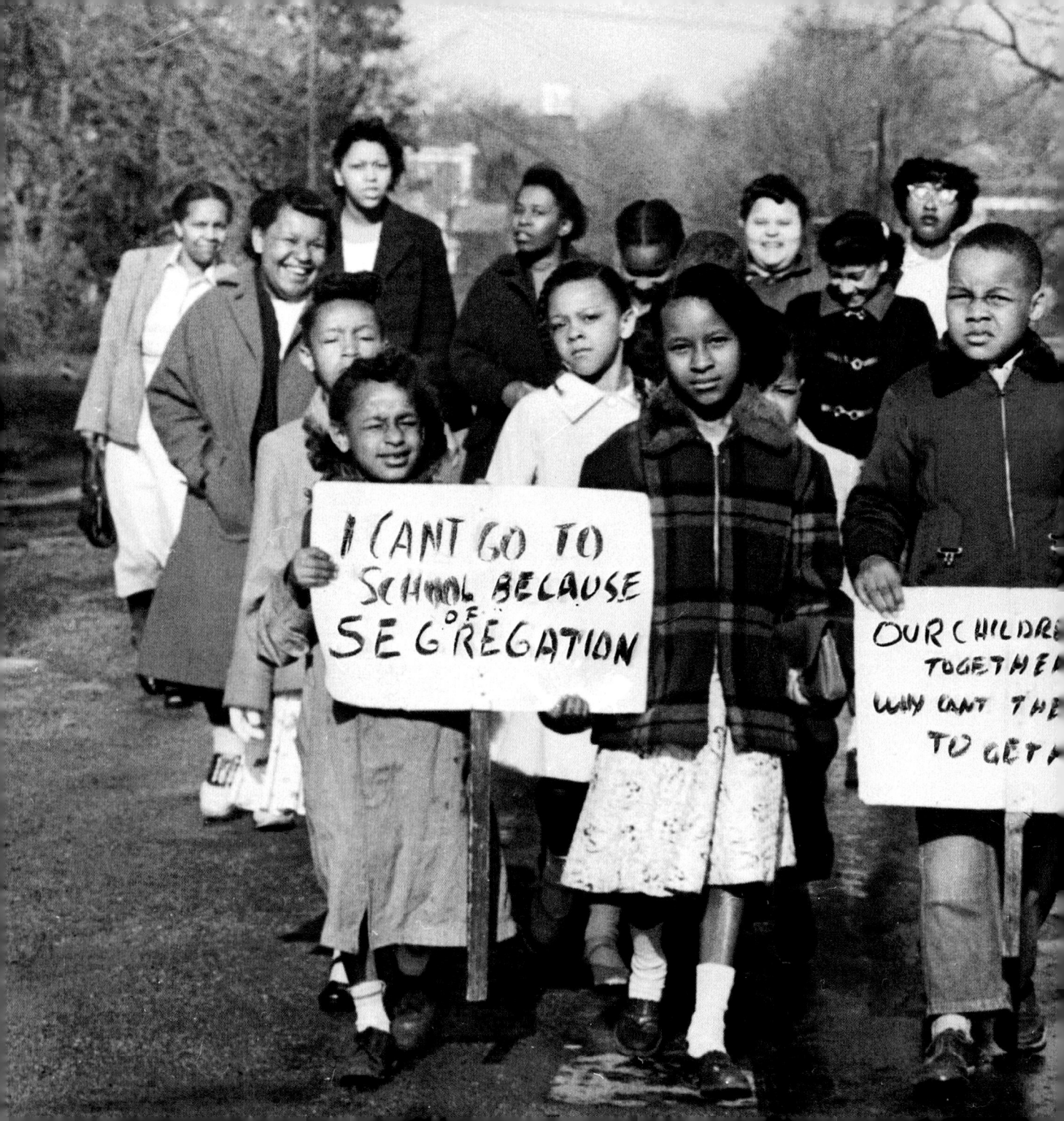

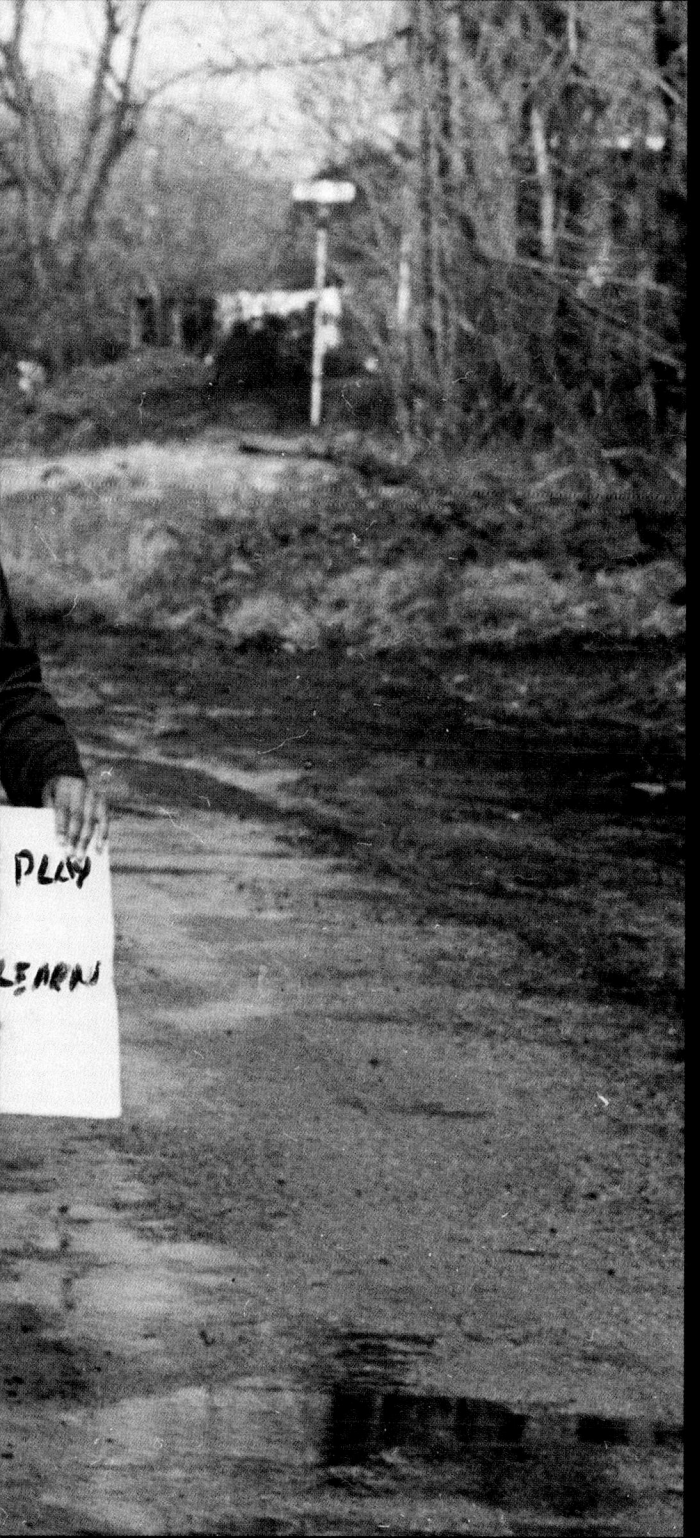

MARCHING MOTHERS

JESSICA VIÑAS-NELSON

*Neither wind nor rain could stop
a band of Ohio mothers from securing
the education their children deserved.*

In 1956, threatened by imprisonment and tormented by racial epithets and a burned cross, schoolchildren marched for integration. Despite conjuring images of the Deep South, this happened in the small town of Hillsboro, Ohio, two years after *Brown v. Board of Education* was supposed to have ended school segregation.

Newspapers nicknamed Hillsboro "Little Dixie," but in truth the town wasn't unique. Hillsboro's all-white school board stalled on desegregating its schools like nearly all schools across the nation. The actual work of integration fell on Black students and parents. The puddles of water underscore that rain or shine, every morning for two years mothers and children marched for education equality in this tiny Ohio town.

In 1954, all of Hillsboro's seventy Black elementary students attended Lincoln School. Many had to walk past the two all-white schools, Washington and Webster, to reach the all-Black school, Lincoln. In a nearly century-old building where snow blew inside in the winter, six grades shared two rooms, two teachers, and books discarded from white schools.

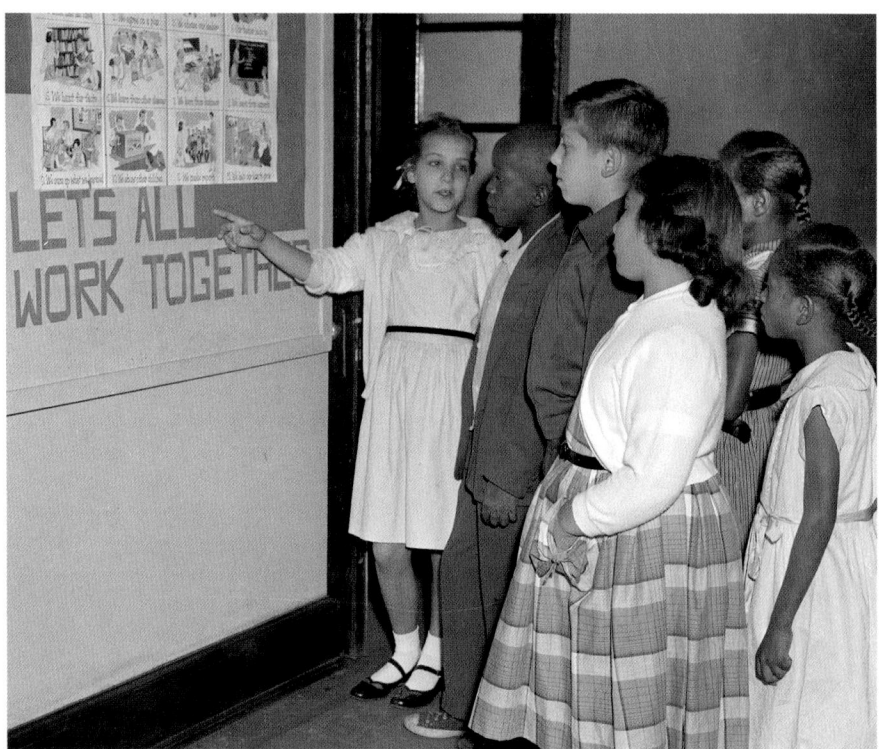

A fire—set by a white man in a misguided effort to end segregation—badly damaged Lincoln that summer but did nothing to convince the school board to integrate. Classrooms were freshly painted, while Black parents feared the building would collapse.

The state's first public schools only allowed funding for "white youths." In 1848, Black Ohioans won the right to be taxed for the education of Black children. After another hard fight, the state repealed a provision allowing segregation in 1887. A Black father in Oxford, Ohio, tested this in court that same year and won. Similar battles continued and courts repeatedly reaffirmed that Ohio's laws banned segregation.

Nevertheless, many Ohio schools remained segregated. By 1954, the fight for integrated education was over a century old and school segregation had been illegal in the state for seventy years. Hillsboro's schools, segregated since at least 1869 when Lincoln opened, formalized segregation in 1939.

The summer after *Brown*, Imogene Curtis, Gertrude Clemons, and several other mothers drafted a petition demanding integration of Lincoln's students and teachers into Washington and Webster. When they delivered it with the signatures of nearly all the Black Hillsboro residents, a board member insisted they were "asking the impossible."

Undeterred, fifty Black students accompanied by their parents arrived at Washington and Webster on the first day of school. Segregation seemed like it might come to an anticlimactic end as they were enrolled and assigned classrooms.

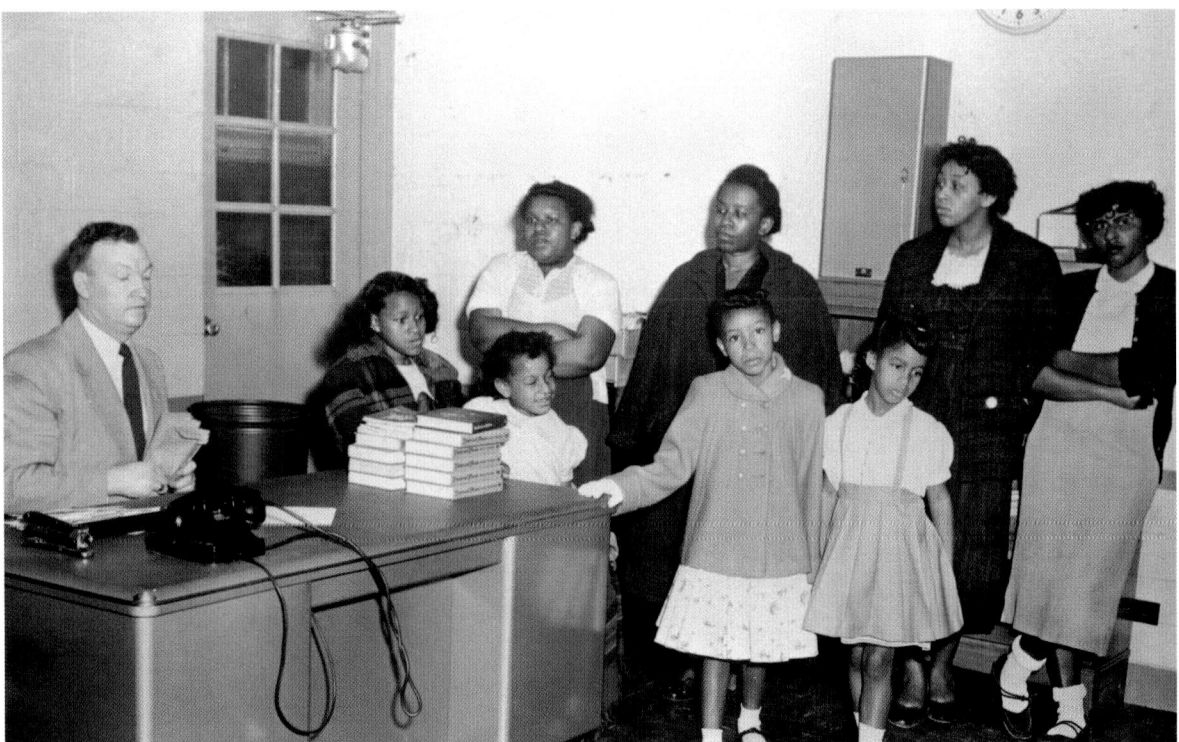

Within days, however, under the guise of overcrowding, the school board redrew district lines. The resulting map, which officials refused to show in court, had been so gerrymandered that only a handful of Black children were assigned to Washington and Webster. Lincoln remained all Black. A board member later told the court that White students would be insulted if assigned to Lincoln.

Unwilling to accept this charade, the mothers began marching their children to Washington and Webster each day only to be rebuffed. Blinds were tightly drawn to prevent white students from seeing as their would-be classmates were turned away. The school board threatened to arrest the mothers if the "truant" children didn't enroll at Lincoln. But the mothers refused to send their children to a school they feared was structurally unsound and instead homeschooled their children with assistance from a nearby Quaker college.

The situation attracted the attention of the NAACP, which brought a case against the district in September 1954. Constance Baker Motley, who worked on the *Brown* decision, served as lead counsel, and Thurgood Marshall led oral arguments one day. The judge insisted the case was "premature" as the Supreme Court had not yet provided a timetable for *Brown*. After the Supreme Court urged schools to comply with "all deliberate speed" in 1955, the judge continued to stall.

Every delay meant another morning march for some twenty mothers and forty children. Throughout the 1954–55 and 1955–56 school years they marched every day without fail.

These photos capture images of these brave mothers and their children. But in its silence, we cannot hear the racial epithets hurled at them as they marched, or the threats mothers received from white employers. One child's sign asks, "Our children play together / Why can't they learn together," but the children recalled being rejected by white would-be playmates.

The marching mothers changed their route after white construction workers exposed themselves to the kids. Even when a cross was burned in a Black family's yard, they maintained their path past the charred remains.

On April 2, 1956, the Supreme Court declined to review the decision of a lower court siding against the school board. That night, Imogene Curtis waited hours at a school board meeting to ask about getting the children placed in the appropriate grades immediately. The board postponed their decision until fall. They marched on.

These pictures were taken the morning after that school board decision. Except for the increased press presence, the march occurred much as it had every day of the long two years. On April 11, the school board voted to integrate only after the Ohio Board of Education, weary of growing press attention, threatened to withhold state funding.

On April 17, 1956, the children were finally allowed to enter their classrooms at Washington and Webster. An editorial in the Hillsboro *Press-Gazette* claimed

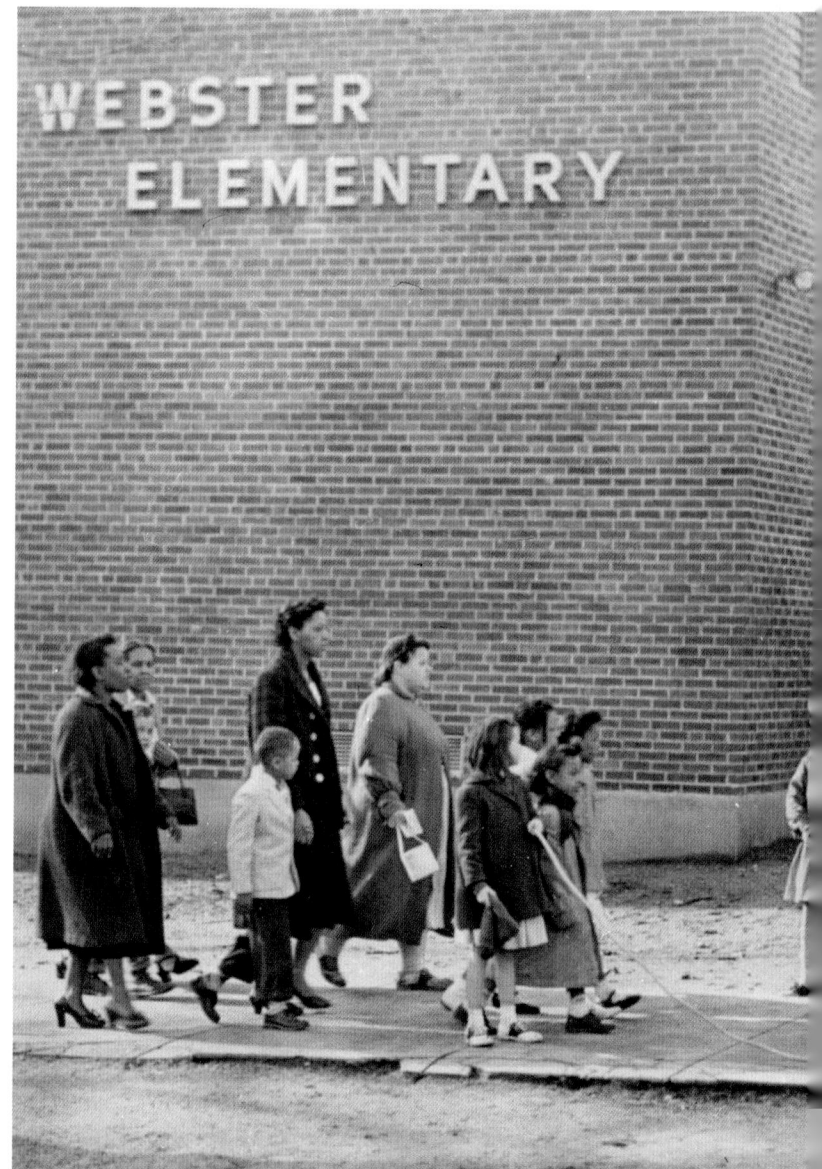

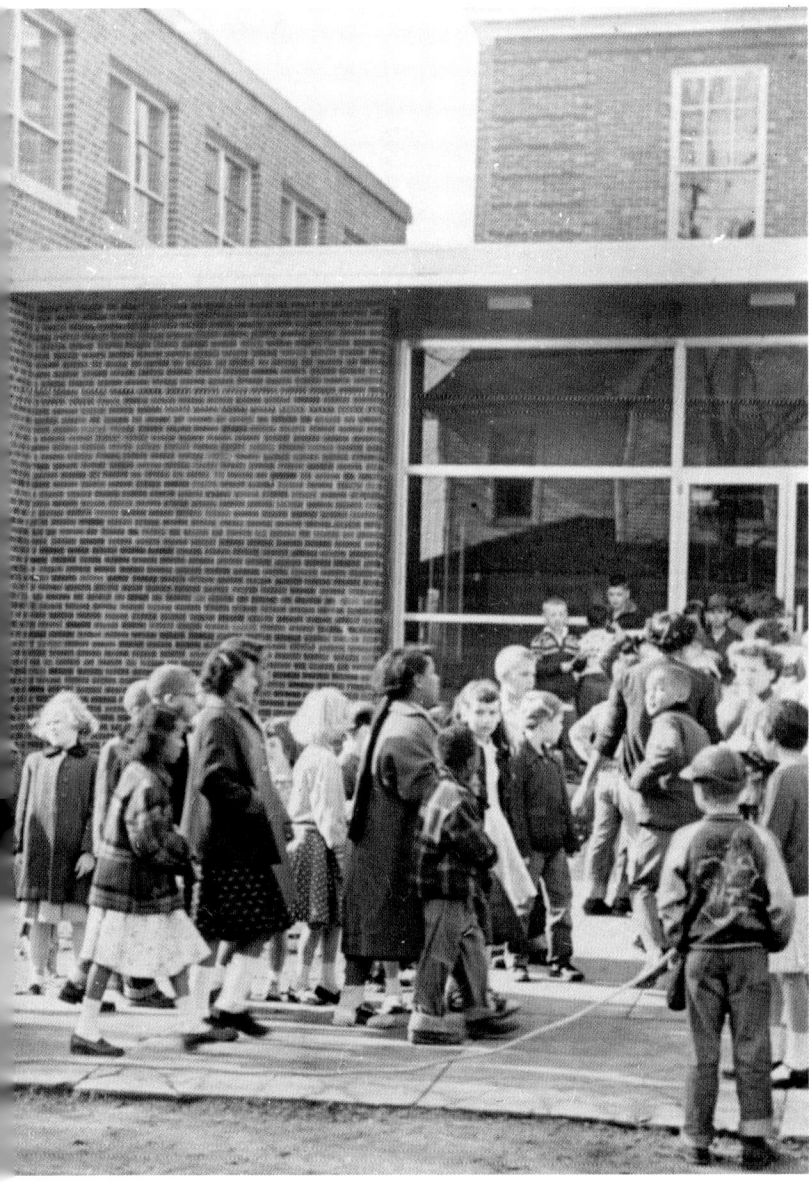

the mothers hurt their children by their actions, but Imogene Curtis retorted, "Many of our people died freeing us and our descendants, but it didn't make the victory any worse."

Once national attention drifted, Hillsboro's schools devised new ways to thwart integration. Students who protested were held back two grades in what their parents believed was punishment for their activism. White teachers glared at their new pupils, white students largely avoided them, and they were bored in grades behind where they should have been. Only recently has the town started to commemorate instead of hiding this history.

Brown receives a lot of praise for ending school segregation, but the ruling didn't make it a reality. The actions, sacrifices, and persistence of Black communities gave *Brown* meaning, as does their continuing fight today. The burden of enforcement was borne on the backs (and marching feet) of Hillsboro students and parents in what became the first Northern test case of the *Brown* decision.

Parents nationwide lamented the year of remote education during the COVID-19 pandemic, but in Hillsboro, Ohio, Farmville, Virginia, and many other places, Black students endured remote education, long before Zoom, in their fight for equality.

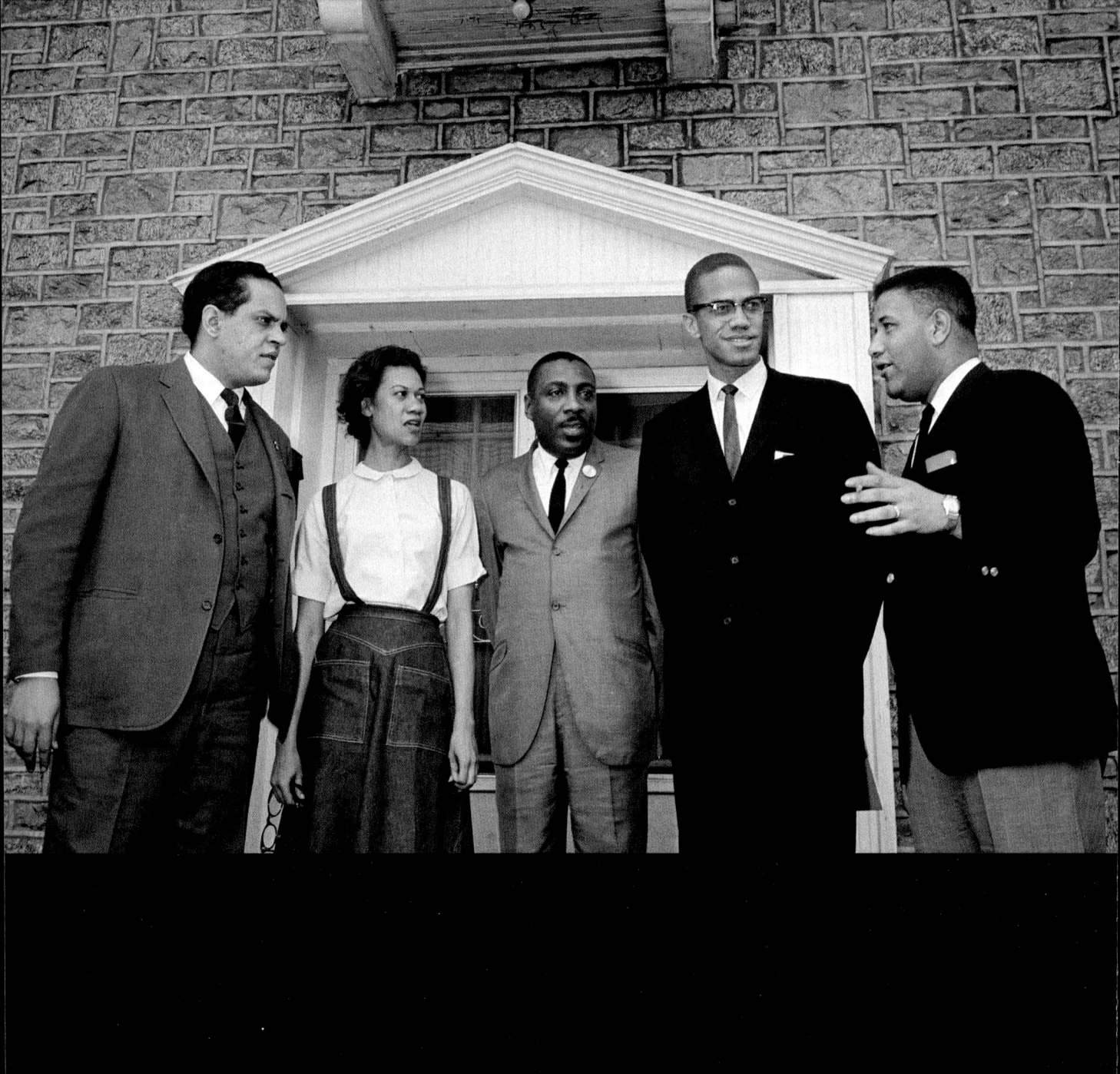

GLORIA RICHARDSON: ACT IN THE FREEDOM STRUGGLE

JASMIN A. YOUNG

*Gloria Richardson's local organizing in
Cambridge, Maryland, influenced a nationwide
movement for armed Black self-defense.*

Between 1962 and 1964, Gloria Richardson led the struggle for better jobs and housing for Black people in Cambridge, Maryland. In 1964, she began organizing more widely, and the Cambridge movement attracted national attention because Black people practiced armed self-defense against violent segregationists.

Richardson became a highly controversial leader for her refusal to publicly denounce armed resistance. As one of a few Black women activists at that time to support armed self-defense and openly reject nonviolence as the sole viable tactic available to Black people, Richardson found herself in good company with like-minded activists including Malcolm X.

As a self-described "radical revolutionary," Richardson collaborated with other Black political radicals. Along with several notable activists, Richardson established a new national organization, ACT, which was not an acronym but rather a call to action.

ACT's founding meeting was held on March 14, 1964, at the Eastern Light Masonic Lodge in Chester, Pennsylvania. Among the organization's founders were DC activist Julius Hobson; NAACP leader Stanley Branche; Rev. Milton Galamison, leader of school boycotts in New York City; Jesse Gray, organizer of the Harlem rent strikes; Lawrence Landry, leader of the Chicago school boycotts; and his fellow Chicagoan Nahaz Rogers.

The group's central purpose was to support activists across the country, mainly in the North and on the West Coast. In contrast to Southern movements, which focused on access to voting rights as a mechanism for improving African American socioeconomic conditions, Black people in the Northern urban movement developed social movements to fight for better schools, better housing, and better job opportunities.

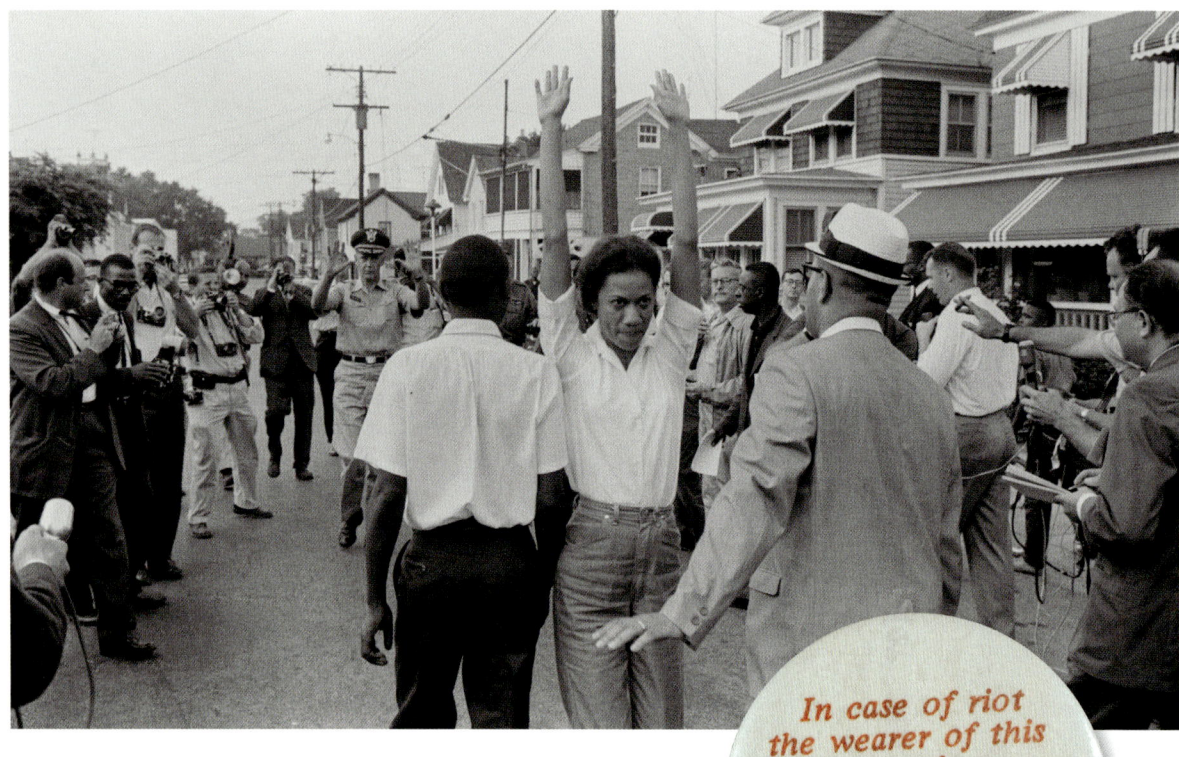

In its May 7, 1964, issue, *Jet* magazine, the nation's first Black weekly, referred to ACT as a "third force" action group, because they were dissatisfied with the established civil rights organizations' polite fight against white bigotry.

The founding members of ACT supported direct action strategies to attack racial inequality and opposed gradual approaches to integration and equal rights. In the same issue of *Jet*, they promised militant action in the fight for equality and proclaimed that it would "not function in a manner that is acceptable to white people. It will do things that are acceptable to Negroes."

ACT's founders all specialized in community organizing, each bringing their unique local experiences to the table. Landry served as ACT's chairman and was a Chicago native. He had been organizing boycotts of Chicago public schools, which treated Black students with racism and contempt.

In case of riot the wearer of this button is an
Honorary Negro
H. Rapp Brown

PREVIOUS SPREAD, LEFT: Civil rights leaders gathered in Chester, Pennsylvania, in 1964 to strategize, and Gloria Richardson was among them, standing with Lawrence Landry, comedian Dick Gregory, Malcolm X, and Stanley Branche.

ABOVE: Gloria Richardson raises her arms to stop a march in Cambridge, Maryland, in July 1963. The town was under limited martial law and the marchers then dispersed.

RIGHT: Though a town of only 12,000 people, Cambridge, Maryland, sent a delegation to the March for Jobs and Freedom in Washington, DC, in August 1963.

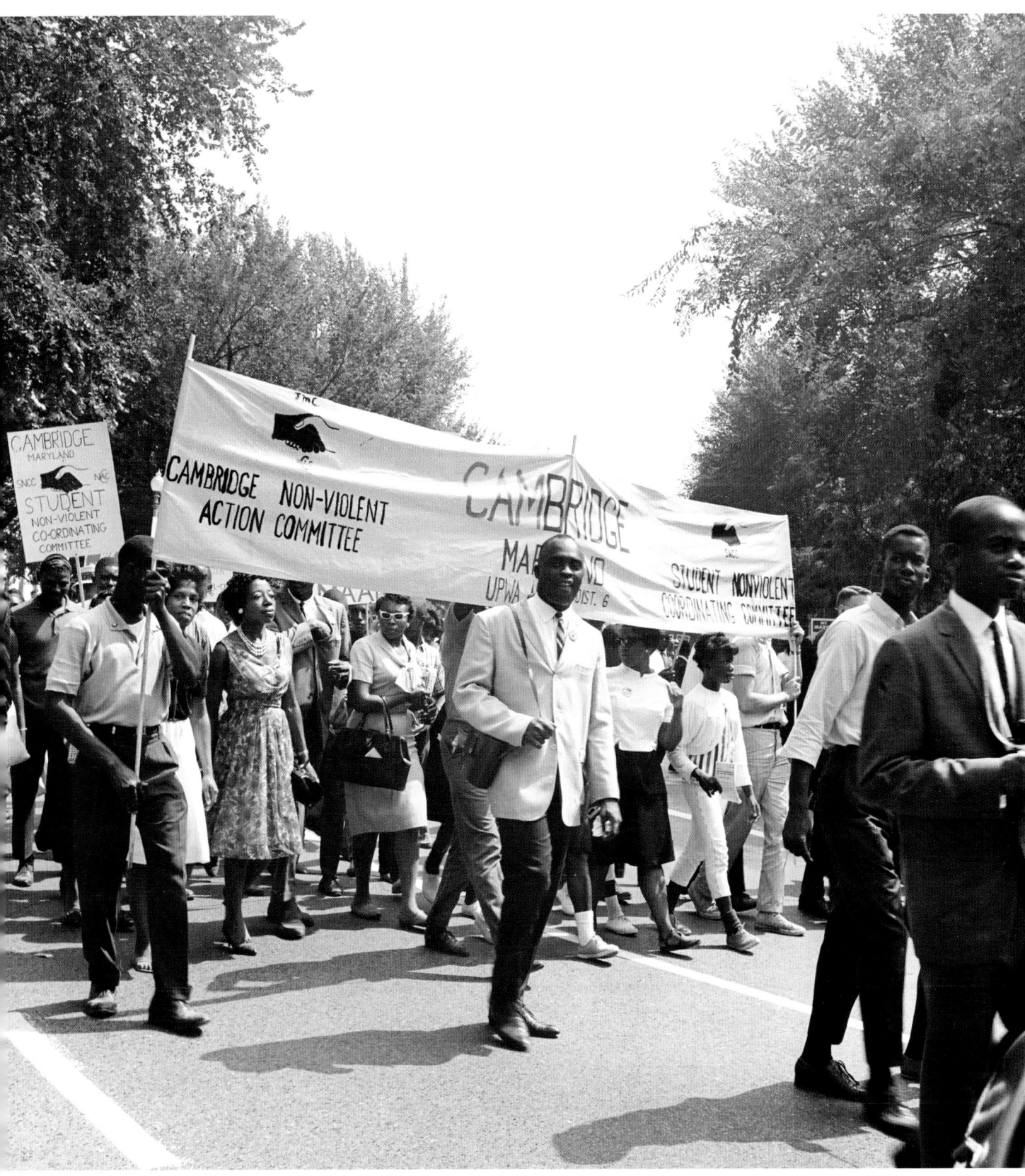

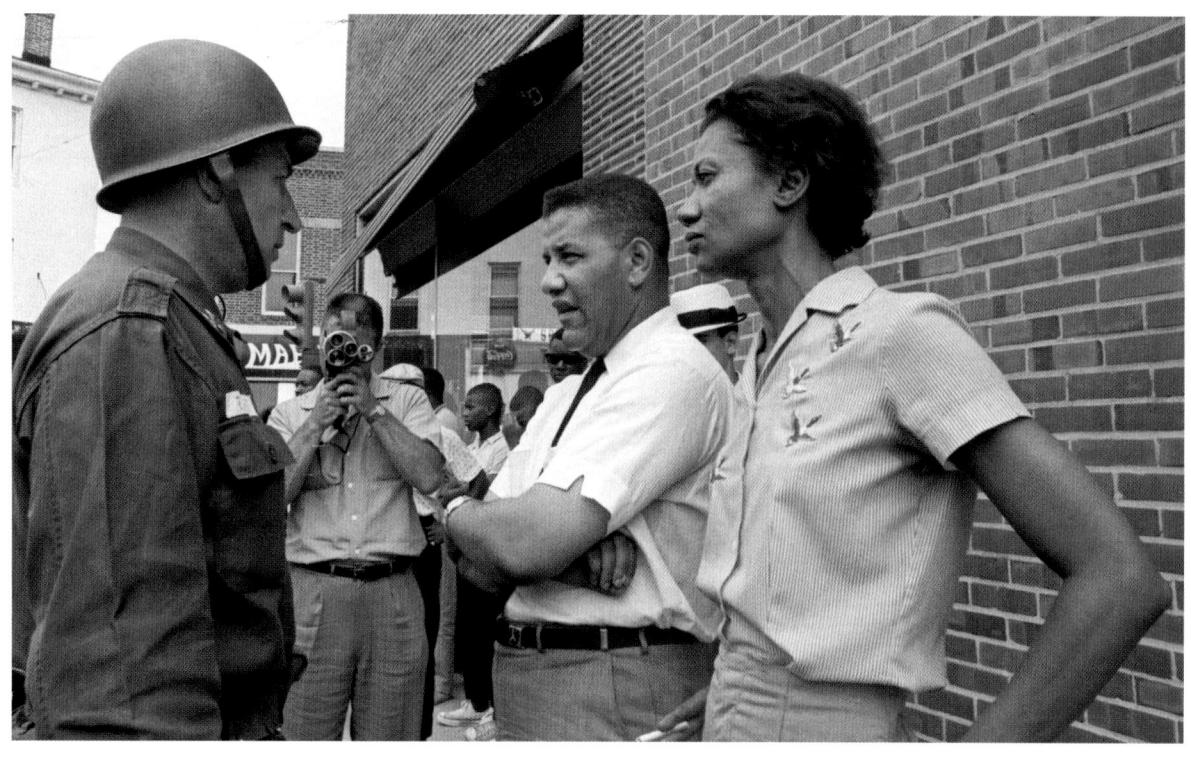

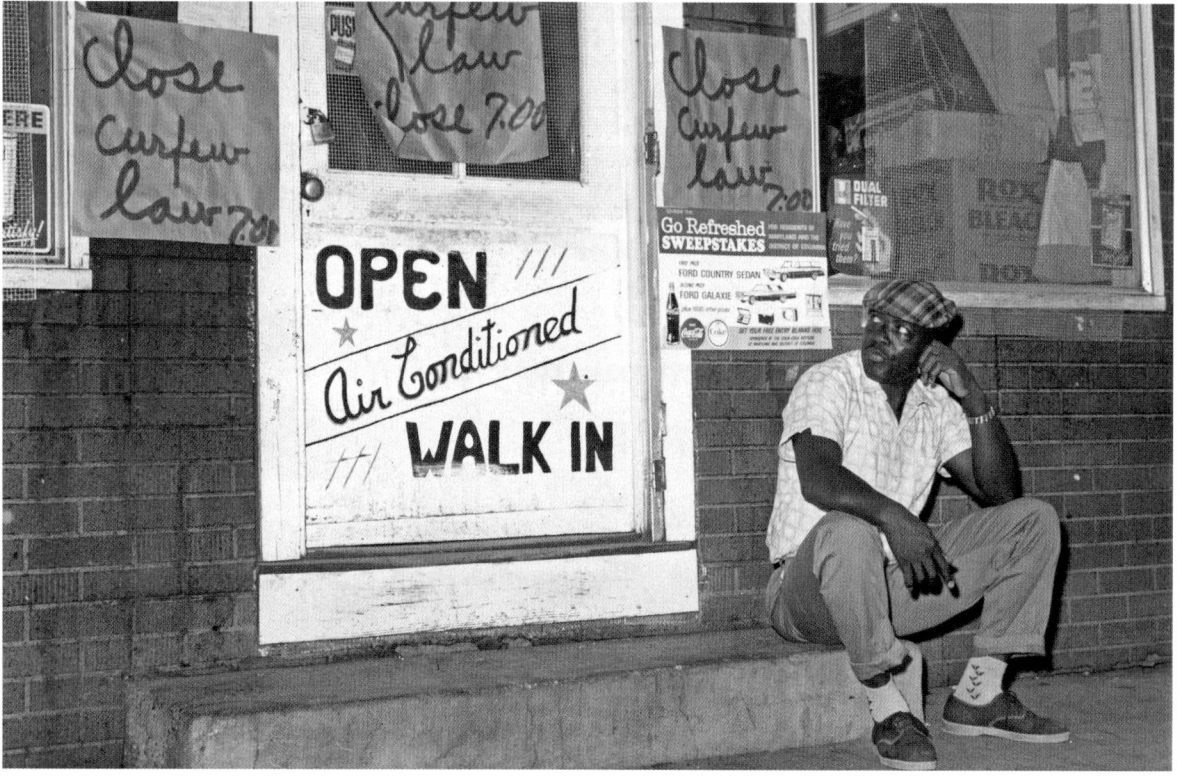

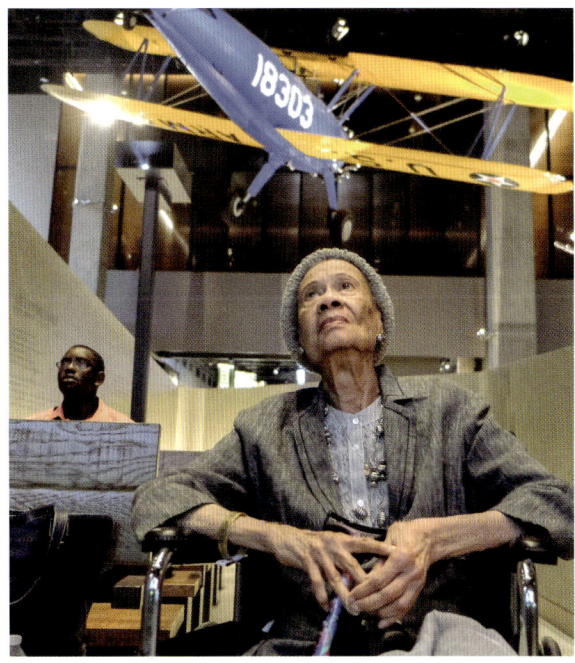

Similarly, Rev. Galamison led a successful student boycott that involved nearly half a million students in New York City just weeks before the founding of ACT. Richardson brought her negotiation and leadership skills to the group, while Dick Gregory and Malcolm X agreed to serve as consultants to the new organization.

Shortly before ACT's founding meeting, Malcolm X left the Nation of Islam. As an independent political leader, he established two separate organizations, the religious Muslim Mosque Inc. and the political Organization of Afro-American Unity.

William Worthy, writing for the *Baltimore Afro-American* on March 10, 1964, reported that "Mrs. Gloria Richardson today became the first civil rights leader to accept an offer of cooperation from Malcolm X." Richardson also invited Branche into the fold. Branche was Landry's brother-in-law and led a group, Chester Committee for Freedom Now, in Chester, Pennsylvania.

A year after Richardson stepped away from ACT, the leadership went on to form the Organization of Black Power (OBP), whose members included left-wing theorists James and Grace Lee Boggs; Maxwell Stanford and Don Freeman, founders of Revolutionary Action Movement (RAM); and Detroit-based activist General Baker.

But through her work with ACT, Richardson masterfully wove together a unique group of "firebrand militants" to bring about this Black revolution. ACT offered the Black freedom movement an alternative to the moderate organizing style of groups like the National Association for the Advancement of Colored People (NAACP). In fact, in many ways the group's organizing strategies, political agenda rooted in a race-first politics, and their position on controversial subjects such as Black people defending themselves against white segregationists set them apart and made them forerunners to the Black Power movement.

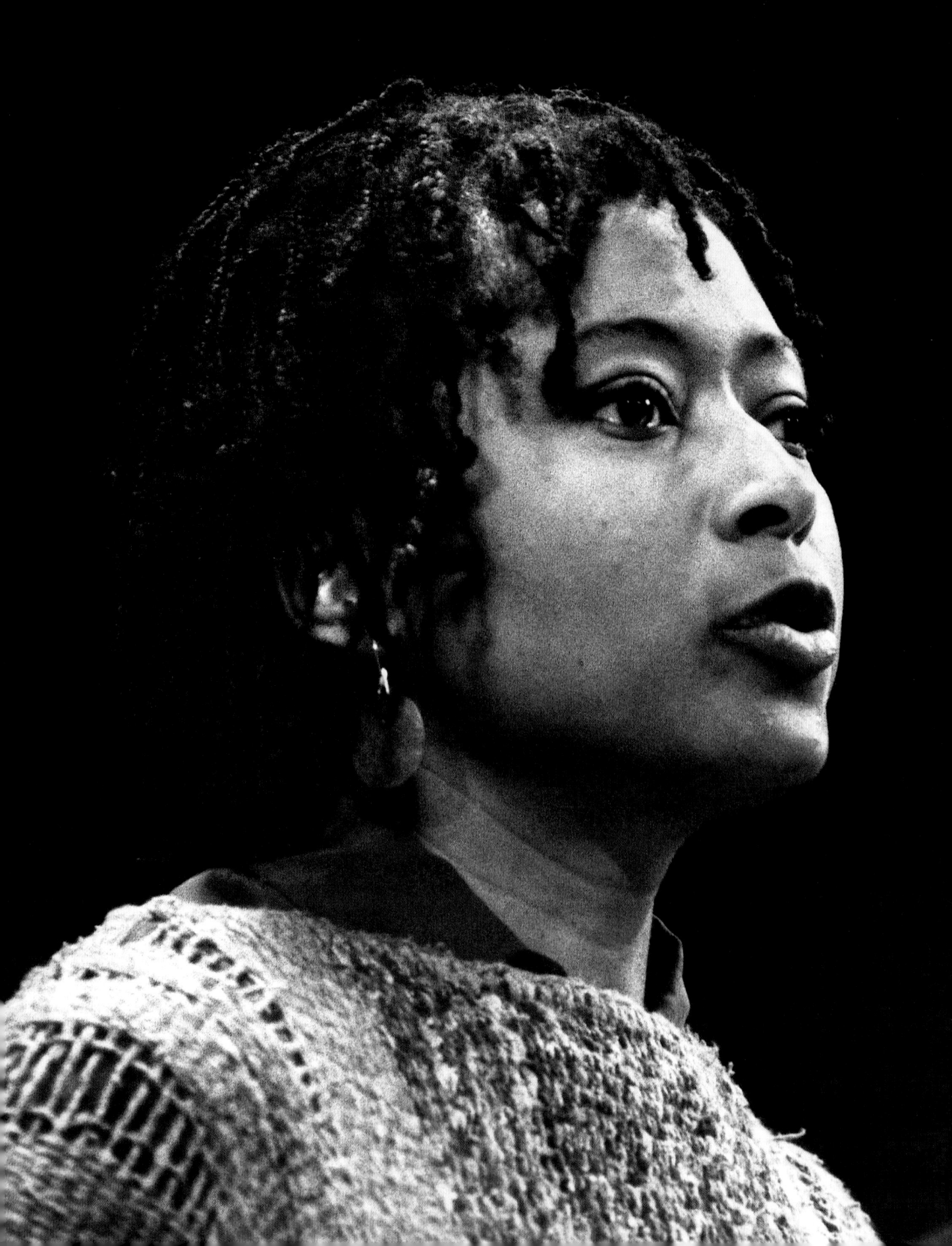

REMEMBERING ALICE WALKER'S *THE COLOR PURPLE*

LORNA M. CLOSEIL

Alice Walker's act of generosity in writing **The Color Purple** *forever revolutionized Black women's literature.*

In 1978, Barbara Smith, a Black feminist writer and organizer, published her groundbreaking text, *Toward a Black Feminist Criticism*, which she ended by expressing her desire to read one book, just *one book*, that would reflect the experiences of Black lesbians loving one another affirmatively.

This yearning exemplified the state of Black literature in the 1960s, up until the late 1970s. Black lesbian relationships, though a well-known presence within Black communities, were almost nonexistent in mainstream Black literature. Such remained true until the publication of Alice Walker's *The Color Purple* in 1982.

Though *The Color Purple* was a silent entry in the literary world upon its publication, it represented a shift in what was possible in the realm of trade publishing for Black women's literature. Not only did it become possible to publish a Black feminist protest novel, but the book marked a turning point in which a protest novel could be Black, feminine, and explicitly queer.

Walker stands tall as she reads letters from *The Color Purple*, her elegance and audaciousness piercing through. It is October 1985, two months before Steven Spielberg's movie adaptation of the book would be released. Walker's gaze is tender yet fearless, commendable given the act of bravery writing her novel had required.

In fact, Walker wrote *The Color Purple* just as Black queer feminist organizing was gaining its footing.

By 1977, the Combahee River Collective, a Black lesbian socialist group from Boston, had already released its famous statement emphasizing the need for Black women to define their own political agendas. Other active Black feminist organizations like the National Alliance of Black Feminists, the Third World Women's Alliance, and the National Black Feminist Organization helped create a sociopolitical environment where Black feminists had arrived.

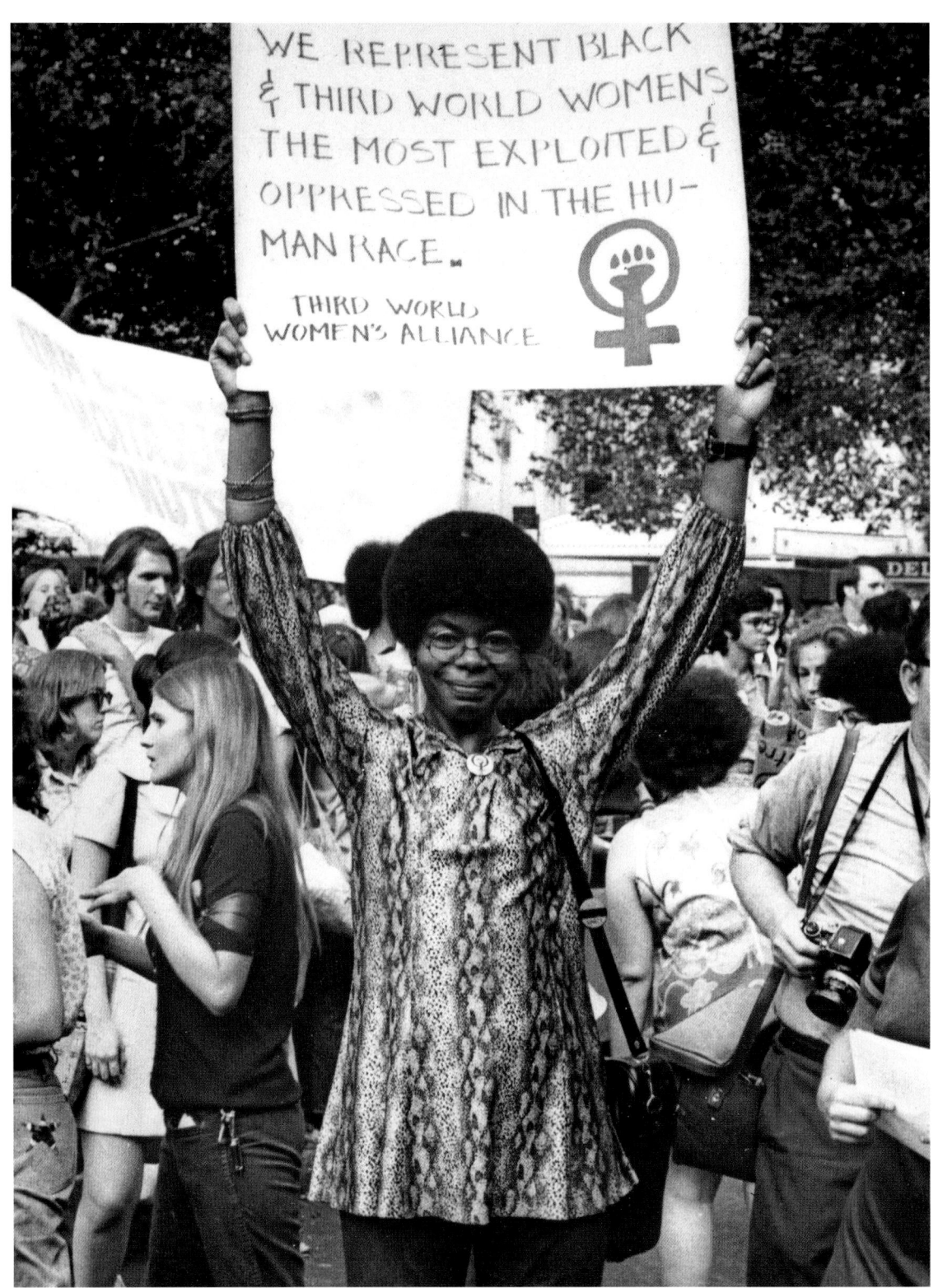

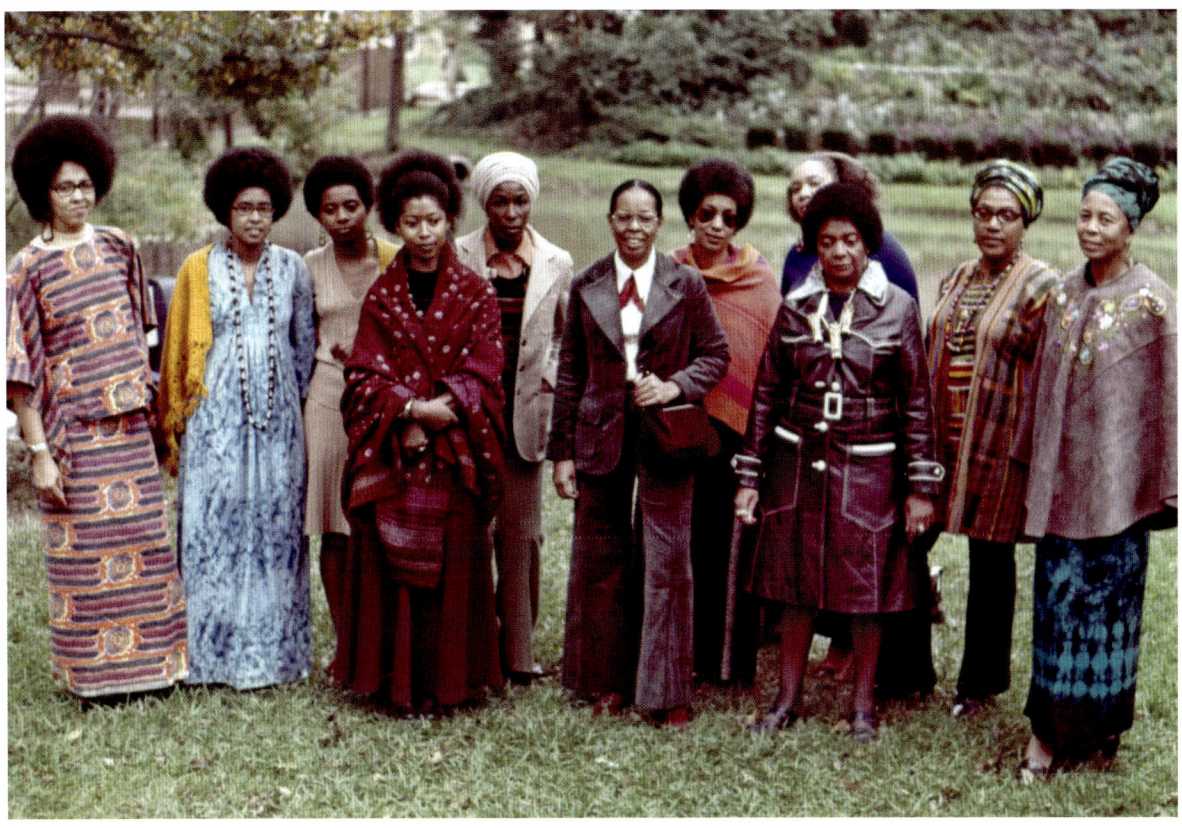

Undeniably, by the 1970s the movement was here. But a longing for storytelling that reflected Black women's lived experiences at the intersections of their Blackness, womanhood, and sexuality characterized its aspirations.

The Color Purple is a coming-of-age story about a Black woman named Celie who writes letters to God as she grapples with poverty, rape, and incest at the hands of her "Pa," and then the violence of her husband "Mr. ___." The story follows Celie as she leans on her relationships with other Black women—Nettie, Shug, and Sofia.

Celie's relationships with these women, romantic and platonic, provide her with a model for living as if she were already free. By the end of the novel, Celie no longer writes letters to God, and instead finds respite in knowing that nothing but the relationships that enable our capacity for rebellion can save us.

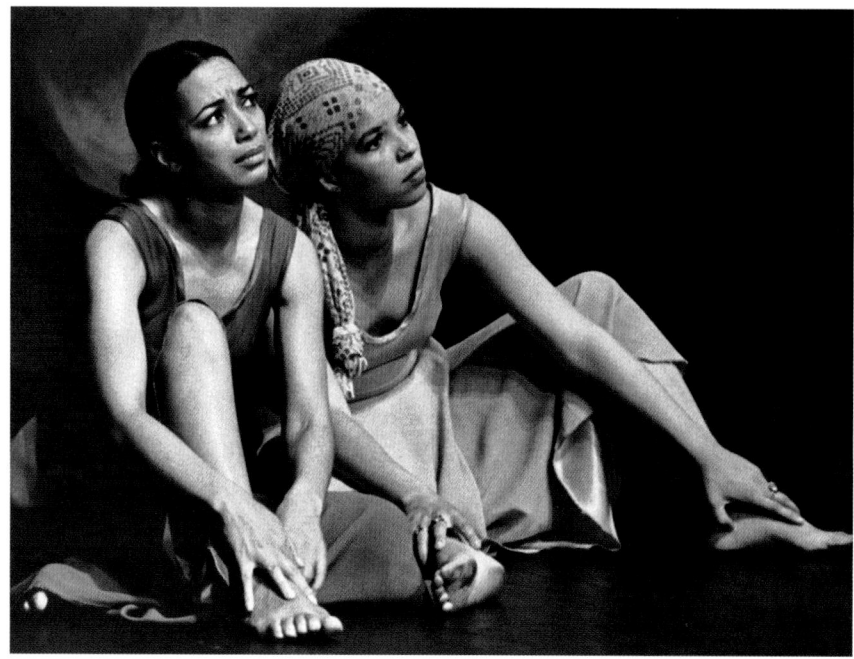

LEFT: Ntozake Shange (right) performs in her play *for colored girls who have considered suicide / when the rainbow is enuf* in 1977. The seven-woman ensemble was nominated for a Tony Award.

RIGHT: These are contact sheets from a photo shoot by *Vogue* magazine of Lorraine Hansberry in her Greenwich Village apartment in April 1959.

FOLLOWING SPREAD: At the National Women's Conference held in Houston in 1977, Coretta Scott King helped bring forward a resolution on minority women's rights. The conference adopted the resolution.

By 1983, the book had met critical acclaim, winning the Pulitzer Prize and a National Book Award. However, it was not until the release of Spielberg's 1985 movie adaptation that Walker faced backlash from many Black male critics.

These Black male critics argued that the film—and by extension the book, Walker, and all Black women—had allied with the white-male establishment to depict Black men as rapists and savages. Some even went so far as to compare the representations of Black men in *The Color Purple* to those in D. W. Griffith's 1915 film, *The Birth of a Nation*.

The backlash Walker faced was typical of reactionary responses to Black women writers whenever they dared to write about the realities of intracommunal violence. Before *The Color Purple*, written works by other Black women like Ntozake Shange's *for colored girls who have considered suicide / when the rainbow is enuf* (1976) and Michele Wallace's *Black Macho and the Myth of the Superwoman* (1979) received similar forms of criticism.

The backlash also represented the suspicion and misconception that some Black people had about Black feminism. Many believed that Black feminists were race traitors, man-hating, and lesbians. The film reified those fears, despite the ways the book had sought to hold on to the complexities of Black social life and the relations that constitute it.

Despite the controversy, *The Color Purple* continues to resonate because of Black feminists' willingness to bear witness to the truth behind Walker's work. The Black feminist movement created a space for the emergence of Walker's book, and in turn, *The Color Purple* created an opening for a lineage of other Black women writers like Octavia Butler, Gloria Naylor, and Audre Lorde.

This act of generosity in writing *The Color Purple* forever revolutionized Black women's literature. No longer are we desperately searching for one another. We have arrived, and we are here to stay.

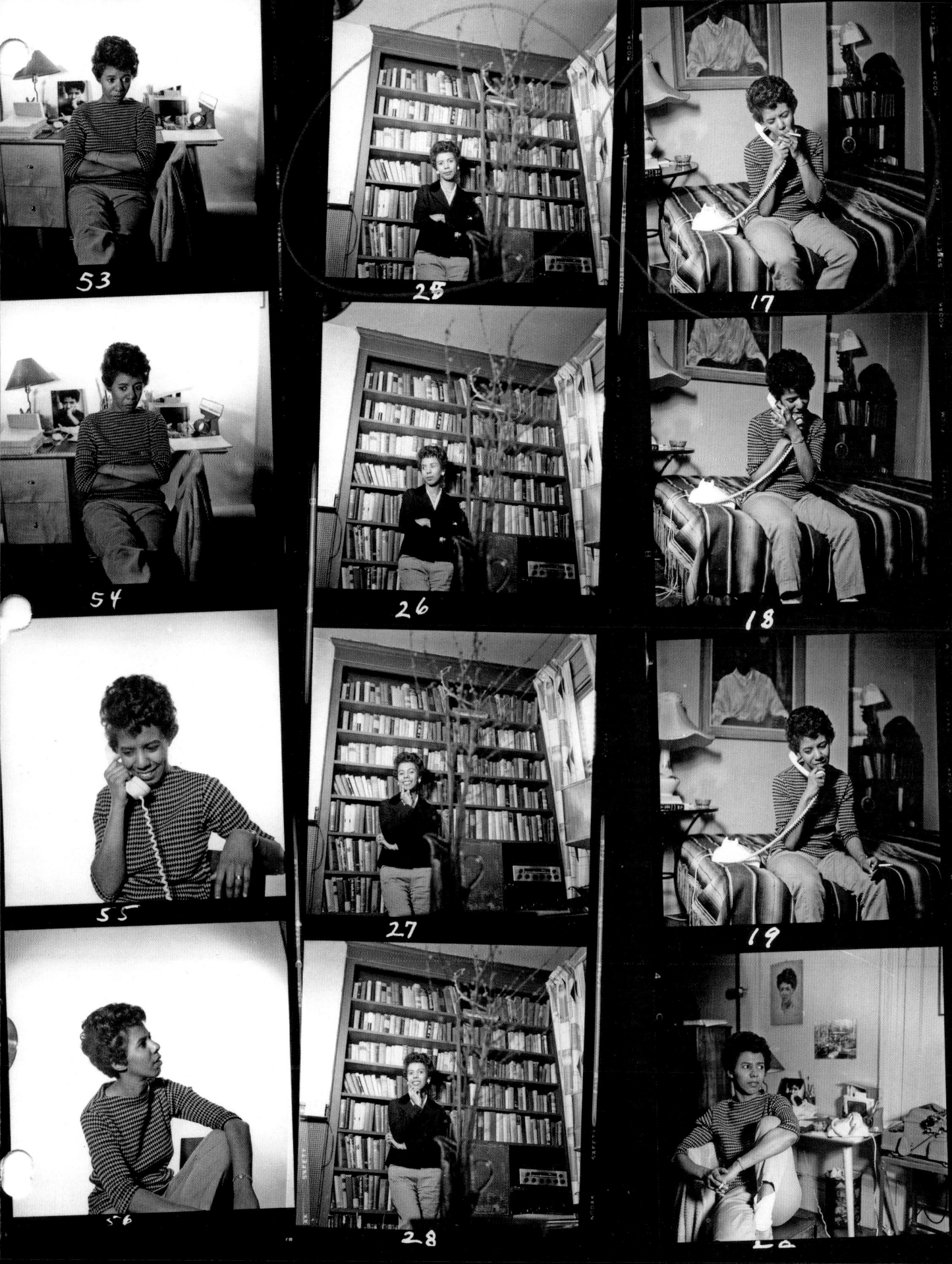

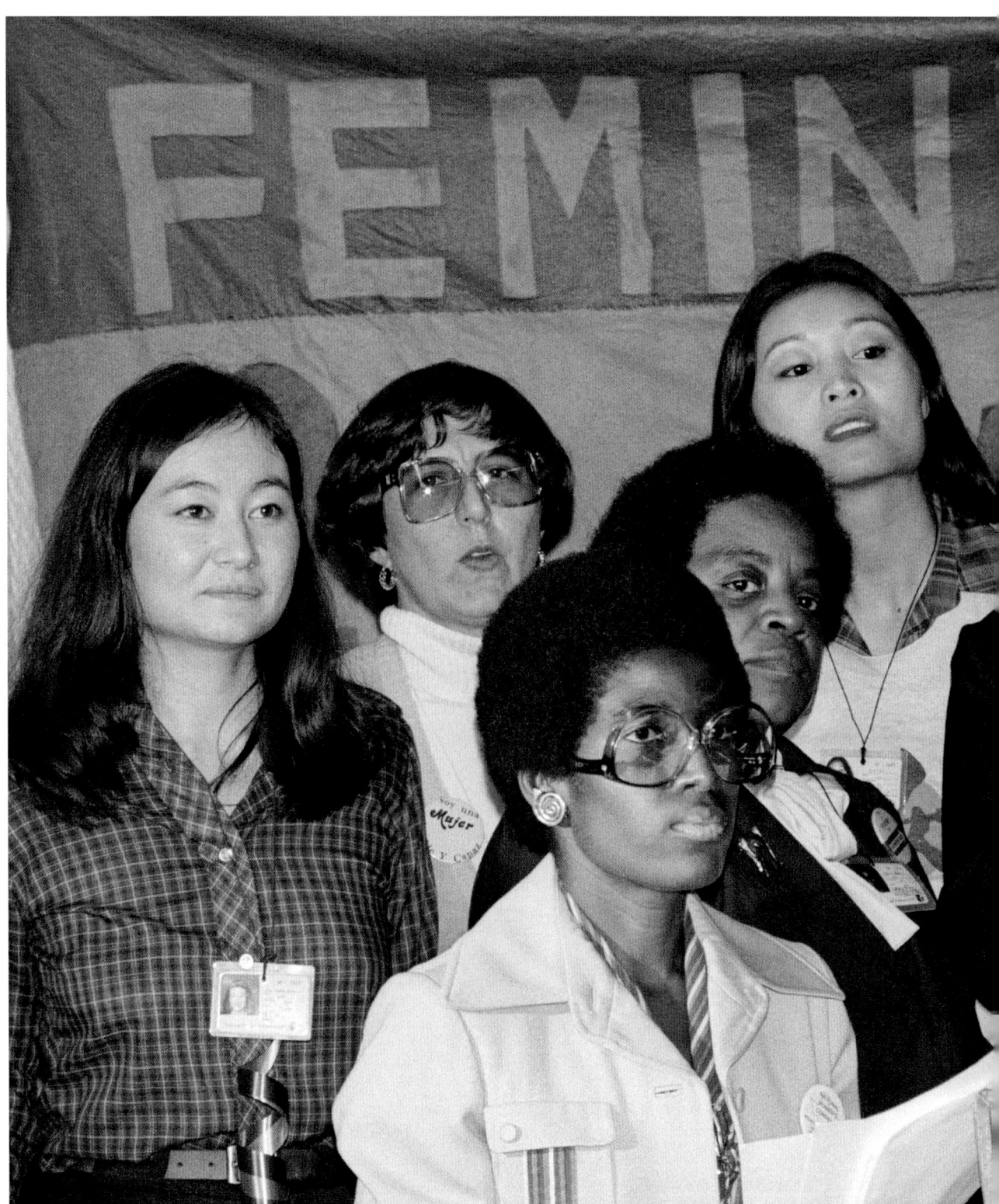

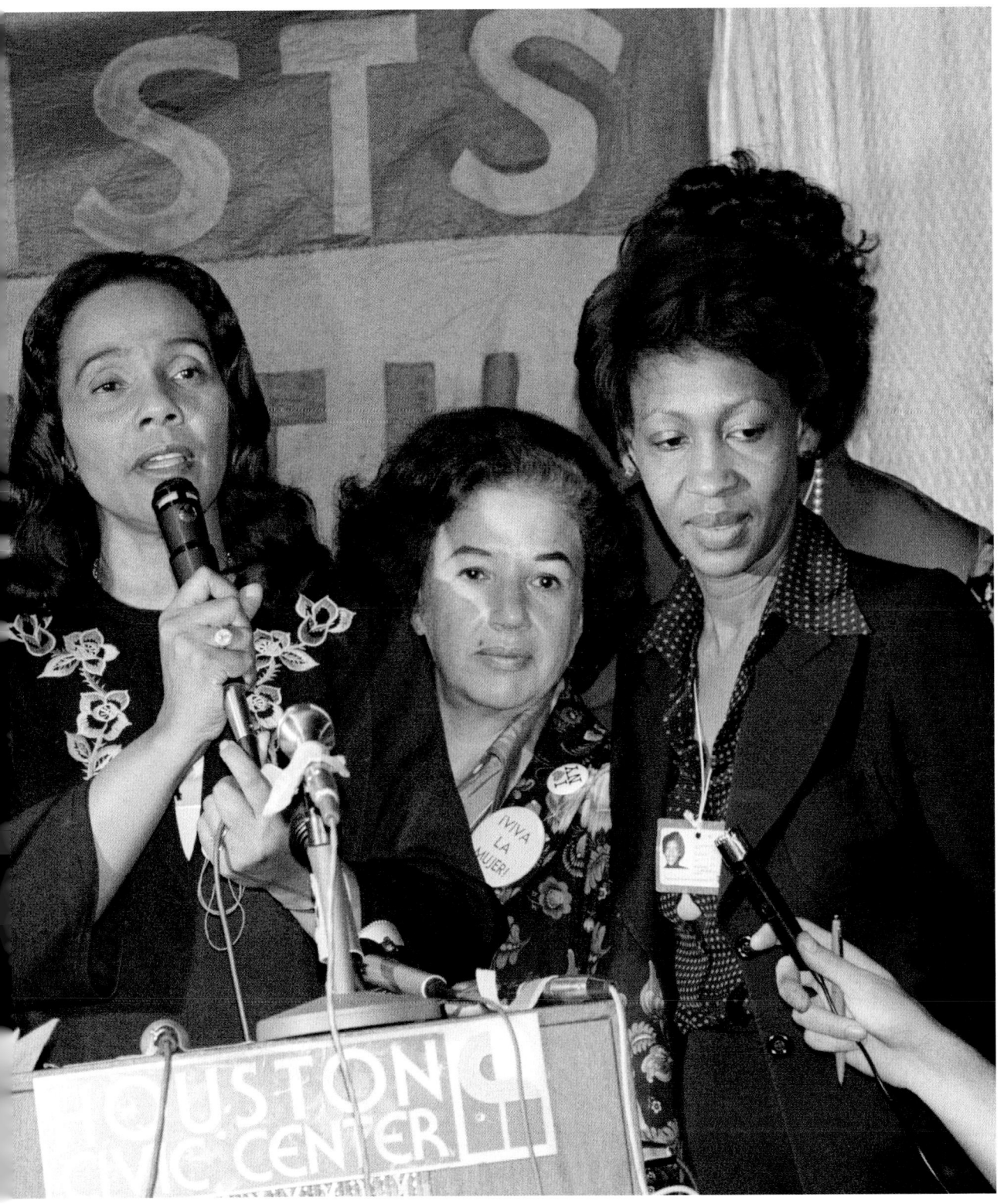

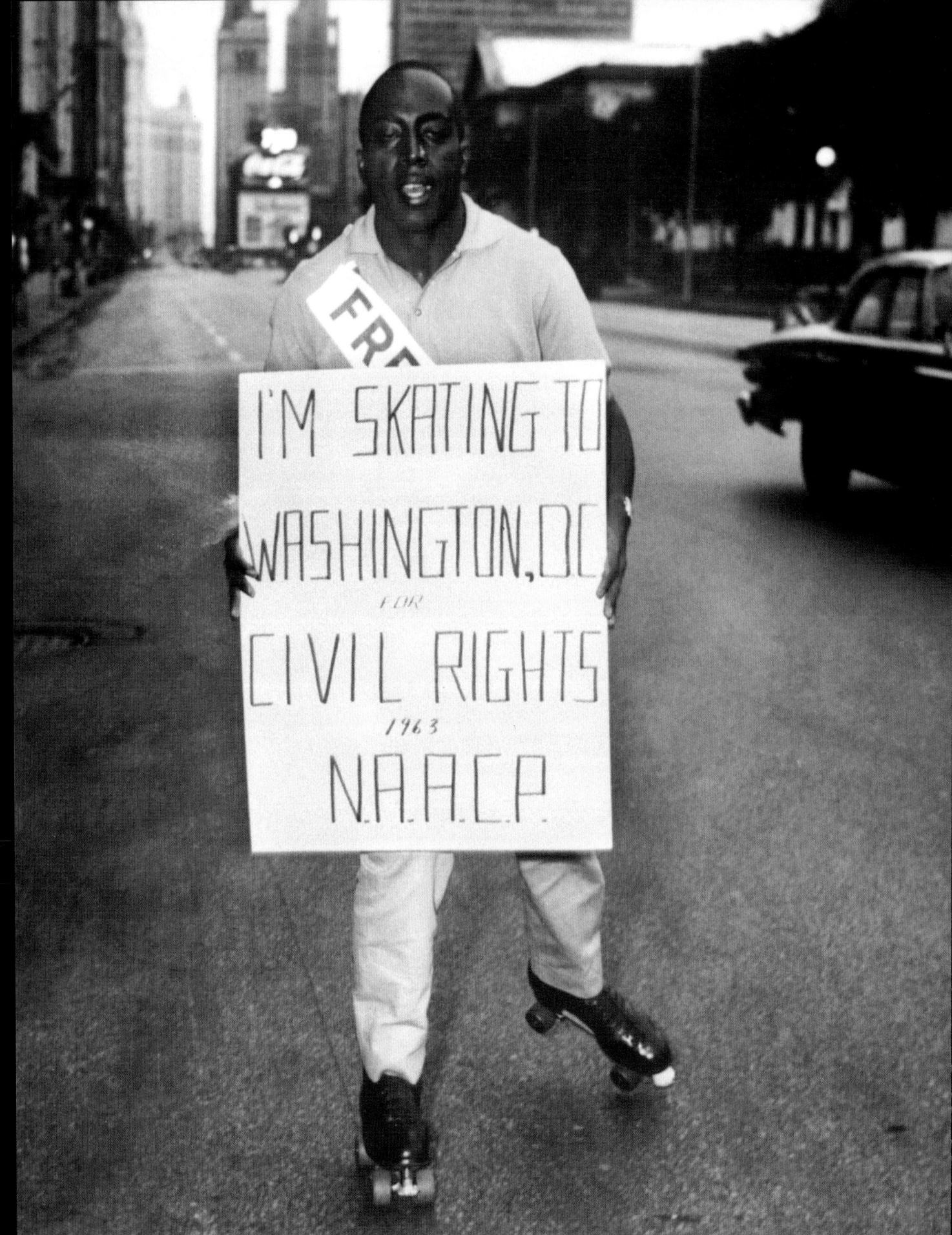

III.

SPACES AND PLACES OF BLACK POLITICS

BLACK POLITICS HAS HISTORICALLY INVOLVED DEMANDING ACCESS TO THE ELECTORAL PROCESS. But electoral participation is only one strategy among many that African Americans adopted to achieve citizenship rights and access to dominant institutions in American society. In fact, African American political movements were inspired by a broader vision of Black humanity than proximity or integration with white Americans.

These political movements were—and are—animated by everyday people. Inspired by a collective vision of self-determination and empowerment, they have directed their energies to transform their local communities. Within these spaces, Black people have wielded their power to produce change in American society.

OPPOSITE: Ledger Smith starts his journey to travel seven hundred miles on roller skates from Chicago to the March on Washington in 1963.

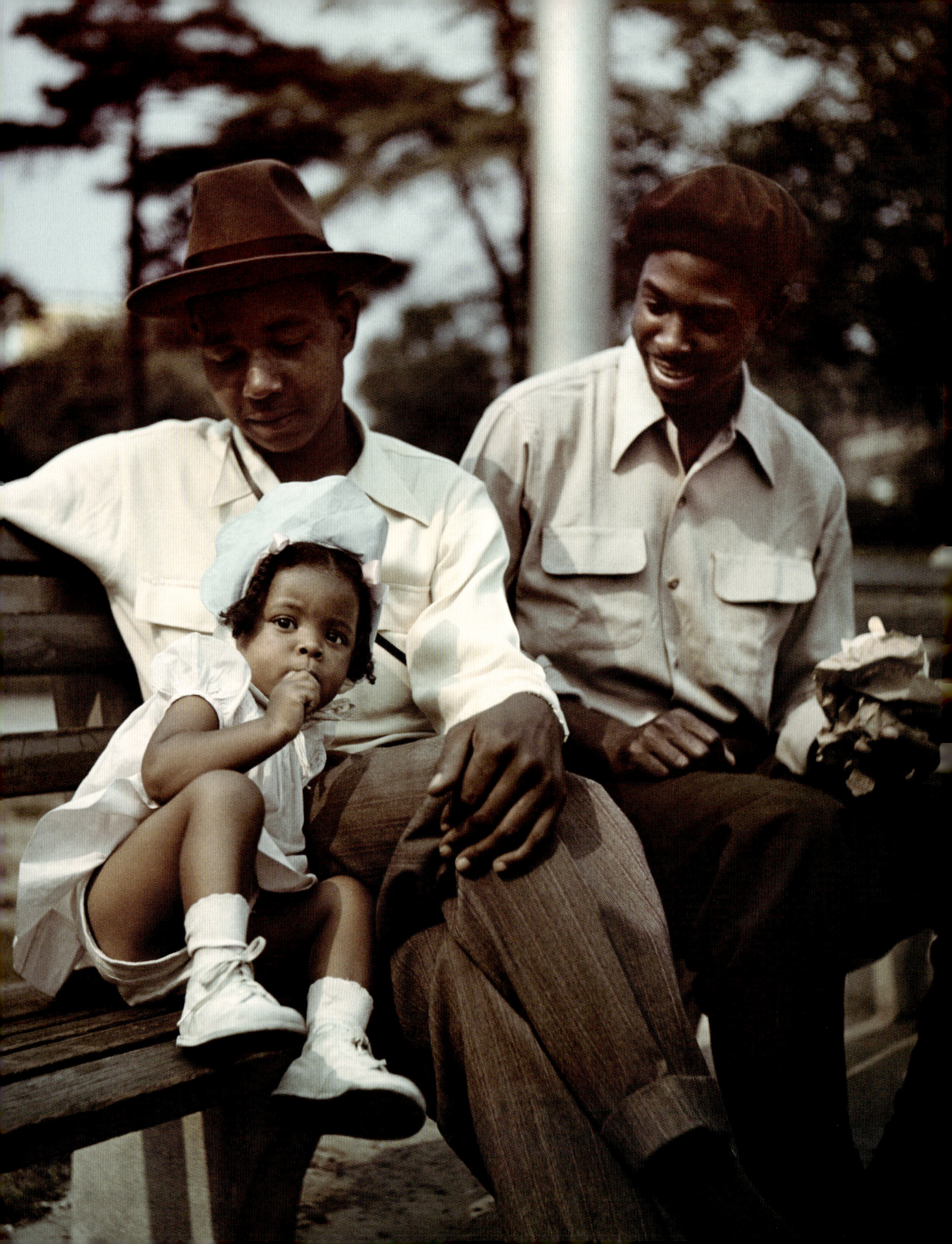

FREE ᴛʜᴇ LAND, FREE ᴛʜᴇ PEOPLE

JOCELYN IMANI

Public spaces in the United States have been sites of both exclusion and violence as well as joy, rest, and community.

Black folks have a complicated history with public land in the United States.

Public lands are created by the citizenry and managed by federal, state, and local governments. In their earliest form, parks were established as agricultural lands for livestock. However, since the mid-nineteenth century, the modern concept of public land has provided a setting for recreation, interpersonal connection, health improvement, and personal development. These spaces range in size and scale from national parks to city playgrounds; what they have in common is an expressed intent of access for all.

But for Black people, public lands have also been sites of exclusion, terror, and denial of rights. Many of the earliest public parks in the country deliberately excluded Black people, and local communities erected legal or social barriers to prevent Black access. Over sixty of the nation's oldest public parks—such as Boston Common and DC's National Mall—were established during the official period of American enslavement (1619–1865) and reflected the era's discriminatory biases.

Public parks frequently were sites of lynching because their public nature allowed for the act of domestic terrorism to become spectacles. Also, because access to the nation's public parks was restricted, they have been transformed into sites of significant Black civil rights demonstrations.

Still, Black folks have long used and engaged with public land, especially from the beginning of city park systems. Houston's Emancipation Park (1872) and Nashville's Hadley Park (1912) are two of the oldest Black parks in the country. The former was purchased by a group of Black businessmen who pooled their money to secure a permanent home for Juneteenth celebrations less than a decade after the holiday was first marked. The latter tract of land was secured by city officials as the first public park in the nation created specifically for Black people under the "separate but equal" doctrine established by the 1896 *Plessy v. Ferguson* Supreme Court ruling.

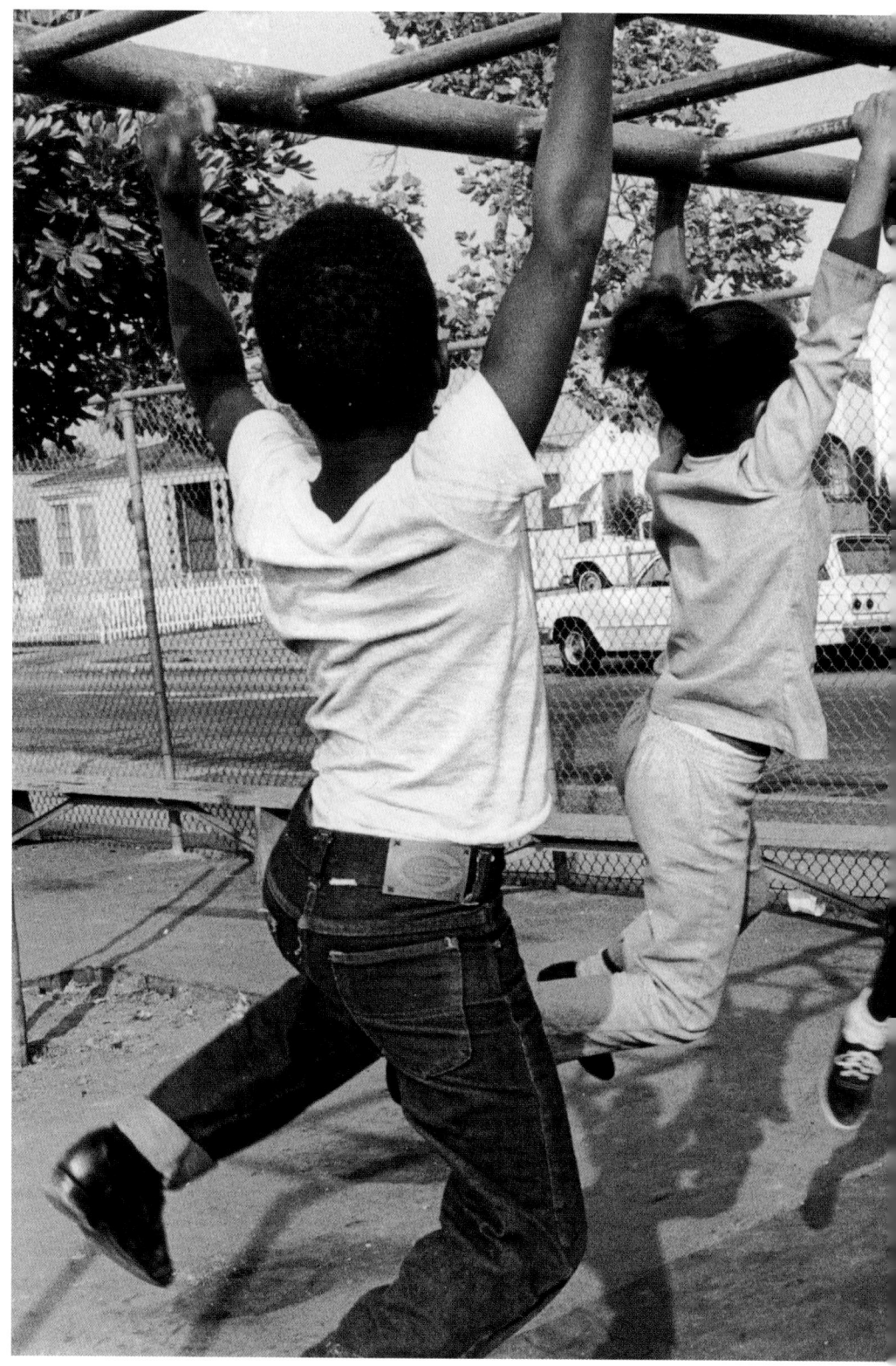

PREVIOUS SPREAD, LEFT: Slim Aarons took this shot of a father and daughter enjoying time on a park bench in New York's Central Park in 1948.

RIGHT: Kids have always loved playing on the monkey bars, including these three in 1975.

SPACES AND PLACES OF BLACK POLITICS

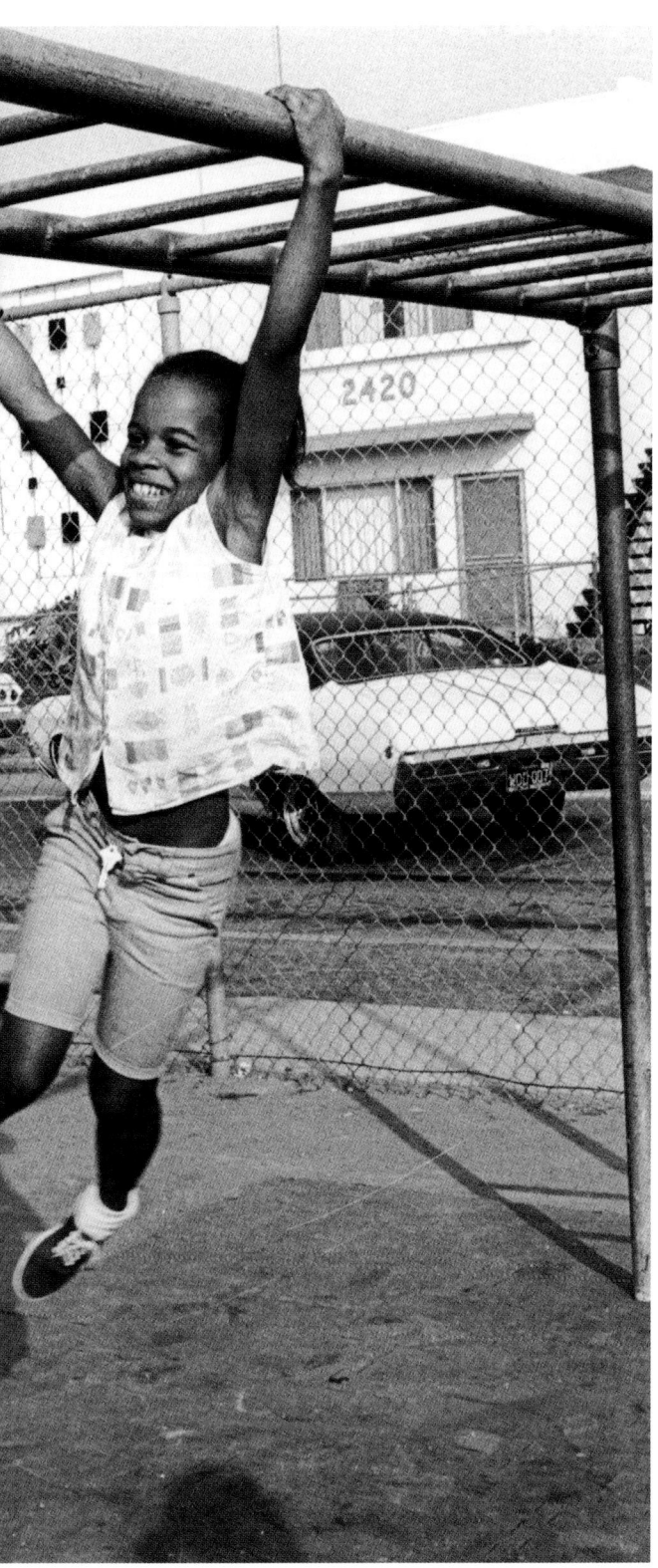

In 1960, the privately owned Glen Echo Park in Maryland—today managed by the National Park Service—became the battleground of a major desegregation struggle. There, local Black college students fought for access to the popular amusement park. Local white residents as well as law enforcement and government officials responded with ferocious repression. Some of the students were arrested and removed from riding the park's famous carousel. This sparked a series of heated protests that eventually required intervention from U.S. Attorney General Robert Kennedy to force desegregation.

When equal access is established, public parks foster community on shared lands for residents. Parks have enabled Black people to engage in cultural connection and community-building from the late nineteenth century to the present.

This 1975 image of three Black children hanging from the monkey bars at an outdoor playground perfectly embodies some of the first engagements many African Americans had with public land. Although all children interact with playgrounds as leisure spaces, their types of play are shaped by their cultural heritage. For example, the tradition of African American clapping games like Miss Mary Mack and Slide and Double Dutch have circulated within African American communities—and beyond into other communities.

That childlike wonder and awe that come from exploring the vast yet contained world of possibilities on the playground are unmatched. The playground is the setting for some of the most pivotal moments of childhood when children get to know themselves and one another. Quick wit is sharpened on the playground via verbal contests in Black vernacular English like "the dozens" or "joning." Conflicts are resolved on the playground, sometimes with the help of older siblings called in for backup. The playground is also the site of some of the earliest experimentation with attraction and rejection by exchanging handwritten notes asking, "Do you like me? Check yes or no." The playground is good for the physical health of children, but it is also a necessary space for psychological and social development.

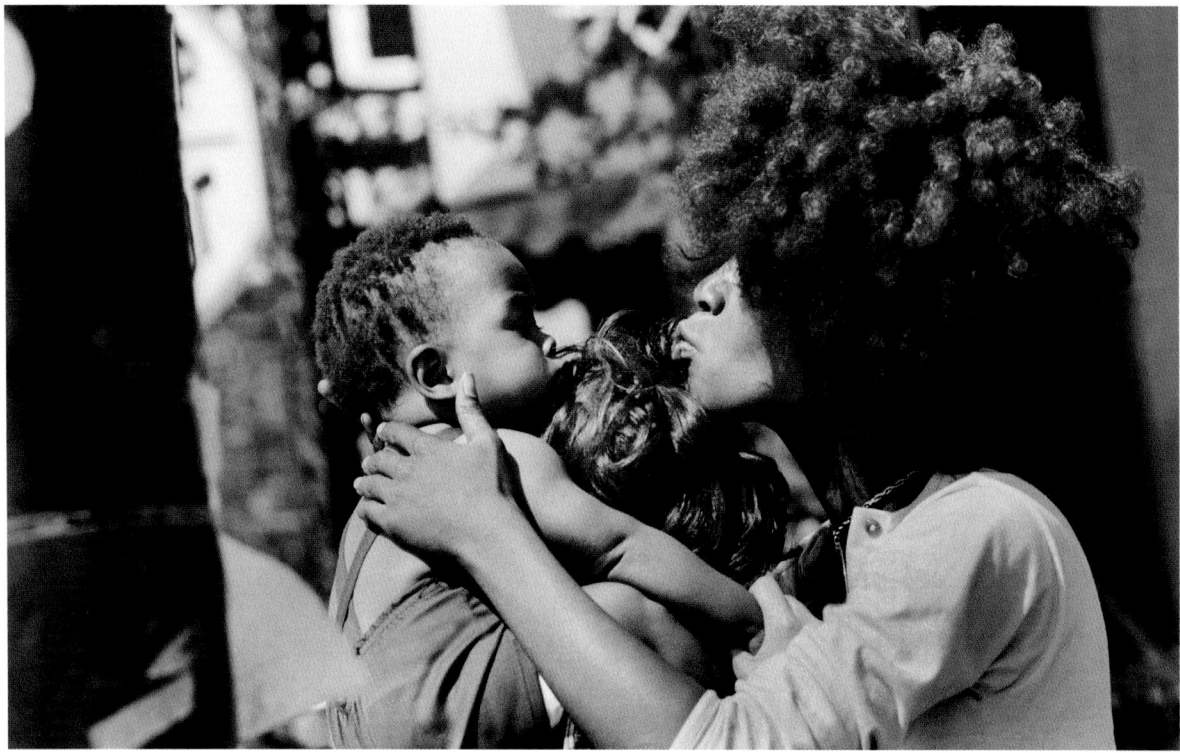

This mother and her child with baby doll in tow at a street fair is a visual recreated generation after generation in parks across the country. The photograph represents some of the most consistent ways in which African Americans interact with public land: Street festivals, church picnics, and family reunions were all often held in public spaces. The setting of the park breaks down the silos of the art gallery, museum, and performance venue and allows everyday Black folks to have access to cultural performances and community events.

Outdoor art festivals, African street fairs, and jazz festivals are hubs of culture where everyday people directly engage with performance art—all happening within the public arena. The street fair is a venue where artists can directly reach the people in their communities who likely inspired their art. Oftentimes, a street festival gives a platform to artists who may not be considered by white establishments. It is also a place where the people can see their own beautiful reflections and share that beauty with the next generation.

The park is also a space where community and politics intertwine. In the photograph to the right, the New Haven, Connecticut, chapter of the Black Panther Party for Self Defense (BPP), a local branch of the national party formed in Oakland, California, in 1966, distributes food to community members. Point 10 of the Black Panther Party's platform states: "We Want Land, Bread, Housing, Education, Clothing, Justice and Peace."

The BPP understood the necessity of meeting people's basic needs, and they very often used public lands as venues for First Amendment demonstrations, political education, and direct service to community members. Ongoing fights for land access for politics, leisure, and culture for the whole Black community remain critical to the Black struggle from slavery to freedom.

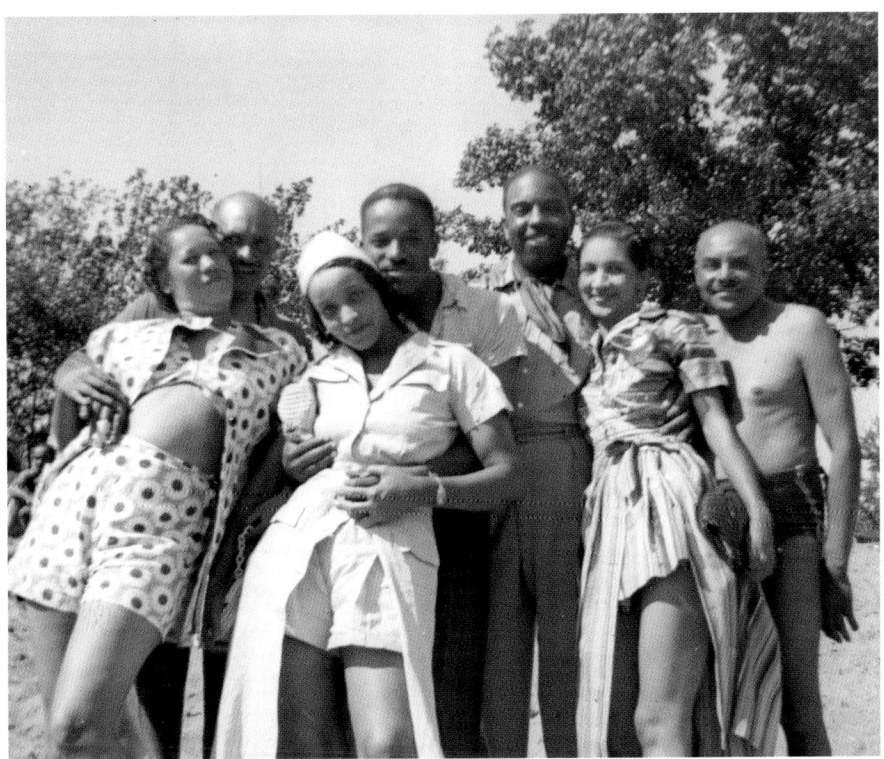

OPPOSITE: A mom and her baby at an outdoor art fair in Chicago in the 1970s.

LEFT: This group was photographed at the Idlewild Resort in Idlewild, Michigan, a Black club known as "Black Eden." Taken in 1938, this image is a reminder that such recreation was still segregated even in the North.

BELOW: Black Panthers distributed free hot dogs to people in a park in New Haven, Connecticut.

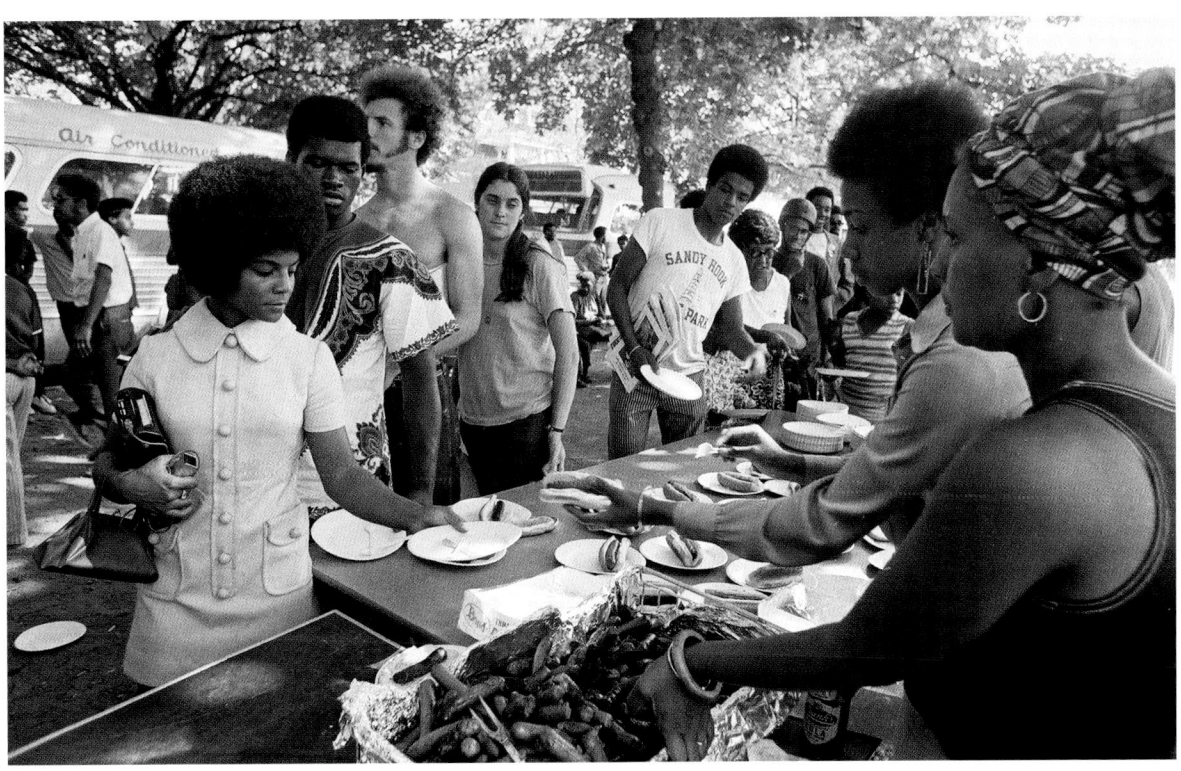

CHILDREN OF THE MISSISSIPPI FREEDOM SUMMER

ALLISON MASHELL MITCHELL

*Black children played a central role
in the Civil Rights Movement.*

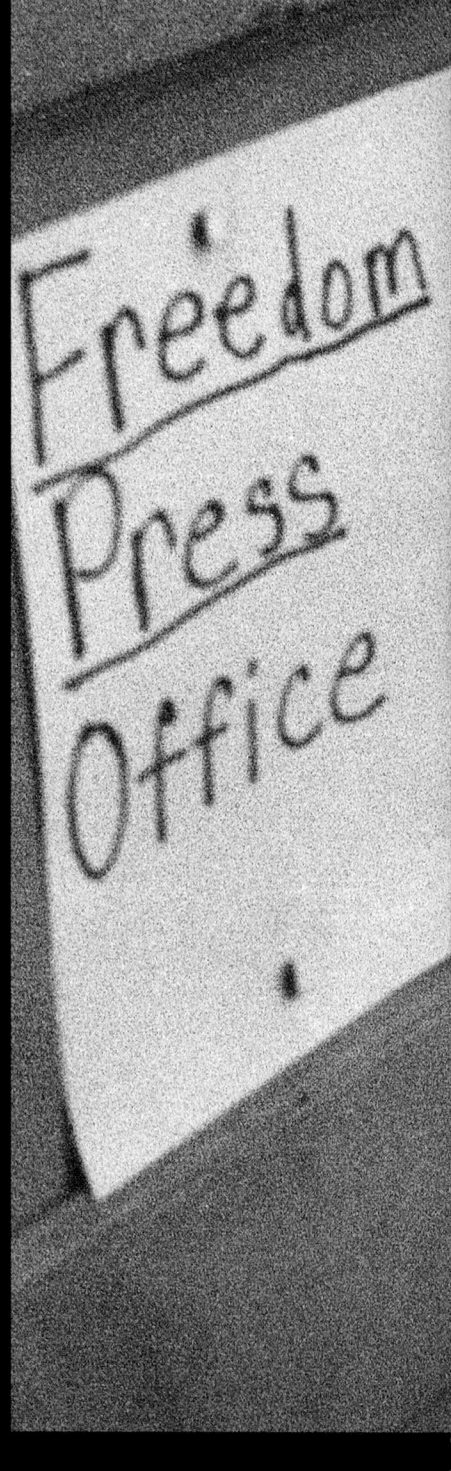

I n the summer of 1964, Mississippi became the focus of the Voter Education Project, an effort to increase Black voter registration across the state. The events of that summer garnered national headlines because the Project recruited Northern white middle-class college students as volunteers, and for the intense violence used by local whites to oppose it.

Known as Freedom Summer, the 1964 program was part of the Council of Federated Organizations' (COFO) greater Mississippi Freedom Project. Activists quickly realized that Black Mississippians needed viable community institutions that could be maintained long after out-of-state volunteers left. Children, though often overlooked, were a prominent presence in this community institution–building drive during the Mississippi Freedom Summer.

Black children contributed to the Civil Rights Movement through organizing, but their presence also shaped organizing objectives and activist and volunteer engagement with Black communities. Black children worked on the *Mississippi Free Press*, attended Mississippi Freedom Schools, and through their interactions with adults, shaped how volunteers established relationships with local Black communities.

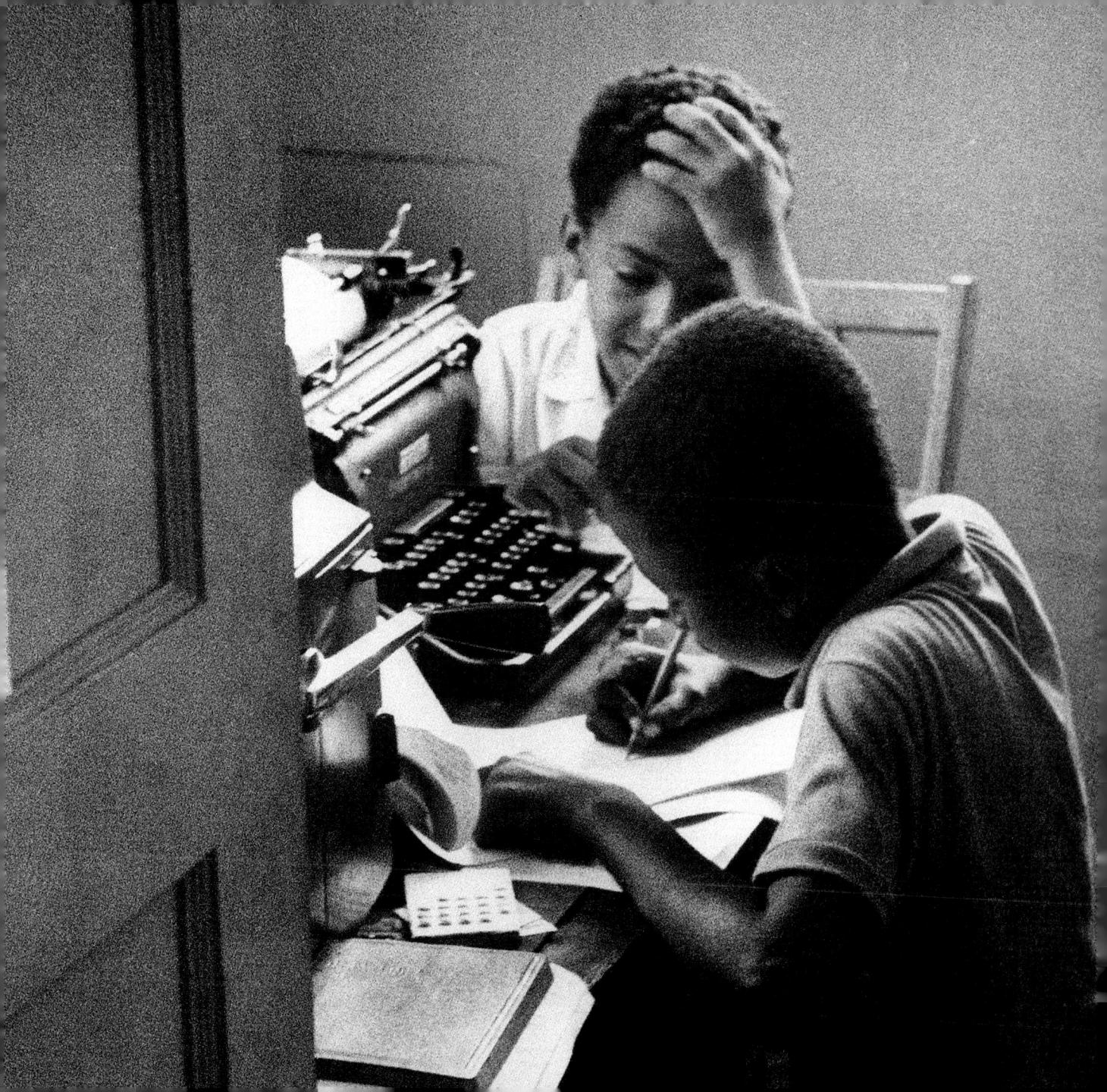

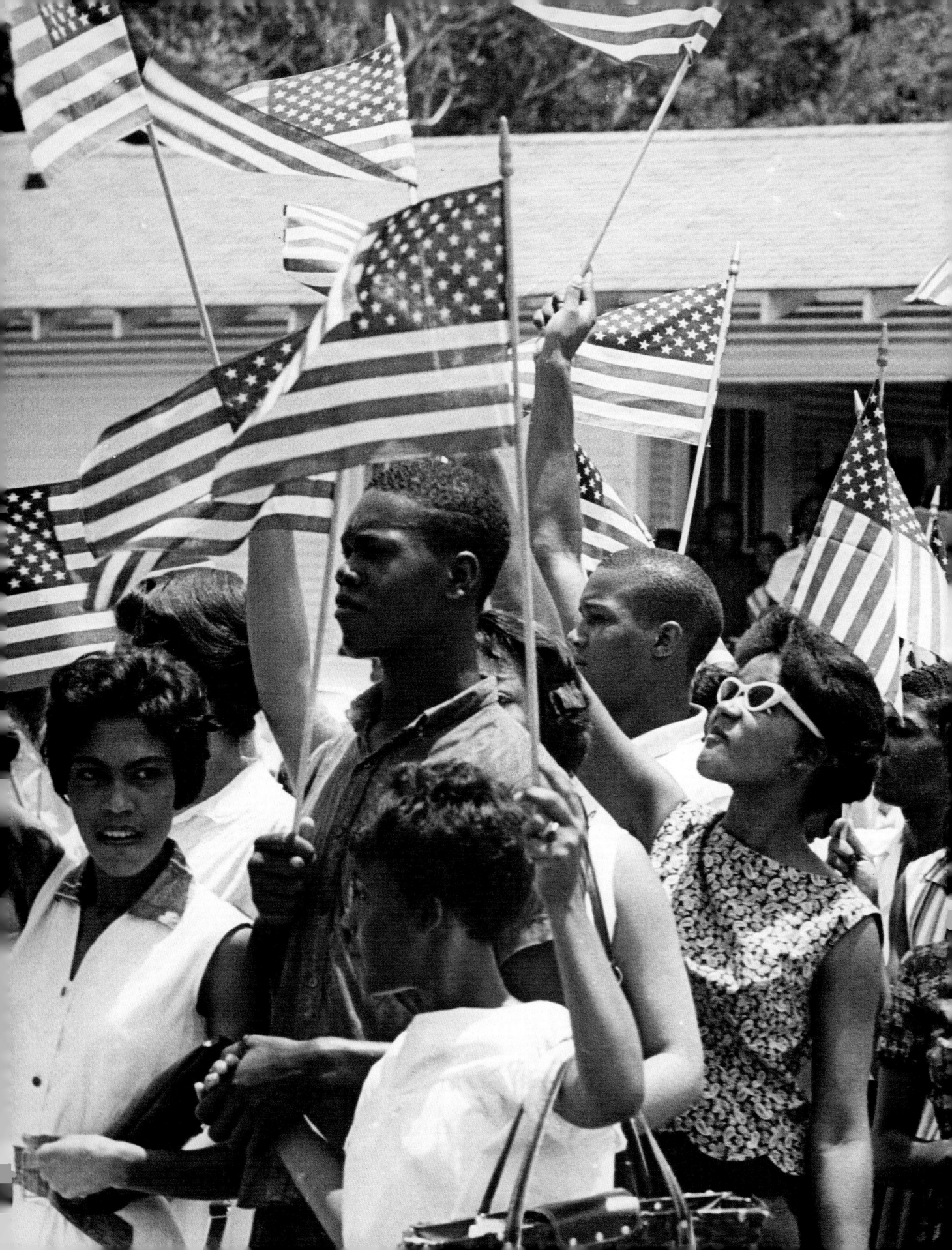

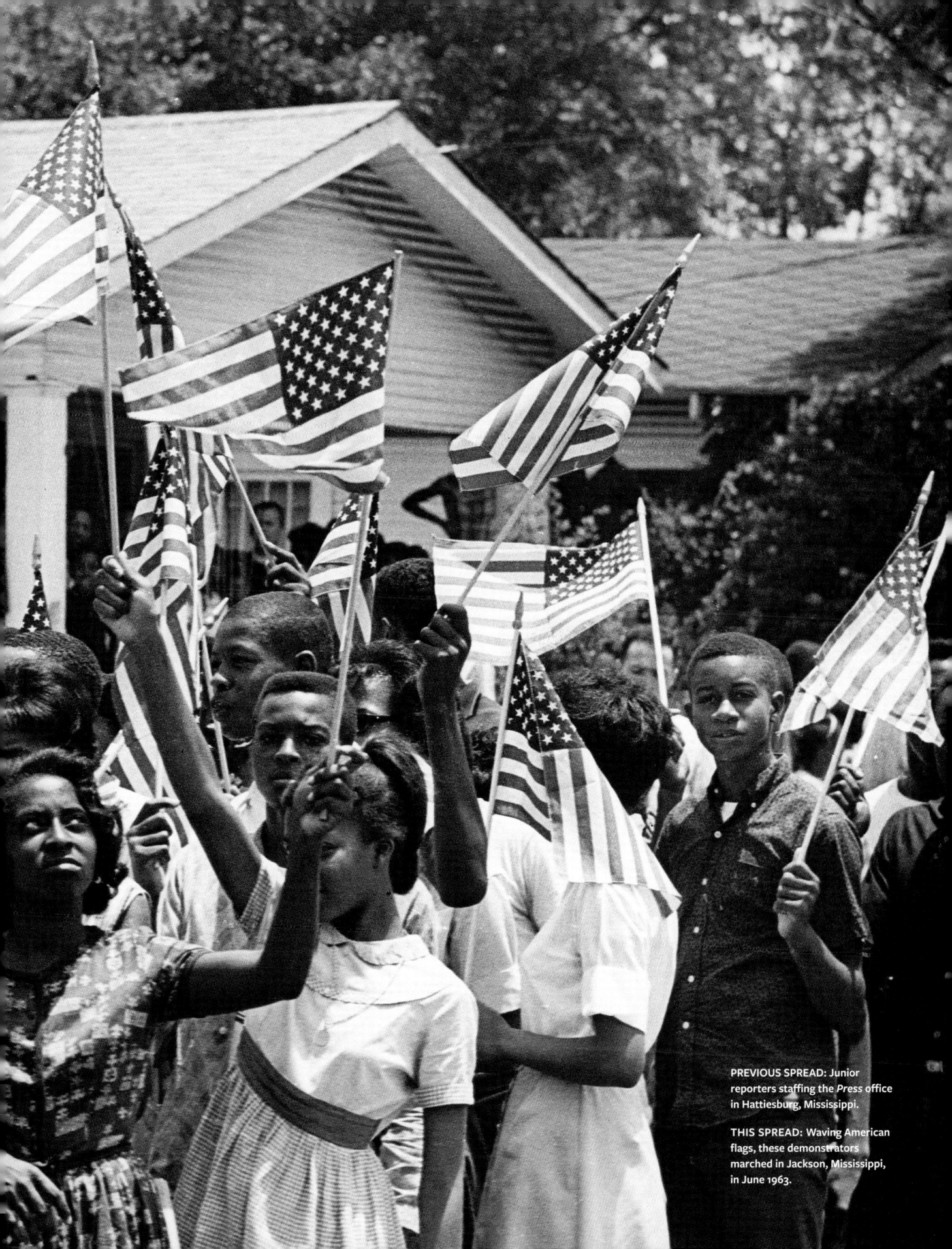

PREVIOUS SPREAD: Junior reporters staffing the *Press* office in Hattiesburg, Mississippi.

THIS SPREAD: Waving American flags, these demonstrators marched in Jackson, Mississippi, in June 1963.

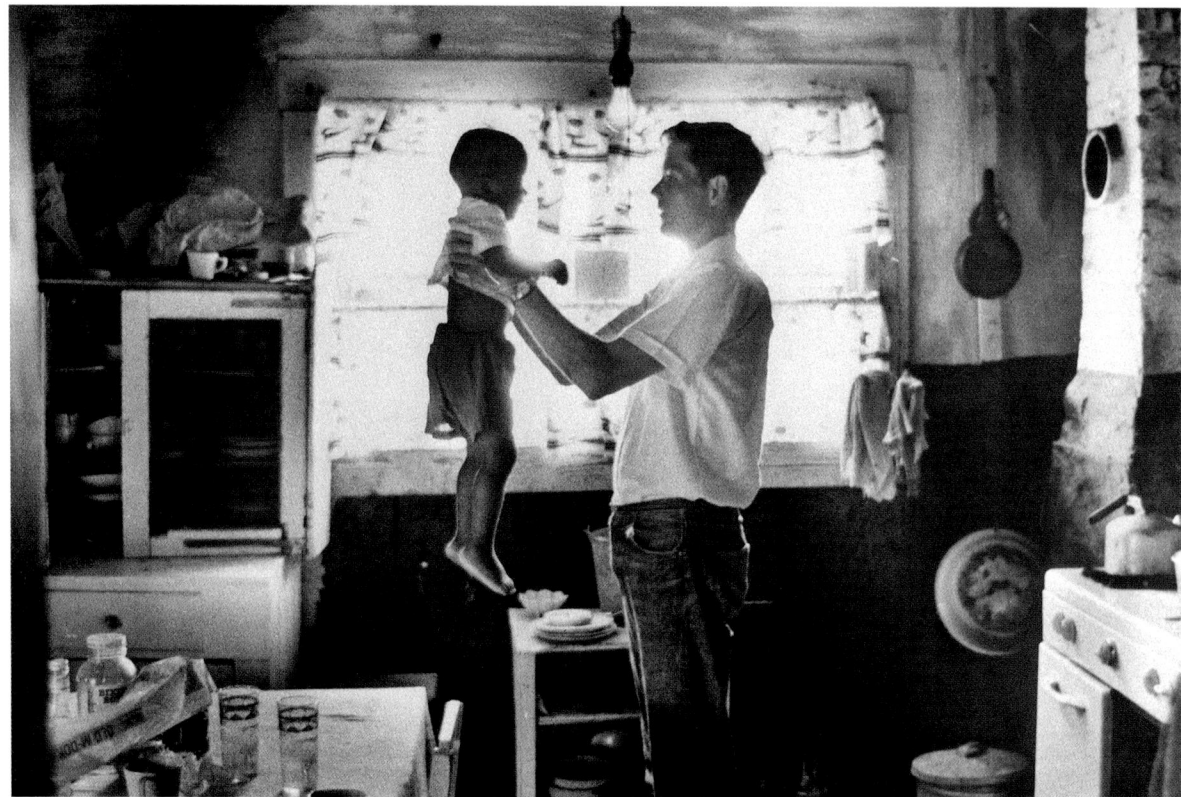

From 1961 to 1964, organizers disseminated information about the state of local and national movement through the *Mississippi Free Press*. These movement-oriented newspapers served as crucial sources for those who wanted to be informed and read the news from the perspective of those supporting the Civil Rights Movement.

Two boys, captured in the image on pages 112–13, are working in the *Mississippi Free Press* office in Hattiesburg, Mississippi. Whether working on a task for the publication or simply practicing their writing skills, these boys were learning how important documenting and sharing information was to the movement's efforts.

Illiteracy was a big concern for activists and community members. Immense disparities between Black and white schools even years after *Brown v. Board of Education*

necessitated the Mississippi Project's critical work with children to ensure they could read and write.

Freedom Schools were spaces whose origins derived from a desire to improve Black children's education. COFO's Mississippi Freedom Schools opened on July 2, 1964, and quickly became an integral part of Freedom Summer. Hattiesburg, where these boys resided, had over six hundred Black students enrolled. The boys in the *Press* office show us how expansive the Mississippi Freedom Project's goals became, moving beyond COFO's initial interest in voter education.

The boys working in the office were learning from a curriculum that instilled a sense of pride in them as Black people and encouraged them to become active citizens in the Black Freedom Struggle, which many children later

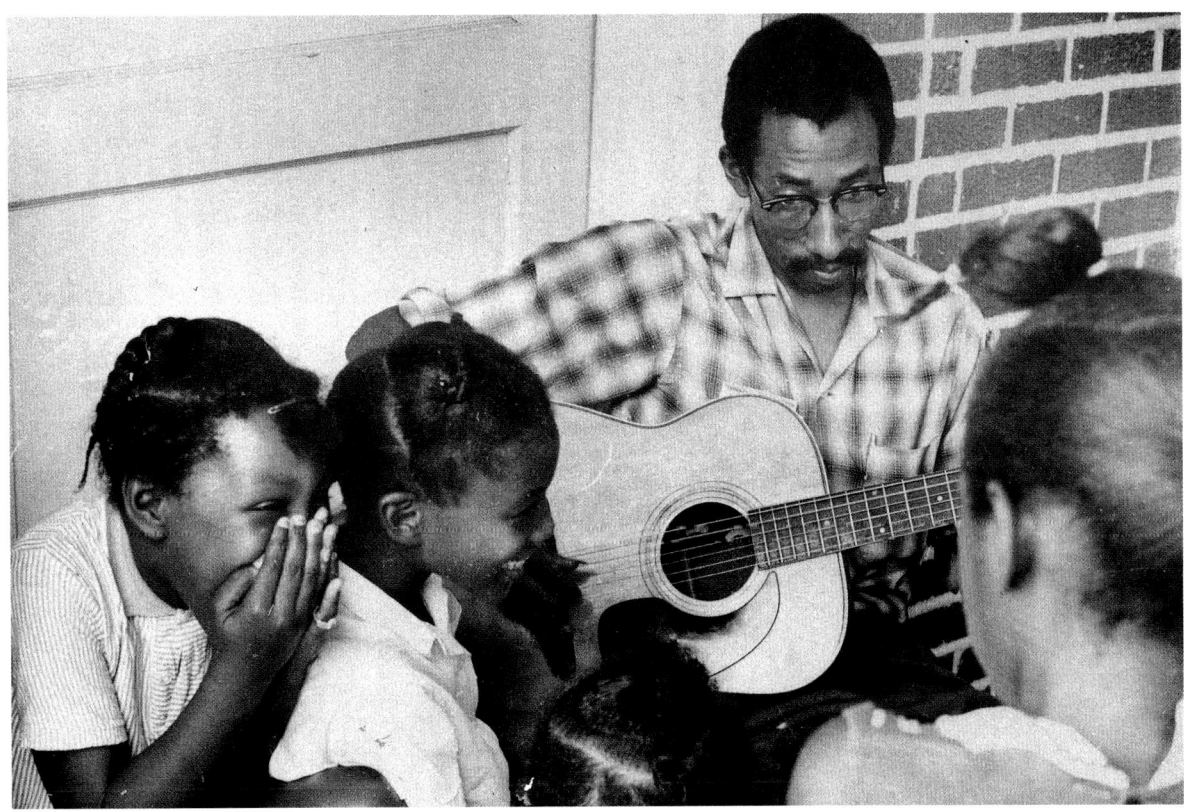

did. Several students who went to Freedom Schools participated in later protests in Mississippi towns, including Indianola, Cleveland, and Shaw.

Black children also shaped how volunteers navigated going into Black communities with the hopes of increasing adult participation in Freedom Summer. Volunteers, including white activists, went door-to-door in Black neighborhoods to increase voter participation in their designated areas, explaining the importance of voter registration.

By allowing white workers in their homes, Black Mississippians knew that they risked reprisal from local whites. Nevertheless, parents and guardians recognized that they needed to expose Black children to a key component of community organizing: trust.

OPPOSITE: This white Freedom Summer volunteer plays with a small child after talking with his parents about registering to vote.

ABOVE: These children giggle as they are entertained by a Freedom Summer worker playing guitar.

FOLLOWING SPREAD: In 1966, Martin Luther King Jr. helped escort Black children to a newly integrated school in Grenada, Mississippi. The kids were also accompanied by Hosea Williams (right center), Andrew Young (left of King), and Joan Baez.

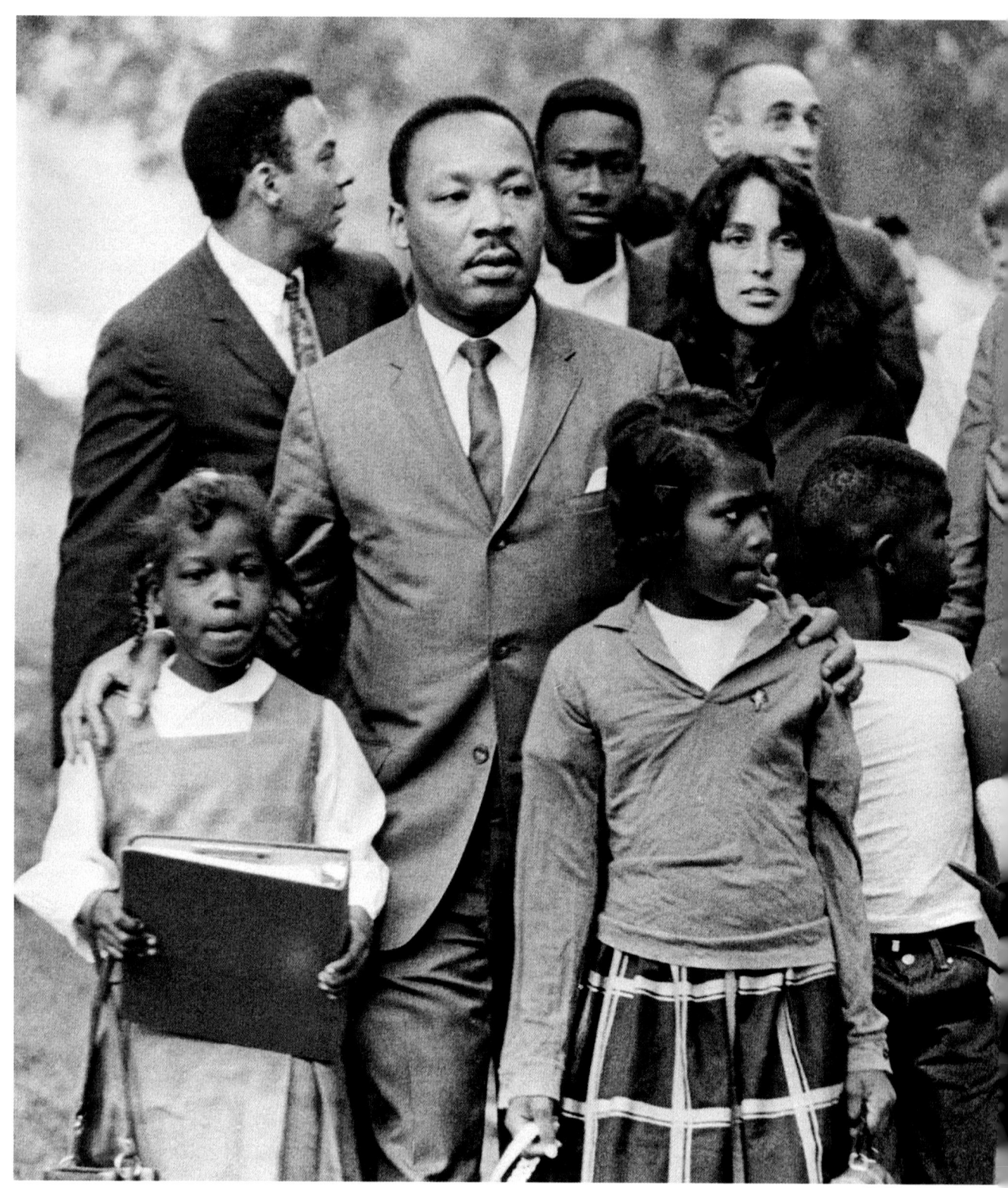

SPACES AND PLACES OF BLACK POLITICS

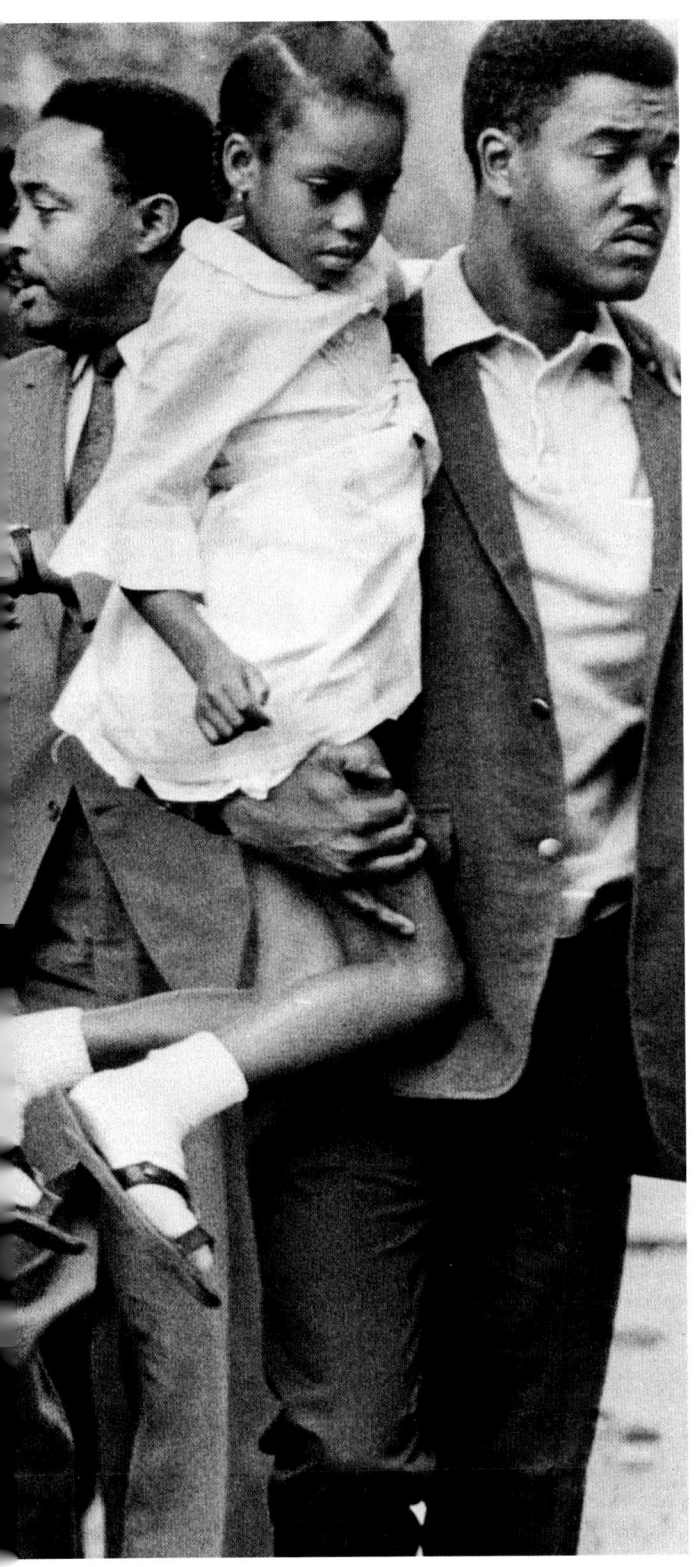

As shown in the image on page 116, after talking to this child's parents about voting, a white worker plays with a small Black child. While the worker's hold is awkward and distanced, it is also firm. This interaction depicts how many volunteers lacked familiarity with Black communities. However, it is also symbolic of the trust and commitment required to advance voting rights in Mississippi. It is unknown whether the child's parents decided to register to vote, but their decision to expose their child to volunteers would not have been made lightly.

The *Mississippi Free Press*, Freedom Schools, and voter registration drives could not have succeeded without establishing genuine relationships between activists and Black communities. Organizers fostered these relationships through social gatherings, and though this was not a new tactic, it was an effective one that can be traced back to union organizing in the 1930s.

Singing freedom songs and other forms of musical expression were important in creating community, and fellowship between community members and volunteers was a vital component of the project. Many parents took their children to Freedom Summer community gatherings with the goals of increasing local participation, further organizing, and taking the opportunity to socialize as a group. Time and time again, children became the center of movement work, as well as active participants in shaping their communities. These photos highlight elements of movement work that activists did not always document in organizational papers.

Children worked and learned, but also established trust and built genuine relationships with one another, other members of their communities, and organizers at large. These aspects of community organizing were crucial to Mississippi Freedom Summer but remain essential tools in contemporary activist movements and organizing efforts.

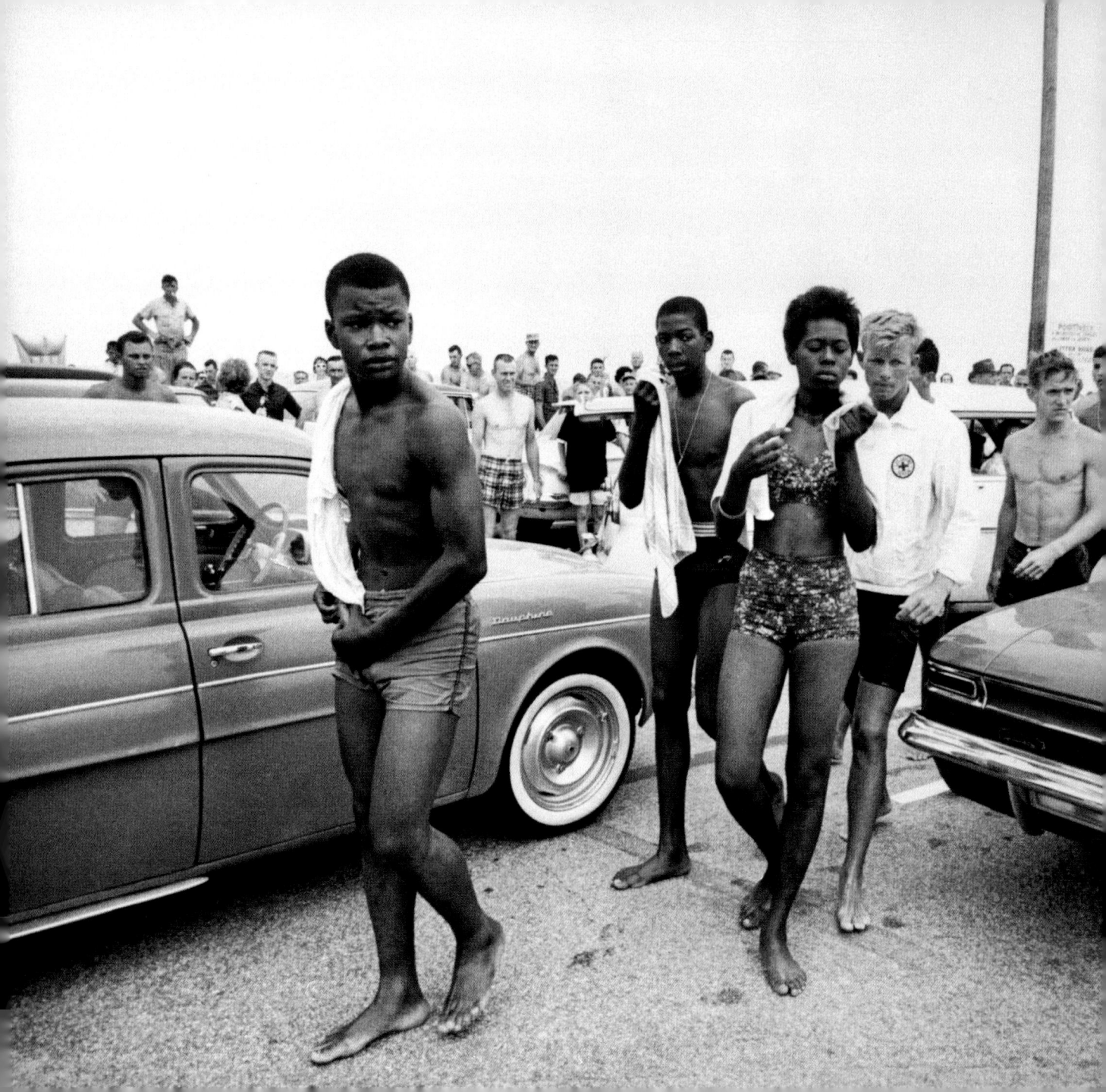

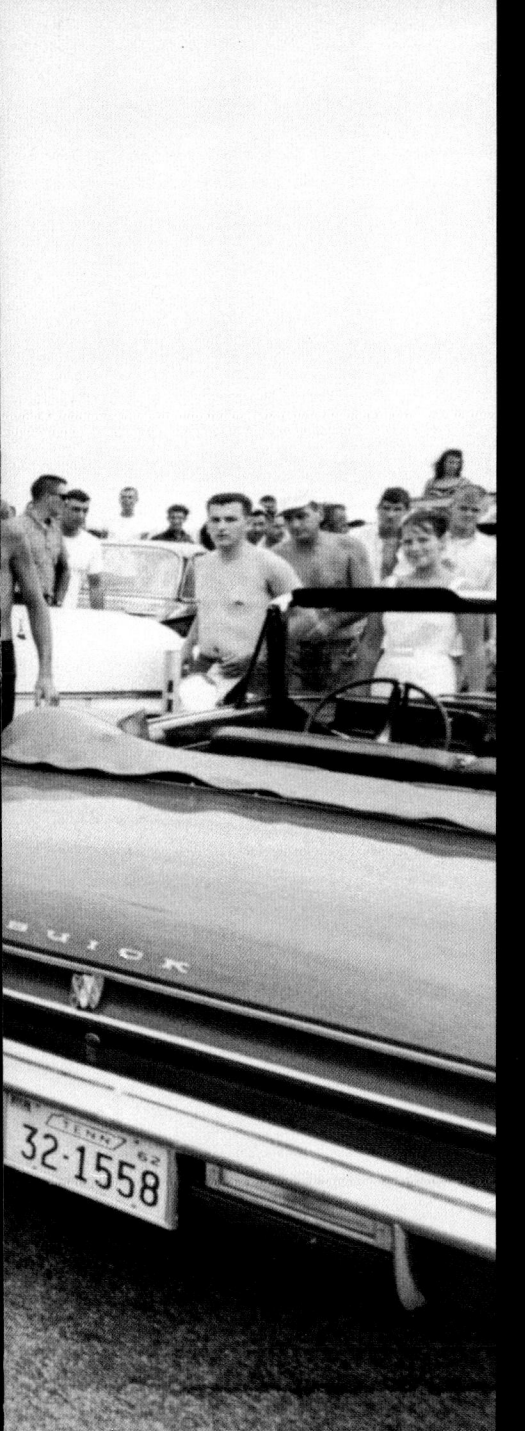

WADE IN THE WATER

DUSTIN MEIER

The fight to desegregate Savannah Beach.

Driving across Georgia in August 1960, eleven students from Atlanta's Morehouse College passed the time singing "Wade in the Water," an African American spiritual said to have been sung by Harriet Tubman on the Underground Railroad. It was a long drive to Savannah, where they planned to wade into the water off the coast of Tybee Island to desegregate the beach.

Inspired by the success of recent lunch counter sit-ins that began in Greensboro, North Carolina, African American activists organized wade-ins along the Atlantic and Gulf coasts throughout the early 1960s. In Savannah, the white population assailed them with racial slurs until police escorted the Black protestors to jail. African Americans continued to stage wade-ins in Savannah for the next two summers, finally forcing the city to desegregate the beach in 1963.

Photographs of this wade-in highlight the complexities of the Black Freedom Struggle and Jim Crow segregation of the era. The mob's anger reveals how the struggle for leisure and access to nature accompanied similar issues of voting rights and economic freedom. For whites, upholding a segregated landscape and regulating the sexuality of the activists' seminude bodies were paramount.

In the photograph to the right, Savannah's white beach-goers exhibited a range of emotions from anger to glee as they flanked and outnumbered the young African Americans they sought to banish. The state's involvement in Jim Crow segregation is also on full display in the local police officers escorting the activists to jail. Such unified opposition reveals just how strongly the white population and local government did not want African Americans to enjoy Savannah Beach.

Civil rights activists in the early 1960s fought to integrate spaces like buses and lunch counters, each integral to daily life, but they also maintained that African Americans deserved equal access to leisure and recreation. Summer days at the beach were a part of life in Savannah and other coastal cities, and activists considered wade-ins central to their wider struggle for basic dignity and citizenship rights.

The rows of cars lining the beach remind us of the important role that mobility played in the Black Freedom Struggle, and specifically in the environmental injustices plaguing Savannah. The nearest beach to which African Americans had access was in Hilton Head, South Carolina, about twice the distance from downtown Savannah as Tybee Island. Driving was never completely safe for African Americans, but longer journeys made going to the beach that much more dangerous and inaccessible.

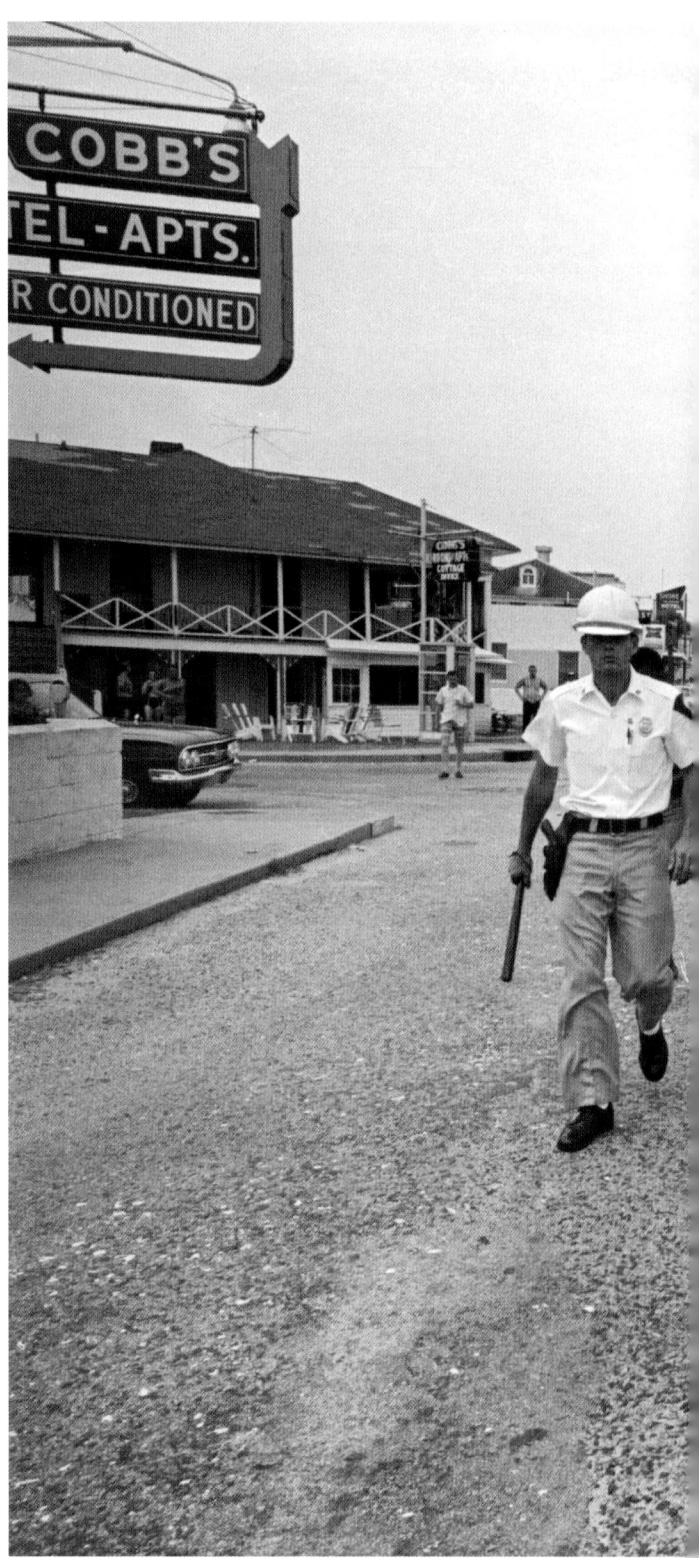

PREVIOUS SPREAD: These three Black bathers were forced off the beach and arrested after trying to integrate the "whites only" Savannah Beach, Georgia.

RIGHT: As they were arrested and taken away, the Black swimmers were jeered by a crowd of white beachgoers.

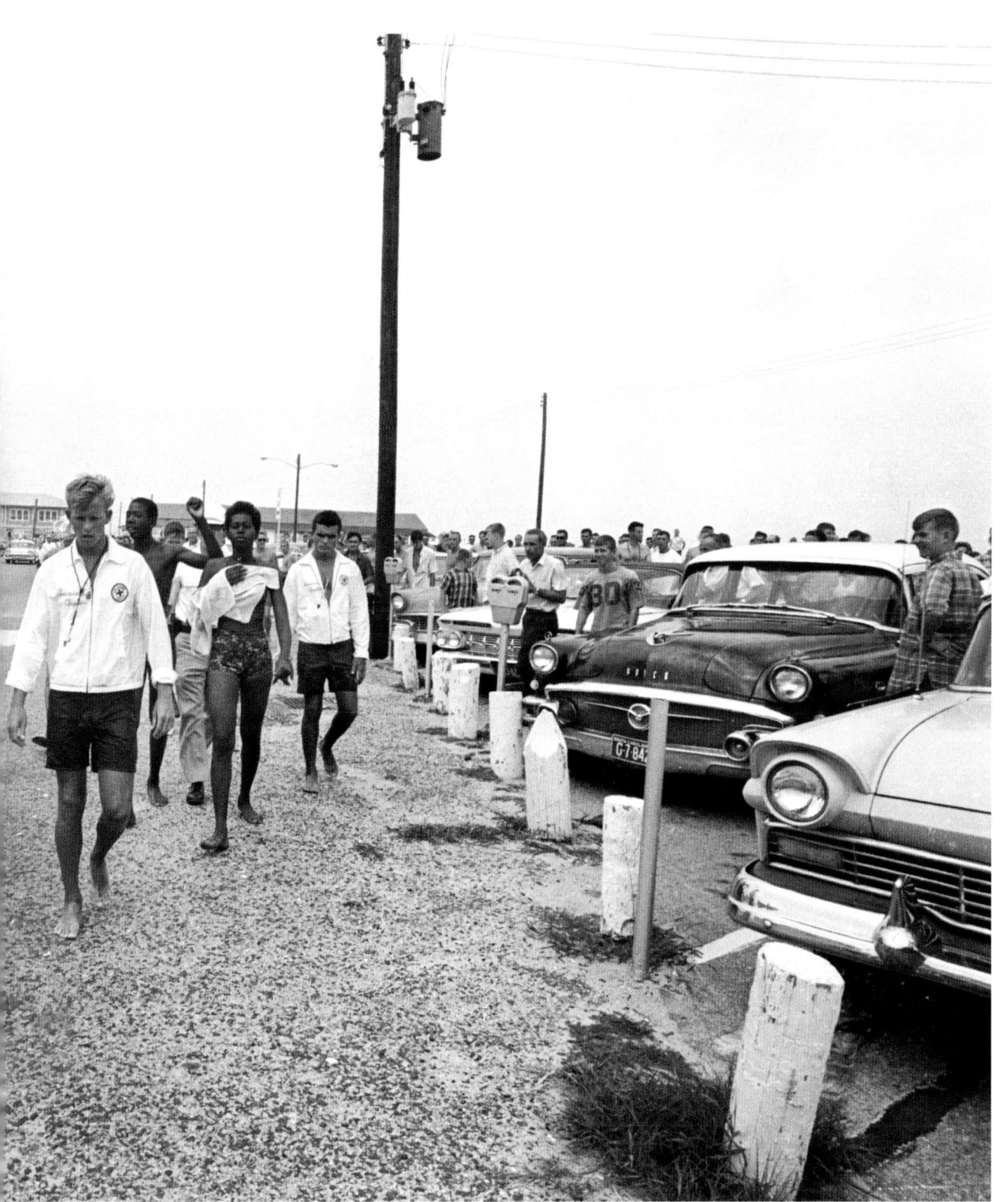

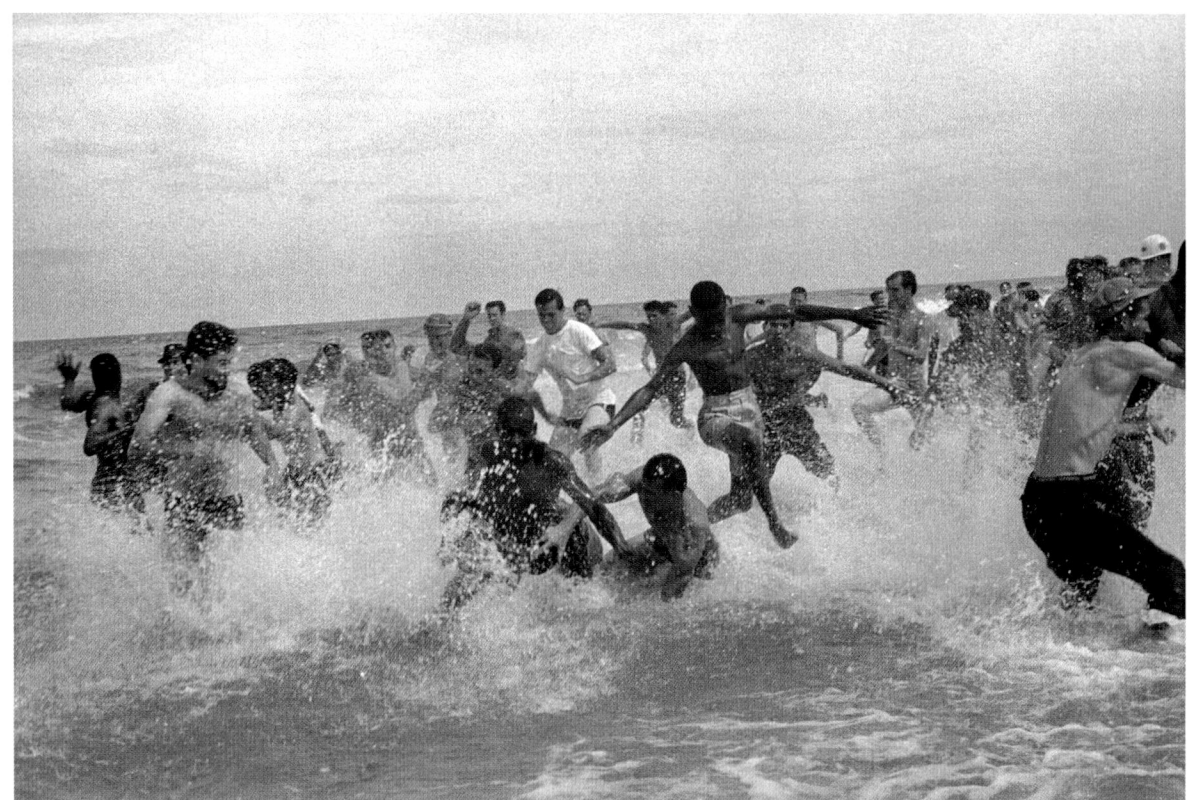

THIS PAGE: These 1964 images capture the moment when whites began to attack Black swimmers trying to integrate St. Augustine Beach in Florida and police intervened.

OPPOSITE, LEFT: A father and his daughter play in the surf at Daytona Beach, Florida, in 1983.

OPPOSITE, RIGHT: Friends greet each other on Highland Beach, Maryland. The Black beach resort was founded in 1893 by Frederick Douglass's son Charles after he retired from the U.S. Army with the rank of major.

FOLLOWING SPREAD: A group of Black women wade into the ocean at Asbury Park, New Jersey, in 1920 holding on to a rope. Those suits were probably made of wool.

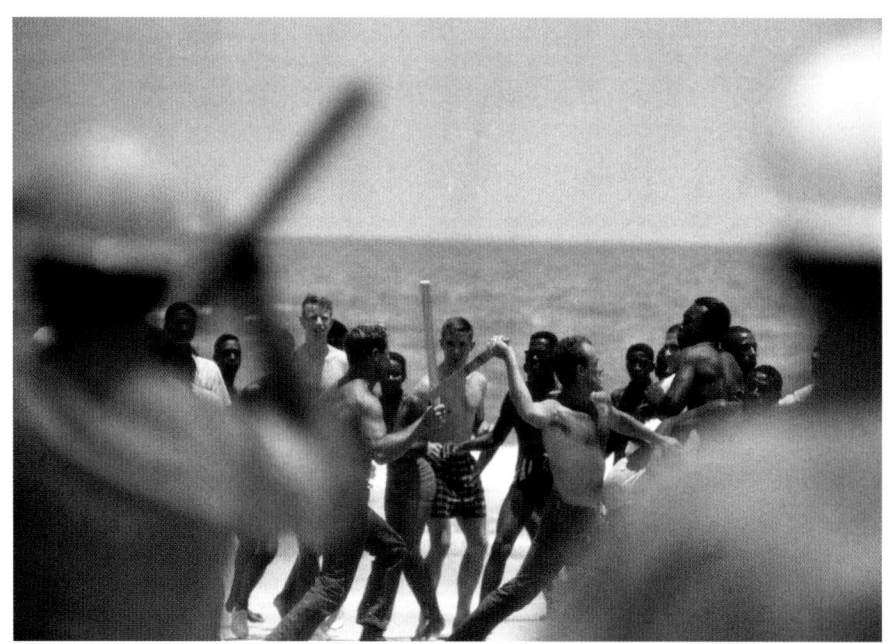

SPACES AND PLACES OF BLACK POLITICS

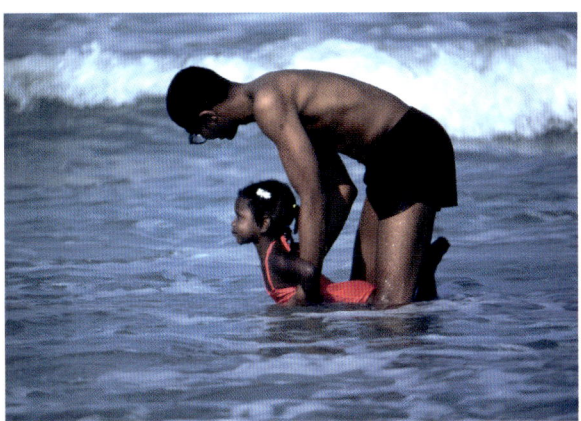
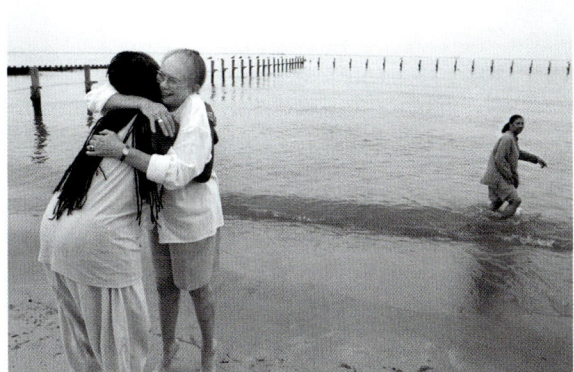

Beaches and other natural spaces provided a much-needed place for Southerners to cool off during the summer. Excluded from beaches, African American children often swam in streams polluted by industry or parks overcome with runoff, contributing to disproportionately higher death rates. Desegregating the natural spaces of Savannah Beach represented a step toward greater access to relaxation and environmental justice.

Dressed only in swim trunks and bikinis, the wade-in activists drew the ire of white beachgoers and provide the focal point of both photographs. White anxiety regarding interracial sexuality played a central role in upholding segregation. Whites maintained stereotypes of Black men as sexual predators preying on white women, whom they considered emblematic of racial purity. They cast Black women as sexually promiscuous figures who took advantage of white men. More than anything, they feared interracial sex and marriage. At Tybee Island and other beaches, these threats became terrifyingly real with the risk of white and Black bodies intermingling daily.

Singing "Wade in the Water" as they fought to desegregate Savannah Beach, these young activists participated in a struggle for freedom that reached back to the eighteenth century. The beach had been there before anyone, white or Black.

When slave traders first brought West Africans to Georgia in the eighteenth century, Tybee Island served as a quarantine station. Following the treacherous Middle Passage, enslaved men and women were forced into a nine-story *lazaretto*, an Italian word meaning "pest house," alongside rats and other vermin. They remained quarantined for days to protect Savannah's population from infectious diseases. Slave traders and plantation owners eschewed any sort of dignified burial procession for those who died, burying them on Tybee Island.

Today, Black college students host their annual Orange Crush spring break celebration on Tybee Island. Still, Savannah officials have taken efforts to limit the event's success by increasing policing and denying permits, promoting narratives of the event as loud, dirty, and dangerous. On Tybee Island, the struggle for racial equality is far from over.

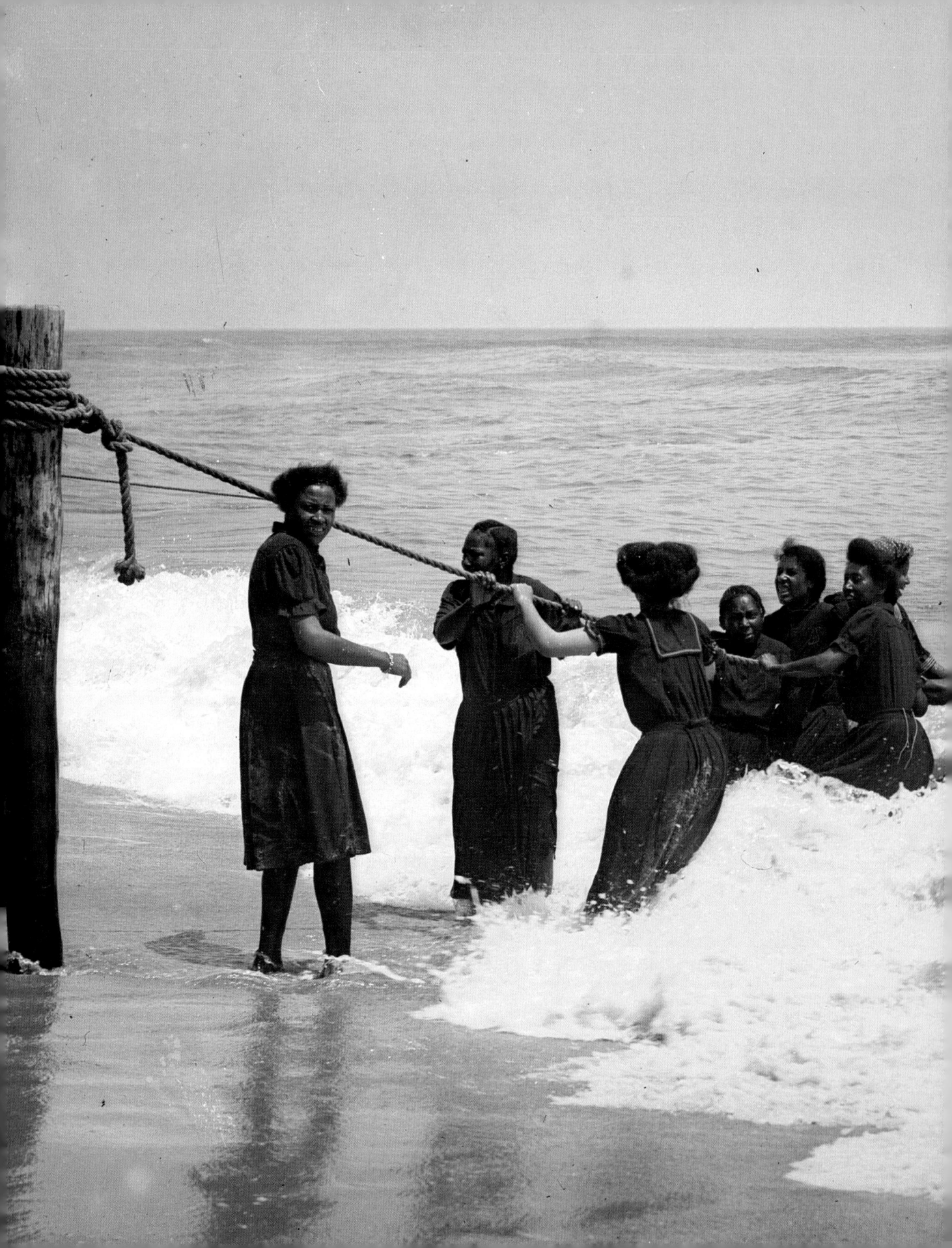

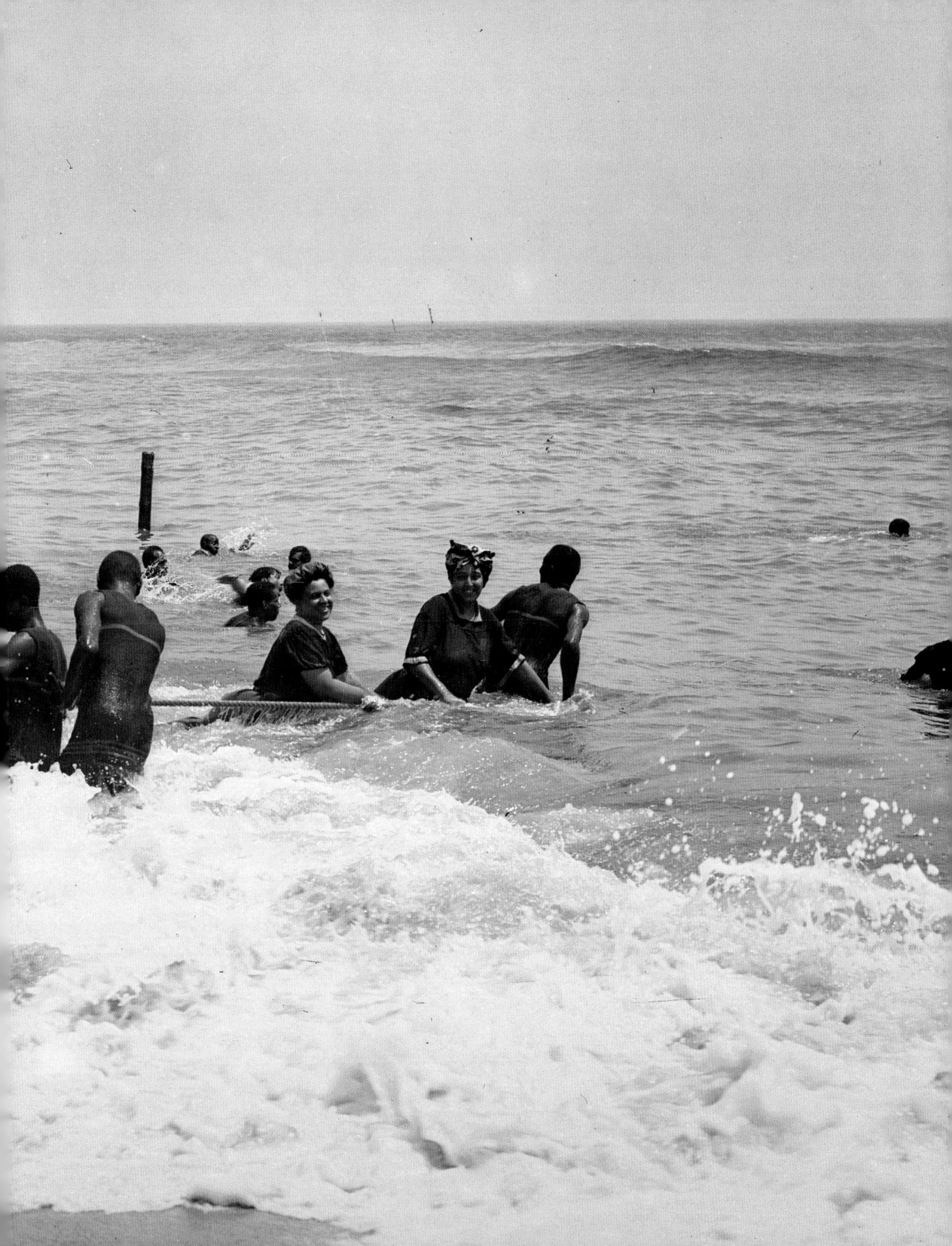

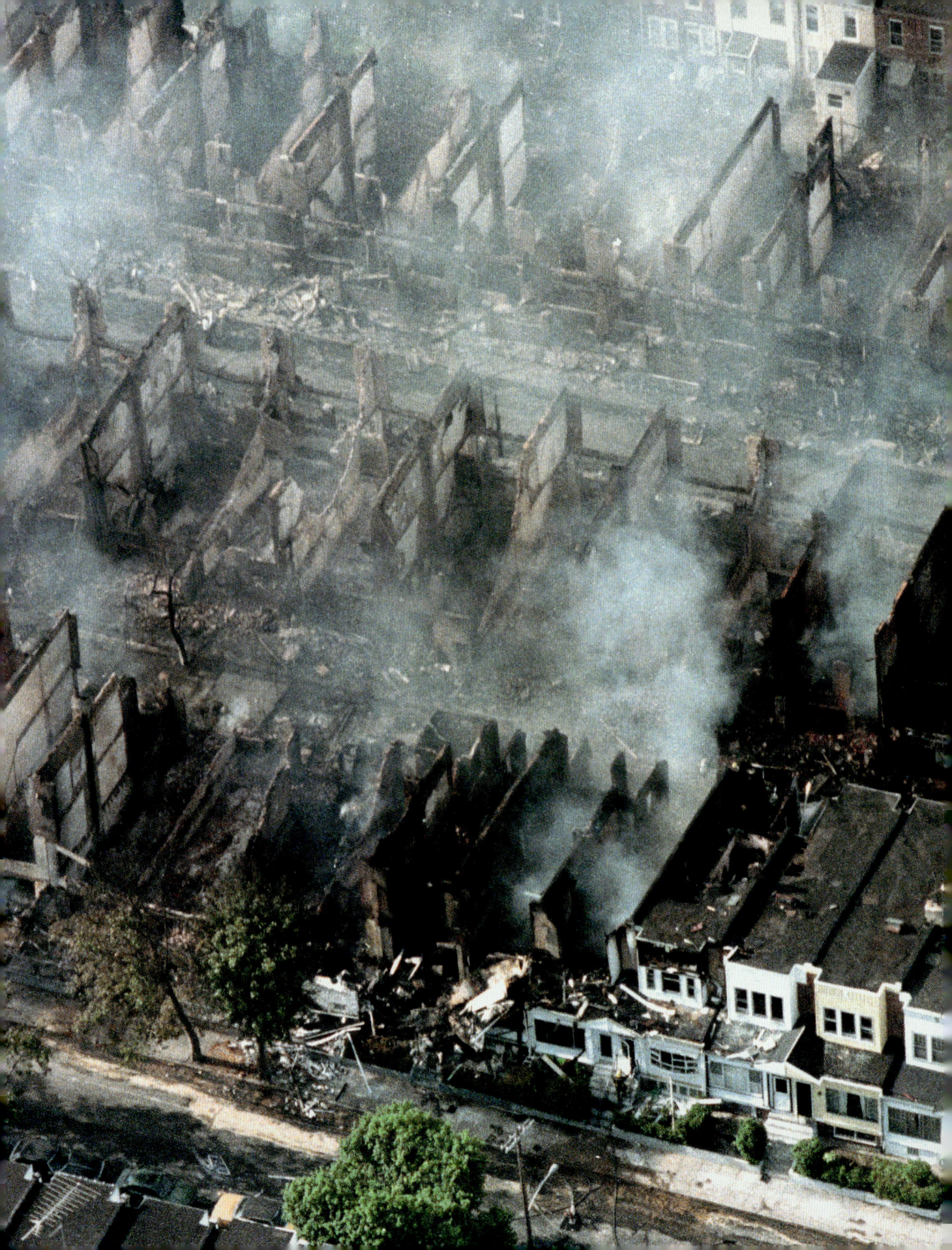

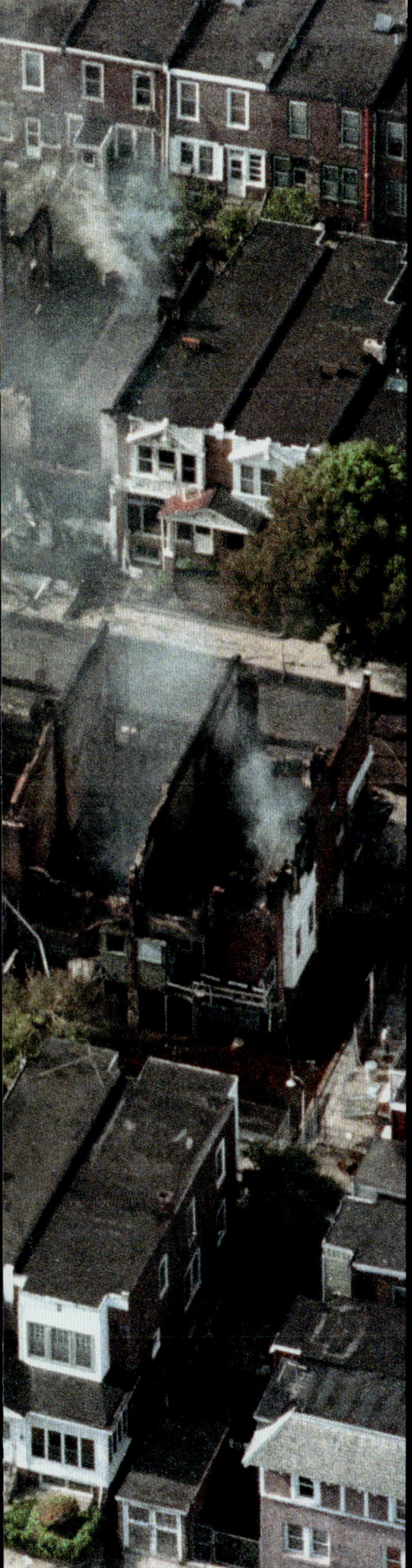

BOMBING MOVE

SHENEESE THOMPSON

What constitutes terrorism?
How the Philadelphia police turned a
neighborhood to ashes and the desecration
of the remains of the dead that followed.

This photograph captures the widespread destruction unleashed in West Philadelphia when the police bombed the MOVE organization on May 13, 1985. The image was originally captioned, "[a]erial view of smoke rising from smouldering [*sic*] rubble where some 60 homes were destroyed by fire after a shootout and bombing at the back-to-nature terrorist group MOVE's house in West Philadelphia where police were trying to force the group's eviction."

The caption takes a clear position in justification of the gratuitous violence the Philadelphia police employed to remove the group from their home as well as how the day's events should be remembered. It also reflects not just the individual bias of the archivist who cataloged the photograph, but also the broader anti-Black bias that shaped public perceptions of the bombing and the MOVE organization itself. In an updated version of the caption, only the word "terrorist" is removed.

The caption does not, however, address what is obscured from the photograph. The responsibility for the decision to drop a satchel bomb on a residential neighborhood that day sits squarely on Mayor Wilson Goode, the City of Philadelphia, and complicit institutions like the Philadelphia Police Department and University of Pennsylvania.

MOVE, a political and religious organization founded in 1972, has focused on human and animal rights, and often engaged in direct-action protests against war, over-policing, and the inhumane treatment of animals. Though largely nonviolent in its operations, the organization had tenuous relationships with the police and surrounding communities. While many of the organization's neighbors found their lifestyle to be a nuisance, Philadelphia authorities, especially Mayor Frank Rizzo, worked diligently to disband MOVE throughout the 1970s.

The bombing was not the organization's first run-in with the Philadelphia Police Department, but rather the culmination of a series of antagonisms. When a deal MOVE struck with the city to release imprisoned members required them to vacate their Powelton Village compound, it resulted in a standoff that ended in a raid on August 8, 1978, where both MOVE members and the police exchanged gunfire. One officer was killed, and consequently, nine MOVE members were convicted and sentenced to life in prison.

In May 1985, after MOVE relocated to Osage Avenue, the Philadelphia Police Department tried again to evict people from one home. This time, the police were directly

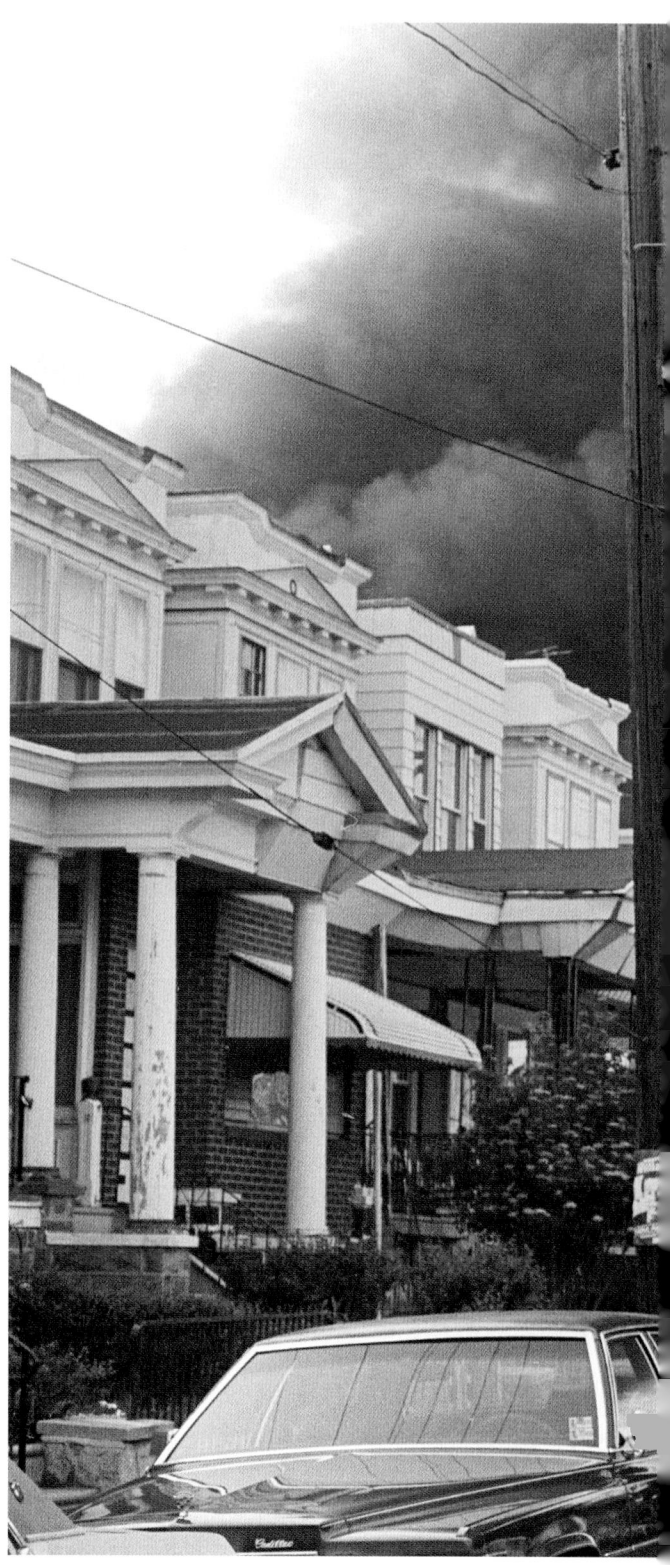

PREVIOUS SPREAD: This aerial photo was taken on May 14, 1985, and shows the devastation that the bombing of the MOVE house had on an entire neighborhood.

RIGHT: Smoke begins to billow over the row houses in the West Philadelphia neighborhood where MOVE lived.

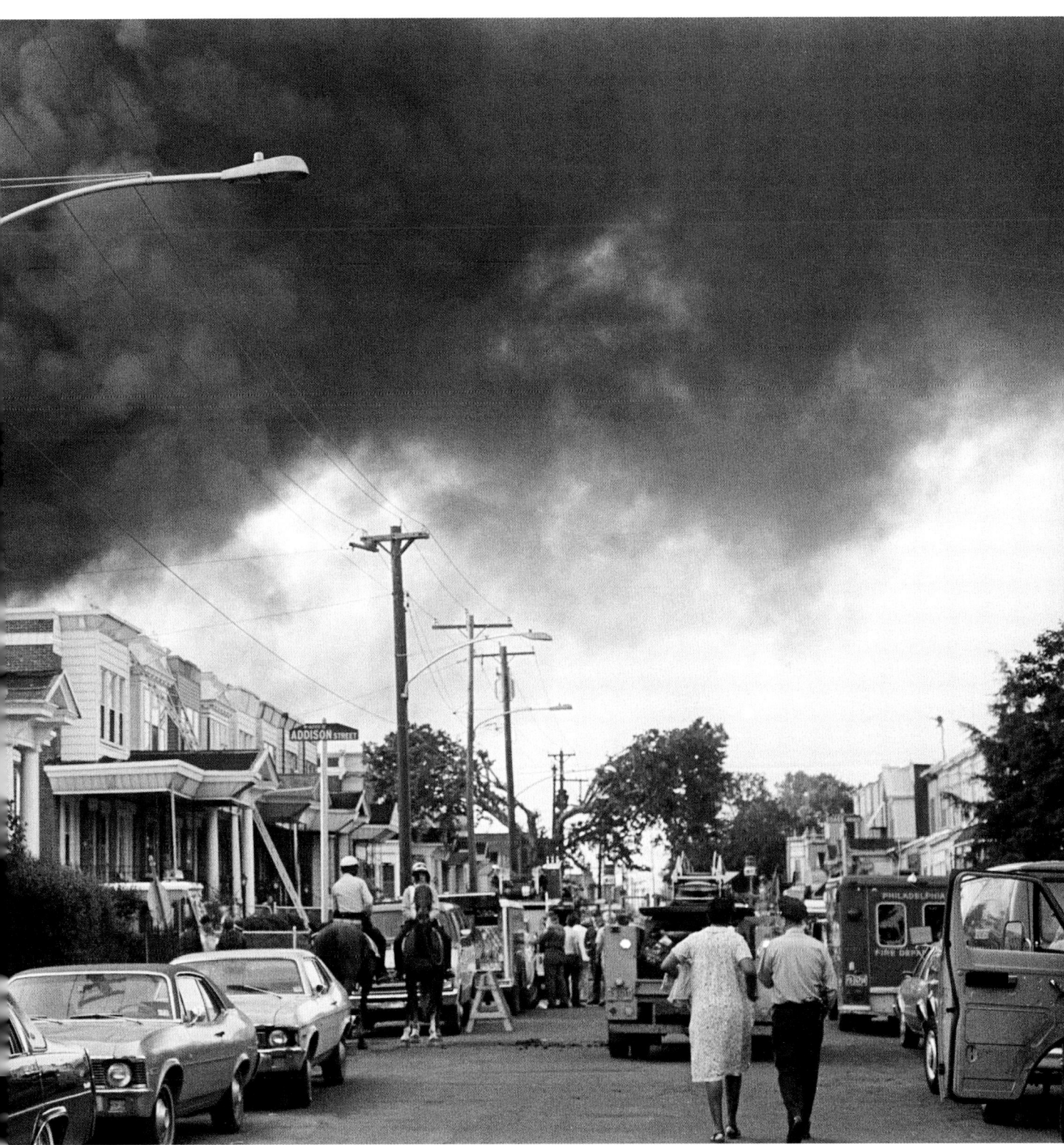

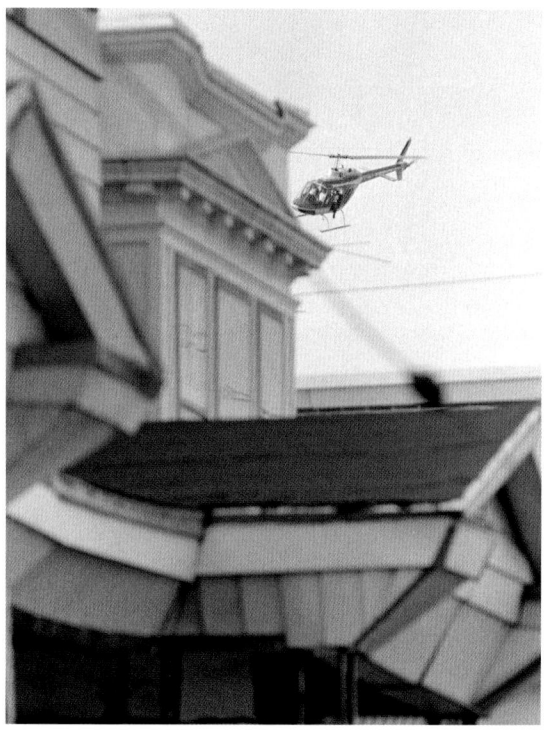

responsible for the destruction of entire city blocks and the unhousing of over 250 people as they insisted that the fire burn even after the Philadelphia Fire Department was dispatched.

Eleven people were killed in the fire including five children, while two survivors, Ramona and Birdie Africa, were badly burned. For years following the incident, the City of Philadelphia claimed that the remains of the MOVE victims were cremated.

However, it was discovered in April 2021 that the University of Pennsylvania Museum has been in possession of the remains of Delisha Africa and Katricia Dotson (also known as Tree Africa), twelve and fourteen years old respectively at the time of their death, and they had been using them as props in a Coursera online forensics course taught by Janet Monge. Their remains were returned to family members on July 6, 2021, after protests erupted in West Philadelphia.

Further investigation found a separate set of remains in the Philadelphia Medical Examiner's Office that the medical examiner, Tom Farley, had ordered destroyed without notifying the family of the deceased. The surviving members of the MOVE organization were only able to lay their lost loved ones to rest in Bartram's Garden thirty-six years after their deaths.

The treatment of the bodies raises the question: What constitutes terrorism? Political and religious civil disobedience and self-determination, which are constitutional rights of all American citizens? Or the bombing of American citizens in a residential neighborhood and the decades-long desecration of the remains of those killed in an unjustified act of violence?

The homes destroyed on 62nd Street and Osage Avenue remain largely vacant, since many of the families never returned to the neighborhood even after homes of questionable quality were erected in place of the houses lost in the fire. The ghost town on Osage Avenue, which used to be a thriving middle-class Black neighborhood, is itself a memorial to the terrorism that occurred on May 13, 1985.

Osage Avenue also represents the continued antagonism between the Philadelphia Police Department and Black communities in the city. And while most Philadelphia residents are aware of the MOVE bombing, if for no other reason than the huge scar it left on the city, it remains largely forgotten in national memory.

These photographs and the events they do and do not capture should be remembered and memorialized nationwide as the first domestic bombing of its kind, as well as another event establishing the disposability of Black lives in the quest for law and order.

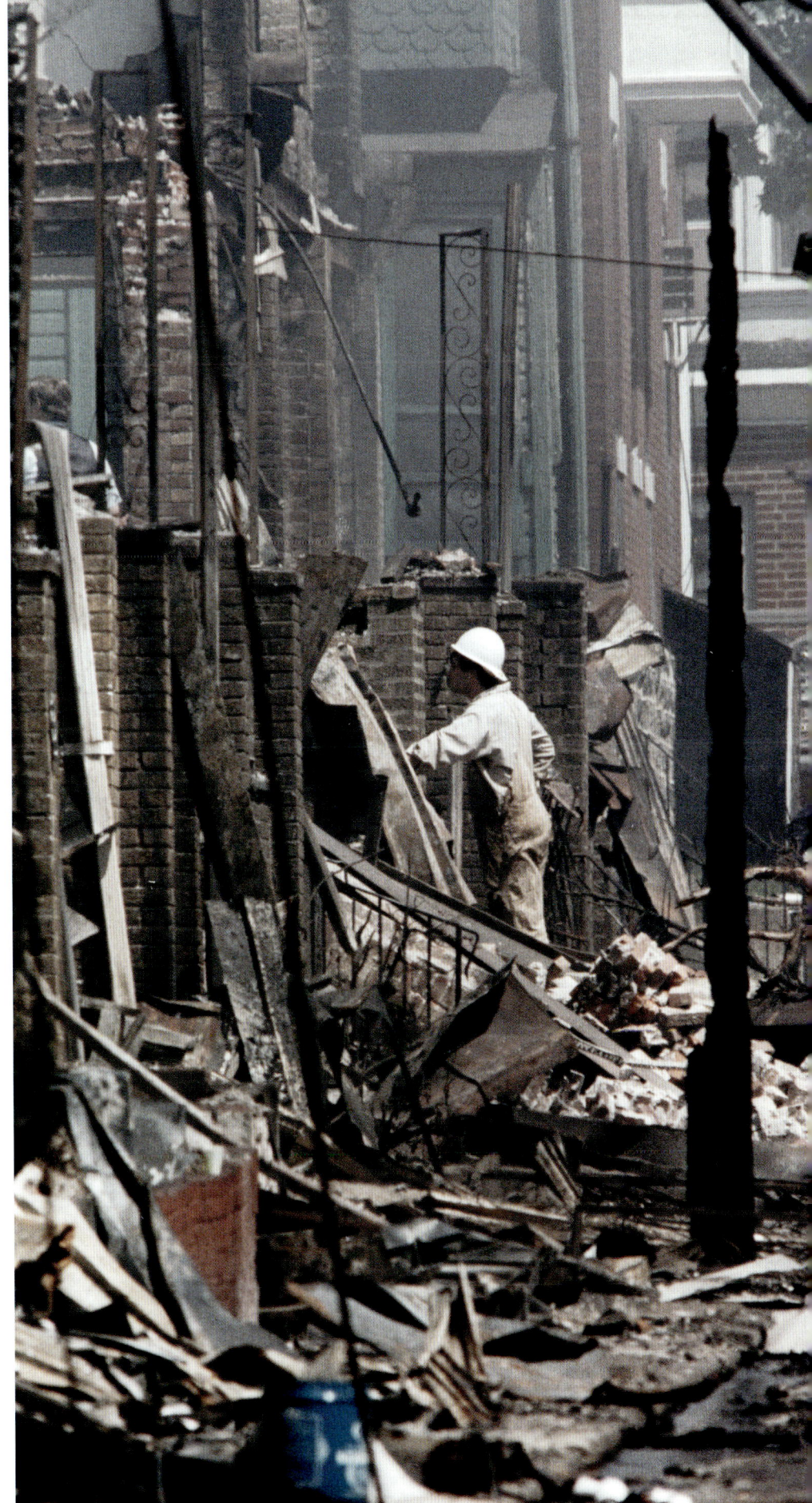

OPPOSITE: A state police helicopter circles over the houses as it prepares to drop an incendiary device on the MOVE house.

RIGHT: Philadelphia firemen hose down the remains after bombing destroyed more than sixty homes.

FOLLOWING SPREAD: Supporters of MOVE raise a Black Power salute during the funeral procession of John Africa in December 1985.

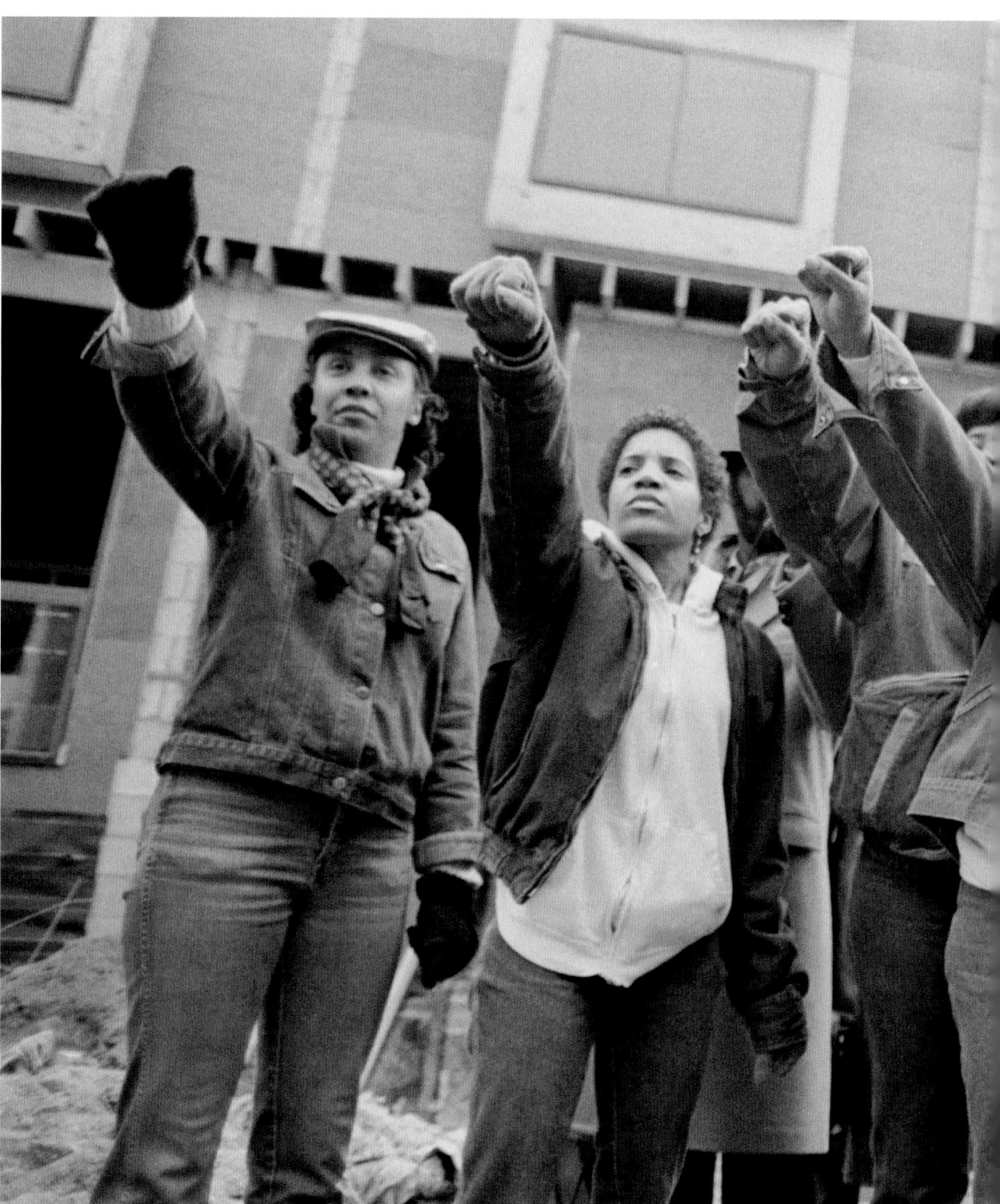

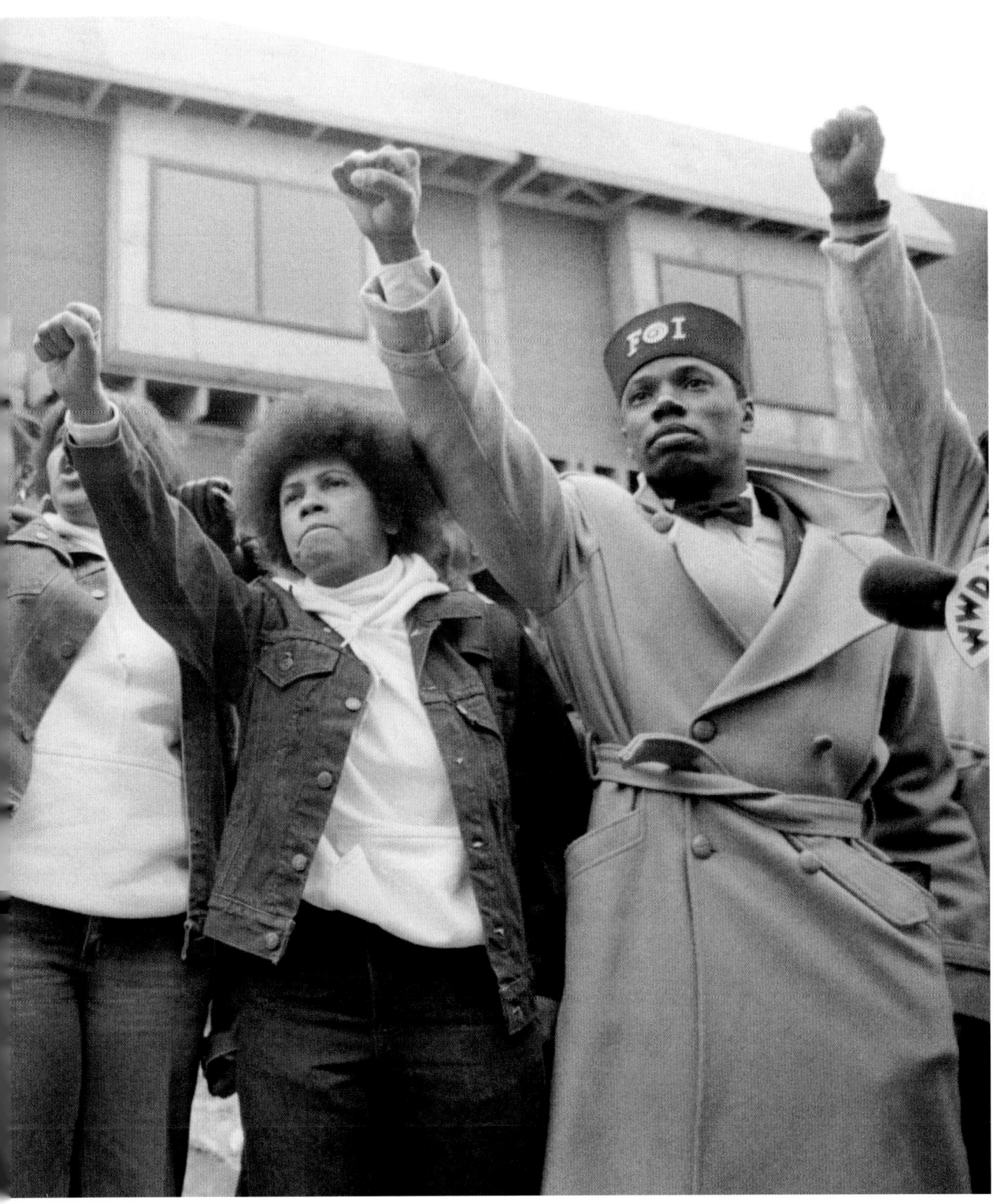

THE LOCKED OUT

JOSHUA MYERS

Jesse Jackson and the radicalism of 1980s Black presidential politics.

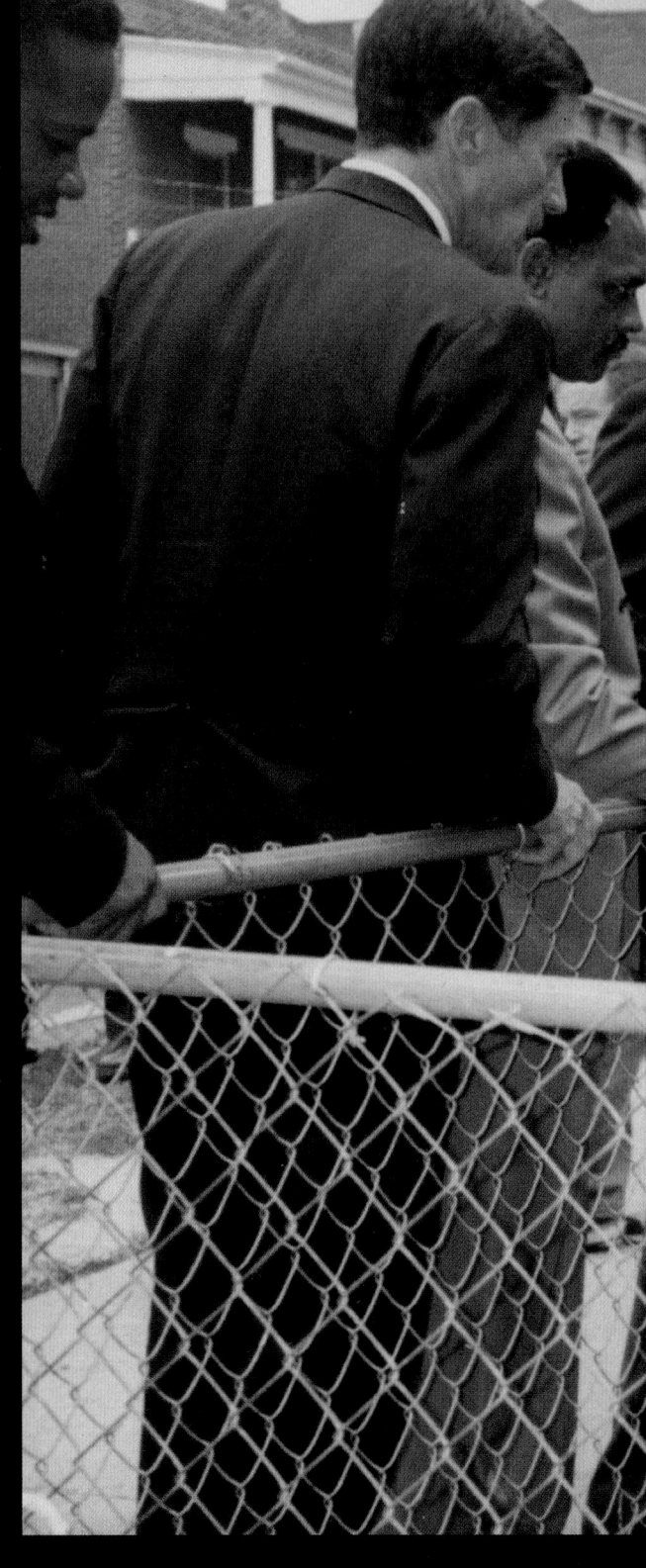

T he year is 1984. Jesse Jackson is running for president in the Democratic primary. It is easy to conclude that this image is merely another example of a politician taking advantage of a photo opportunity, an orchestrated projection of the idea that politicians represent the marginalized.

But this is Jesse Jackson, so there is more in this photo than immediately meets the eye.

Jesse Jackson was not a politician. Though many political analysts called him inexperienced, he seemed personally to attract the very constituencies his campaign sought to reach. Here he is engaging with a Black mother and her children in inner-city Chicago (and though we do not know the details of their financial circumstances, we do know that in general, Black women faced almost impossible odds as workers, as mothers, and as citizens during the Reagan era).

Particularly, city centers enfeebled by economic neglect, the withdrawal of resources, and deep poverty were the order of the day in Black communities across the country. The Jackson campaign directly addressed these folk. It directly focused on the nature of the system that could produce such suffering, exposing how the plight of urban Black people was minimized by the Democratic Party and pathologized by the conservative movement.

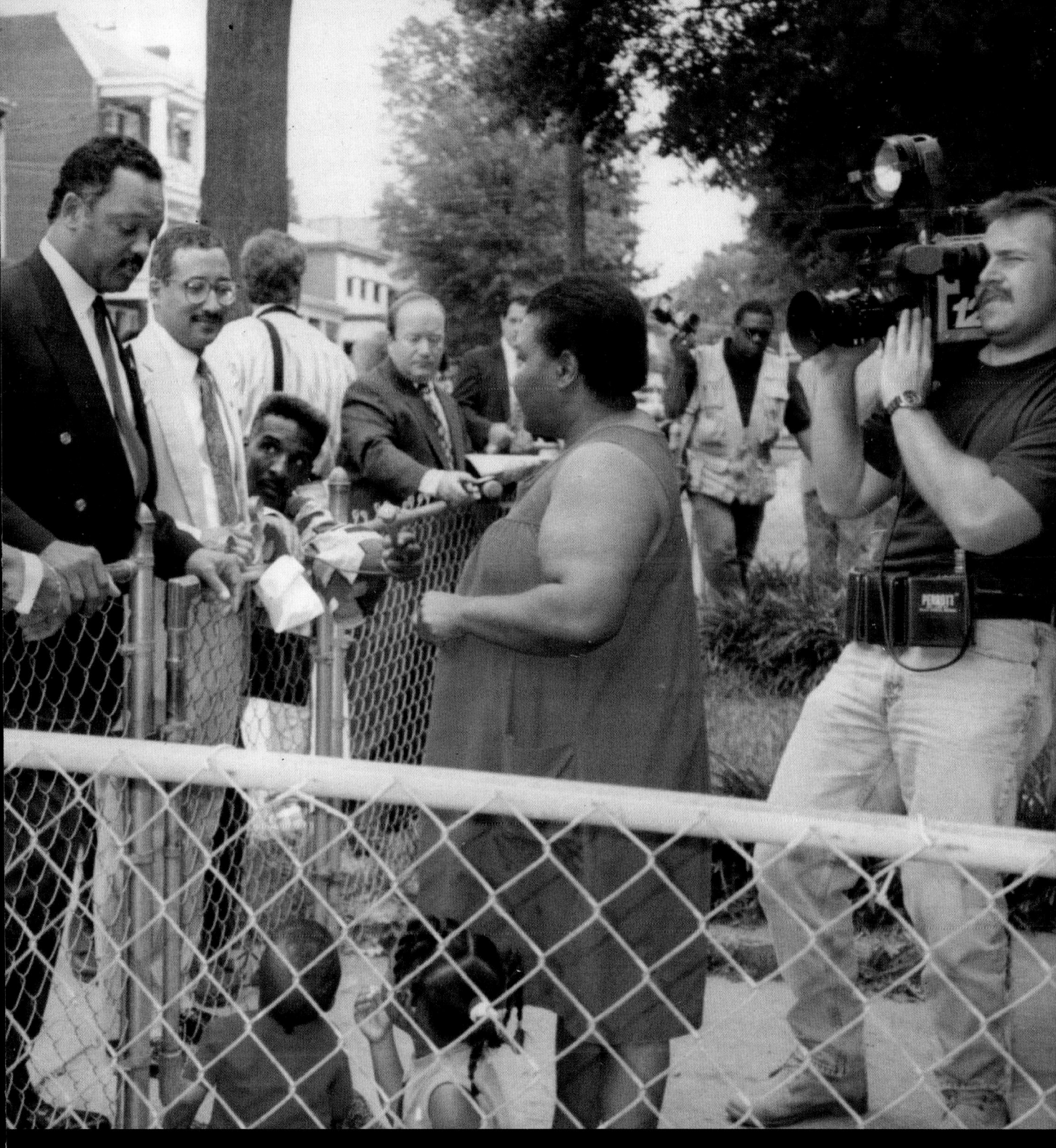

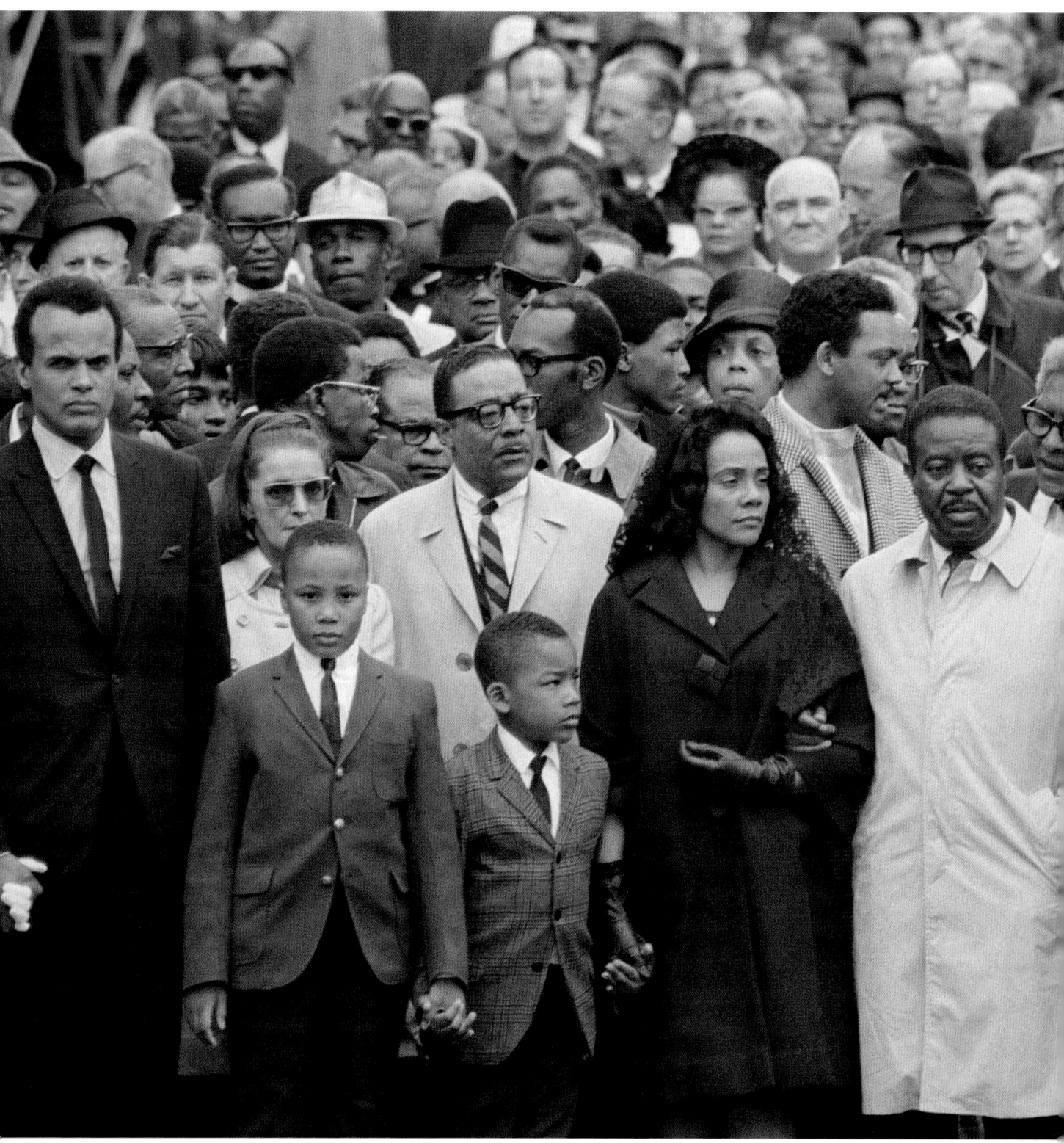

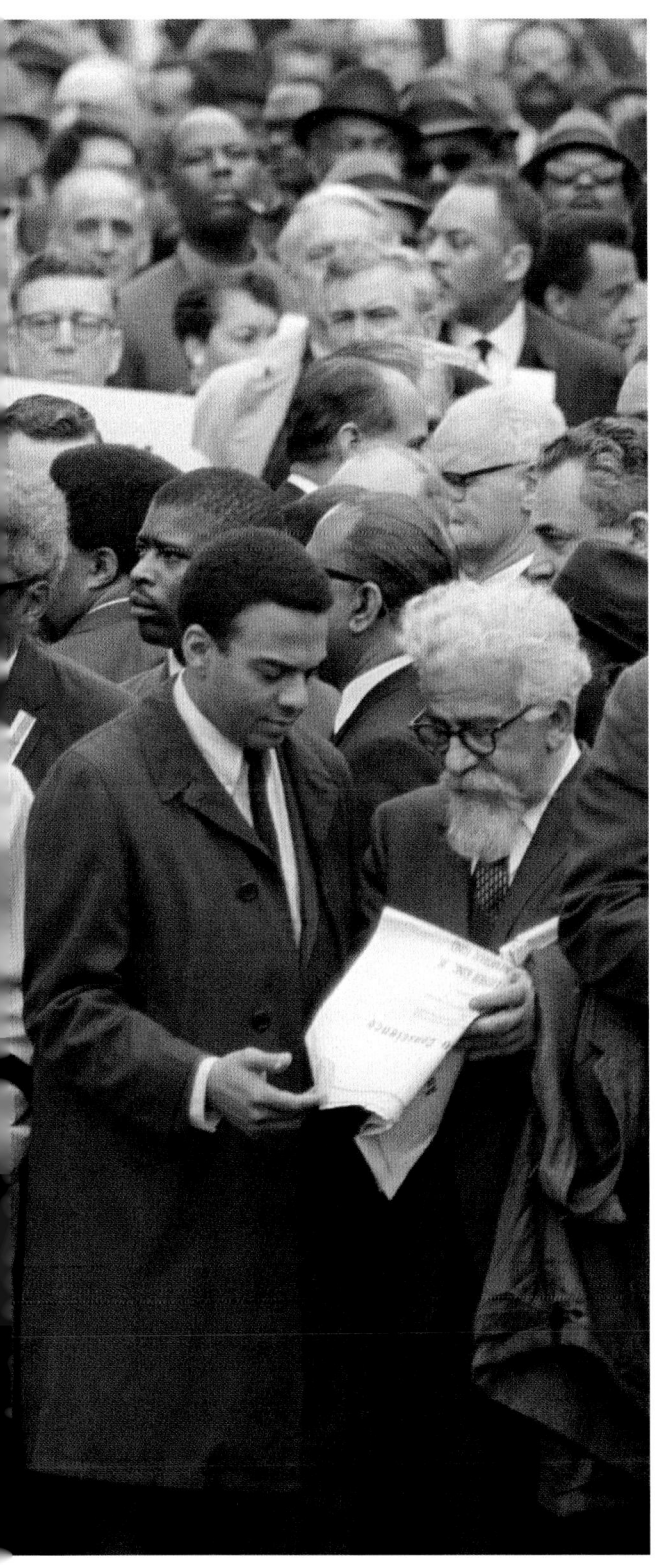

In his own imagination, and in the imagination of many Black working-class people, Jackson had always been their advocate. A former football star, the Greenville, South Carolina, native was a veteran of the Southern Black Freedom Struggle. He had been a staffer for the Southern Christian Leadership Conference (SCLC) and director of its Operation Breadbasket.

An initiative of Martin Luther King Jr., Operation Breadbasket, based in Chicago, aimed to ensure that corporations that directly benefited from their business operations in Black communities reinvested in those communities.

Under Jackson's leadership, Operation Breadbasket led successful boycotts of large corporations unwilling to accede to its demands and executed what it called "covenants" where businesses like A&P Grocery agreed to hire and train Black employees for managerial positions, stock Black-created consumer items, utilize Black-owned service agencies, and invest funds in Black-owned banks.

After he ran afoul of the SCLC's leadership in the wake of King's assassination—a controversy that haunted his efforts—Jackson branched out on his own by developing Operation PUSH (People United to Save Humanity, later changed to "Serve").

Often appearing in a dashiki, leather jacket, Afro, and wearing a medallion of King's likeness, Jackson frequently invoked the slogan "It's nation time!" made famous by his comrade Amiri Baraka. Appearing at the legendary Wattstax concert in 1972, he roused the crowd with his now famous cry of "I am somebody!"

PREVIOUS SPREAD: Jesse Jackson visits Chicago residents during his 1984 run for the presidency.

LEFT: Civil rights leaders including Harry Belafonte, Ralph Abernathy, and Andrew Young join Coretta Scott King at the head of a memorial march for Martin Luther King Jr. on April 8, 1968, in Memphis, four days after King's assassination. Jesse Jackson talks to Bayard Rustin behind Coretta Scott King.

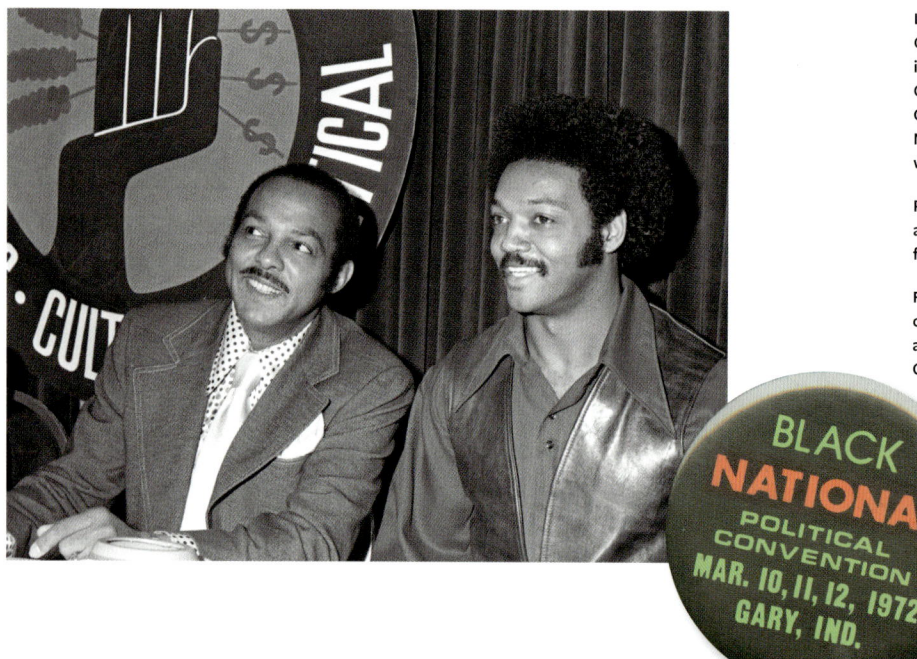

LEFT: Jesse Jackson headed Operation Breadbasket, and here is seated with Cleveland mayor Carl Stokes at a convention in Chicago in 1972. That same year the National Black Political Convention was held in Gary, Indiana.

RIGHT: In August 1972, Jackson attended the Wattstax music festival in Los Angeles.

FOLLOWING SPREAD: In front of a sea of supporters, Jackson addressed the Democratic National Convention held in Atlanta in 1988.

These experiences attracted movement folk to the presidential campaign. Organizers like Ron Walters and Jack O'Dell were critical members of the campaign team. Ardent supporters Baraka and Frances Beal, as well as Black churches and social organizations, backed Jackson.

Jackson's personal sensibilities often rankled Chicago's machine politicians, the media, and other civil rights activists, but among the Black masses his message resonated. Together with progressive whites, college students, farmers, and Arab Americans, they were a composite portrait of those who had been effectively "locked out."

With the exception of white feminists, most of the traditional segments of "captured" Democratic voters were moving closer and closer to the Jackson column. The old deals made behind closed doors among establishment figures were now being called into question, if not dismissed.

The foundation of Jackson's campaign was radical and leftist, part of a long-used strategy of Black presidential politics. Jackson's campaign drew from the 1972 National Black Political Convention in Gary, Indiana, which rejected mainstream liberalism and Democratic Party politics in favor of radical redistributive economic policies, reparative justice, anti-colonialism, and elements of the radical welfare movement. Black women's political struggles around sexual exploitation and labor joined this broad array of concerns.

Thus, when the National Black Independent Political Party was founded in 1980, there was already a concerted effort to address issues facing Black men and women within a radical political movement.

Jackson lost the primary in 1984 and again in 1988. Yet the lesson here is not about electoral victory. It is about what kind of movements—rather than political campaigns—can be sustained by taking seriously the plight of people like the women and children in the opening photo, the lives of the locked out.

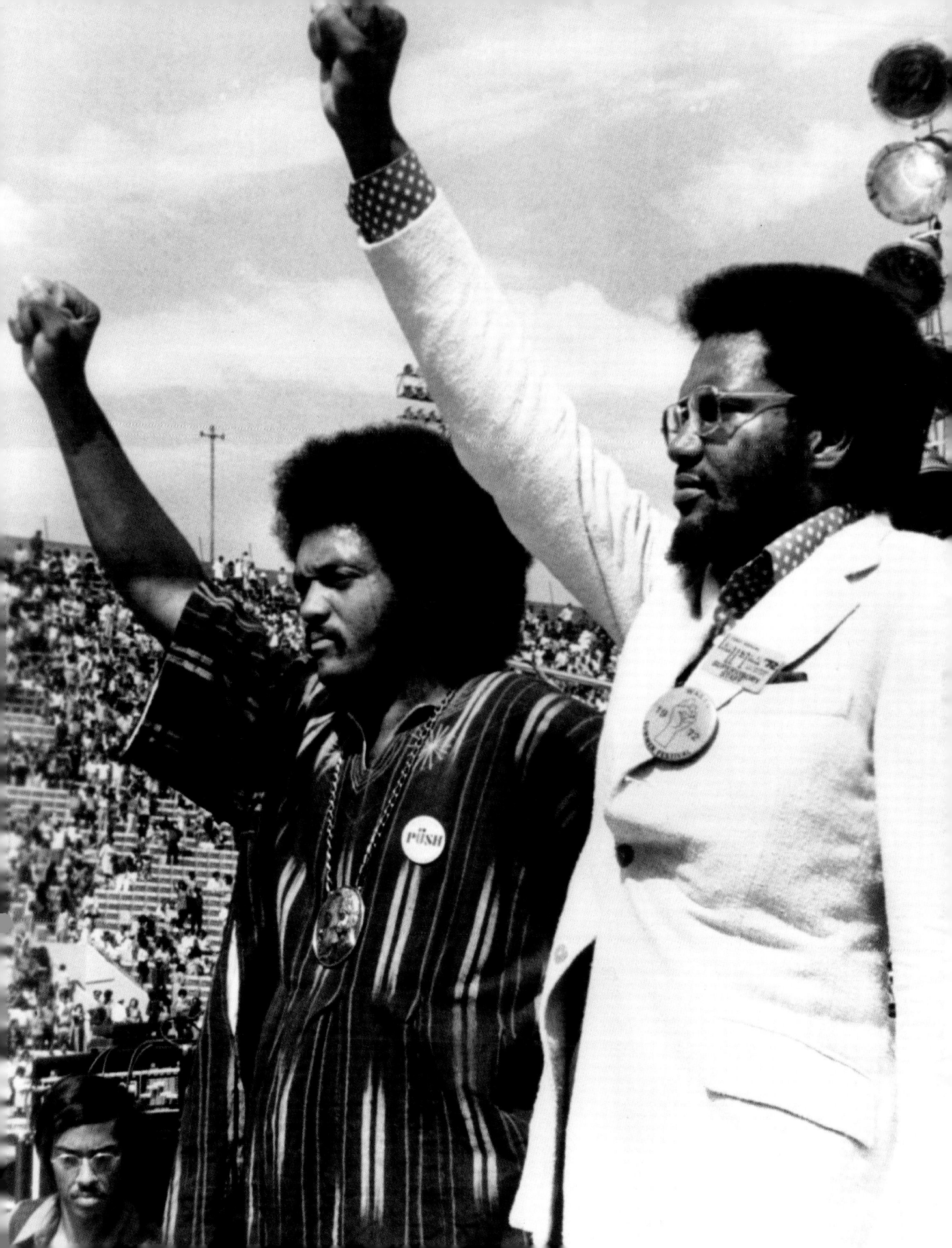

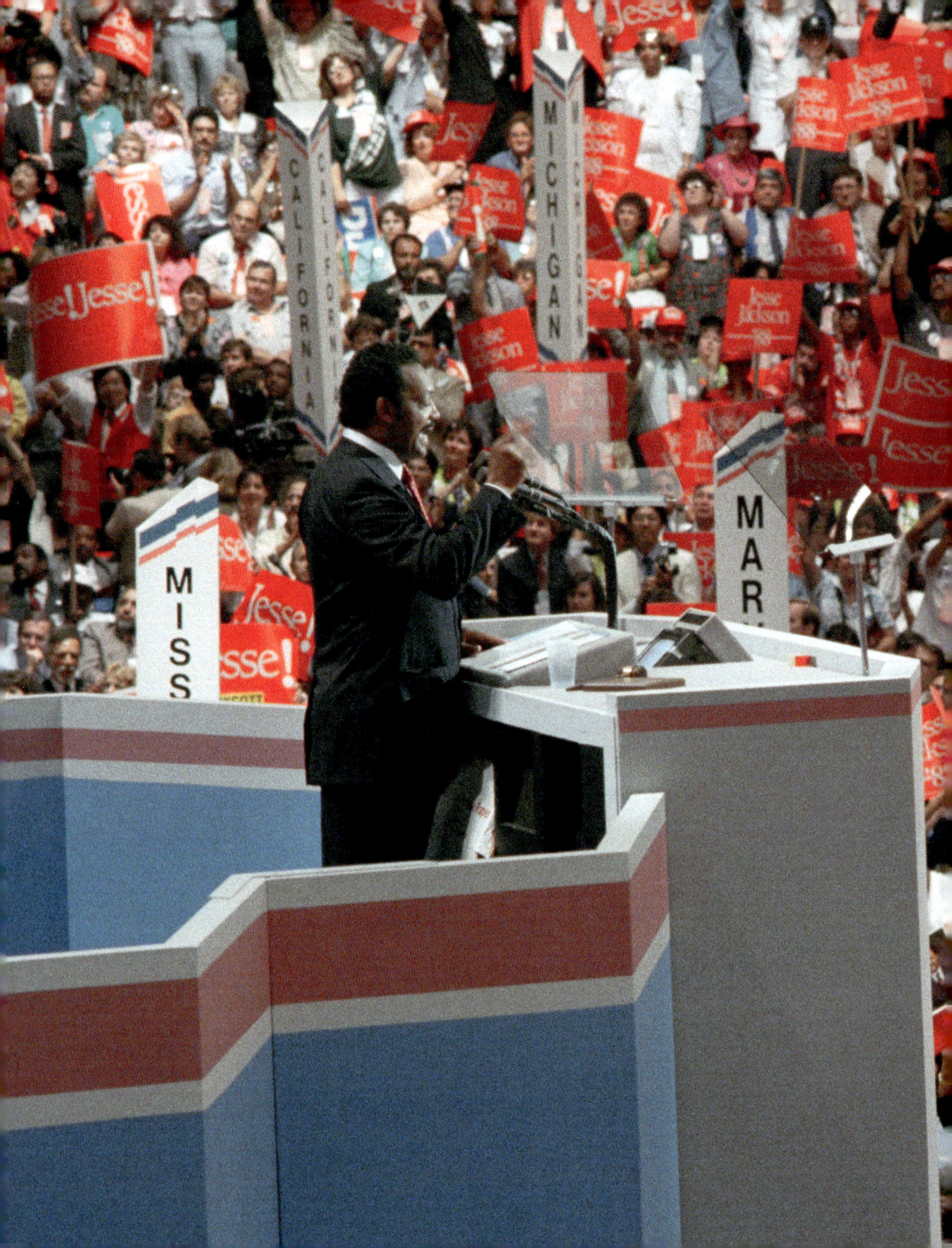

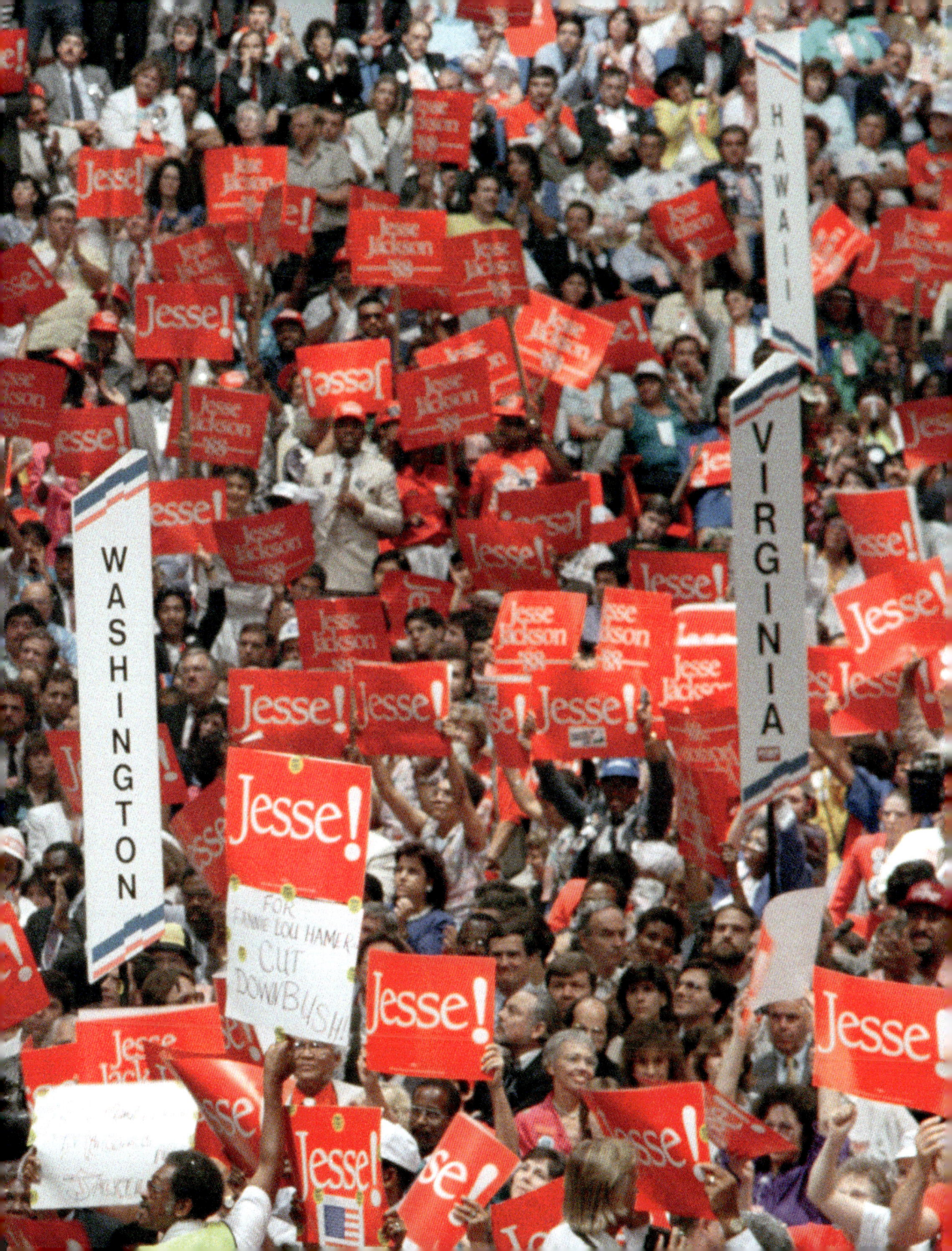

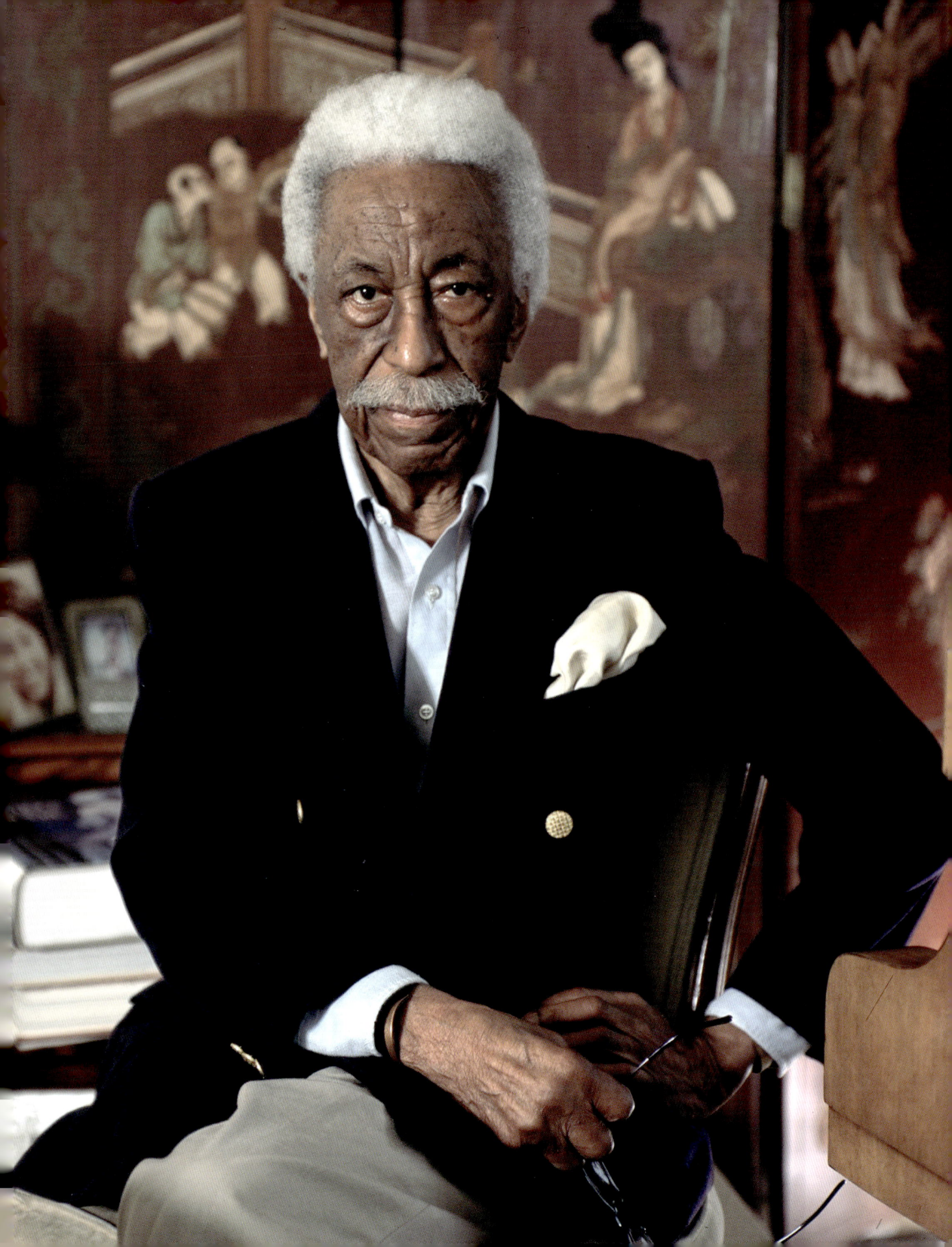

IV.

BLACK CULTURE AS PEOPLE POWER

BLACK CULTURE HAS PLAYED A TRANSFORMATIVE ROLE IN AMERICAN SOCIETY. Sports, music, dance, literature, film, fashion, style, and more have been used by Black individuals as avenues for exploring and reinforcing their identities in the face of oppression. Cultural production has been critical in answering what it means to be "Black" through expressions that resist narratives of the dominant culture and create new ways for Black people to assert self-determination.

In this sense, Black culture encourages Black self-love, community empowerment, and an appreciation of the historical legacy from which these individuals emerged. These essays remind us of the essential role of Black culture in sustaining and empowering Black communities and influencing American society.

OPPOSITE: Photographer Gordon Parks spent his career behind the camera taking astonishing pictures. In 2005 he sat to have his own photograph taken.

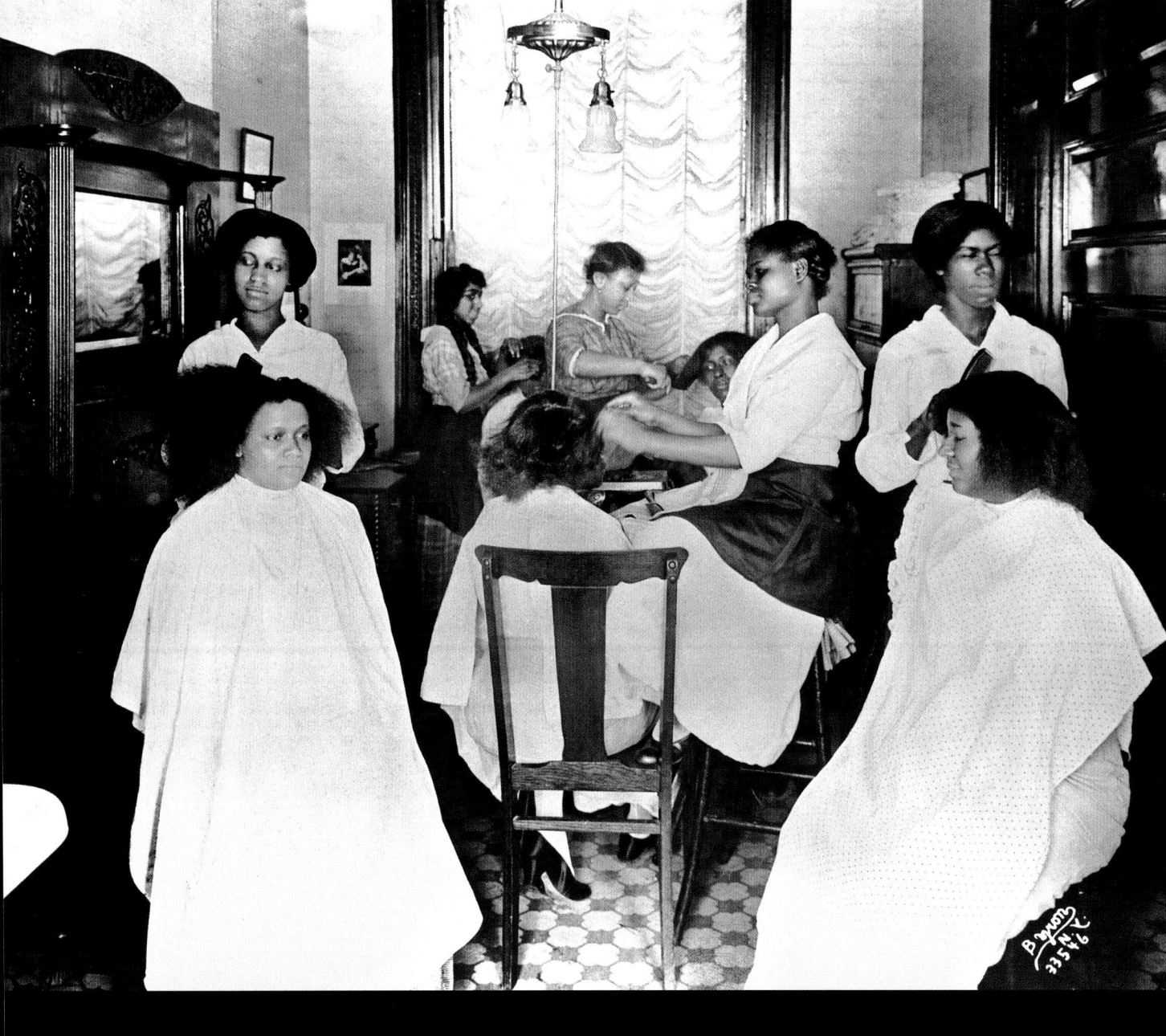

BEAUTY SALONS AS SACRED SPACE IN BLACK AMERICA

BY BLAIR BANKS

*Black women created hair salons and beauty parlors
as communal gathering spots to offer professional beauty services and
community to one another during segregation.*

It's early—a Saturday morning in mid-August. Instead of your favorite cartoons, you're watching as your family's hairdresser swipes petroleum jelly around the perimeter of your older sister's hair. Using the end of a rattail comb, she parts her thick hair into four quadrants, twisted up and secured with metal hair clips. Section by section, she retouches the hair near the roots, coating her curls with creamy relaxer.

At the appointment's end, your hair and your sister's hair fall pin-straight around your faces. Handing her folded bills, your mother thanks your hairdresser and ushers the two of you toward the door into the afternoon sun.

Hair salons, beauty parlors, shops—beloved spaces of Black beauty—have existed for well over a century in African American communities. Black women created these gathering spots to offer professional services at a time when segregation restricted access to white-owned establishments.

As Black beauty salons grew popular during the early twentieth century, it became apparent they offered Black women more than simply hairstyling. Amid community and acts of service, these cherished spaces provided Black women the chance to visualize a different future for themselves—one of entrepreneurship and the possibility of financial success without white patronage.

Before Black women came to dominate the Black beauty industry at the turn of the twentieth century, they served a white clientele during the antebellum period. These women, some known to history and others lost to time, laid the foundation for women like Annie Malone and Sarah Breedlove, aka Madam C. J. Walker, to thrive in their own ventures. By 1920 Malone and Walker had two competing hair product lines, several beauty salons, cosmetology schools, and an expansive payroll compensating thousands of Black women for selling their products door-to-door.

147

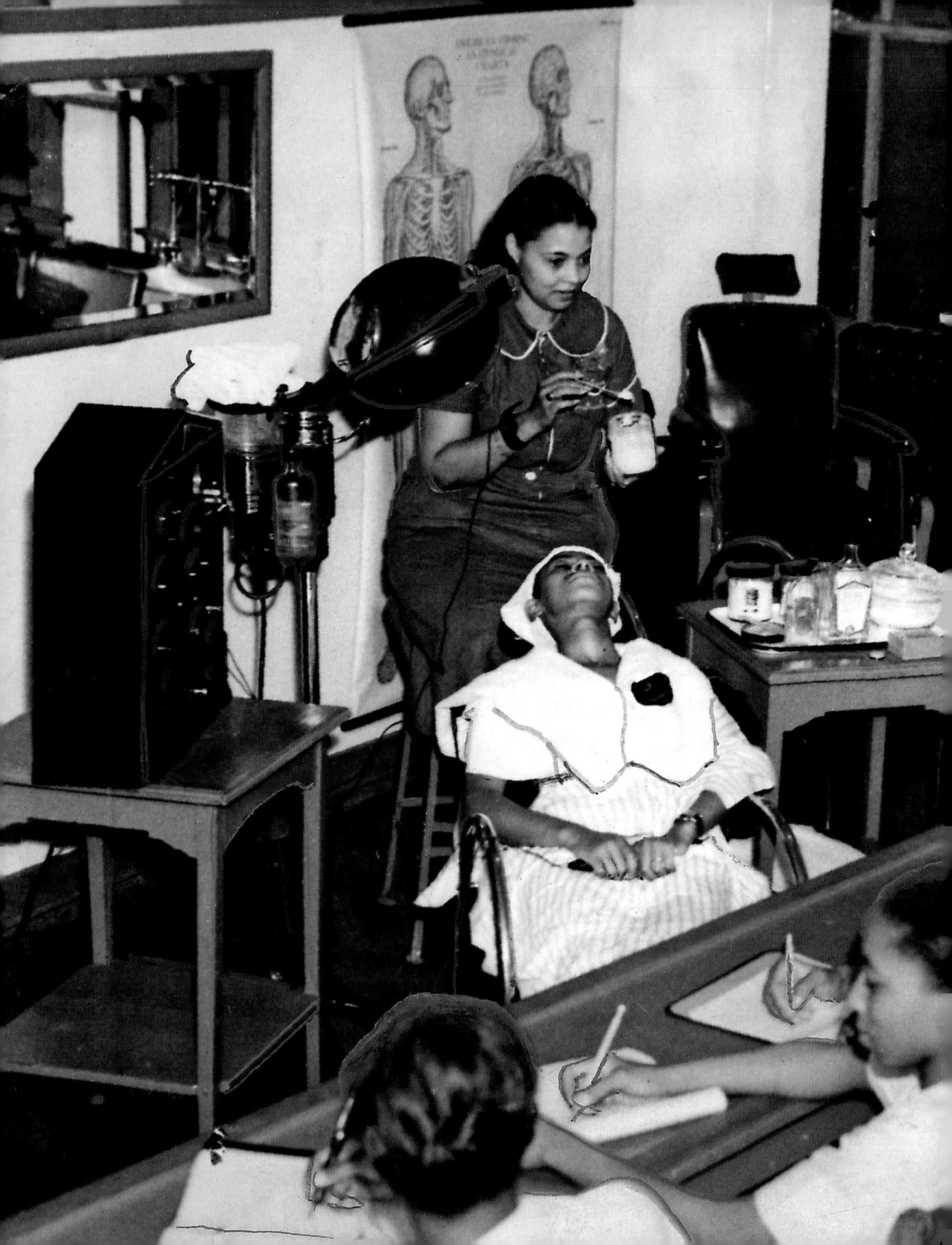

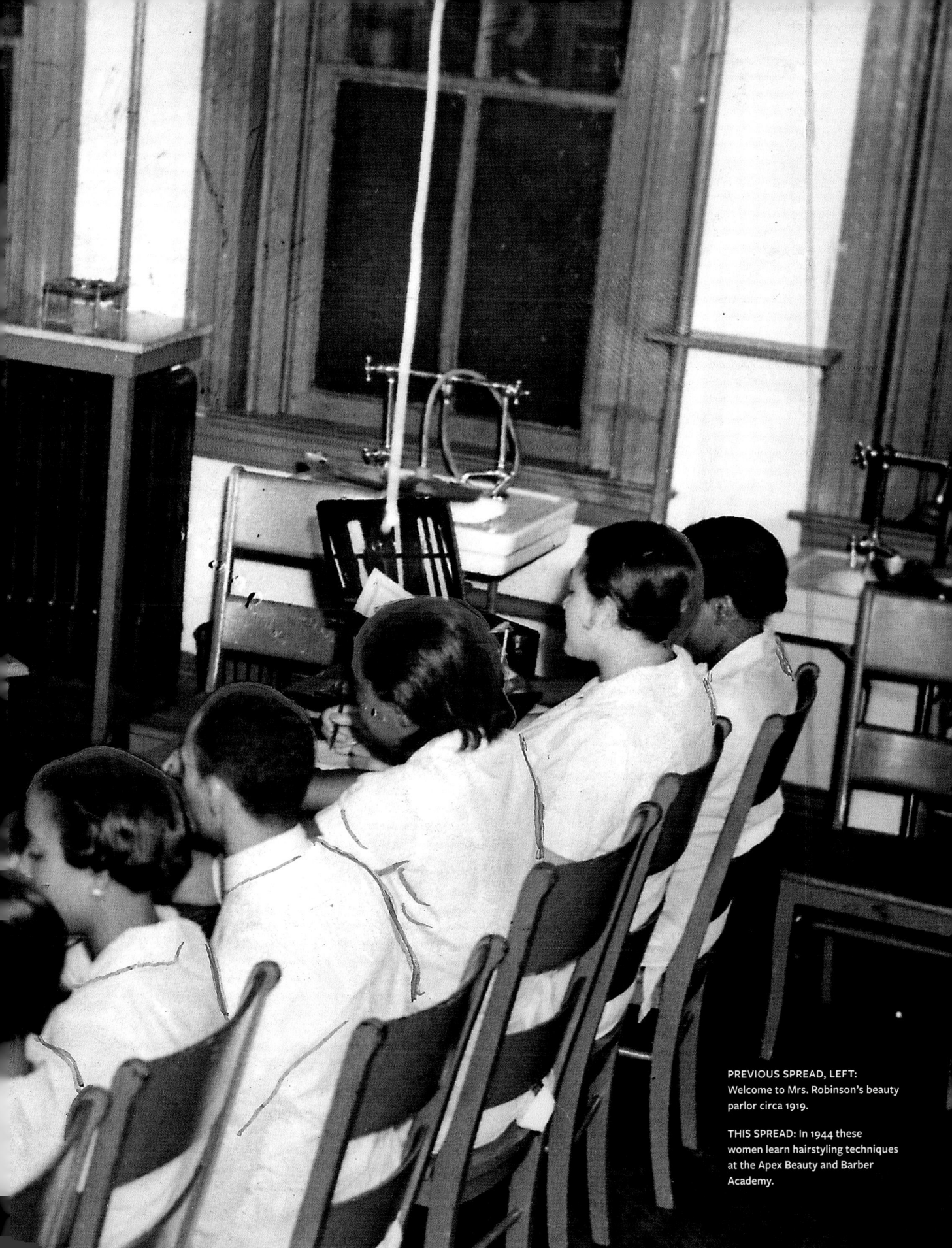

PREVIOUS SPREAD, LEFT:
Welcome to Mrs. Robinson's beauty parlor circa 1919.

THIS SPREAD: In 1944 these women learn hairstyling techniques at the Apex Beauty and Barber Academy.

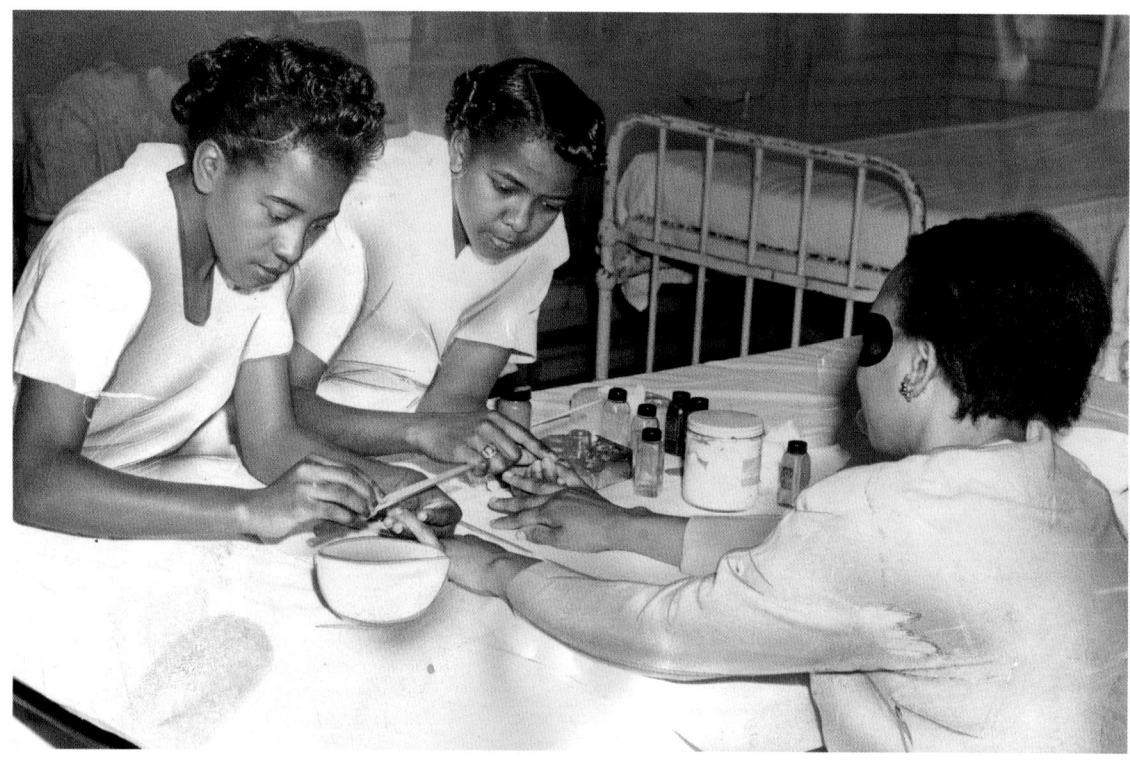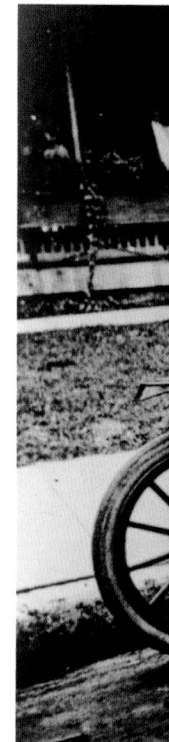

As the industry grew and proved profitable, more Black women took the entrepreneurial plunge and began opening their own home-based salons. Take Mrs. A'Lelia Walker Robinson, owner of the beauty parlor (seen in the opening photograph of the chapter). Her employees, aprons draped around their waists, part and comb through their clients' textured hair at their own makeshift stations, operating in a cramped space.

Forming their own community—bounded by their Blackness, womanhood, and penchant for self-care—one can easily imagine the conversations they shared and the similarities they might have to those that occur in salons today: family drama, gossip from around town, recipes, beauty secrets.

With their businesses flourishing, many Black women outgrew their home-based salons, and required

storefronts as well as skilled employees. Those who did so took advantage of the influx of beauty school graduates entering the workforce in the early 1900s.

Producing hundreds of beauticians each year, Malone's Poro College in St. Louis and Walker's Lelia College in Indianapolis attracted young women who aspired to the success and wealth of their founders. Others enrolled at franchised institutions like Apex Beauty and Barber Academy, which had eleven locations in Black communities across the United States and abroad. Founded as the educational arm of Sara Spencer Washington's Apex News and Hair Company, the schools provided training to both women and men on Black beauty services utilizing Washington's own product line.

Classes at Apex consisted of hairstyling demonstrations like the one featured in the photograph on the previous

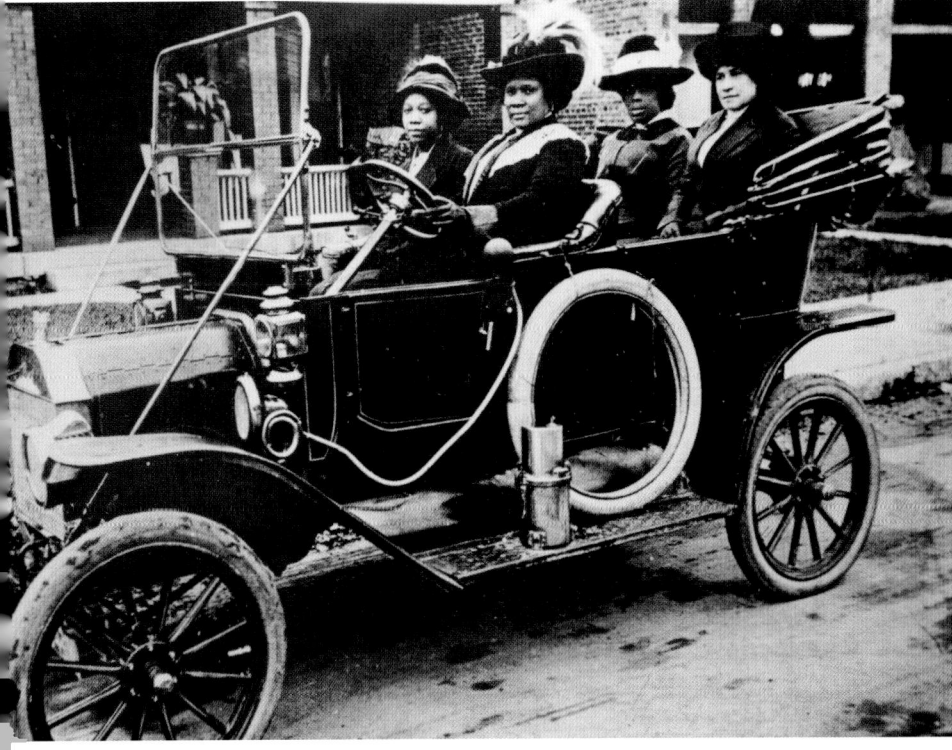

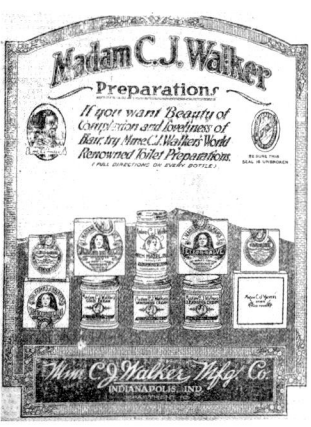

spread. Situated in a room with sinks lined against a wall, an instructor holds a jar of product while sitting in front of a poster of human anatomy. Seated before her is a row of students diligently taking notes on the product and its usage in haircare. The model for the day's lesson, a young woman with her head leaned back and eyes closed, waits patiently—leaving the viewer to wonder if she herself is another student, or is perhaps taking advantage of a discounted service.

While most new graduates sought work in hair salons and beauty parlors like those from their youth, others chose to work in unconventional spaces—like the beauty salon at Crownsville State Hospital in Maryland. Opened in 1949 by Mayme Tilghman, president of the Master Beauticians Association, the beauty salon at Crownsville served a clientele of Black patients admitted to the psychiatric facility for mental health treatment and long-term care.

Hiring skilled cosmeticians like Evelyn Bradford and her companion, Tilghman sought to treat patients to the same beauty services they'd receive outside of the hospital. Recreating the look and feel of a home-based salon, the two cosmeticians sit across from their client, buffing her nails in preparation for a fresh manicure.

From home-based salons of the early 1900s to multimillionaire beauty brands of the twenty-first century, Black beauty culture has proven to be not only a pathway to financial success, but an avenue by which Black women can love on themselves freely. As a physical embodiment of that love, beauty parlors continue to serve as cherished spaces where Black women can be in community.

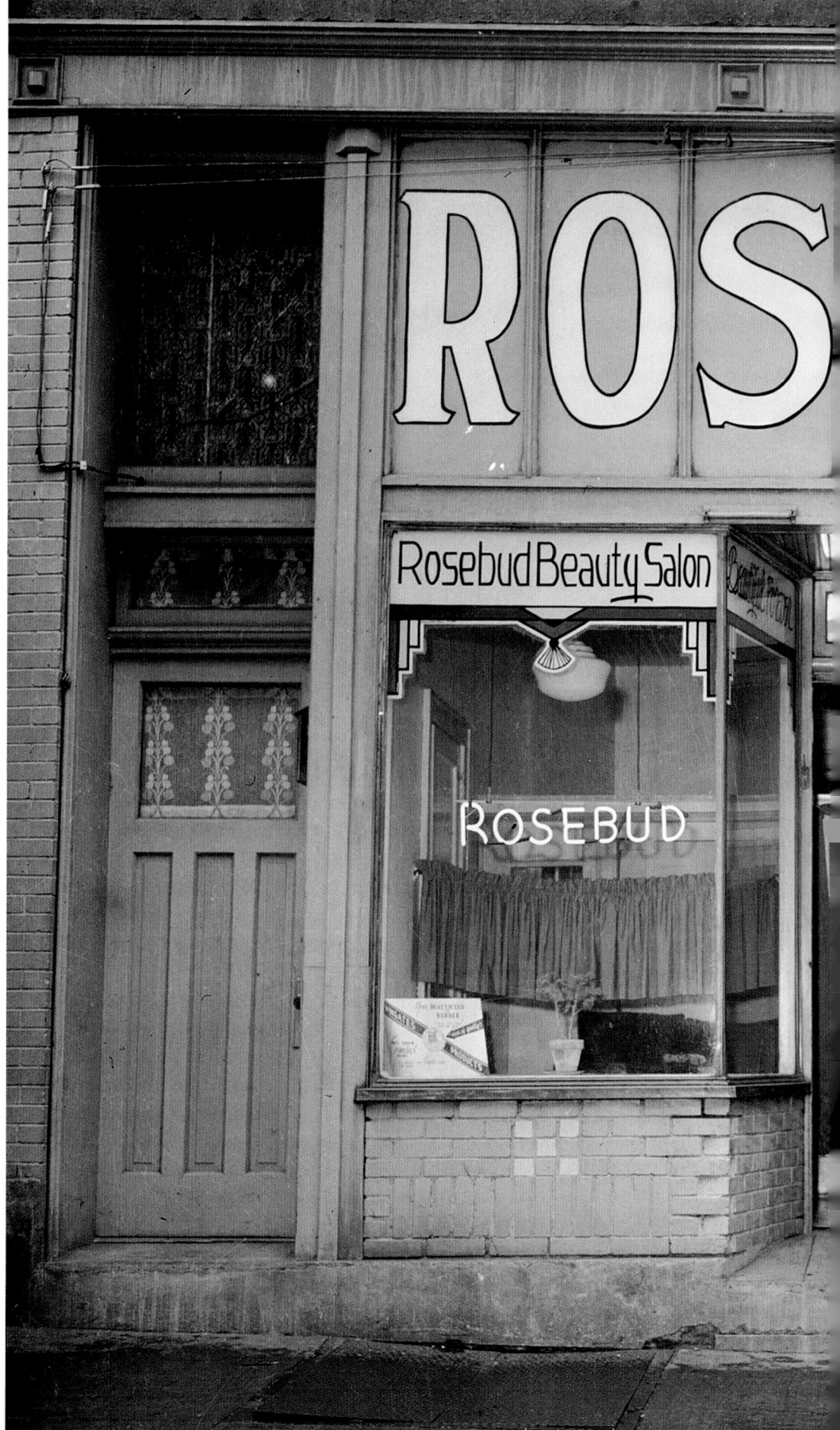

The Rosebud salon in the
Hill District neighborhood of
Pittsburgh, photographed by
Teenie Harris.

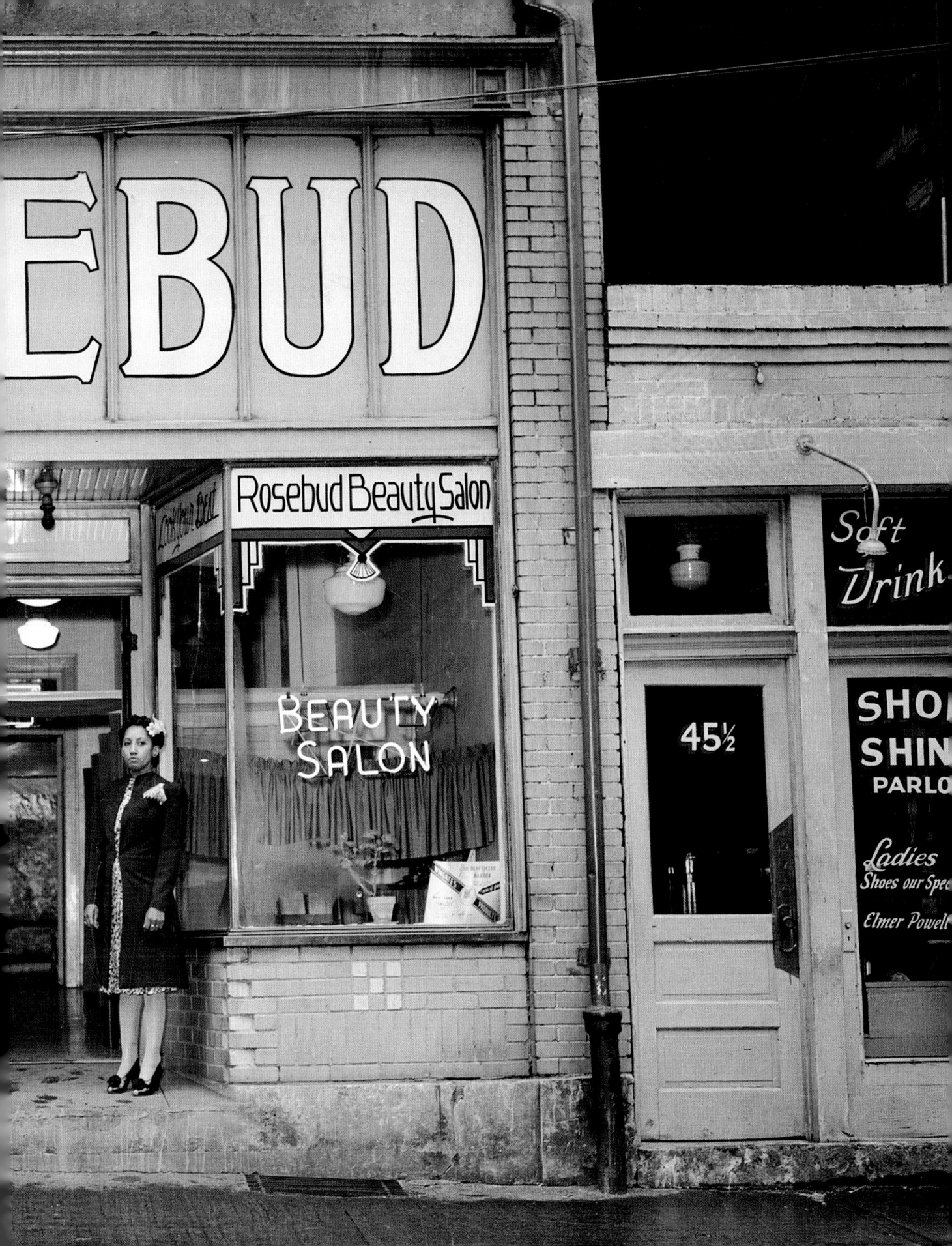

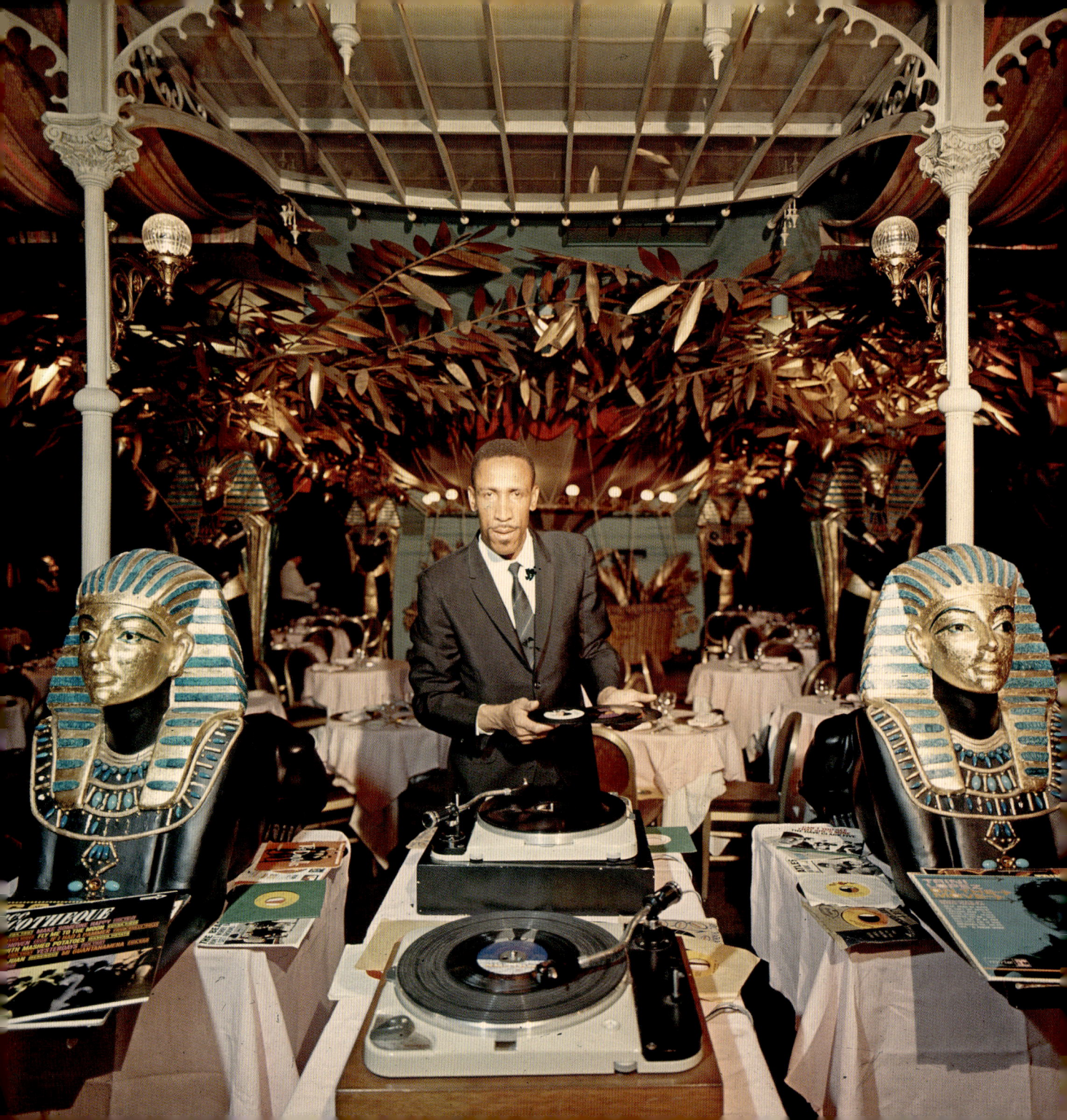

SLIM HYATT: DISQUAIR EXTRAORDINAIRE

SHAWN WALDRON

A pioneer in spinning recorded music in dance clubs, Slim Hyatt played a critical role in the development of New York's legendary nightclub and DJ culture.

In 1964, the World War II combat journalist turned lifestyle photographer George "Slim" Aarons was on assignment for *Holiday* magazine. He had been sent to "Velvet New York" to photograph what the magazine described as New York City's "elite establishments," along with "some velvet personalities."

Among the personalities was George "Slim" Hyatt, a thirty-four-year-old Panamanian DJ who manned three turntables from inside a closet-sized booth at Shepheard's nightclub in the Drake Hotel. It's not every day two men born as George but known as "Slim" find themselves in the same room, never mind one filled with Egyptian-themed nightclub decor.

A furniture maker by trade, Hyatt, known as Flacco in his native Panama, had a gift for music and a keen ear for popular song. He also had a fondness for American jazz and during the late 1950s began drumming with small nightclub acts around Panama City.

While playing the circuit he encountered Peter Duchin, son of the American pianist and bandleader Eddy Duchin. Peter was stationed in the Canal Zone and had formed the Stablemates, an off-duty jazz orchestra with players from the local U.S. military bands, to combat the boredom of peacetime military life. The band began to gain some notoriety around the city and a dedicated following, including the six-foot-one Hyatt.

The two men bonded over their mutual love of jazz and cultivated a lifelong friendship. Hyatt began helping Duchin recruit local players for the Stablemates and became his driver and a jack-of-all-trades. Duchin returned to New York in 1960 and sponsored Hyatt's entry to the United States.

That same year, a Frenchman named Olivier Coquelin, a.k.a. Disco Daddy, opened New York's first discotheque, Le Club, in a former underground garage on 55th Street in Sutton Place. While social dancing was hardly new, the concept of a DJ (then known by the French term *disquair*) playing recorded music specifically for that purpose was novel in the United States.

People joined the club, but Coquelin struggled to get them on the dance floor. He hired a series of local musicians to entice the crowd with both live and recorded music, but none were able to whip the clientele into a frenzy. Coquelin contacted his friend Peter Duchin for help; Duchin suggested his musical friend Slim for the task.

Hyatt had never spun records for a crowd, and one music historian described his first night as "catastrophic." But his innate gift for finding the beat, recognizing pop trends, and enchanting a crowd soon overcame any technical limitations. Hyatt's undeniable talent and charisma were quickly recognized by Le Club's owners and patrons alike; within a few months he was the heartbeat of the city's hottest venue.

As he told the New York *Daily News* in the winter of 1964–65, "Before I knew what happened, I'm the disquair for private affairs in Tuxedo Park, the West Side Tennis Club, and Lake Placid. They asked me to open discotheques in Montreal and Mamaroneck and Stamford. I'm booked for private parties through July Fourth."

Le Club's success spawned dozens of imitations in New York City and beyond. This was a time when dance floors were dominated by, and continually producing, new popular dances such as the Waddle, the Frug, the Mashed Potato, the Watusi, and the Twist, which was created at New York's legendary teenage hot spot the Peppermint Lounge.

Given Hyatt's fame among jet-setters—and reminiscent of the modern celebrity DJ trend—Hyatt was soon in demand among new club owners looking to make a splash in the competitive confines of New York.

In 1963, he left Le Club for L'Interdit, a new club in the Gotham Hotel. The following year Hyatt toted his growing collection of two thousand records to Shepheard's nightclub in the basement of the Drake Hotel on Park Avenue. It was here that he had a small booth with a pillbox slit for monitoring the dance floor, and was photographed by Slim Aaron. The club took its name (and decor) as an homage to Englishman Samuel Shepheard's nineteenth-century luxury hotel in Cairo.

A typical night at Shepheard's began with paying a $2–$4 cover (depending on the night) followed by seated dinner service. Hyatt's set began around 10 p.m.; he generally took it slow and easy for the first hour or so. For the first few years, the recorded music was accompanied live by a jazz trio; the odd arrangement was the result of a compromise between club ownership and the local musicians' union, which saw the playing of canned music as a threat to their careers.

The dancing began in earnest around 11 p.m. as Hyatt cranked up the tempo and the volume. In his view, table chatter equaled death in a nightclub. As he told *Variety* (in the April 1, 1964, edition), "They have more fun if they're up there dancing and if they start to talk, I make the music noisier." With Hyatt at the helm, the fun typically lasted until 3 or 4 a.m.

By 1964, the discotheque craze had swept across the United States to intense media coverage. The boldface headline of the April 1 issue of *Variety* boasted of the

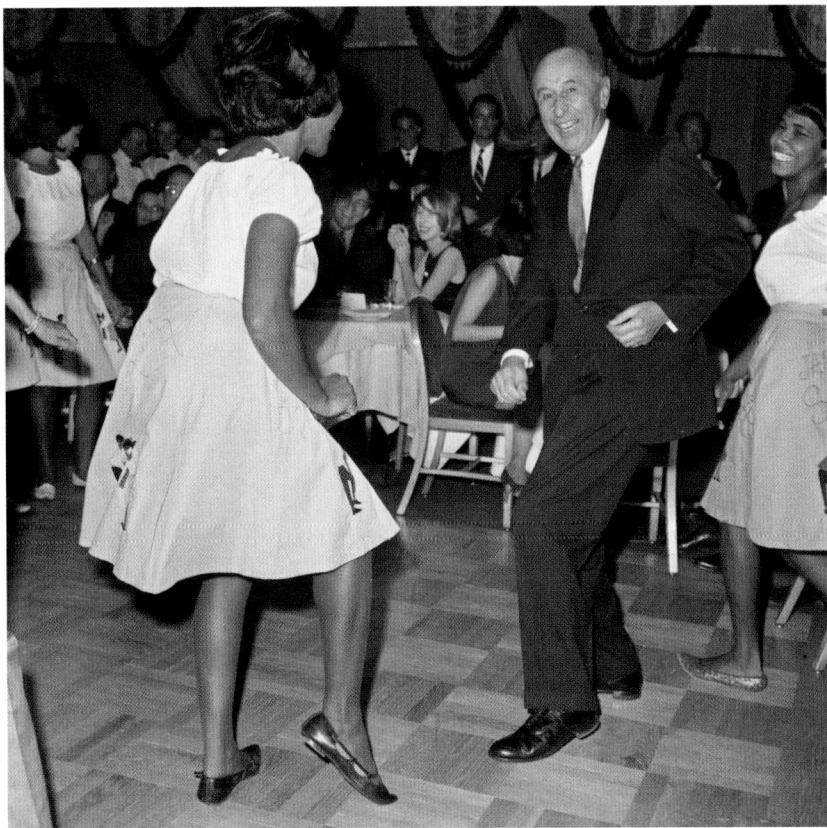

JUMPING JET SET'S DISK DEN, while the *Daily News* ran a fawning profile of Hyatt on New Year's Day 1965.

Hyatt was routinely name-checked in trend pieces in *Women's Wear Daily*, *Look*, *Newsweek*, *Holiday*, and the *New York Times*. Each spoke of his mastery and skill at controlling the crowd, but *Variety* said it best: "By judicious admixture of tunes and tempos geared to the tide and timing of the customers he keeps the room vibrant and jumping."

The demand proved too much for one man, so with an entrepreneur's instinct Hyatt trained a cadre of young protégés to fill in for him and was paid a cut of their fees. He also launched a side business that provided a team of engineers to assist nightclubs with setting up sound systems.

The discotheque trend naturally caught the attention of the recording industry. In 1964, Hyatt was hired by Decca Records to supervise the production of *Dance Discotheque*, an LP record designed to support fast-tempo steps such as the Frug and Hully Gully and slower dances like the merengue and bossa nova. It was the first time a DJ had been hired to produce a record.

Slim Hyatt remained active on the New York club scene for decades, including a long run at Doubles supper club in the Sherry-Netherland Hotel from 1984 to 1995. Hyatt and his wife Alice settled on New York's Upper West Side in the 1960s and raised two daughters there. Largely unknown today, Hyatt's critical role in the development of New York's legendary nightclub and DJ culture deserves broader recognition.

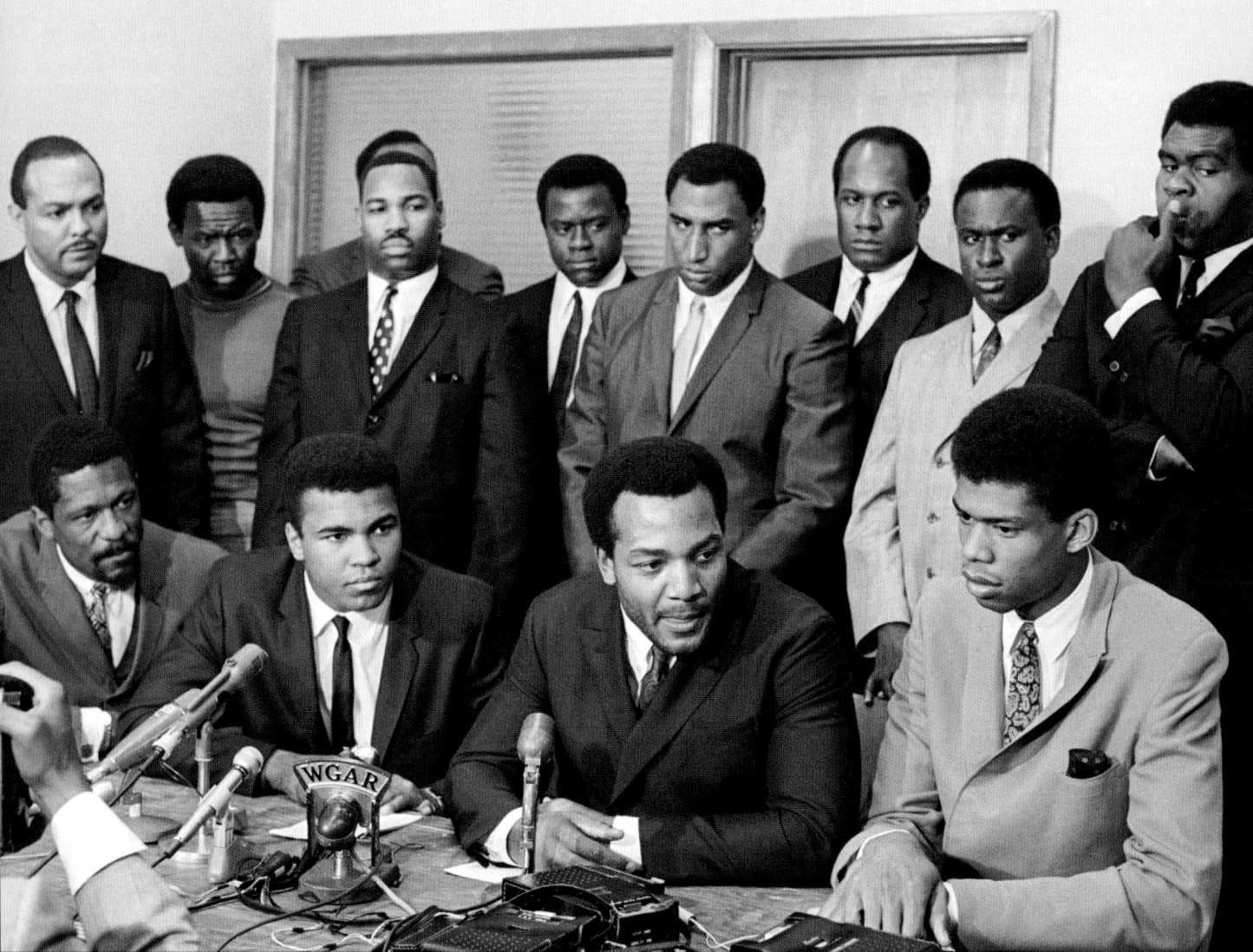

"I AM NOT WORRIED ABOUT ALI": BILL RUSSELL, JIM BROWN, AND THE NEGRO INDUSTRIAL ECONOMIC UNION

RAJA MALIKAH RAHIM

How the nation's most influential Black athletes organized the 1967 Cleveland Summit to talk about the power of the Black dollar.

On June 4, 1967, some of the greatest Black athletes in the United States gathered at the Negro Industrial Economic Union (NIEU) headquarters in Cleveland, Ohio. What became known as the Cleveland Summit or Ali Draft Summit was about more than providing a site for Black athletic solidarity and a space for Muhammad Ali to express his religious and anti–Vietnam War views. It was also about the promotion of Black capitalism.

Former Cleveland Browns star Jim Brown organized the summit as an opportunity for Ali to explain his positions directly to the media and a group of powerful Black athletes, including Bill Russell, who was the founding officer of the NIEU and had both public influence and star power.

In the mid-1960s, Russell—a close friend of Ali—was one of the nation's most visible Black athletes, having won multiple NBA championships with the Boston Celtics and becoming the organization's head coach in 1966. By then, he was also an outspoken Black civil rights activist who denounced racism and white supremacy, criticized the lack of progress in the struggle for racial equality, and believed that Black athletes had a responsibility to use their sporting platform as a catalyst for change.

"We have to do more than just play basketball and run track," Russell said in a 1966 *Sports Illustrated* interview. "We have to let people know we are here, and that we are a part of the community. We have to make them aware of the problems and show them what we can do to help solve them."

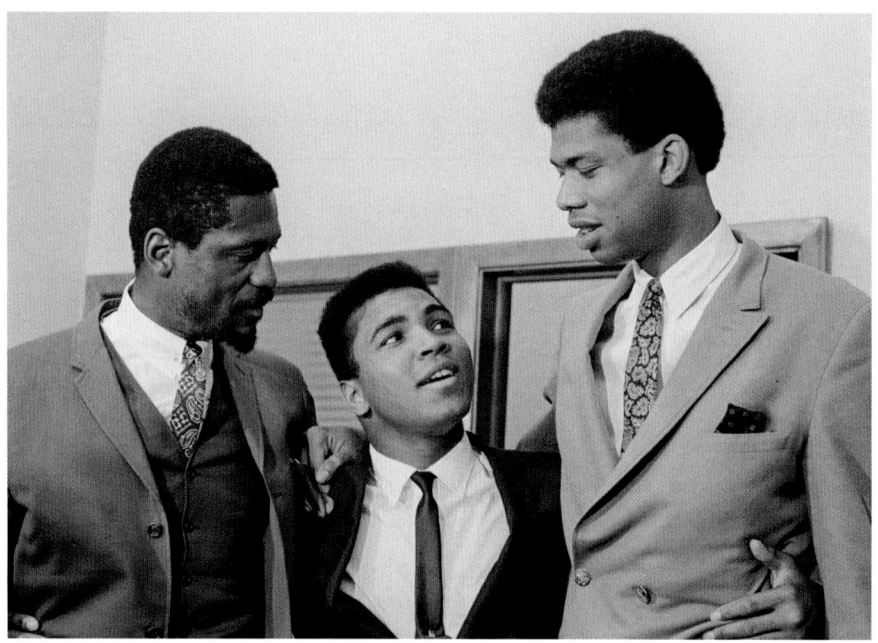

For Russell, Brown, and the other Black athletes, the NIEU became a significant vehicle for Black political, economic, and social awareness. Founded in 1966 by Brown, the nonprofit operated as a network of Black athletes, businessmen, politicians, and community activists who believed Black power and equality went hand in hand with Black economic autonomy.

Under the motto "produce, achieve, and prosper," the NIEU—later renamed the Black Economic Union—provided finances to establish and promote Black businesses throughout the nation. Bill Russell, for instance, owned a barbecue restaurant—Slade's—in Boston's Black community of Roxbury. During its eight years in existence, the NIEU also trained Black entrepreneurs and held economic self-sufficiency programs for Black youth.

On that Sunday afternoon in June, Russell, Brown, Kareem Abdul-Jabbar, and other Black athletes met with Muhammad Ali and discussed his stance as an anti-war conscientious objector. At the time, Ali—the heavyweight champion of the world and one of the most well-known athletes in the country—had recently been stripped of his title and banned from boxing for refusing to be drafted into the military during the Vietnam War.

By June 1967, Ali—who had recently joined the Nation of Islam and changed his name—faced charges of draft dodging and had become the most controversial and criticized man in the country by both white and Black Americans, including Willie Davis of the Green Bay Packers, who attended the meeting despite initially believing Ali's anti-war stance was unpatriotic.

While the press and Black residents from the Hough neighborhood lingered outside of the closed meeting, Russell, Ali, and the other Black athletes engaged in a long, heated discussion that extended beyond a show of support for Ali. They also discussed the importance of economic empowerment for Black people and communities.

BLACK CULTURE AS PEOPLE POWER

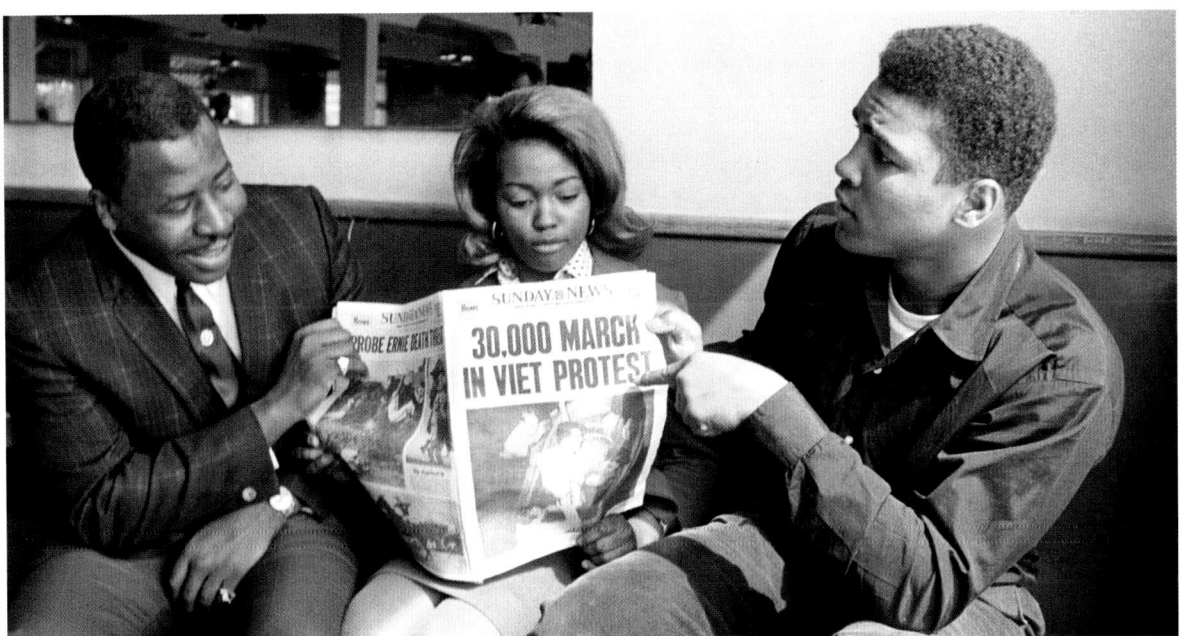

For Russell, the economic oppression of Black people and their systematic elimination from the mainstream economy were the nation's greatest problems.

By 1967, as economic power became synonymous with Black Power and civil rights, the NIEU and Black athletes saw their athletic talents and successes as a pathway to financial freedom—not only for themselves, but also for their people and communities. They also saw Ali's quick return to boxing as a key to Black capitalism and economic independence.

As part of the discussions, Brown attempted to convince Ali to take a deal that would dismiss the charges and allow his return to boxing. Though their urging was not without some ulterior motive--at the time, Brown and the NIEU had economic ties with Main Bout, a Black-owned entertainment company with television rights to Ali's fights. While on the surface Brown organized the summit to discuss and garner support for Ali's religious rights and moral stance against the Vietnam War, Brown aimed to capitalize on Ali's boxing talent to advance the economic goals and ambitions of the NIEU and Main Bout.

Yet, despite the pressure and numerous questions, Ali remained steadfast, praising the virtues of the Nation of Islam and refusing to compromise his principles for war and money. After five hours, they ended their private session to address the media—captured in the opening photograph—with Bill Russell seated to Ali's right.

Following the Cleveland Summit, the mainstream media criticized the group of Black athletes for failing to persuade Ali. Russell, however, when interviewed in *Sports Illustrated* on June 19, 1967, stood by the convictions of his friend. "He has something I have never been able to attain and something very few people I know possess. He has an absolute and sincere faith," Russell wrote. "I'm not worried about Muhammad Ali."

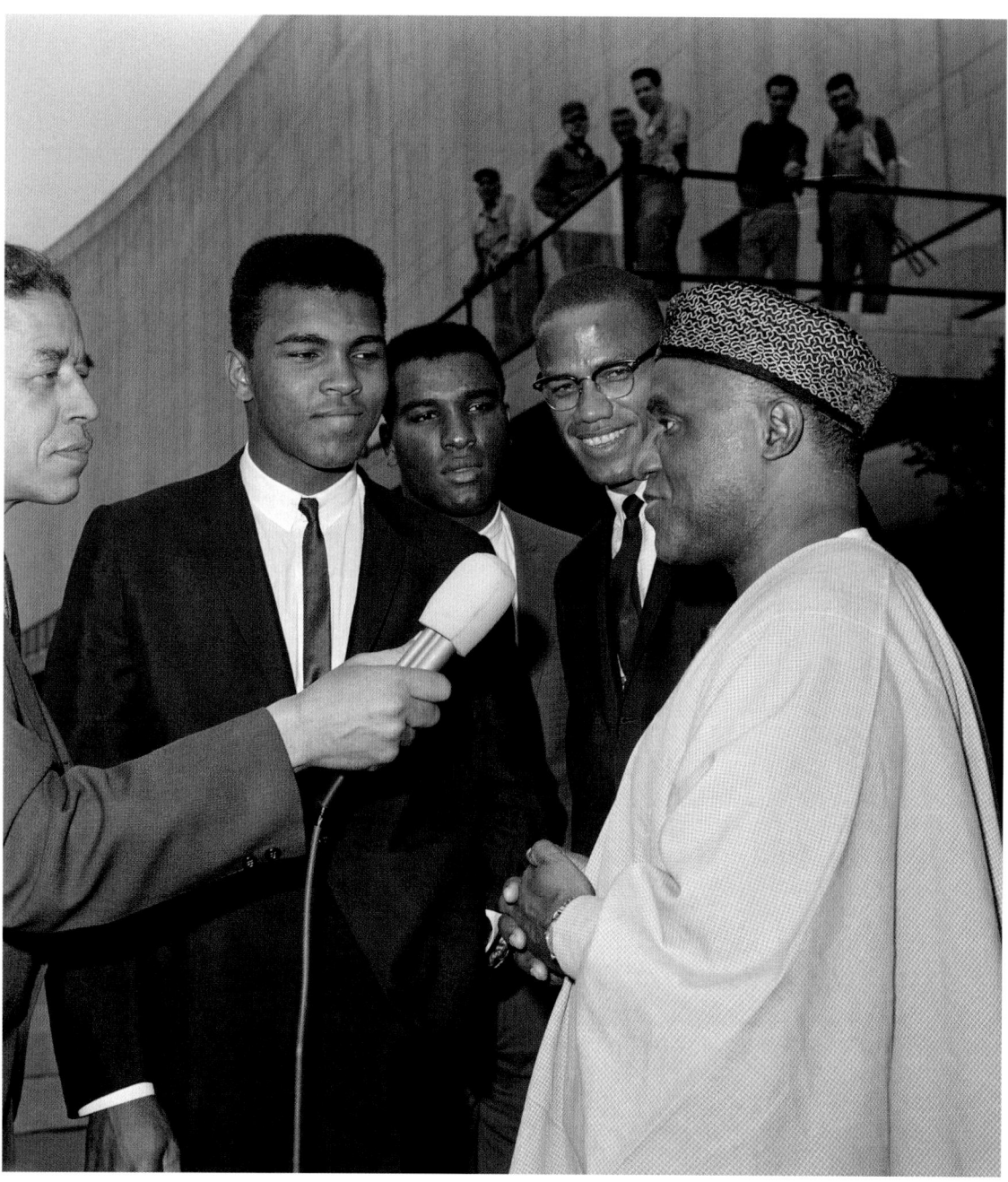

ABOVE: Cassius Clay changed his name to Muhammad Ali in March 1964 when this photo was taken. Here, he's at the United Nations with Malcolm X and the Nigerian ambassador S. O. Adebo.

RIGHT: Bill Russell demonstrates an impressive reach with his right. He and Ali posed in front of Russell's restaurant Slade's Original Barbeque in Boston in 1964.

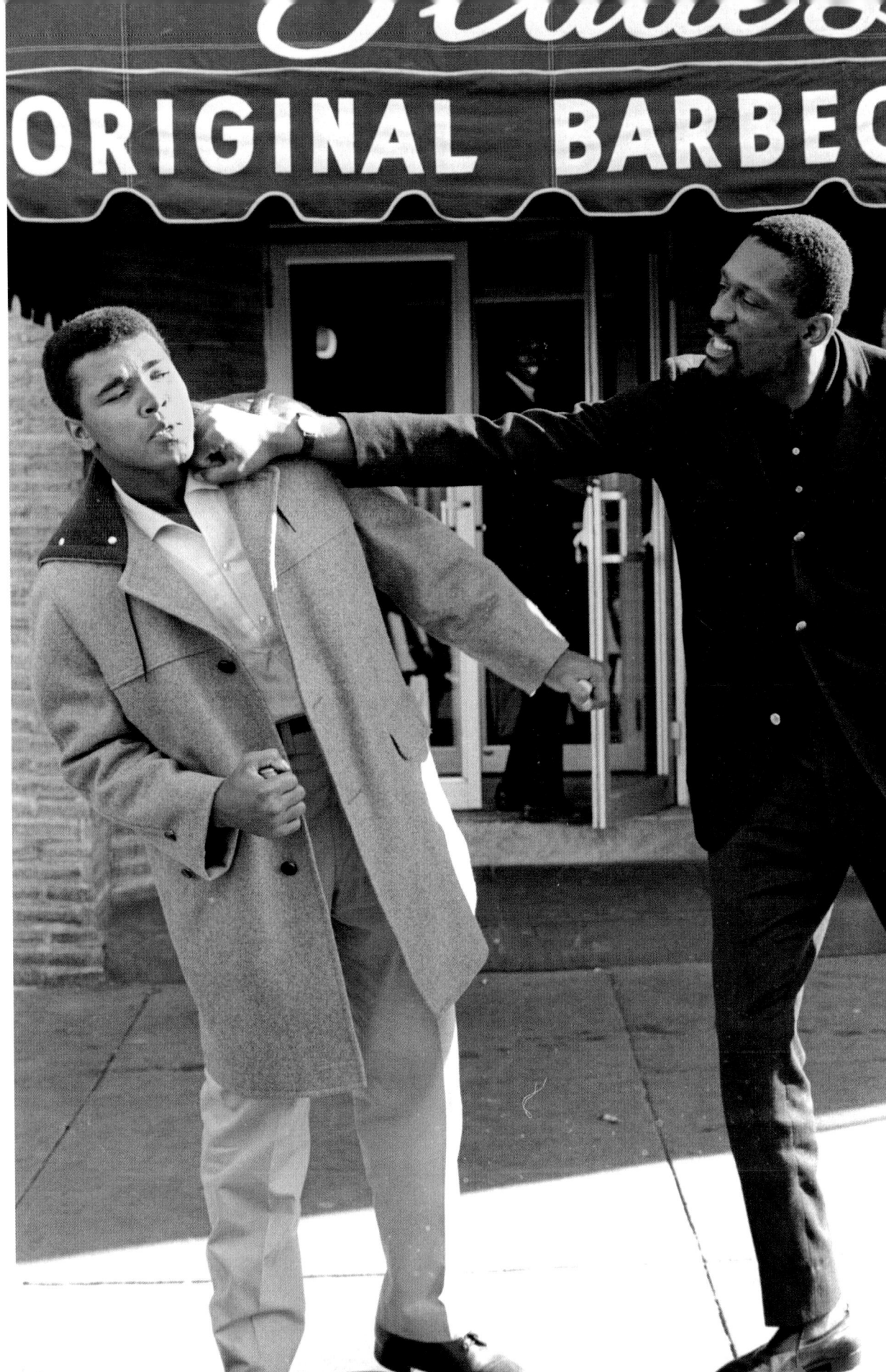

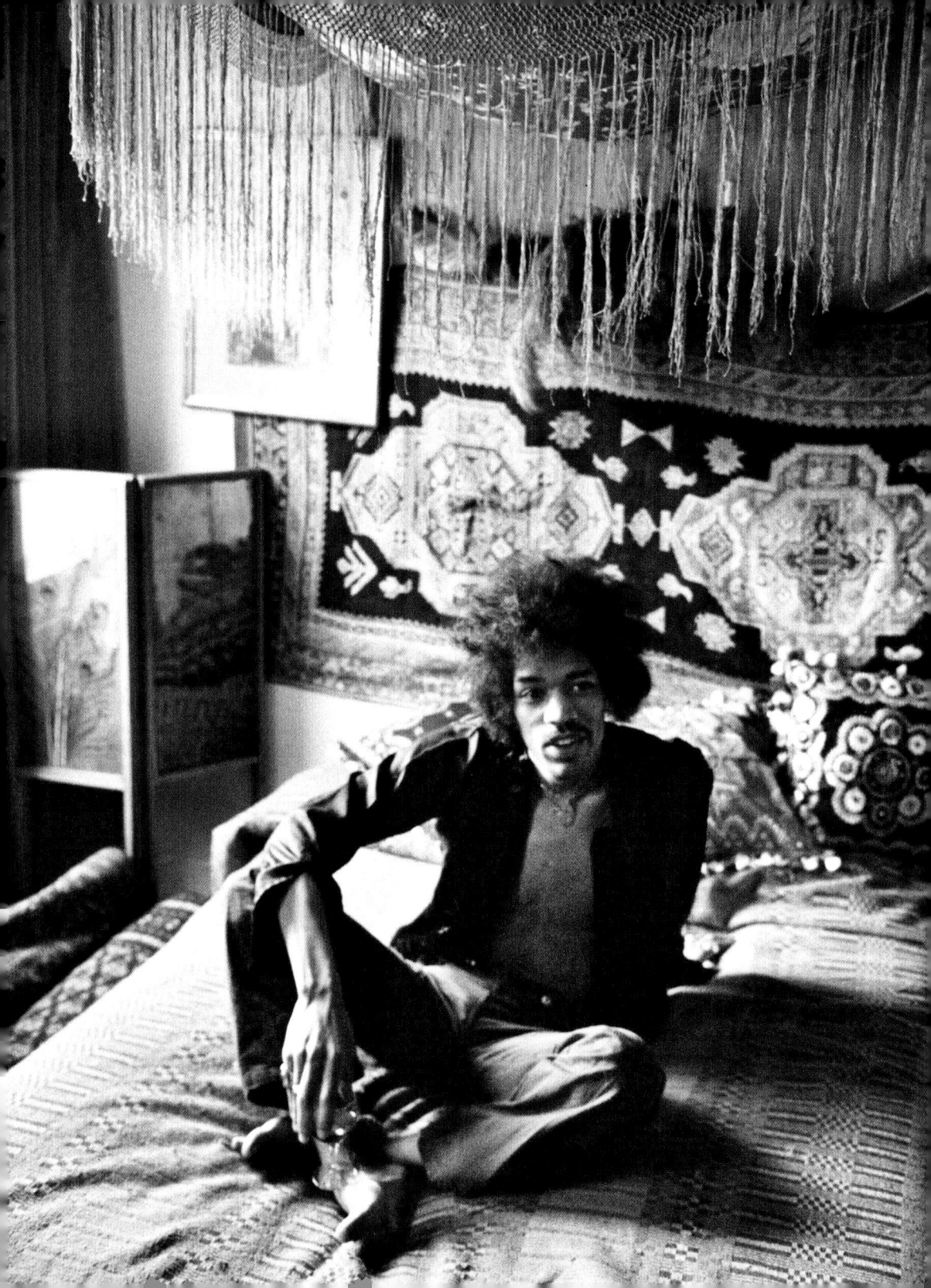

BOHEMIAN MESSIAH: JIMI HENDRIX FINDS FREEDOM IN LONDON

TAMMY L. BROWN

How could a Black musical genius in 1960s America confront and transcend the racism of the time to create the music and life that he wanted? Exit to London.

Sitting cross-legged with bare feet before a backdrop of Middle Eastern–styled tapestries in his London flat, rock and roll virtuoso Jimi Hendrix presents himself as a quintessential bohemian, an artistic free spirit. His curious smile and whimsical gaze set to the right of the photographer's lens suggest the subject knows something that we, the viewers, do not yet know.

For Hendrix, London symbolized creative freedom and professional opportunities. London was where he could escape the cultural typecasting that had frustrated his career in the United States.

When he arrived in September 1966, Hendrix had already achieved fame as a songwriter and guitarist who electrified the blues in ways no one had ever heard before. However, Hendrix's star could only rise so high in the United States. Racist white radio executives refused to play his music, while Black music executives dismissed his sound as too weird or too white because it veered so far from Motown rhythm and blues.

What to do with a Black bluesman inspired by Bob Dylan?

Hendrix had always struggled to fit in. Triangulating numerous anecdotal accounts of his tenure as a backup guitarist for bands like the Isley Brothers and Ike & Tina Turner, it seems that Hendrix kept getting fired for arriving too late to rehearsal, missing the tour bus, or riffing on his guitar in live performances. Little Richard apparently fired him for wearing a shirt that was too flamboyant.

In every regard Hendrix sought freedom of expression and could never resist taking creative license. In other words, he refused to be boxed in. So how could a Black musical genius in 1960s America confront, break free, or even transcend the racism of the time to create the music, career, and life that he wanted to live? Exit to London.

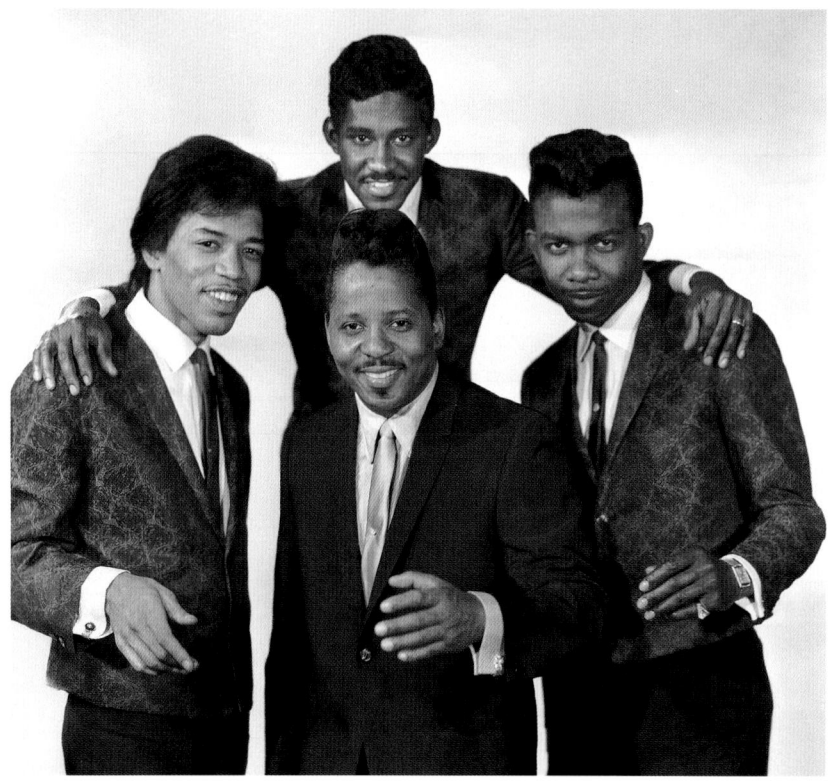

At the time, the U.S. music industry's narrow notions of "Black music" conspired to limit Hendrix's success; meanwhile, white British musicians' love for and even fetishism of Black American blues music fueled Hendrix's decision to move to London in 1966. He had met the white British bass player of the Animals, Chas Chandler, while performing at Cafe Wha? in Greenwich Village, New York. Chandler encouraged Hendrix to travel with him back to London to explore the possibility of recording a series of albums.

Hendrix sought out professional and personal freedom there. In interviews he gave from the time of his arrival in England through his untimely death at age twenty-seven, four years later, Hendrix repeated over and over that London served him as a place of creative and personal freedom.

In the tradition of Black literary, visual, and performance artists who found a greater sense of personal freedom and professional success in Europe—including Josephine Baker, Paul Robeson, James Baldwin, and Nina Simone—Hendrix pursued his own vision of freedom in London.

In a 1969 interview printed in *Hullabaloo* magazine, Hendrix praised music industry employees with whom he worked in London:

[T]hey have less equipment and it's not as good as the equipment they have [in the United States]. Therefore, they work twice as hard. Even the engineers are involved in getting the best for you . . . They have more imagination over there. It's groovy. Even the limitations are beautiful because they make people really listen—and the people are very, very, very good. They're almost critics themselves. It's all very positive.

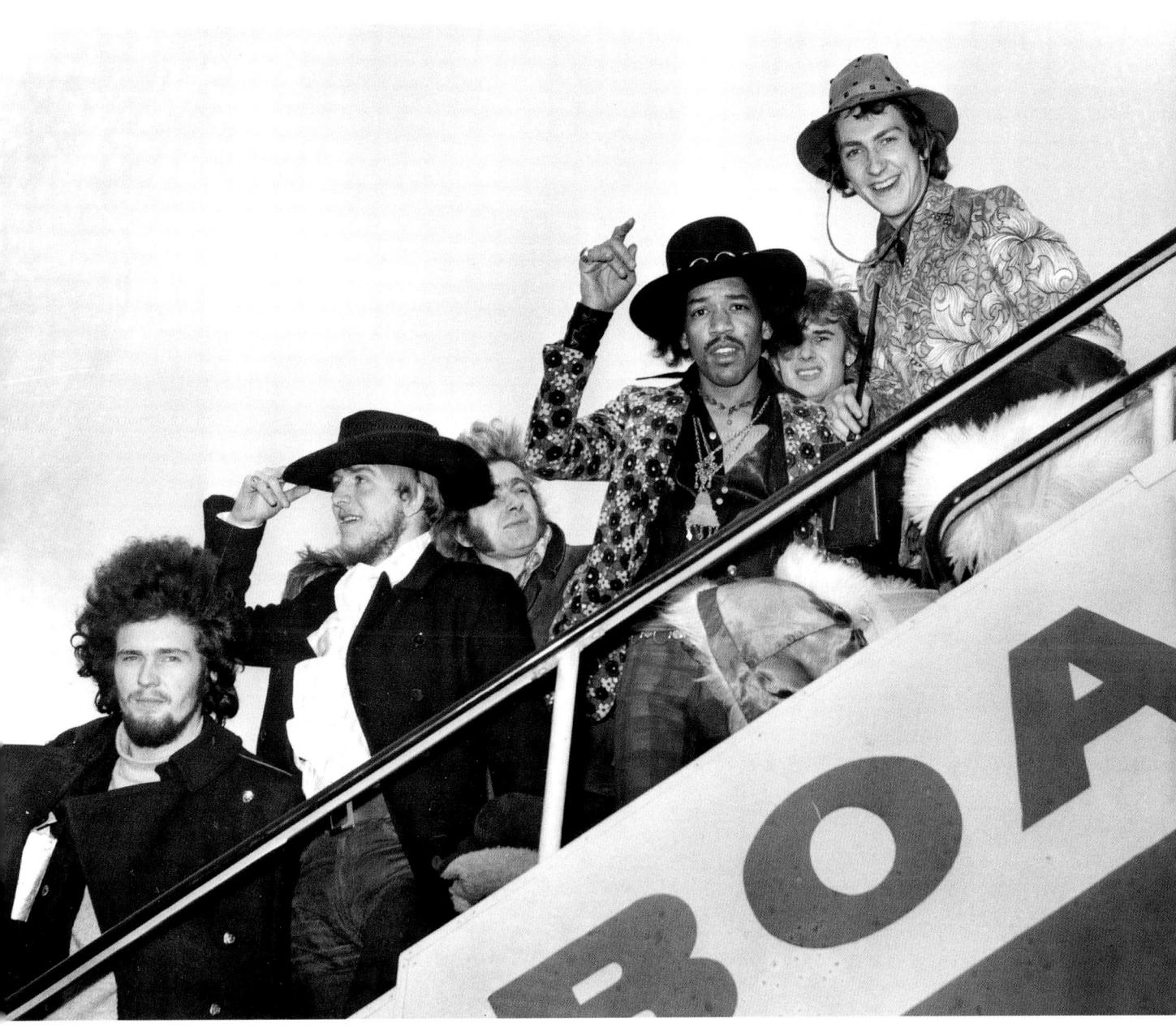

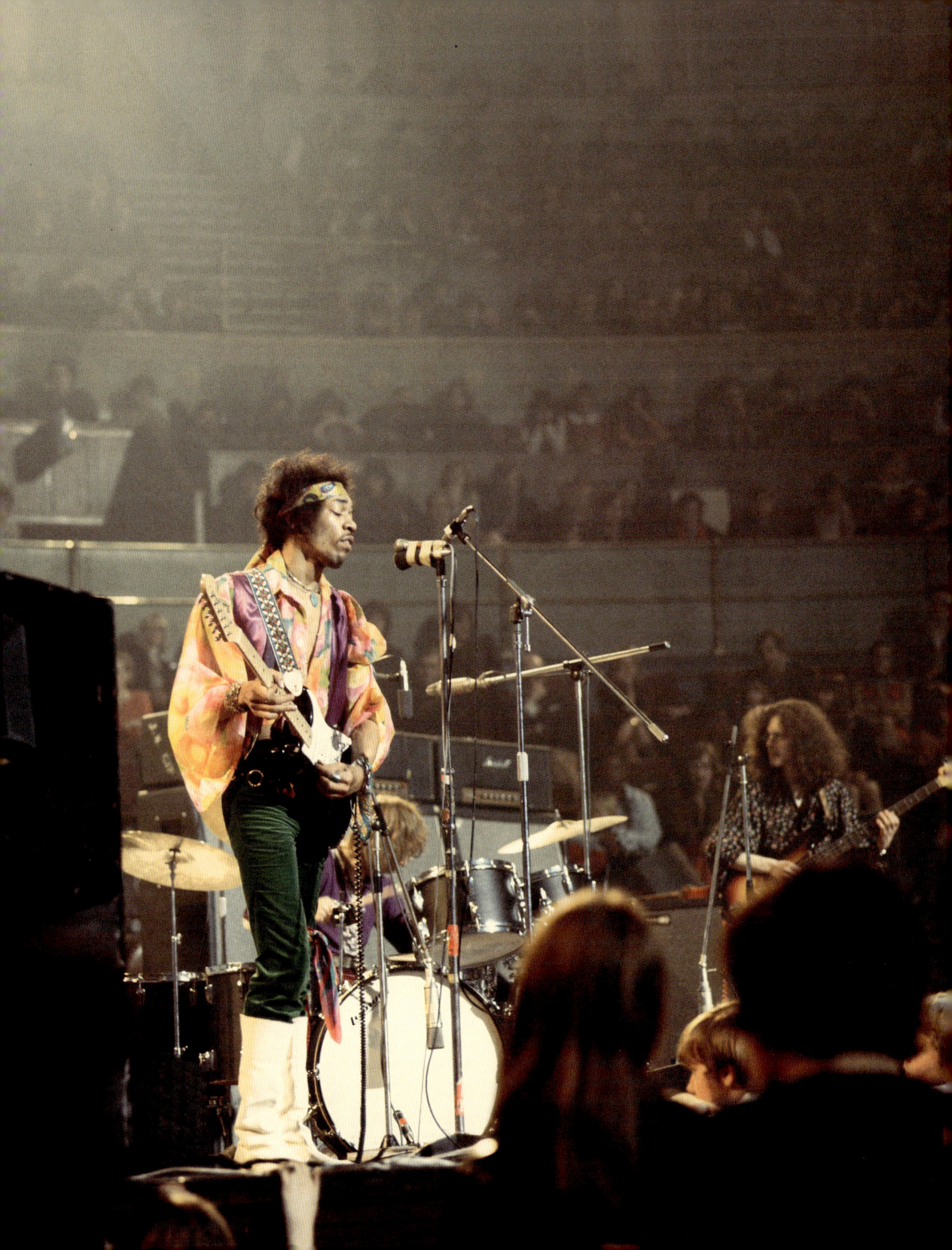

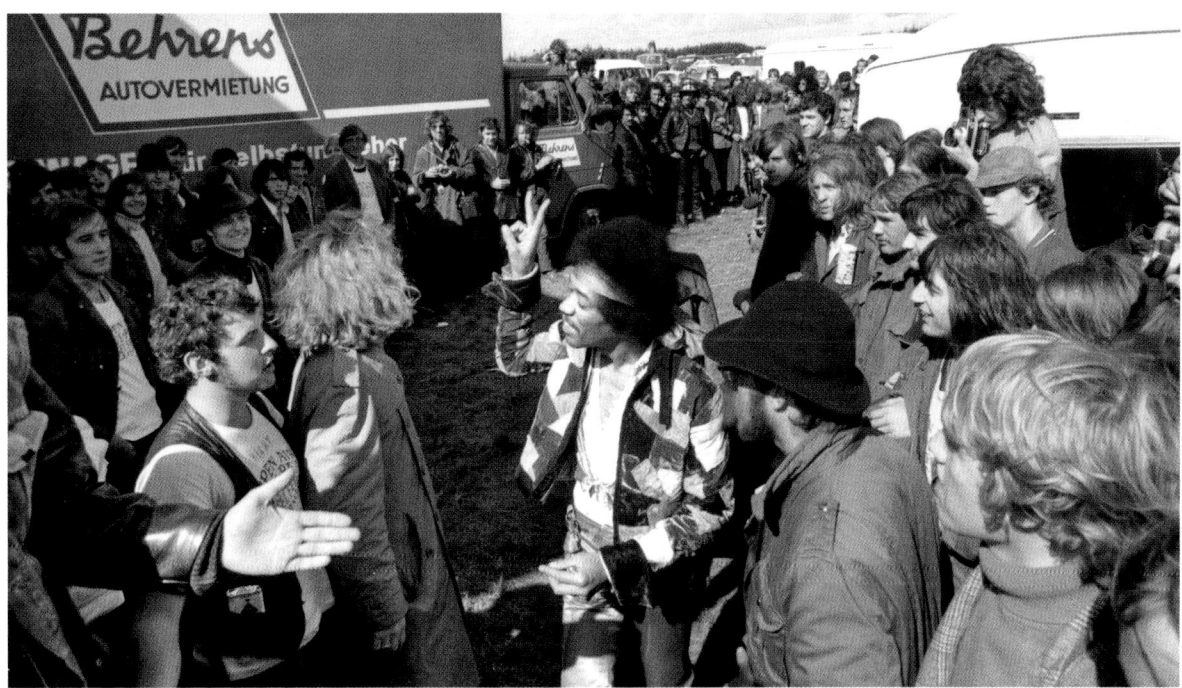

Within one week of his arrival in London, Hendrix was jamming with leading white British musicians—including the band Cream, with guitarist Eric Clapton. These musicians admired Hendrix; they saw him as an authentic Black American bluesman, and they were blown away by his musical virtuosity.

But even with his success, Hendrix did not entirely escape racism in London. British music critic Charles Shaar Murray's 1989 biography *Crosstown Traffic* includes many quotes by white male musicians who used the N-word to denigrate Hendrix, jealous as they were of his talent and success.

Taken on January 7, 1969, the photo of Hendrix in repose (page 164) emphasizes the importance of London as a locale that offered Hendrix a multilayered sense of freedom. His relaxed pose is a deliberate self-presentation of calm amid the culture wars of his time—the ongoing battle for civil rights, Black Power, women's equality, the anti-war movement, and burgeoning activism around LGBTQ intersectional identities and empowerment.

Hendrix displays his agency, bohemian attitude, and spiritual fortitude here, clad in bell-bottoms and an unbuttoned shirt with a fly-away collar, gently holding a glass of wine (or is that whiskey?) in his Mayfair apartment—one of the poshest neighborhoods in London.

Today, Jimi Hendrix's London flat is a museum. He was inspired to move to this apartment in 1968 because the prolific and renowned classical musician George Frideric Handel had lived there more than two centuries prior to his arrival; so, Hendrix wanted to dwell with the spirit of musical genius that the building once sheltered.

Hendrix's musical imagination reached across genres and national borders. His imagination also spanned past eras and spiritual traditions, offering music as a vehicle to elevate listeners' consciousnesses to more expansive existential freedoms.

ABOVE: Hendrix arrived on the Isle of Fehmarn, Germany, on September 6, 1970. It would turn out to be his last performance.

OPPOSITE: Hendrix and his band the Jimi Hendrix Experience played a sold-out show in London's Royal Albert Hall on February 24, 1969.

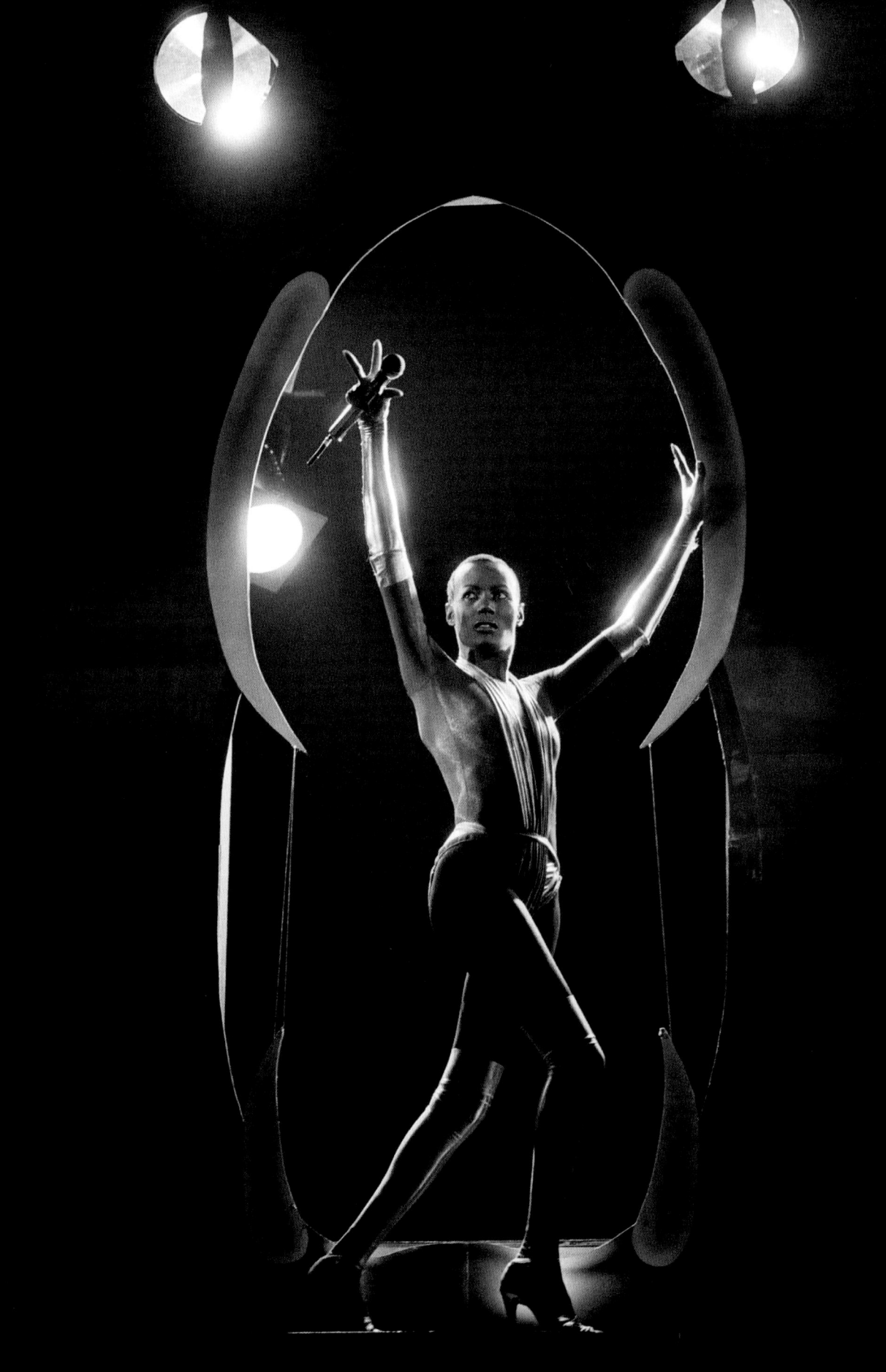

LOVE IS THE MESSAGE

SAI ISOKE

Blackness, queerness, and disco.

On June 6, 2021, FX's *Pose* aired its series finale. *Pose* was renowned for thoughtfully and vividly showcasing the stories of Black and Brown queer and trans folx of the 1980s and '90s.

One scene in particular captured the zeitgeist. The sixth episode of the first season, titled "Love Is the Message," is named after MFSB's song of the same name. In the episode, the character Pray Tell requests that the song be played on a loop during several balls. The significance of his choice is later revealed in a conversation with his lover, who is dying of AIDS complications:

I didn't tell them what it was like in 1980 when we danced all summer to that song. There wasn't none of this AIDS mess going on. We were truly free. Free to love. Free to fuck. Free to be our gay ass selves in this beautiful shithole of a little town.

Through Pray Tell's story, viewers are given an opportunity to witness the balm that disco provided the queer community.

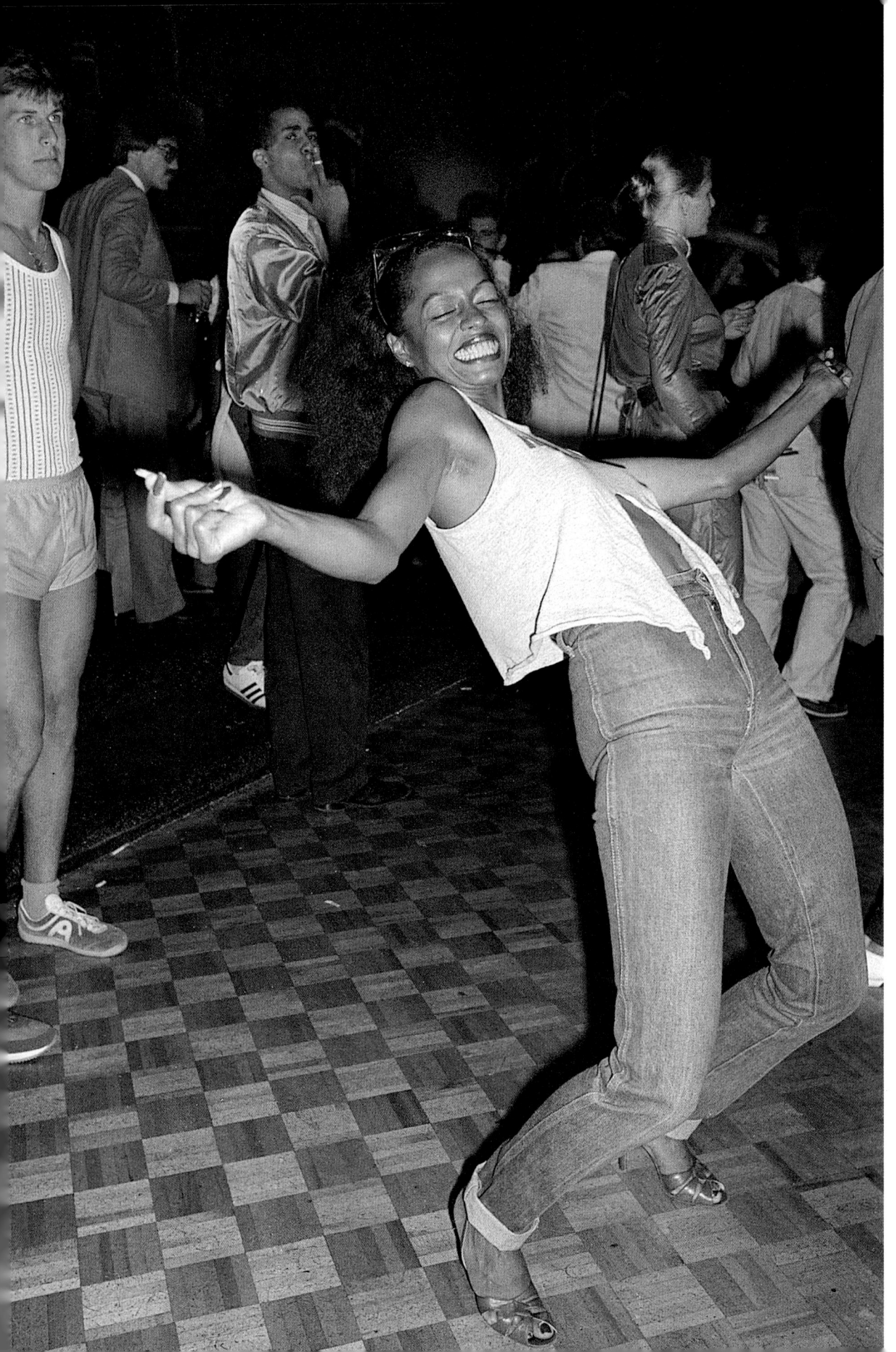

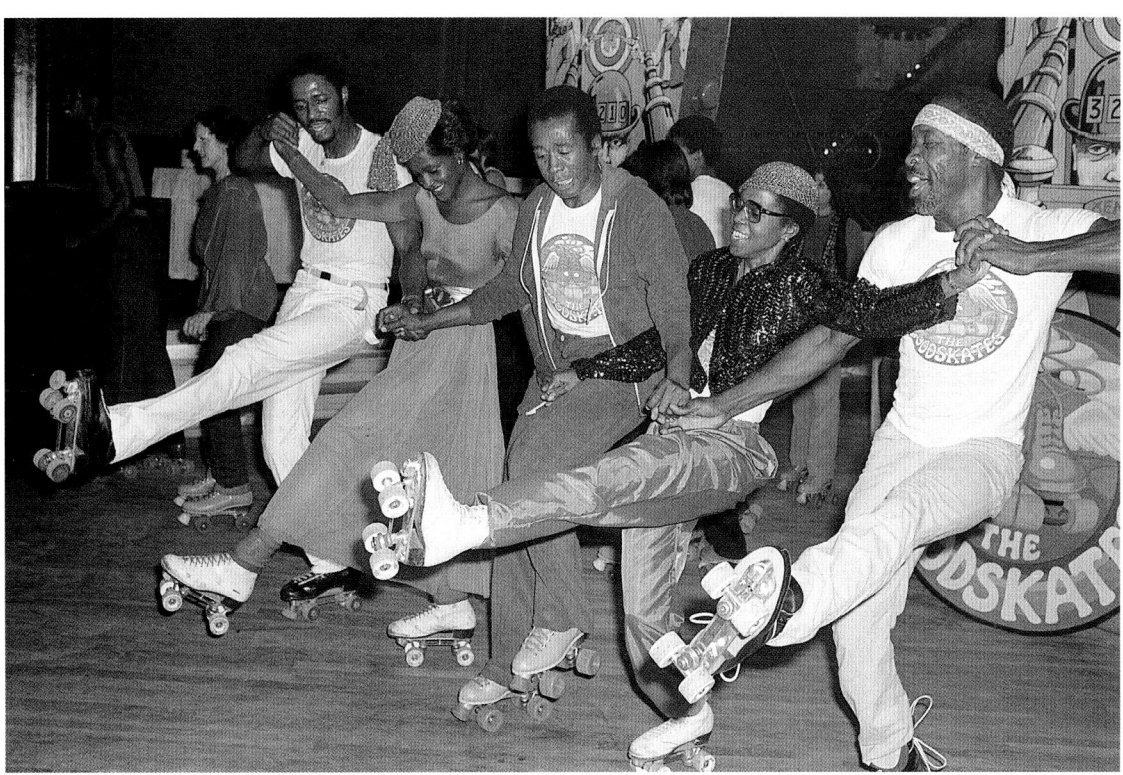

PREVIOUS SPREAD, LEFT: Grace
Jones performs at New York's
Studio 54 on New Year's Eve 1977.

LEFT: Diana Ross gets down at
Studio 54 in August 1979.

ABOVE: Actor, dancer, and singer
Ben Vereen tries to master the art
of roller dancing with the regulars
at the Xenon nightclub in New
York City.

BLACK AND QUEER AT THE DISCO

Disco music was the perfect soundtrack for queer bars and clubs during that era. For many Black queer and trans people who felt alienated from the Black church, discos were spaces of freedom and acceptance. Disco, with its underlying gospel influences, married the secular and the sacred.

Though disco was created by Black and Brown queer and trans folx, the commercialization of disco centered on whiteness and produced pop culture institutions like 1977's famed *Saturday Night Fever*. By then disco had been turned into a cash machine for record companies and pop culture conglomerates alike. Yet, even in its fervent whitewashing, disco remained a sonic and social environment for folx at the margins.

Artists like Sylvester, the unsung original Queen of Disco, asserted disco's queerness as an openly gay Black man. Sylvester sang unapologetically about his desires in a high-pitched voice that demanded attention. His androgynous fashion was ahead of his time, making way for other musicians, both contemporary and future, to queer their art.

Nightlife scenes and disco were an important part of modern queer and trans life and were especially havens for queers of color. We can look back to Jewel's Catch One in Los Angeles, for example, as a landmark disco for Black queers in the 1970s.

Even artists who were not queer became purveyors of the original values of the genre. Grace Jones developed a space at the intersection of Blackness and androgyny. Her performances provided a disco soundtrack to the avant-garde movements of her body, her wardrobe, and her expressions of sex and sensuality. These elements encouraged those in attendance to grapple with the intersections of race, gender, and desire.

DISCO NEVER DIED

The unapologetically queer style of disco may have been a refuge for marginalized people—Black, Brown, queer, trans, sexual, free, and joyful—but it was seen as a threat to mainstream America's values during the 1970s. On July 12, 1979, Steve Dahl, a Chicago shock jock DJ on WLUP, hosted what would be called "Disco Demolition Night" during a Chicago White Sox and Detroit Tigers doubleheader. The price of admission? Ninety-eight cents and a disco record to demolish during the break.

Dahl was disgruntled with the genre because the classic rock radio station he worked for had recently changed its format to disco. In his frustration with this, Dahl worked to create a narrative that disco was the antithesis of what Americans needed and wanted. To Dahl, disco was corny and vapid and held no place in the American music pantheon.

In between the doubleheader, Dahl blew up thousands of disco records brought by attendees in center field at Comiskey Park. Though this event was an attempt to increase attendance at the ballpark, it helped create a narrative that disco was dead—a story that was propelled by the media. Disco became the butt of jokes and declined over time, but the truth is: disco never died. The culture of disco, rooted in the expressed liberation of Black and Brown queer folx, has shape-shifted over the years, serving as inspiration for many modern acts and spawning new genres. Keep listening to disco. Continue getting free.

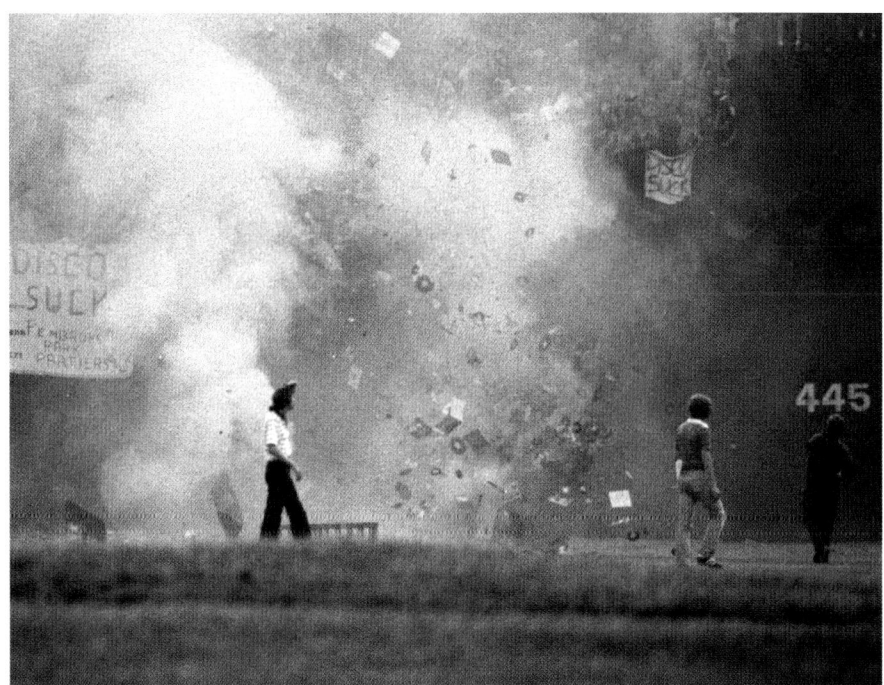

LEFT: Disco generated a backlash by the late 1970s, and on July 13, 1979, fans were invited to Comiskey Park in Chicago to blow up disco records. Chaos ensued, and the second game of the doubleheader had to be called off.

BELOW: Sylvester and Two Tons O′ Fun (Martha Wash, left, and Izora Rhodes [Armstead], right) present Merv Griffin with a gold *Step II* album during a 1978 appearance on Griffin's show.

FOLLOWING SPREAD:
LEFT: Sylvester performs in 1972 at the Los Angeles club Whiskey a Go Go.

RIGHT: An undated, unidentified photo of Sylvester.

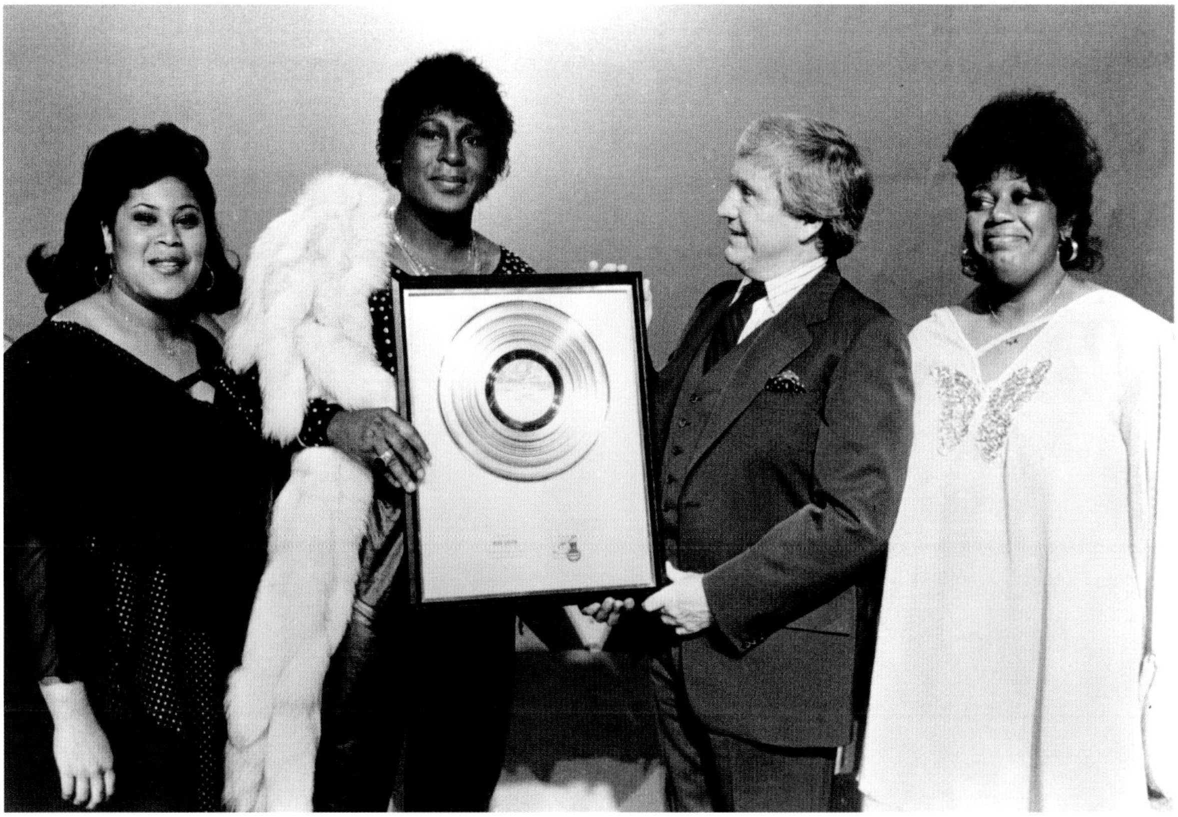

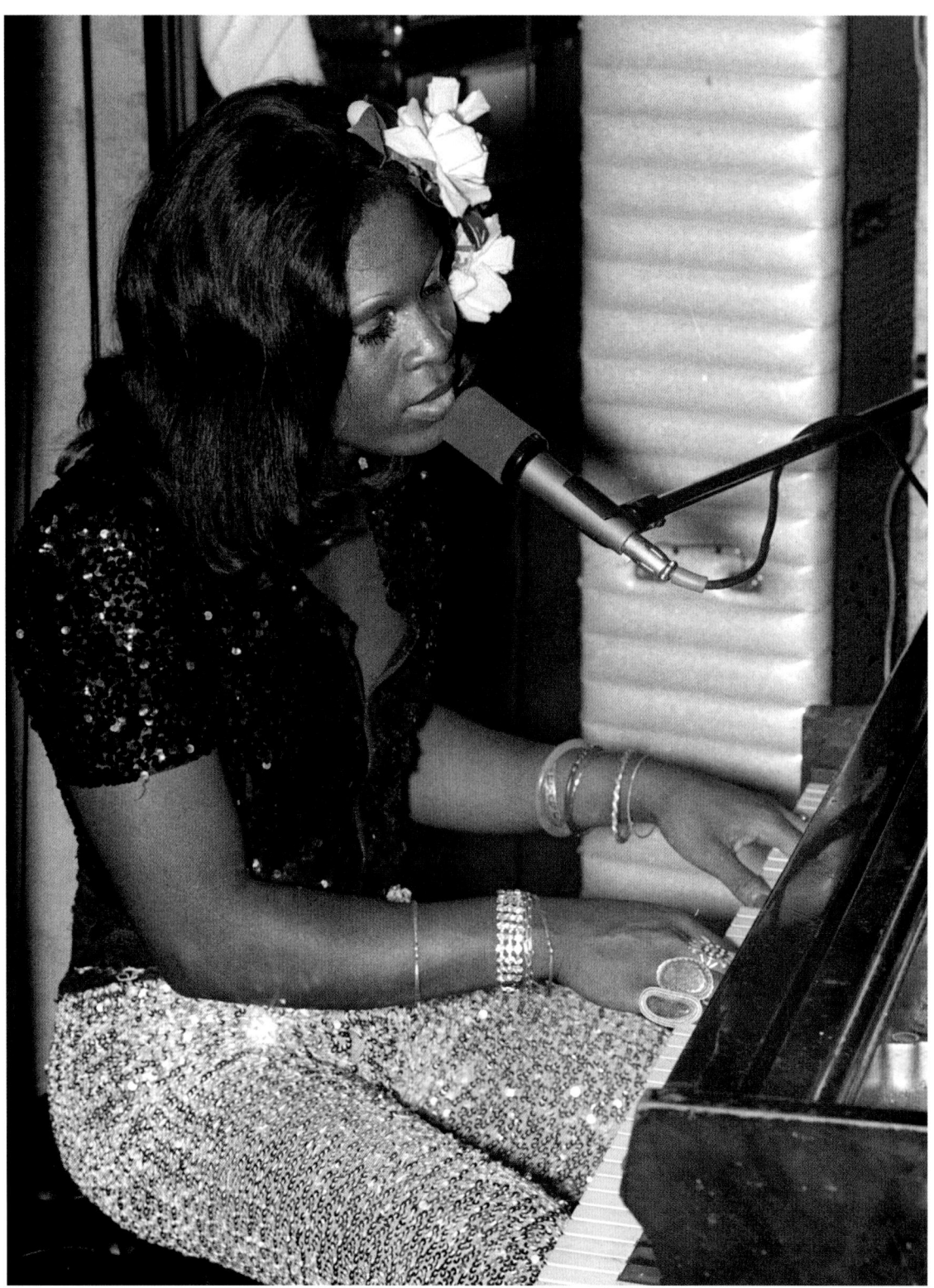

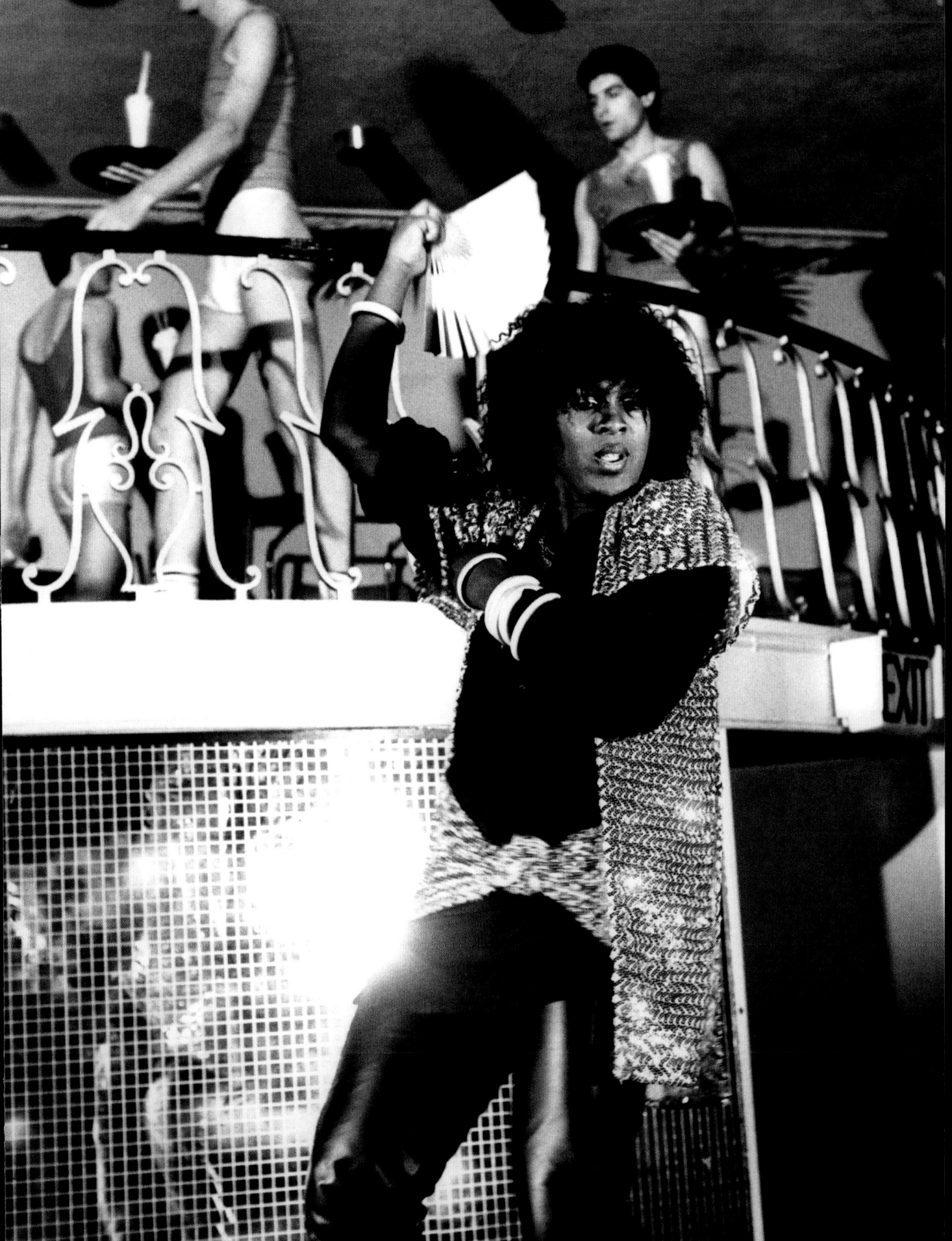

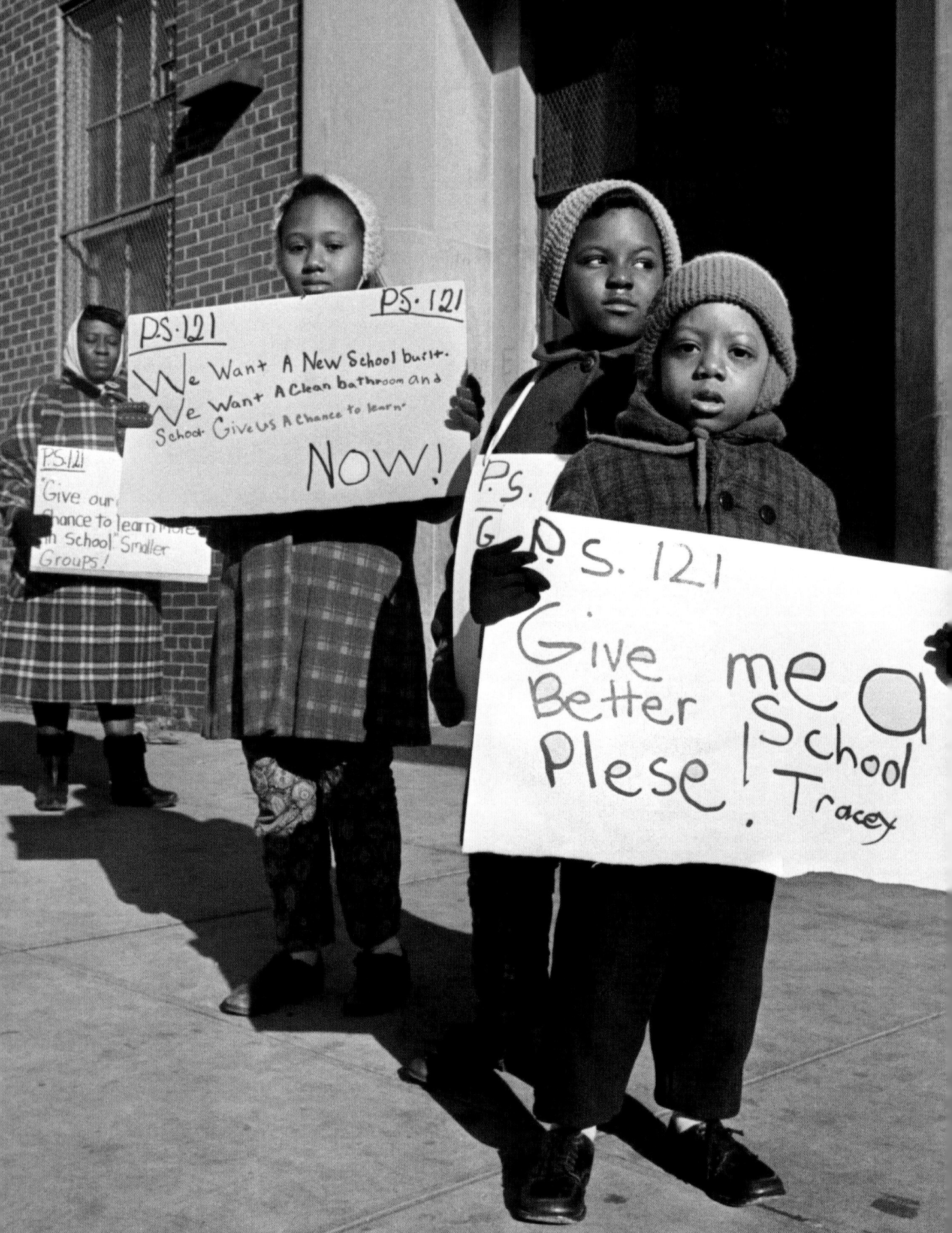

V.

BLACK EDUCATION AS RESISTANCE

BLACK EDUCATION IS A SPECIFIC MANIFESTATION OF A LONG TRADITION OF BLACK SELF-DETERMINATION AND COMMUNITY EMPOWERMENT. These traditions preserved and transmitted family histories, cultural literacy, pragmatic survival skills, and curricular knowledge across generations of African American life in the United States.

For the entirety of African American history, from enslavement to the present, the pursuit of formal education in American schools and universities was tempered by the active opposition of white supremacists who sought to block educational access. Despite this opposition, proponents of Black education sustained informal and formal educational institutions to nurture the conditions for African American survival and liberation.

These essays investigate the role of educational institutions and Black youth—schoolchildren, college students, community members—in creating and transforming educational spheres in ways that made space for Black students and Black history in American society.

OPPOSITE: Children participated in mass demonstrations to protest de facto segregation in New York City schools, 1964.

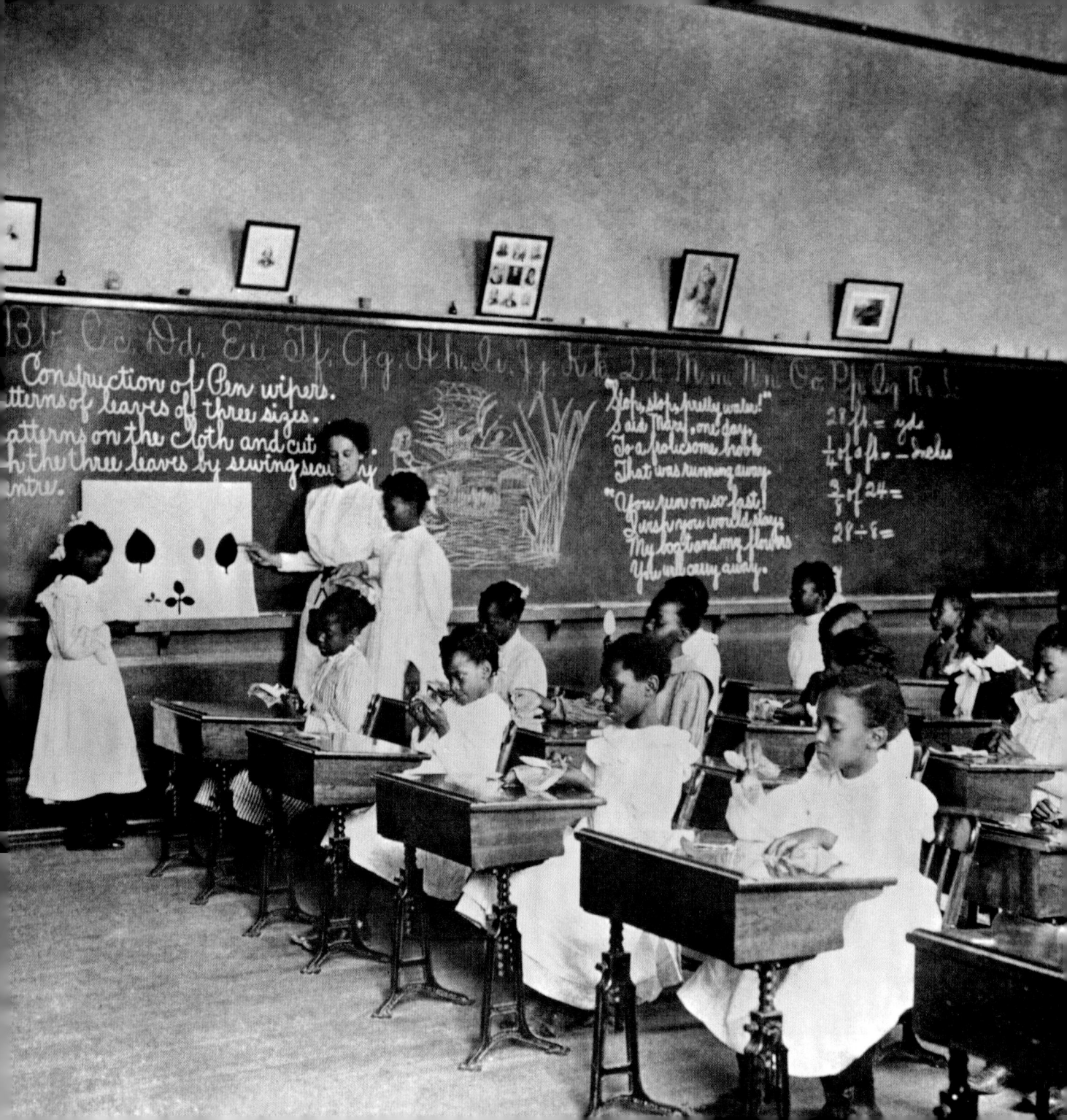

LEARNING IN SECRET PLACES

DAWN CHITTY

Susie Baker and the drive for education equality
before Brown v. Board of Education.

Many Americans have been taught that the fight for equal education in the United States started in the 1950s with the Supreme Court's decision in *Brown v. Board of Education*. While the families in that case were certainly courageous, efforts to redress unequal education for African Americans had started much earlier.

Enslaved persons in the nineteenth century struggled to educate themselves despite legal barriers and threats to their lives and well-being. These efforts were a form of protest as well as a forceful push toward freedom.

On December 11, 1829, police in Savannah, Georgia, seized sixty copies of Black abolitionist David Walker's book *Appeal to the Colored Citizens of the World*, published three months earlier. A scathing critique of racist white institutions, the essay collection became so popular that some Southern states criminalized its mere possession. In Georgia, persons caught smuggling the literature into its ports or across its borders could be executed, and undercover police officers were deployed to ferret them out.

Perhaps Walker's *Appeal* was inflammatory due to its promoting education as the means to overturn oppression in America. An enslaved person's ability to read and write contradicted the idea that African Americans were intellectually inferior and revealed to them ideas of human equality that might induce slave rebellion. Walker wrote that slavery was destined to end, whether peacefully or violently.

Within a year of the *Appeal*'s publication, North Carolina exemplified the link between literacy and freedom by prohibiting free and enslaved Black persons from learning to read and write. Georgia passed a similar law in 1833, and other Southern states followed suit. Despite the roadblocks to education for African Americans, the desire to learn didn't diminish, and some found ways to circumvent the law.

Susie Baker was one of those people. The eldest of nine children, Susie was born enslaved in 1848 in Georgia's Sea Islands. She was raised by her grandmother in Savannah. Every day, young Susie and her brother were sent to a widow and friend of her grandmother named Mrs. Woodhouse, who lived on Bay Lane in Savannah.

The school in Mrs. Woodhouse's home became the first of two secret schools Susie would attend in her community. "We went every day about nine o'clock, with our books wrapped in paper to prevent the police or white persons from seeing them," she recounted in her memoir.

If any of the educators were ever caught, they might have received a fine or, worse, a whipping, which was mandated by a Georgia law passed before Susie was born.

Her literacy would prove invaluable not only to her but to other African Americans she educated during and after the Civil War.

During the battle at Fort Pulaski at the mouth of Savannah's harbor (April 1862), Susie escaped with her uncle and his family, and they made their way to Union military lines. Susie quickly found herself teaching both children and adults to read and write while she herself was only fourteen years old.

For a time, Susie served as a laundress with the 33rd U.S. Colored Troops while finding the time to teach soldiers. The photo of Susie King Taylor (opposite page, top right) was taken sometime between 1890 and 1902

and was printed in her memoir, *Reminiscences of My Life in Camp with the 33d United States Colored Troops Late 1st S.C. Volunteers.*

Susie's commitment to and passion for teaching continued after the war, and she opened schools for both children and adults in Savannah.

After the war, some states established public school systems that, at first, accorded only miserly space to African American students. The Freedmen's Bureau, established in 1865, provided some educational resources. Freedmen's schools like the one pictured here (opposite page, bottom) were built all over the South after the Civil War ended. This photograph, likely taken between 1865 and 1870, shows mostly female students with their teachers at a Freedmen's School in Beaufort, South Carolina.

The Bureau did not build enough schools to meet demand. Even in the poorest rural communities, African American men and women hosted fundraisers and donated land to build schools. In the later years of the Reconstruction Era (1865–77), a dual system of public schools started to form in many municipalities. A single education board offered separate public education to African Americans and white people in different school systems. These new public schools made it hard for Susie to sustain enrollment at her private schools, forcing her to close all of them by the 1870s.

Although fraught with challenges and faced with closure, Susie's schools and her story exemplify the struggles and lengths Black citizens traversed for equal education. Her journey left a lasting legacy on generations of activism, culminating at last in the 1954 U.S. Supreme Court determination that separate education is not equal.

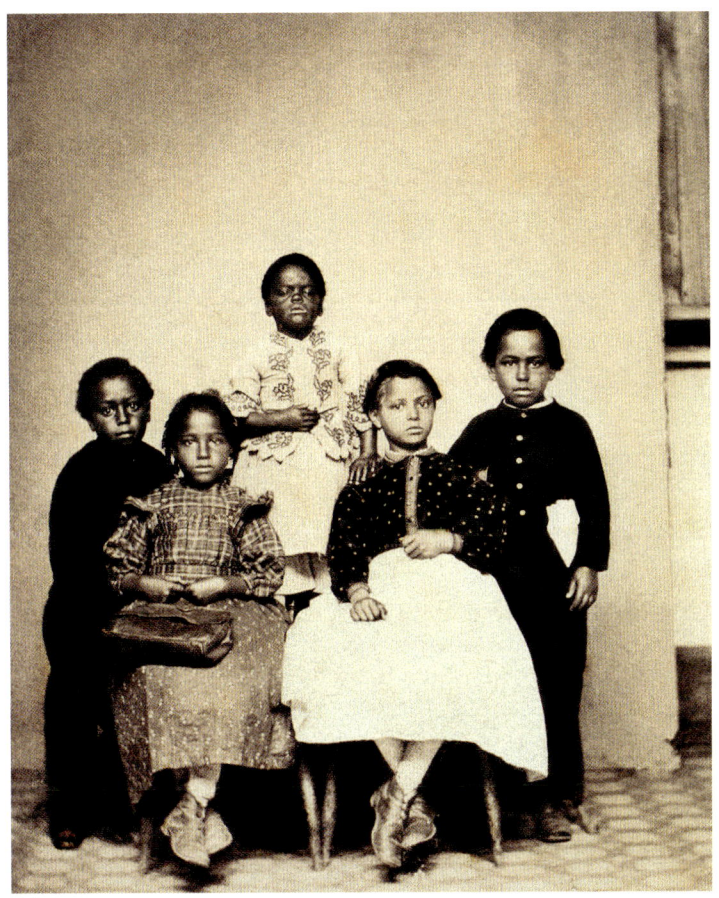

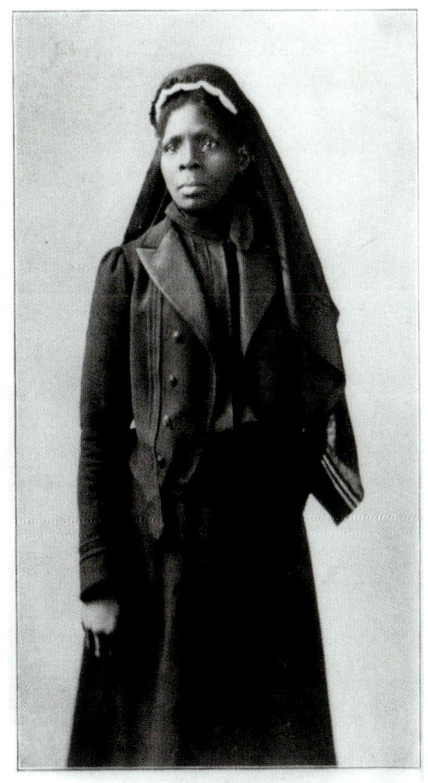

Susie King Taylor.

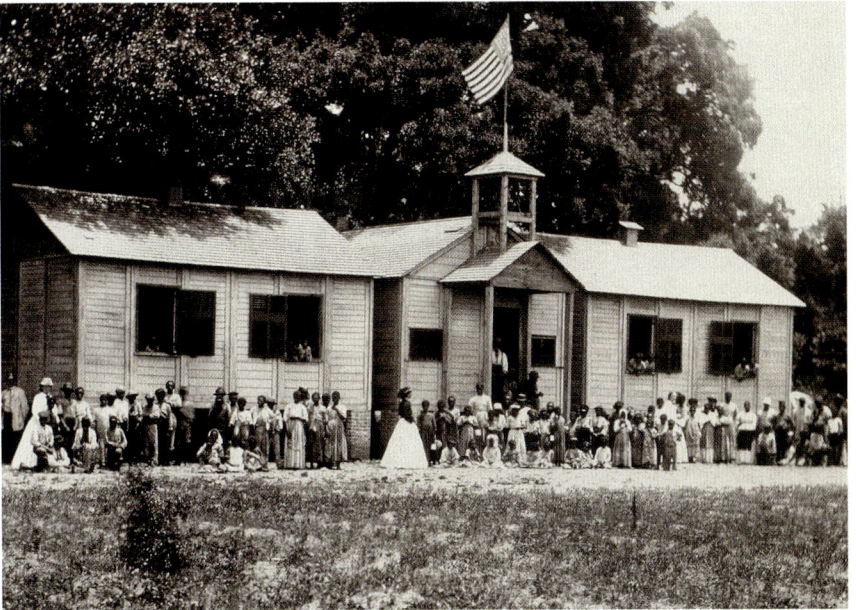

PREVIOUS SPREAD, LEFT: Black girls study plants in this 1899 photo from Washington, DC.

ABOVE, LEFT: A portrait of Black schoolchildren in North Carolina taken in the 1860s.

ABOVE, RIGHT: Susie King Taylor served as the first Black nurse in the U.S. Army during the Civil War before she became a teacher.

LEFT: The Pennsylvania Freedmen's Relief Association helped fund this school on St. Helena Island, South Carolina.

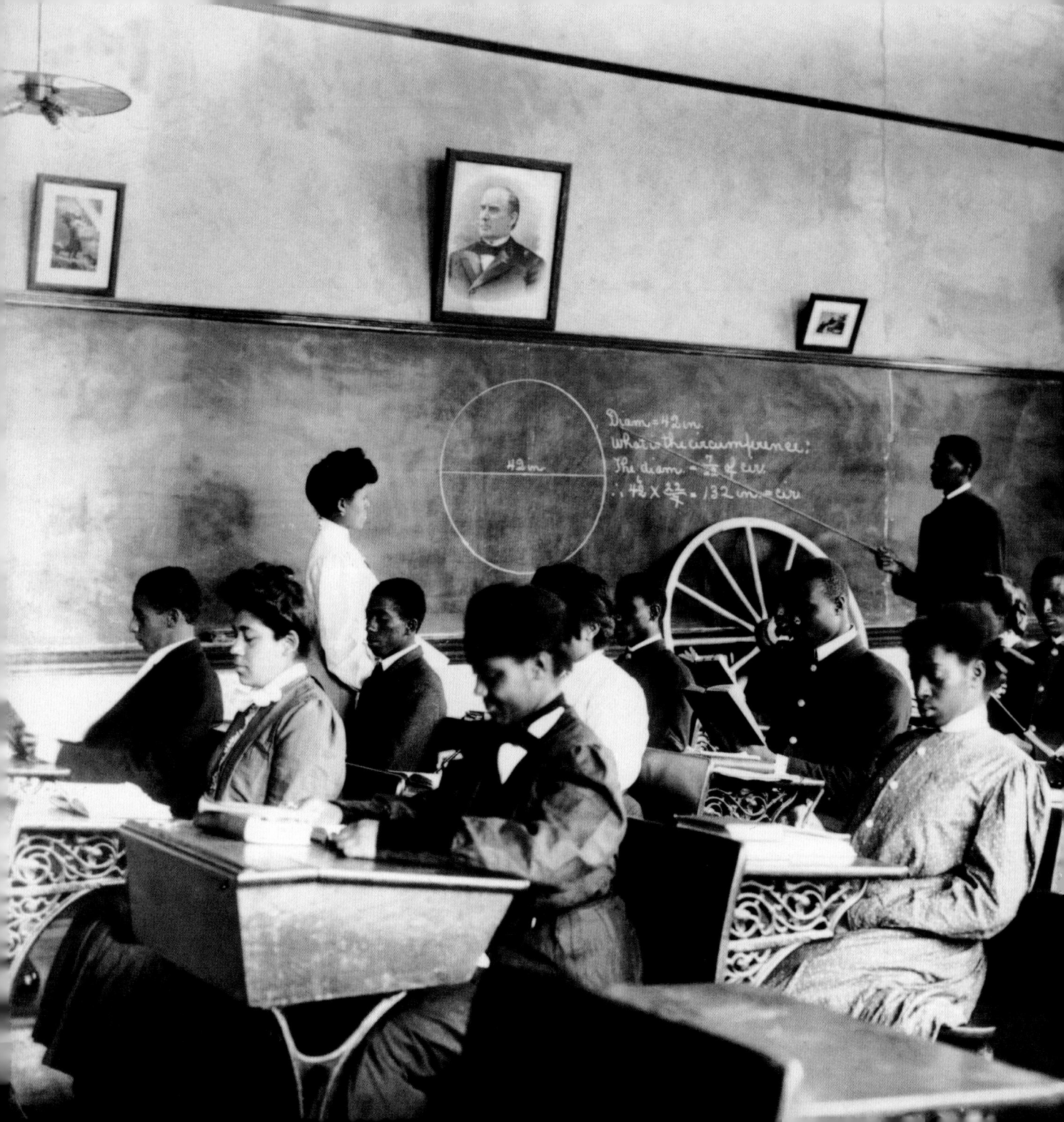

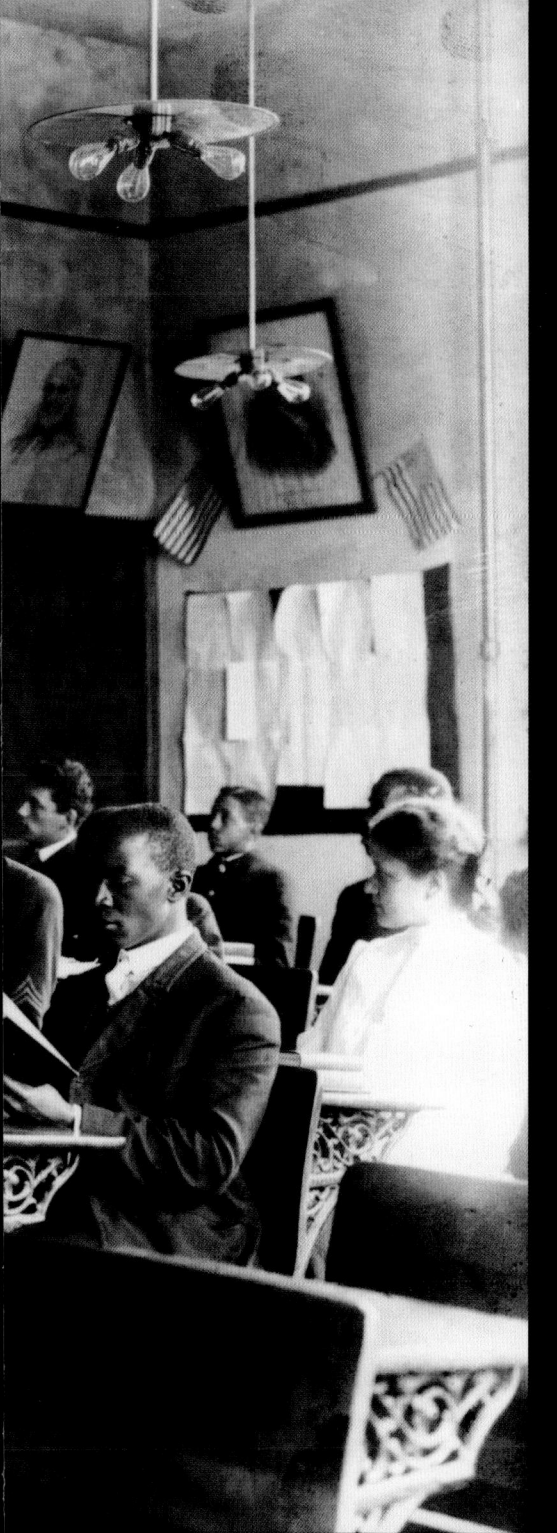

TWENTY-TWO DIVIDED ^{BY} SEVEN, GEOMETRY ^{AT} TUSKEGEE

KWABENA SLAUGHTER

A 1906 photograph of a mathematics classroom illustrates how the Tuskegee Institute used "correlation" theory and the Sloyd system to teach applied mathematics.

During the early twentieth century, the Tuskegee Institute was harshly criticized by many African American scholars and activists, most famously W. E. B. Du Bois in his 1903 essay "Of Mr. Booker T. Washington and Others," as being an anti-intellectual learning environment that trained students in the same manual labor skills that had been forced on them during enslavement.

That critique became the conventional wisdom. But this photograph, which depicts Tuskegee's intersection of manual labor informed by specialized intellectual knowledge, complicates that perception.

During a math class at the Tuskegee Institute in 1906, a circle 42 inches in diameter has been drawn on the chalkboard. Its dimensions come from the wagon wheel that is leaning against the wall. That wheel is being used as an object lesson because Tuskegee's curriculum operates on a pedagogic theory of "correlation."

Mathematical equations—such as the geometric relationships to determine the circumference of a circle—were taught in the context of their practical use in daily life rather than as abstract concepts learned in isolation.

For much the same reason that the alphabet is taught as a song––aiding the brain to remember and create a material association with the letters––the technique of correlation is an example of Booker T. Washington's concept of "head and hands together."

The method more familiar in the twenty-first century for teaching the calculation of the circumference of a circle is to use the equation $C = \varpi(d)$. In this math class, instead of writing the Greek symbol ϖ (pi), they use the fraction $^{22}/_7$, which equals 3.14285714286. When that number is rounded down to 3.14, as is commonly used for ϖ today, the answer yielded by this alternate form of the equation still holds true to the arithmetic laws of geometry.

In the third line on the chalkboard the diameter is written as being equal to $^7/_{22}$ of the circumference. The three dots at the beginning of the fourth line are a shorthand symbol for the word "therefore." The students know that the carriage wheel's diameter is 42 inches, and the teacher has informed them that the diameter is equal to the circumference times $^7/_{22}$; therefore, they can multiply 42 inches by $^{22}/_7$. The answer to this math problem is that the wagon wheel has a circumference of 132 inches (or 11 feet).

Use of the $^{22}/_7$ fraction to represent ϖ was first created by the ancient Greek mathematician and engineer, Archimedes in the third century BCE. It likely became part of Tuskegee's curriculum via a system of manual training called Sloyd, founded in Sweden in the mid-1800s on the classic principles of geometry.

In the 1890s, industrial training schools in the United States started incorporating Sloyd into their curriculum. Sloyd's creators pictured the system's role in mathematics education as building a road between the brain and the fingers.

In 1907, Dudley W. Woodard, one of the first African Americans to receive a PhD in mathematics, was appointed to lead Tuskegee's mathematics curriculum. In his 1911 book *Practical Arithmetic* (Tuskegee Institute edition), he explains how the educational theory of correlation is represented in this photograph:

> The diameter of the front wheels of a wagon made in the Institute Shops was 42 [inches] . . . In the Blacksmith Shop iron tires are put on the wheels of the vehicles built in the Institute Shops. In estimating, the amount of iron required for the tire of a wheel, it is necessary to find the circumference of a circle . . . [which] is found by multiplying the diameter by 3⅐.

The goal of Woodard's lesson was to teach the students how to "find the cost of the iron used in making the four tires" before they set to work, as pictured in the photo on the following spread of students in the Tuskegee wheelwright shop from the same period. The correlation theory framed the teaching of applied mathematics in the Tuskegee classroom.

In the history of Western and Eastern culture, respect for geometry has been considered an indicator of advanced civilization. In his 1904 book *Working with the Hands*, Booker T. Washington argued that "there is a vast difference between working and being worked. Being worked means degradation; working means civilization."

These photographs illustrate Washington's contribution, as it was described by his secretary and biographer Emmett J. Scott, as a "builder of a civilization."

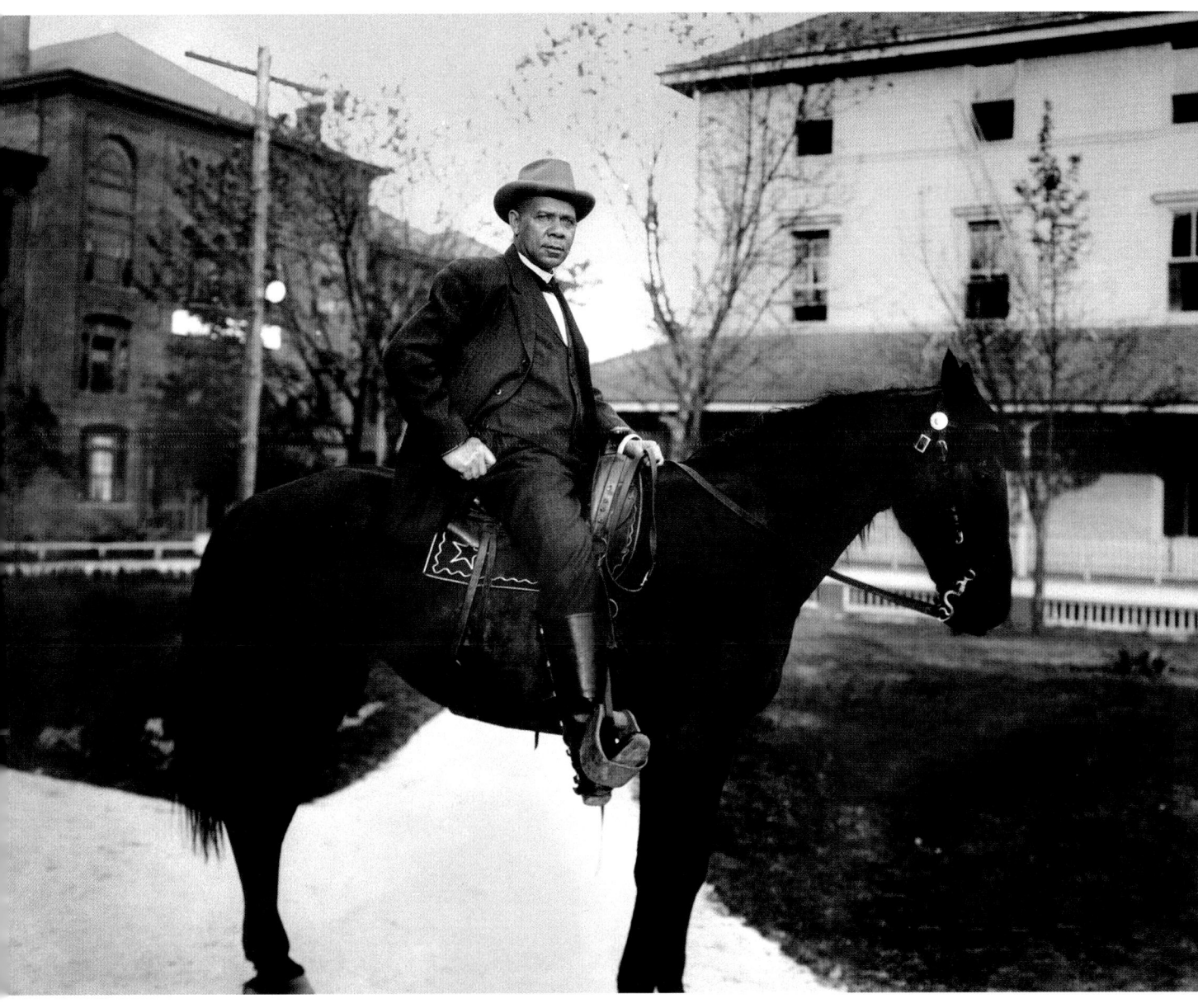

PREVIOUS SPREAD: A math class at
Tuskegee in 1906. Notice that the
class is coed.

FOLLOWING SPREAD: Geometry
put to practical use in the
wheelwright's shop at Tuskegee.

ABOVE: Booker T. Washington
came to Tuskegee in 1881 and built
it into a remarkable institution.

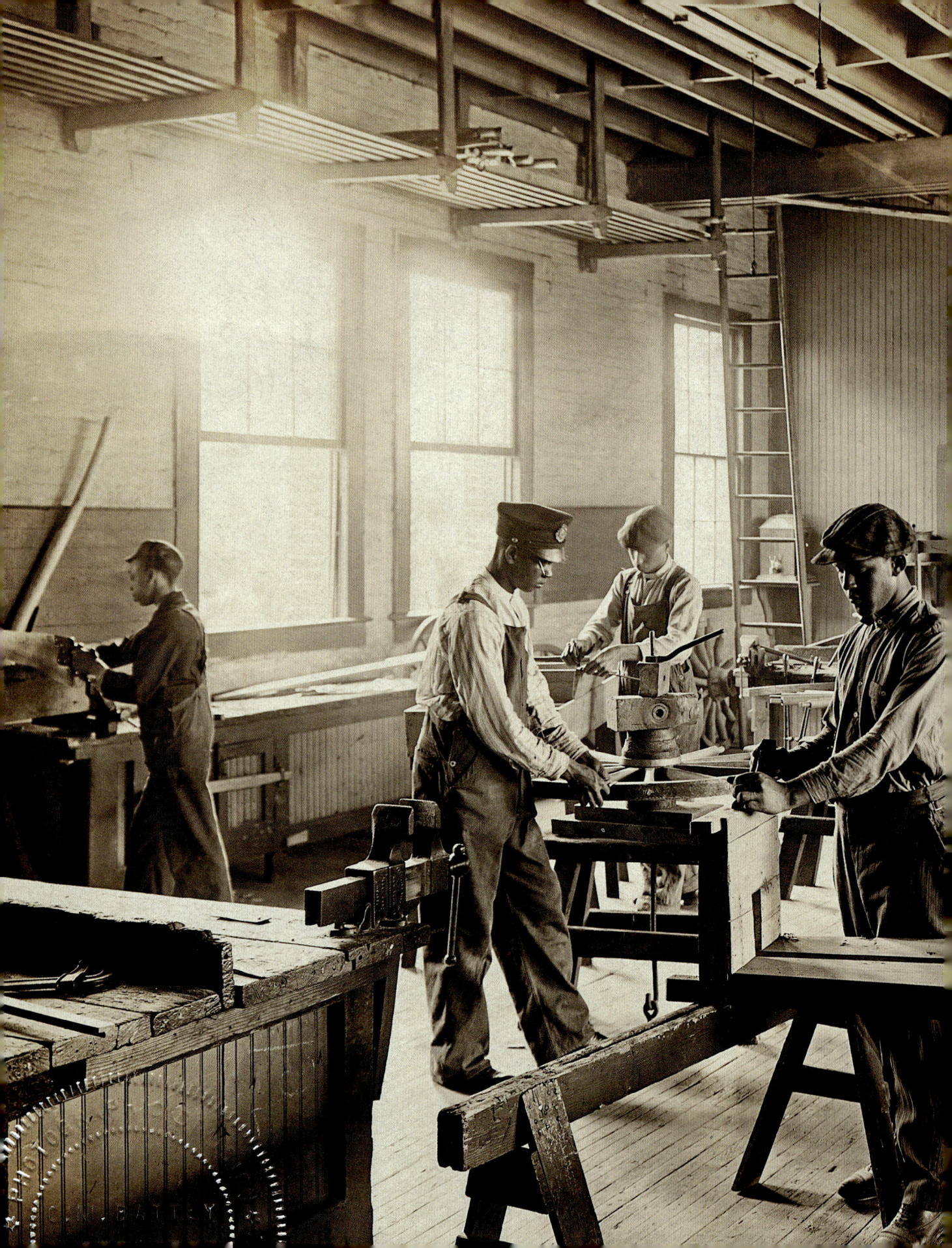

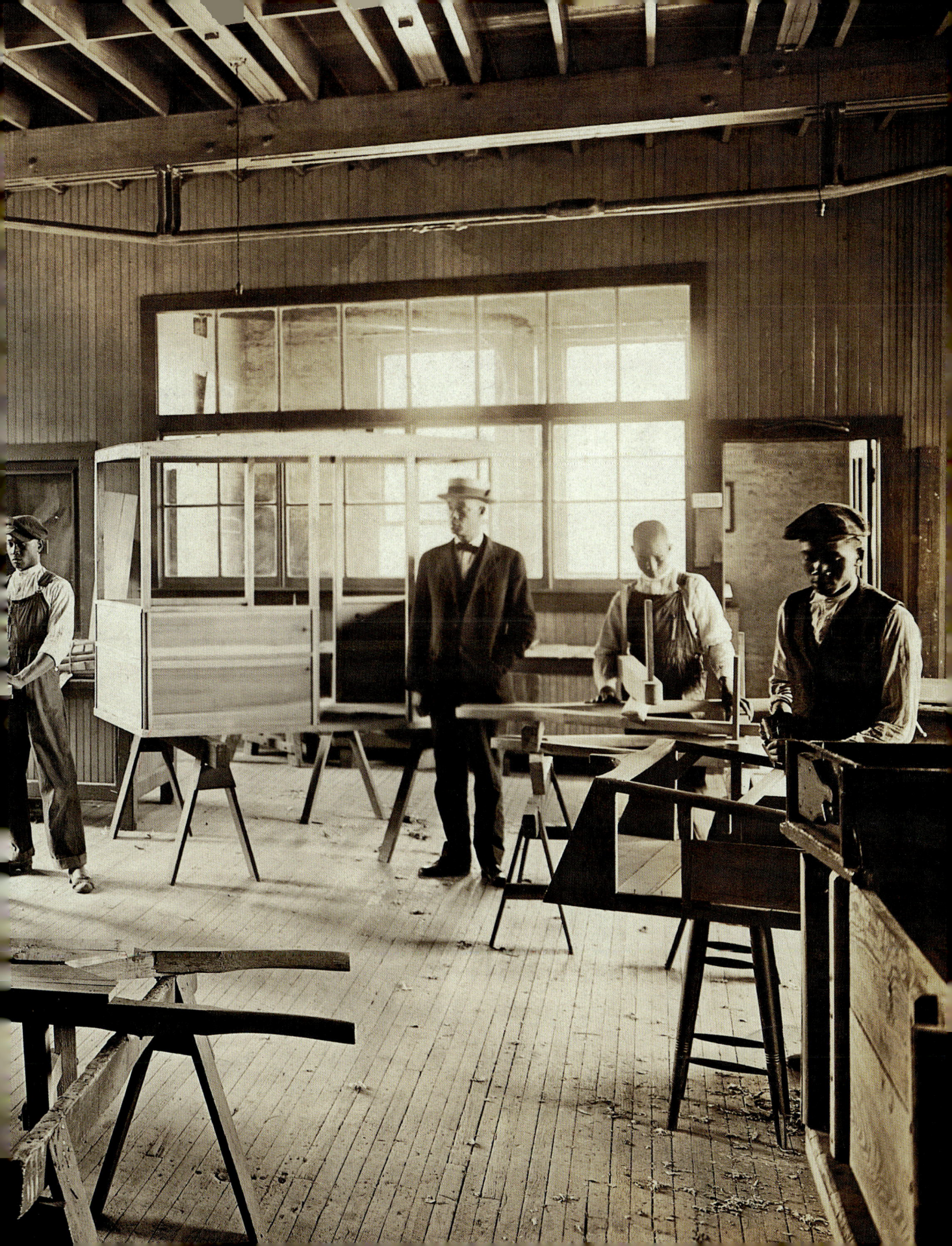

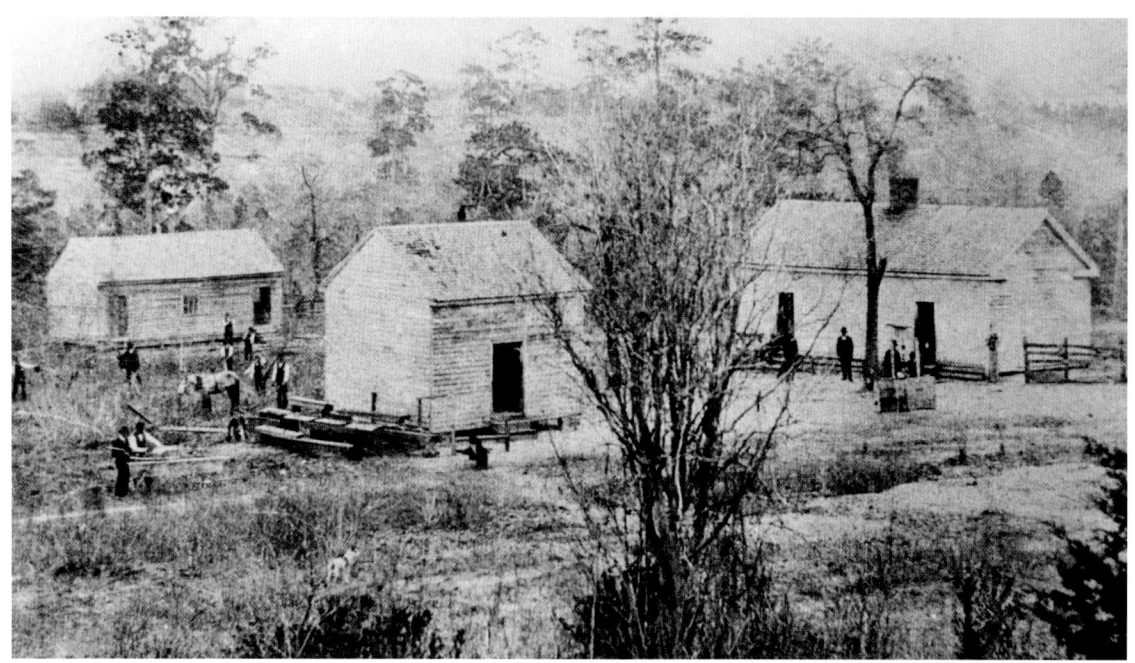

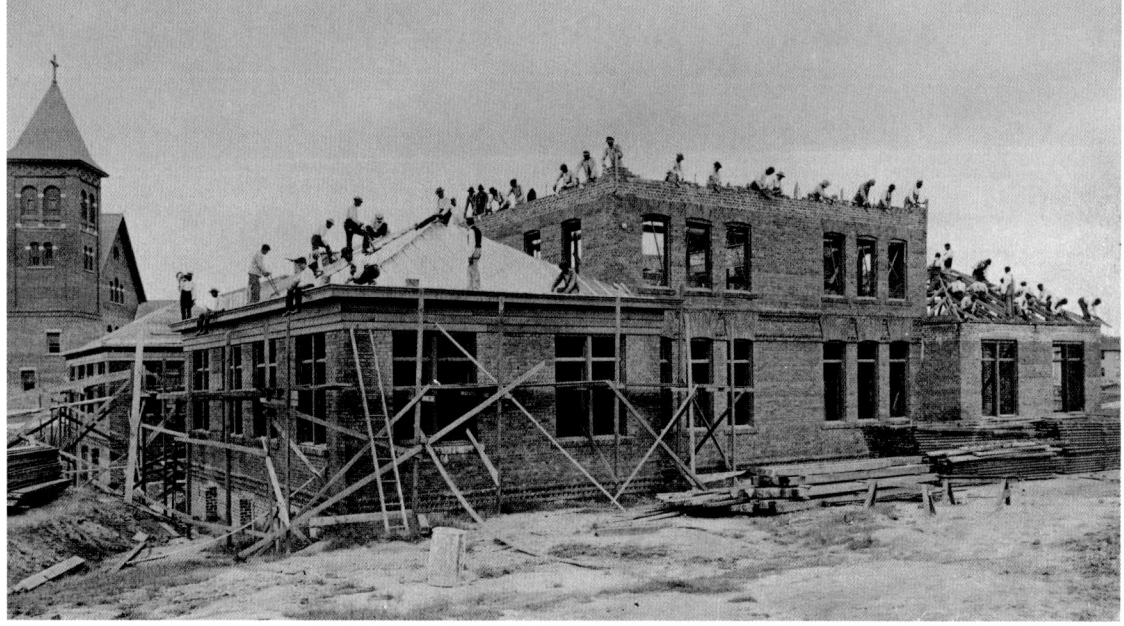

TOP: The Tuskegee Institute sometime in the 1880s.

BOTTOM: Tuskegee students put their learning to use, erecting this building in 1915.

RIGHT: An arial view of the Tuskegee Institute sometime in the mid-twentieth century. Together, these three photographs show the remarkable growth of the Tuskegee Institute.

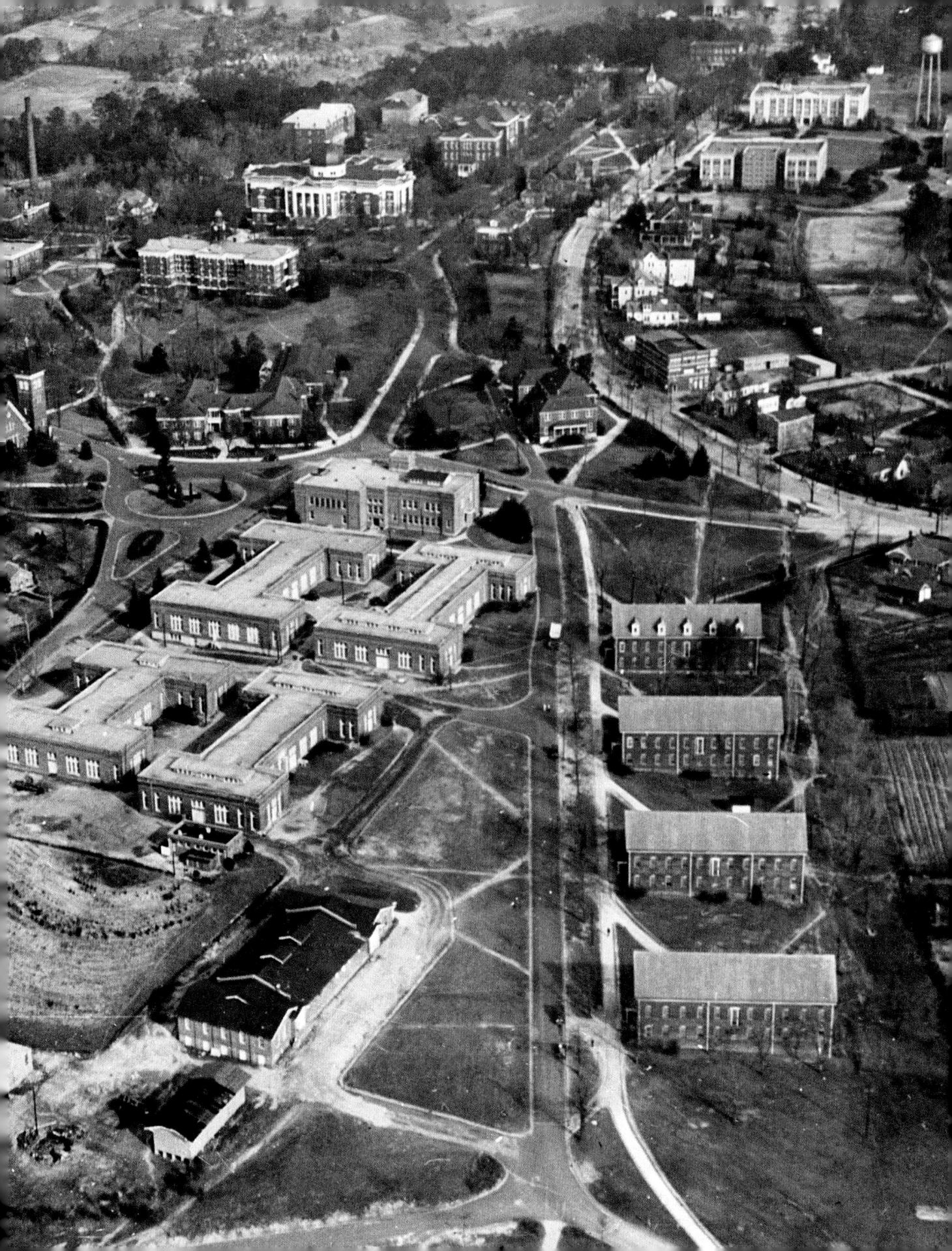

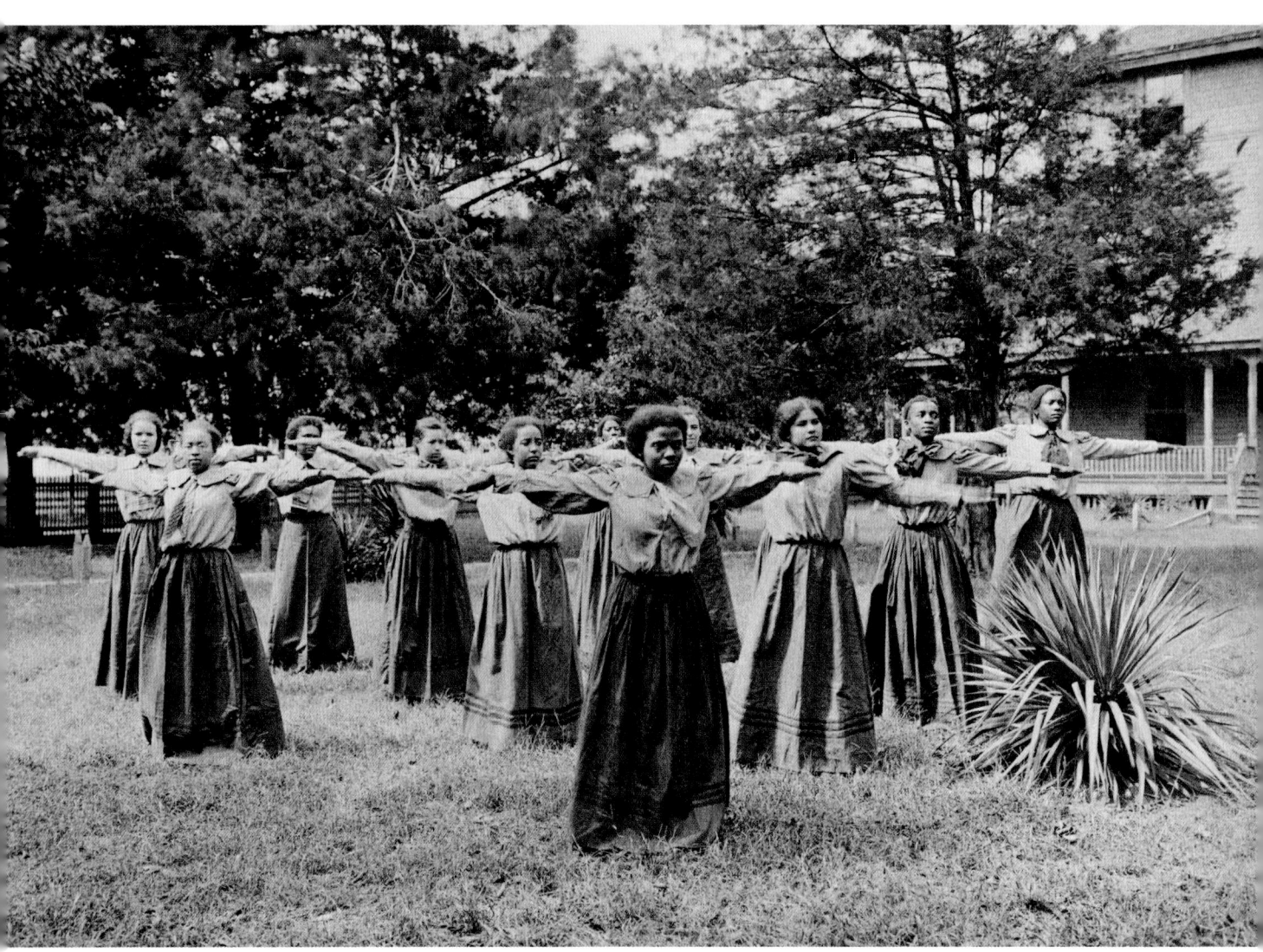

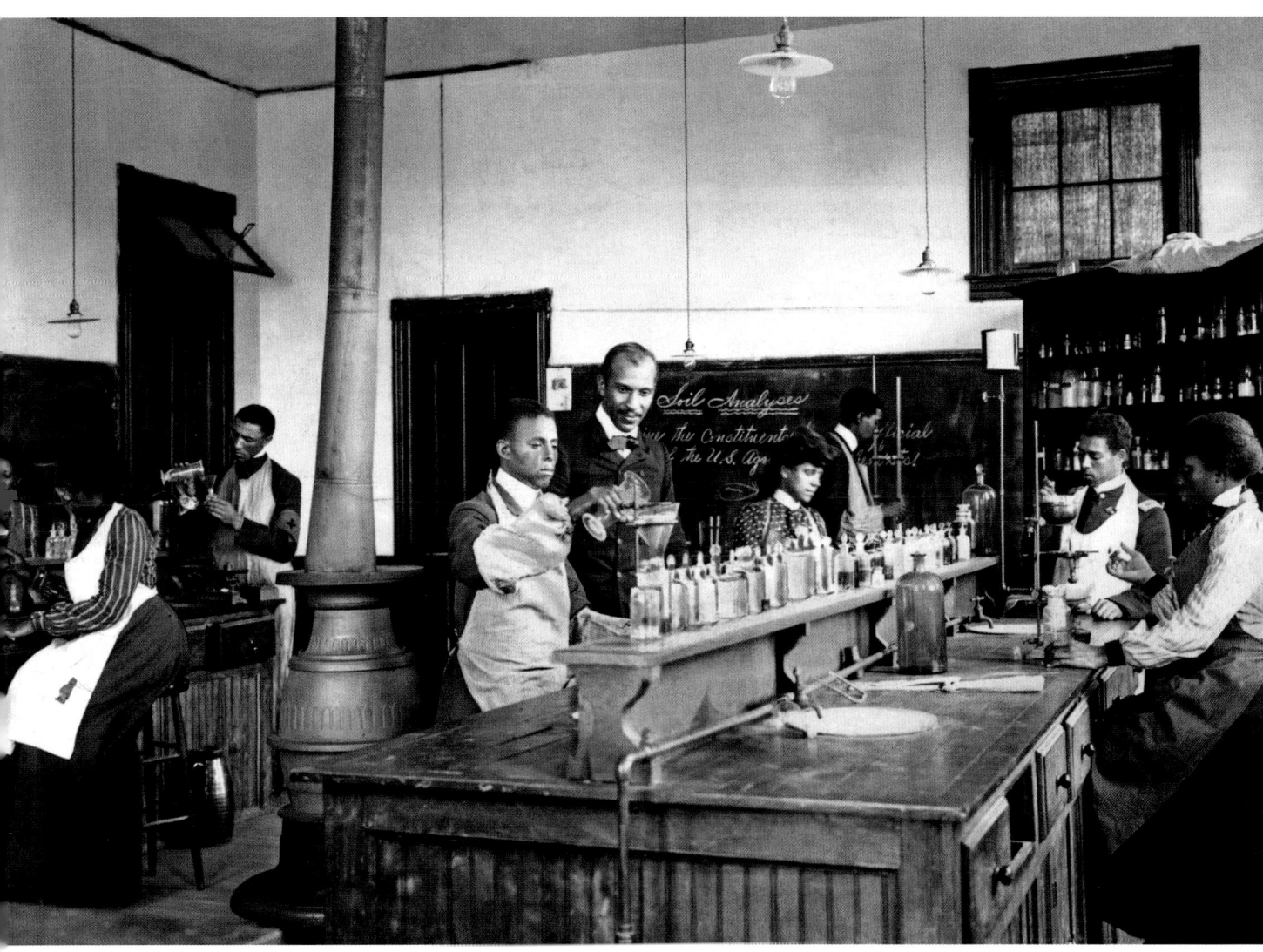

OPPOSITE: Training the body and
the mind, even if in very long skirts.

ABOVE: George Washington
Carver in his laboratory at
Tuskegee. The photo has no date,
but Carver taught there from 1896
until 1943.

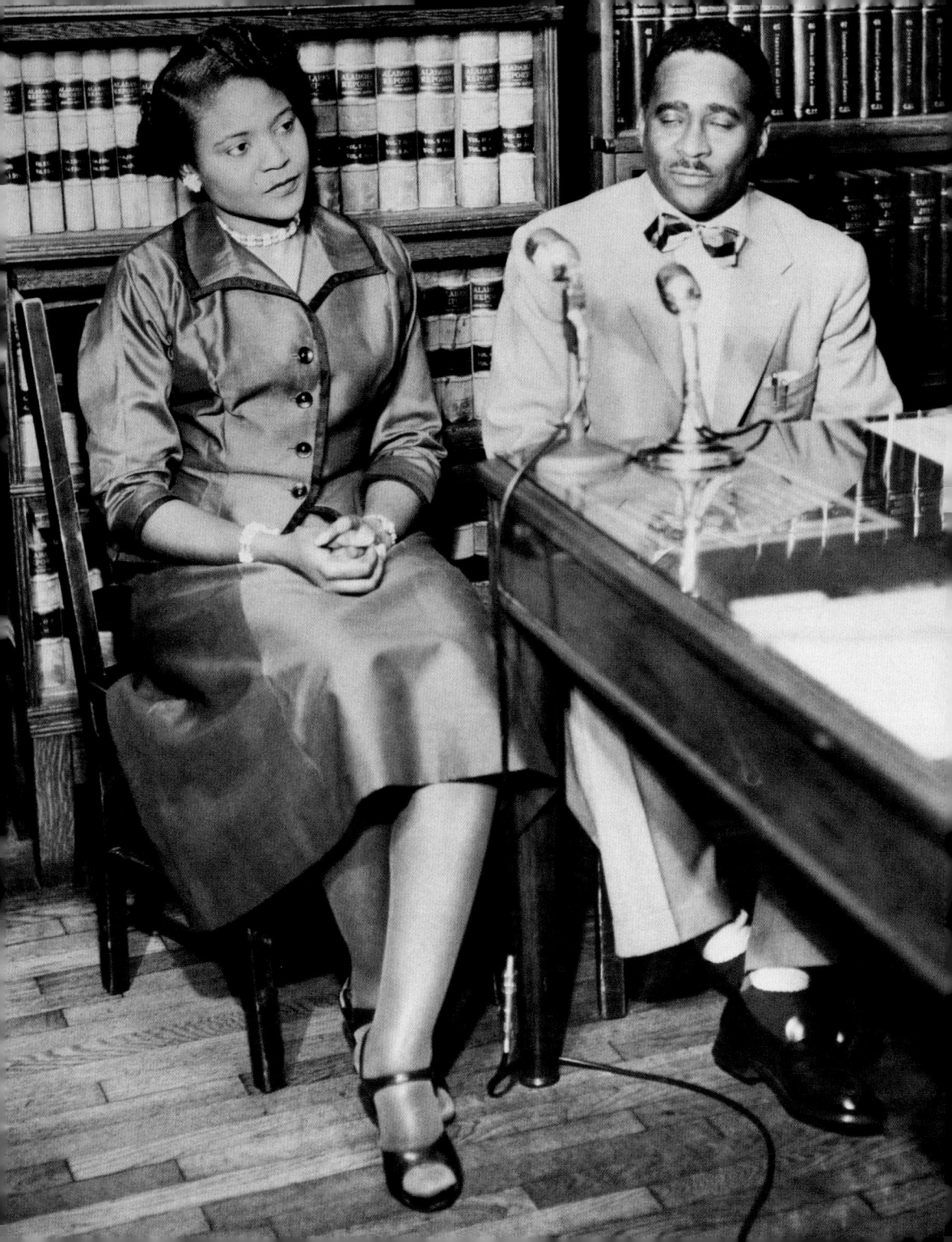

POISE <u>AND</u> PERSEVERANCE

SARÁJANÉE O. DAVIS

How Autherine Lucy, Charlayne Hunter, and Vivian Malone desegregated higher education in the American South.

For many, the story of school desegregation in the United States starts with the Supreme Court ruling in the *Brown v. Board of Education* case in 1954. While Oliver and Linda Brown, Ruby Bridges, and the Little Rock Nine deserve every accolade for their courage, the struggle to desegregate higher education was just as difficult and at least as significant.

It also began before the *Brown* decision in 1954. The legal strategies that proved successful in the 1950s for schools had been crafted and refined at the university level in the first half of the twentieth century. They began to pay off in a series of court rulings that opened all-white state universities to Black students. As the images in this chapter remind us, Black women were at the center of the struggle to integrate higher education.

Autherine Lucy applied and was accepted to attend the University of Alabama in 1952. However, university administrators rescinded her acceptance after learning she wasn't white. Three years and a lawsuit filed by the National Association for the Advancement of Colored People were necessary for her finally to secure her spot.

Lucy attended two days of classes in February 1956 before white mobs rioted on the campus for three days, at which point university officials suspended her, allegedly for her own safety. Lawyer Arthur Shores, pictured with Lucy, oversaw her second case against the University of Alabama. The microphones on the table indicate the national media attention on the case, which drew the ire of university officials.

PREVIOUS SPREAD, LEFT: Autherine Lucy had her acceptance to the University of Alabama in 1952 revoked when officials discovered she wasn't white.

RIGHT: After being expelled from the University of Alabama, Autherine Lucy flew to New York, accompanied by NAACP attorney Constance Motley.

OPPOSITE: Charlayne Hunter was forced to leave campus "for her own safety." She clutches a Madonna statuette.

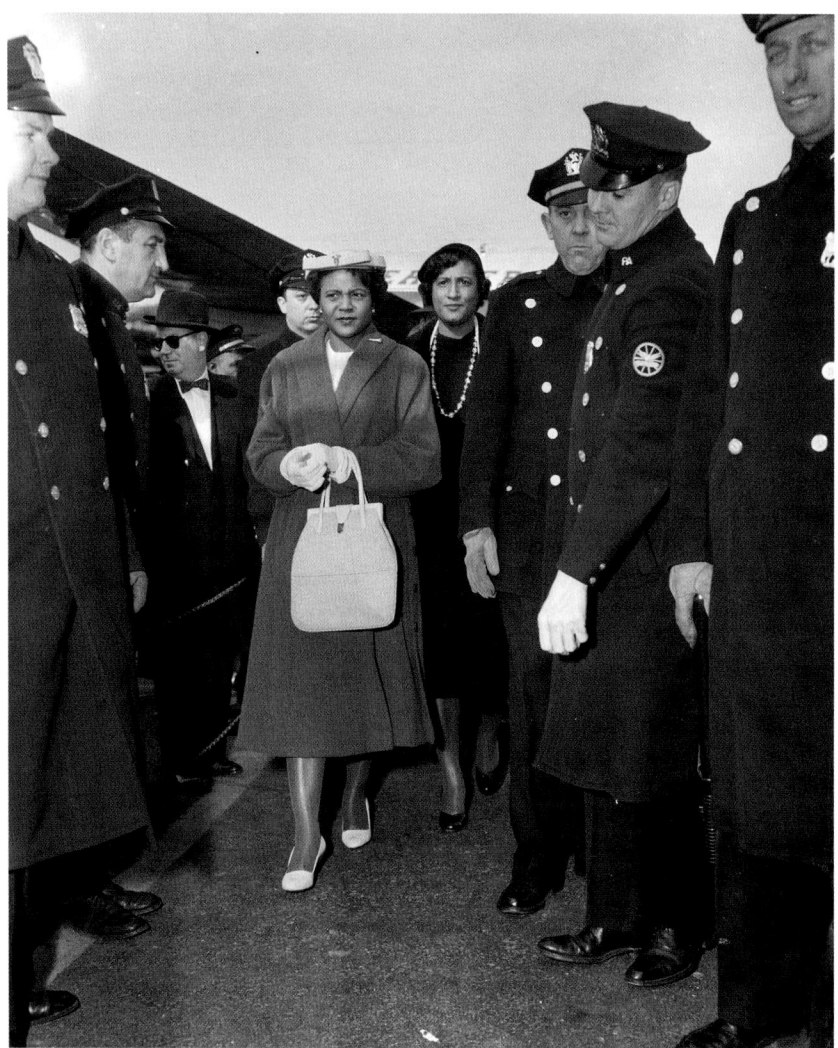

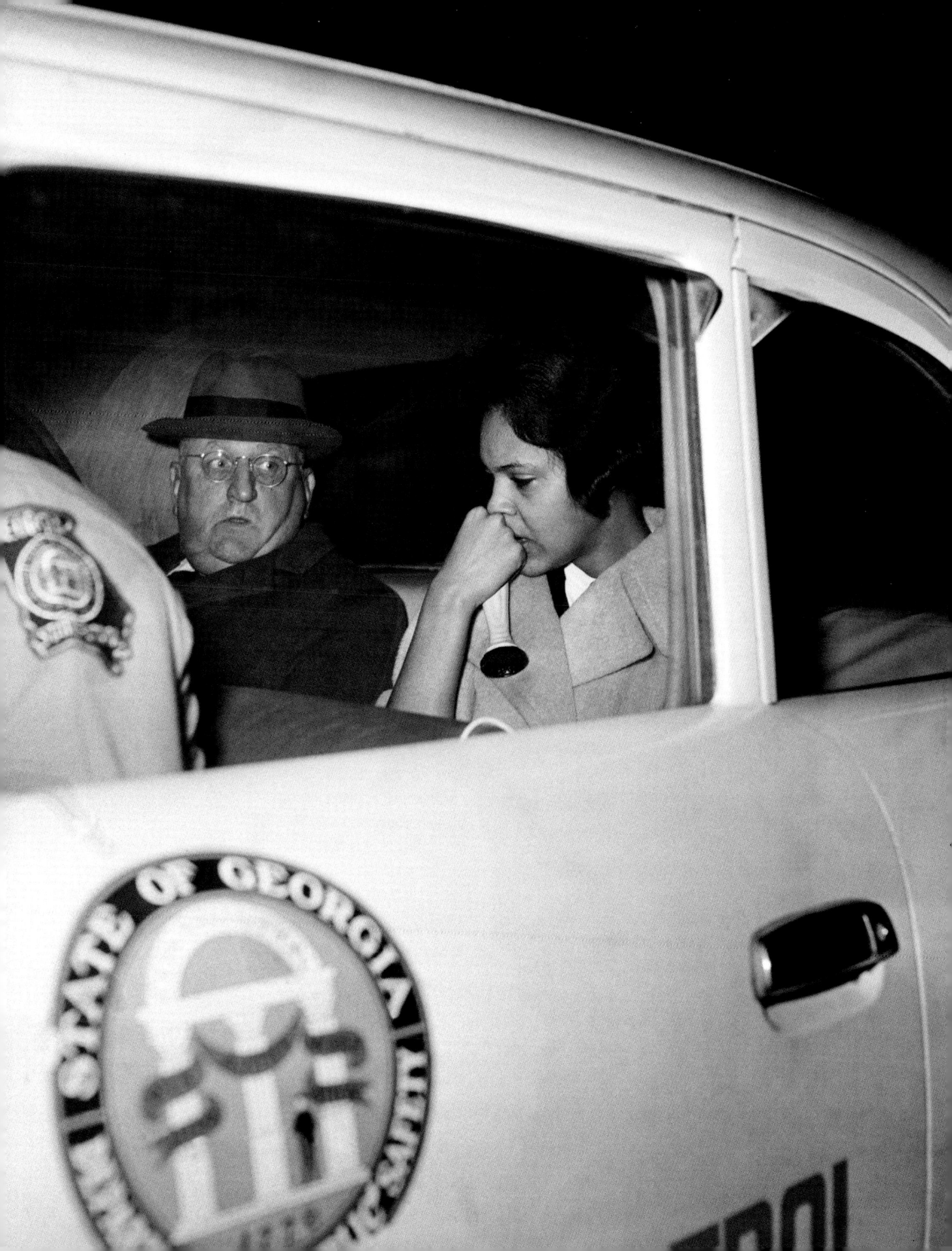

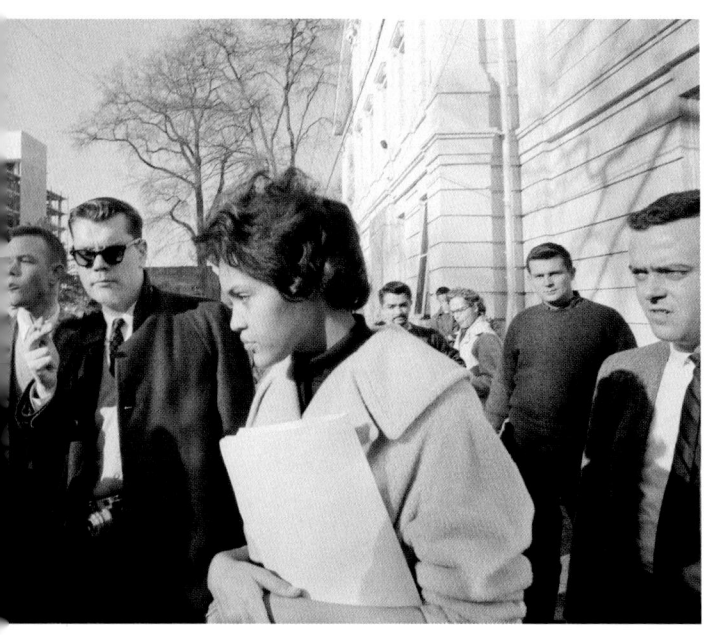
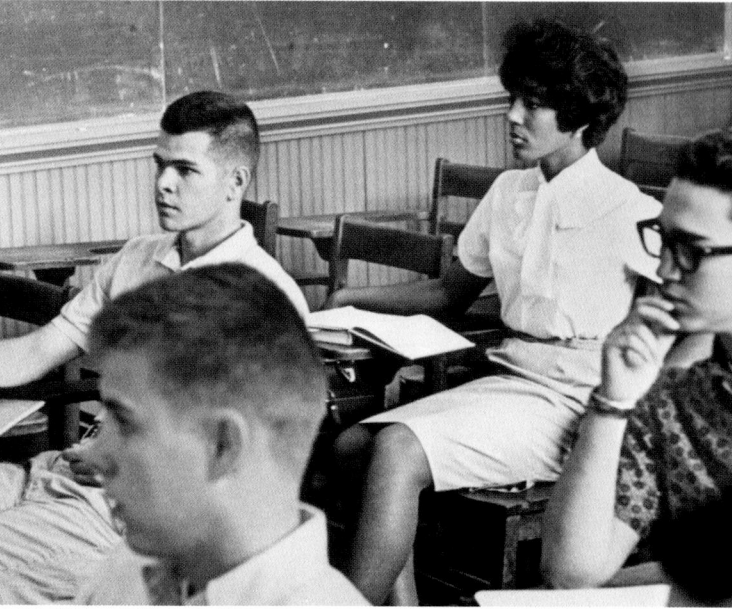

Autherine Lucy's courage made her a target of white supremacists and she temporarily relocated to New York City. Lucy married Hugh Foster in the spring of 1956 and toured the country with the NAACP telling her story and agitating for access to higher education. By the end of the year the pair returned to the South full-time. Lucy remained committed to education. Like many educated Black women, Lucy became a career teacher whose legacy lived on through her students.

The admittance of Charlayne Hunter (now Hunter-Gault) to the University of Georgia (UGA) offers proof that previous pressure cracked the system of Jim Crow that structured the South. When Hunter enrolled alongside Hamilton Holmes in 1961, the pair became UGA's first African American students. This photograph captured Hunter as she left the registrar's office after officially enrolling.

The small crowd seen here pales in comparison to the angry mob that surrounded her dorm two days later.

While racists were able to express their dissatisfaction with her presence freely and violently, Hunter had to remain stoic and composed. Though UGA officials followed Alabama administrators' model by suspending Hunter and Holmes, a court order allowed them to return to campus and resume classes. She graduated in 1963 with a journalism degree and embarked on an illustrious career. Hunter's persistence and success inspired and encouraged those who came next.

Vivian Malone may have been one of those people Hunter invigorated. Years later, at her University of Alabama Commencement Address in 2000, Malone named Autherine Lucy's persistence as a source of inspiration as she and James Hood faced down Governor George Wallace to enroll at the University of Alabama in 1963. She graduated in 1965 with a degree in business management.

Even though Malone completed the mission Lucy began, her success at Alabama carried its own cost. The range of cold indifference to close stares from the university

198

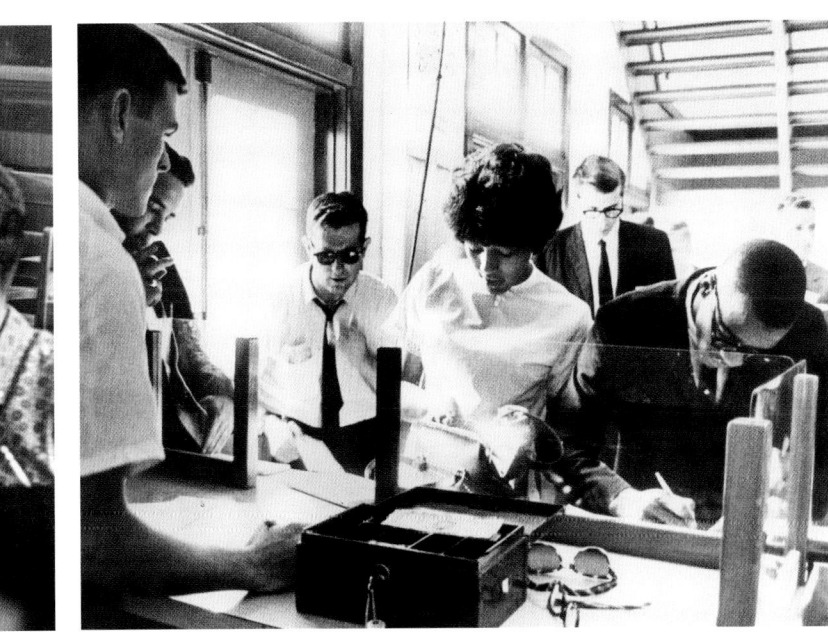

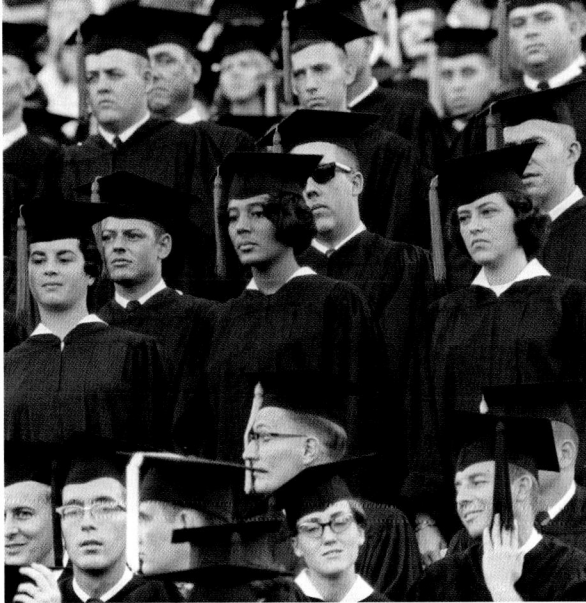

registrar's staff captures her experience on campus. Simultaneously ignored and placed under a microscope, Malone had to remain poised and was acutely aware of what her presence represented. Malone's attire, like that of Lucy's and Hunter's, communicated her preparedness and decorum, two qualities necessary to counter prevailing stereotypes about Black women and claim their dignity and autonomy.

This history illuminates the long struggle for educational equity in the United States. Greater attention to these three stories prompted long-overdue formal acknowledgment. Alabama awarded Malone an honorary doctorate in 2000 to commemorate her career dedicated to advancing civil rights. The university recognized Autherine Lucy's contributions with an honorary doctorate in 2019. UGA announced an annual lecture in Hunter's name in 2021. Each woman's journey highlights the incredible and lasting difference one individual can make.

LEFT TO RIGHT: Charlayne Hunter leaving the registrar's office as the first Black woman to enroll at the University of Georgia.

Vivian Malone sitting in class at the University of Alabama.

Vivian Malone next to James Hood as they both paid their registration fees.

Vivian Malone graduated from the University of Alabama in May 1965.

FOLLOWING SPREAD: Walking past a gauntlet of university officials and press photographers, Vivian Malone registers for class at the University of Alabama on July 11, 1963.

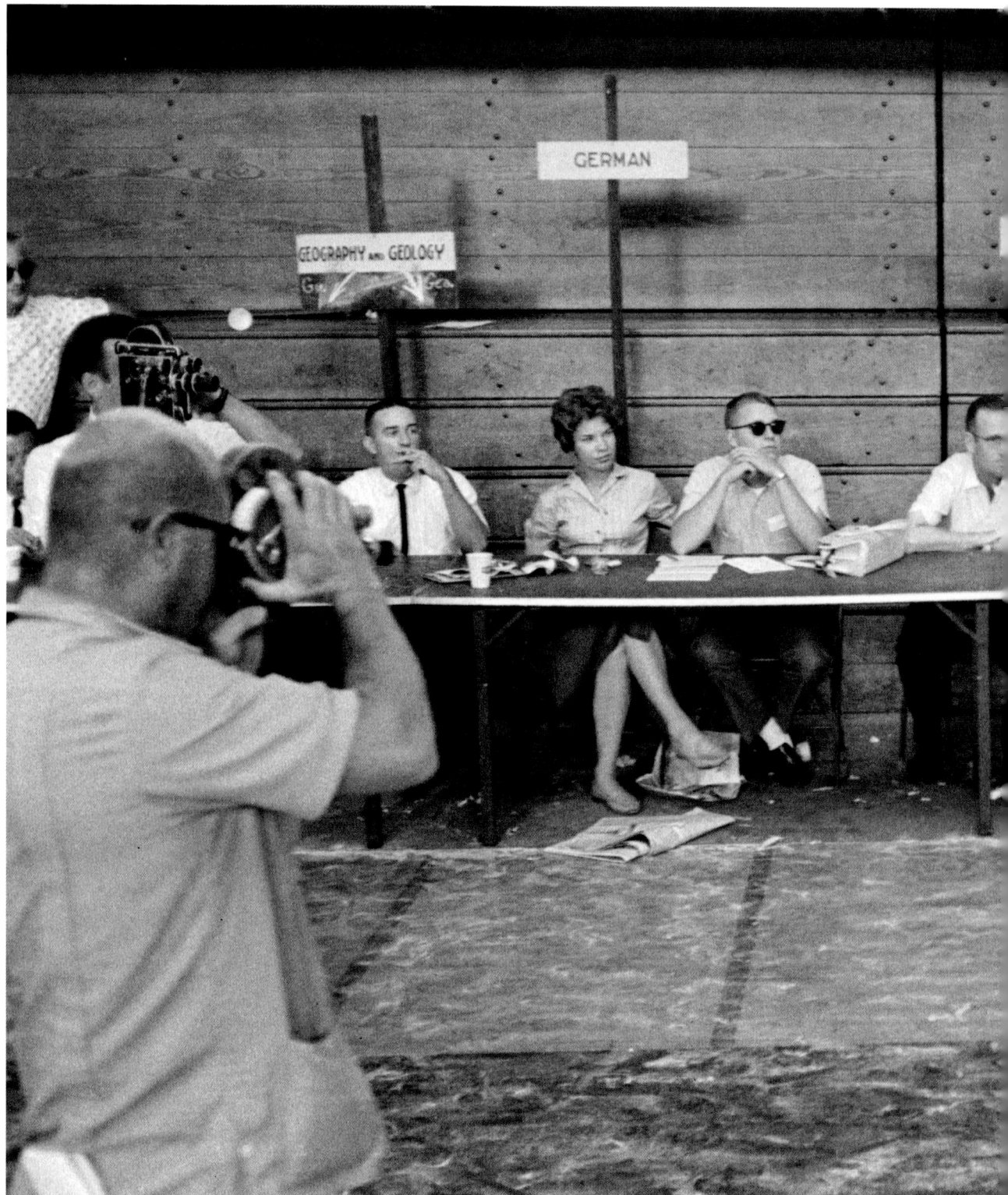

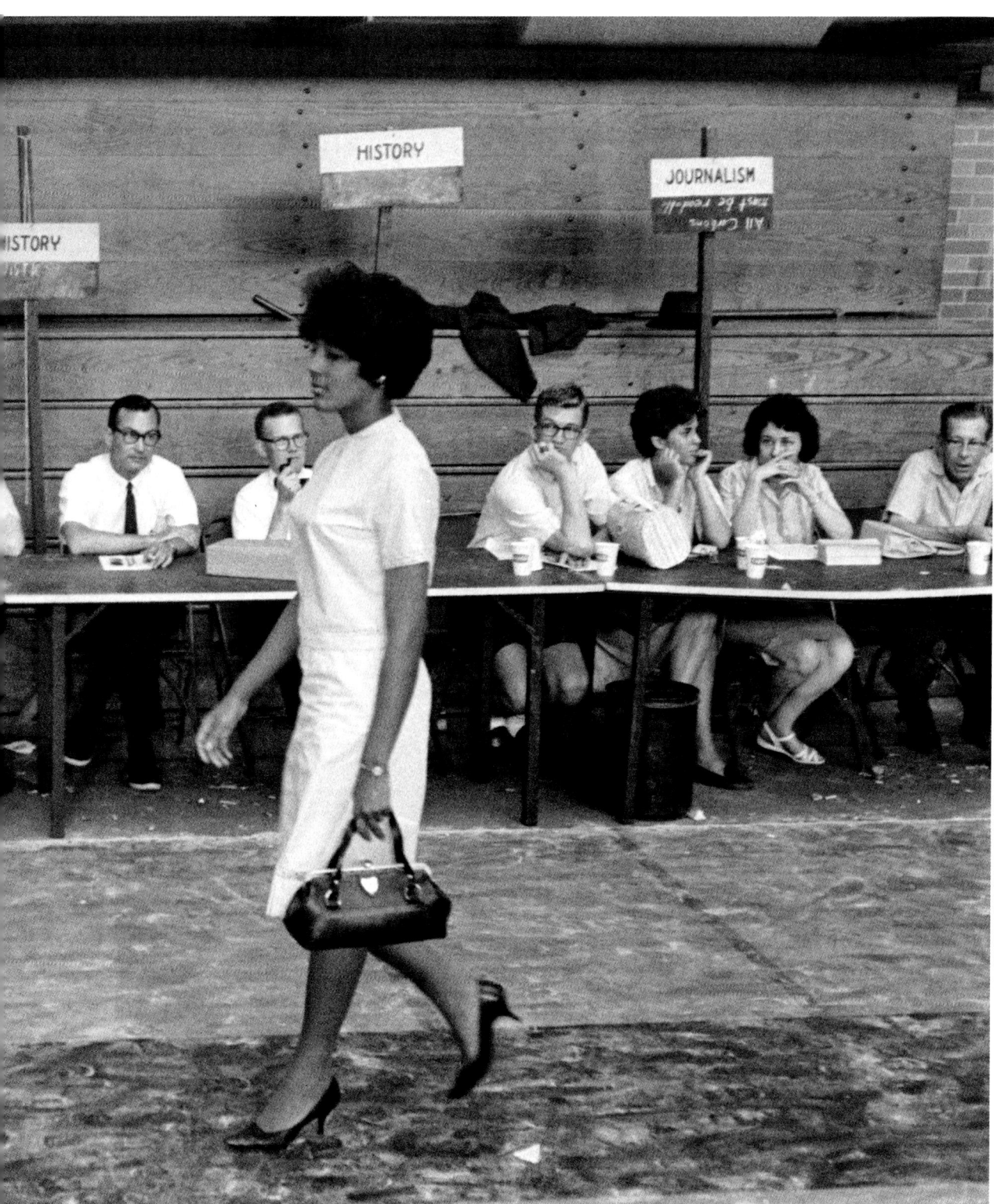

YOUTH LEADERSHIP MEETING
SHAW UNIVERSITY

RALEIGH, N. C. – APRIL 15-17, 1960

W H Y   THIS   MEETING?

Recent lunchcounter Sit-ins and other nonviolent protests by students of the South are tremendously significant developments in the drive for Freedom and Human Dignity in America.

The courageous, dedicated and thoughtful leadership manifested by hundreds of Negro students on college campuses, in large cities and small towns, and the over-whelming support by thousands of others, present new challenges for the future. This great potential for social change now calls for evaluation in terms of where do we go from here. The Easter week-end conference is convened to help find the answers. Together, we   chart new goals and achieve a mo   unified sense of direction for training and a ion in Nonviolent Resistance.

W H O   WILL   ATTEND?

Representation is invited from all areas of recent protest. However, to be effective, a leadership conference should not be too large. For this reason, each community is being asked to send a specified number of youth leaders. Adult Freedom Fighters will be present for counsel and guidance, but the meeting will be youth centered.

S C H E D U L E:

The opening session will be Friday, April 15 at 7:30 o'clock. Saturday will be devoted to workshops, buzz-sessions and committee work. There will be a public meet-ing Saturday night, and the conference will close at lunchtime Sunday.

E X P E N S E S :

We believe that your community will want to help share your travel expenses; and the Southern Christian Leadership Conference hopes that housing and meals will be underwritten. The total cost for six (6) meals and housing for two (2) nights will be $6.30 per person.

FOR FURTHER INFORMATION, Contact the Southern Christian Leadership Conference, 208 Auburn Avenue, N. E., Atlanta, Ga..

Dr. Martin L. King, Jr.
President

Ella J. Baker
Executive Director

THE TUMULTUOUS DAYS OF SNCC

BEN ST. ANGELO

Students formed the Student Nonviolent Coordinating Committee from their conviction that lasting change required aggressive action.

In the spring of 1960, Dr. Martin Luther King Jr. and Ella Baker of the Southern Christian Leadership Conference (SCLC) organized a youth leadership meeting at Shaw University in North Carolina. King and Baker recognized that nonviolent tactics like the lunch counter sit-ins prepared college students to win the battle for civil rights. They hoped to create a youth wing of the SCLC committed to nonviolent resistance.

However, shortly after the meeting convened, the students decided that the SCLC's values did not fully align with how they saw their role in the Civil Rights Movement. Rather than join the SCLC, the young leaders formed a new organization, the Student Nonviolent Coordinating Committee (SNCC), to better reflect their conviction that lasting change required aggressive action.

Several students who later rose to prominence in the Civil Rights Movement, including John Lewis, Diane Nash, Chuck McDew, and Julian Bond, attended the Shaw meeting. They listened to Dr. King preach that nonviolence was the only acceptable way to combat American racism, but many students at Shaw disagreed.

When student activists sat down to order food in a "whites only" space, organized white counter-protestors responded with verbal and physical abuse.

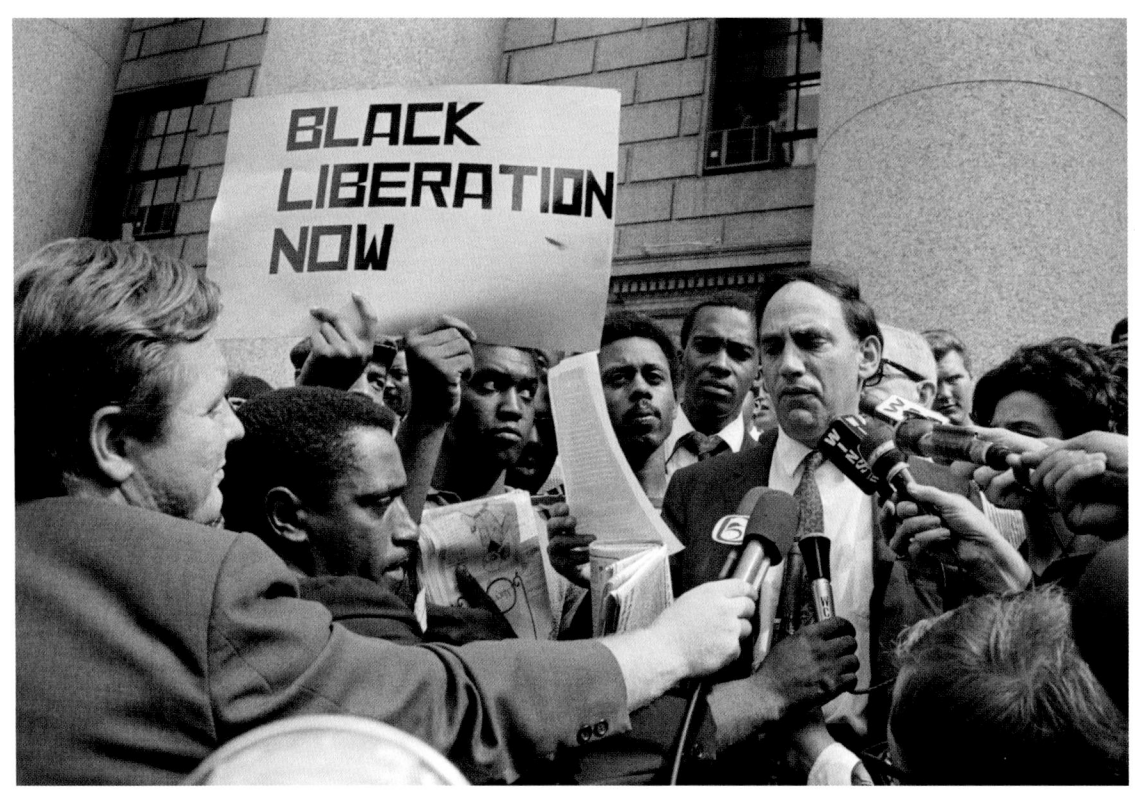

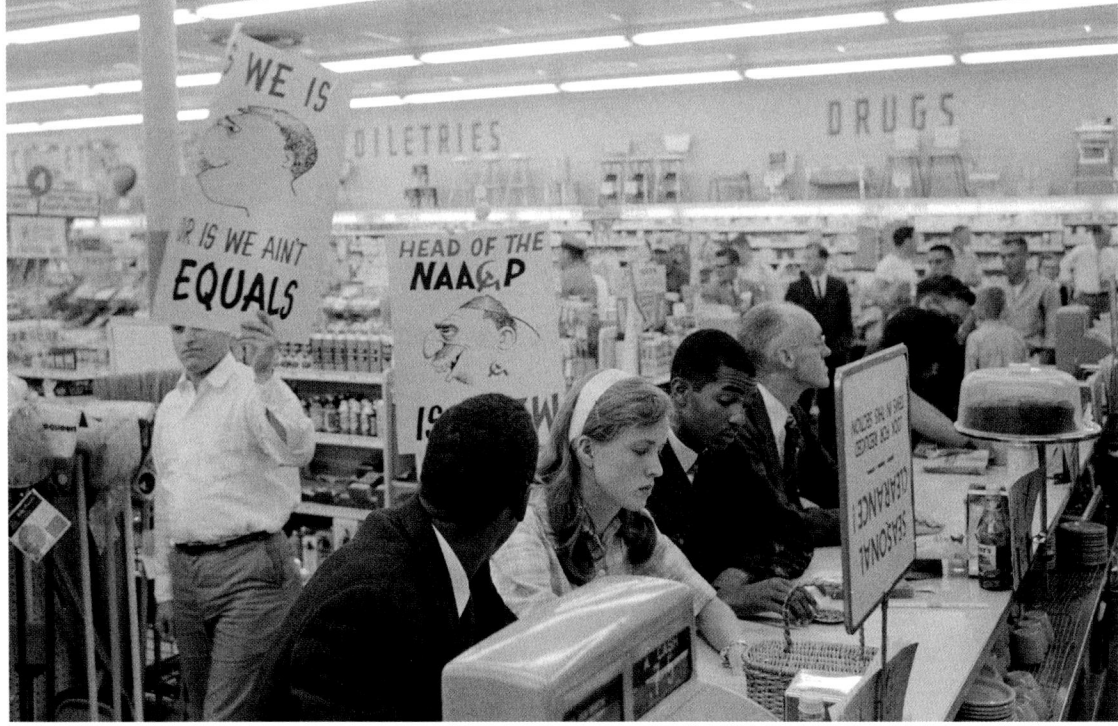

As desegregation gained momentum as a political cause, white supremacists attacked its proponents by appealing to antisemitism and anti-communism because Jews and communists worked with Black Americans to advance civil rights. The men harassing the customers in the photo (opposite, bottom) designed the caricatures on the posters to dehumanize protestors. In an environment like this, many students found nonviolence insufficient.

McDew explained SNCC's desire to retain self-defense as an option. He recalled an event in which Gandhi stopped trains by having protestors lay on the tracks. Gandhi gambled that a train engineer's respect for humanity would prevent them from running over protestors. On June 4, 2011, McDew told a Library of Congress interviewer he believed that if you applied that same tactic in the United States, "a train would run you over and back up to make certain you're dead."

While the young protestors chose to remain outside SCLC, they maintained a close partnership. Shortly after the Shaw meeting, SNCC affirmed their collaborative relationship with the SCLC by agreeing to coordinate "in all possible and appropriate ways." They also established SNCC's headquarters in the SCLC's Atlanta offices and listed King as an advisor.

While SNCC understood that legitimacy came through aligning with the SCLC, the group also realized that there was an ideological divide between themselves and established freedom fighters like King. Nevertheless, as SNCC matured, so too did its strategy. Throughout the early 1960s, its members wrestled with the merits of nonviolence versus armed self-defense.

The photo above captures Selma police dragging SNCC member Willie Lawrence McRae to jail for blocking the sidewalk. Unjust and constant police harassment targeting African Americans was a primary reason why many SNCC members began to turn away from nonviolence.

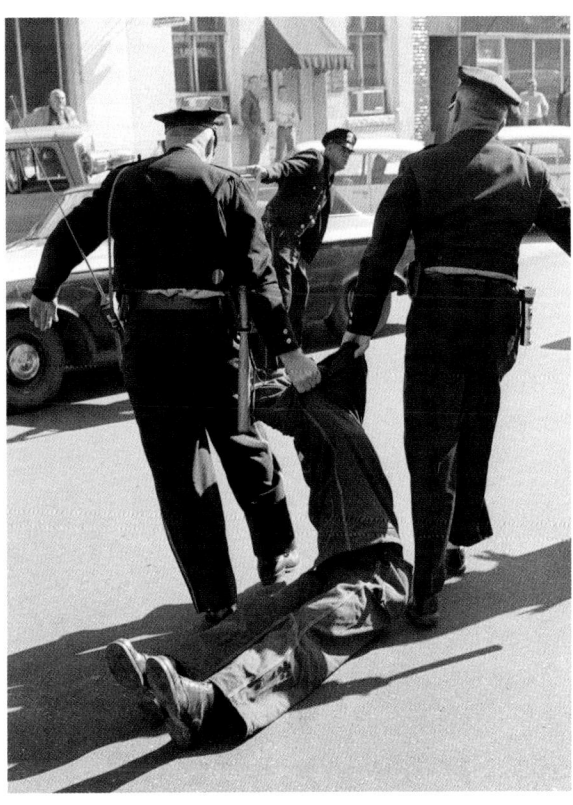

PREVIOUS SPREAD, LEFT: Flyer for a youth leadership meeting held at Shaw University organized by Martin Luther King Jr and Ella Baker of SCLC.

OPPOSITE, TOP: William Kunstler, attorney for Black Power activist H. Rap Brown (Jamil Al-Amin), gives a press conference following Brown's release from jail.

OPPOSITE, BOTTOM: 1960 sit-in at Arlington, Virginia, picketed by the American Nazi Party.

ABOVE: Willie Lawrence McRae, a member of the SNCC Atlanta branch, dragged by two police officers.

During John Lewis's term as chairman from 1963 to 1966, the organization favored provocative—yet nonviolent—direct action. When the Supreme Court outlawed segregated interstate busing in December 1960, SNCC joined the Congress of Racial Equality on a series of "Freedom Rides" throughout 1961 to test the decision.

In 1964, SNCC took part in "Freedom Summer," a multi-organizational effort to expand voting and civil rights in Mississippi. In 1965, Lewis led marchers across the Edmund Pettis Bridge during the famous Selma to Montgomery march to protest the police murder of activist Jimmie Lee Jackson.

White supremacists responded with violence. They firebombed a bus carrying Freedom Riders in Anniston, Alabama, murdered Freedom Summer workers, and assaulted marchers—fracturing Lewis's skull. It became clear that recalcitrant whites intended to do everything they could to keep Black citizens subjugated. This helped radicalize SNCC's membership and solidified their belief that African Americans needed political power to achieve self-determination.

In 1965, SNCC launched voter registration and political education projects in places like Lowndes County, Alabama. Lowndes was such a notoriously violent place for African Americans that SNCC leaders like Stokely Carmichael believed they would have free rein to experiment with more radical methods. As in much of the rural South, many Blacks there already carried guns. When SNCC arrived, the county became a test case for the efficacy of armed self-defense. Harassment continued, but SNCC activists working alongside local Black citizens achieved their goals with little physical harm.

When they finished their work, Lowndes County had a slew of new Black voters, candidates, and an independent political party (the Lowndes County Freedom Party). The picture on pages 210–11 shows the fruits of their labor—Black hands casting a vote to place a Black candidate on the ballot. Before SNCC's involvement, it would have been an audacious and suicidal act in the county known as Bloody Lowndes.

Shortly after the departure from Lowndes County, SNCC fell into a sharp decline. Their successes emboldened members who believed in militant principles tied to the emerging Black Power movement of the late 1960s. In 1966, many SNCC members came to doubt that white liberals could be counted on to fight for Black liberation, and after a close vote, whites were expelled from the organization.

SNCC at first had been known for prolonged and honest deliberation, often holding multiday meetings until they reached consensus on movement strategies. But after Lowndes, majority rule became the norm, and votes often split narrowly, with sometimes a single vote deciding major issues.

Divides among SNCC's leadership reflected those among the rank and file. Exhausted from years of organizing, many members became radical or disenchanted. By 1973, SNCC had dissolved as an organization.

Still, SNCC's brief time at the forefront of the Civil Rights Movement remains a success. Its founders' initial goal was to create a body meant to ease student involvement in the broad fight for justice. From lunch counter sit-ins to voter registration, SNCC's members met those challenges and consistently inspired positive social change.

RIGHT: Packages of napkins have been placed on nearby stools to discourage other protesters from joining the lunch-counter sit-in.

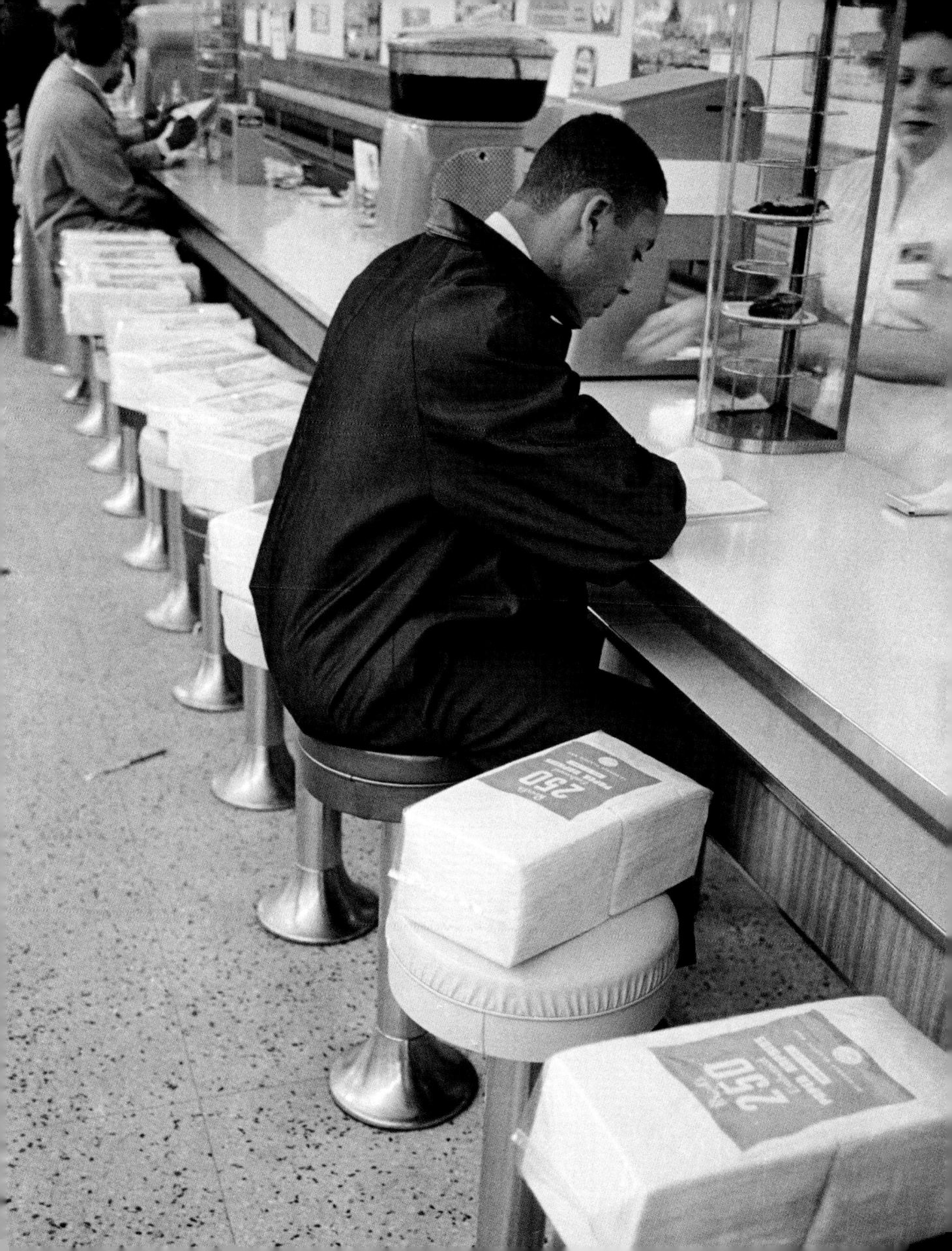

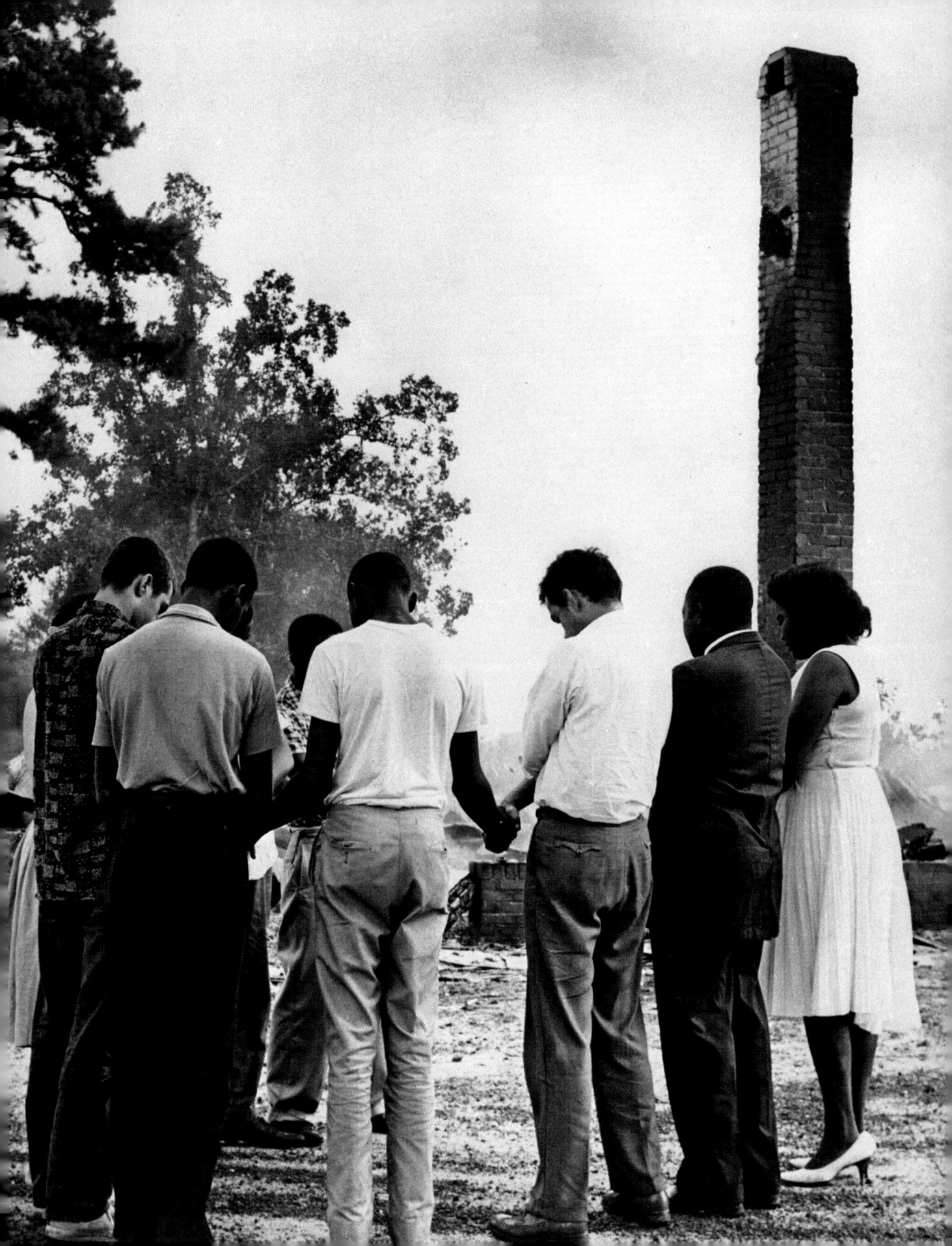

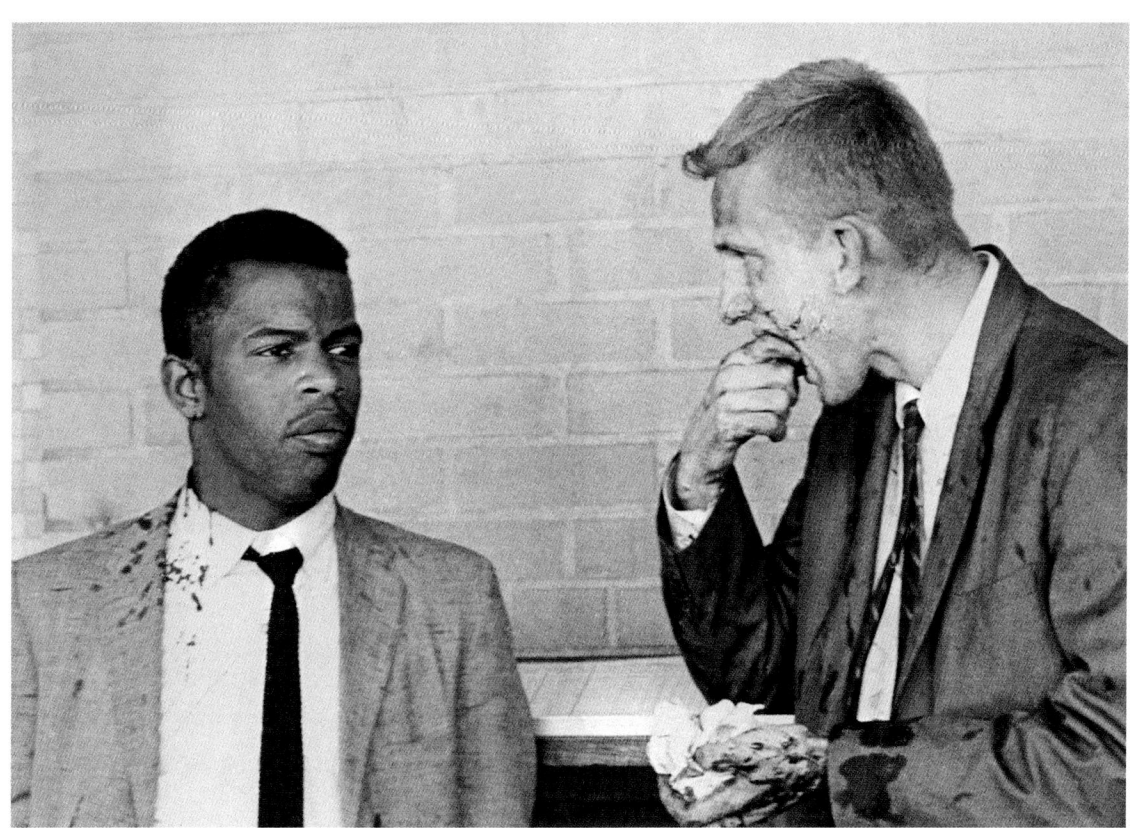

LEFT: SNCC members gather in a prayer circle near ruins of the Mount Mary Church at the Chickasawhatchee community near Dawson, Georgia.

ABOVE: John Lewis stands alongside Freedom Rider James Zwerg after being attacked by segregationists in Montgomery, Alabama, on May 20, 1961.

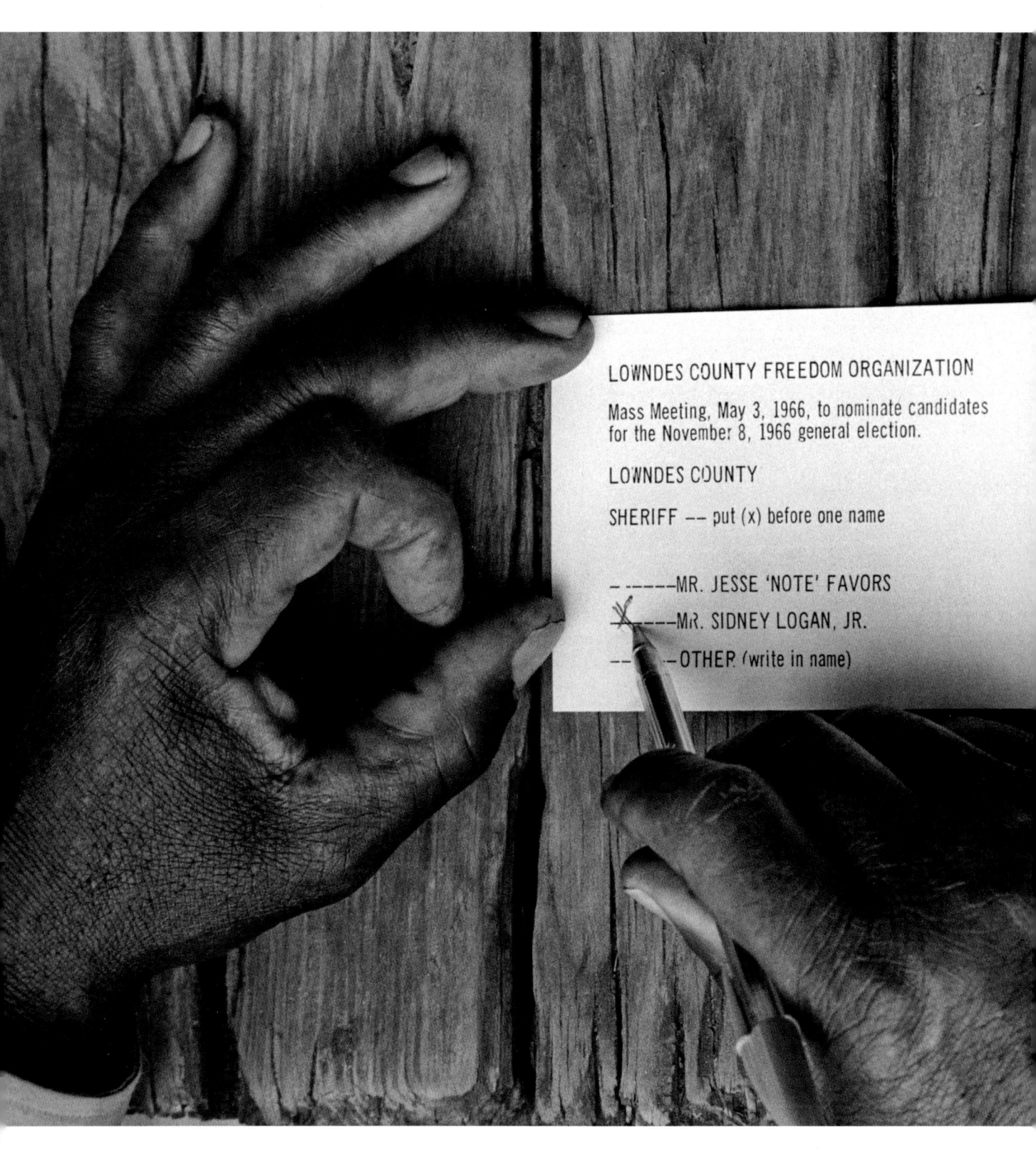

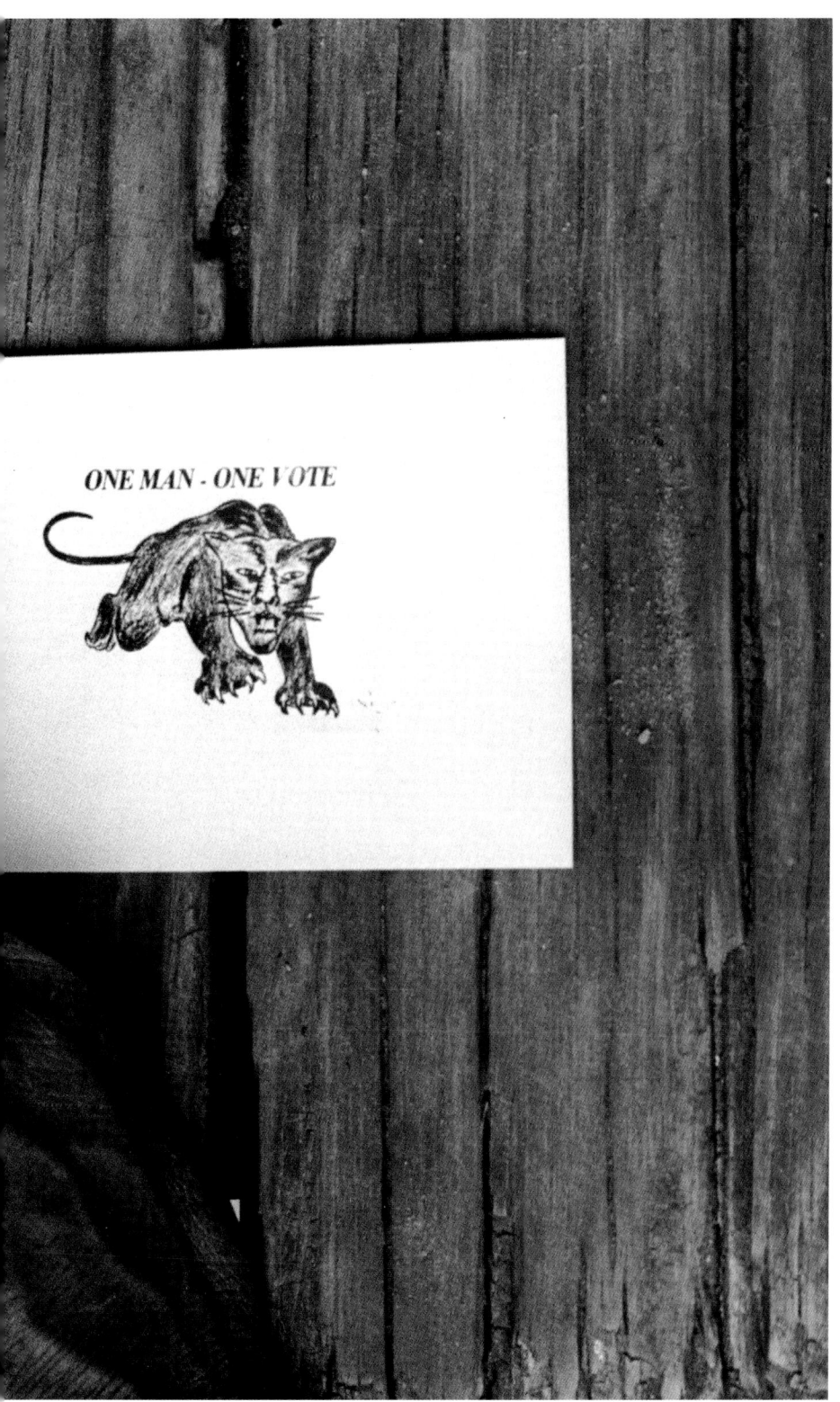

LEFT: A newly registered voter fills out a Black Panther Party sample ballot.

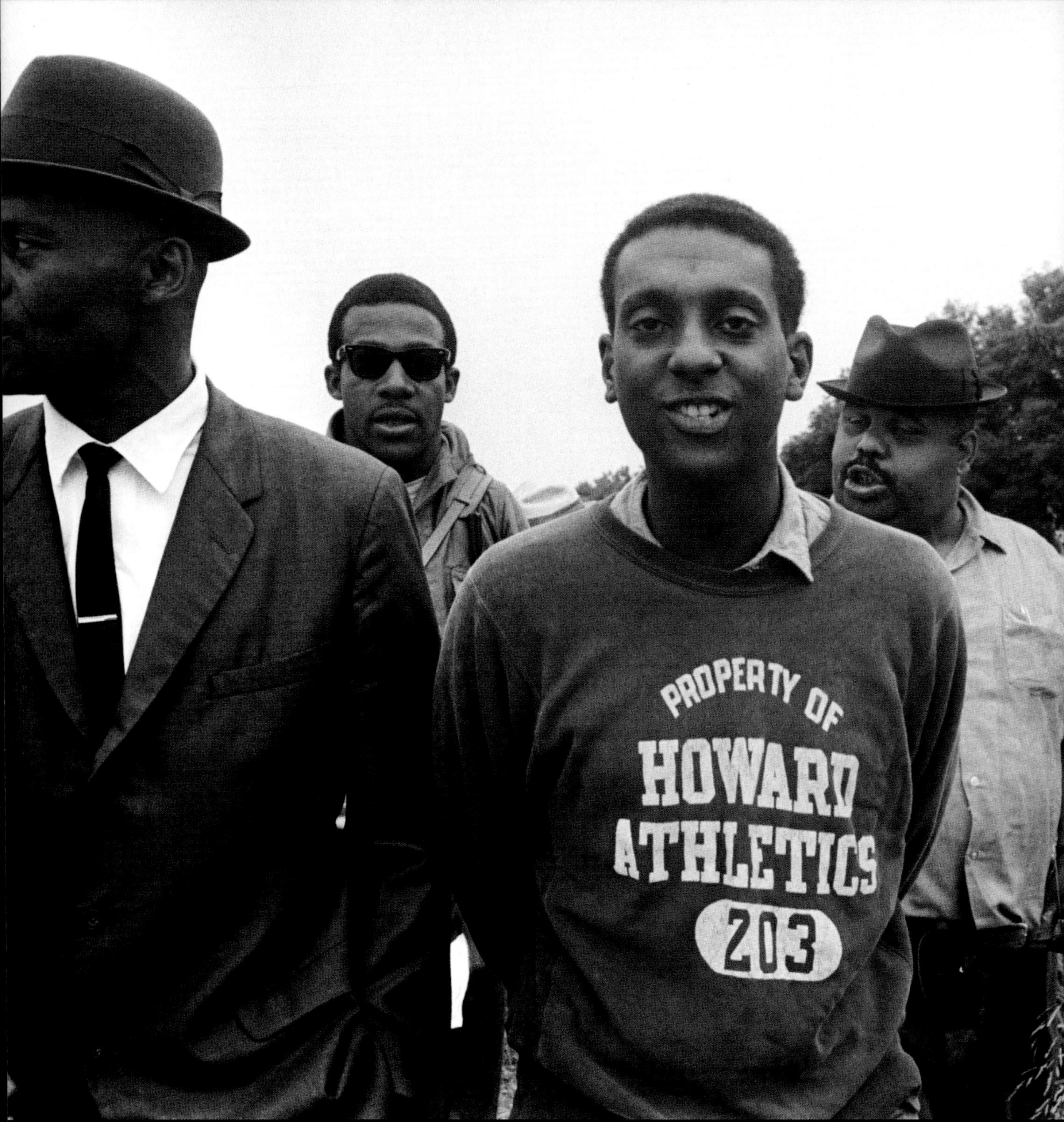
PROPERTY OF
HOWARD
ATHLETICS
203

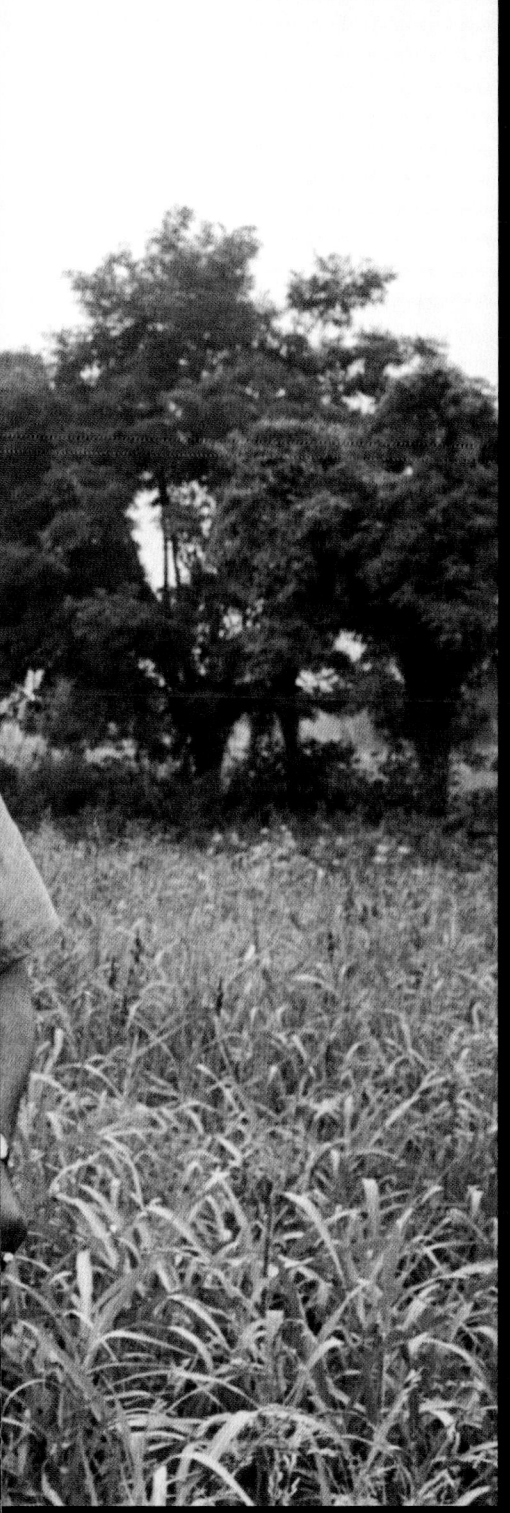

STUDENT ACTIVISM AND THE RISE OF BLACK STUDIES

KIMBERLY F. MONROE

The struggle of university students to build Black Studies on campus, in their communities, and throughout the nation.

From ship revolts to maroon communities, from abolition to civil rights, from Black Power to Black Lives Matter, through the intellectual labor of Anna Julia Cooper, Carter G. Woodson, and W. E. B. Du Bois, the major goal of Black Studies has been strategic action to maintain the dignity and humanity of Black people.

In his conception of the Black radical tradition in his influential 1983 book, *Black Marxism*, Cedric Robinson described it as an effort to resist structures rooted in slavery, imperialism, and capitalism. Further, he argued that the Black radical tradition is built on a foundation of cultural traditions, beliefs, and values.

PREVIOUS SPREAD: Stokely Carmichael (also known as Kwame Ture), SNCC chairman, at the 1966 March Against Fear in Sardis, Mississippi.

RIGHT: Students and faculty at present-day San Francisco State College discuss student demands for Black Studies (November 18, 1968).

BELOW: Howard University student takeover of the administration building during the 1968 protest.

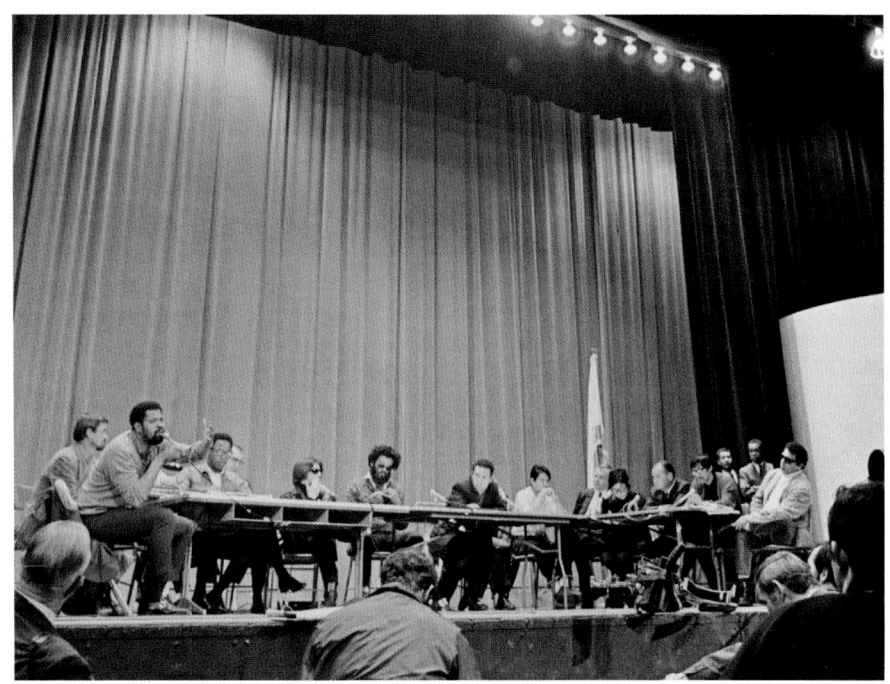

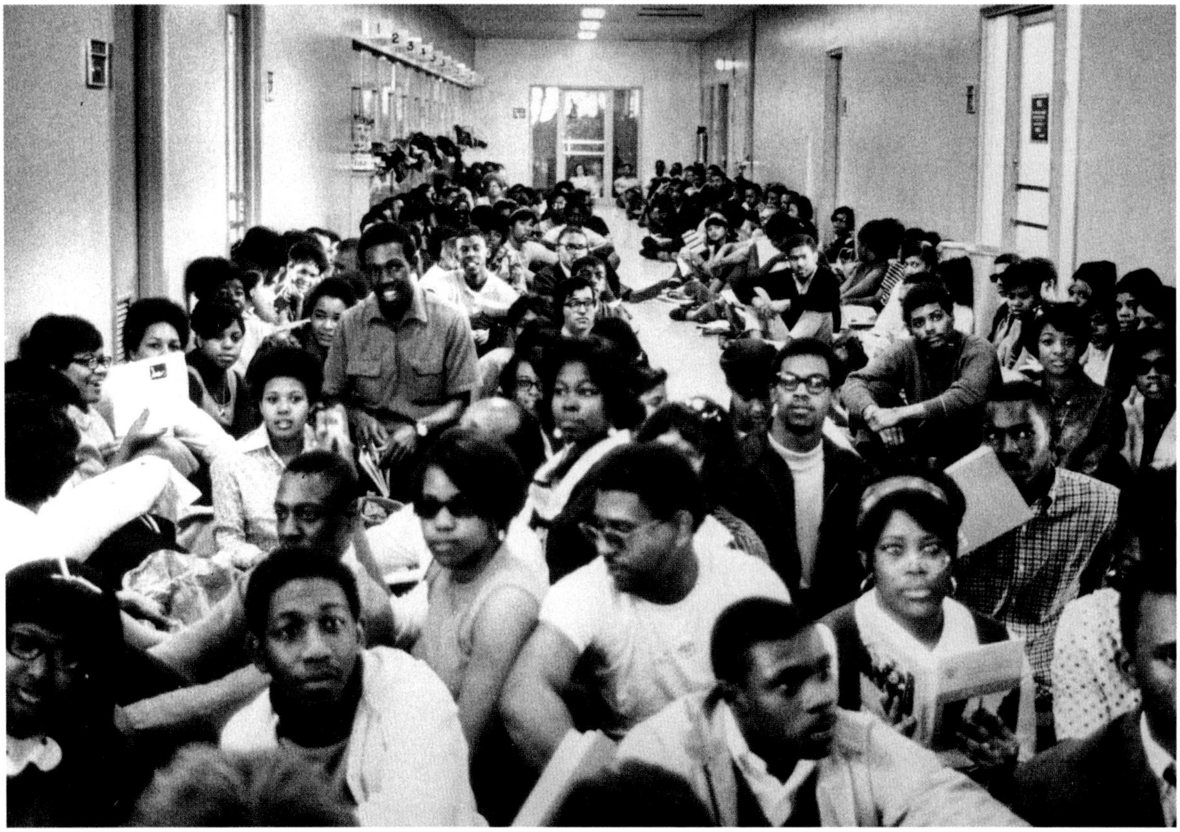

Focused on self-determination, Black radicalism, and Black pride, university students from the 1960s demanded that administrators address the lack of Black culture on campus and within the curriculum. In an interview with A. B. Spellman in March 1964, civil rights activist Malcolm X said he believed that Black students were the ones to bring radical change to their universities and the United States. His call to college students was "to launch their own independent studies of the race problem" so they could devise an "action program geared to their thinking." Malcolm X viewed young people as a vanguard of revolutionary force.

Student organizations often invited Malcolm X to speak on campus. In 1962, at Michigan State University, Ayo Azikiwe, leader of the African Student Association and son of Nigerian President Nnamdi Azikiwe, invited Malcolm to speak. One of Malcolm's most famous campus visits was in 1961 at Howard University, where he debated civil rights activist Bayard Rustin. Kwame Ture, a Howard student then known as Stokely Carmichael, sat in the front row.

Ture and the student body were left amazed after the debate between Malcolm and Rustin. Ture, who became chairman of the Student Nonviolent Coordinating Committee (SNCC) in 1966, is seen in the opening photo participating in the Mississippi Freedom March, during which he called for the pursuit of "Black power."

Ture's exposure to Black civil rights leaders, including Malcolm X and many others during his time as a student, provided a foundation to his radical activism, and he became the symbol of Black student activism. The work and tragic murders of civil rights leaders created a mass eruption of Black consciousness at colleges and universities across the country.

Student activists influenced three sites: the local campus, elite institutions, and the institutions that set policy for colleges and universities. In 1968, after a diverse, student-led protest, San Francisco State College (SFSC), now San Francisco State University, founded the first Black Studies Department, now known as the Africana Studies Department.

In the photo (opposite, top) from November 18, 1968, at SFSC, students and faculty are seen during a public convocation discussing student demands. These included separate facilities on campus, a Black Studies curriculum, and more Black students, faculty, coaches, athletes, and administrators. They were engaged in both study and praxis.

Students and alumni from various Historically Black Colleges and Universities (HBCUs) played a major role in the Civil Rights Movement. For instance, SNCC was founded in 1960 after Ella Baker, Shaw University alumna, and other Black students in North Carolina organized sit-ins challenging segregation in public spaces. Sisters Joyce and Dorie Ladner, while still Tougaloo College students, were organizers in SNCC and worked alongside civil rights activist Medgar Evers. These are just a couple of examples of student activists working to address issues on campus, in their communities, and throughout the nation.

Black students across the United States protested by occupying buildings, listing demands, and launching rallies to ensure that higher education became more relevant to their history, culture, and needs. HBCUs like Howard also addressed the needs and aspirations of Black college students in their national-level fight against predominantly white university administrations that did not include Black Studies in their curricula.

In 1968, Howard students occupied the Administration Building from March 19 to 23 (photo opposite, bottom). Students insisted on changes in the student disciplinary policy and that courses be offered in African American Studies as two conditions for vacating the building. One thousand students held a rally in front of Douglass Hall, again pushing for a Black Studies curriculum. The facial expressions of students showed that they were unified and unruffled. Despite missing class, students still found time to study.

As several Africana Studies programs developed after the 2020 protests against the murders of George Floyd, Ahmaud Arbery, Breonna Taylor, and others, it is important to understand the history of Black Studies—born of student and faculty activism. Ture, Black Panther Party founder Huey P. Newton, and others exemplify Black Studies' contributions to the freedom struggle inside and outside of the university. Today, that mission is carried on by a new generation.

Students across the United States continue to challenge their administrations and policies. Whether graduate students at Columbia University demanding stipend increases, Northwestern University students attempting to abolish campus police, or Howard students sleeping in tents to address housing issues, the struggle continues.

Black Studies goes beyond the walls of the university. Black Studies is a livelihood that is grounded in how we connect to our communities and how we struggle collectively toward liberation.

RIGHT: Police descend upon student protesters at the City College of New York (May 8, 1969).

FOLLOWING SPREAD: Howard University closed during student protest at the administration building (March 20, 1968).

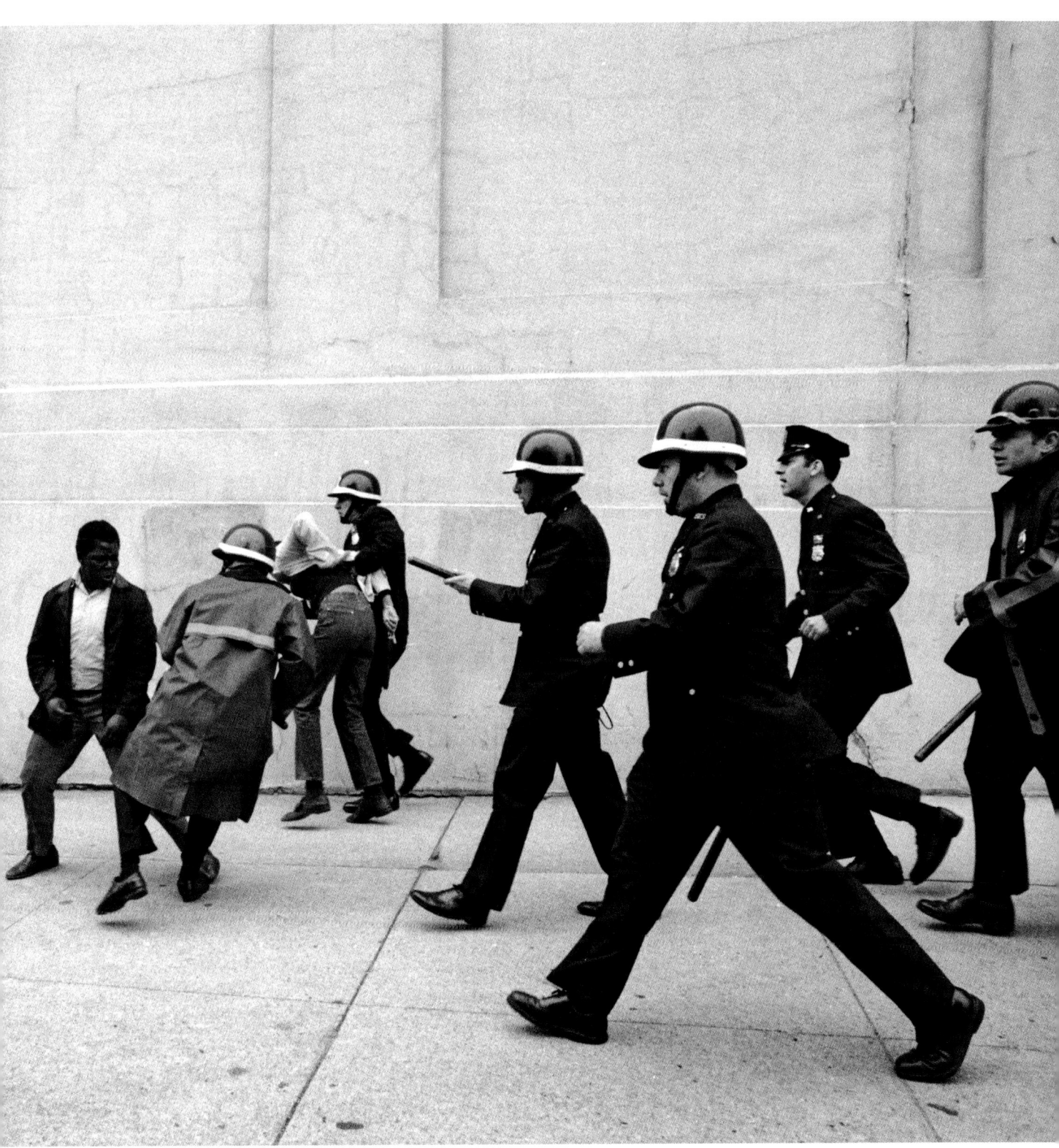

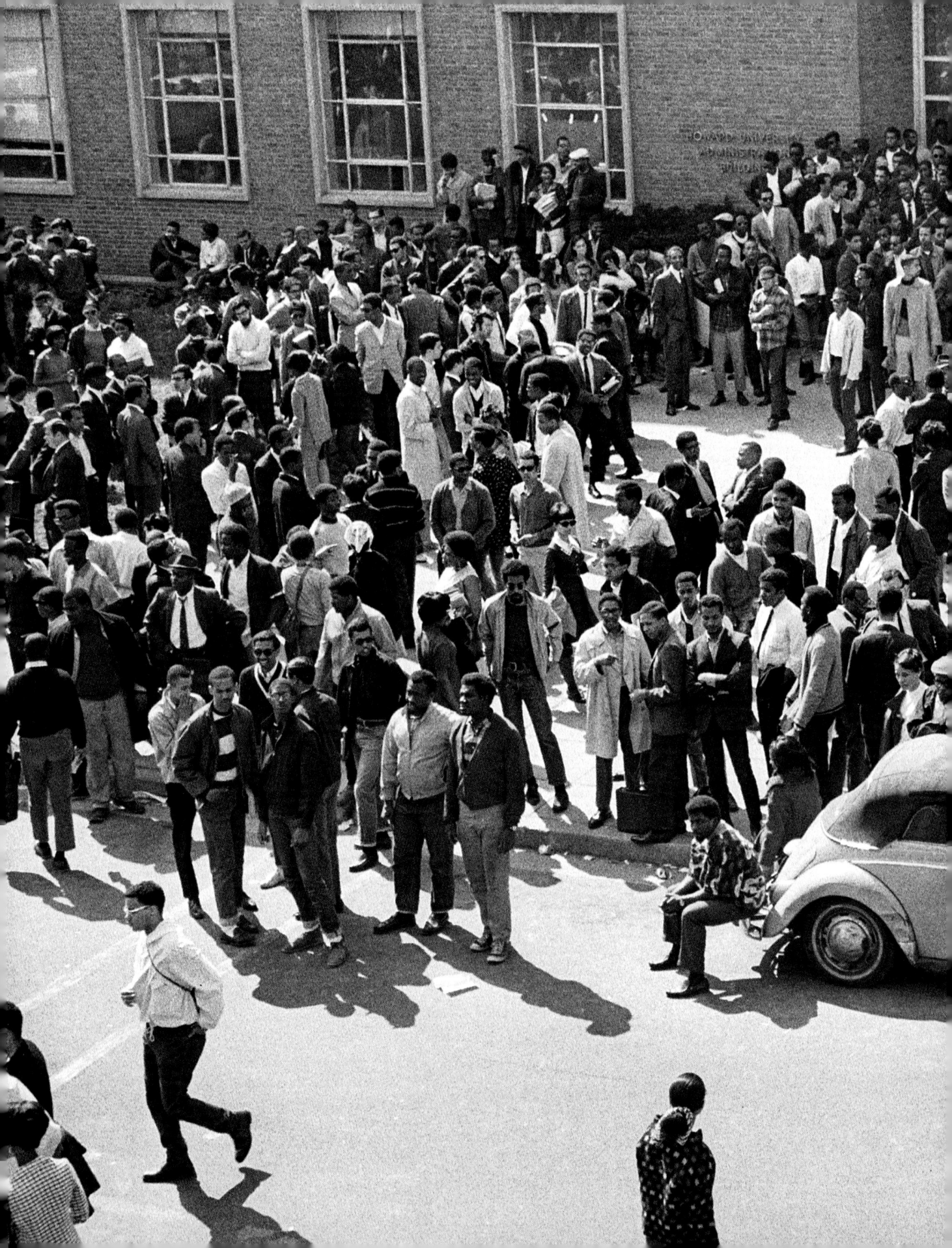

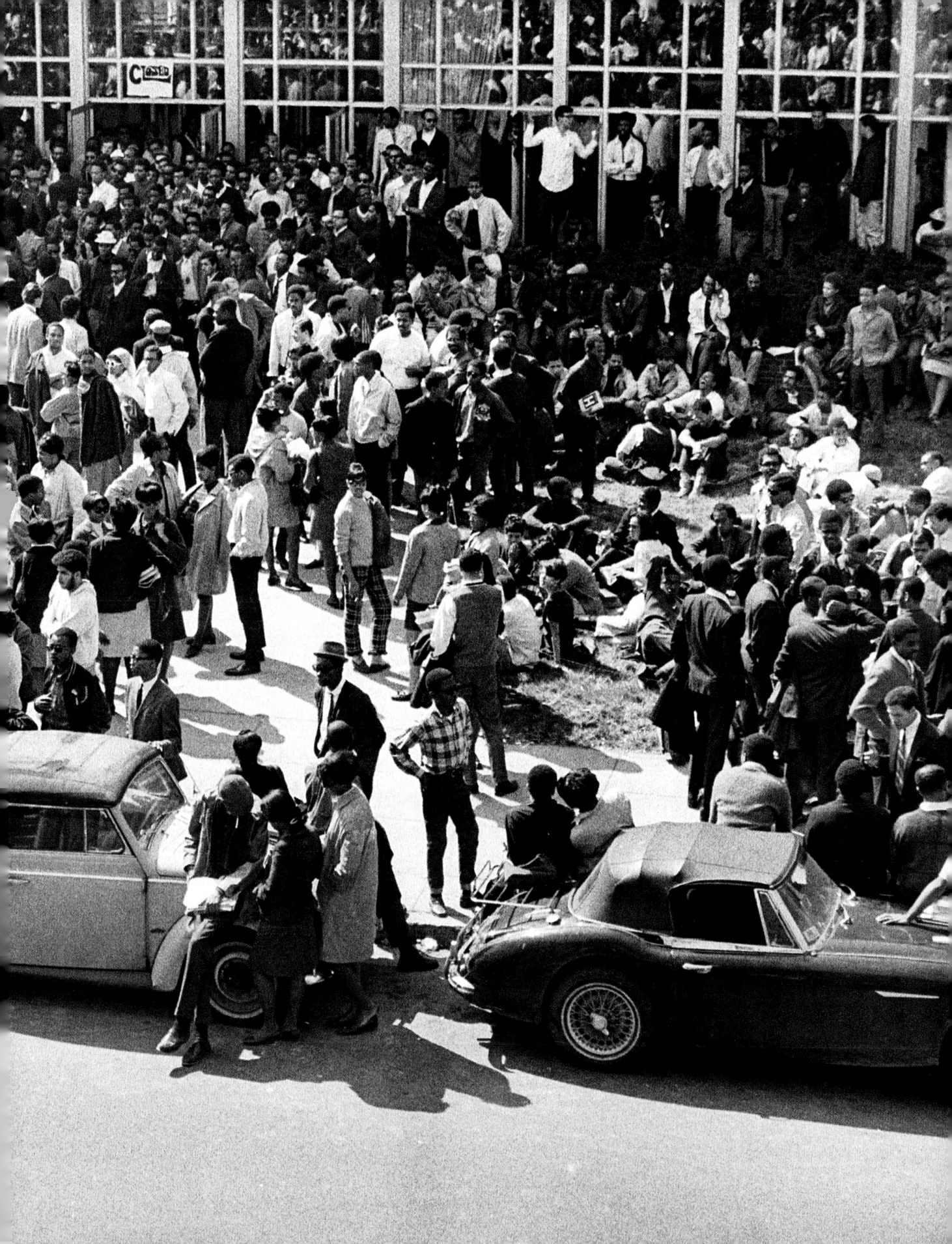

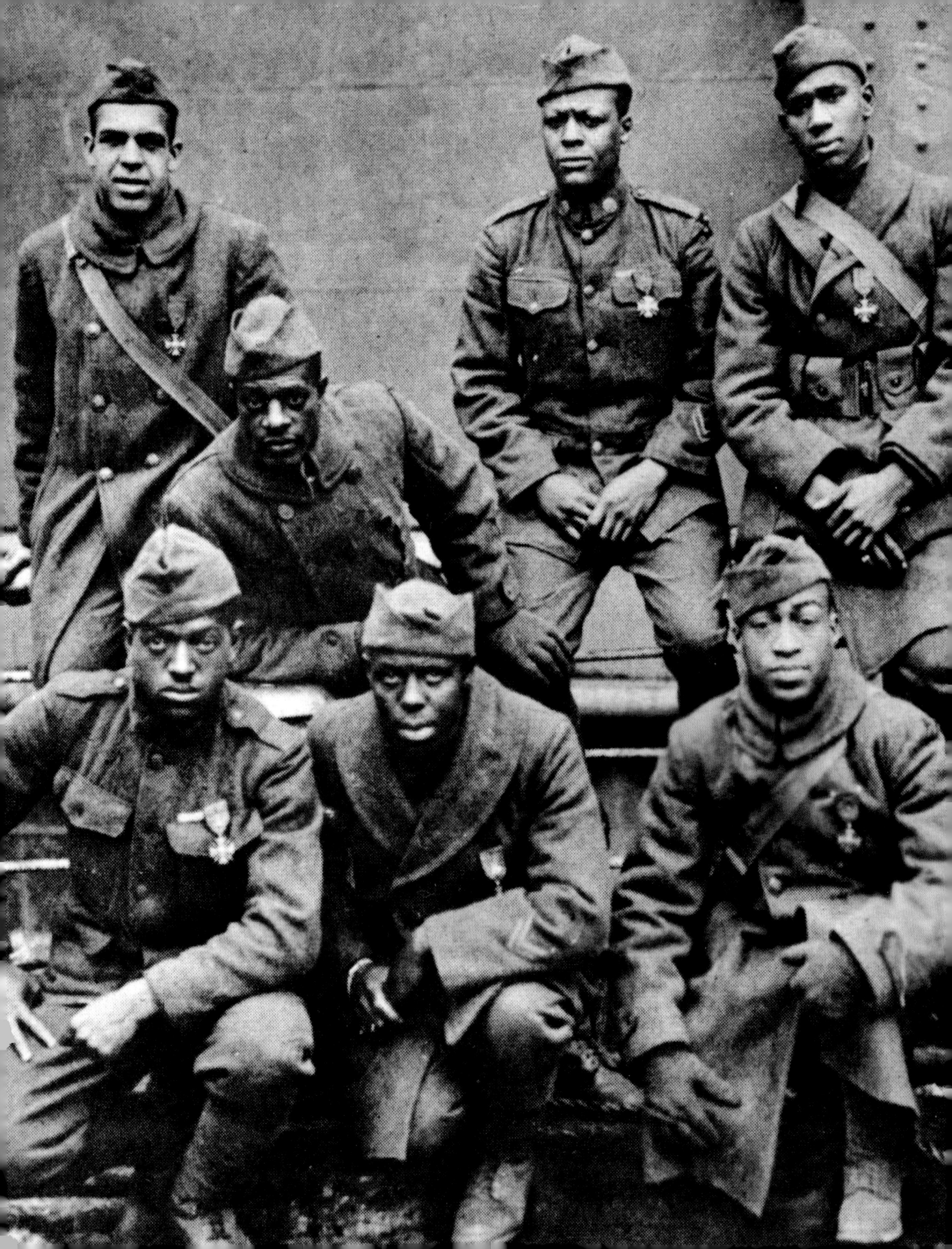

VI.
BLACK AMERICA IN WARTIME

BLACK AMERICANS HAVE HAD CHALLENGING RELATIONSHIPS WITH THE UNITED STATES DURING WARTIME. While African-descended peoples have fought in every American war as far back as the American Revolution, there has often been a disconnect between the "blood debt" earned by these contributions and the failed recognition of their sacrifices by a larger American public. The culmination of this irony even found a name in the "Double V Campaign" of World War II, where Black Americans returning from war mobilized against white supremacist violence across the nation in an effort to fight for both democracy abroad and equal rights at home.

These essays consider moments of war that shone spotlights on international relations, and, just as frequently, exposed domestic tensions and anxieties.

OPPOSITE: African American soldiers, wearing the *Croix de Guerre* (War Cross), return from World War I in Europe.

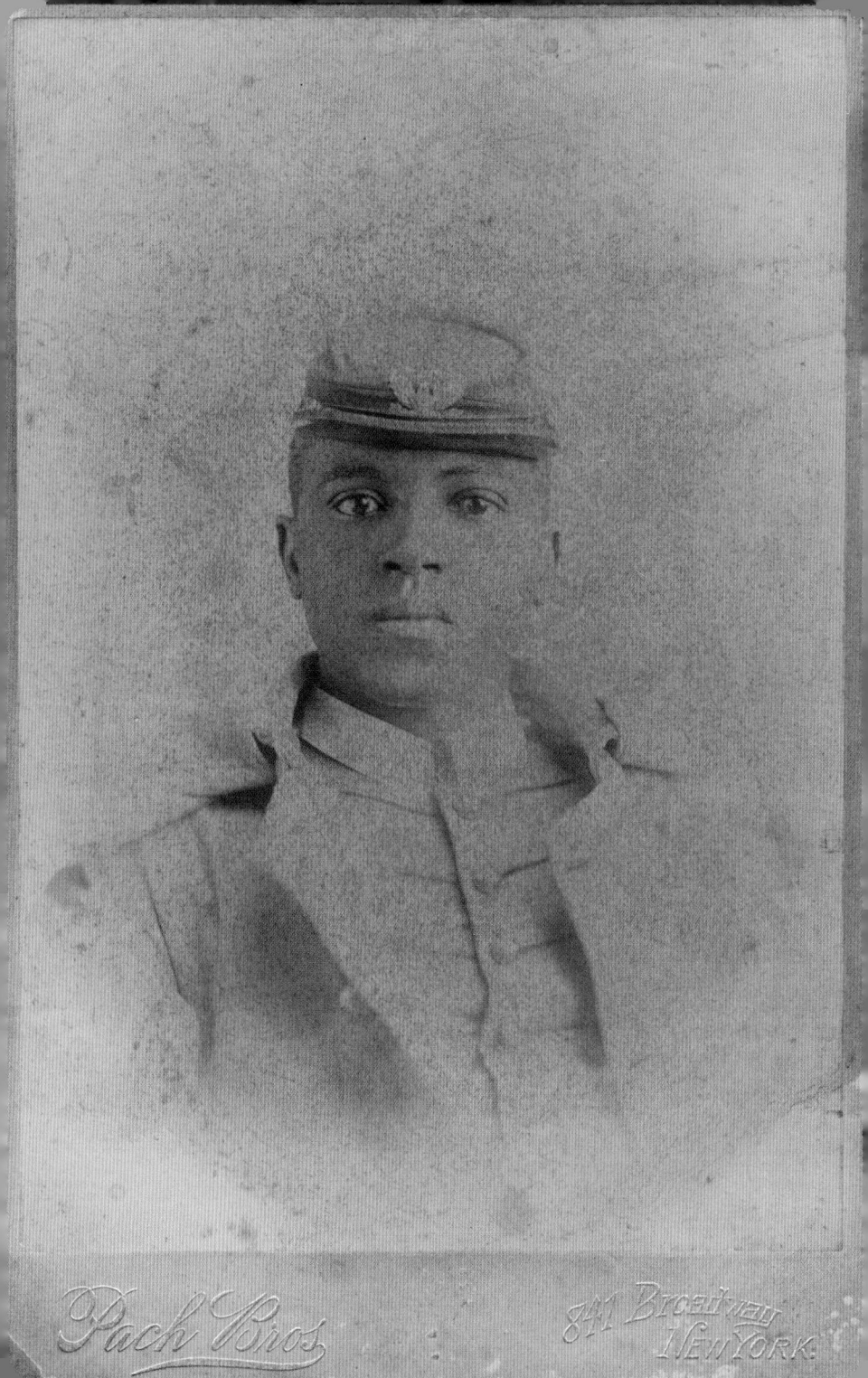

CHARLES YOUNG: THE LIFE OF A SOLDIER

PAUL L. MCALLISTER

*A remarkable career of selfless service to country
and struggle for racial equality.*

I n June 1917, as it prepared to fight in World War I, the U.S. Army forcibly retired Charles Young, one of its most senior and accomplished officers. Why? It did not want any Black officer in command of white soldiers, and the outbreak of war combined with Young's rank and experience would have made this inevitable.

A notable Black leader during the late nineteenth and early twentieth centuries, Young is perhaps the most important figure in African American military history. Born enslaved, he lived through the Civil War, the promise and eventual failure of Reconstruction, and the rise of Jim Crow. Despite tremendous obstacles, he eventually rose to the rank of colonel in the U.S. Army and forged what remains one of the most remarkable military careers of the era.

Young was born in Kentucky in 1864. His father was a Civil War veteran who had escaped slavery to serve with the U.S. Colored Troops. He instilled in his son a strong racial pride and a desire to serve. His mother was literate and imbued him with a love of learning.

Their influence pushed Young to excel in high school, particularly in the study of music and foreign languages, and test for entrance into the U.S. Military Academy at West Point. He scored perfectly on the written exam and second overall. After the first-place candidate withdrew, twenty-year-old Charles Young was nominated and accepted into the academy.

In this photograph, we can see Young as a cadet at West Point. He entered the academy in 1884, only the ninth African American ever admitted up to then. He was exceptional among his peers in several respects— he had no powerful patron pushing for his admission, and he had neither previous college experience nor an upper-class background.

Thus, his acceptance, while a fantastic accomplishment, also brought further challenges. While he excelled in the humanities, Young struggled in mathematics and, as a result, had to repeat his first year. He also suffered through harsh racial abuse and social ostracization. Steadfast and resilient, he gained the respect of some of his white peers over time, and the abuse diminished. However, it never desisted, and he constantly faced racism throughout his schooling and career.

Despite these difficulties, Young found military life very fulfilling. He graduated from West Point in 1889 and was assigned to the Ninth Cavalry, one of the four Black regiments in the U.S. Army more commonly known as the Buffalo Soldiers. He served with the unit on several missions in the western United States and during the Philippine-American War. In 1894, he went on detached service to Wilberforce University to teach military science, and he stayed as a professor (until 1898).

In 1903, Young became the first Black National Park superintendent. He was sent to Haiti in 1904 and became one of the first military officers in the United States to be a military attaché. He also served as military attaché to Liberia twice, first in 1912 and then in 1919. His final field assignment came in 1916 when he led the Tenth Cavalry in several actions in Mexico during the "punitive expedition" launched in a failed attempt to capture the Mexican revolutionary Pancho Villa.

Young served with a high degree of intelligence, skill, and vigor. He believed in military service and recognized its importance as a vehicle of uplift for African American men. His rank and status established Young as one of the foremost torchbearers of the African American demand for the rights of full citizens. W. E. B. Du Bois and the NAACP recognized his efforts with the 1916 Spingarn Medal.

Paradoxically, America's imperial ambitions marred his service. Many of his assignments, particularly those in Haiti, Liberia, and the Philippines, were directed at the suppression of Black and Indigenous populations.

Young's forced medical retirement sparked outrage in the Black community, and he undertook a highly publicized trip to protest the decision, riding his horse 497 miles from his home in Wilberforce, Ohio, to Washington, DC. His trip itinerary, shown in the photograph bottom left, demonstrates just how physically demanding his journey was. Eventually he was reinstated but not until five days before the armistice between the Allies and Germany, denying him the chance for wartime service and further promotion.

In this final image (bottom right), we see Young traveling to Liberia for his second stint as military attaché. It was his last assignment. While on a mission in Nigeria in 1921, Young fell ill and died in early 1922. His body was returned to the United States in 1923 and buried in Arlington National Cemetery. In 2013, his home in Wilberforce was designated as the Charles Young Buffalo Soldiers National Monument, a testament to his selfless service and struggle for racial equality.

PREVIOUS SPREAD, LEFT: Pach Brothers' cabinet card of Colonel Charles Young at West Point.

CLOCKWISE FROM TOP LEFT: Sergeant Henry Johnson receives the French *Croix de Guerre* for his bravery during World War I (February 12, 1919).

A soldier injured in World War I watches a parade in New York, 1919.

Colonel Charles Young aboard SS *Orduña*, en route to Liberia, on January 3, 1920.

Itinerary for Colonel Charles Young's trip from Wilberforce, Ohio, to Washington, DC, 1918

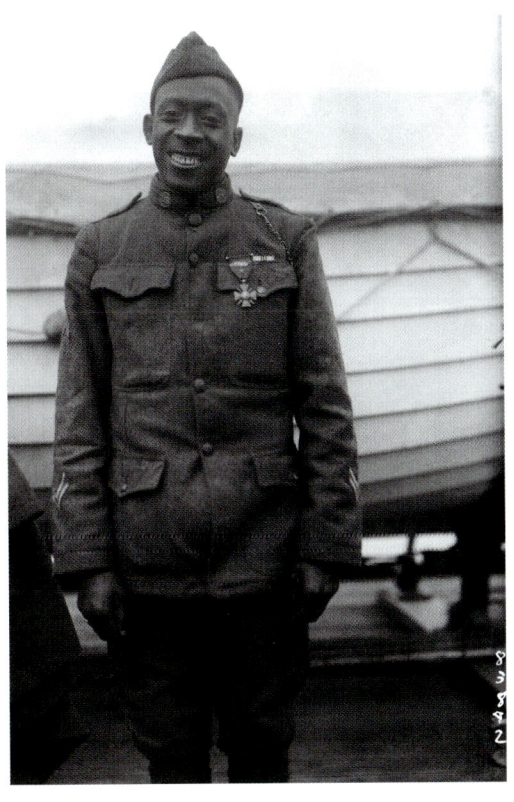

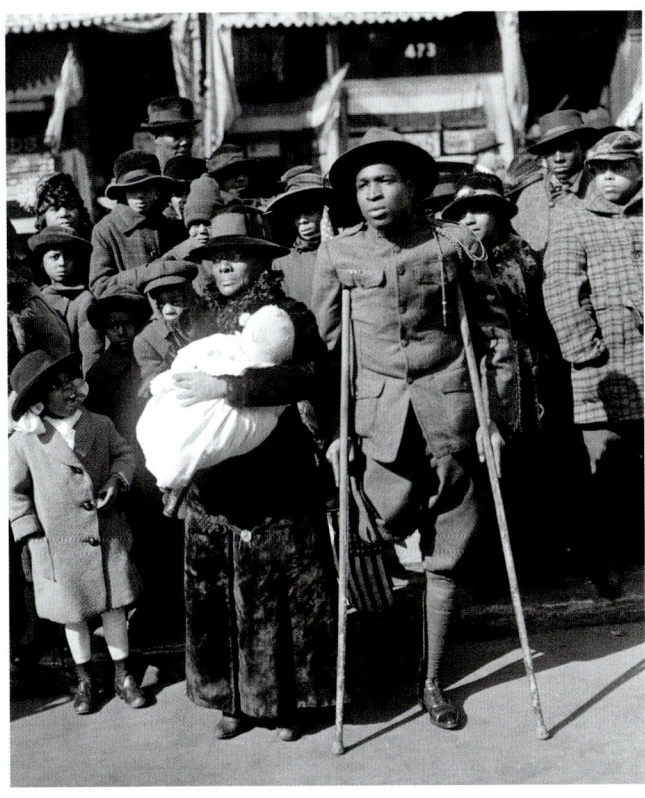

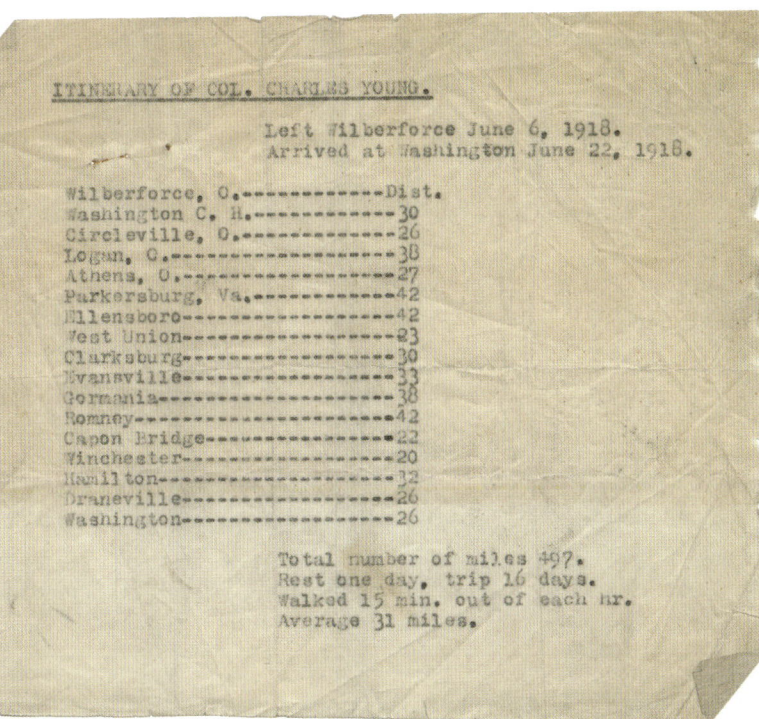

ITINERARY OF COL. CHARLES YOUNG.

Left Wilberforce June 6, 1918.
Arrived at Washington June 22, 1918.

Wilberforce, O.------------Dist.
Washington C. H.------------30
Circleville, O.------------26
Logan, O.------------38
Athens, O.------------27
Parkersburg, Va.------------42
Ellensboro------------42
West Union------------23
Clarksburg------------30
Evansville------------33
Gormania------------38
Romney------------42
Capon Bridge------------22
Winchester------------20
Hamilton------------32
Draneville------------26
Washington------------26

Total number of miles 497.
Rest one day, trip 16 days.
Walked 15 min. out of each hr.
Average 31 miles.

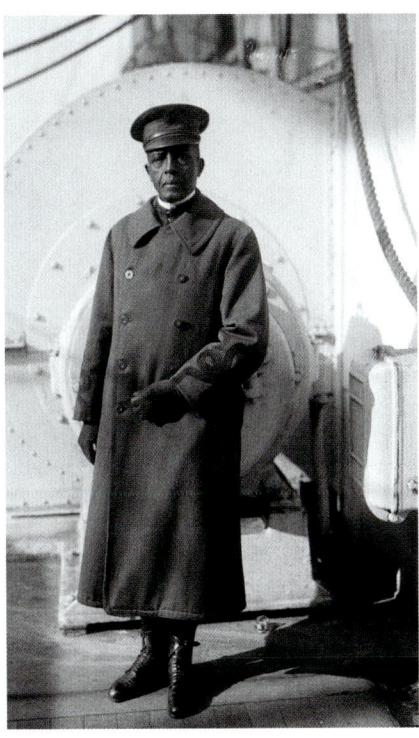

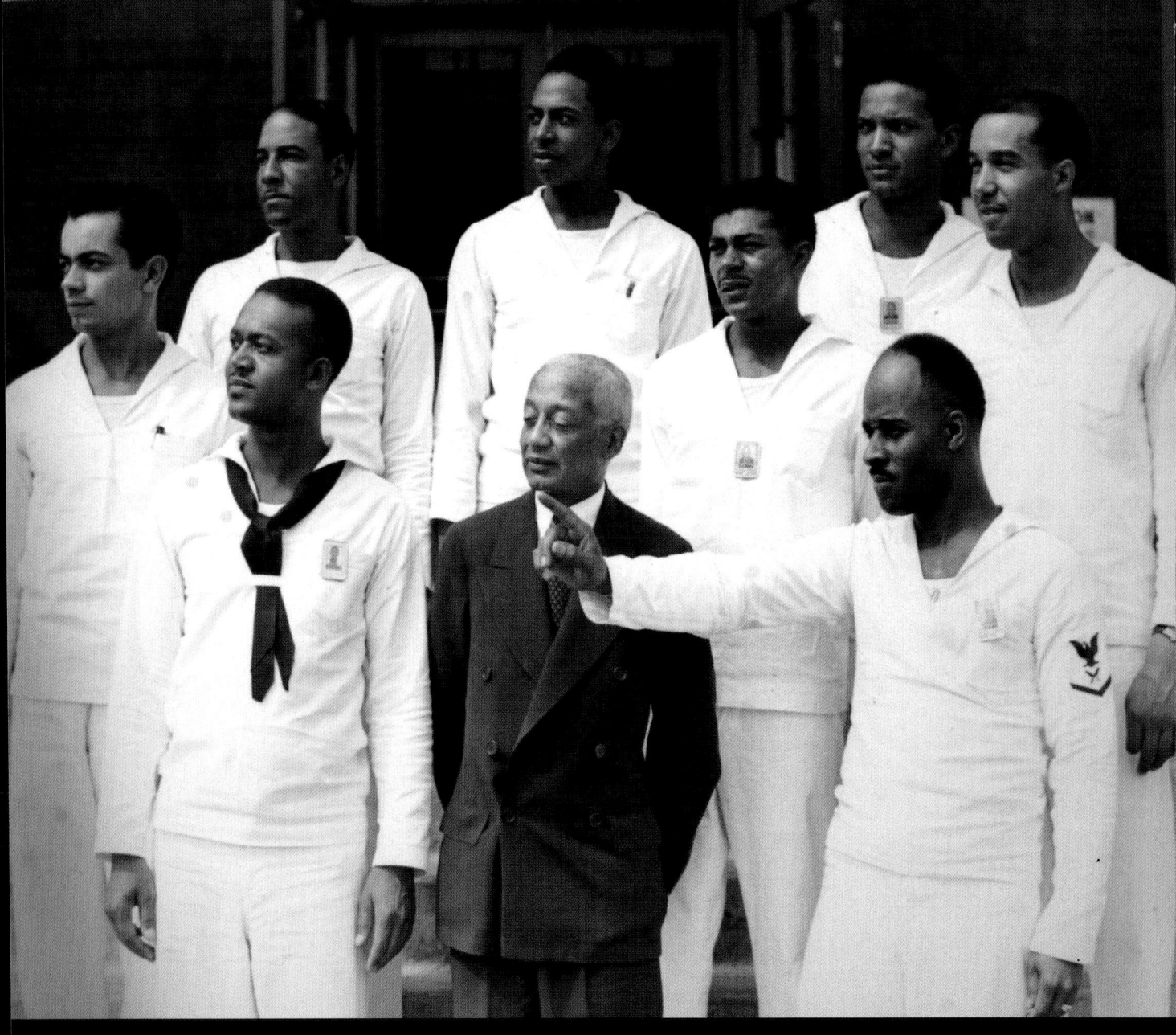

MAKING AND MOBILIZING ART IN TIMES OF WAR

JOVONNA JONES

*Black painters and intellectuals crafted a powerful
artistic vision during World War II.*

During the Great Depression, Franklin D. Roosevelt, Eleanor Roosevelt, and philanthropic leaders prioritized art, literature, culture, and public discourse. They funded a variety of projects from art centers and exhibitions to books, studies, and journals. African American art and writing thrived in these years of fiscal support, and artists and intellectuals found a variety of employment including as muralists, instructors, and editors.

World War II upended those efforts, drawing the nation's attention and economic support elsewhere. Still, it was not uncommon for African American artists and intellectuals to be involved in war efforts or to enlist themselves, and many found ways to continue their artistic work.

In a photograph entitled *Black Soldiers*, a group of young sailors in crisp white uniforms and an older man in a suit all gaze in unison. They appear to watch something in the distance as the sailor in front directs their vision. Who or what could they be looking at?

This photograph was taken on August 15, 1942, at the height of World War II. Their faces offer a variety of expressions: curiosity, bewilderment, amusement. The man in the suit, Dr. Alain LeRoy Locke, must have blinked the moment the photograph was taken; still, he is poised and grounded at the center of this group. He is immersed in the event, quietly observant with his arms folded behind his back.

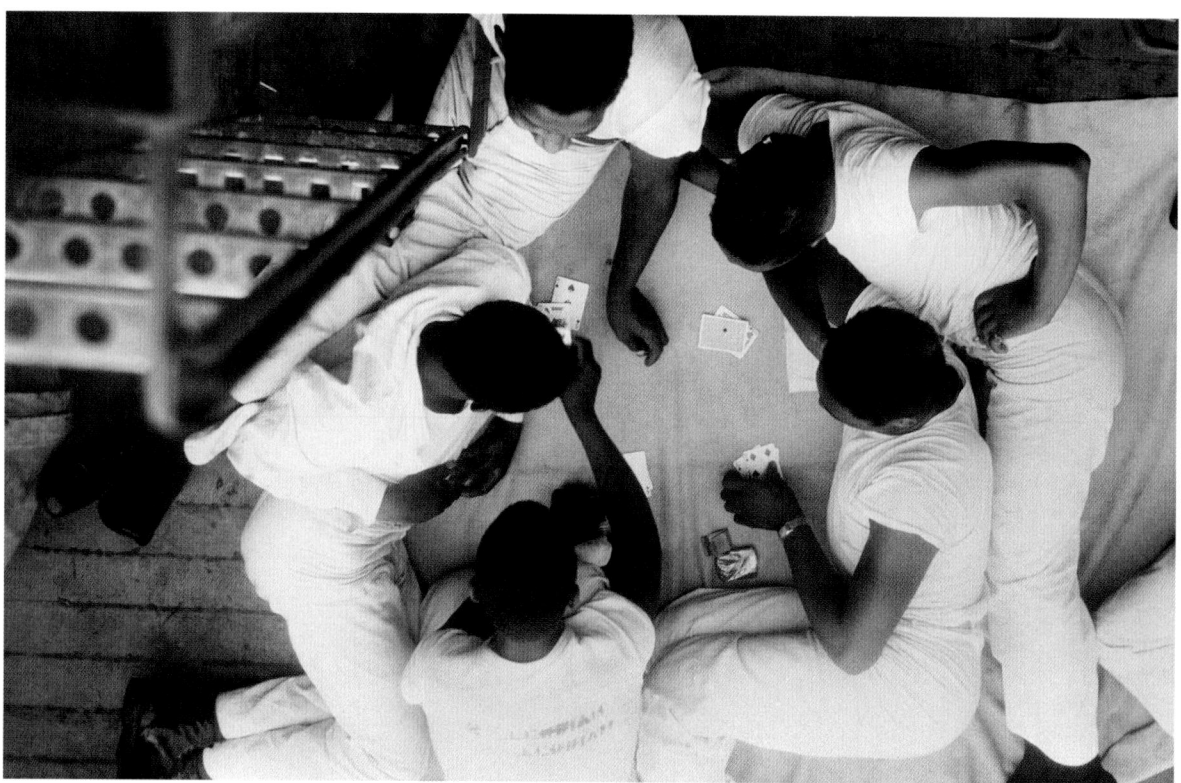

Locke was an African American philosopher, patron of the arts, and educator once heralded as the "Father of the Harlem Renaissance." During the height of the war, Locke visited and toured the U.S. Naval Station Great Lakes in Illinois. He poses here with a group of sailors from West Virginia, Illinois, Massachusetts, Texas, Indiana, Pennsylvania, Florida, and Michigan. How did Locke, a visionary for Negro arts and letters, find himself with a group of sailors at a midwestern military training center?

He had just met the First Lady at the South Side Community Art Center in Chicago and secured her support for future initiatives for Black art and artists when World War II began. The war halted whatever federal support he might have received. President Roosevelt mobilized the U.S. economy to support war efforts, which meant that most new opportunities were connected to the war.

PREVIOUS SPREAD, LEFT: 1942 photograph of Alain Locke pictured with World War II sailors.

ABOVE: U.S. Navy sailors gather to play cards, 1944.

RIGHT: Serviceman and painter Frederick D. Jones displays his artworks, 1942.

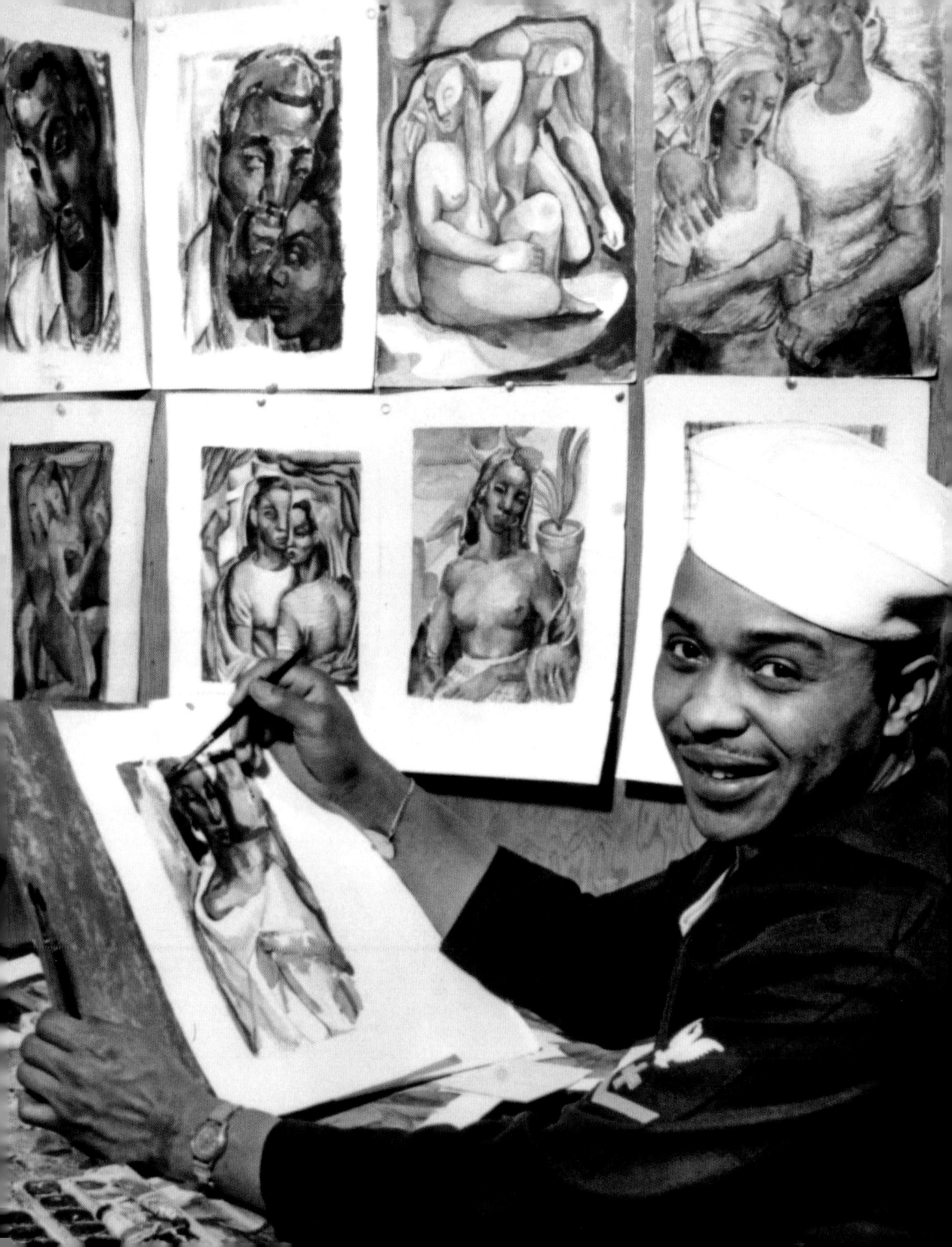

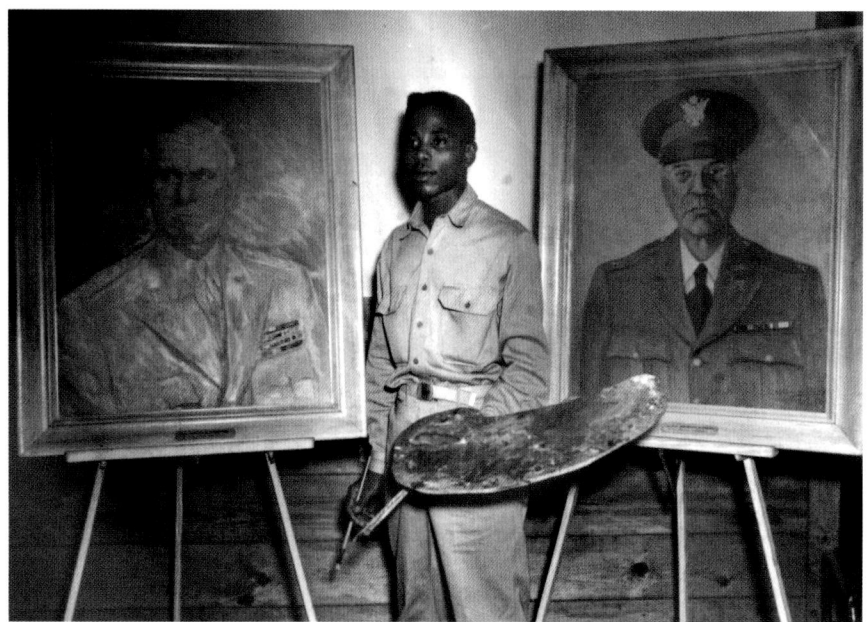

LEFT: Clarence Williams displays two paintings of General George Marshall (left) and Brigadier General Benjamin O. Davis (right).

OPPOSITE: Painter Horace Pippin receives the J. Henry Scheidt Memorial Prize. Pippin wears the Purple Heart he received from the armed services.

Some soldiers entered the service as skilled painters and continued their practice on base. In the photograph above entitled *Enlisted Man Displays Art*, Clarence Williams presents two elegant military portraits.

He stands at the center of the image, "flanked on one side by a painting of General George Marshall"—who was the chief of staff of the U.S. Army under Roosevelt—and "on the other side by an art study of Brigadier General Benjamin O. Davis," commander of the Tuskegee Airmen and later the first African American brigadier general in the U.S. Air Force. With a slight smile, Williams steadies his large artist's palette against his hip. He holds his paintbrush firmly and gracefully in his hand like a craftsman with his favorite tool.

Frederick Jones was a prolific painter who trained at the Art Institute of Chicago. Jones paused his studies to enlist in the U.S. Navy and worked as a pharmacist's mate but continued to paint as if he had never left his studio. In the photograph on the previous page, the artist is surrounded by portraits of African American figures embracing, faces nestled into each other or limbs intertwining.

Although it is not visible in black-and-white photos, Jones liked to play with bold colors and textures, using bright jewel tones for flowing drapes and clothing and rich brown tones that made his painted figures appear vivid and full-bodied, as if they were sculpted from clay. Jones wanted to present Black life in fantastical ways, and was drawn to fluidity as a technique to invoke beauty and sensitivity and combat the harsh realities of Black struggle.

While artists continued to make work while serving in the war, Locke found a way to channel a new political vision through an artistic lens. His trip to the base might have inspired him to do so. Locke was invited to guest-edit a special edition of the journal *Survey Graphic* "in response to the issue of race, Negroes, and the American war mobilization," as biographer Jeffrey C. Stewart writes.

The war was supposed to provide more employment opportunities for African Americans, but they were hired in limited capacity. At Naval Station Great Lakes, African American sailors were trained at a segregated camp and could take on only noncombat roles. Even as they demonstrated their willingness to sacrifice their lives for their

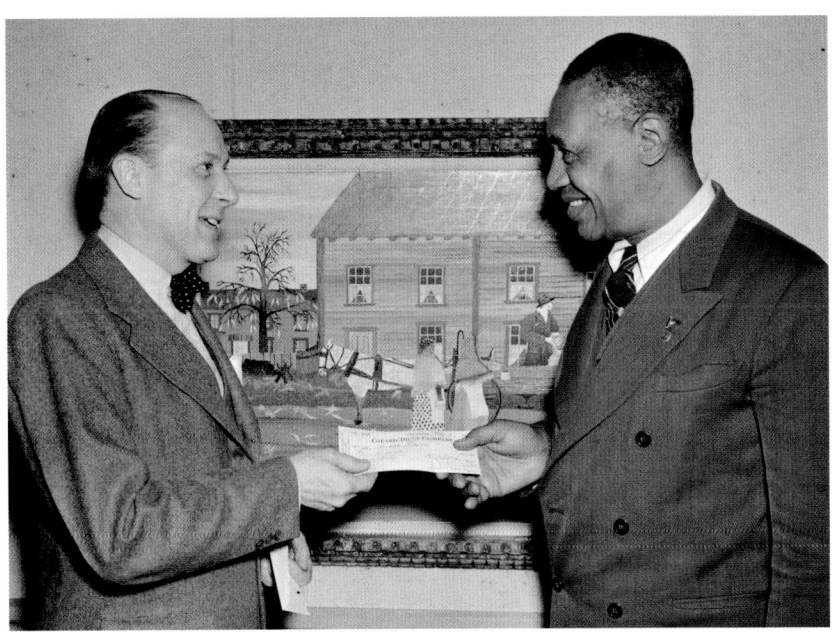

country, Black sailors and soldiers still faced as much discrimination in the service as they did as civilians.

Locke's task was to help expose the hypocrisy undergirding America's fight for global democracy while demeaning their own citizens. In his opening essay of 1942's "Color: Unfinished Business of Democracy," the title of a special issue of *Survey Graphic*, Locke turns to the language of art—specifically collage and sculpture—to help his readers visualize what a different world could be:

> Significantly enough, the phalanx of the United Nations unites an unprecedented assemblage of the races, cultures, and peoples of the world. Could this war-born assemblage be welded by a constructive peace into an effective world-order—one based on the essential parity of peoples and a truly democratic reciprocity of cultures—world democracy could be within reach of attainment.

Ultimately, in Locke's vision articulated through art, global democracy can only be achieved through the people of the world coming together and establishing a shared commitment to peace, equality, and reciprocity within and between nations.

Locke's presence with the sailors at Naval Station Great Lakes reveals another dimension of life on the base. Artists like Clarence Williams and Frederick Jones did not leave their talents and training at home when they committed to serve. Rather, their gifts of artistry may have created spaces of mental, physical, and emotional solace for themselves and for their peers.

Williams, through military portraiture, took the opportunity to honor an African American officer leaving a new legacy through the Tuskegee Airmen. Jones brought the spirit of home to the base by painting his people—whether family members, friends, lovers, or imagined figures—and surrounding himself with their likenesses. Locke channeled the language of artistry into poignant social and political commentary.

Two artists and an esteemed intellectual each found ways to craft and mobilize an artistic vision in times of turmoil at home and abroad.

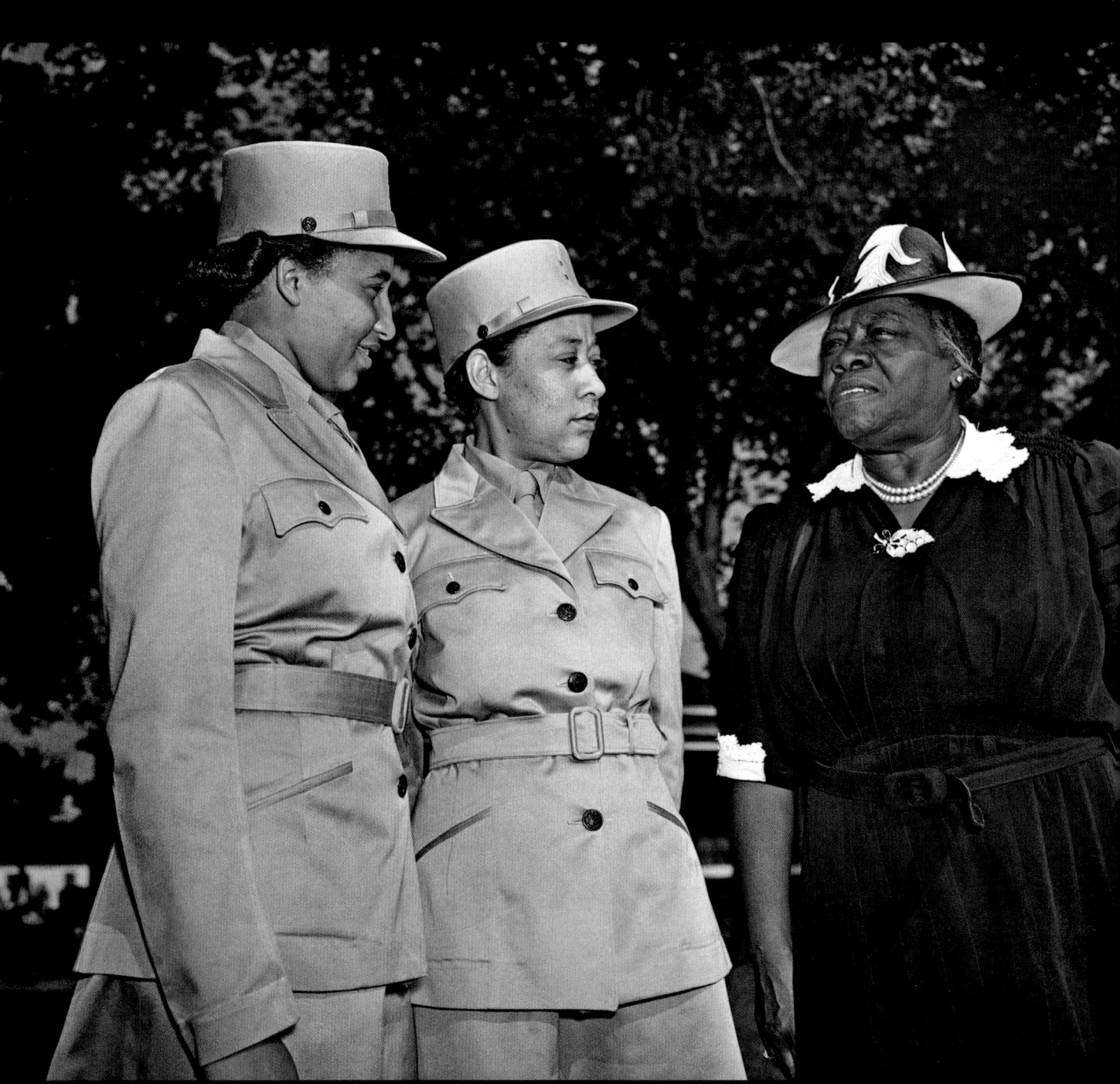

MARY MCLEOD BETHUNE

ASHLEY ROBERTSON PRESTON

Black servicewomen and the
winning of World War II.

Conversations about World War II focus heavily on the efforts of men, ignoring the importance of the women who served and those left behind, whose home front work provided critical support. At a time when much of the world was focused on Axis and Allied forces, Mary McLeod Bethune saw military service and defense-related jobs as an opportunity for Black women to become a part of history.

When the Women's Army Auxiliary Corps (WAAC) was created in 1942, it allowed women to serve in the army in roles other than as nurses for the first time. Bethune, pictured here at right, worked tirelessly to ensure that Black women were a part of the corps.

Having worked closely with the Roosevelt administration as director of the Division of Negro Affairs for the National Youth Administration, Bethune was one of the most influential leaders of her time. As founder of the National Council of Negro Women and president of Bethune-Cookman College, she was a fierce advocate for civil rights, and she used her voice to bring attention to issues of inequality and discrimination.

As African Americans fought in World War II, they also sought to challenge white supremacy at home. The "Double V Campaign" called for victory abroad and victory at home as African Americans strategically linked the need to eliminate the evils of Jim Crow with the need to end fascism across the world.

233

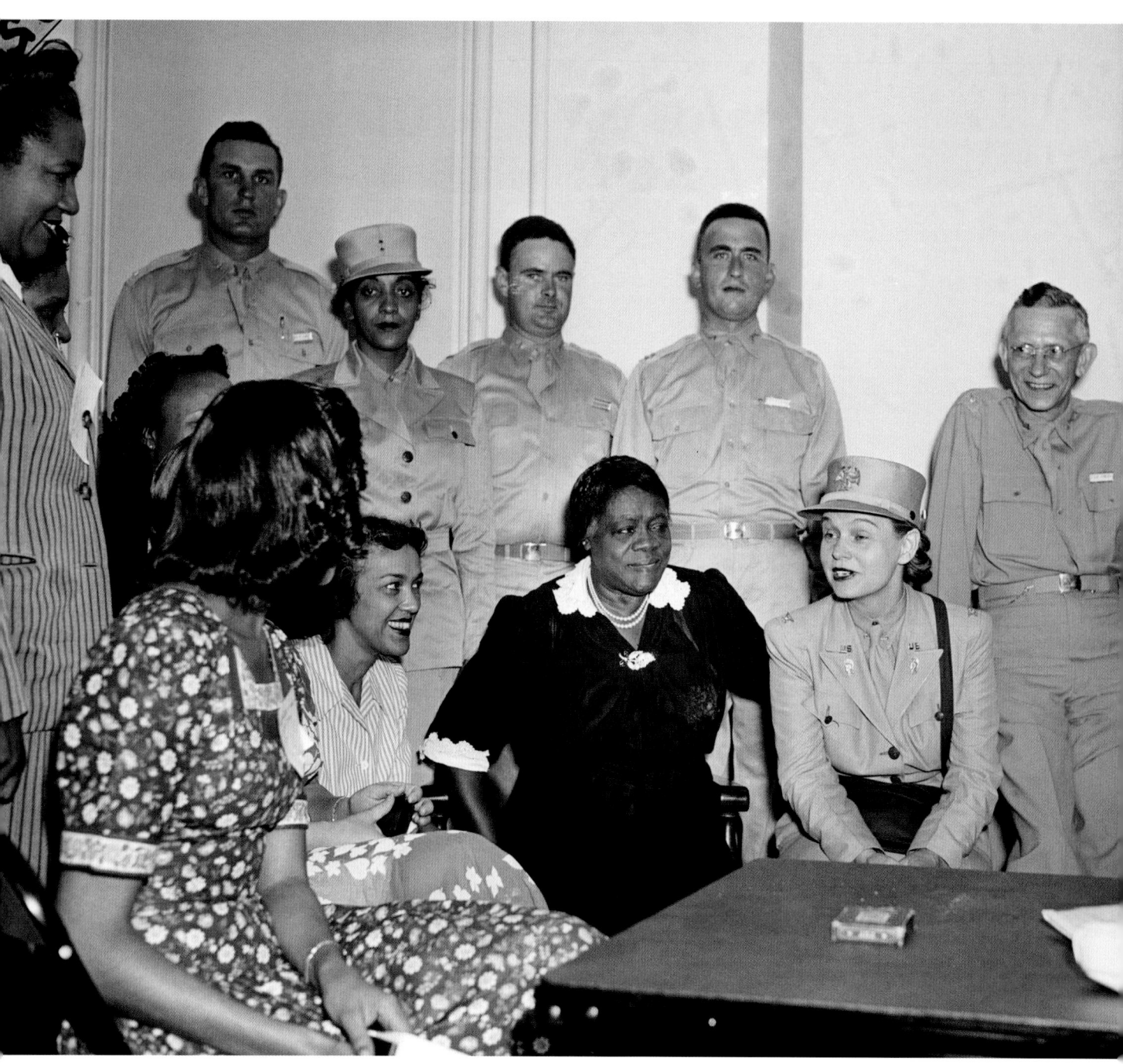

Despite the discrimination they faced at the hands of the United States, African Americans served their country valiantly. Bethune urged Black women to rise to the occasion of wartime activities, and in 1942 she accepted the position of special assistant to the secretary of war for the selection of candidates for the WAAC Officer Training School. She carefully handpicked the first forty women of the corps. With Bethune's persistence, some 6,500 African American women served as WAAC members over the course of World War II.

One of those women was Dovey Johnson Roundtree. In her autobiography, *Justice Older than the Law: The Life of Dovey Johnson Roundtree*, Roundtree wrote: "Watching Dr. Bethune fight so hard over so many months for a place for [B]lack women in the military, I came to the conclusion that for all my reservations and fears, I couldn't turn away from her challenge."

For many of the WAAC members it was a daunting experience to assume roles that had not previously existed. There was also the extra layer of pressure of being the first Black women to serve in this capacity. In their non-combat positions the women served as clerical workers, cooks, phone operators, and medical staff.

The two women in the opening photo, Vera Harrison of Wilberforce, Ohio, and Mary Bordeaux of Louisville, Kentucky, were members of the first graduating class of officer candidates in the WAAC. Harrison later was deployed to England and France along with 817 other women as a part of the 6888th Central Postal Directory Battalion, as she rose to the rank of commanding officer of Company C. The 6888th was the only African American women's military unit to go overseas during World War II.

In her role as the president of the National Council of Negro Women, Bethune ensured that the Black community supported the WAAC. The organization's *Aframerican Woman's Journal* featured important articles on the WAAC, which included stories about the director, Oveta Culp Hobby, an outline of the daily activities of the WAAC, and the historical significance of their positions. The organization urged journal readers to support the women by writing them letters and sending care packages, and published their mailing addresses.

Throughout the war, Bethune continued to make herself available to the women of the corps, and those whom she selected remained able to call on her if they needed her assistance. She inspected living conditions in training camps in Des Moines, Iowa, and she kept herself abreast of the overall well-being of the women.

The photographs (opposite and on page 232) show Bethune speaking with women during a visit to Des Moines. Remembering the sobering effect of Bethune's visit, Roundtree wrote: "She gathered her *girls* about her . . . and reminded us of our place in history . . . Dr. Bethune transformed the atmosphere of those uneasy hours with a few carefully chosen words."

African American women rose to the occasion of participating in World War II. As a visionary leader, Mary McLeod Bethune saw entrance into the corps as an opportunity to make history and take a major step toward creating a more inclusive military.

PREVIOUS SPREAD, LEFT: Mary McLeod Bethune speaks with WAAC officers Vera Harrison (left) and Mary Bordeaux (center) upon their arrival at Fort Des Moines in 1942.

LEFT: Mary McLeod Bethune (center) meets with Oveta Culp Hobby (seated right) at Fort Des Moines in 1942.

FOLLOWING SPREAD:
LEFT: Mary McLeod Bethune meets with Bethune-Cookman students in 1943, one year after resigning as university president.

RIGHT: Mary McLeod Bethune greets St. Louis WAAC enlistee Inna McFadden.

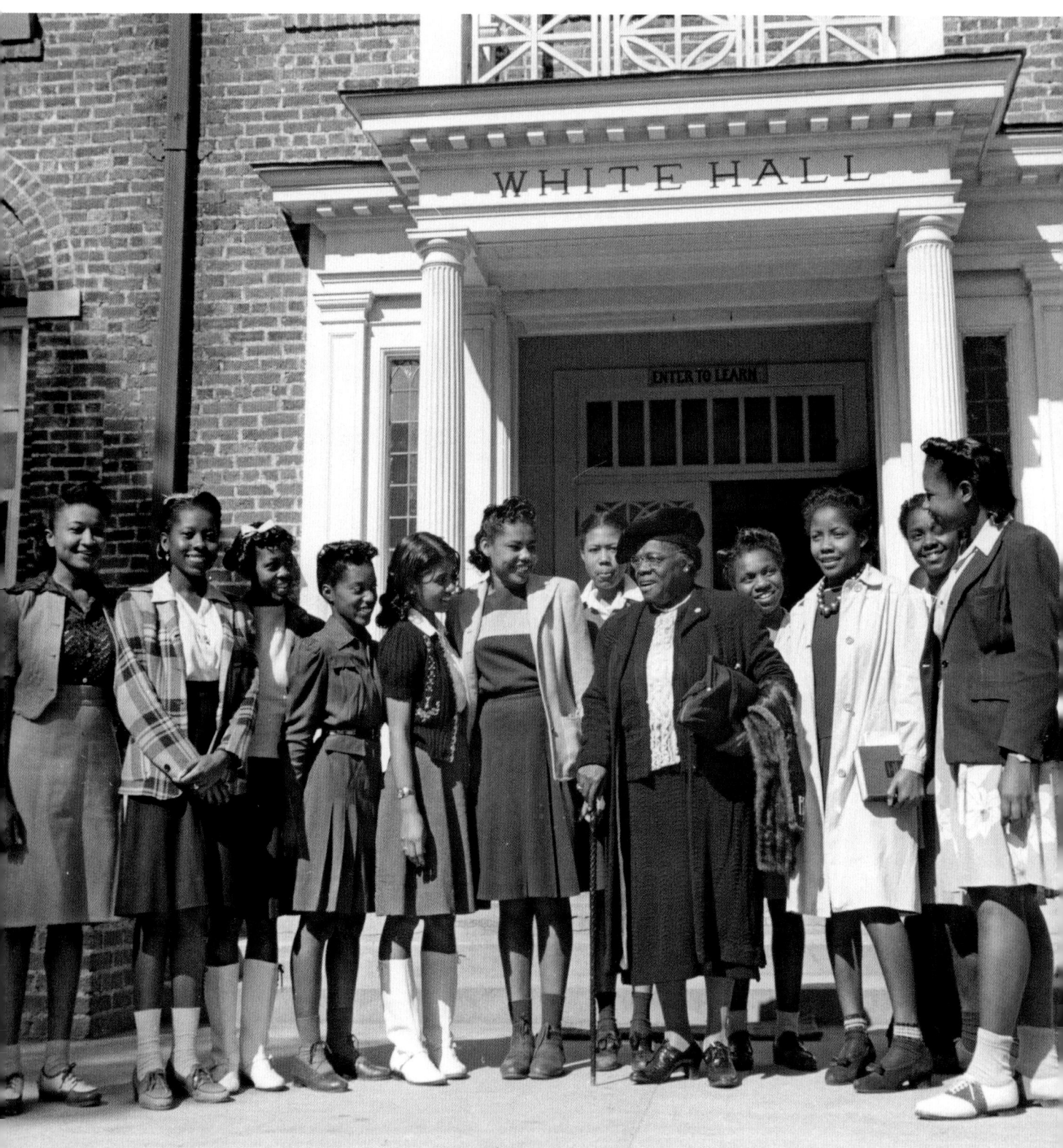

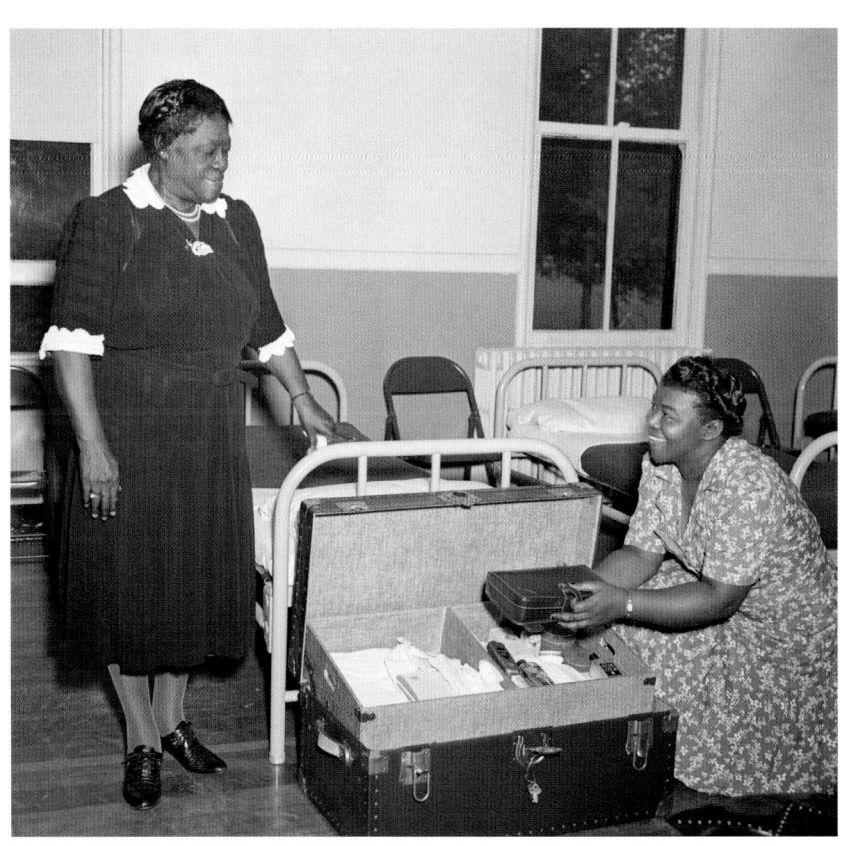

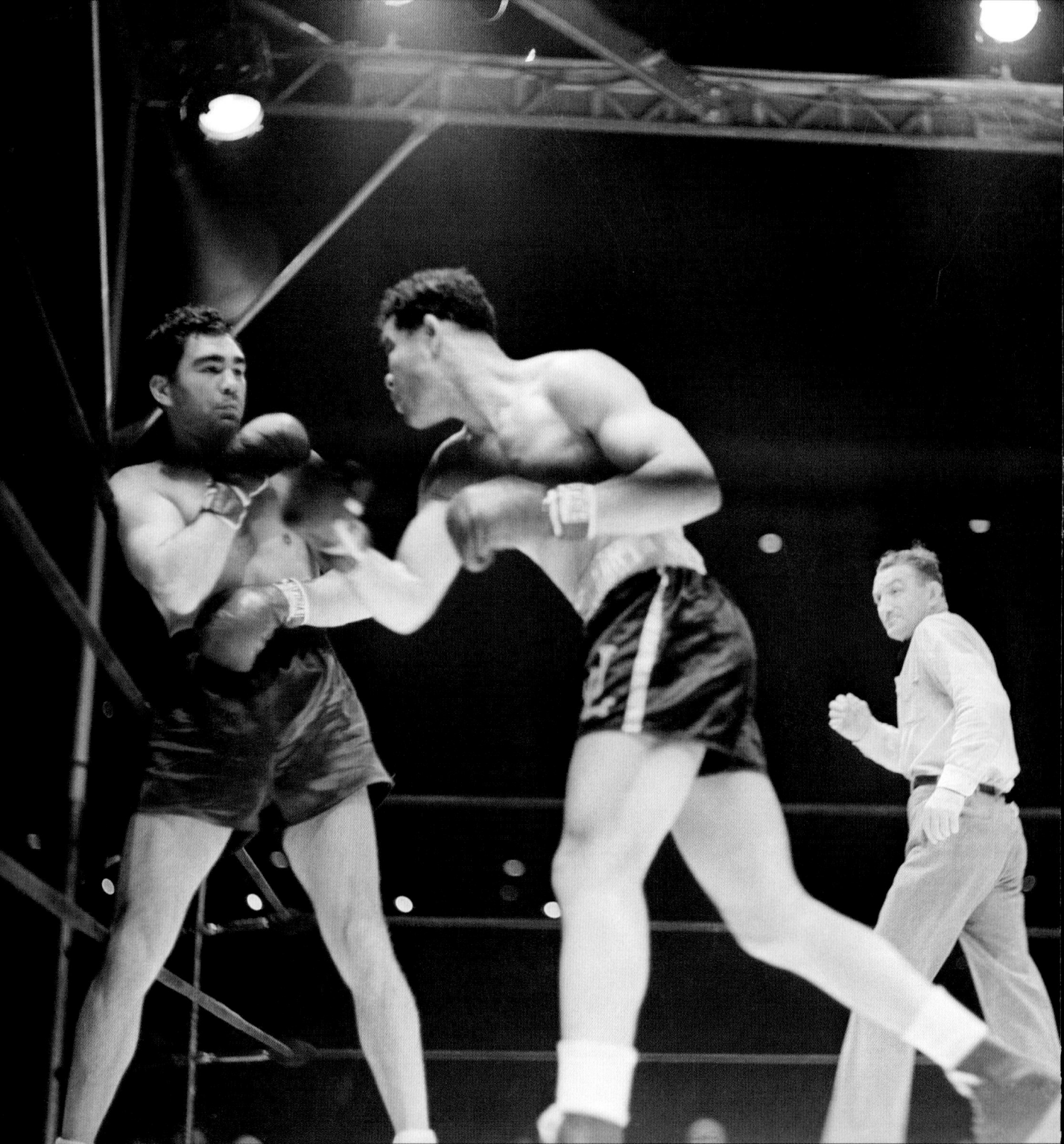

JOE LOUIS: THE BLACK FACE OF MILITARY PROPAGANDA

BRIAN C. DAVIS JR.

During World War II, Joe Louis became the representative of military propaganda to Black Americ as an attempt to sway racial attitudes toward the U.S. military.

American involvement in World War II started, symbolically, when Joe Louis fought German Max Schmeling for the heavyweight boxing title in 1938. After having lost to Schmeling in 1936, Louis knocked him out during their 1938 rematch.

The American public saw this win as the United States of America's emblematic defeat of Hitler's Germany. Not only was Louis the undisputed heavyweight champion of the world, but he was America's champion.

Joseph Louis Barrow was born in Lafayette, Alabama, on May 13, 1914. His parents were cotton sharecroppers, and he and his seven brothers and sisters often worked the fields. After migrating to Detroit with his mother and siblings, Louis used boxing to financially support his family during the Great Depression.

As Louis's boxing career blossomed in the 1930s, reporters called him the most famous Black man in the country. A massive crowd of Black fans celebrated his win over Schmeling in the streets of Harlem (see photo on page 242), though Louis was cheered by Americans of all races.

Even before his military career began, Louis was pressed into service. On January 9, 1942, he was asked to fight in a Navy Emergency Relief Department benefit and donated 40 percent of his winnings to the U.S. Navy.

Many within the Black community were unhappy with his participation due to the ongoing discrimination and segregation in the American military. Plenty of Black Americans recognized the bitter irony of being asked to fight a war against fascism overseas while being denied citizenship rights at home. For them the war could only be fought for "Double V": victory abroad and victory at home.

239

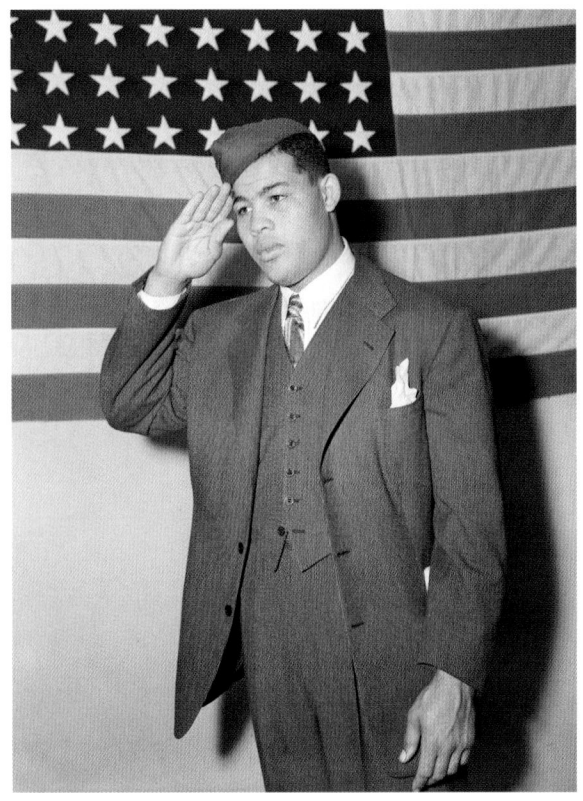

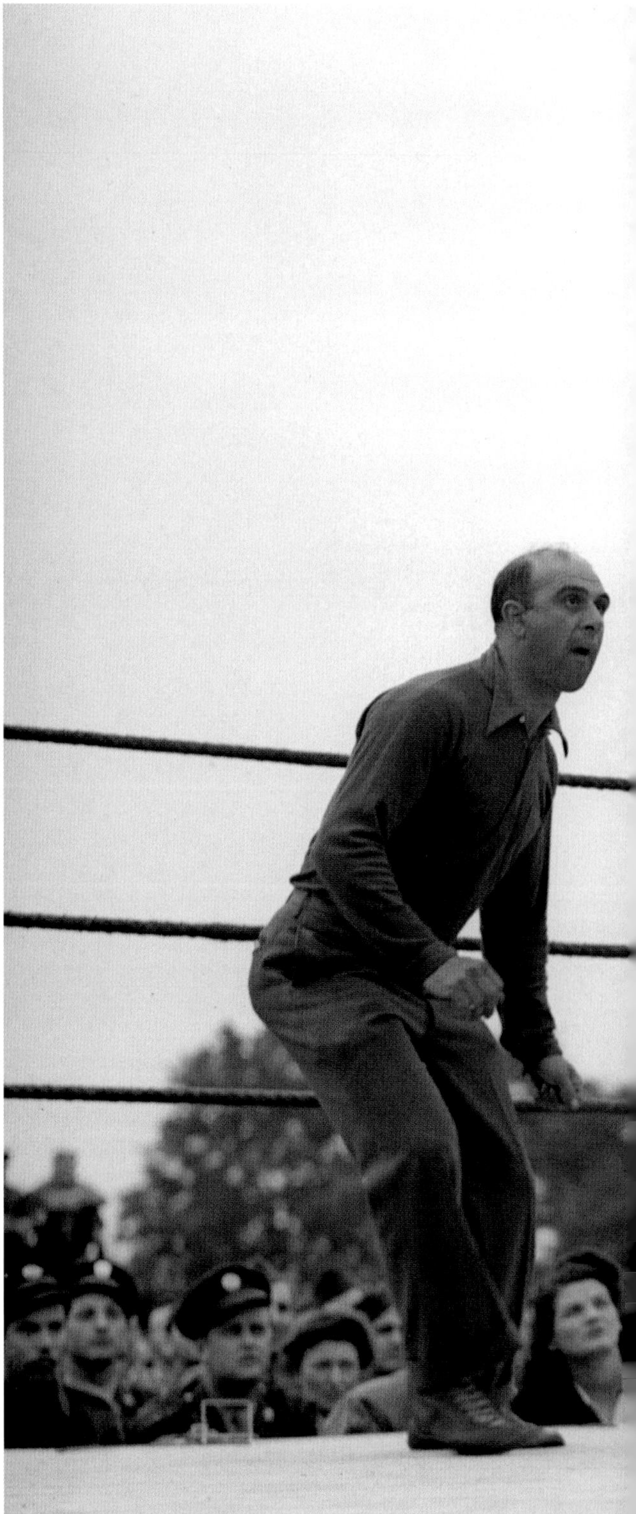

PREVIOUS SPREAD, LEFT: Max Schmeling (left) in a 1938 bout with Joe Louis.

ABOVE: Joe Louis, at the Camp Upton, New York, draft board, is inducted into the Morale Division of the U.S. Army.

RIGHT: Joe Louis fights in an exhibition match while in London with the U.S. Army.

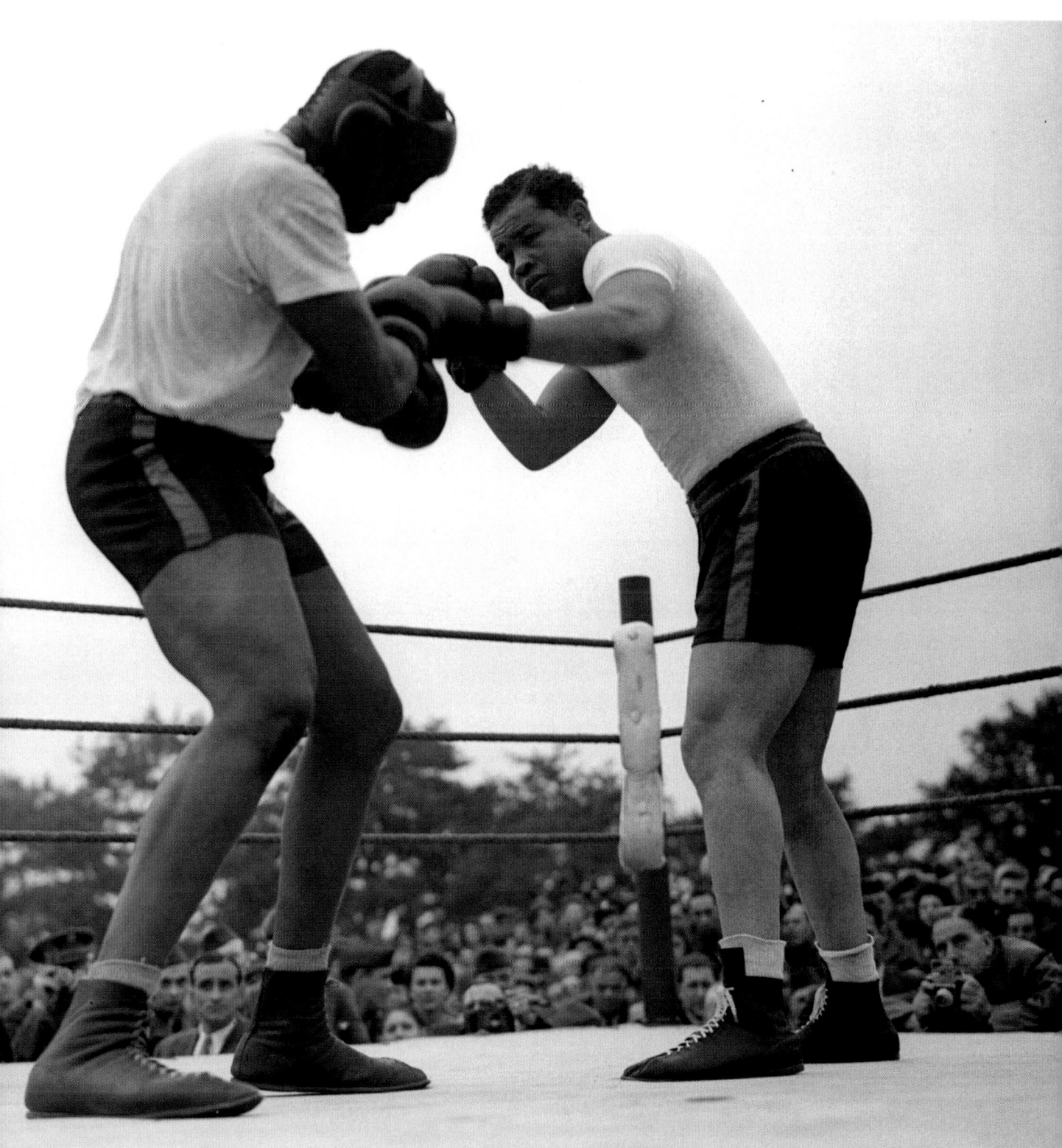

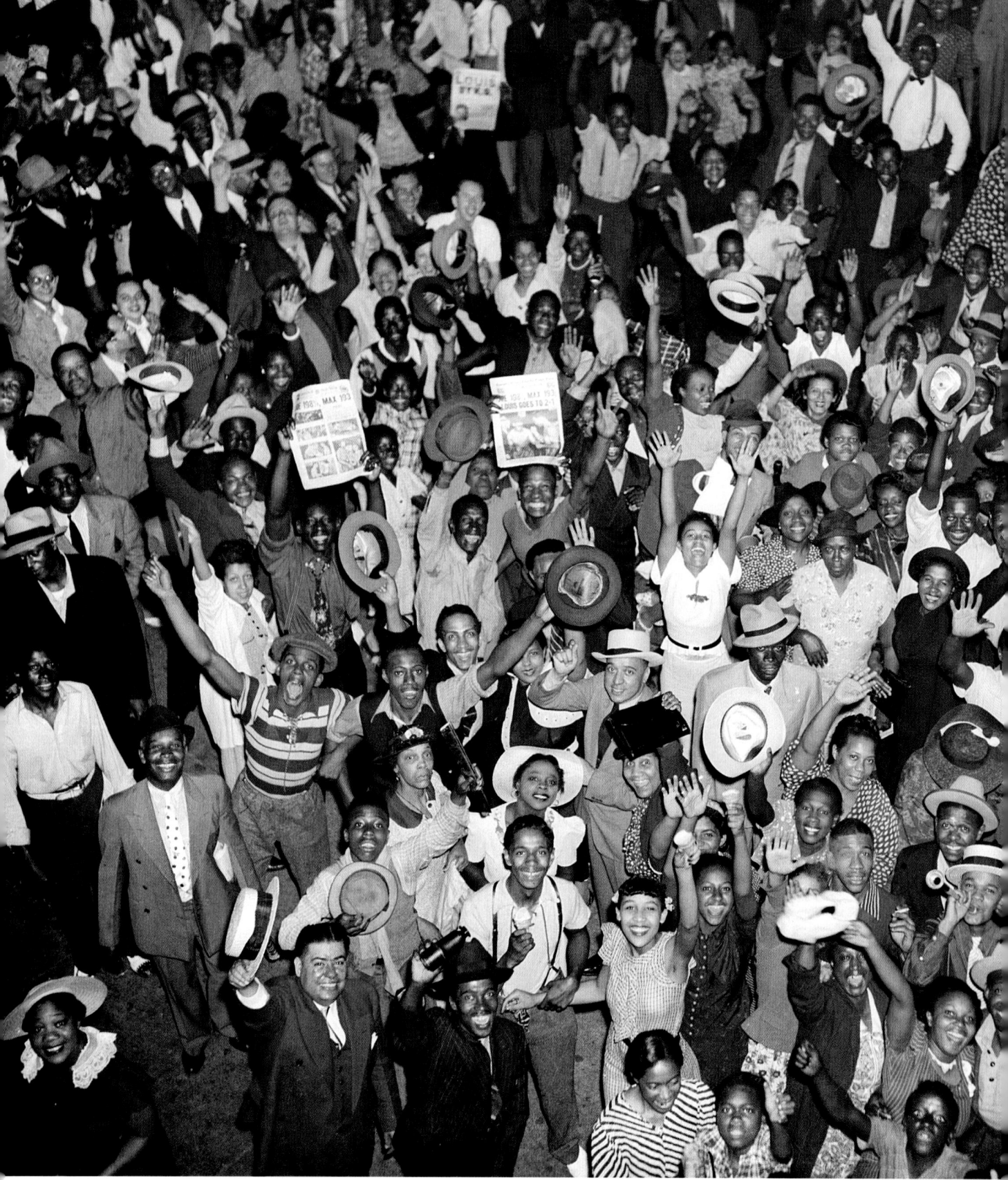

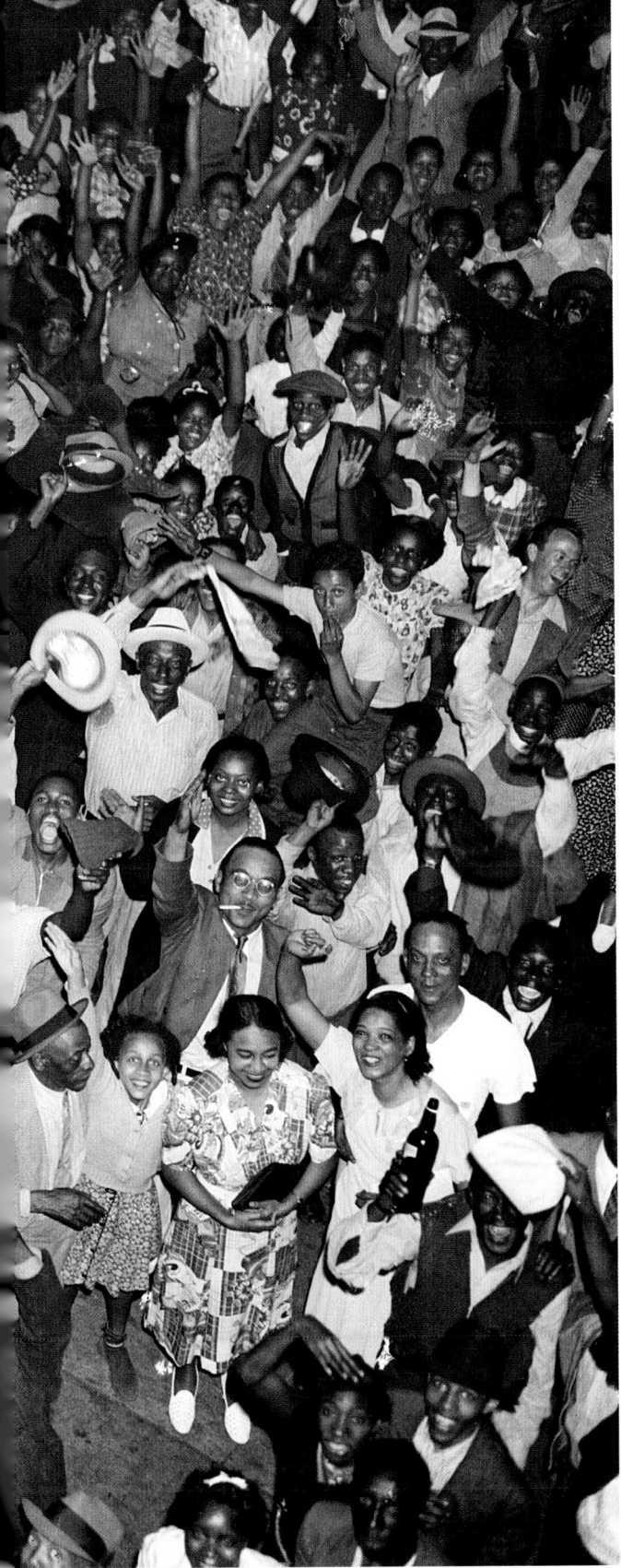

Louis, however, was clear about his sense of patriotism, telling the *Cleveland Gazette* on January 3, 1942: "I am very glad to do what I can to help America in the war." Louis was drafted into the U.S. Army later in 1942, at the apex of his boxing career.

Government officials enlisted Private Joe Louis to the cause, hoping to improve enthusiasm for the war among Black Americans and to raise the morale of Black troops serving in the still-segregated military ranks.

His squeaky-clean public persona, carefully cultivated by his manager, made Louis the perfect candidate to promote the U.S. military to the Black community. In the photo on page 240, he salutes with an American flag behind him, conveying an image of Black patriotism designed to defuse racial tensions.

Louis never saw the battlefield. Instead, the army kept him boxing.

In 1944, Truman K. Gibson Jr., civilian aide to the secretary of war; Colonel Stanley J. Gorgan, director of the War Department's Bureau of Public Relations; and Sergeant Joe Louis met to organize a world boxing tour. These exhibition matches took Louis around the world to entertain, boost morale, and raise funds for the U.S. Army.

In the image on pages 240–41, Louis is fighting in a 1944 exhibition in London. The photo shows a predominantly white group of military troops and civilians intensely focused on the world champion fighting. Photographers are front row to ensure they can capture an image of Louis for newspapers worldwide and military propaganda.

LEFT: Harlem crowds celebrate Joe Louis's victory over Max Schmeling, 1938.

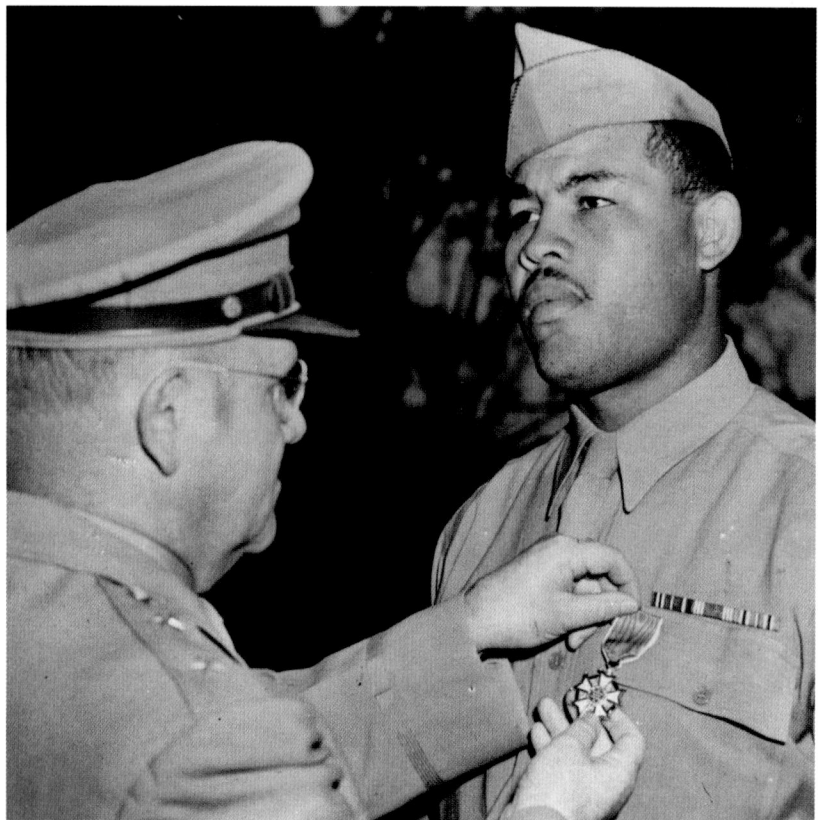

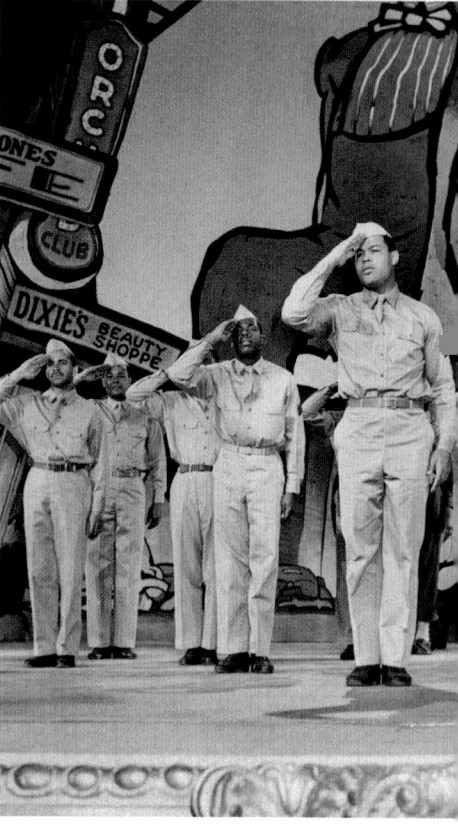

Perhaps most remarkably, World War II made Louis a screen star. The poster (see page 247) for the 1944 war documentary *The Negro Soldier* demonstrates how the War Department utilized Louis to present an image of a racially united American nation. The film was created specifically for an African American audience to persuade them that they should also consider the World War II their war. By one estimate, almost all Black servicemen saw it.

The film showed Black military experiences throughout American history but left out any mention of segregation, racism, slavery, and discrimination. The message was clear: the military needed Black troops and endorsed "America's Joe Louis" not just as a Black American but as a true American hero who was protecting his country against Nazi Germany.

By the end of the war, Louis had fought in ninety-six boxing exhibitions worldwide while participating in various morale and fundraising engagements, all of which worked to advance the military's racial agenda.

According to the National WWII Museum's website, the War Department awarded Louis the Legion of Merit in 1945 for his contribution to its war efforts. The citation reads in part: "Staff Sergeant Barrow has entertained two million soldiers by frequent boxing exhibitions which entailed considerable risk to his boxing future as the champion heavyweight of the world, but he willingly

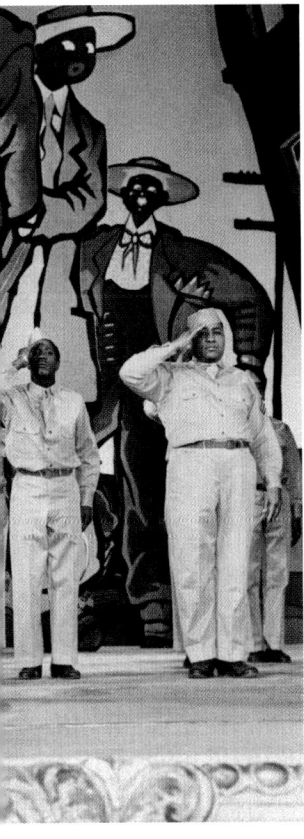

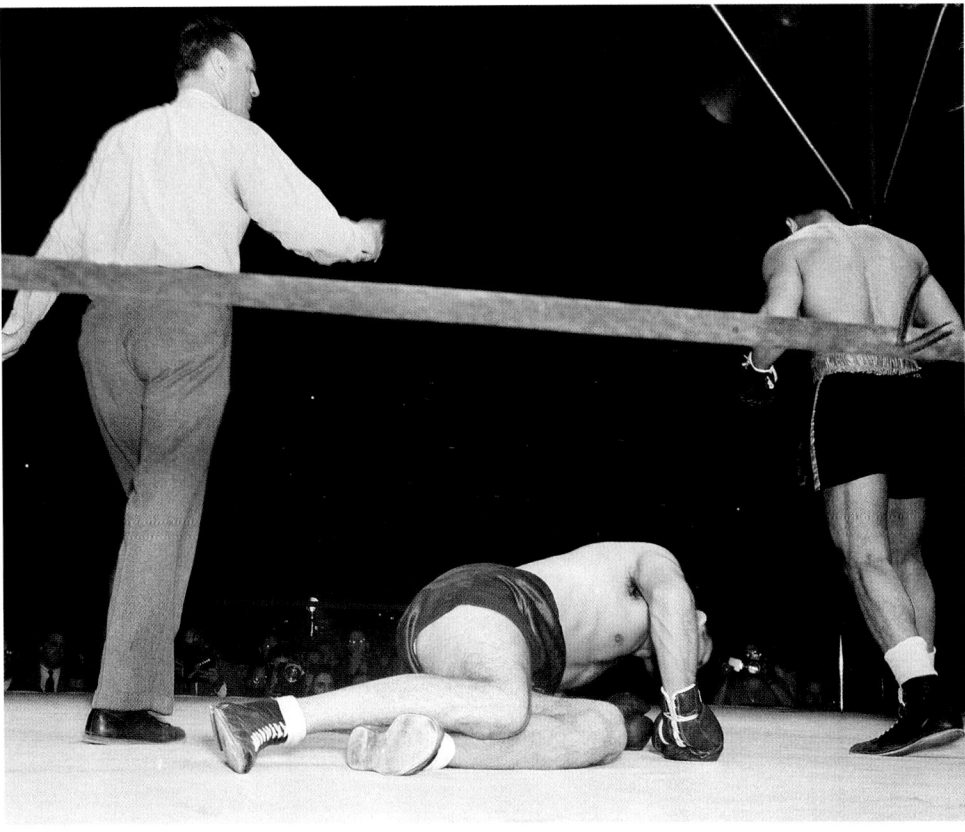

volunteered such action rather than disappoint the soldiers who desired to see him in the ring."

In his memoir, *My Life Story*, he reflects on his time as a soldier. Louis wrote that regardless of race, every soldier deserves to be treated like an American, and that he "felt very proud of having a chance to help my country and do my part." Louis is often remembered for his time as the world heavyweight champion and extensive boxing career, but just as often overlooked is the War Department's use of his image to craft a sanitized view of the Black military experience during World War II.

LEFT TO RIGHT: Joe Louis is presented with the Legion of Merit medal by Major General Clarence H. Kells during a ceremony at Port Hamilton (September 1945).

Joe Louis salutes alongside Black enlistees during a performance of "The Well-Dressed Man in Harlem."

Joe Louis knocked out Max Schmeling two minutes into the first round of their second fight (1938).

FOLLOWING SPREAD:
Joe Louis fans gather to celebrate his victory over Tom Farr on August 30, 1937.

Circa 1942 poster of Joe Louis in a combat uniform and helmet, pointing a rifle with a bayonet.

A movie poster advertises *The Negro Soldier*, a military documentary directed by Frank Capra and starring boxer Joe Louis (1944).

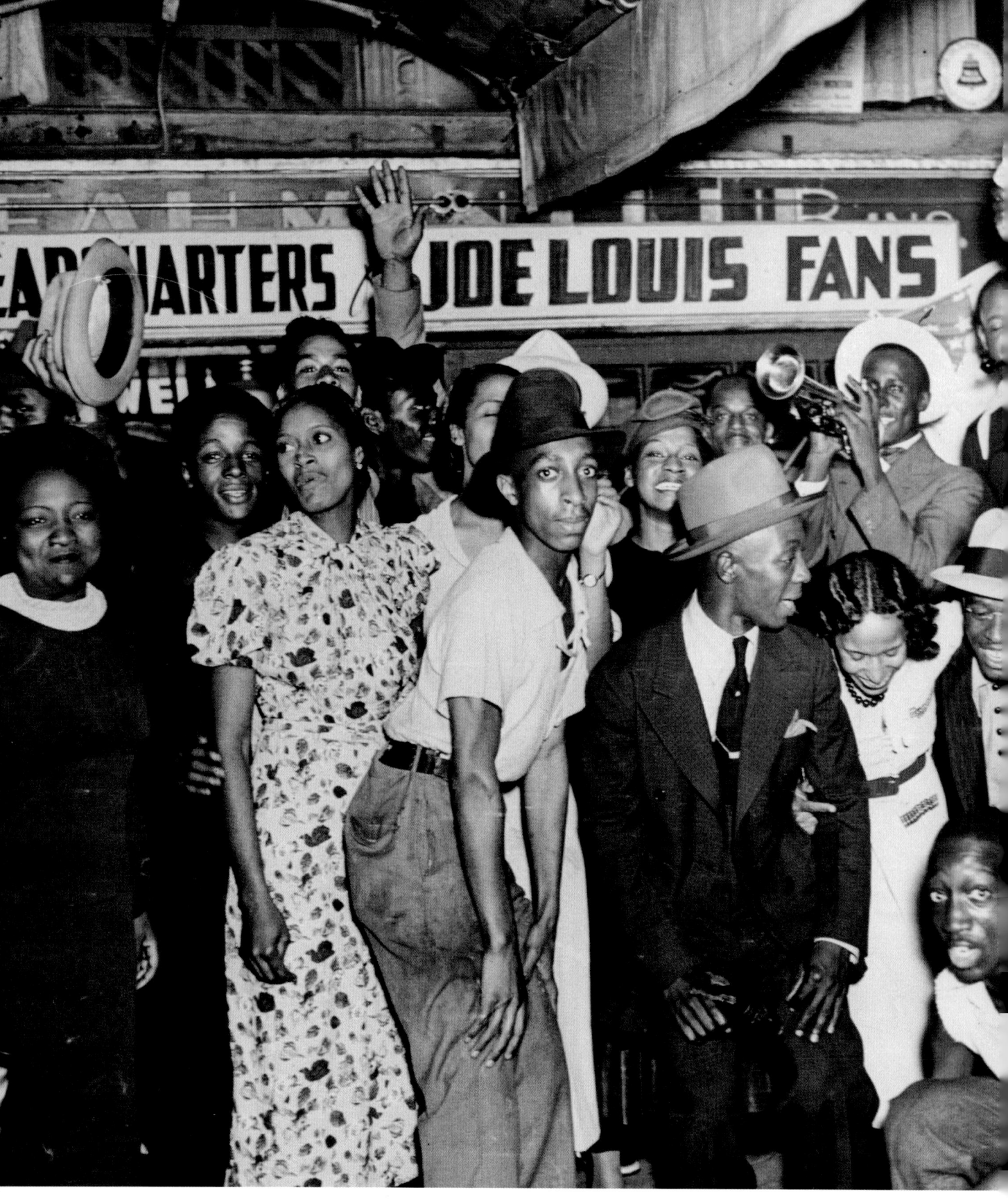

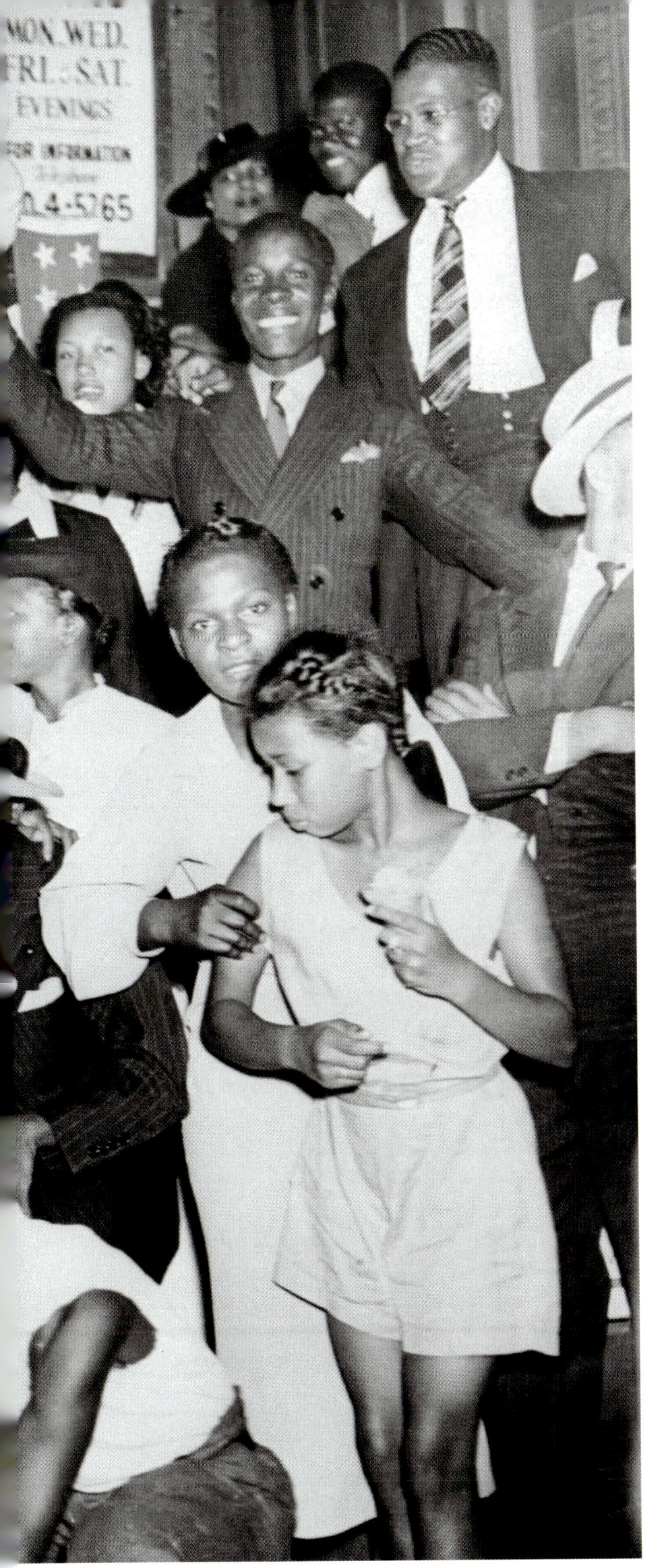

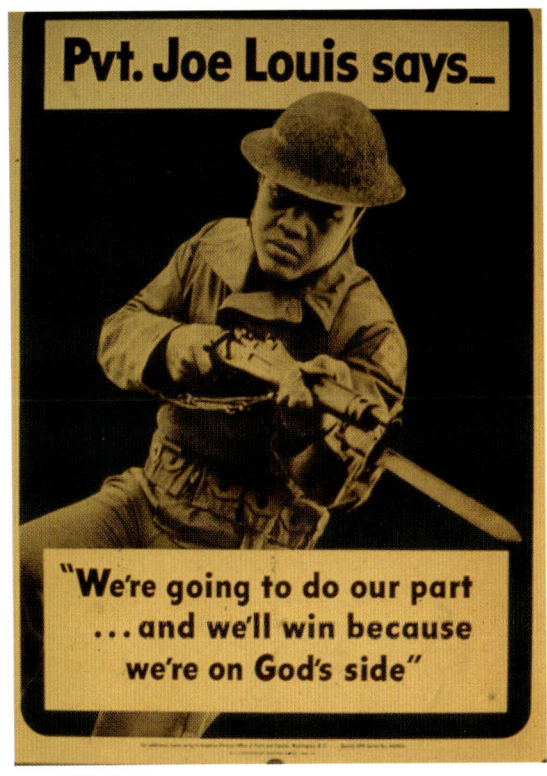

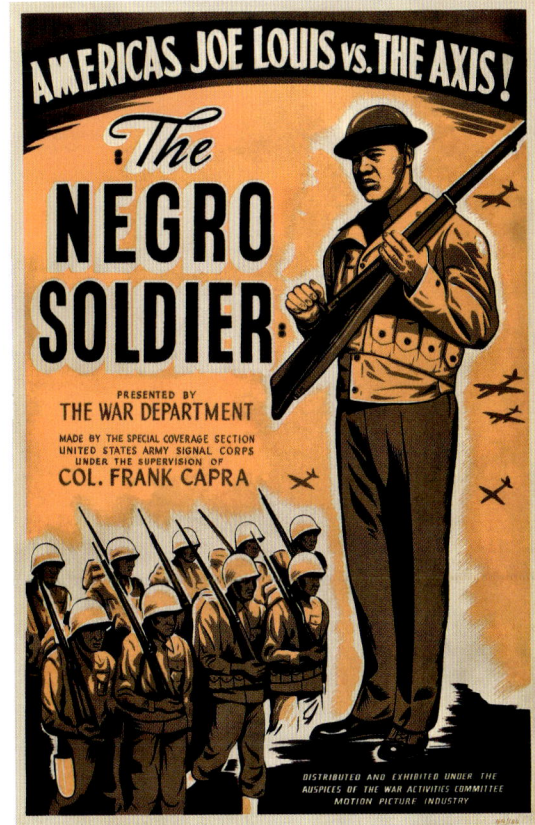

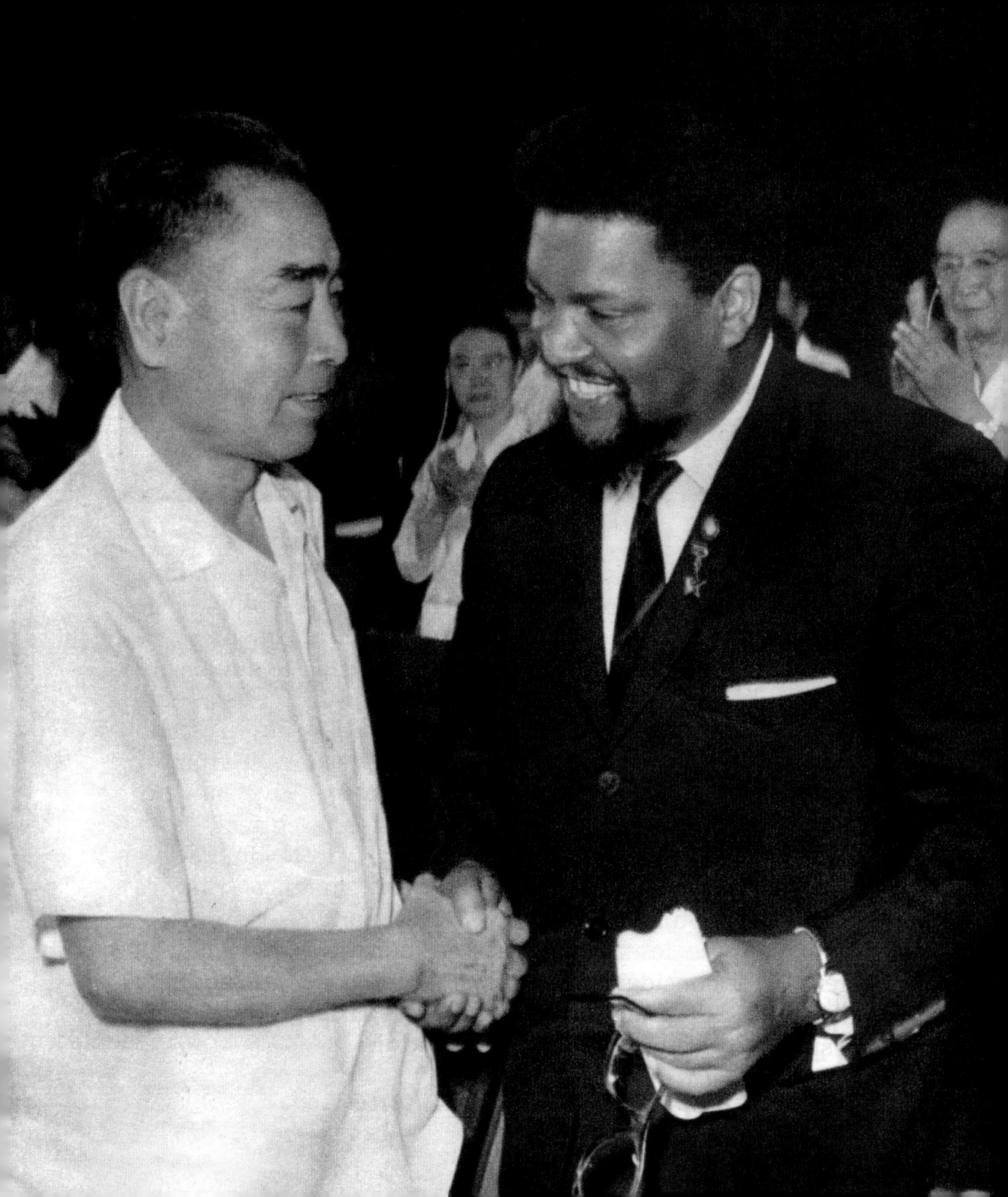

PANTHERS <u>AND</u> <u>THE</u> PREMIER: BLACK INTERNATIONALISM <u>AND</u> COLD WAR CHINA

MELVIN BARNES JR.

*From Robert F. Williams and Huey Newton to President
Richard Nixon, three moments where Black liberation movements
converged, and diverged, with revolutionary China.*

Malcolm X's 1964 speech at Cory Methodist Church in Cleveland, Ohio, has become famous for its juxtaposition of the "ballot or the bullet." Less remembered, however, is Malcolm's call midway through his speech to "expand the civil-rights struggle to the level of human rights" and take it to China, where 800 million Chinese citizens were "waiting to throw their weight on [their] side."

Malcolm was referring to the "Statement Supporting the Afro-Americans in Their Just Struggle against Racial Discrimination by U.S. Imperialism," issued by Chinese leader Mao Zedong on August 8, 1963.

With anti-colonial revolutions in full swing, African Americans increasingly turned abroad for inspiration and support, and while they found many allies around the globe, the People's Republic of China became a vital source of solidarity for Black dissidents and revolutionaries during the 1960s and early 1970s.

But even before Malcolm X's appeal to the crowd in Cleveland, activist Robert F. Williams had already turned his attention to China.

Williams is best known for calling on African Americans in Monroe, North Carolina, as president of the local branch of the NAACP in 1959, to "meet violence with violence." However, by the mid-1960s, the revolutionary lived in exile in China, via Cuba, after fleeing kidnapping charges in the United States.

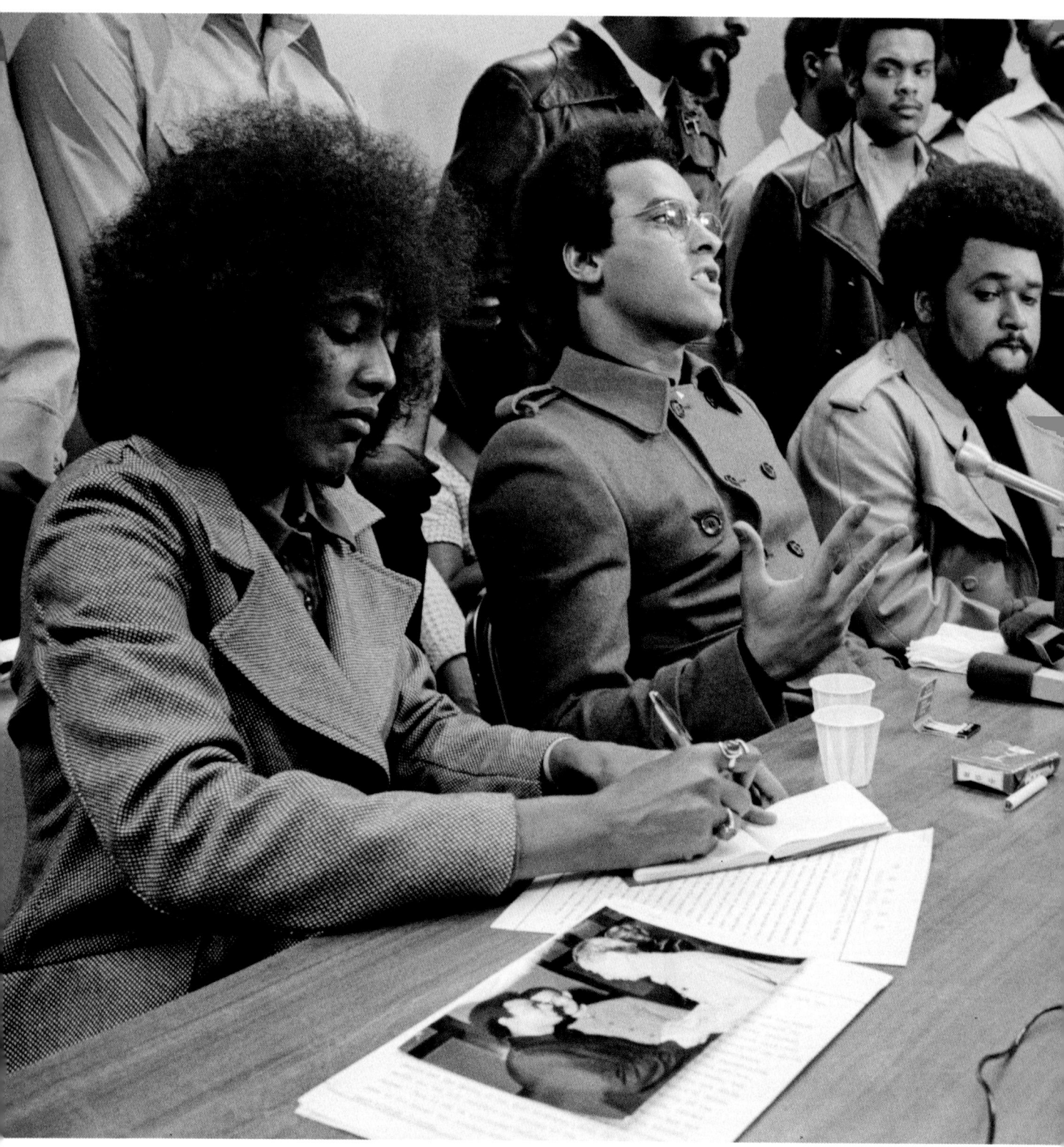

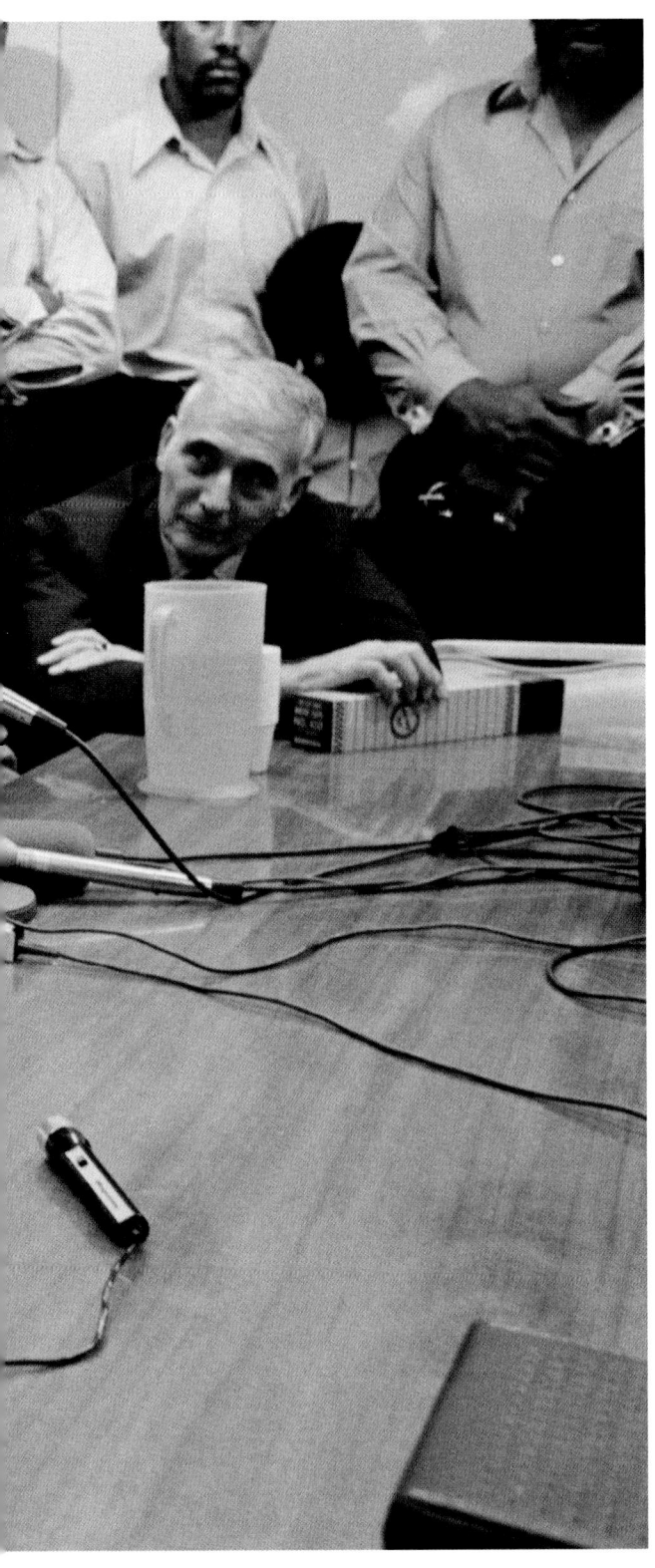

Williams had just given a speech at a rally in Beijing celebrating the third anniversary of Mao Zedong's statement of support and is seen in the photograph on page 248 shaking hands with the Chinese premier, Zhou Enlai, on August 8, 1966. (This image was reprinted in the *Peking Review* on August 12.) Bolstered by Zhou's support, Williams declared that President Lyndon B. Johnson "can no more intimidate the Afro-American people with his threat of unleashing his great hordes of mad-dog racists than he can intimidate the Chinese people with the threat of unleashing a nuclear attack. The day when brutal white racist oppressors and imperialists can frighten colored peoples into submission by threats of savage violence are gone forever!" For the Chinese leadership, Williams was their first high-profile African American ally since W. E. B. Du Bois, who had died in 1963.

While the photograph suggests cordial friendship, it fails to capture the political turmoil beginning to grip Chinese society and its political institutions. The Cultural Revolution had just begun, and four days earlier, at an enlarged meeting of the Politburo Standing Committee, Mao accused political leaders of "standing on the side of the bourgeoisie to oppose the Great Proletarian Cultural Revolution." The Cultural Revolution brought about the downfall of high-ranking Chinese officials like Deng Xiaoping, Liu Shaoqi, and Lin Biao, but it elevated Williams and other Black radicals in the years following this photo.

Williams's call to meet violence with violence and his strong stance against the U.S. government made him a popular figure in China, while arguably more moderate activists like Martin Luther King Jr. came to be widely despised there. Williams returned to the United States three years after this photograph was taken, but he was not the last African American leader to look to China for support.

PREVIOUS SPREAD, LEFT: Chinese premier Zhou Enlai (left) congratulates Robert F. Williams following the latter's speech in Beijing, China, August 8, 1966.

LEFT: October 8, 1971: Huey P. Newton during a press conference following his visit to China, where he met with Zhou Enlai.

In 1971, Zhou Enlai again greeted African American activists when Black Panther Party founder Huey Newton visited China. On the table at this press conference in San Francisco, is a photograph of Newton meeting Zhou in Beijing. The image is strikingly similar to the photograph of Williams's meeting five years earlier.

At the time, Newton teetered upon a political tightrope. The press conference was held roughly six months following his party's split with more radically minded revolutionaries like Eldridge Cleaver and just five months before President Richard Nixon's visit to China. At the conference, Newton spoke vaguely of gaining China's support. Meanwhile, Zhou was balancing his own political challenges. The Cultural Revolution had raged on for six years, restoring Mao's grip over the party, but at a grave cost of Chinese lives, economic growth, and social stability. China's relationship with the Soviet Union had also grown increasingly antagonistic, marred by border conflicts that risked all-out war.

Although Zhou agreed to meet with Newton and other Black Panther Party members in October 1971, Chinese political leaders were already moving to foster better relations with the U.S. government. While hosting a banquet on October 5, Zhou encouraged Newton and other Black Panther Party delegation members to drop their revolutionary rhetoric and promote cordial relations between the U.S. and China.

Zhou's meeting with Newton ultimately became a part of his country's efforts to normalize relations with the United States. The Chinese support that Newton alluded to at this press conference would never materialize.

RIGHT: American president Richard Nixon inspects assembled Chinese soldiers with Chinese premier Zhou Enlai, February 26, 1972.

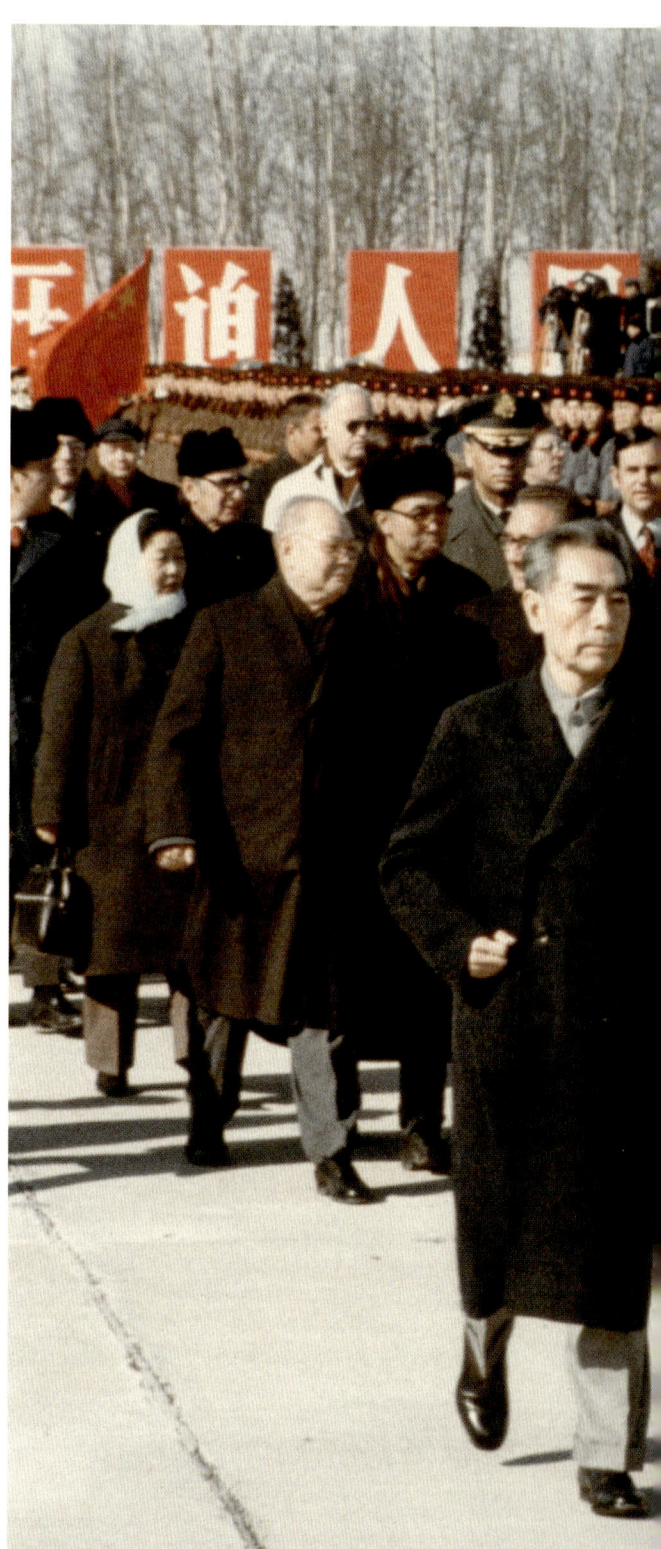

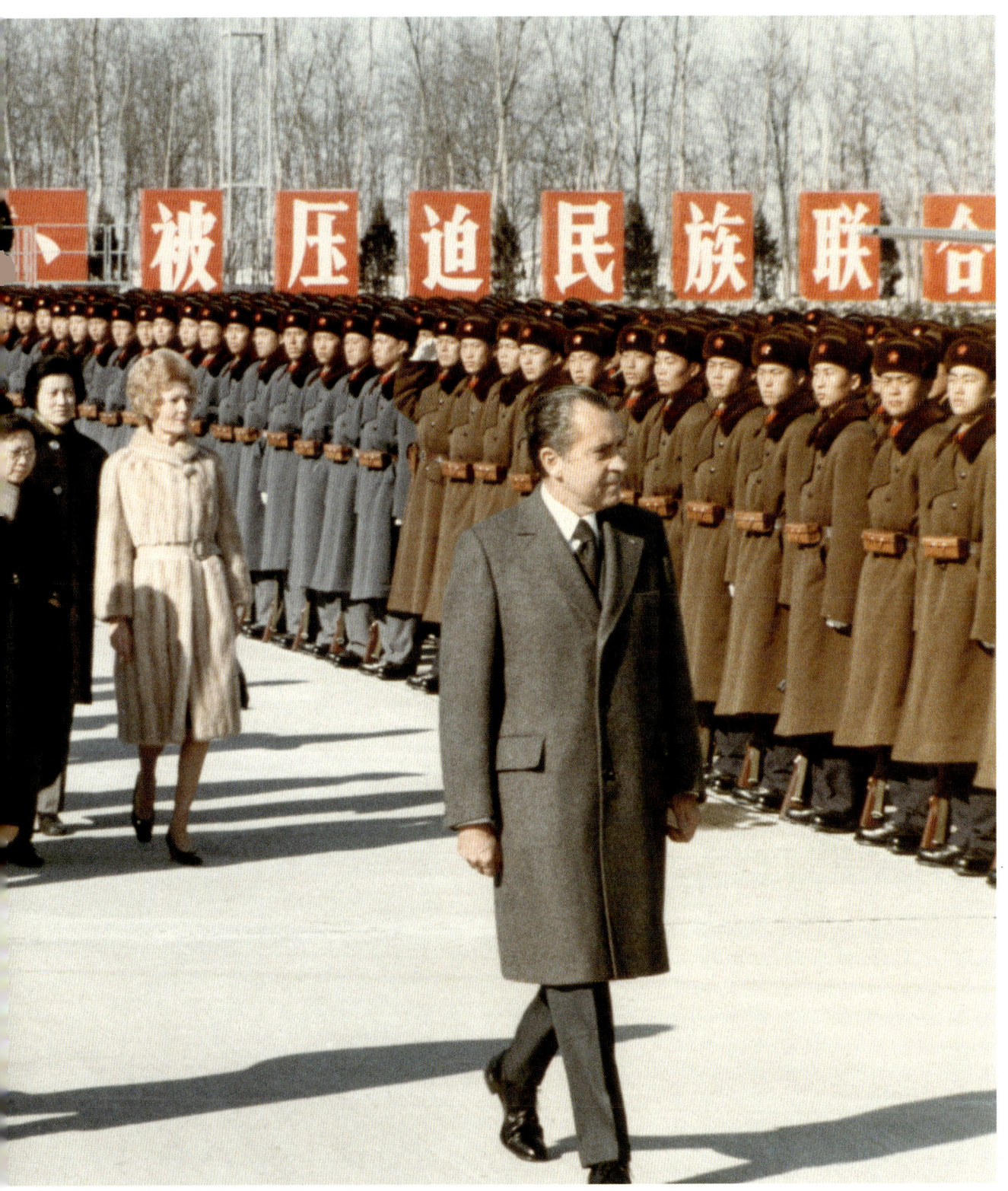

被 压 迫 民 族 联 合

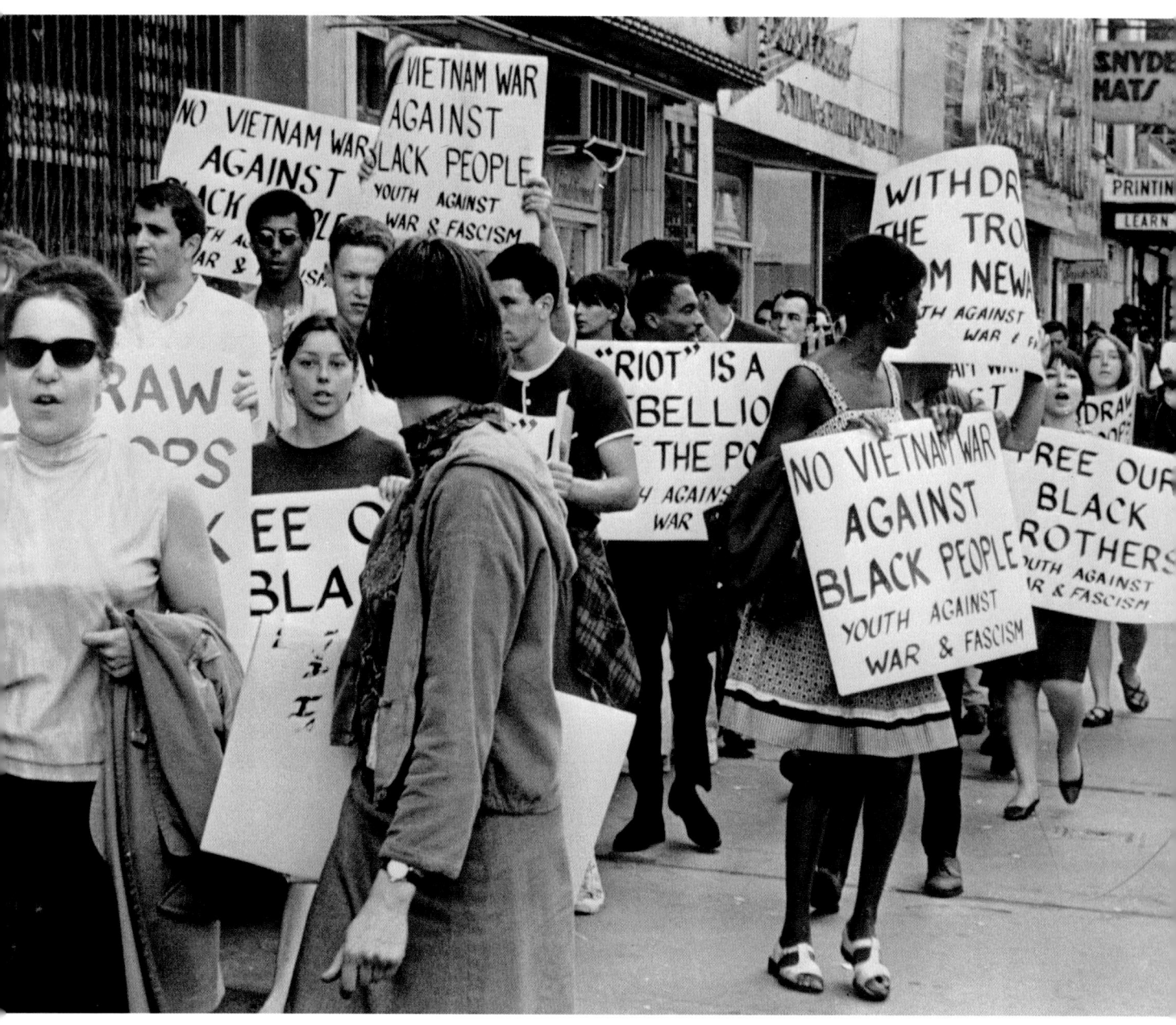

Just months after the banquet with the Black Panthers, and against the backdrop of the Vietnam War, China openly began the process of normalizing relations with the U.S. government and embedding itself in international systems. Nothing symbolized that more than President Richard Nixon, seen in the photo on the previous spread at the end of his trip to China, reviewing Chinese troops. Meanwhile, many African Americans believed that those international systems contributed to their problems.

Mao hoped to check the Soviet Union's territorial ambitions by forming an alliance with the United States. For his part, Nixon hoped that normalizing relations with China would speed the U.S. exit from Vietnam. The racial discrimination faced by African Americans was not of significant concern for either party in 1972.

While this photograph of Nixon and Zhou Enlai represented a nascent friendship between two countries, it also represented a betrayal for many revolutionary-minded African Americans. Still barred from expressing the fullest extent of their rights, this change in political winds highlighted that while many African Americans invested considerable energy abroad, foreign allies often proved ready to divest themselves from their cause.

Ironically, the visible characters on the upper right-hand side of the photograph read, "oppressed peoples of the world unite." Although the first two photographs captured moments when revolutionary Black liberation movements met the Chinese revolution, the third picture highlighted their divergence.

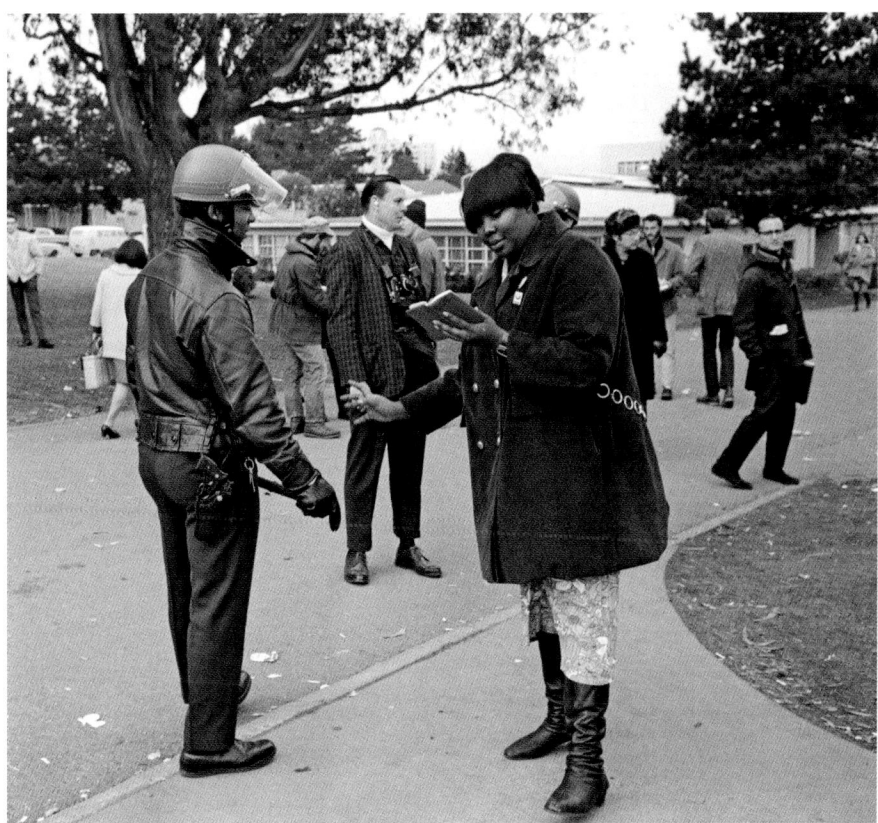

OPPOSITE: Youth protest deployment of the National Guard during the 1967 Newark Race Riots.

LEFT: A demonstrator reads *The Quotations of Mao Tse-tung* during a 1969 protest at San Francisco State University.

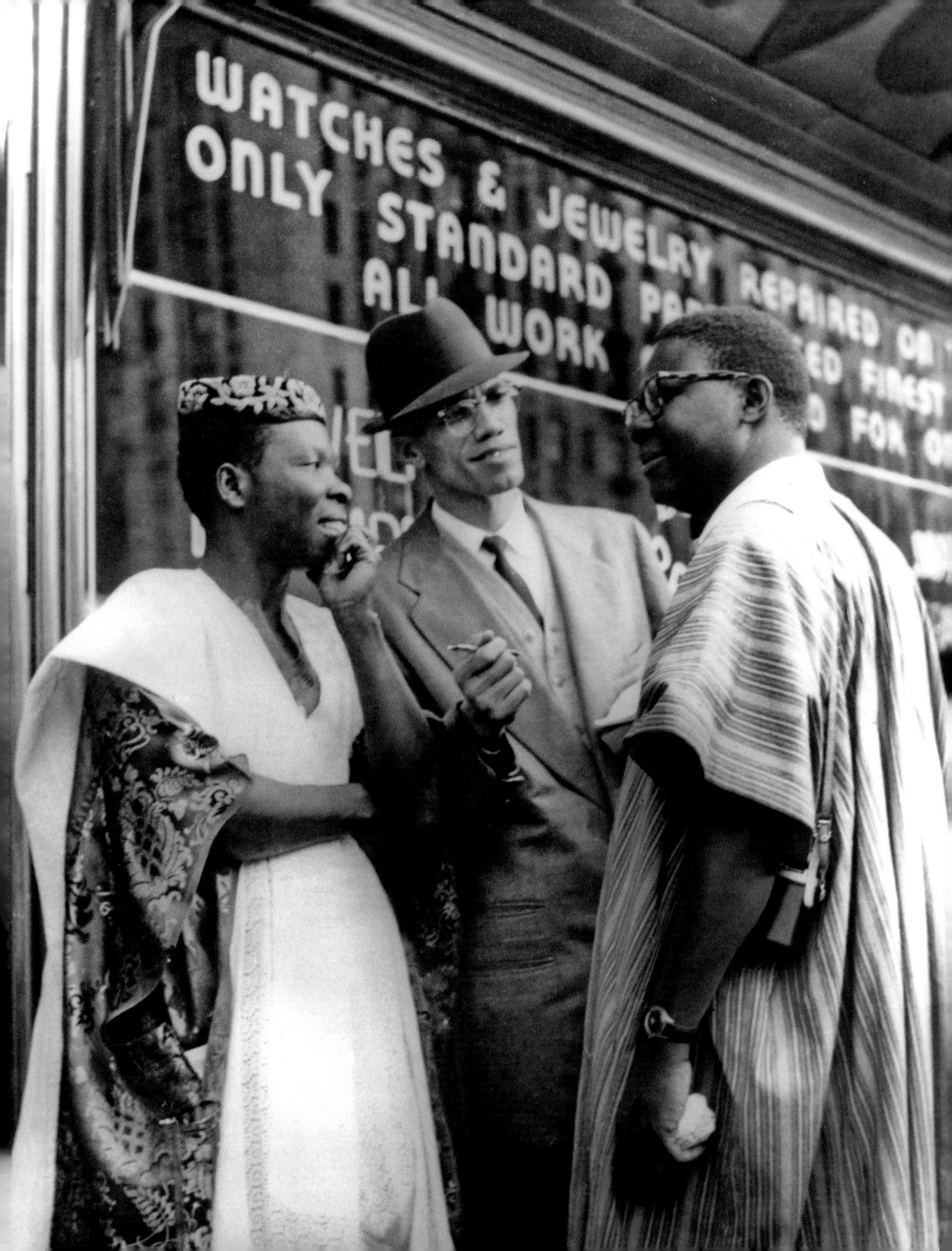

VII.

GLOBAL DIMENSIONS OF BLACK HISTORY

AFRICAN AMERICAN HISTORY HAS OFTEN BEEN INTERTWINED WITH INTERNATIONAL EVENTS. In the earliest days, students of Black history were keen to investigate the interconnections, commonalities, and shared struggles of African Americans with continental Africans, the African diaspora, and other historically marginalized people around the world. These collaborations produced coalitions that linked African American social movements to broader currents against European imperialism, and to other ethnic communities facing racial discrimination. African Americans participated as international actors even as they were shaped by both domestic and international affairs.

This section presents the expansiveness of Black history into Africa, Asia, Latin America, and Europe to explore the possibilities and constraints of social movement formation and social change within the United States and abroad.

OPPOSITE: Malcolm X (center) talking to Babatunde Olatunji, a Nigerian educator and musician (left) and a Nigerian student, on the day Nigeria declared its independence, October 1, 1960.

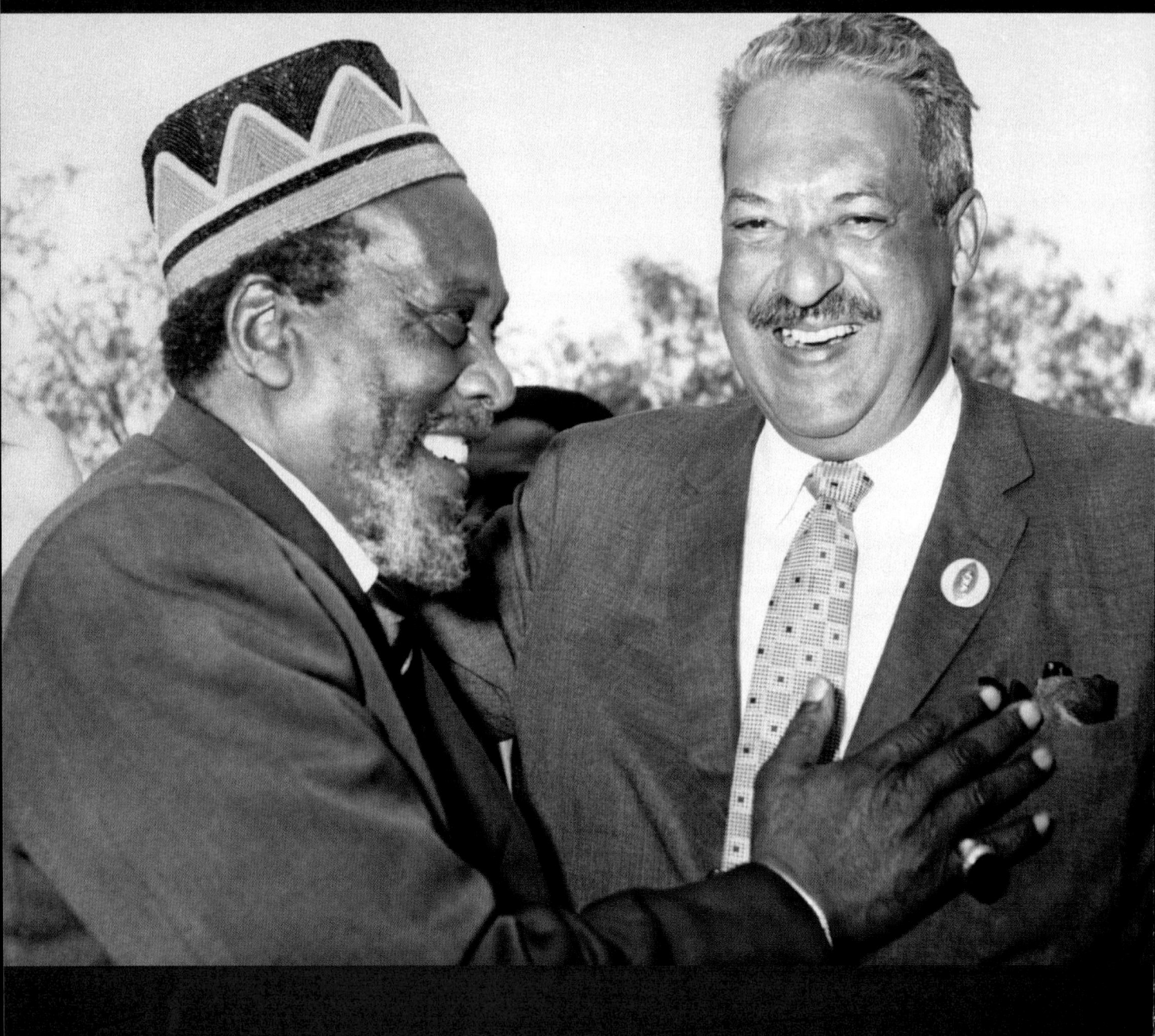

INTERNATIONAL LEGACIES <u>OF</u> AFRICAN AMERICAN CIVIL RIGHTS ACTIVISM

DAMARIUS JOHNSON

Thurgood Marshall, Malcolm X, and Stokely Carmichael are torchbearers of an American Civil Rights Movement with international significance.

The conventional history of the Civil Rights Movement details a series of legal victories from 1954 to 1968 that improved access to voting rights, economic opportunity, and social participation for African Americans in the United States.

A lesser-known aspect of civil rights activism is that the struggle for domestic social progress was inseparable from international political movements. Civil rights activists often looked abroad to establish coalitions with other marginalized communities, build moral and material support for their causes, and develop strategies to pursue their goals. The American Civil Rights Movement was a human rights struggle on an international stage.

Federal district judge Thurgood Marshall had been sympathetic to the Kenyan decolonization struggle in the 1950s and he had defended African students as a lawyer for the NAACP. In 1960, Marshall participated in the first of three Lancaster House Conferences that ultimately produced the first constitution of independent Kenya.

At the 1960 Lancaster House Conference, Marshall drafted a "Kenyan Bill of Rights" that protected Kenyan minorities (White, Asian, and African) from discriminatory treatment. Jomo Kenyatta, inaugural president of post-independence Kenya, embraced Marshall's view of equality under the law during the early days of his administration.

By July 1963, Kenya achieved full independence from Britain, and Kenyatta invited Marshall to witness the practical impact of the earlier constitutional debates. Here the two men share a light moment during Marshall's short visit to Kenya.

Marshall's legal framework for justice and equality in independent Kenya articulated the vision of social justice that guided his legal career in the United States. In 1963, African politicians formed the Organization of African Unity (OAU) to promote mutual aid and consolidate material resources across newly formed African nations. Civil rights activist and Muslim minister Malcolm X spoke at the African Summit Conference, the second gathering of the OAU, in July 1964. The Quran, as held by Malcolm X in the photograph at right, established a framework for global Muslim community that shaped his evolving vision of international political activism and racial progress.

In a memorandum delivered at the African Summit on July 17, Malcolm X emphasized the shared struggle and common emancipatory visions of diasporic and continental African communities. He defined racial violence, discrimination, and bigotry in the United States as an extension of colonial and imperial governments in continental Africa. Furthermore, he petitioned OAU delegates to propose a United Nations investigation into American racial violence as a violation of African Americans' human rights.

Following this speech, which reinforced the political networks that linked African Americans to continental Africa and condemned American racism before the international community, the FBI intensified electronic surveillance of Malcolm X and his family.

Kwame Ture (previously known as Stokely Carmichael) arrived in Hanoi, North Vietnam, on August 18, 1967, to celebrate the International Day of Solidarity with members of the Black Panther Party. This ceremonial event reflects the global expansion of U.S. civil rights activism to include alliances in Asia and South America.

Ture's appearance in Hanoi deepened the Afro-Asian affiliation that began more than a decade earlier at the 1955 Bandung Conference, which fostered economic and political collaboration between governments in Africa and Asia. Black Power activists participating in high-profile gatherings with communists in the global south ran tremendous risks, particularly state surveillance and disruption of organizing activities. In the case of Kwame Ture, along with activists Essie and Paul Robeson, the United States withheld passports to prevent their involvement in socialist causes throughout the Cold War.

Each of these photographs captures the international scope of American civil rights activism in the 1960s. Civil rights leaders understood that their domestic concerns in the United States gained recognition, authority, and legitimacy by attracting international press and collaborations. The activism of the civil rights era included demands for African Americans' citizenship rights and denunciations of America's role as an imperial and colonial force across the world. African Americans also contributed their activist labors to support anti-colonial struggles across the Global South.

These efforts at coalition-building provided a playbook for contemporary social movements to convey their local struggles within a much broader community of international support.

PREVIOUS SPREAD, LEFT: Kenyan Premier Jomo Kenyatta (left) shares a laugh with U.S. federal judge Thurgood Marshall during a visit to Nairobi, Kenya, on July 11, 1963.

RIGHT: Malcolm X (left) holds an open copy of the Quran as he speaks to an unidentified man at the African Summit Conference in Cairo, Egypt, July 1964.

FOLLOWING SPREAD: Kwame Ture (Stokely Carmichael), center left, with officials at the International Day of Solidarity with the American Black Power movement in Hanoi, North Vietnam, 1967.

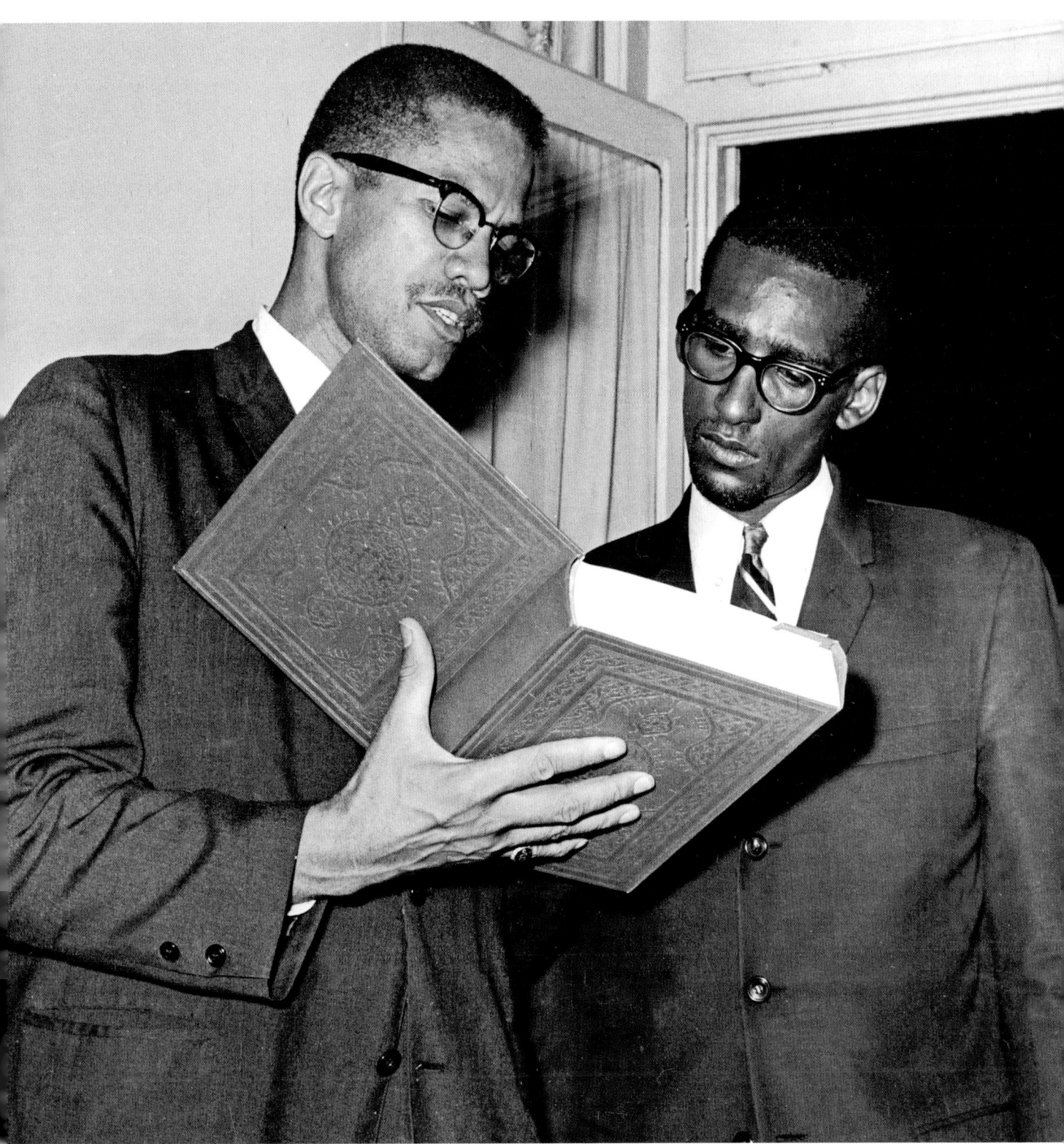

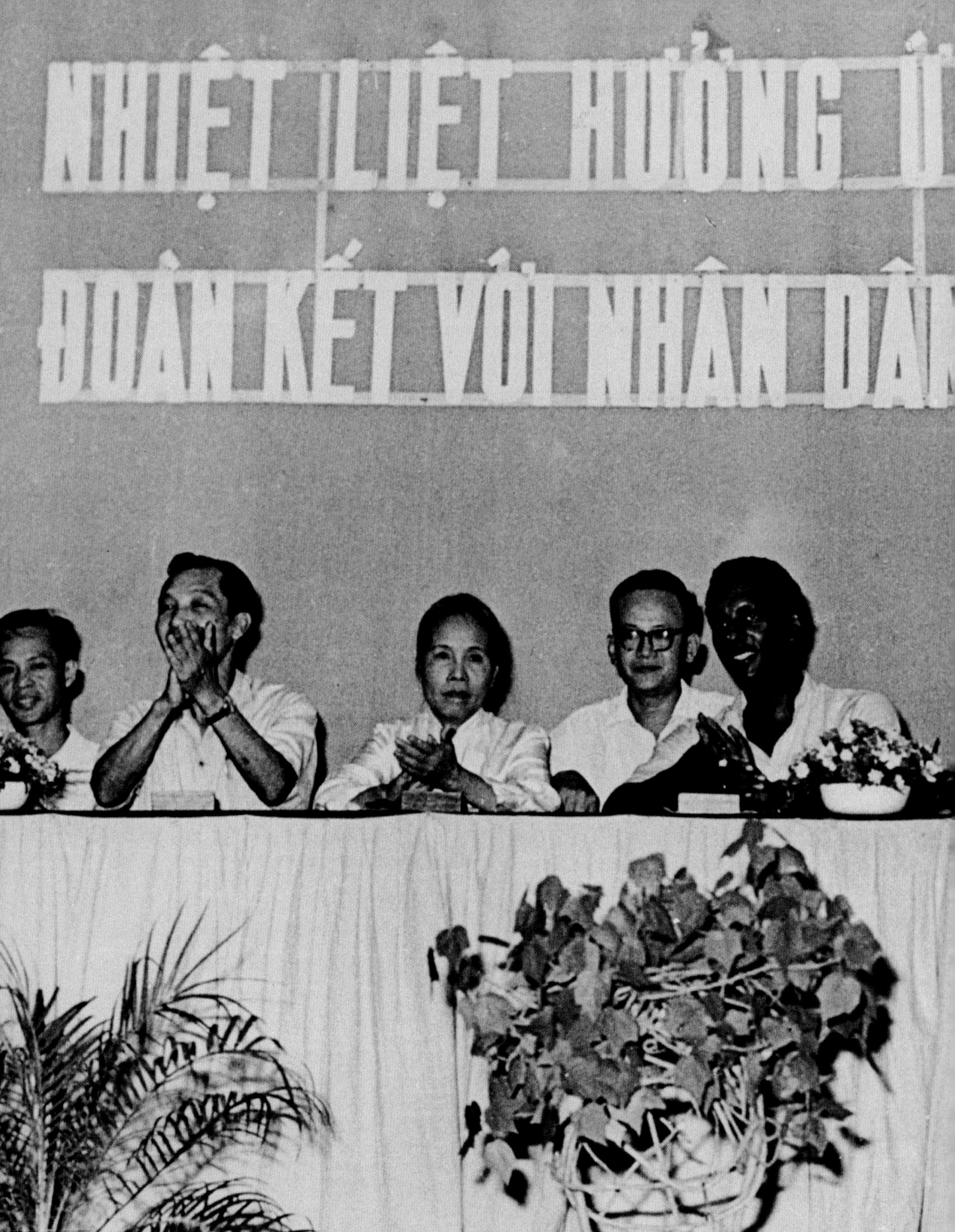

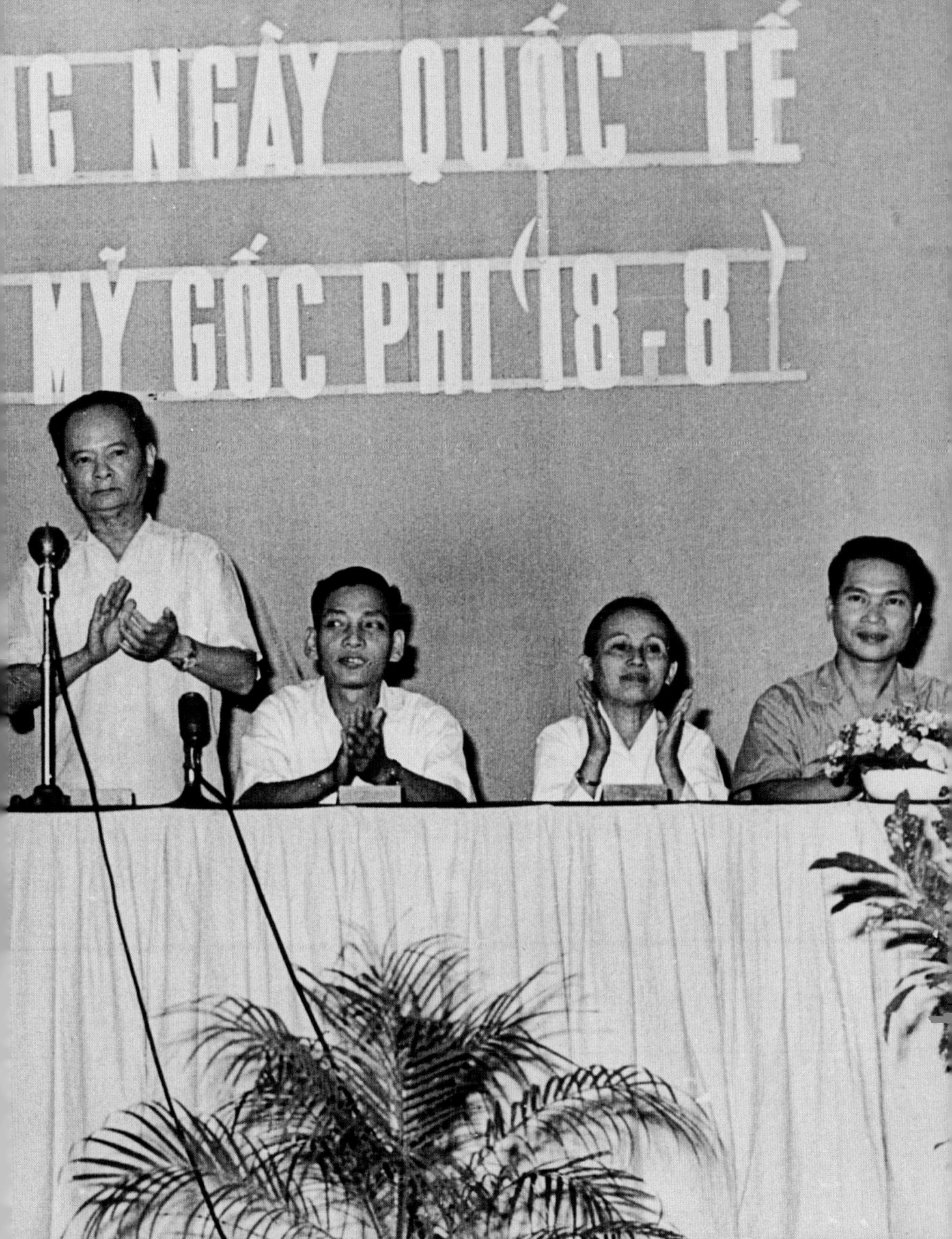

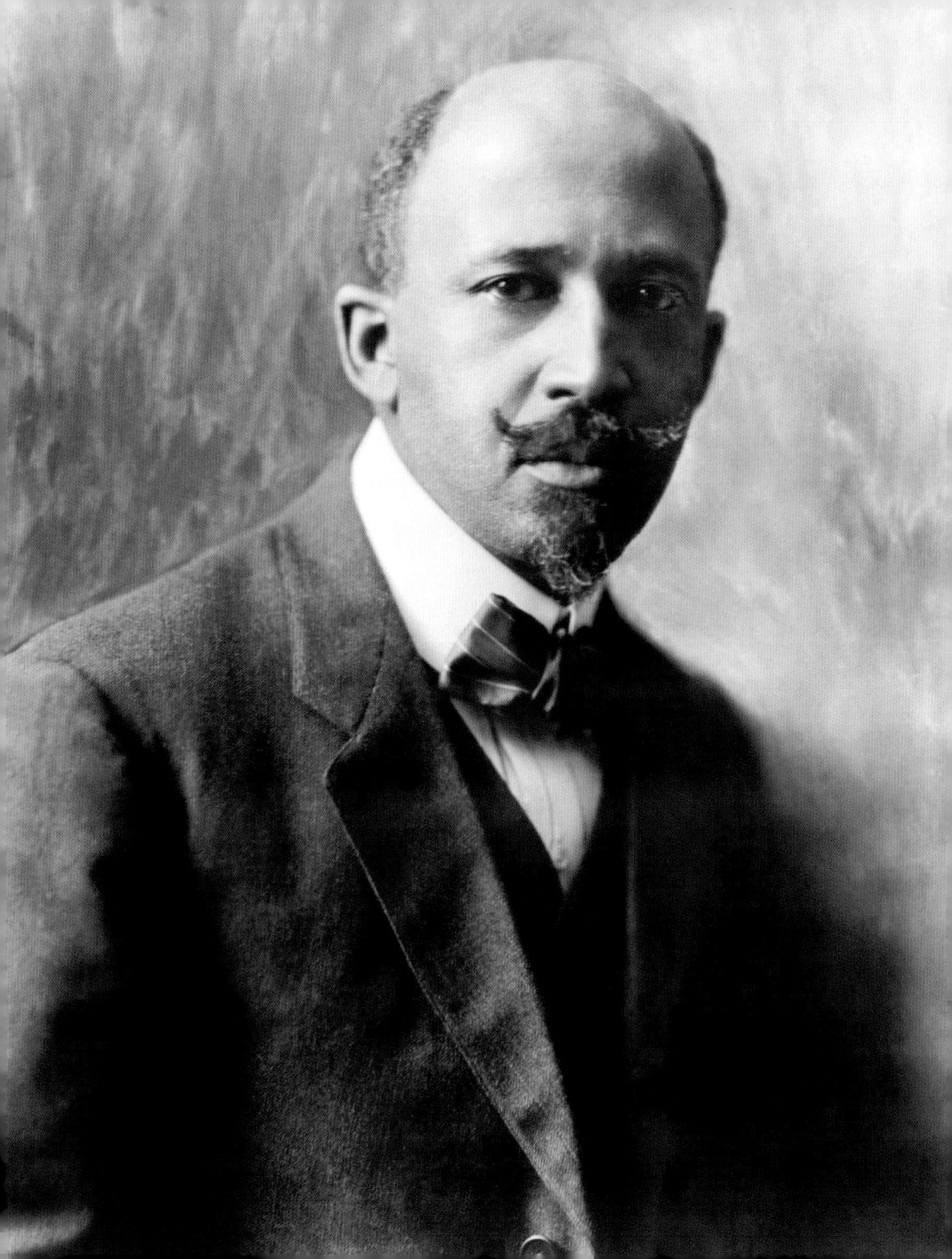

W. E. B. DU BOIS
AND THE PAN-AFRICAN CONGRESS

JAMES R. MORGAN III

*W. E. B. Du Bois contributed to the global dimensions
of the African American freedom struggle that continues today.*

From the beginning, William Edward Burghardt (W. E. B.) Du Bois knew that the problems of racial inequality were global. Jim Crow racism in the United States and European imperialism, he well understood, oppressed people of color around the world. Du Bois envisioned that, through a new international Black solidarity, African Americans might see an end to their second-class citizenship under American laws. But he was also very clear that the fate of Africans in the diaspora was connected to the fate and status of Africans in Africa itself.

Educated at Fisk University, then at Harvard, where he became the first Black person awarded a PhD, and then at Friedrich Wilhelm University in Berlin (now Humboldt University), Du Bois was among a generation of "race men and women," in the language of the era, who positioned themselves to fight against the historical injustices done against African people internationally. Before the twentieth century, it was hard for organizers of African descent to build up a struggle against European imperialism. During the so-called Scramble for Africa, the continent's people had been subjugated by seven different European powers. By 1914 only Ethiopia and Liberia remained independent.

This would all begin to change with the globalization brought by World War I. The war's end resulted in the dissolution of several major empires. Equally important, World War I created the first major opportunity for many working-class Africans from across the world to interact with one another. This exchange of personal experiences offered windows into similarities and differences in African people's lived experiences and reinforced a Pan-African destiny of liberation.

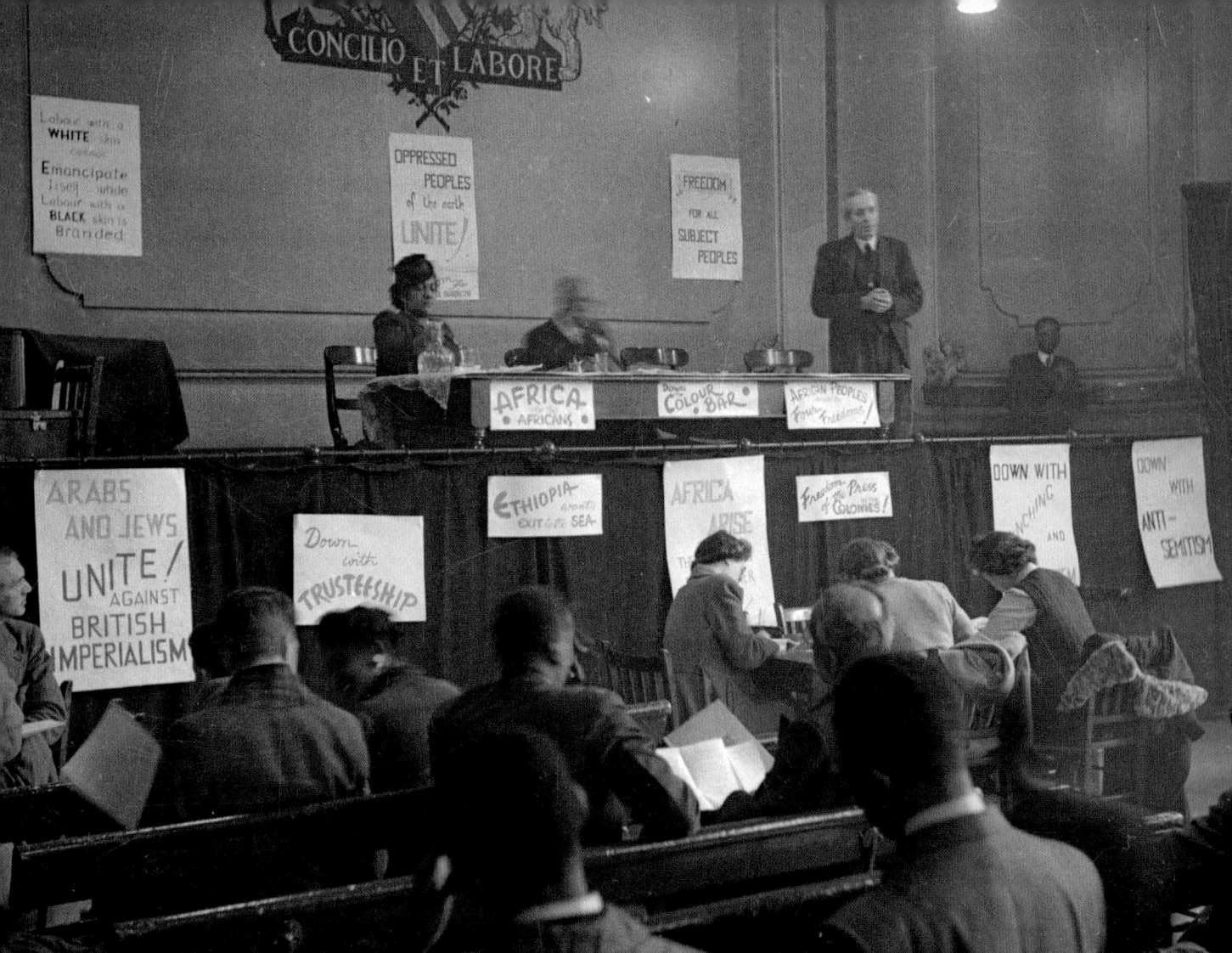

Du Bois had taken part in international efforts for racial justice prior to World War I, such as the First Pan-African Conference in July 1900, which sought to establish a coordinated opposition to colonial regimes that oppressed African people across the globe. However, the postwar period presented a new opportunity for African people to grasp their liberation as colonial power shifted at the conclusion of the conflict.

Du Bois and other political activists decided to capitalize on this new synergy and sense of connectivity by organizing the Pan-African Congress in February 1919 in Paris. The timing of the Congress aligned with the Paris Peace Conference, where representatives from thirty-two countries met to decide how postwar Europe would function after defeating Germany and the other Central Powers. Du Bois and other Pan-Africanist thinkers believed that organizing their own Pan-African Congresses on the state of the African world, and presenting their case to the European powers, would start talks leading to the independence of African nations from European rule.

The inaugural Pan-African Congress allowed Du Bois to interact with other leading minds of African descent such as John Archer (Britain), Anna Julia Cooper (United States), Rayford Logan (United States), Amy

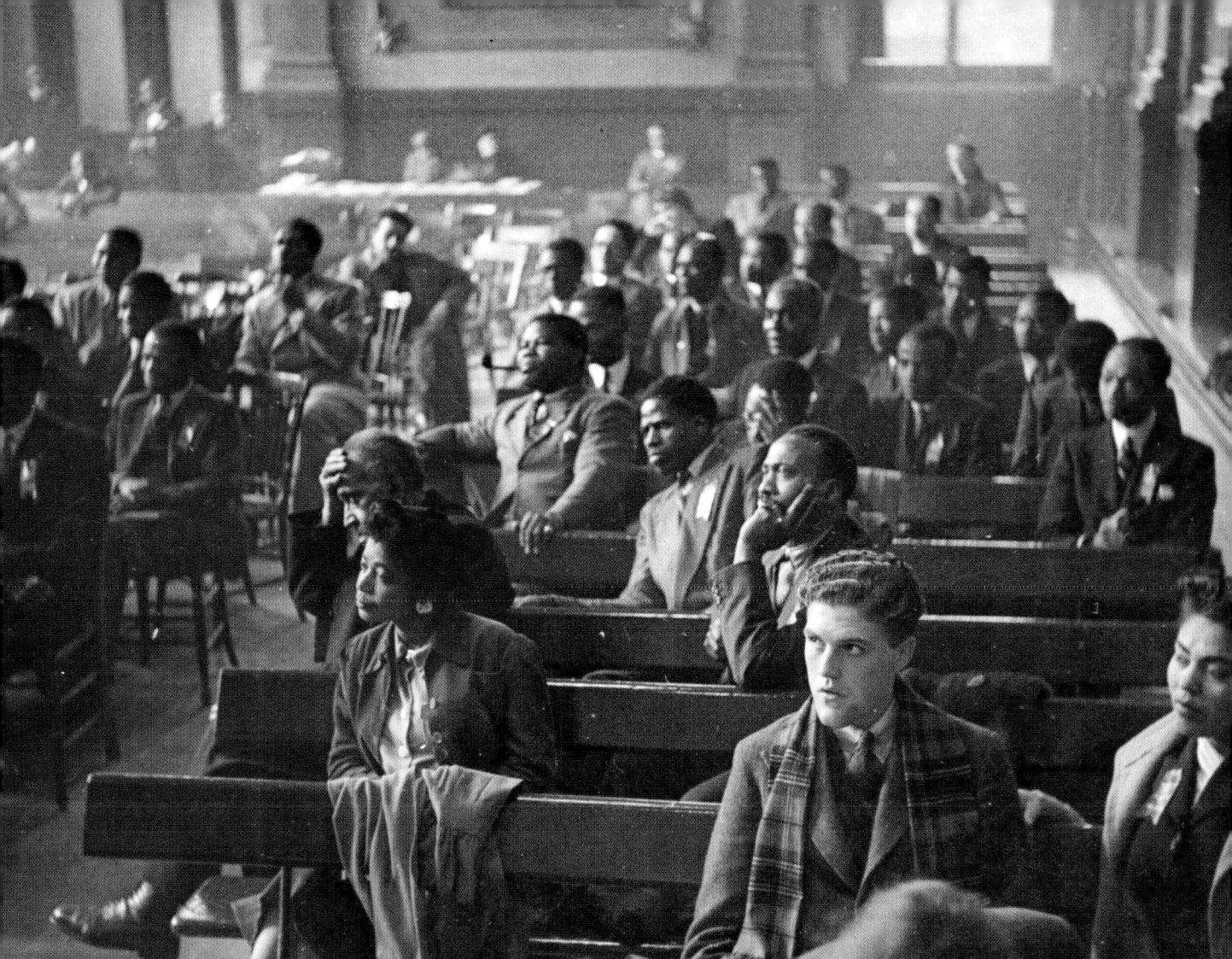

Jacques Garvey (Jamaica), and Blaise Diagne (Senegal). Continental African delegates attended in smaller numbers than diasporic Africans due to travel bans, and the U.S. government blocked many African Americans from receiving passport approvals.

Delegates to the Congress believed their case for liberation was strengthened due to Black soldiers from African colonies and African Americans fighting on the side of the victorious Allies. They hoped that such loyalty might allow for Africans around the world to share in the spoils of war, if not monetarily, then certainly to loosen the chains of oppression and exploitation.

PREVIOUS SPREAD, LEFT: A 1918 portrait of political organizer, educator, historian, and sociologist W. E. B. Du Bois.

OPPOSITE: John McNair, general secretary of the Independent Labour Party (right), shares the stage with Amy Ashwood Garvey (left) at the Fifth Pan-African Congress.

ABOVE: The audience listens intently to the proceedings at the Fifth Pan-African Congress in Manchester, United Kingdom, October 15–21, 1945.

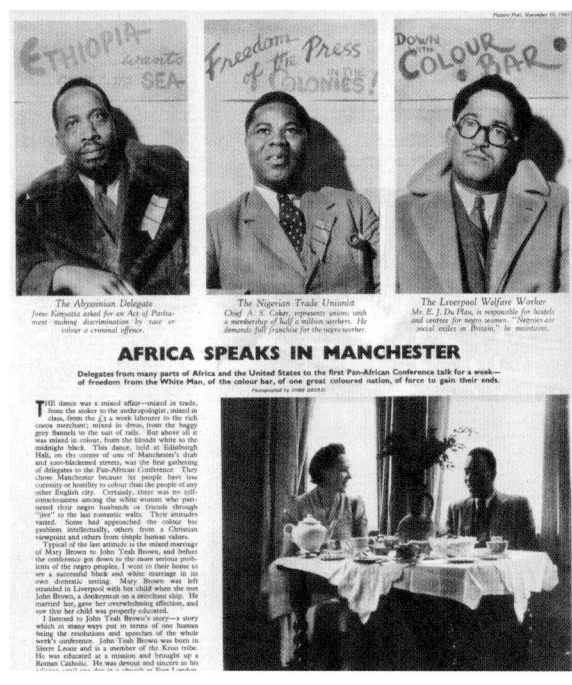

AFRICA SPEAKS IN MANCHESTER

The 1919 Pan-African Congress resulted in several resolutions. One called for a new international journal entitled the *Black Review* to be published in each of the major languages spoken by African people around the world. The Congress also demanded legal protections for African people and for the supervision of African colonies by the newly minted League of Nations.

Delegates believed that European powers had abused Africans to such a degree that international oversight was needed until African colonies developed the infrastructure to govern themselves in the modern world, independent of their functional dependency on European colonial administration.

Du Bois personally forwarded a copy of the resolutions to Winston Churchill, then British secretary of state for the colonies, and to the administration of American president Woodrow Wilson, thus serving as a messenger of the entire African world to leading politicians in the two most powerful Allied nations.

The birth of the Pan-African Congresses was one of the earliest seeds of the African independence movement. At the conclusion of the first Pan-African Congress in 1919, attendees decided to continue meeting to deliberate the global concerns of African peoples.

With the advent of newer technologies such as radio and television, African people began to see and hear one another in real time, reinforcing their commonalities and shared commitments by linking the domestic American Civil Rights Movement with African independence movements in the 1950s and 1960s, just as Du Bois intended.

Pan-African Congresses continued across the twentieth and twenty-first centuries to meet in Europe, the United States, and continental Africa: 1919 in Paris; 1921 in Brussels, London, and Paris; 1923 in Lisbon and London; 1927 in New York City; 1945 in Manchester; 1974 in Dar es Salaam; 1994 in Kampala; and 2014 in Johannesburg.

Each of the Pan-African Congresses testifies to the undying dream of those who, like Du Bois, realized that by liberating Africans from their oppressions in continental Africa and the African diaspora, the entire world would be liberated from the oppressions of old.

LEFT: Newspaper coverage of the Fifth Pan-African Congress featuring Kenyan Jomo Kenyatta (left), Nigerian chief A. S. Cohen (center), and Liverpool Labor organizer E. J. Du Plau (right).

RIGHT: Amy Ashwood Garvey (left) attends a demonstration in Trafalgar Square (London) to demand the lifting of the British arms embargo against Ethiopia.

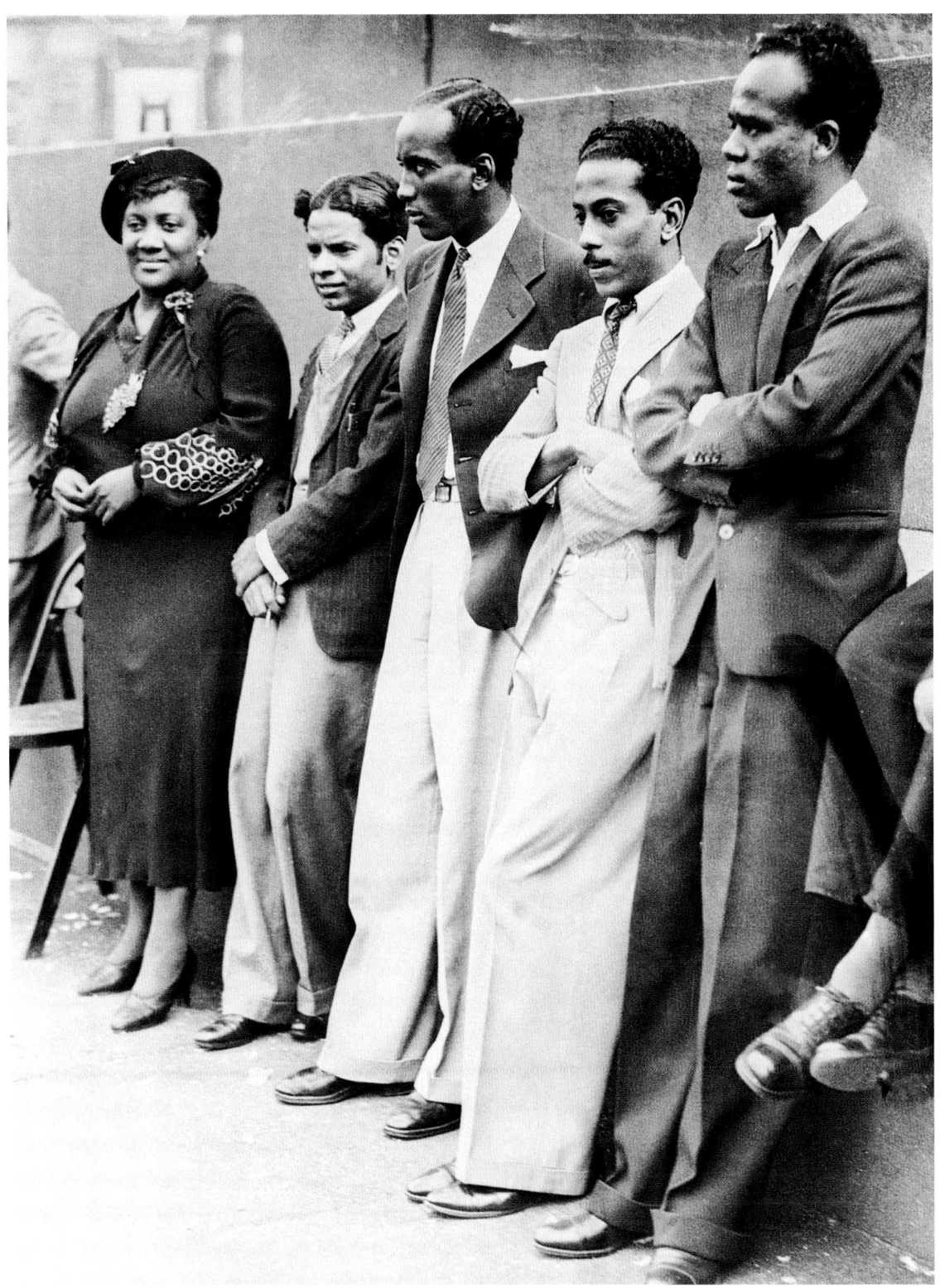

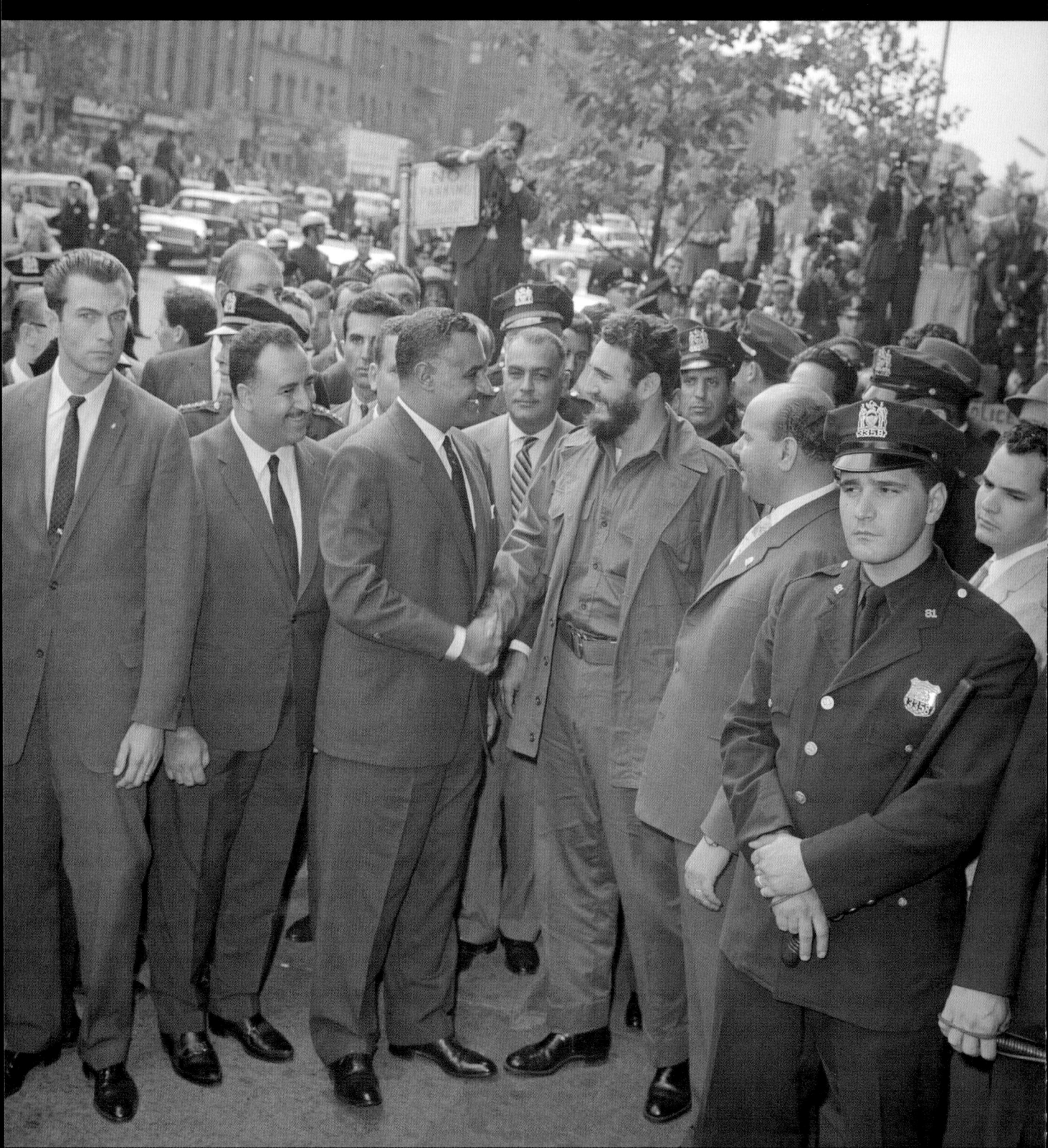

CASTRO COMES <u>TO</u> HARLEM

KEVIN MCGRUDER

*Fidel Castro spent ten days at the Hotel Theresa in Harlem,
meeting world leaders and spotlighting the
racial discrimination faced by Blacks in New York City.*

In September 1960, some eighteen months after he had come to power as Cuba's premier, Fidel Castro announced plans to attend the 15th session of the United Nations General Assembly in New York City.

This was notable as the General Assembly serves as the policymaking body of the UN. Naturally, amid the Cold War, questions regarding whether Castro would ally Cuba with the Soviet Union made his visit a matter of curiosity and concern for the American press.

While many Americans viewed Castro with suspicion, his vigorous denunciation of colonialism and racial oppression worldwide excited many Latino and Black New Yorkers who anticipated his visit. In photograph on the following spread, an excited crowd of New Yorkers, many with Cuban flags and banners in Spanish, gathered to welcome Castro's motorcade on the evening of Sunday, September 18, as it made its way from Idlewild Airport (now JFK) to Manhattan.

The U.S. State Department confined Castro to the island of Manhattan, but Manhattan's racially segregated hotels refused to provide Castro's delegation, which included many Afro-Cuban and Taino/European members, with lodging. Only after the intervention of the State Department and the United Nations was lodging finally secured at the Hotel Shelburne on Lexington Avenue in midtown Manhattan. Even so, the hotel's owner, Edward Spatz, refused to allow the delegation to eat in the hotel dining room.

Soon after they arrived at the Shelburne, Castro had a dispute with the hotel's management, and the Cuban delegation left. Castro threatened that the Cuban delegation would instead camp out in the courtyard of the UN or in Central Park, but according to his obituary in the *New York Times* on May 30, 1967, Love B. Woods, the Black manager of the Hotel Theresa in Harlem, offered the delegation rooms, noting "we don't discriminate against anybody."

Castro enthusiastically accepted Woods's offer, undoubtedly understanding that the move would provide him with an opportunity to highlight the hypocrisy of the United States' supposed commitment to freedom for all, by bringing a media focus to the poor housing conditions, police brutality, struggling schools, and other manifestations of racial discrimination that Harlem residents regularly experienced.

Built in 1913 by the German-born stockbroker Gustavus Seidenberg, the Hotel Theresa, a white brick, thirteen-story building, spans the block from 124th to 125th Streets on Seventh Avenue. When the hotel opened, Harlem was a predominantly white neighborhood, although Black people had begun moving there in greater numbers. The Theresa did not accept Black lodgers until 1940, by which time Central Harlem was a predominantly Black neighborhood.

The Theresa's owners then hired Black management, who marketed the hotel to Black celebrities and professionals unable to stay in midtown Manhattan's segregated hotels. By 1946, an *Ebony* magazine article described the Theresa as "the Waldorf of Harlem" after the exclusive Waldorf Astoria Hotel in midtown Manhattan.

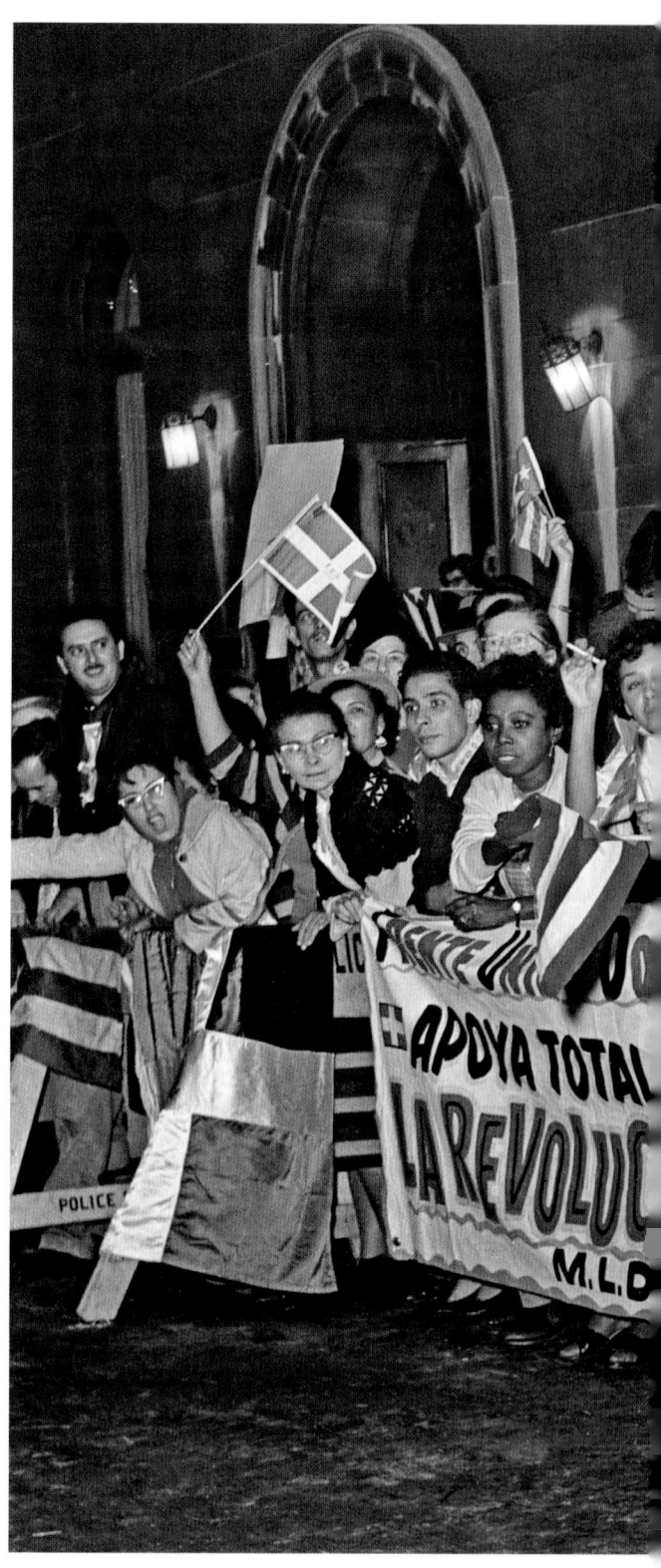

RIGHT: Crowd of Castro critics and supporters await his arrival to New York International Airport in 1960.

PREVIOUS SPREAD, LEFT: Gamal Abdel Nasser, president of Egypt, and Fidel Castro met at the Hotel Theresa during Castro's Harlem visit.

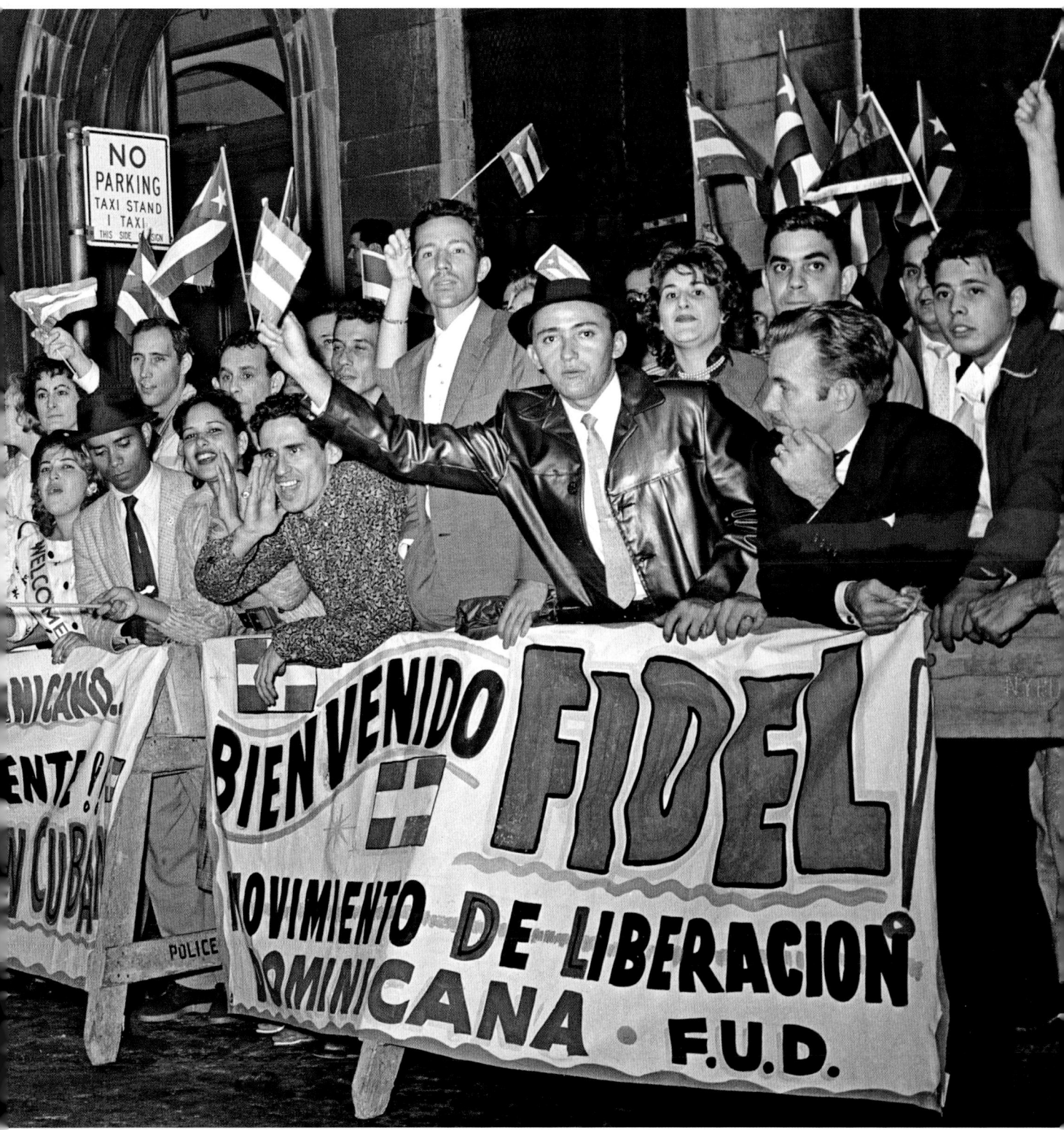

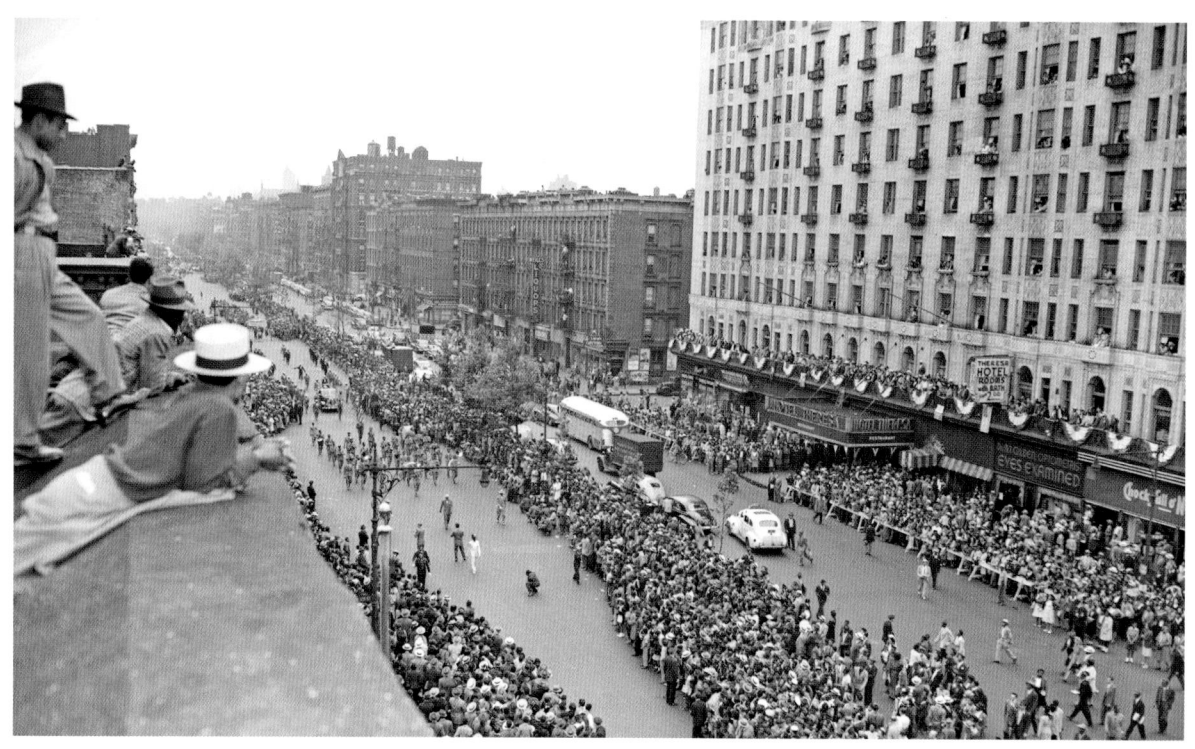

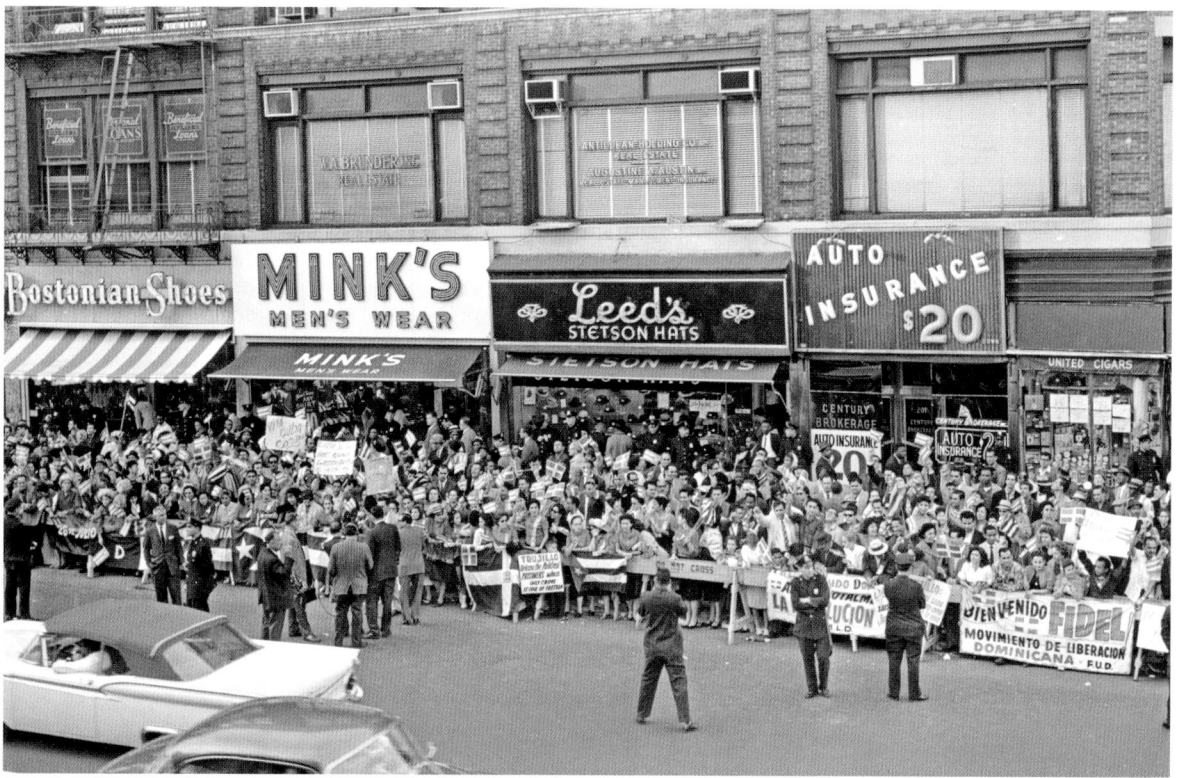

OPPOSITE, TOP: Aerial view of
a parade in honor of Joe Louis
passing the Hotel Theresa (right).

OPPOSITE, BOTTOM: A crowd
gathers outside the Hotel Theresa
to greet Fidel Castro (October
6, 1960).

RIGHT: 1960 photo of Fidel Castro
and Malcolm X

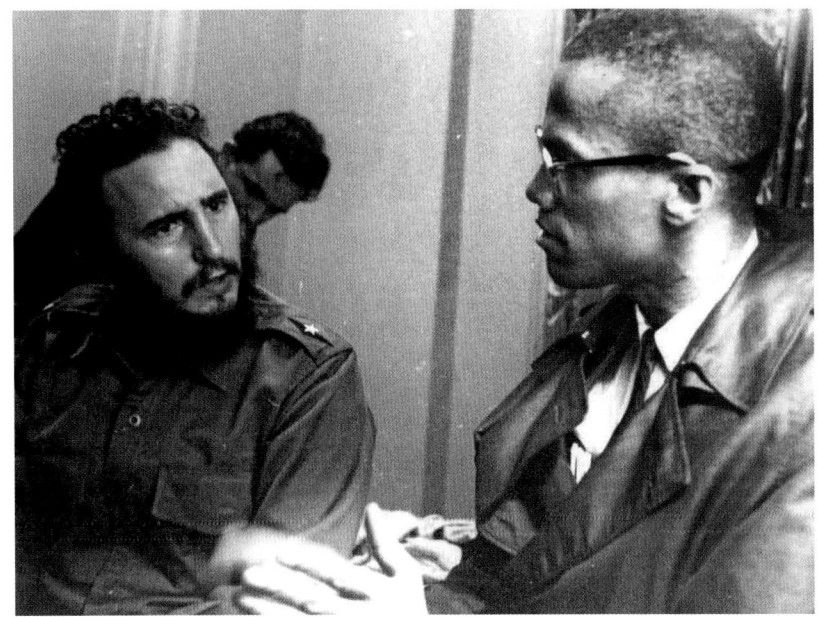

Seventh Avenue in Harlem was a magnet for public events, making the hotel a backdrop for major social gatherings, like this parade (opposite, top) honoring heavyweight champion Joe Louis, which passed in front of the Hotel Theresa in 1946.

During his time in New York, Castro's delegation quickly made themselves at home at the hotel, where the management welcomed them graciously. Castro's move to Harlem was met with excitement by residents. Hundreds flocked to the hotel hoping to catch a glimpse of him, like the crowd that gathered around the corner from the hotel on 125th Street and gave Castro a hero's welcome (opposite, botom).

Maya Angelou, a member of the Harlem Writers Guild, whose members also included John Henrik Clarke, Julian Mayfield, and John Oliver Killens, described how they interrupted a guild meeting to rush to the Hotel Theresa, where "on a Monday evening, we were unable to get close to the hotel. Thousands of people filled the sidewalks and intersections, and police cordoned off the main and side streets."

Over the next ten days local, national, and international leaders made their way to the hotel to meet with Castro.

Just after 1 a.m. on Tuesday, September 20, several hours after the delegation had checked in, Malcolm X, the spokesman for the Nation of Islam, still wearing his trench coat, met with Castro in his suite for approximately thirty minutes. According to an FBI informant, they sympathized over their shared belief that the United States was threatened by people like them who sought to challenge American racial and imperialist oppression.

The informant reported that, as Malcolm X prepared to leave, he observed, "No one knows the master better than his servants. We have been servants ever since we were brought here. We know all his little tricks. Understand? We know what he is going to do before he does." To which Castro, laughing, responded, "Si, si."

Later that afternoon, Soviet premier Nikita Khrushchev made an unannounced visit to Castro at the Hotel Theresa. The Cubans had offered to meet at the Soviet

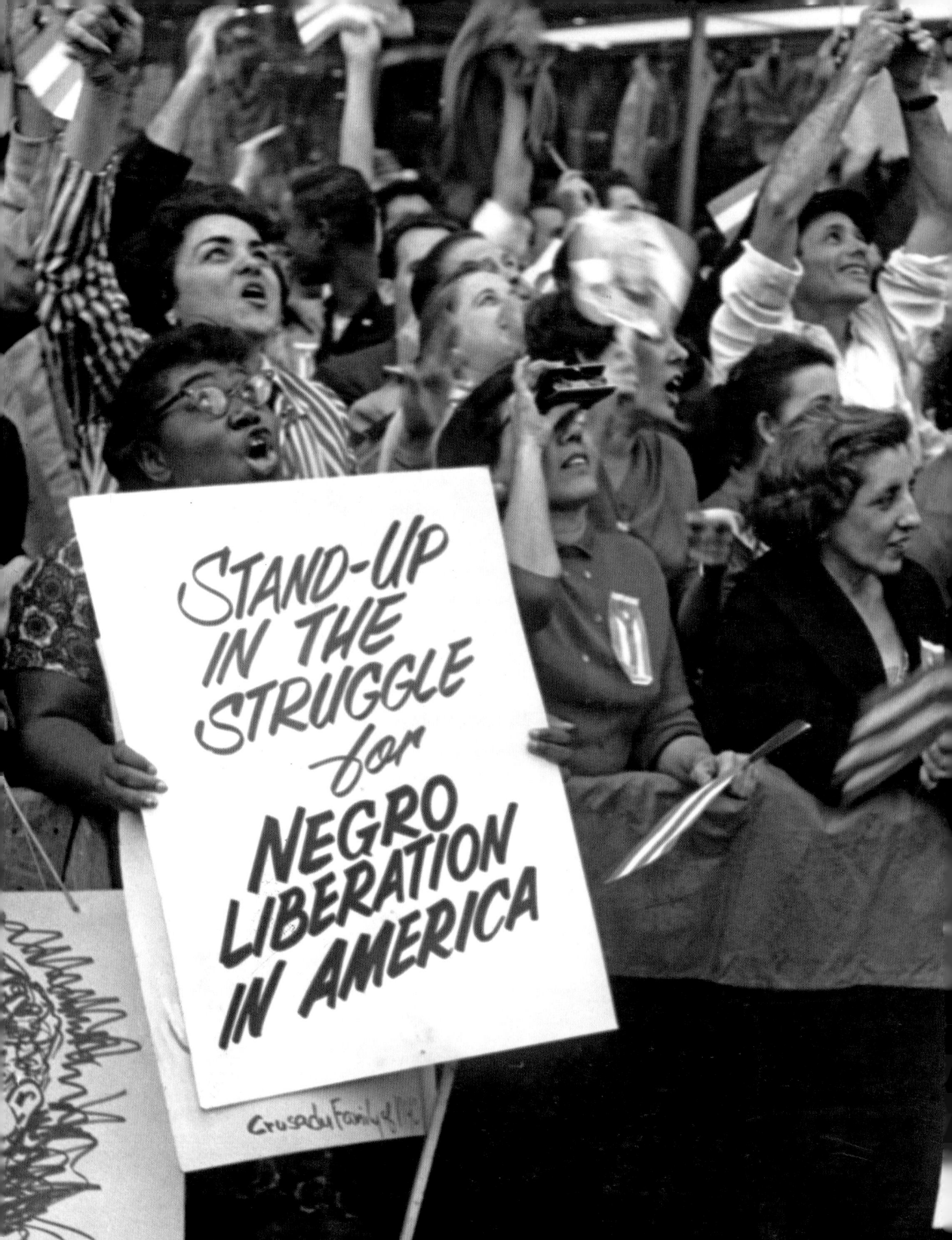

LEFT: Crowds gather outside Hotel Theresa to greet the Castro delegation.

RIGHT: Love B. Woods speaks with the press following Castro's visit.

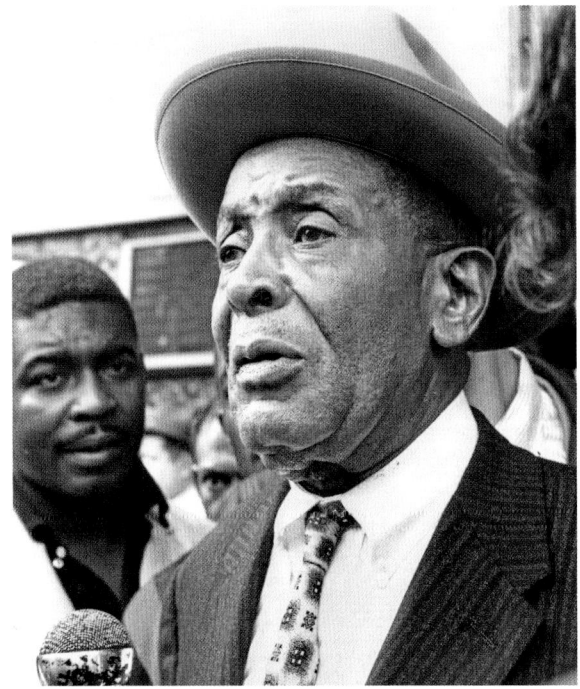

mission elsewhere in Manhattan, but Khrushchev had insisted on coming to them, observing that "by going to a Negro hotel in a Negro district, we would be making a double demonstration against the discriminatory policies of the United States toward Negroes as well as toward Cuba."

This was the first meeting between the two leaders, during which they noted that they shared similar views on several of the issues that would be discussed during the UN 15th General Assembly.

In one photo of their meeting, the two men are smiling for the camera, most likely in an interior hallway at the Hotel Theresa, Khrushchev with medals pinned to the breast pocket and lapel of his dark business suit and Castro in his standard military fatigues.

Several days later, on Sunday morning, September 25, Gamal Abdel Nasser, president of the United Arab Republic—an alliance between Egypt and Syria, from which Syria would withdraw in 1961—traveled to Harlem to meet with Castro for over an hour. In the photograph that begins this essay, the men look at each other eye to eye as they shake hands on the sidewalk outside the hotel, surrounded by members of their delegations and police officers.

In Castro's suite, they discussed, among other topics, the common histories of exploitation experienced by their nations, what their future trade relations might be with Communist bloc countries, the best approach for Cuba regarding Guantanamo Bay, the idea of Arab unity, and the challenges facing Latin America.

Reflecting on the impact of Castro's stay in Harlem, a Havana radio station noted that Harlem residents understood that his stay there "had pulled aside the screen, showing the world that the Negroes, kept apart in a quarter as if they had the plague . . . know that only a revolution can save them."

ANTI-RACIST COMRADES: AFRICAN AMERICANS IN CUBA

CHRISTOPHER M. SHELL

Fidel Castro, Joe Louis, Angela Davis,
and Jesse Jackson navigate the complicated relationship
between Black America and Communist Cuba.

I n 1959, Fidel Castro succeeded in his years-long revolution in Cuba, overthrowing the rule of Fulgencio Batista. As Castro turned Cuba into the Western Hemisphere's first Communist state, he also made the bold promise of uprooting racial discrimination in Cuban society. Literacy campaigns, agrarian land reforms, and increased employment opportunities were initiatives extended to Afro-Cubans to transform Cuba into an "anti-racist" country.

While the United States did not take kindly to the creation of a Communist state in its backyard, African American opinions about Communist Cuba were rather different. African Americans were already engaged in their own fight against American racism and were particularly interested in a nation whose leaders were vocal about undoing systemic racism.

Several months before Castro made his historic trip to Harlem and met with Malcolm X at the Hotel Theresa, he courted another prominent African American figure: boxing legend Joe "the Brown Bomber" Louis. In January 1960, Louis traveled to Cuba to speak with Castro about developing an avenue for African American tourism in Cuba. This meeting was opportune for both parties. African Americans faced severe racial discrimination when traveling in the United States, especially in the Southern states.

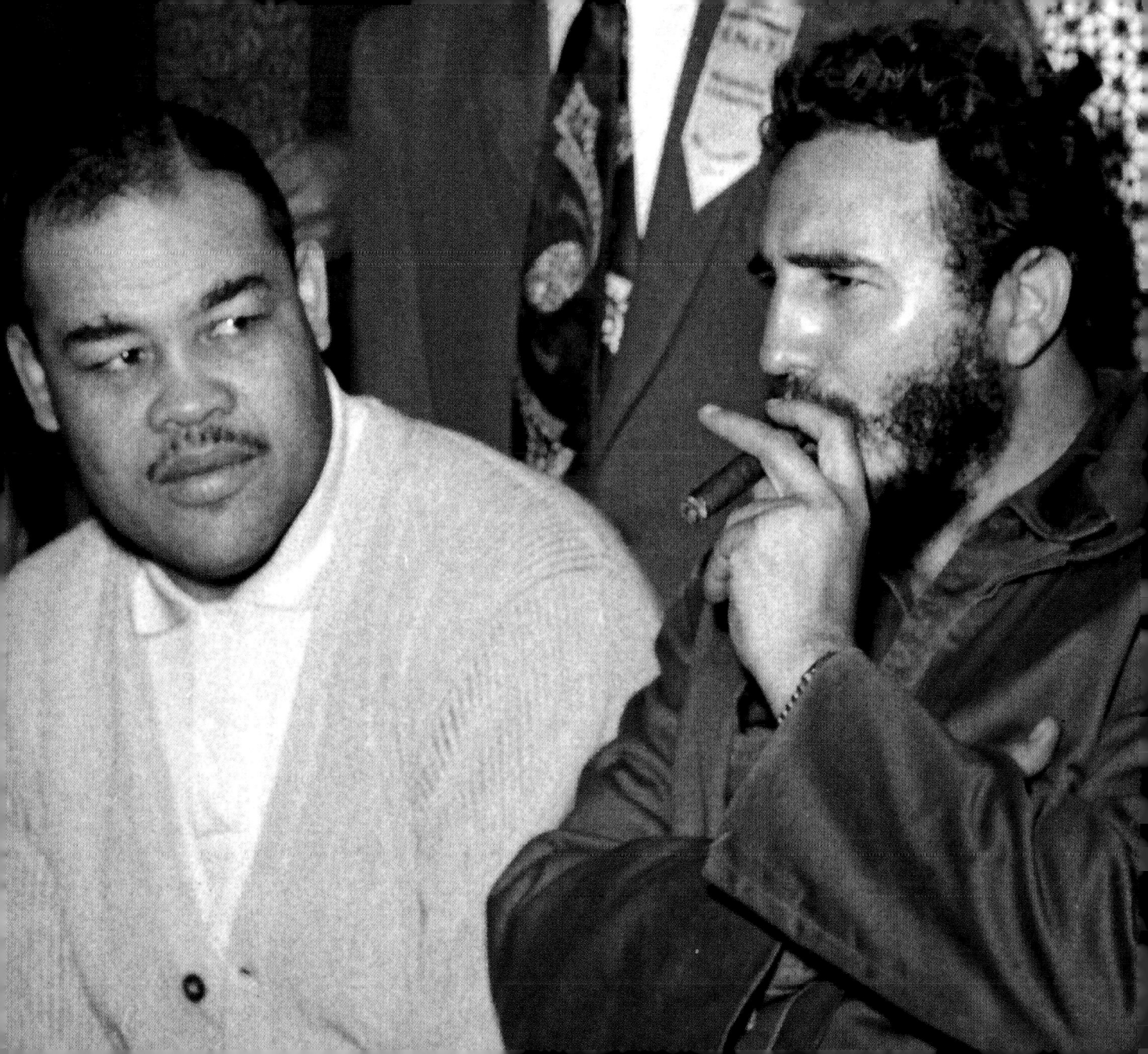

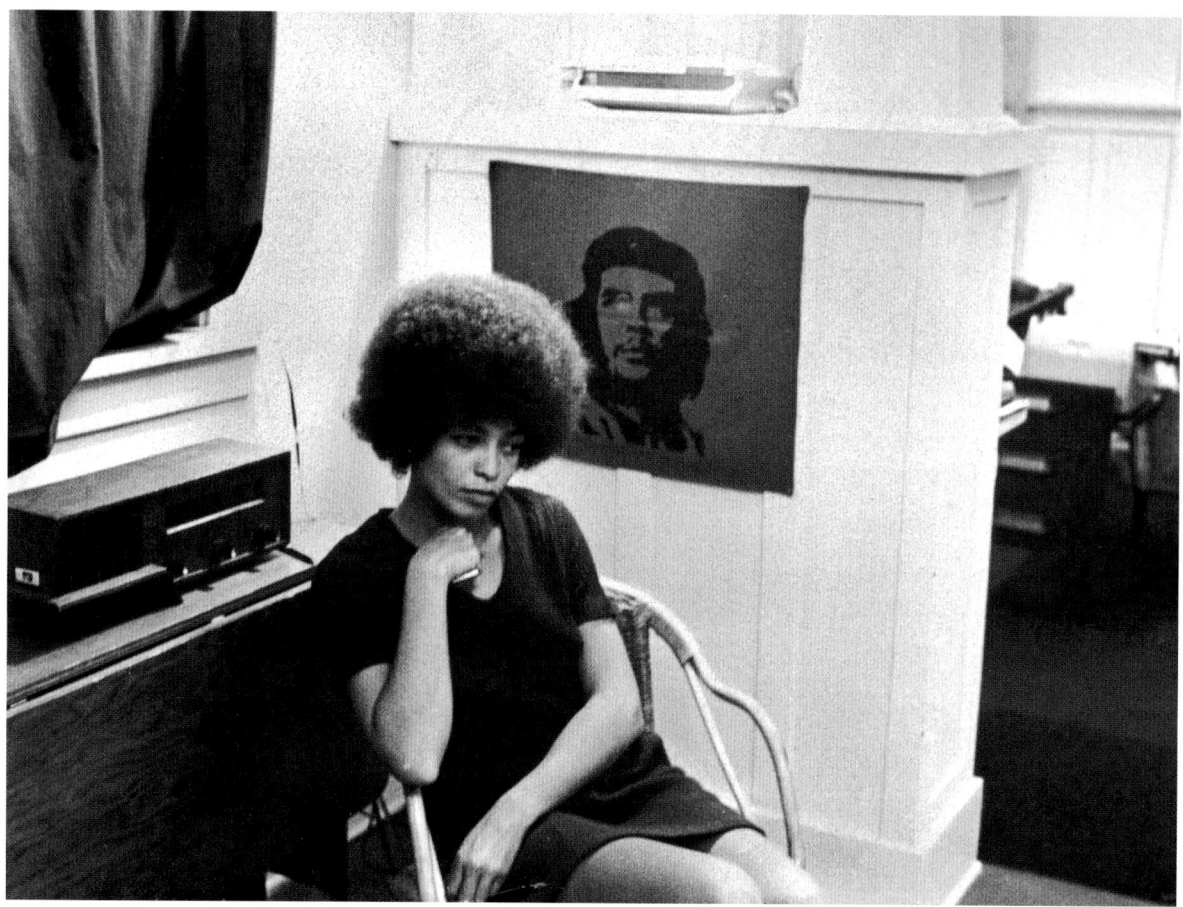

Conversely, Castro had kicked out major U.S. hotel and casino companies from Cuba and was searching for another way to fill the tourist void. At their meeting, Castro and Louis discussed plans for middle-class African Americans to travel to Cuba and experience first-hand the "anti-racist" society that Castro was shaping.

Unfortunately, the 1962 embargo enacted by President John F. Kennedy snuffed out any plans of establishing an African American travel network with Cuba. However, that did not sever the transnational relationship between African Americans and Communist Cuba. One instance of this was Cuba's relationship with the Black Panther Party (BPP).

The BPP was founded in 1966, in East Oakland, California. A self-help organization committed to Black self-determination, the BPP looked to Communist China and Communist Cuba as models for bringing revolutionary change in the United States. The Cuban government also established official partnerships and provided domicile to the Black Panther Party and other Black radical activists.

This sign in Havana in 1971 in the photograph on the following spread reads "Freedom for Angela Davis." Davis was a prominent Black Panther and her trial and subsequent imprisonment garnered international attention. Two individuals who appear to be of African descent walk in front

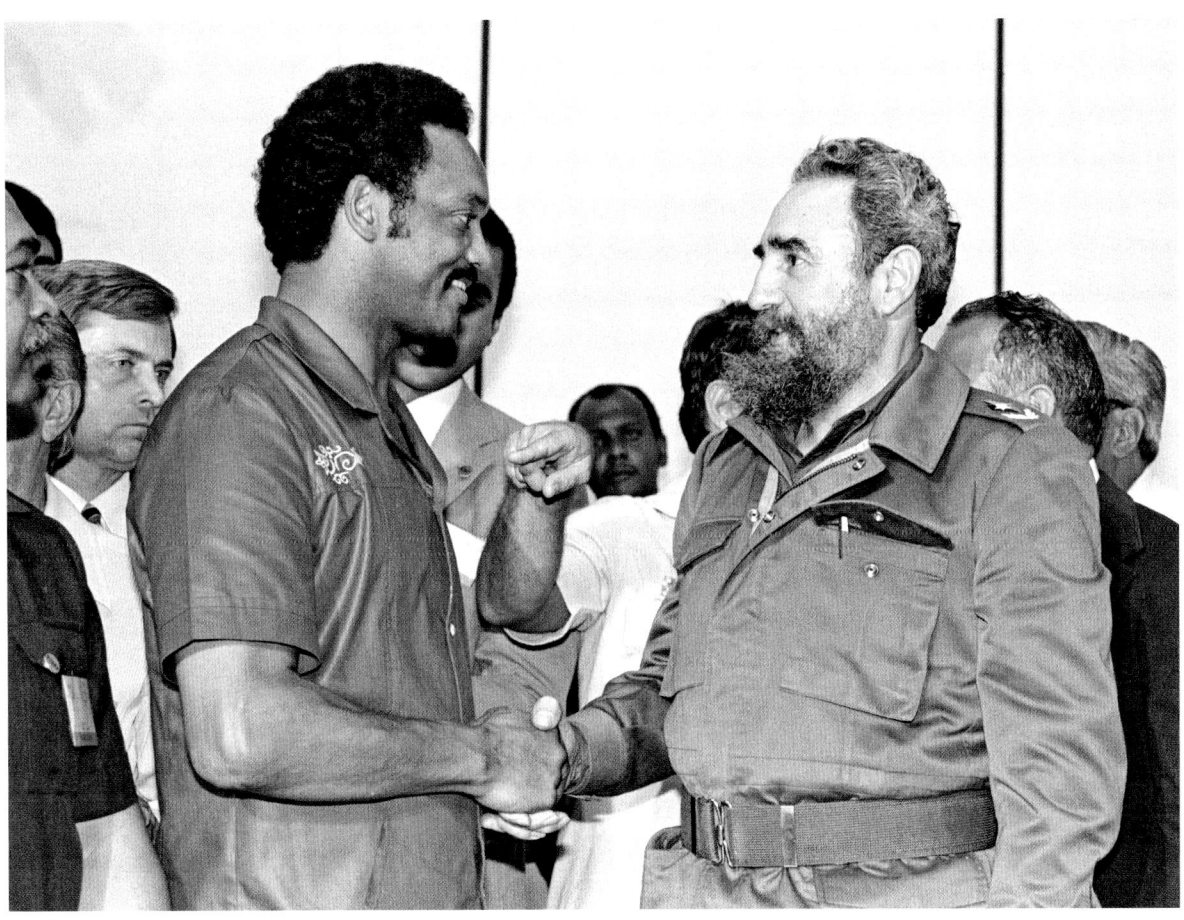

of the sign as a reminder that American racial politics were visible to everyday Afro-Cubans.

In 1984, twenty-four years after Joe Louis had visited Cuba, civil rights activist Jesse Jackson ran for the Democratic Party presidential nomination. In order to bolster his knowledge of international affairs, he made the trip to Havana to meet with Fidel Castro. The meeting between Jackson and Castro culminated in Jackson securing the freedom of twenty-six Cuban political prisoners and twenty-two American citizens, which government officials thought was a near impossible task. Jackson's success led him to denounce U.S. policy toward Cuba at a press conference on June 29,

PREVIOUS SPREAD, RIGHT:
Joe Louis and Fidel Castro meet in Havana, Cuba, during a visit by the Joe Louis Commission in January 1960.

OPPOSITE: Angela Davis photographed shortly after her 1969 firing from UCLA. A poster of Che Guevara appears behind her.

ABOVE: Jesse Jackson meets with Fidel Castro in Havana, Cuba, June 27, 1984.

1984, when he told reporters, "a no-talk policy does not work. We must talk with the Cubans."

This put Jackson at odds with many Americans and certainly with the Reagan administration, which pursued an aggressive anti-communist agenda in Latin America broadly and against Cuba in particular.

Jackson secured the freedom of people whom the Castro administration had labeled as "terrorists" and "enemies of the state." Ironically, in the same year, Cuba offered political asylum to a Black Panther member, Assata Shakur, whom the United States had deemed "an enemy of the state."

Since the 1959 Cuban Revolution, the United States has had a fraught relationship with Cuba. As these images remind us, however, African Americans have at times viewed Cuba differently: as a nation fighting to dismantle a legacy of systemic racism, never mind that it was a Communist country.

RIGHT: Pedestrians pass a billboard in Spanish that reads "Libertad Para Angela Davis" ("Freedom for Angela Davis") in Havana, Cuba, August 26, 1971.

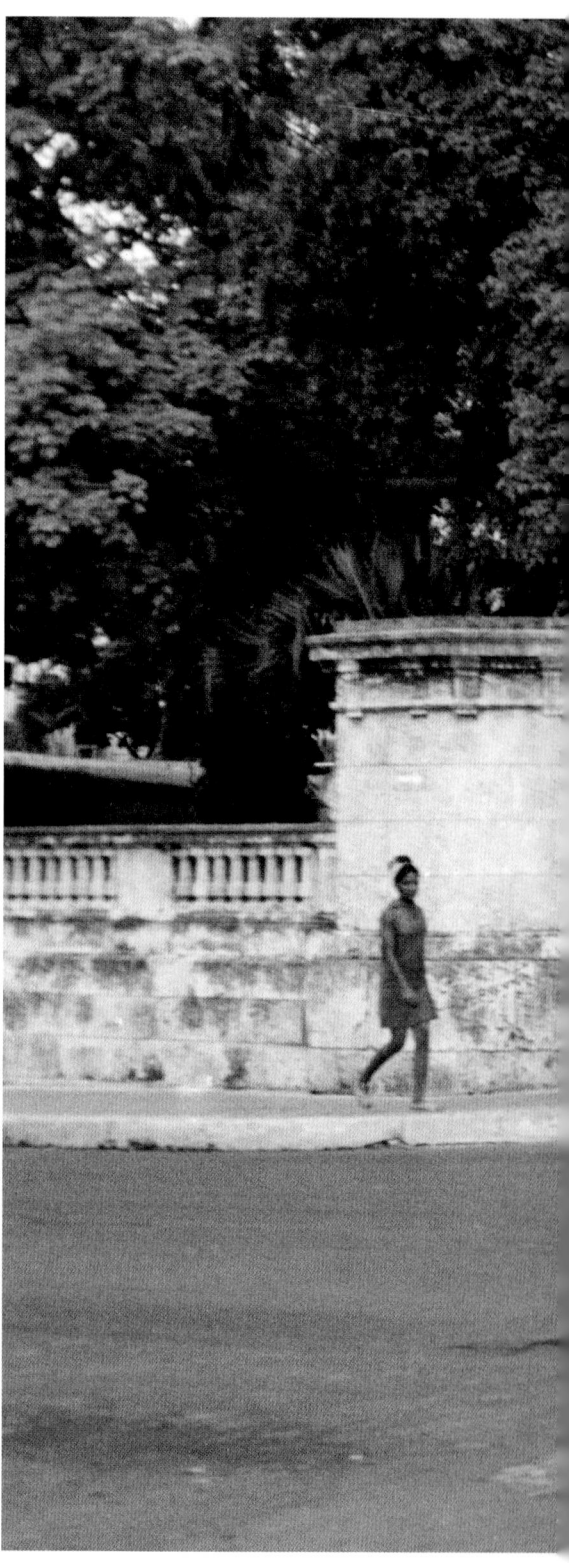

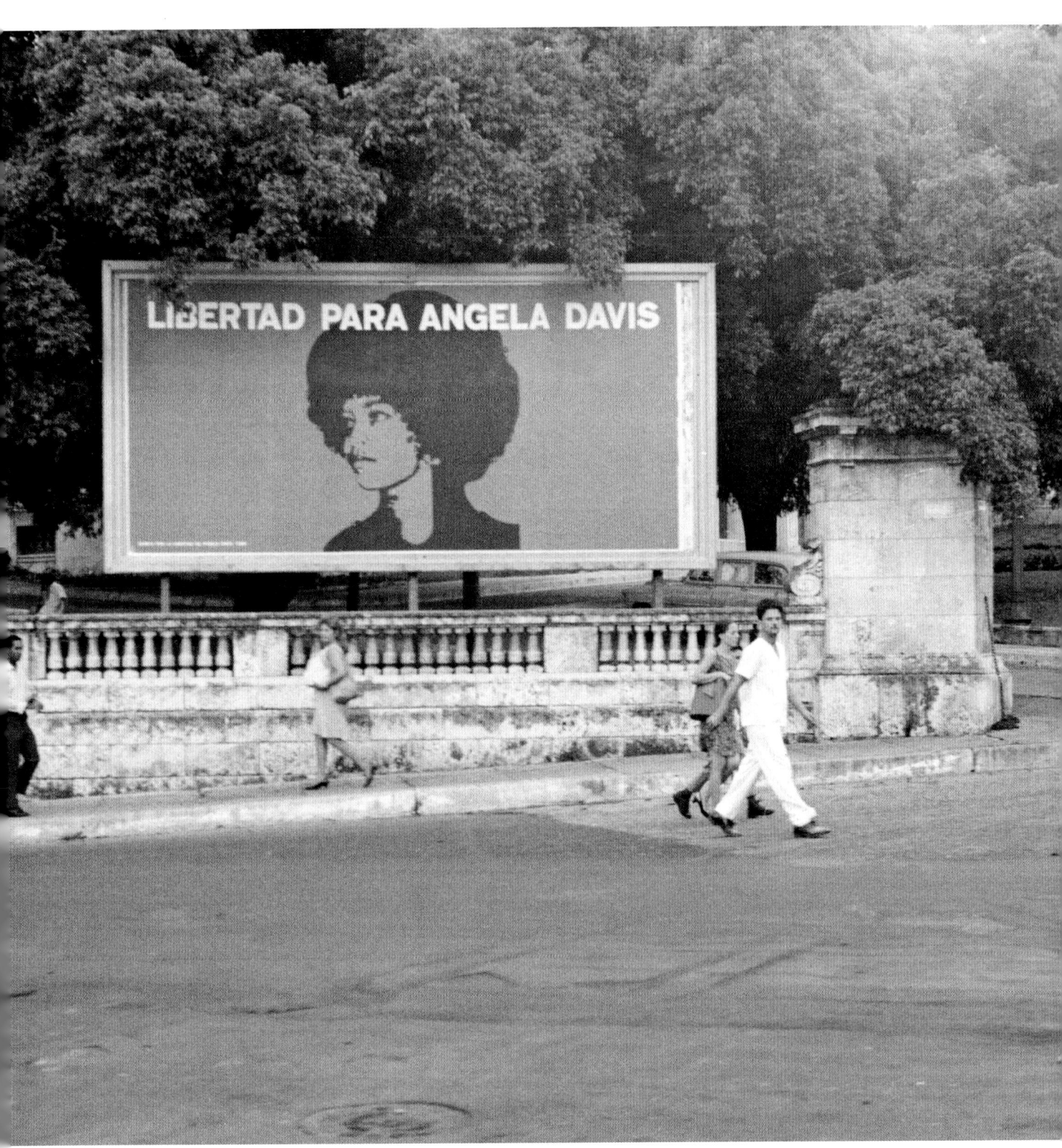

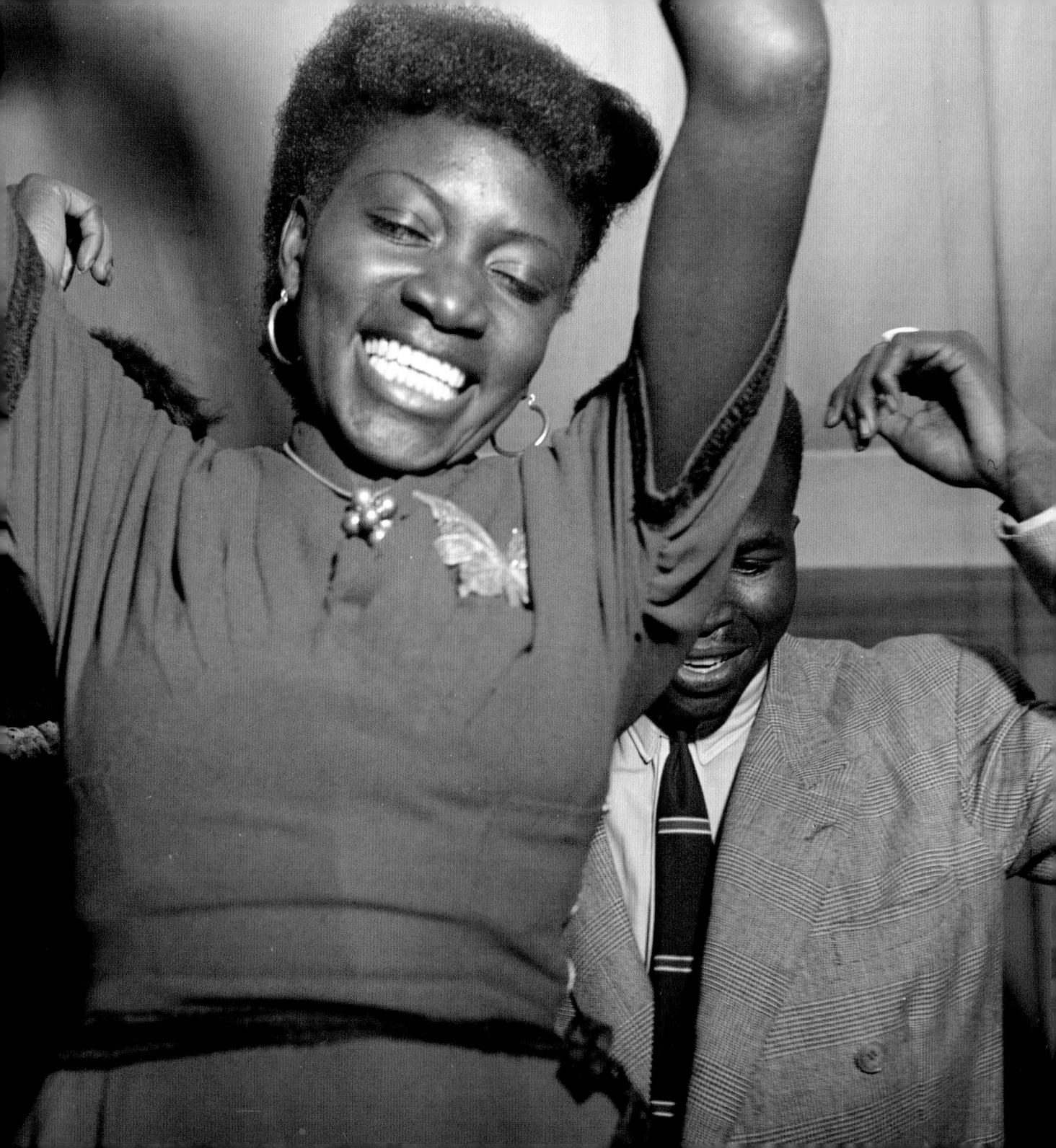

REFUGE AND REVOLUTION FOR BLACK AMERICANS IN FRANCE

DANIELA EDMEIER

*In twentieth-century France, Black Americans found
a racial sanctuary of sorts and a racialized French culture,
which they ultimately helped to transform.*

France claims to be color-blind. Since 1978, for example, French censuses have prohibited the collection of racial and ethnic data. Yet, this belief in a color-blind society overlooks France's deep history with slavery and colonialism, and obscures how that history affects the nation's contemporary relationship with ethnic and racial minorities.

France has offered the illusion of racial integration while concealing the harsh social and cultural subtleties that support its color-blind fantasy. This is particularly vivid in the relationship between Black Americans and France. During the twentieth century, France welcomed Black Americans—as soldiers to fight in its wars or as musicians and artists to enrich its cultural environment—but only insofar as they posed no threat to France's colonial hierarchy.

In the decades after World War I, France proved a racial refuge, welcoming Black Americans as well as their cultural offerings. But the French did not fully comprehend the type of political aspirations this immigration would produce once the U.S. Civil Rights Movement looked beyond its borders and contributed to agitation in the French Empire. By the late 1960s, the real racial limits of the French imagined nation were readily apparent.

During World War I, many Black soldiers fighting in France found that they were treated with a surprising level of respect—certainly more than they felt at home in the United States. For the two hundred thousand Black American servicemen who fought in Europe, romantic relationships with white French women and racial solidarity with French colonial troops, among other experiences, revealed the possibility of a world beyond Jim Crow.

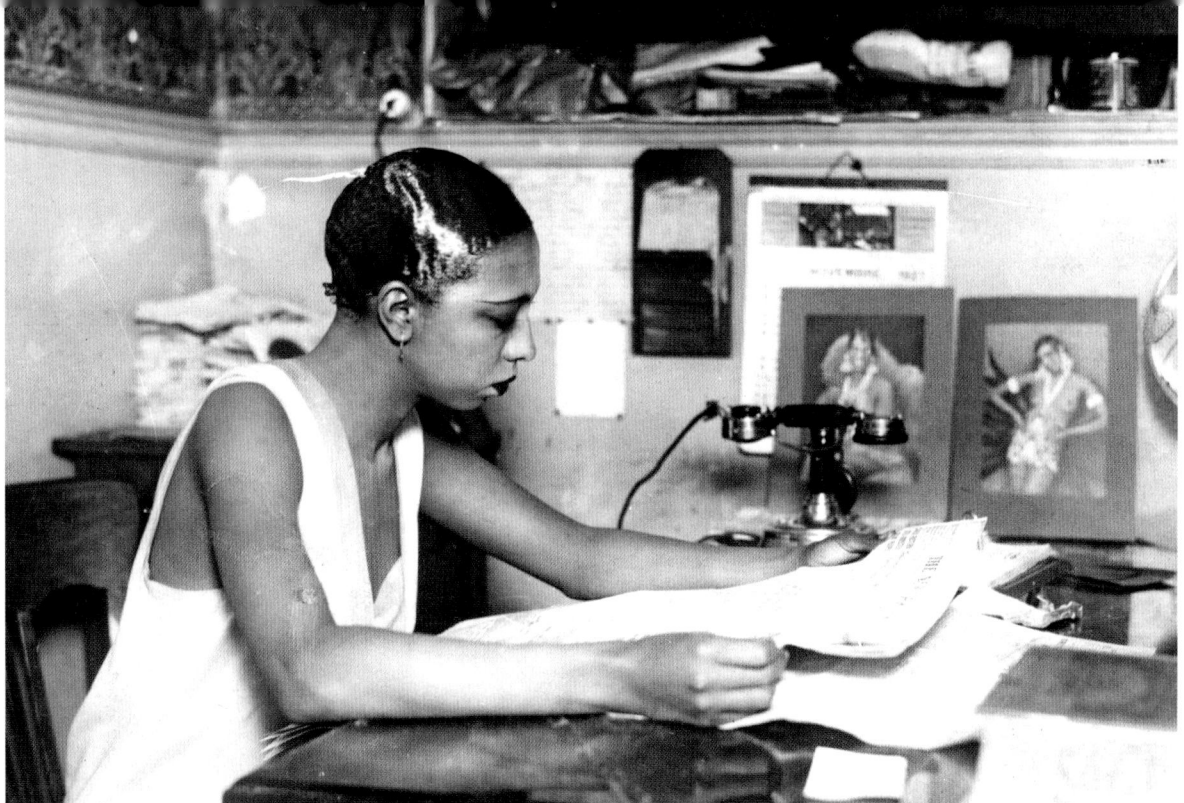

Black American soldiers brought back not only a rising political consciousness, but also stories about France and the possibilities there for people of color. Equally important, Black military musicians primed France for the reception of Black culture and entertainment, namely through jazz.

The influx of Black artists during the interwar period satisfied France's craving for the "exotic." However, the warm cultural reception of Black Americans in France frequently required Black entertainers to play into racialized stereotypes in order to provide white French audiences the entertainment they wanted.

The most famous example of this paradoxical trade-off was the stellar rise of St. Louis native, actress, and dancer Josephine Baker. This 1928 photo of *la Vénus Noire* (the Black Venus), as she was called, working at the desk of her own cabaret in Paris, demonstrates the level of stardom and financial success that some Black Americans could attain in France. The seminude, racially stylized photos behind her reveal the origins of her success.

PREVIOUS SPREAD, LEFT: A couple dances at La Rose Rouge, 1948.

ABOVE: Josephine Baker, directrice of her own cabaret, circa 1928.

RIGHT: Josephine Baker in costume for her famous banana dance, circa 1925.

FOLLOWING SPREAD: The crowded bar at La Boule Blanche, a much-frequented Paris nightclub, circa late 1920s.

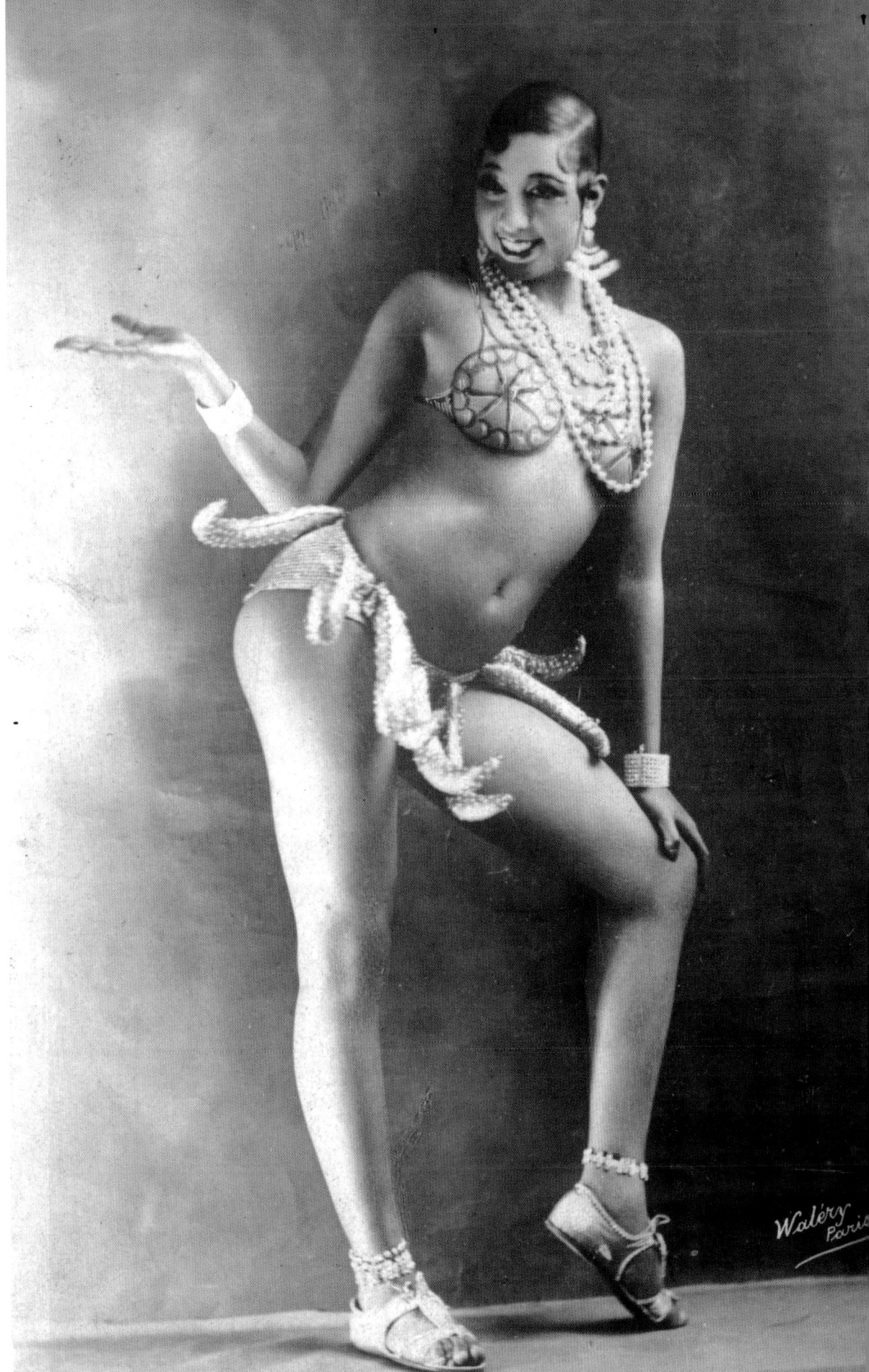

Waléry Paris

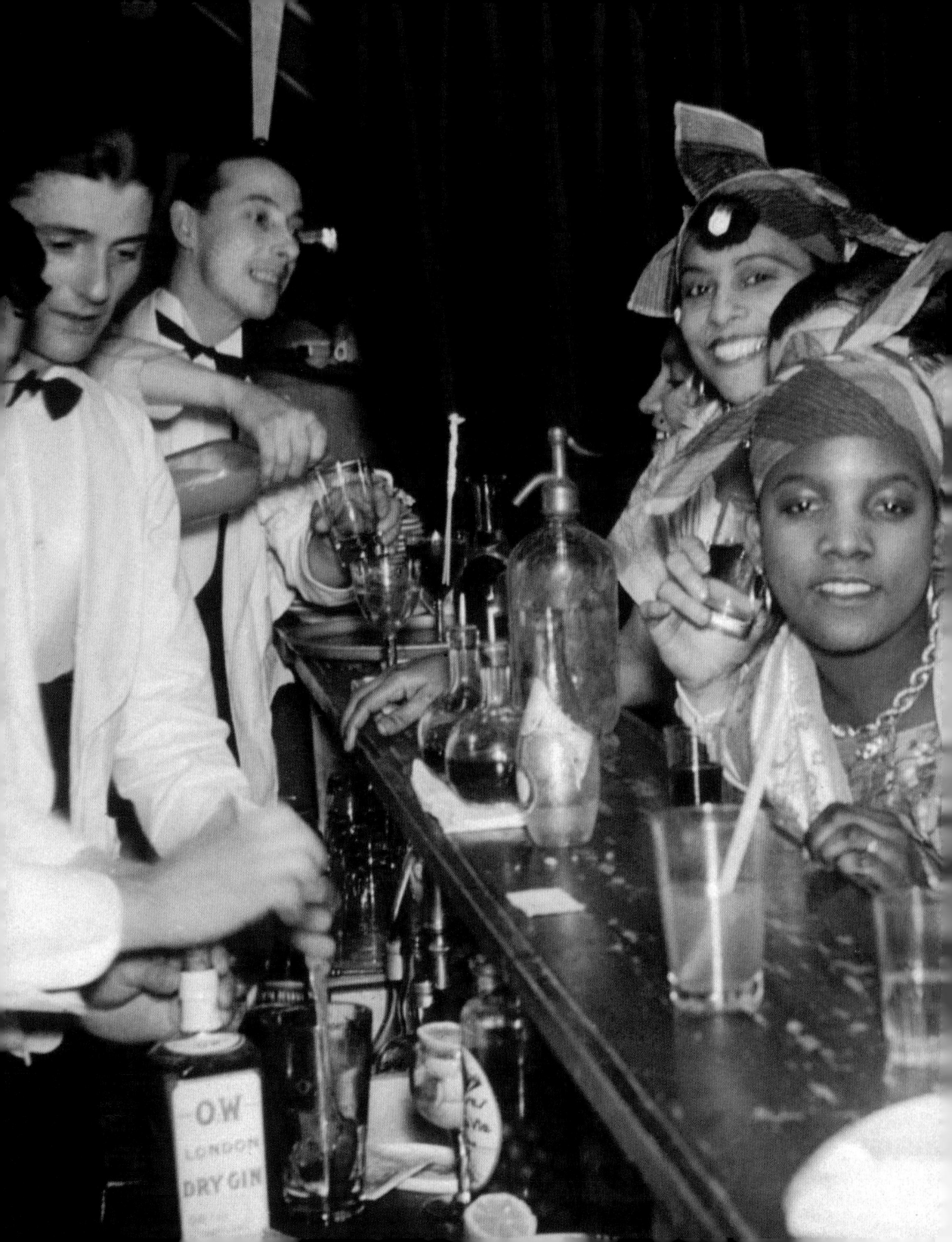

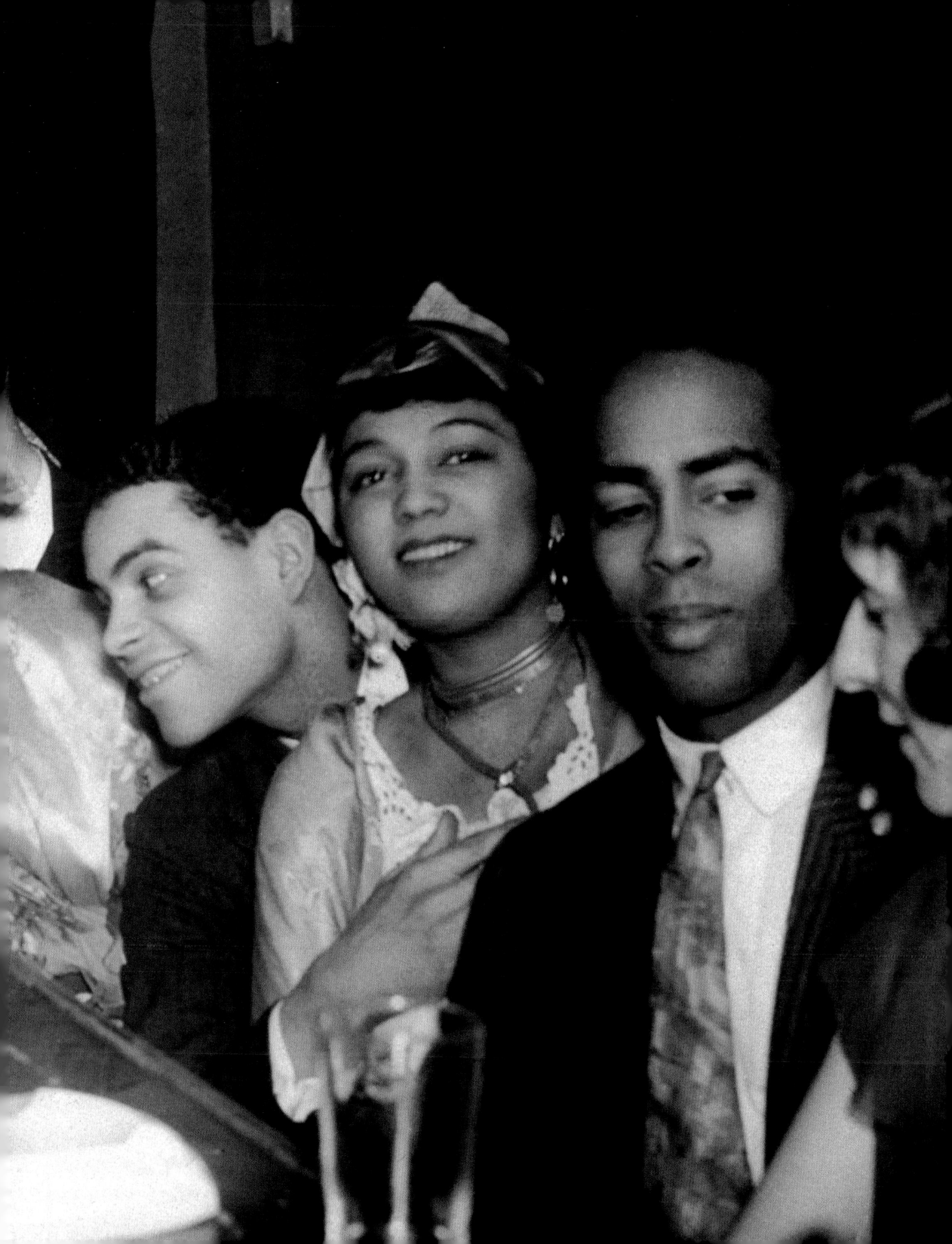

Baker strategically offered white French audiences their ideal, imagined experience of the "African continent." The photo of Baker on page 287 demonstrates their racialized expectations of Black American performers, and the way Baker exploited these expectations for her own success. Whether in performance or advertisement, viewers wanted the "authentic" from Black performers—and that meant drawing on racist caricatures.

Nevertheless, Black artists and intellectuals did find a certain kind of haven in France. Interracial socialization in Parisian clubs and cafés often upended many of the racial barriers upheld in the United States.

In 1925 and 1926, thousands of robed and unmasked Ku Klux Klan members marched down Pennsylvania Avenue in Washington, DC, to promote white supremacy. In contrast, in the photo on the previous spread taken in the same year, we see Black men and women in *haute couture* not only mingling with white patrons but also being served by white bartenders in France. A scene like this was almost unimaginable in the United States, and the image would have shocked many Americans.

Interracial socialization, particularly between Black men and white women, continued through the twentieth century, as this 1948 photo of Americans at a Parisian "Black and Tan" club attests. The joy on many Black patrons' faces implies a freedom of expression through movement without fear of racial retaliation.

After World War II, Black creative expats were joined in France by civil rights activists who were more politically active, militant, and transnational in their outlook. Such new arrivals raised French officials' concerns about how such ideas might undermine the empire and implicate its own colonial subjects.

During the 1960s, Black American civil rights leaders and activists engaged with decolonization politics in Africa and Asia, and many French intellectuals, like

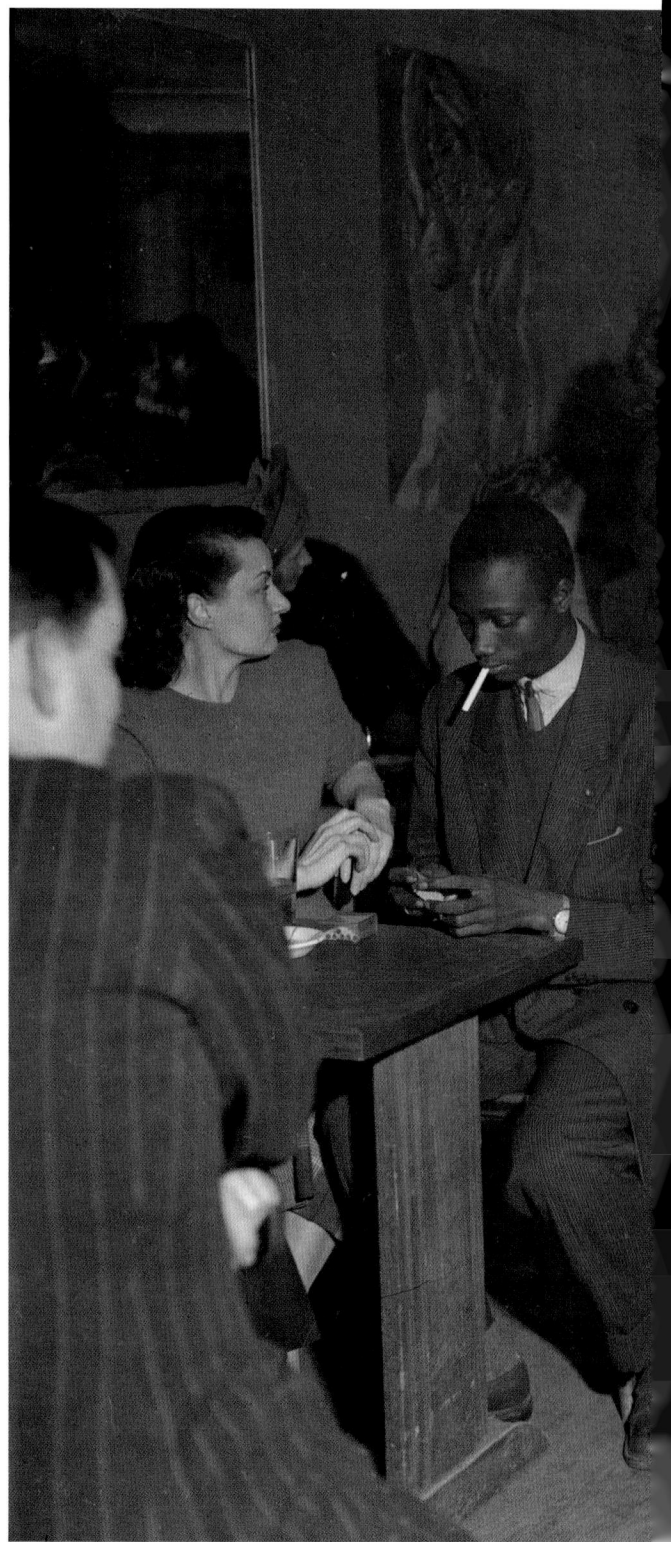

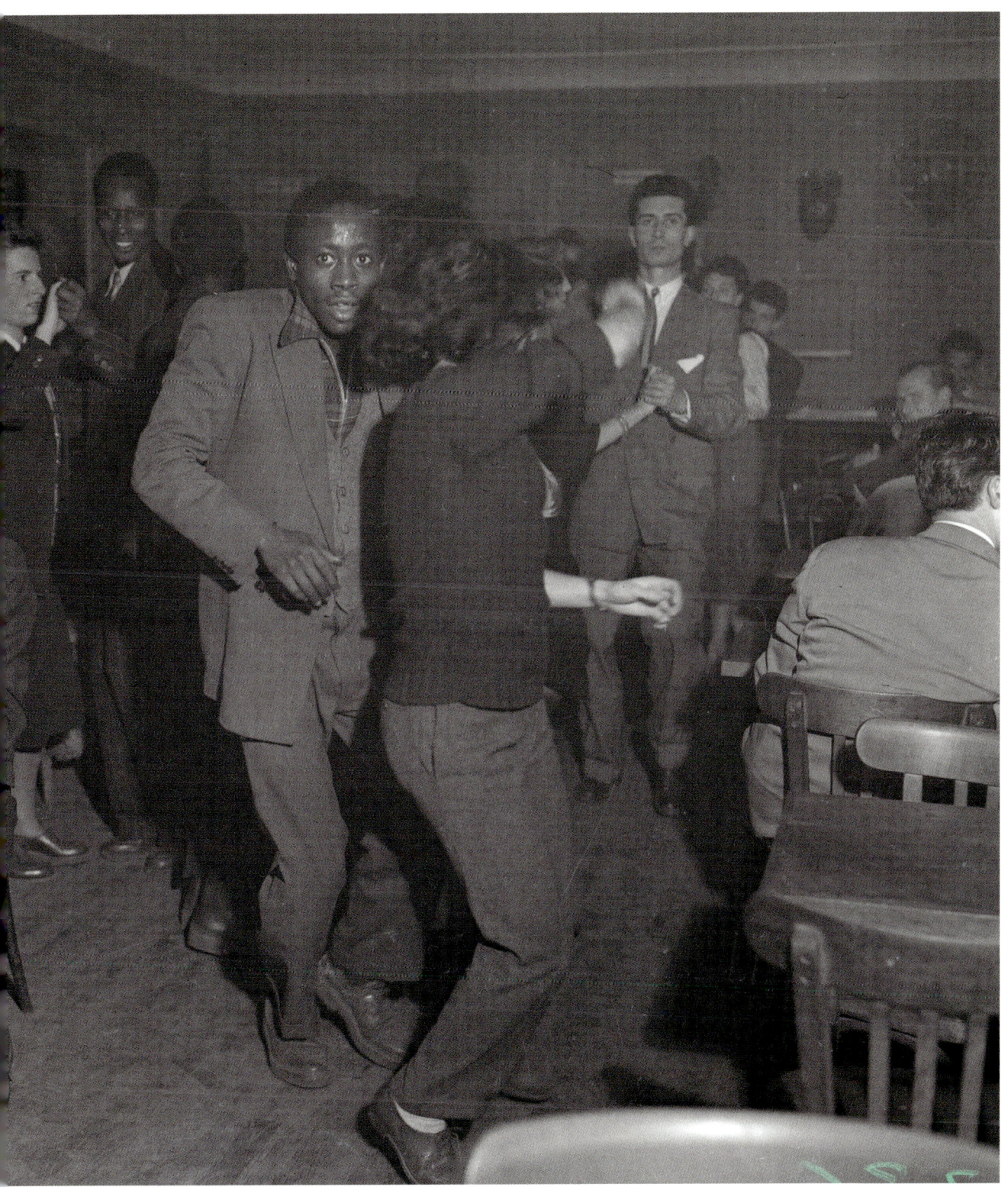

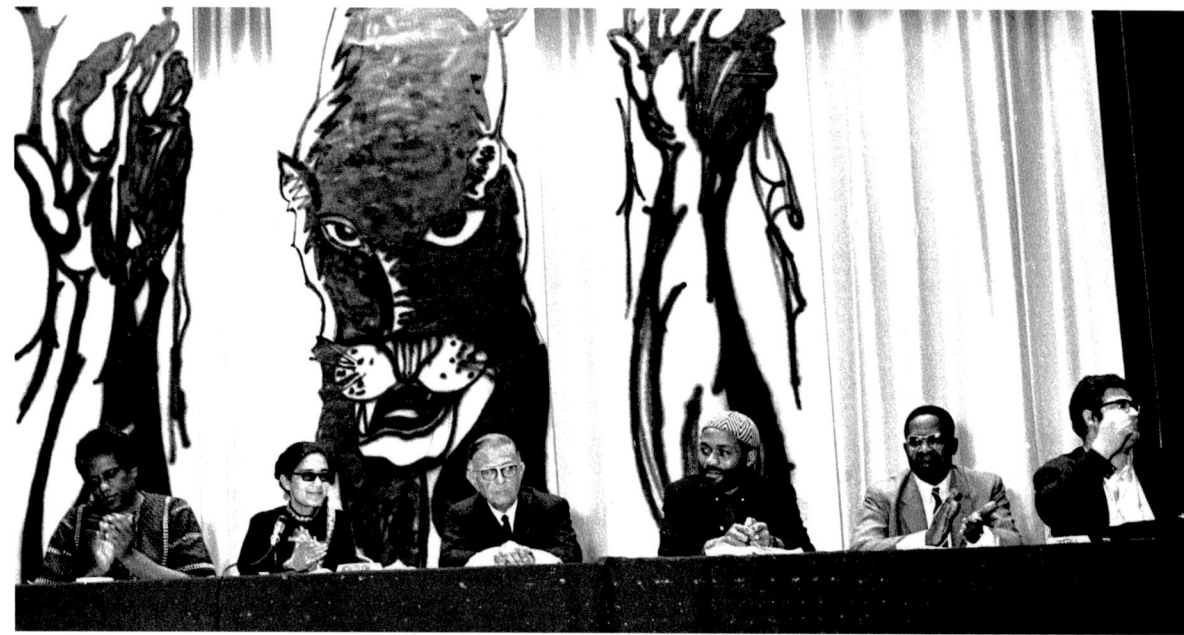

those pictured in the photograph above, joined in solidarity with Black civil rights organizations fighting in the United States.

Organizations like the NAACP, the Southern Christian Leadership Conference, and the Student Nonviolent Coordinating Committee supported common French theories of integration, which argued that the success of formerly colonized peoples depended on assimilation into French society—aligning unproblematically with France's universalist tradition.

Others, however, like Malcolm X and Kwame Ture (originally Stokely Carmichael), opposed integrationist discourse. These activists promoted self-reliant and autonomous Black communities in the United States, and, more importantly, emphasized solidarity and Third World nation-building that defied national borders. These beliefs posed an active threat to the French government, which in the 1960s was grappling with independence movements in its former colonies and an influx of Black and brown migrants to the metropole.

At times, French officials actively sought to prevent American activists from spreading Black consciousness among France's growing populations of color. After giving a speech at Paris's La Maison de la Mutualité to an audience of mostly French Caribbean and African students in November 1964, Malcolm X was later denied entry to France at the Orly Airport in February 1965. Similarly, in 1967, French police attempted to detain and remove Kwame Ture during his visit to the country but ultimately released him.

Through the latter decades of the twentieth century, France continued to distance itself from radical Black American politics that might influence their formerly colonized populations.

But for most of the twentieth century, France benefited from the narrative that it was a refuge for Black Americans, and a beacon of republican egalitarianism. However, once Black Americans began to help reveal France's paradoxical relationship with racial minorities, the fantasy of France as a republican racial refuge unraveled.

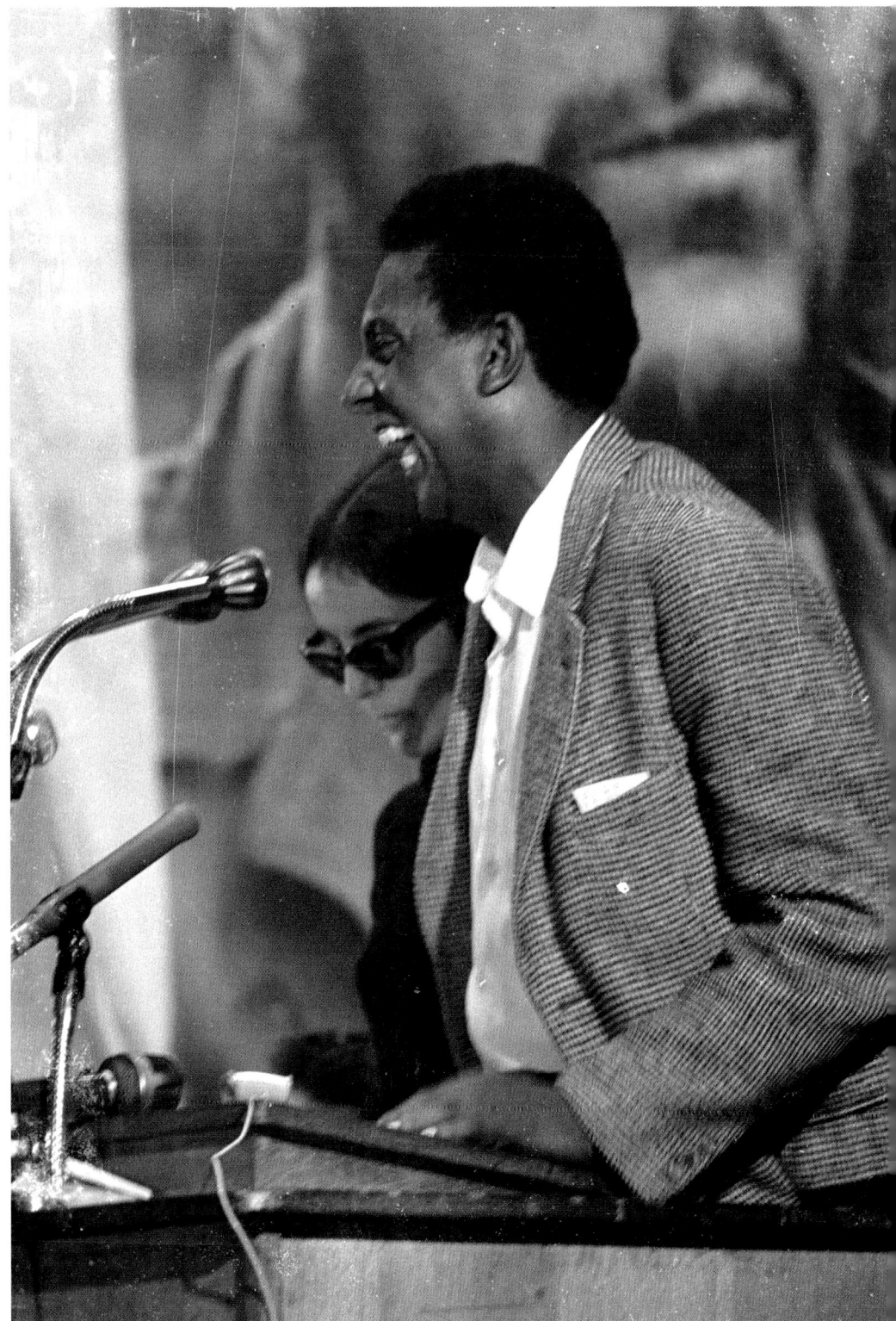

PREVIOUS SPREAD: La Rose Rouge, the Parisian equivalent to a "Black and Tan" nightclub, invited interracial mingling.

OPPOSITE, TOP: Paris gathering of intellectuals in support of the Black Power movement (left to right): James Forman of SNCC; Julia Wright, daughter of novelist Richard Wright; philosopher Jean-Paul Sartre; activist Ted Joans; novelist Aimé Césaire; and activist Nicolas Boulte.

RIGHT: Kwame Ture (Stokely Carmichael) addresses a rally of the leftist National Vietnam Committee in Paris alongside militant activist Elaine Mokhtefi.

FOLLOWING SPREAD, LEFT: Thousands gathered for a Black Lives Matter rally at the Place de la République in Paris on June 13, 2020.

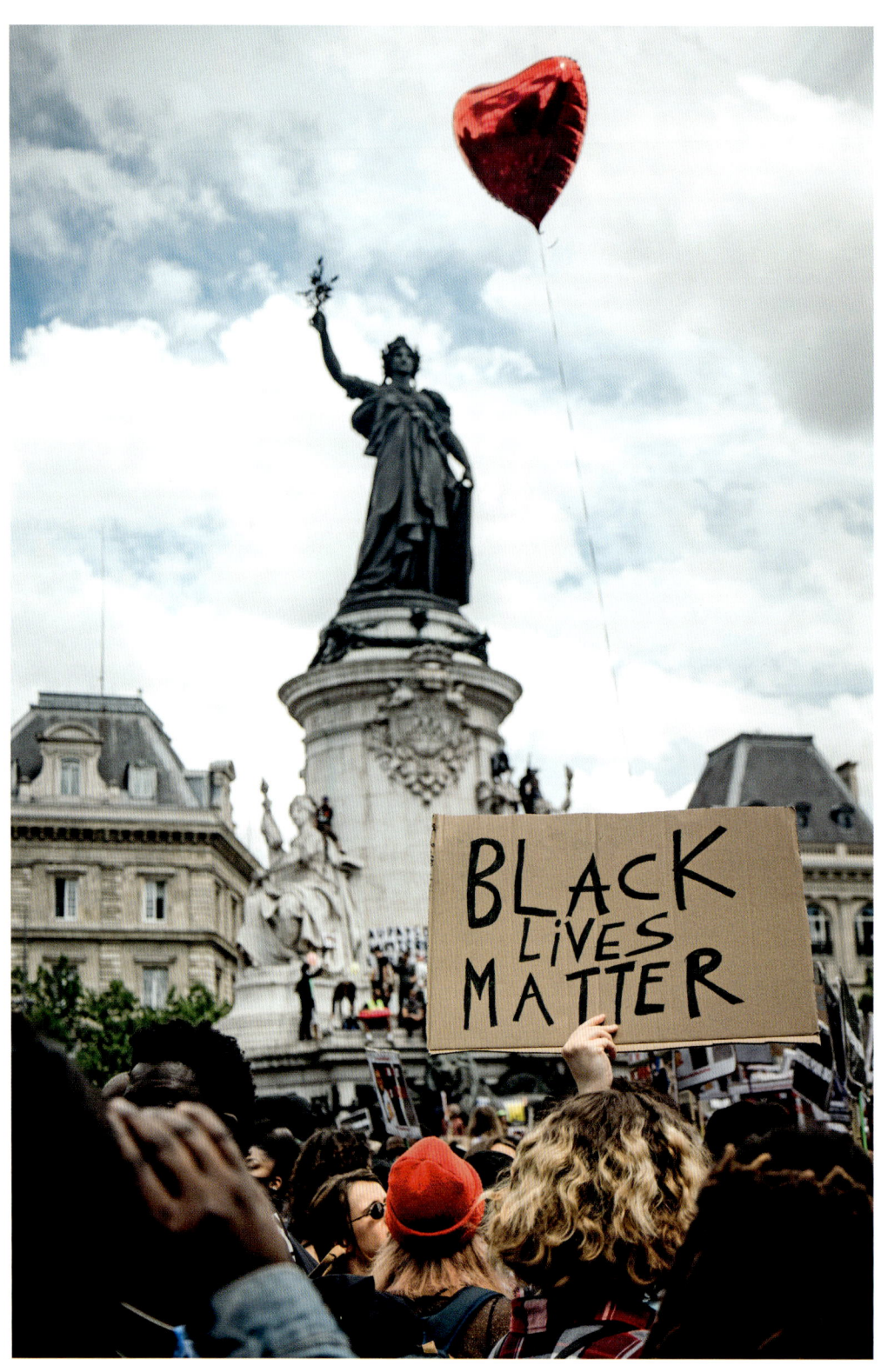

BIBLIOGRAPHY

THE POWER OF IMAGES AND STORIES

Franklin, John Hope. *From Slavery to Freedom: A History of African Americans.* Edited by Evelyn Brooks Higginbotham. 10th ed. New York: McGraw Hill, 2020.

Givens, Jarvis R. *Fugitive Pedagogy: Carter G. Woodson and the Art of Black Teaching.* Cambridge, MA: Harvard University Press, 2021.

Kaepernick, Colin, Robin D. G. Kelley, Keeanga-Yamahtta Taylor, eds. *Our History Has Always Been Contraband: In Defense of Black Studies.* New York: Haymarket Books, 2023.

Marable, Manning, and Leith Mullings. *Freedom: A Photographic History of the African American Struggle.* New York: Phaidon Press, 2005.

Painter, Nell Irwin. *Creating Black Americans: African-American History and Its Meanings, 1619 to the Present.* Oxford: Oxford University Press, 2006.

Willis, Deborah. *Reflections in Black: A History of Black Photographers, 1840 to the Present.* New York: W. W. Norton, 2000.

I. PORTRAITS OF BLACK HISTORY

THE BLACK FOUNDERS OF THE UNITED STATES OF AMERICA

Bennett, Lerone. *The Shaping of Black America: The Struggles and Triumphs of African-Americans, 1619–1990s.* New York: Penguin Books, 1993.

Bernstein, Richard B. *The Founding Fathers Reconsidered.* Oxford: Oxford University Press, 2009.

King, LaGarrett J. "More Than Slaves: Black Founders, Benjamin Banneker, and Critical Intellectual Agency." *Social Studies Research and Practice* 9, no. 3 (2014): 88–105.

Nash, Gary B. *The Forgotten Fifth: African Americans in the Age of Revolution.* Cambridge, MA: Harvard University Press, 2006.

Newman, Richard S. *Freedom's Prophet: Bishop Richard Allen, the AME Church, and the Black Founding Fathers.* New York: New York University Press, 2009.

PORTRAITS OF A BLACK DAGUERREOTYPIST

Ball, James Presley. *J.P. Ball, Daguerrean and Studio Photographer.* Edited by Deborah Willis. New York: Garland Publishing, 1993.

Ketner, Joseph D. II. "Struggles Many and Great: James P. Ball, Robert Duncanson, and Other Artists of Color in Antebellum Cincinnati." *The Magazine ANTIQUES*, November/December 2011. Accessed November 3, 2023. https://www.themagazineantiques.com/article/ketner-james-p-ball-robert-duncanson-antebellum-cincinnati/.

Leininger-Miller, Theresa. Review of *An American Journey: The Life and Photography of James Presley Ball*, by Cincinnati Museum Center. *Nineteenth-Century Art Worldwide* 10, no. 2 (Autumn 2011). Accessed November 3, 2023. https://www.19thc-artworldwide.org/autumn11/review-of-an-american-journey-the-life-and-photography-of-james-presley-ball.

Stauffer, John, Zoe Trodd, and Celeste-Marie Bernier. *Picturing Frederick Douglass: An Illustrated Biography of the Nineteenth Century's Most Photographed American.* New York: Liveright Publishing Corporation, 2015.

Thompson, Shona. "Representing Race and Spectacular Violence in the Work of J.P. Ball." *Epoch* 1 (September 2020). Accessed November 6, 2023. https://www.epoch-magazine.com/thompsonrepresentinggrace.

Wallace, Maurice O., and Shawn Michelle Smith, eds. *Pictures and Progress: Early Photography and the Making of African American Identity.* Durham, NC: Duke University Press, 2012.

A SHARECROPPER'S FAMILY

Ben Shahn: Passion for Justice. New Jersey Public Broadcasting Authority, 2001. 57 minutes. https://cambridge.films.com/id/4990?TrackingID=FMK.

Honey, Michael K. *Sharecropper's Troubadour: John L. Handcox, the Southern Tenant Farmers' Union, and the African American Song Tradition.* New York: Palgrave Macmillan, 2013.

Kester, Howard. *Revolt among the Sharecroppers.* Knoxville: University of Tennessee Press, 1997.

Meister, Sarah. *Dorothea Lange: Words & Pictures.* New York: MOMA, 2019.

Natanson, Nicholas. *The Black Image in the New Deal: The Politics of FSA Photography.* Knoxville: University of Tennessee Press, 1992.

Shahn, Ben. *The Photographs of Ben Shahn.* Washington, DC: Library of Congress, 2008.

TWICE BURIED

Brown, Ras Michael. *African-Atlantic Cultures and the South Carolina Lowcountry.* New York: Cambridge University Press, 2012.

Edgar, Walter. *History of Santee Cooper, 1934–1984.* Columbia, SC: R. L. Bryan Company, 1984.

Schulman, Bruce. *From Cotton Belt to Sunbelt: Federal Policy, Economic Development &*

The Transformation of the South, 1938–1980. Durham, NC: Duke University Press, 1994.

Thompson, Robert Farris. *Flash of the Spirit: African & Afro-American Art & Philosophy.* New York: Vintage Books, 1984.

PHOTOGRAPHING HISTORY IN THE MAKING

Lewis, John, and Michael D'Orso. *Walking with the Wind: A Memoir of the Movement.* New York: Simon and Schuster, 1998.

Lewis, John, Andrew Young, and Kabir Sehgal. *Carry On: Reflections for a New Generation.* New York: Grand Central Publishing, 2021.

II. BLACK WOMEN: ACTIVIST LIVES AND LEGACIES

THE REVOLUTION OF BEING

Bridges, Ruby. *This Is Your Time.* New York: Penguin Random House, 2020.

Epstein, Rebecca, Jamilia Blake, and Thalia González. "Girlhood Interrupted: The Erasure of Black Girls' Childhood." SSRN, July 18, 2017. http://dx.doi.org/10.2139/ssrn.3000695.

Lee, Spike, director. *4 Little Girls.* 40 Acres and a Mule Filmworks, 1997. 102 minutes. https://www.hbo.com/movies/4-little-girls.

Lorde, Audre. *The Cancer Journals.* San Francisco: Aunt Lute Books, 1980.

Lorde, Audre. *Sister Outsider: Essays and Speeches.* New York: Crossing Press, 1984.

Simone, Nina. *I Put a Spell on You: The Autobiography of Nina Simone.* Boston: Da Capo Press, 1992.

A MOTHER'S POWER

"Battered Body of Till Boy Arrives Here. Murdered Youth's Kin Hysterical at Station." *Chicago Sun-Times,* September 2, 1955, 3. Reprint: https://chicago.suntimes.com/1955/9/2/23837892/emmett-till-news-battered-body-of-till-boy-arrives-here-murdered-youths-kin-hysterical-at-station.

Beauchamp, Keith, director. *The Untold Story of Emmett Louis Till.* ThinkFilm, 2005. 70 minutes.

Gorn, Elliott. *Let the People See: The Story of Emmett Till.* Oxford: Oxford University Press, 2018.

Till-Mobley, Mamie. *Death of Innocence: The Story of the Hate Crime That Changed America.* Los Angeles: One World Print Press, 2004.

MARCHING MOTHERS

Meier, August, and Elliott Rudwick. "Early Boycotts of Segregated Schools: The Case of Springfield, Ohio, 1922–23." *American Quarterly* 20, no. 4 (Winter 1968): 744–58. https://doi.org/10.2307/2711405.

Stankorb, Sarah. "The Long Walk." *The Atavist Magazine,* no. 104 (June 2020). Accessed November 6, 2023. https://magazine.atavist.com/the-long-walk-civil-rights-hillsboro-ohio-segregation-black-lives-matter/.

Torrice, Andrea. *The Lincoln School Story: A Battle for School Integration in Ohio.* Torrice Media, 2017. 30 minutes.

Williams, Heather Andrea. *Self-Taught: African American Education in Slavery and Freedom.* Chapel Hill: University of North Carolina Press, 2005.

Williamsen, Pat. "Fire of Justice: The Battle for School Desegregation in Hillsboro." *Pathways* (Spring 2017): 14–19. http://www.ohiohumanities.org/wp-content/uploads/2020/06/Fire-of-Justice-SP17-Article.pdf.

GLORIA RICHARDSON: ACT IN THE FREEDOM STRUGGLE

"Announce Formation of New Super-Militant Group." *Jet,* May 7, 1964.

Fitzgerald, Joseph R. *The Struggle Is Eternal: Gloria Richardson and Black Liberation.*

Lexington: University Press of Kentucky, 2018.

Marable, Manning. *Malcolm X: A Life of Reinvention.* New York: Penguin Books, 2011.

Williams, Rhonda Y. *Concrete Demands: The Search for Black Power in the 20th Century.* London: Routledge, 2014.

Worthy, William. "Mrs. Richardson Okeys Malcolm X." *Baltimore Afro-American,* March 10, 1964, 16.

REMEMBERING ALICE WALKER'S THE COLOR PURPLE

Bobo, Jacqueline. *Black Women as Cultural Readers.* New York: Columbia University Press, 1995.

Walker, Alice, and Valerie Boyd. *Gathering Blossoms under Fire: The Journals of Alice Walker.* New York: Simon & Schuster, 2022.

Walker, Alice. *The Color Purple.* Reprint, New York: Penguin Books, 2022.

III. SPACES AND PLACES OF BLACK POLITICS

FREE THE LAND, FREE THE PEOPLE

Bloom, Joshua, and Waldo E. Martin Jr. *Black against Empire: The History and Politics of the Black Panther Party.* Berkeley: University of California Press, 2013.

Finney, Carolyn. *Black Faces, White Spaces: Reimagining the Relationship of African Americans to the Great Outdoors.* Durham, NC: University of North Carolina Press, 2014.

Glave, Dianne D. *Rooted in the Earth: Reclaiming the African American Environmental Heritage.* Chicago: Lawrence Hill Books, 2010.

Kahrl, Andrew W., Malcolm Cammeron, and Brian Katen. *African American Outdoor Recreation Theme Study: Historical Context and National Historic Landmark Survey.* Washington, DC: National Park Service, Department of the Interior, 2022.

CHILDREN OF THE MISSISSIPPI FREEDOM SUMMER

Carson, Clayborne. *In Struggle: SNCC and the Black Awakening of the 1960s.* Cambridge, MA: Harvard University Press, 1995.

Franklin, V. P. *The Young Crusaders: The Untold Story of the Children and the Teenagers Who Galvanized the Civil Rights Movement.* Boston: Beacon Press, 2021.

Payne, Charles M. *I've Got the Light of Freedom: The Organizing Tradition and the Mississippi Freedom Struggle.* Berkeley: University of California Press, 1997.

Sturkey, William. "The 1964 Mississippi Freedom Schools." *Mississippi History Now,* May 2016. Accessed November 6, 2023. https://mshistorynow.mdah.ms.gov/issue/The-1964-Mississippi-Freedom-Schools.

WADE IN THE WATER

Finney, Jeffery, and Amy Potter. "'You're Out of Your Place': Black Mobility on Tybee Island, Georgia from Civil Rights to Orange Crush." *Southeastern Geographer* 58, no. 1 (2018): 104–24.

Kahrl, Andrew. *The Land Was Ours: African American Beaches from Jim Crow to the Sunbelt South.* Cambridge, MA: Harvard University Press, 2012.

O'Brien, William. *Landscapes of Exclusion: State Parks and Jim Crow in the American South.* Amherst: University of Massachusetts Press, 2016.

BOMBING MOVE

Anderson, John, and Hilary Hevenor. *Burning Down the House: MOVE and the Tragedy of Philadelphia.* New York: W. W. Norton, 1990.

Beckman, Karen. "Black Media Matters: Remembering *The Bombing of Osage Avenue.*" *Film Quarterly* 68, no. 4 (Summer 2015): 8–23. https://doi.org/10.1525/fq.2015.68.4.8.

Muhammad, Abdul-Aliy A. "Decades after Philadelphia's MOVE Bombing, Penn Museum Still Keeps Secrets on the Remains of 12-Year-Old Girl."

Hyperallergic, April 20, 2022. Accessed November 6, 2023. https://hyperallergic.com/725976/philadelphia-move-bombing-penn-museum-still-keeps-secrets-on-the-remains/.

Osder, Jason, director. *Let the Fire Burn.* Zeitgeist Films, 2013. 95 minutes.

THE LOCKED OUT

Barker, Lucius J., and Ronald W. Walters, eds. *Jesse Jackson's 1984 Presidential Campaign: Challenge and Change in American Politics.* Urbana: University of Illinois Press, 1989.

Beal, Frances. "U.S. Politics Will Never Be the Same." *The Black Scholar* 15, no. 5 (September/October 1984): 10–18.

Early, James. "Rainbow Politics: From Civil Rights to Civil Equality: An Interview with Jack O'Dell." *The Black Scholar* 15, no. 15 (September/October 1984): 50–56.

Morris, Lorenzo, ed. *The Social and Political Implications of the 1984 Jesse Jackson Presidential Campaign.* Westport, CT: Praeger, 1990.

Smith, Robert C., and Joseph P. McCormick II. "The Challenge of a Black Presidential Candidacy (1984): The Question of Political Independence." *New Directions* 12 (July 1985): 22–25.

IV. BLACK CULTURE AS PEOPLE POWER

BEAUTY SALONS AS SACRED SPACE IN BLACK AMERICA

Byrd, Ayana, and Lori Tharps. *Hair Story: Untangling the Roots of Black Hair in America.* New York: St. Martin's Griffin, 2014.

Gill, Tiffany M. *Beauty Shop Politics: African American Women's Activism in the Beauty Industry.* Urbana-Champaign: University of Illinois Press, 2010.

SLIM HYATT: DISQUAIR EXTRAORDINAIRE

Duchin, Peter. *Ghost of a Chance: A Memoir.* New York: Random House, 1996.

Green, Abel. "Jumping Jet Set's Disk Den: Panama Cuts an East Side Canal," *Variety,* April 1, 1964, 1.

Poschardt, Ulf. *DJ-Culture.* Translated by Shaun Whiteside. London: Quartet Books, 2000.

"I AM NOT WORRIED ABOUT ALI": BILL RUSSELL, JIM BROWN, AND THE NEGRO INDUSTRIAL ECONOMIC UNION

Eig, Jonathan. "The Cleveland Summit and Muhammad Ali: The True Story." *Andscape,* June 1, 2017. https://andscape.com/features/the-cleveland-summit-muhammad-ali/.

Goudsouzian, Aram. "The House That Russell Built: Bill Russell, the University of San Francisco, and the Winning Streak That Changed College Basketball." *California History* 84, no. 4 (Fall 2007): 4–25. https://doi.org/10.2307/25161913.

Goudsouzian, Aram. *King of the Court: Bill Russell and the Basketball Revolution.* Berkeley: University of California Press, 2010.

McGraw, Dan. "50 Years Ago: Ali Summit in Cleveland with Jim Brown, Others Shows How Landscape Has Changed in Sports." *The Athletic,* June 4, 2017. https://theathletic.com/64694/2017/06/04/ali-summit-mcgraw/.

Russell, Bill, with William McSweeny. *Go Up for Glory.* New York: Coward-McCann, 1966.

BOHEMIAN MESSIAH: JIMI HENDRIX FINDS FREEDOM IN LONDON

Altham, Keith. "New to the Charts: Wild Jimi Hendrix." *NME,* January 14, 1967.

Atlas, Jacoba. "Interview with Jimi Hendrix." *Hullabaloo,* February 1969.

Henderson, David. *'Scuse Me While I Kiss the Sky: Jimi Hendrix: Voodoo Child.* Reprint, New York: Atria, 2009.

Murray, Charles Shaar. *Crosstown Traffic: Jimi Hendrix and the Post-War Rock & Roll Revolution.* New York: St. Martin's Griffin, 1991.

Roby, Steven, and Jimi Hendrix. *Hendrix on Hendrix: Interviews and Encounters with Jimi Hendrix*. Chicago: Chicago Review Press, 2012.

Tate, Greg. "The Black Male Show: Jimi Hendrix." In *Flyboy 2: The Greg Tate Reader*. Durham, NC: Duke University Press, 2016.

Tate, Greg. *Midnight Lightning: Jimi Hendrix and the Black Experience*. Chicago: Chicago Review Press, 2003.

LOVE IS THE MESSAGE

Fikentscher, Kai. *"You Better Work!": Underground Dance Music in New York*. Middleton, CT: Wesleyan University Press, 2000.

Gamson, Joshua. *The Fabulous Sylvester: The Legend, the Music, the Seventies in San Francisco*. New York: Macmillan Publishing, 2006.

Green, Kai M. "Catching the Incurable Contagion: Black Los Angeles' Disco Queers." *PBS SoCal*, May 19, 2013. http://www.kcet.org/arts/artbound /counties/los-angeles/los-angeles-disco -queers.html.

Lawrence, Tim. *Love Saves the Day: A History of American Dance Music Culture, 1970–1979*. Durham, NC: Duke University Press, 2004.

Murphy, Ryan, Brad Falchuk, and Steven Canals. *Pose* (FX Network TV series), June 3, 2018–June 6, 2021.

V. BLACK EDUCATION AS RESISTANCE

LEARNING IN SECRET PLACES

Anderson, James D. *The Education of Blacks in the South, 1860–1935*. Chapel Hill: University of North Carolina Press, 1988.

New-York Historical Society Museum & Library. "Life Story: Susie Baker King Taylor (1848–1912)." Accessed October 26, 2023. https://wams.nyhistory.org/a -nation-divided/reconstruction/susie -baker-king-taylor/.

Taylor, Susie King. *Reminiscences of My Life: A Black Woman's Civil War Memoirs*. Reprint, Princeton, NJ: Markus Wiener, 1989.

Walker, David. *David Walker's Appeal to the Colored Citizens of the World*. Reprint, Hartford, CT: Martino Fine Books, 2015.

TWENTY-TWO DIVIDED BY SEVEN, GEOMETRY AT TUSKEGEE

Beckmann, Petr. *A History of ϖ (Pi)*. 2nd ed. New York: St. Martin's Press, 1971.

Scott, Emmett Jay, and Lyman Beecher Stowe. *Booker T. Washington, Builder of a Civilization*. Garden City, NY: Doubleday, 1916.

Washington, Booker T. *Working with the Hands: Being a Sequel to "Up from Slavery," Covering the Author's Experiences in Industrial Training at Tuskegee*. New York: Doubleday, Page & Company, 1904.

Woodard, Dudley Weldon. *Practical Arithmetic*. Tuskegee Institute edition. Tuskegee, AL: Tuskegee Normal & Industrial Institute, 1911.

POISE AND PERSEVERANCE

Ford, Tanisha. *Liberated Threads: Black Women, Style, and the Global Politics of Soul*. Oxford: Oxford University Press, 2015.

Journal of Blacks in Higher Education. "Key Events in Black Higher Education." Accessed March 20, 2021. https://www .jbhe.com/chronology.

National Museum of African American History and Culture at the Smithsonian Institution. "An Indomitable Spirit: Autherine Lucy." In *Our American Story*. Accessed March 23, 2021. https:// nmaahc.si.edu/blog-post/indomitable -spirit-autherine-lucy.

Richmond, Krista. "Holmes and Hunter-Gault: They Followed Their Dreams." *UGA Today*, February 1, 2019. Accessed November 6, 2023. https://news.uga .edu/holmes-hunter-gault-georgia -groundbreakers/.

THE TUMULTUOUS DAYS OF SNCC

"Charles F. McDew Oral History Interview Conducted by Joseph Mosnier in Albany, Georgia, 2011 June 04." Library of Congress. https://www.loc.gov /item/2015669120/.

Payne, Charles M. *I've Got the Light of Freedom: The Organizing Tradition and the Mississippi Freedom Struggle*. Berkeley: University of California Press, 1997.

Robinson, Phil Alden, director. *Freedom Song*. Warner Brothers, 2007. 150 minutes.

Umoja, Akinyele Omowale. *We Will Shoot Back: Armed Resistance in the Mississippi Freedom Movement*. New York: NYU Press, 2014.

STUDENT ACTIVISM AND THE RISE OF BLACK STUDIES

Alkalimat, Abdul. *The History of Black Studies*. London: Pluto Press, 2021.

Carr, Gregory. "What Black Studies Is Not: Moving from Crisis to Liberation in Africana Intellectual Work." *Socialism and Democracy* 25, no. 1 (2011): 178–91. https://doi.org/10.1080/08854300.2011 .569201.

Kendi, Ibram. *The Black Campus Movement: Black Students and the Racial Reconstitution of Higher Education, 1965–1972*. London: Palgrave Macmillan, 2012.

Myers, Joshua M. *We Are Worth Fighting For: A History of the Howard University Student Protest of 1989*. New York: NYU Press, 2019.

Spellman, A. B., and Malcolm X. "Interview with Malcolm X." *Monthly Review: An Independent Socialist Magazine*, March 19, 1964. Reprint, February 1, 2005. https:// monthlyreview.org/2005/02/01 /interview-with-malcolm-x/.

VI. BLACK AMERICA IN WARTIME

CHARLES YOUNG: THE LIFE OF A SOLDIER

Clegg, Claude A. "'A Splendid Type of Colored

American': Charles Young and the Reorganization of the Liberian Frontier Force." *International Journal of African Historical Studies* 29, no. 1 (1996): 47–70. https://doi.org/10.2307/221418.

Donaldson, Le'Trice D. *Duty beyond the Battlefield: African American Soldiers Fight for Racial Uplift, Citizenship, and Manhood, 1870–1920.* Carbondale: Southern Illinois University Press, 2020.

Kilroy, David P. *For Race and Country: The Life and Career of Colonel Charles Young.* Westport, CT: Praeger, 2003.

MAKING AND MOBILIZING ART IN TIMES OF WAR

Duis, Perry R. "Great Lakes Naval Training Station." *Encyclopedia of Chicago.* Accessed September 30, 2022. http://www.encyclopedia.chicagohistory.org/pages/543.html.

Langley, Jerry L. "The Fantasy World of Fred D. Jones: Re-discovering His Life in Art." *IRAAA+: The International Review of African American Art Plus.* Accessed November 6, 2023. https://web.archive.org/web/20230531042310/http://iraaa.museum.hamptonu.edu/page/The-Fantasy-World-of-Fred-D%3E-Jones.

Locke, Alain. "The Unfinished Business of Democracy." *Survey Graphic*, November 1942.

Stewart, Jeffrey C. *The New Negro: The Life of Alain Locke.* Oxford: Oxford University Press, 2018.

MARY MCLEOD BETHUNE

Evans, Stephanie Y., Andrea D. Domingue, and Tania D. Mitchell. *Black Women and Social Justice Education: Legacies and Lessons.* Albany: State University of New York Press, 2019.

Jones, Ida. *Mary McLeod Bethune in Washington, D.C.: Activism & Education in Logan Circle.* Washington, DC: Arcadia Publishing, 2013.

McCabe, Katie, and Dovey Johnson Roundtree. *Justice Older Than the Law: The Life of Dovey Johnson Roundtree.* Jackson: University Press of Mississippi, 2009.

Robertson, Ashley N. *Mary McLeod Bethune in Florida: Bringing Social Justice to the Sunshine State.* Washington, DC: Arcadia Publishing, 2015.

JOE LOUIS: THE BLACK FACE OF MILITARY PROPAGANDA

Cripps, Thomas. *Making Movies Black: The Hollywood Message Movie from World War II to the Civil Rights Era.* New York: Oxford University Press, 1993.

Hietala, Thomas R. *The Fight of the Century: Jack Johnson, Joe Louis, and the Struggle for Racial Equality.* Armonk, NY: M. E. Sharpe, 2002.

Louis, Joe, Chester L. Washington, and Haskell Cohen. *My Life Story.* New York: Duell, Sloan and Pearce, 1947.

"Louis Signs For Benefit Bout." *Cleveland Gazette*, January 3, 1942, 1.

Martin, Kali. "Joe Louis: From Boxing Gloves to Combat Boots." National WWII Museum, April 9, 2000. https://www.nationalww2museum.org/war/articles/joe-louis-boxing.

Roberts, Randy. *Joe Louis: Hard Times Man.* New Haven, CT: Yale University Press, 2010.

PANTHERS AND THE PREMIER: BLACK INTERNATIONALISM AND COLD WAR CHINA

Brown, Keisha A. "Blackness in Exile: W. E. B. Du Bois' Role in the Formation of Representations of Blackness as Conceptualized by the Chinese Communist Party (CCP)." *Phylon* 53, no. 2 (2016): 20–33.

Clemons, Michael L., and Charles E. Jones. "Global Solidarity: The Black Panther Party in the International Arena." In *Liberation, Imagination and the Black Panther Party: A New Look at the Panthers and Their Legacy.* Edited by Kathleen Cleaver and George Katsiaficas. New York: Taylor & Francis, 2014.

Frazier, Robeson Taj. *The East Is Black: Cold War China in the Black Radical Imagination.* Durham, NC: Duke University Press, 2015.

Gallicchio, Marc. *The African American Encounter with Japan and China: Black Internationalism in Asia, 1895–1945.* Chapel Hill: University of North Carolina Press, 2000.

Gao, Yunxiang. *Arise Africa, Roar China: Black and Chinese Citizens of the World in the Twentieth Century.* Chapel Hill: University of North Carolina Press, 2021.

Malloy, Sean L. *Out of Oakland: Black Panther Party Internationalism during the Cold War.* Ithaca, NY: Cornell University Press, 2017.

Stout, David. "Robert F. Williams, 71, Civil Rights Leader and Revolutionary." *New York Times*, October 19, 1996, 52.

VII. GLOBAL DIMENSIONS OF BLACK HISTORY

INTERNATIONAL LEGACIES OF AFRICAN AMERICAN CIVIL RIGHTS ACTIVISM

Breitman, George, ed. *Malcolm X Speaks: Selected Speeches and Statements.* New York: Grove Press, 1990.

Dudziak, Mary L. *Exporting American Dreams: Thurgood Marshall's African Journey.* Princeton: Princeton University Press, 2011.

Slate, Nico, ed. *Black Power beyond Borders: The Global Dimensions of the Black Power Movement.* New York: Palgrave Macmillan, 2012.

W. E. B. DU BOIS AND THE PAN-AFRICAN CONGRESS

Adi, Hakim. *Pan-Africanism: A History.* London: Bloomsbury Academic, 2018.

Blain, Keisha N. *Set the World on Fire: Black Nationalist Women and the Global Struggle for Freedom.* Philadelphia: University of Pennsylvania Press, 2018.

Kelley, Robin D. G. *Freedom Dreams: The Black*

Radical Imagination. Boston: Beacon Press, 2002.

Rabaka, Reiland, ed. *Routledge Handbook of Pan-Africanism*. New York: Taylor & Francis, 2020.

Walters, Ronald W. *Pan Africanism in the African Diaspora: An Analysis of Modern Afrocentric Political Movements*. Detroit: Wayne State University Press, 1997.

CASTRO COMES TO HARLEM

Cohen, Steven. "When Castro Came to Harlem." *The New Republic*, March 21, 2015.

Goldstein, Brian. *The Roots of Urban Renaissance: Gentrification and the Struggle over Harlem*. Cambridge, MA: Harvard University Press, 2017.

Hall, Simon. "Fidel Castro Stayed in Harlem 60 Years Ago to Highlight Racial Injustice in the U.S." *Smithsonian*, September 18, 2020. https://www.smithsonianmag.com/history/fidel-castro-harlem-60-years-ago-180975863/.

Hall, Simon. *Ten Days in Harlem: Fidel Castro and the Making of the 1960s*. London: Faber & Faber, 2020.

"Love Woods Dies; Ran the Theresa," *New York Times*, Tuesday, May 30, 1967, 19.

"The Waldorf of Harlem." *Ebony*, April 1946.

ANTI-RACIST COMRADES: AFRICAN AMERICANS IN CUBA

Benson, Devyn Spence. *Antiracism in Cuba: The Unfinished Revolution*. Chapel Hill: University of North Carolina Press, 2016.

Guridy, Frank Andre. *Forging Diaspora: Afro-Cubans and African Americans in a World of Empire and Jim Crow*. Chapel Hill: University of North Carolina Press, 2010.

REFUGE AND REVOLUTION FOR BLACK AMERICANS IN FRANCE

Ambar, Saladin. "The Din of Malcolm: Projections of Islam in France and the United Kingdom, 1964–1965." *Journal of Africana Religions* 3, no. 1 (2015): 18–30. https://doi.org/10.5325/jafrireli.3.1.0018.

Boittin, Jennifer Anne. *Colonial Metropolis: The Urban Grounds of Anti-Imperialism and Feminism in Interwar Paris*. Lincoln: University of Nebraska Press, 2010.

Germain, Félix. "French Fears of African-Americanization in a Historical Context." *Contemporary French and Francophone Studies* 26, no. 4–5 (2022): 429–38. https://doi.org/10.1080/17409292.2022.2107277.

Gillett, Rachel. "Jazz and the Evolution of Black American Cosmopolitanism in Interwar Paris." *Journal of World History* 21, no. 3 (2010): 471–96. https://doi.org/10.1353/jwh.2010.0000.

"Malcolm X Barred by French Security." *New York Times*, February 10, 1965.

McCormack, Donald J. "Stokely Carmichael and Pan-Africanism: Back to Black Power." *Journal of Politics* 35, no. 2 (1973): 386–409. https://doi.org/10.2307/2129075.

Murphy, David. "The Emergence of a Black France, 1985–2015: History, Race and Identity." *Nottingham French Studies* 54, no. 3 (2015): 238–52. https://doi.org/10.3366/nfs.2015.0124.

Rojas, Don. "Celebrating the Life and Legacy of Kwame Ture aka Stokely Carmichael." IBW21.org, July 31, 2023. https://ibw21.org/editors-choice/celebrating-the-life-and-legacy-of-kwame-ture-aka-stokely-carmichael/.

Stovall, Tyler. *White Freedom: The Racial History of an Idea*. Princeton, NJ: Princeton University Press, 2021.

ACKNOWLEDGMENTS

The great force of history comes from the fact that we carry it within us, are unconsciously controlled by it in many ways, and history is literally present in all that we do. It could scarcely be otherwise, since it is to history that we owe our frames of reference, our identities, and our aspirations.

—JAMES BALDWIN

Picturing Black History is a testament to Black history that is not past. An ongoing collaborative effort between Getty Images, *Origins: Current Events in Historical Perspective*, and the History Departments at the Ohio State and Miami Universities, *Picturing Black History* seeks to uncover untold stories and rarely seen images of the Black experience by providing new context around culturally significant moments. Through the collective work of our contributors, we recognize the contributions of prominent figures and everyday people in African American life to contextualize the past and envision the future.

Picturing Black History emerged in the wake of national and international Black Lives Matter protests following the murder of George Floyd at the hands of four Minneapolis police officers in 2020. We recognize that Black Lives Matter is a contemporary outgrowth of a long history of Black racial protest in the United States. For more images and stories of Black history, go to www.picturingblackhistory.org.

It is a great pleasure to recognize and thank all the many people and institutions that have assisted us in the production of this book.

Heartfelt thanks to our friends and partners at Getty Images who have worked so generously and passionately with us to create *Picturing Black History*, in both its digital and its book forms: Bob Ahern, Shawn Waldron, Leslie Stauffer, Sarah Kubiak, and Melanie Llewellyn. This has been the true embodiment of joyful collaboration.

Deep thanks our colleagues and supporters at the Ohio State University who have worked with us at various stages of this project—Paul McAllister, Ben St. Angelo, Laura Seeger, David Steigerwald, Sarájanée Davis, Lauren Henry, Scott Levi, Brian Rzepka, Missie Hathaway, Steve McCann, and the *Origins: Current Events in Historical Perspective* team. We are especially thankful for the financial support of Ohio State's Department of History, College of Arts and Humanities, Global Arts and Humanities Discovery Theme, East Asian Studies Center, Center for Latin American Studies, and Stanton Foundation, which have collectively made this publication possible. A shout-out to our editorial board for their guidance and support: Tammy Brown, Jocelyn Imani, Hasan Kwame Jeffries, LaGarrett King, Treva Lindsey, and Kaye Whitehead. Our deep appreciation goes to the fabulous team at Abrams Books, especially Zack Knoll and Laura Dozier, who have made the publication process so easy.

Damarius Johnson gives thanks to the Black communities that shaped him. Libations pour to the living presence of ancestors, known and unknown, whose energetic activity fortifies his physical presence. Enduring gratitude to the Kwame Ture Society and Department of Afro-American Studies at Howard University for their invitation and introduction to the spirit and truth of Africana Studies. Finally and ultimately, he is humbled by the loving support of immediate family, friends who've become family, colleagues, and Naptown neighbors who share the expectation that the study of the African past shapes possibilities for Black community life.

Daniela Edmeier would like to honor the community whose unwavering belief in her, even when those feelings were difficult to muster for herself, continued to light her path. Her mom, Vivian; sister, Julianna; brother, Gabriel; dad, Daniel; and sister-in-spirit, Claire, remain the unshakable foundation of her life. To her friends who have become family—too many to name—a million thanks over. Opportunities are frequently the result of someone else's trust in your abilities. As such, Daniela would like to thank the team of intelligent, compassionate academic mentors who have been true role models in the deepest sense of the term: Drs. Alice Conklin, Robin Judd, Theodora Dragostinova, Sarah van Beurden, and Mytheli Sreenivas. Being not only accepted but cherished for your authentic self is a precious and rare gift, so finally, Daniela would like to thank her partner, Chad, for choosing to love and grow together in this weird cosmic dance called life (*Ready, partner? Giddy up!*).

Steven Conn has never had so much fun working on a collaborative project, and he wants to thank Nick, Daniela, Damarius, and the Getty team in particular for teaching him so much. He worked on this book with his children, Olivia and Zachary, always in mind. They, too, have taught him a great deal about race and justice and reminded him of the fierce urgency of now. And as always, his wife, Angela Brintlinger, who laughs with him and at him in equal measure.

It has been a marvelous adventure working on the *Picturing Black History* project, from its humble beginnings to the website and now on to this book. Nick Breyfogle passes on profound thanks to Daniela, Damarius, Steve, Bob, Shawn, Leslie, Sarah, and Mel for all their brilliance, camaraderie, and humor at every step. Thanks also to the amazing group of friends and visionaries at NYU's Center for Black Visual Culture for bringing me into their Black Rest Project. I have learned so much from all of you. Boundless hugs and love to Jillian, Charlie, Sam, and Oakley. I hope this book will be one small step toward a more just, inclusive, and peaceful world. As Toni Morrison said in her 2004 Wellesley College commencement address: "I am a teller of stories and therefore an optimist, a believer in the ethical bend of the human heart."

Two fonts are used in this book: Marsha and Freight. Marsha was developed by Vocal Type (founded by Tré Seals). As their website describes: "This typeface is inspired by the vertical sign that once hung outside of Stonewall, and named after Marsha P. Johnson. Marsha was an African-American, transgender woman from New Jersey, whose activism in the 1960s and '70s made her one of the most prominent figures in the Stonewall uprising of 1969" (www.vocaltype.co/history-of/marsha). Freight was developed by Joshua Darden, the first known Black typeface designer (www.letterformarchive.org /news/darden-type-design-archive/).

RIGHT: African American writer James Baldwin (New York, 1975).

PAGE 305: Three young men wait for a breakdancing competition to begin, Hayward, California, 1985.

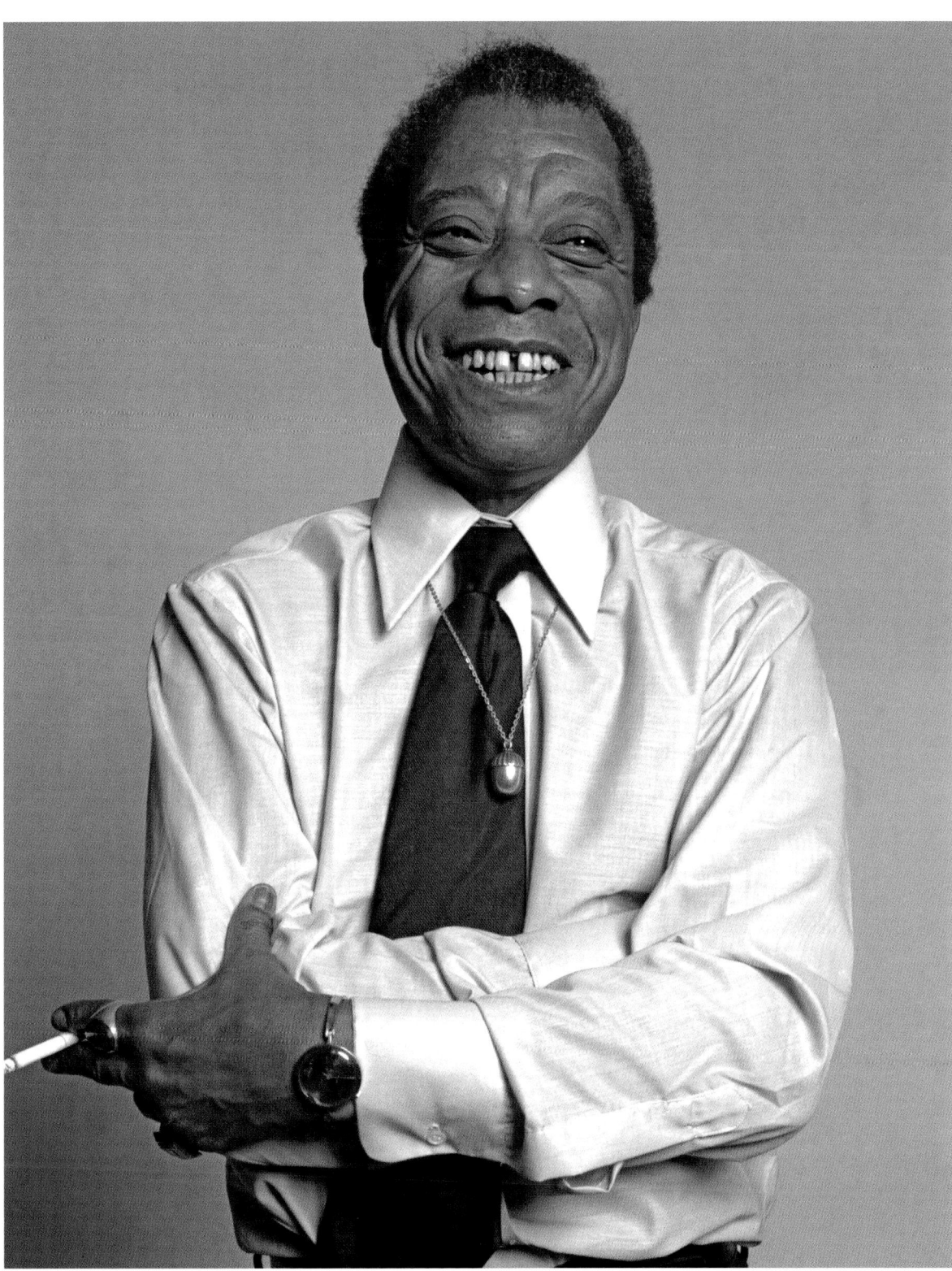

ABOUT THE AUTHORS

EDITORS

Daniela Edmeier is a managing editor of *Picturing Black History*. She is a PhD candidate in history at the Ohio State University, where she studies immigration, race and ethnicity, and settler colonialism in French Algeria.

Damarius Johnson is a PhD student at the Ohio State University. He is a public historian whose research examines intersecting traditions of Black museum-building in the United States and West Africa.

Nicholas B. Breyfogle is a coeditor of *Origins: Current Events in Historical Perspective* and *Picturing Black History*, professor of history at the Ohio State University, and director of the Harvey Goldberg Center for Excellence in Teaching.

Steven Conn is a coeditor of *Origins: Current Events in Historical Perspective* and *Picturing Black History* and W. E. Smith Professor of History at Miami University.

AUTHORS

Blair Banks is a proud metro Atlanta native and graduate of Georgia State's Africana Studies program currently working as a DEI specialist in her hometown.

Melvin Barnes Jr., PhD, is a teacher-scholar specializing in East Asian, transnational, and African American history.

Tammy L. Brown, PhD, is associate professor of Black world studies, history, and global and intercultural studies at Miami University.

Dawn Chitty, EdD, is the director of education at the African American Civil War Museum, where she has worked since 2010.

Lorna M. Closeil is a Black feminist scholar and practitioner whose research interests include Black women's literature, radical Black feminisms, and exploring Black childhood as it intersects with anti-Blackness.

Brian C. Davis Jr. is a second-year history PhD student at Florida State University who researches Black military experiences during the Cold War era.

Sarájanée O. Davis, PhD, is an educator and historian who is committed to preserving Black historical perspectives and amplifying them in pursuit of an equitable future.

Daniela Edmeier is a PhD candidate in history at the Ohio State University, where she studies immigration, race and ethnicity, and settler colonialism in French Algeria.

Jocelyn Imani, PhD, is a storyteller, educator, and community builder with over a decade of experience as a public historian and is currently the National Director of Black History and Culture for the Trust for Public Land.

Sai Isoke is an educator, facilitator, and creative living in Los Angeles, California.

Damarius Johnson is a PhD student at the Ohio State University. He is a public historian whose research examines intersecting traditions of Black museum-building in the United States and West Africa.

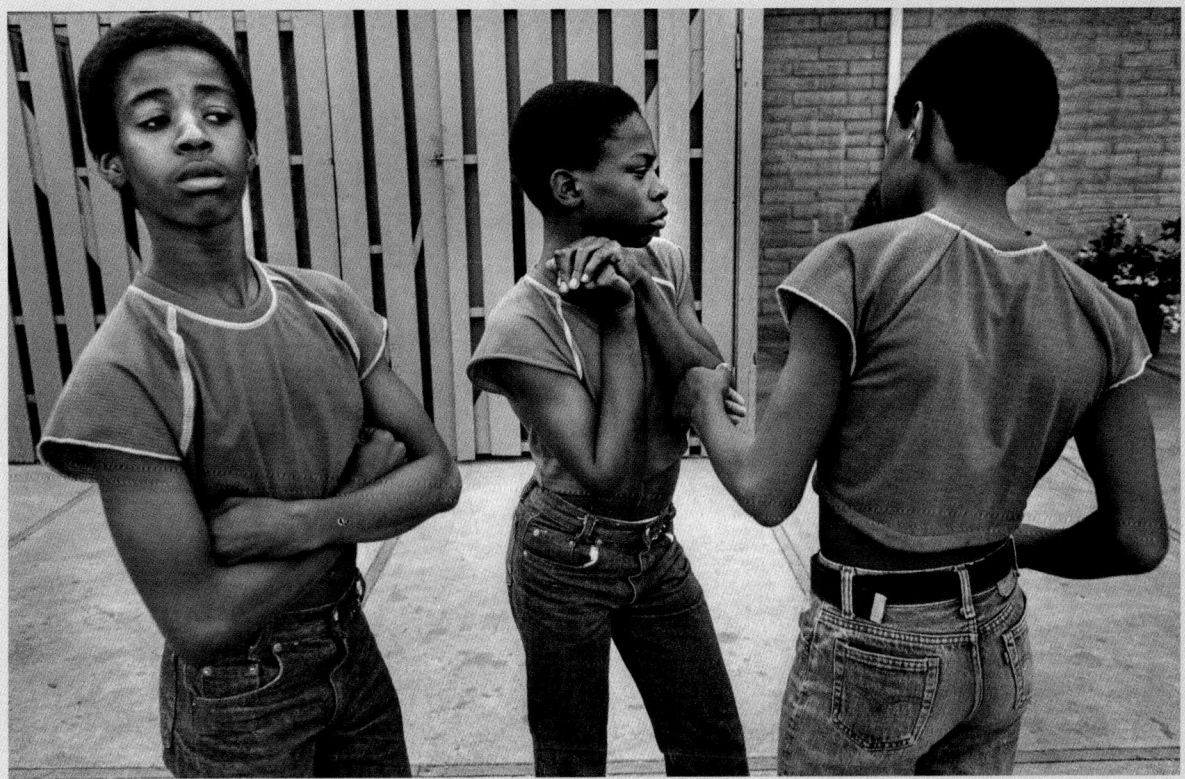

Jovonna Jones, PhD, is an assistant professor of African American literature and culture at Boston College, specializing in photography and visual studies, space and place, and Black feminist criticism.

LaGarrett King, PhD, is an associate professor of social studies education in the Department of Learning and Instruction in the Graduate School of Education at the University at Buffalo.

Alex Lichtenstein, PhD, is professor of history and American studies at Indiana University, Bloomington.

Paul L. McAllister is a PhD candidate at the Ohio State University, where he studies military history, specifically the experience of African American soldiers from the late nineteenth to the mid-twentieth century.

Kevin McGruder, PhD, is associate professor of history at Antioch College and is the author of *Race and Real Estate: Conflict and Cooperation in Harlem, 1890–1920* and *Philip Payton: The Father of Black Harlem.*

Dustin Meier, PhD, is an urban and environmental historian who teaches at John Jay College of Criminal Justice.

Allison Mashell Mitchell is a doctoral candidate in the Corcoran Department of History at the University of Virginia studying Black electoral politics and political organizing in the twentieth-century U.S. South.

Kimberly F. Monroe, PhD, is a native of southern Louisiana and is assistant professor of Africana Studies at Trinity Washington University in Washington, DC, and the advisor of the Black Student Alliance.

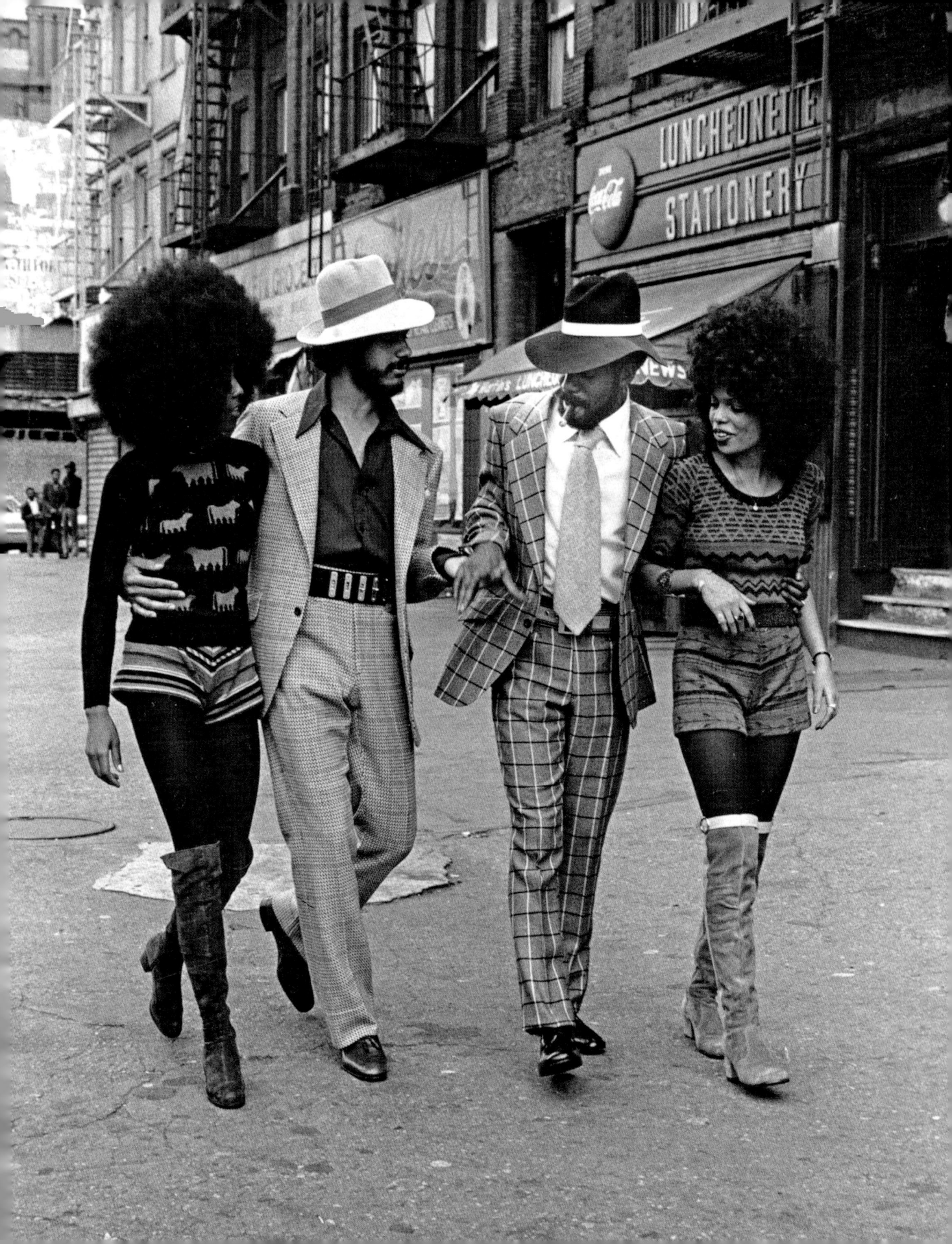

Kelsey A. Moore is a PhD candidate in the History Department at Johns Hopkins University and a proud Black South Carolinian invested in telling more robust stories about Black Southern life.

James R. Morgan III holds degrees from Howard University and Morgan State University, where he is currently pursuing doctoral study in African American history.

Joshua Myers, PhD, is a writer based in the Washington, DC, area.

Sierra L. Phillips is a Minneapolis native and history PhD student at the Ohio State University, where she studies Black women's activism, urban history, and the Civil Rights Movement.

Ashley Robertson Preston, PhD, is an assistant professor of history at Howard University and the author of *Mary McLeod Bethune the Pan-Africanist*.

Raja Malikah Rahim, PhD, is an academic and acommunity-trained social and cultural historian, a professor, and a scholar-activist with an anti-racist and anti-sexist agenda whose current research centers on the intersection of race, culture, politics, and sports at Historically Black Colleges and Universities in the twentieth century.

Cedric Rose is a writer and researcher and a librarian at the Mercantile Library in Cincinnati, Ohio.

Michael M. Santiago is a staff news photojournalist with Getty Images based in Brooklyn, New York.

Chet'la Sebree, PhD, is a creative writing professor at George Washington University and the author of *Field Study* and *Mistress*.

Kwabena Slaughter is an artist and a PhD candidate in the Department of American Studies at George Washington University whose writing has appeared in *Critical Inquiry* and in the *Journal of Popular Music Studies*, and his photography and video artworks are in public and private collections in the United States and Europe.

Christopher M. Shell, PhD, is a fellow in the American Statecraft Program at the Carnegie Endowment for International Peace.

Ben St. Angelo is a PhD candidate in modern American history at the Ohio State University whose research focuses on working-class people and the strategies they employed when faced with exploitation and oppression.

Sheneese Thompson, PhD, is an assistant professor in language, literature, and culture at Bowie State University who specializes in African traditional religions in Black popular culture and loves teaching her students.

Jessica Viñas-Nelson, PhD, is an assistant professor of African and African American Studies at Arizona State University focusing on Black intellectual history.

Shawn Waldron is Getty Images' curator for print sales and exhibitions and manager of the Slim Aarons Archive.

Jasmin A. Young, PhD, is a historian of Black women's history, intellectual history, resistance, and radical Black feminism.

OPPOSITE: A summer stroll in New York City, 1970s.

PHOTOGRAPHY CREDITS

Pages 200–201: Bettmann Archive/ VCG/Getty Images

Page 202: Smith Collection/Archive Photos/Getty Images

Page 204, top to bottom: Bettmann Archive/VCG/Getty Images; Wally McNamee/Corbis Historical/VCG/ Getty Images

Page 205: Bettmann Archive/VCG/ Getty Images

Page 207: Bettmann Archive/VCG/ Getty Images

Page 208: Bettmann Archive/VCG/ Getty Images

Page 209: Bettmann Archive/VCG/ Getty Images

Pages 210–11: Flip Schulke/Corbis Historical/VCG/Getty Images

Pages 212–213: Bettmann Archive/VCG/ Getty Images

Page 214, top to bottom: Garth Eliassen/Archive Photos/Getty Images; Bettmann Archive/VCG/Getty Images

Pages 216–17: Bettmann Archive/VCG/ Getty Images

Page 218–19: Bettmann Archive/VCG/ Getty Images

Page 220: Hulton Archive/Archive Photos/Getty Images

Page 222: Pach Bros/Heritage Images via Getty Images

Page 225, top, left to right: Bettmann Archive/VCG/Getty Images; Bettmann Archive/VCG/Getty Images; bottom, left to right: Heritage Art/Heritage Images via Getty Images; Bettmann Archive/VCG/Getty Images

Page 226: Afro Newspaper/Archive Photos/Getty Images

Page 228: Bettmann Archive/VCG/ Getty Images

Page 229: Afro Newspaper/Archive Photos/Getty Images

Page 230: Afro Newspaper/Archive Photos/Getty Images

Page 231: Bettmann Archive/VCG/ Getty Images

Page 232: Bettmann Archive/VCG/ Getty Images

Page 234: Bettmann Archive/VCG/ Getty Images

Page 236: Corbis Historical/VCG/Getty Images

Page 237: Bettmann Archive/VCG/ Getty Images

Page 238: Bettmann Archive/VCG/ Getty Images

Page 240, left: Bettmann Archive/VCG/ Getty Images

Pages 240–41, right: Express/Hulton Archive/Getty Images

Pages 242–43: Bettmann Archive/VCG/ Getty Images

Pages 244–45, left to right: Keystone/ Hulton Archive/Getty Images; Bettmann Archive/VCG/Getty Images; Bettmann Archive/VCG/Getty Images

Pages 246–47, left: Bettmann Archive/ VCG/Getty Images

Page 247, right, top to bottom: Fotosearch/Archive Photos/Getty Images; John Kisch/Moviepix/Getty Images

Page 248: Apic/Hulton Archive/Getty Images

Pages 250–51: Bettmann Archive/VCG/ Getty Images

Pages 252–53: Corbis Historical/VCG/ Getty Images

Page 254: Three Lions/Hulton Archive/ Getty Images

Page 255: Bettmann Archive/VCG/ Getty Images

Page 256: Lloyd Yearwood/Hulton Archive/Getty Images

Page 258: Bettmann Archive/VCG/ Getty Images

Page 261: Pictorial Parade/Archive Photos/Getty Images

Pages 262–63: Rapho Guillumette/ Archive Photos/Getty Images

Page 264: C. M. Battey/Hulton Archive/ Getty Images

Page 266: John Deakin/Hulton Archive/Getty Images

Page 267: John Deakin/Hulton Archive/ Getty Images

Page 268: John Deakin/Picture Post/ Hulton Archive/Getty Images

Page 269: Bettmann Archive/VCG/ Getty Images

Page 270: Bettmann Archive/VCG/ Getty Images

Pages 272–73: Hulton Deutsch/Corbis Historical/VCG/Getty Images

Page 274, top to bottom: Bettmann Archive/VCG/Getty Images; Keystone/ Hulton Archive/Getty Images

Page 275: Photo 12/Universal Images Group via Getty Images

Page 276: FPG/Archive Photos/Getty Images

Page 277: Bettmann Archive/VCG/ Getty Images

Page 279: Robert Abbott Sengstacke/ Archive Photos/Getty Images

Page 280: Lucas Mendes/Archive Photos/Getty Images

Page 281: Bettmann Archive/VCG/ Getty Images

Pages 282–83: Rudy Suwara/Bettmann Archive/VCG/Getty Images

Page 284: Bettmann Archive/VCG/ Getty Images

Page 286: Bettmann Archive/VCG/ Getty Images

Page 287: Walery/Hulton Archive/ Getty Images

Pages 288–89: Sasha/Hulton Archive/ Getty Images

Pages 290–91: Bettmann Archive/VCG/ Getty Images

Page 292: GERARD-AIME/Gamma-Rapho via Getty Images

Page 293: Bettmann Archive/VCG/ Getty Images

Page 294: Samuel Boivin/NurPhoto via Getty Images

Page 303: Anthony Barboza/Archive Photos/Getty Images

Page 305: Bromberger Hoover Photography/Archive Photos/Getty Images

Page 306: Anthony Barboza/Archive Photos/Getty Images

Page 311: Bettmann Archive/VCG/Getty Images

Pages 318–19: Cecil Williams/Premium Archives/Getty Images

RIGHT: A young boy salutes on a sidewalk in Harlem, 1935.

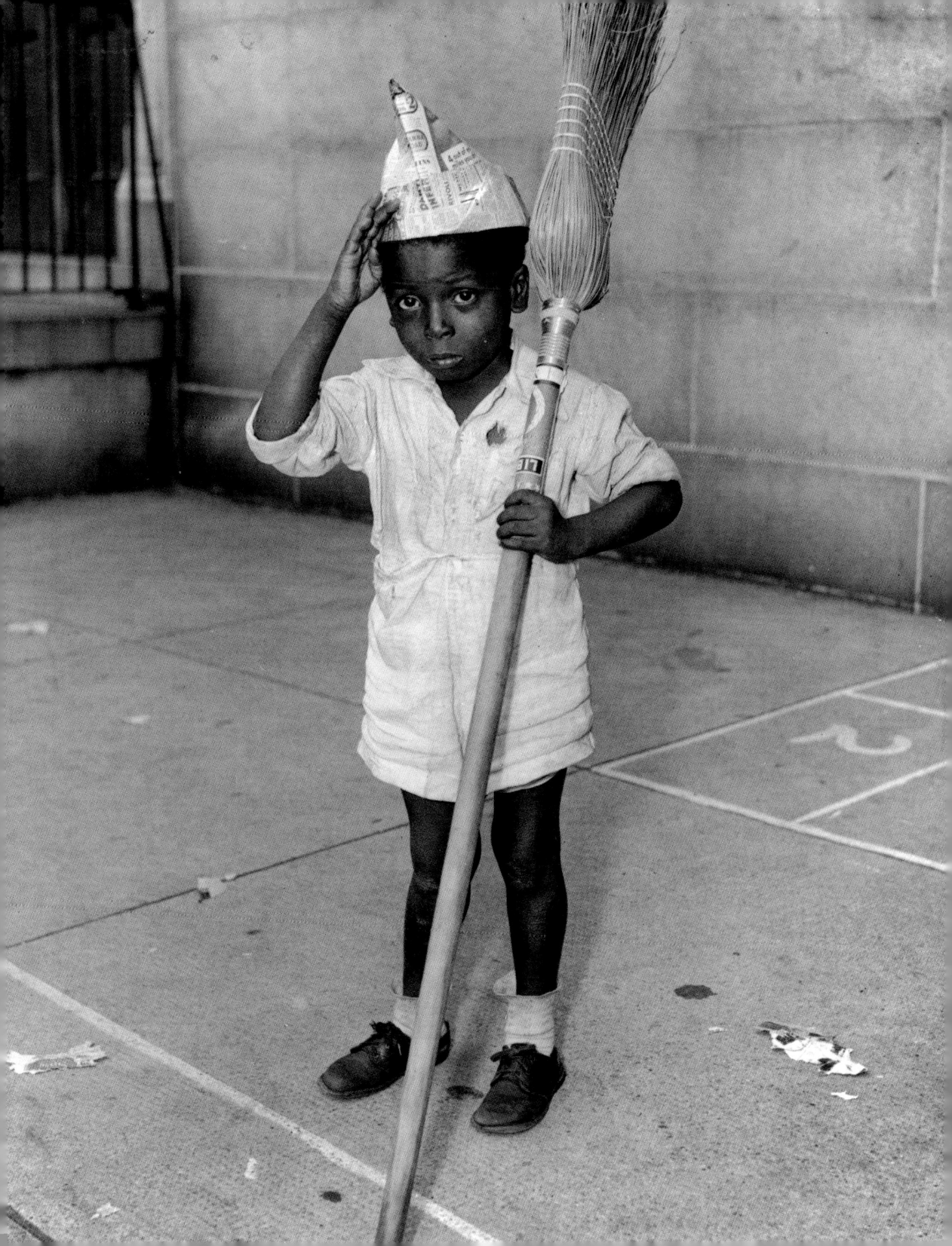

INDEX

FOLLOWING SPREAD: African American photographer John Williamson Goodwin Jr and his wife, Susan, at the beach at Coney Island, New York, 1962.

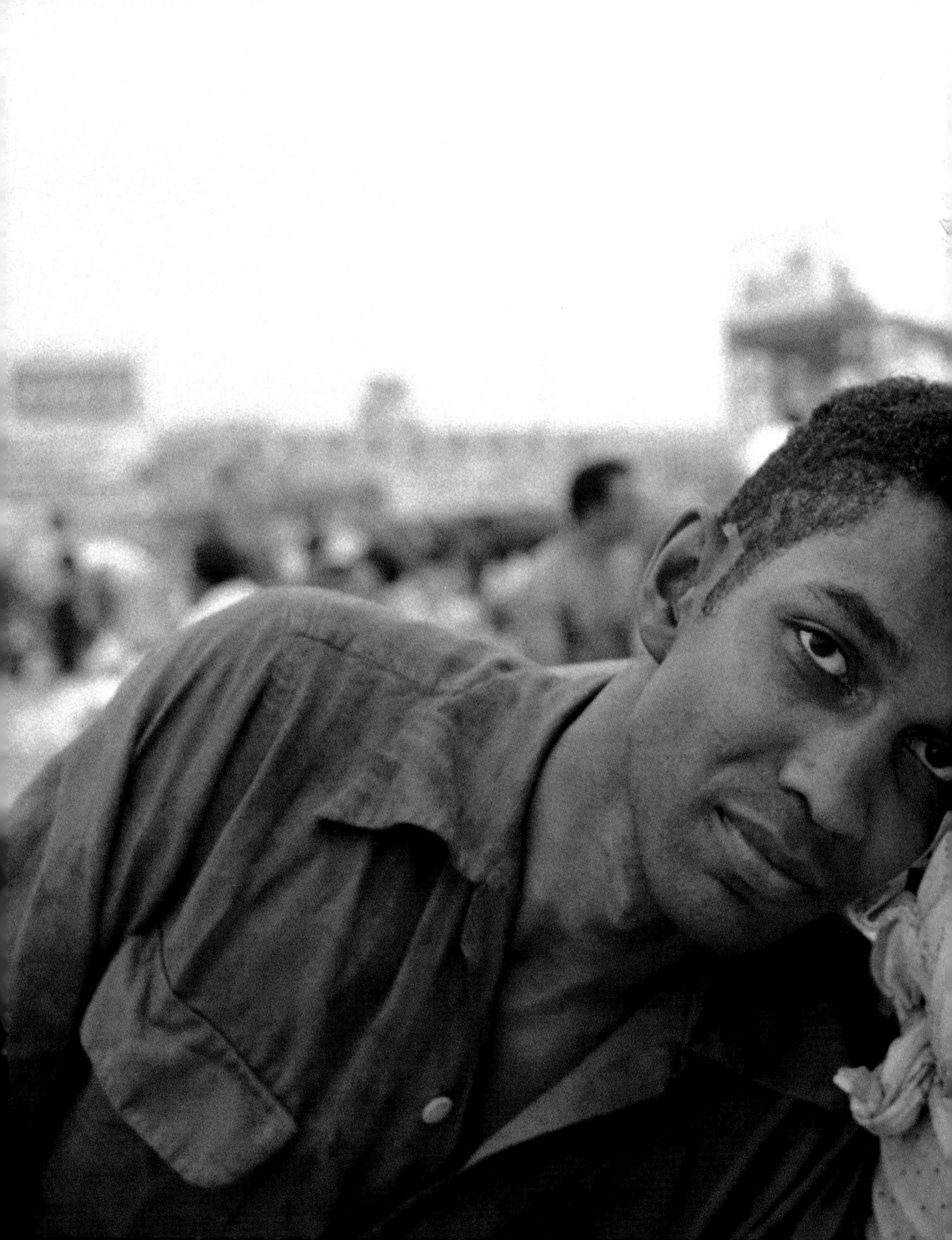

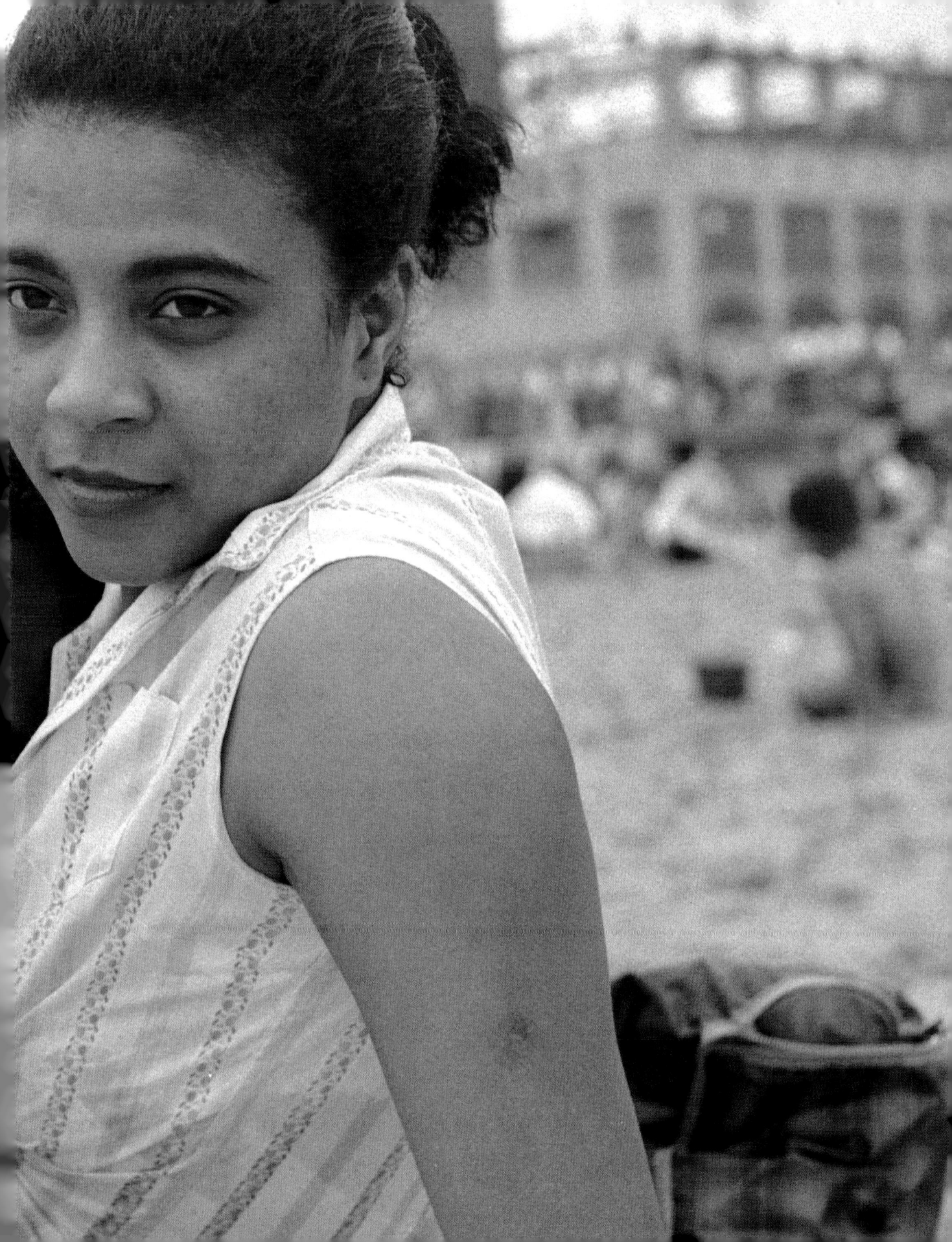

Editor: Zack Knoll
Designer: Diane Shaw
Managing Editor: Logan Hill
Production Manager: Denise LaCongo

Library of Congress Control Number: 2024935812

ISBN: 978-1-4197-6955-9
eISBN: 979-8-88707-094-0

Text copyright © 2024 Ohio State University
See page 308 for photography credits

Cover © 2024 Abrams

Printed and bound in Thailand
10 9 8 7 6 5 4 3 2 1

Abrams books are available at special discounts when purchased
in quantity for premiums and promotions as well as fundraising
or educational use. Special editions can also be created to
specification. For details, contact specialsales@abramsbooks.com
or the address below.

ABRAMS The Art of Books
195 Broadway, New York, NY 10007
abramsbooks.com